Preliminary Edition Notice

You have been selected to receive a copy of this book in the form of a preliminary edition. A preliminary edition is used in a classroom setting to test the overall value of a book's content and its effectiveness in a practical course prior to its formal publication on the national market.

As you use this text in your course, please share any and all feedback regarding the volume with your professor. Your comments on this text will allow the author to further develop the content of the book, so we can ensure it will be a useful and informative classroom tool for students in universities across the nation and around the globe. If you find the material is challenging to understand, or could be expanded to improve the usefulness of the text, it is important for us to know. If you have any suggestions for improving the material contained in the book or the way it is presented, we encourage you to share your thoughts.

Please note, preliminary editions are similar to review copies, which publishers distribute to select readers prior to publication in order to test a book's audience and elicit early feedback; therefore, you may find inconsistencies in formatting or design, or small textual errors within this volume. Design elements and the written text will undergo changes before this book goes to print and is distributed on the national market.

This text is not available in wide release on the market, as it is actively being prepared for formal publication. This may mean that new content is still being added to the author's manuscript, or that the content appears in a draft format.

If you would like to provide notes directly to the publisher, you may contact us by e-mailing studentreviews@cognella.com. Please include the book's title, author, and 7-digit SKU reference number (found below the barcode on the back cover of the book) in the body of your message.

Afrikan American Women

Living at the Crossroads of Race, Gender, Class, and Culture

Preliminary Second Edition

Edited by Huberta Jackson-Lowman

Florida A&M University

SAN DIEGO

Bassim Hamadeh, CEO and Publisher
Carrie Baarns, Senior Manager, Revisions and Author Care
Kaela Martin, Project Editor
Jeanine Rees, Production Editor
Jess Estrella, Senior Graphic Designer
Alexa Lucido, Licensing Manager
Natalie Piccotti, Director of Marketing
Kassie Graves, Senior Vice President, Editorial
Jamie Giganti, Director of Academic Publishing

cognella® | ACADEMIC PUBLISHING
3970 Sorrento Valley Blvd., Ste. 500, San Diego, CA 92121

To my sister and sister friends, daughter, granddaughters, niece, and goddaughters:

May you live your lives knowing, loving, and appreciating all of who you are, expressing your authentic selves with confidence and courage, and using your Divine gifts to enhance the lives of Afrikan people throughout the Diaspora.

Contents

Acknowledgments

The task of expressing gratitude to all those who have helped and supported me through the completion of this first book, and now the second edition, is more than daunting. It is insufficient to simply say that all those who have crossed my path have in one way or another influenced me, although this is certainly true. Stepping out on faith, I offer my sincere expressions of gratitude and appreciation to each of you who has contributed to this achievement. I have done this with an exceptional group of women authors, for women of Afrikan ancestry, and for those who do not know who we really are.

My backers and supporters are extensive. First, I must begin by saying Maferefun Egun (I give praise and honor to the ancestors), *those known and unknown, those that I can name and those that I cannot name, those lost during the Middle Passage, those scattered throughout the Diaspora, those buried in the soil of Afrika*. It is their collective energy, efforts, and struggle for dignity, social justice, liberation, and the sovereignty of Afrikan people that I have called upon, and it is their shoulders on which I stand. I sincerely hope their contributions are adequately recognized and lifted up in this book. Included among them are my parents—Emma (Martin) Jackson and Hugh Jackson—whose lives shaped everything that I am today.

My family, in particular my husband Bill, has stood by me, giving me the space to undertake this work. Without his continuous support, assistance, and willingness to adapt, this book would never have been completed. He filled in wherever he was needed and did so graciously and without hesitation. Other family members—Burrietta, my sister, and my daughter, Awoyunla—have offered feedback to me at various stages during the writing of these first two editions, while still others constantly encouraged me to go forward, enabling me to complete the first edition of this book and thus laying the groundwork for the second edition.

I am particularly grateful to Dr. Kobi Kambon, recently transitioned, who was a friend and *jegna* (trusted advisor) from arrival at Florida A&M University (FAMU) until his passing. He provided valuable feedback to me on the first edition of the book, and his work has been a source of inspiration for me. I also must acknowledge my long-standing jegna, Dr. Jerome Taylor, former Chair of the Africana Studies Department at the University of Pittsburgh and founder of the Center of Family Excellence in Pittsburgh, PA. He has influenced my life directly and indirectly in many countless ways through his support, the work ethic that he modeled, and his style of leadership and interaction. Organizationally, the Association of Black Psychologists (ABPsi) has been my professional extended family and has provided the place for me to test out my ideas and receive critical feedback and encouragement. I am extremely appreciative of all the support that I have received from ABPsi over the years. Librarians Tiger Swan and Elaine McCreary at FAMU's Coleman Library were particularly helpful and efficiently carried out their roles, providing me with the resources that I needed along the way for the first edition.

I began this trek with three friends who were graduate students also in the Department of Psychology at the University of Pittsburgh—Drs. Anita Brown and Beverly Goodwin, and Barbara Hall. Our work together for over 10 years is the basis for what appears in this textbook. As instructors of the first course on the Psychological Experiences of Black Women at the University of Pittsburgh in the mid-1980s, and as partners in Nia Associates, an organization we created to provide training, consultation, and research on the psychological experiences of Black women, we diligently and enthusiastically began to carve out a focus on Black women as worthy subjects of study and investigation. To each of you, I am deeply indebted for helping me to define and clarify a mission that I consider to be integral to my life purpose.

I cannot conclude my acknowledgments without also saying *Eeepa-ooo Obatala*, my father and owner of my head. I know that I have been spiritually guided by the wise and patient hand of Obatala. I am grateful for my godmother, Oshun Gwere egbe kunle, iba'ye, who crowned me over 36 years ago, and my Ojubona, OmiYinka, iba'ye. To them I am deeply indebted for passing this sacred *ashe* on to me. I pray that I will use it well and through it bring light, peace, and healing to Afrikan women and facilitate the restoration of Afrikan women to our esteemed place on the stage of humanity.

Introduction: Why the Need for a Psychology of Black Women

Huberta Jackson-Lowman

Personal Reflection

One of my most prescient memories of being a graduate student in psychology at the University of Pittsburgh in the 70s occurred when I realized that what I was learning had very little to do with who I was as an Afrikan American woman. The nation had just gone through a period of tremendous upheaval as a result of the Civil Rights and Black Consciousness movements, which challenged the legacy of Jim Crow segregation and called for the establishment of Black Studies programs, among other things. Aside from opening its doors to Afrikan American students and hiring two Black professors, the Department of Psychology had done little else to address the needs of this new group of students. Fortunately, the University of Pittsburgh was one of the first institutions to establish a Black Studies program, in response to the demands made by Black students, faculty, and community residents. I took advantage of the opportunity to attend a Black Psychology class, which was my first introduction to psychology from an Afrikan perspective. My professor, Yusef Ali, obviously loved the class, and I was completely enthralled with it. Finally, I was getting what I had been longing for—an opportunity to explore the dynamics of being Black in America. As appealing as this was, though, I wanted more. I began to engage in conversations with some of my friends who were also graduate students in the Department of Psychology. We shared similar views regarding the invisibility of Afrikan American women in the psychology curriculum. Thus, our quest began to create a course on the psychological experiences of the Black female. Our dream was realized in the early 80s. Anita Brown, Beverly Goodwin, Barbara Hall, and I launched the university's first course dealing with the psychology of Black women. The course was initially populated only by Black women. It provided a site where Black women could discuss some of their most personal thoughts and experiences regarding what it meant to be Black and female. We quickly realized the need for and value of this work. This experience led to the formation of a partnership focused on offering consultation addressing the issues of Black women. For over five years, as Nia Associates, we offered workshops, presentations, and retreats, and did radio and TV interviews focused on the psychology of Black women. We also wrote an article that was published in the *Psychology of Women Quarterly* criticizing both the discipline and the existing Psychology of Women[1] textbooks for their lack of inclusion of women of Afrikan descent (Brown et al., 1985). Though we eventually went our separate ways to pursue our various careers, my interest in this field has persisted. Over the 30-plus years since we developed the first course on the psychology of Black women, I have witnessed tremendous changes in the discipline of psychology; however, the need for courses focusing on Black women remains.

---

[1] In this book, capitalized phrases such as "Psychology of Women" and "Psychology of Black Women" refer to specific disciplines, departments, and courses, while uncapitalized phrases such as "psychology of women" and "psychology of Black women" are used more generally and in other contexts.

A Call for Psychology of Black Women

Brown and colleagues' analysis (1985) suggested that Psychology of Women writers needed to confront their racism, ethnocentrism, and classism and to examine the impact of culture, race, and social class on behavior. Other recommendations we offered included the development of courses to address the psychological experiences of women of Afrikan ancestry, as well as women of other racial/ethnic groups, and the development of a more comprehensive and inclusive psychology of women. A decade later, Reid & Kelly (1994) reviewed submissions to the *Psychology of Women Quarterly* and *Sex Roles* journals for the 1986–1988 and 1989–1991 time periods. The majority of submissions did not identify ethnicity, implying that this was not a relevant variable for analysis. Reid critiqued the discipline for its treatment of women of Afrikan ancestry as anomalies, its assumption that Afrikan American women are monolithic, and its failure to consider poor women (Reid, 1993; Reid & Kelly, 1994). Reid also called for a comprehensive Psychology of Women. Recently, some scholars have undertaken efforts to make Psychology of Women textbooks more inclusive (Crawford, 2017; Lips, 2017; Liss et al., 2019). These authors note the complexity of developing a comprehensive Psychology of Women that sufficiently addresses the diversity of women of different races/ethnicities, nationalities, abilities, sexual orientations, religions, and other characteristics. Their attempts, though laudable, reveal the monumental challenge of adequately addressing the complexity of Black women's psychological experiences within a general or "comprehensive" Psychology of Women course. Since the 1980s considerable research has been carried out on women of Afrikan ancestry by researchers, many of Afrikan ancestry themselves; however, still missing from the landscape are courses that focus on the psychology of Black women.

The first chapter of this book: introduces readers to the rationale that underlies the need for the development of courses focusing on the psychology of Black women; delineates goals and principles that should guide these courses; and presents key issues that guide my approach to this endeavor. Thomas's (2004) treatise on the psychology of Black women comprehensively describes those characteristics that distinguish Afrikan American women, essentializing the need for courses that distinctively investigate Black women's experiences from the perspective of Black women. Building on the work of Thomas (2004), I extend her foundational analysis, adding factors that support the crucial place of Psychology of Black Women in Psychology, Africana Studies, and Women's Studies departments.

Rationale for Psychology of Black Women

A number of authors have explored in depth the shortcomings of the discipline of psychology as a whole, Psychology of Women courses, and Black Psychology courses with regard to the treatment of Black women as a group (Reid & Kelly, 1994; Jackson-Lowman, 1998; Thomas, 2004). To sum up their criticisms, these areas of study have been shackled by influences of racism, ethnocentrism, sexism, and/or classism on their analyses or have demonstrated the wholesale exclusion of women of Afrikan ancestry. Psychology's treatment of Black women has often been pejorative, value-laden, and decontextualized. When Black women are studied, typically the focus has been on the poor, and they have been used to represent the entire group (Reid, 1993). In sum, the discipline's treatment of women of Afrikan ancestry and poor women has violated its own standard of external validity or generalizability, which requires the inclusion of Blacks, women, the poor, and other excluded groups in order to make claims of universality (Thomas, 2004). The discipline has fallen significantly short of the standards it set for itself by rarely including Black women in research samples or including them in ways that disguise their uniqueness and differences, and by using evaluation measures that have not been standardized on Afrikan American women.

Psychology of Women, though meant to be the correction for an androcentric psychology, initially repeated this error in its treatment of women of color. In an effort to become more comprehensive, writers have recently attempted to incorporate women of color into the content, but the uniqueness, range, and breadth of the experiences of Black women is not adequately captured in these efforts. Certainly, women of Afrikan ancestry share the patriarchal oppression of European American women; however, the virulence of this oppression is intensely magnified when the dimension of race is added—a factor not typically acknowledged in Psychology of Women texts. The evidence of the potency of the oppressive forces that have affected Afrikan American women is registered in the disproportionate rates of obesity, abuse, violence, rape, incarceration, STIs and HIV/AIDS, and premature deaths. Rarely are these disparate issues addressed in these texts. Without a cultural and historical analysis, these conditions will not be fully understood, nor will interventions designed to address them be effective. Psychology of Women courses, even with a more comprehensive emphasis, are unprepared to unpack these afflictions.

On the other hand, Black Psychology courses that were meant to address the exclusion of Afrikan people from the domain of psychology and to use Africentric perspectives to evaluate the experiences of Afrikan people have given minimal to no attention to the inherited issue of sexism that exists within the group. Consequently, they give unequal and significantly insufficient consideration to the experiences of Africana women and to the role that gender socialization plays in the lives of both men and women.

From a historical perspective there should be little if any need to defend the creation of courses focusing on women of Afrikan ancestry. It is now a well-known fact that an Afrikan woman was the first ancestor of all of humanity. Thus, the reality is that the Afrikan woman is the mother of humanity—the first woman. An accurate study of the psychology of women would ideally begin with Afrikan women and their descendants, if the assumption is made that this is the origin of humanity. Yet, even in Black feminist writings, the fact that Afrikan women are the foremothers of humanity has not been acknowledged.

All of these identified inadequacies have left a significant vacuum with regard to examining the psychological experiences of women of Afrikan ancestry. Courses on Psychology of Black Women and Africana Women's Studies may address these omissions and/or deficiencies, among other things, while also serving as a stimulus for course revisions and for tackling issues of social justice. To be effective, though, these courses need to display certain characteristics.

Defining the Psychology of Black Women

Thomas (2004) suggests that Psychology of Black Women courses need to exhibit four key characteristics in their quest to address the psychological experiences of the Africana woman. Addressing the epistemological question, "How do we know," the first characteristic that she identifies distinguishes Psychology of Black Women from the more traditional focus of the discipline. Thomas stresses the importance of extending the field's narrow emphasis on experimentally designed and/or quantitatively focused approaches for gaining knowledge and advocates instead for the inclusion of qualitatively designed strategies. Qualitatively designed studies allow the voices of women of Afrikan ancestry to be heard and their perspectives to be understood. Thus, the use of *standpoint epistemologies* (Collins, 2000) is emphasized in Psychology of Black Women. Through the use of standpoint epistemologies, both the lived experiences of Afrikan women and their intuitive experiences can be acknowledged and considered. In contrast, the discipline of psychology, steeped in Western Eurocentric philosophy, does not value intuition, in spite of the fact that intuition has unwittingly influenced the direction of much of the research that is purported to be strictly based in logic and reason.

As Thomas (2004) states, Psychology of Black Women must use a *contextual* approach to examine the lives of women of African ancestry. A contextual approach recognizes that survival for Black women requires that they adapt to oppressive settings; thus, their behavior, as Kurt Lewin (Thomas, 2004) specifies in field theory, is a function of "Person X Environment." In defining context, though, both present and past context—one's history individually and collectively—must be considered, not solely the present context, as Lewin suggests. Past context for women of Afrikan ancestry includes their pre-colonial Afrikan experiences as well as their experiences during and after their enslavement. No true understanding of women of Afrikan ancestry will occur without the inclusion of their historical context, which predates enslavement by the Europeans. On this point, Thomas's analysis must be extended to reflect an ecological framework rooted in the pre-colonial history and culture of Afrikan people.

A third notable characteristic of Psychology of Black Women is an appreciation of the diversity that exists among women of Afrikan ancestry. In her landmark book *Tomorrow's Tomorrow*, Ladner (1970) sought to debunk the notion of a monolithic Black woman. Diversity is integral to the experience of the Africana woman and is reflected in the variations in our locations, languages, social classes, educations, incomes, sexual orientations, abilities, and religious preferences. Needless to say, as Ladner has adroitly indicated, the commonalities that bind us are our Afrikan history and the experience of oppression; however, these commonalities are filtered through a range of diverse settings. Reckoning with these diverse settings—and examining how they have affected our adaptations to an oppressive environment—is essential to any investigation of the psychological experiences of women of Afrikan descent.

Having theory that is compatible with the lives and experiences of women of Afrikan ancestry is critical to the study of Africana women. Black feminist theories, along with theories that emerge from social, cultural, and cross-cultural domains, offer the potential of explaining and predicting the behavior of women of Afrikan ancestry (Thomas, 2004). Another framework, which emanates from an Africentric perspective that is also appropriate for use in the study of Psychology of Black Women, is Africana womanism (Hudson-Weems, 2008). Both of these theoretical frameworks, and others not mentioned here, are used to explain and predict the behavior of Afrikan American women. Black feminism provided the theoretical framework for holding the dual identities of being a woman and also being of Afrikan ancestry through the development of the concept of "intersectionality." It also furthered the understanding of Black women's multiple oppressions through the concept of the "simultaneity of oppression," which recognized that women of Afrikan ancestry were oppressed due to their race, sex, and class at once. Black feminism's kinship with Africentric philosophy is evident in its use of an interdisciplinary approach and in its application of a diunital or both/and approach, rather than the Eurocentric either/or dichotomy, to its analyses. Similarly, Africana womanism offers an Africentric analysis in which the criteria associated with the Africana womanist are delineated. In conclusion, an Africentric philosophical lens is needed to fully comprehend women of Afrikan ancestry.

Tasks and Scope of Psychology of Black Women

This textbook addresses three foundational issues first articulated by Franz Fanon (Karenga, 1988). The first issue concerns the importance of knowing who we are—the question of identity. The identity of Afrikan women has been sullied by myths and stereotypes. Our history has been ignored and misrepresented. The first task of Psychology of Black Women must be to bring clarity to the issue of who we are as women of Afrikan ancestry. Consequently, it is essential that history be an integral part of the analysis of Black women's psychology. A foundational assumption that I assert is that Psychology of Black Women must reckon with our disconnection with our Afrikan past imposed on us since 1619, and confront our Afrikan legacy to which our DNA continues to bear witness as expressed through a variety of Afrikan retentions. Integrating ancient cultural and historical experiences of Afrikan women into course content is crucial to clarifying the identity of Afrikan American women.

The second key issue concerns the ability of Afrikan American women to be their authentic selves. This capacity has been mitigated by the *Maafa*/Afrikan Holocaust, which disrupted our connection to Afrika—our culture, languages, traditions, values, customs, clans, and families—and which continues to undermine our capacity to be fully authentic. Psychology of Black Women suggests that the Maafa persists in the form of the continued oppression of Afrikan people, and Afrikan women specifically. Furthermore, it assumes that many of the maladies experienced by Afrikan American women are connected to these wounds, which have not been adequately acknowledged nor healed.

Third, the capacity to be self-determining women and to manifest the divine purpose that all human beings possess depends upon our ability to achieve knowledge of self and to display who we are in authentic ways. Psychology of Black Women courses, by providing a safe space where the complex and deep-seated issues that have been passed from one generation to the next can be deconstructed and resolved, can fulfill a liberating purpose with regard to the minds of Afrikan American women. Thus, addressing these critical issues can point women of Afrikan ancestry toward the achievement of their maximum potential, which in Maslow's terms ultimately leads to self-actualization. In Afrikan-centered thought, actualization of self is grounded in one's connection to community.

The scope of this textbook is Afrikan American women, that is, women of Afrikan ancestry, most of whom descend from ancestors who were enslaved and brought to the United States. While there are numerous similarities between the experiences of Afrikan American women and those of other women of Afrikan ancestry, the limitations of space do not allow for an adequate treatment of the diversity that exists across nationalities and ethnicities. Thus, the term "Afrikan American" is used in this book to refer to this select group of women of Afrikan ancestry. This text will not focus on Afro-Caribbean women, though they may find many parallels between their experiences and those of Afrikan American women, particularly if they have resided in the United States for at least two generations. Books that address the unique experiences of Afro-Caribbean women are also very much needed, and through this book I hope to encourage other authors to develop such texts.

Finally, several terms are used in this textbook to refer to Afrikan women. The term "Black" generally is an inclusive term that references women of Afrikan ancestry throughout the Diaspora and in Africa. The terms "Africana women," "women of Afrikan ancestry," "women of Afrikan descent," and "Black" are used interchangeably. My preference in the spelling of "Afrika" with a "k" rather than a "c" represents my choice to honor the majority of Afrikan languages that do not include the letter "c." In those cases where authors have chosen to use the traditional spelling (Africa), it will not be altered.

Delineating the Goals of Psychology of Black Women

Thomas (2004) identifies seven guiding principles for courses that focus on Psychology of Black Women: Knowledge development, contextuality, connectedness of theory and research, collaboration and cross-fertilization, diversity and equity promoting conceptual and methodological frameworks, dissemination, and advocacy of social justice. Building on these principles, there are three critical goals that courses addressing Psychology of Black Women should consider. These goals reflect both the very real reality that over 500 years of oppression have created, and the importance of courses on Black women dealing directly with the lived experiences of women of Afrikan ancestry. Thus, the content and process of these courses must embrace the following indispensable dimensions: reconstructing the vision of who Afrikan women are, based upon placing content in an historical context that predates enslavement; providing a framework for understanding and confronting the wounds that have resulted from enslavement and continued oppression; and addressing the role of advocacy for social justice in facilitating self-determination.

It is essential that Afrikan American women gain familiarity with the historical context from which they emerged. Again, this historical context places them on the stage of humanity as its foremothers. Through explorations of the history of Afrikan people with a targeted focus on the Afrikan woman, Afrikan American women will gain the necessary tools for debunking persistent, debilitating myths and stereotypes of Afrikan womanhood. A significant and growing body of research supports the destructive effects of myths and stereotypes on self-perception and sense of efficacy, on the perceptions of others, and on others' treatment of those they have stereotyped. Another valuable sequela of infusing Afrikan history in the content of Psychology of Black Women courses is that it facilitates challenging Western norms regarding femininity and womanhood. Furthermore, it serves to cleanse the vision of women of Afrikan ancestry, enabling them to begin to appreciate their unique beauty within an Afrikan-centered context. It is also within an historical context that Afrikan women and others can begin to understand and appreciate the wounds that they have experienced and to see how these wounds—unrecognized, unattended, and unhealed—have affected their health and well-being. Not enough can be said for the models of resistance that are buried in the history of Afrikan women. These stories of resistance foster pride, courage, and commitment to a more authentic way of functioning. The principle of knowledge development serves to motivate both the investigation of the history of Afrikan women across the millennia, and the development of theory and research guided by the insights revealed in that investigation. Through this enterprise, an accurate analysis of women of Afrikan ancestry will occur.

A second goal of relevance to courses in Psychology of Black Women involves the clarification of values associated with our identity, and with our ability to be authentic and self-determining people. This second goal is not independent of the first goal, for through our historical study we are introduced to the values of our foremothers, which can be contrasted with the values that we have assumed. How these values have shaped our choices and decisions and affected the quality of our lives in our families and communities, often contributing to the maintenance of the oppressive conditions that we seek to escape, is a much-needed discussion. Learning about ancient value systems such as the Ma'at (truth, justice, harmony, balance, reciprocity, order, propriety) and about contemporary value systems based in Afrikan culture (e.g., Nguzo Saba) can facilitate greater comprehension of the dilemmas that Afrikan American women face in their relationships, families, communities, and society, and can point the way toward viable solutions.

Theories of Black feminism and Africana womanism both stress the importance of self-definition or *Kujichagulia*/Self-Determination. As defined by Maulana Karenga (1988), *Kujichagulia* entails defining oneself, naming oneself, speaking for oneself, and creating for oneself rather than being defined, named, spoken for, or created for by someone else. As expressed in the Afrikan proverb, *Until the lioness (lion) has her (his) own herstorian (historian), tales of the hunt will always glorify the hunter*, Psychology of Black Women restores women of Afrikan ancestry to the position of being subjects of their own experiences. This particular goal underscores the need for continued knowledge development, for theory development, for additional research, and for social justice advocacy, as Thomas (2004) has suggested, so that Afrikan women can tell their own stories. How this is done necessarily involves interdisciplinary collaboration, and the use of a variety of methodologies inclusive of quantitative, experimentally designed studies, qualitatively designed studies, and spiritually based approaches grounded in Afrikan and Afrikan American religious and spiritual traditions.

Standing on the Shoulders

In the spirit of all those women who have sought to address the challenges of being Black and female in a society where both are considered devalued statuses—Jeanne Noble (1978), Joyce Ladner (1970), bell hooks (1981), Phyllis Giddings (1984), Audre Lorde (1984), La Francis Rodgers-Rose (1980), Kimberly Vaz (1995), Gail Wyatt (1997), Beverly Guy-Sheftall (1995), Patricia Hill Collins (2000), Darlene Clark Hine (1994), Charisse Jones and Kumea Shorter-Gooden (2003), and others too numerous to name—this book builds on this sturdy foundation. Integrating Afrikan and Afrikan American history, including theoretical and empirical articles that are based in both quantitative and qualitative research, and drawing on the work of scholars across different disciplines, this text strives to, in the words of Maria Stewart, "awake, arise, no longer sleep nor slumber…" students, scholars, and researchers whose quest is to gain a better understanding of who the Afrikan American woman is. As Melissa Harris-Perry (2011) so cogently states: "It is African American women, surviving at the nexus of racialized, gendered, and classed dis-privilege, who mark the progress of the nation" (p. 17).

References

Brown, A., Goodwin, B. J., Hall, B. A., & Jackson-Lowman, H. (1985). Review of psychology of women textbooks: Focus on the Afro-American woman. *Psychology of Women Quarterly, 9*(1), 29–38. https://doi.org/10.1111/j.1471-6402.1985.tb00858.x

Collins, P. H. (2000). *Black feminist thought: Knowledge, consciousness, and the politics of empowerment* (2nd ed.). Routledge.

Crawford, M. (2017). *Transformations: Women, gender & psychology.* (3rd ed.) McGraw-Hill.

Giddings, P. (1984). *When and where I enter: The impact of Black women on race and sex in America.* William Morrow.

Guy-Sheftall, B. (Ed.). (1995). *Words of fire: An anthology of African-American feminist thought.* The New Press.

Harris-Perry, M. V. (2011). *Sister citizen: Shame, stereotypes, and Black women in America.* Yale University Press.

Hine, D. C. (1994). *Hine sight: Black women and the re-construction of American history.* Carlson.

hooks, b. (1981). *Ain't I a woman: Black women and feminism.* South End.

Hudson-Weems, C. (2008). *Africana womanism & race & gender in the presidential candidacy of Barack Obama.* AuthorHouse.

Jackson-Lowman, H. (1998). Sankofa: A Black mental health imperative. In R. Jones (Ed.), *African American mental health.* Cobb & Henry.

Jones, C., & Shorter-Gooden, K. (2003). *Shifting: The double lives of Black women.* HarperCollins.

Karenga, M. (1988). *The African American holiday of Kwanzaa: A celebration of family, community & culture.* University of Sankore Press.

Ladner, J. (1970). *Tomorrow's tomorrow.* Doubleday.

Lips, H. M. (2017). *A new psychology of women: Gender, culture, and ethnicity* (4th ed.). McGraw-Hill.

Liss, M., Richmond, K., & Erchull, M. J. (2019). *Psychology of women and gender.* W. W. Norton & Company, Inc.

Lorde, A. (1984). *Sister outsider: Essays and speeches.* Crossing Press.

Noble, J. (1978). *Beautiful, also, are the souls of my Black sisters: A history of the Black woman in America.* Prentice-Hall.

Reid, P. T. (1993). Poor women in psychological research: Shut up and shut out. *Psychology of Women Quarterly, 17,* 133–150.

Reid, P. T., & Kelly, E. (1994). Research on women of color: From ignorance to awareness. *Psychology of Women Quarterly, 18*(4), 477–486. https://doi.org/10.1111/j.1471-6402.1994.tb01044.x

Rodgers-Rose, L. (Ed.). (1980). *The Black woman.* Sage.

Thomas, V. G. (2004). The psychology of Black women: Studying women's lives in context. *The Journal of Black Psychology, 30*(3), 286–306.

Vaz, K. (Ed.). (1995). *Black women in America.* Sage.

Wyatt, G. E. (1997). *Stolen women: Reclaiming our sexuality, taking back our lives.* John Wiley & Sons.

Reflection Activity: Significant Afrikan American Women and Men

How many of the following women and men are you familiar with? Place an "X" by all those with whom you are familiar.

Mary McLeod Bethune	Paul Robeson
Harriet Tubman	Nat Turner
Sojourner Truth	Frederick Douglass
Ida B. Wells-Barnett	Hubert Henry Harrison
Anna Julia Cooper	W. E. B. Du Bois
Maria Stewart	David Walker
Fannie Lou Hamer	Rev. Ralph Abernathy
Ella Baker	James Meredith
Assata Shakur	Stokely Carmichael/Kwame Ture
Septima Clark	Harry T. Moore
Shirley Chisholm	Rev. Jesse Jackson
Amy Jacques Garvey	Marcus Garvey
Rebecca Cox Jackson	Richard Allen
Mary Church Terrell	Booker T. Washington
Angela Davis	Huey Newton
Zora Neale Hurston	Langston Hughes
Barbara Jordan	Malcolm X
Dorothy Height	Elijah Muhammad

Are there significant differences in your knowledge of men vs. women? If so, why do you think this is the case?

Unit I. Defining Who We Are at the Crossroads of Race, Gender, Class, and Culture

Introduction: A Culturally Syntonic Model of Healthy Identity for Afrikan American Women

Huberta Jackson-Lowman

> Each is under the most sacred obligation not to squander the material committed to him, not to sap his strength in folly and vice, and to see at the least that he (she) delivers a product worthy the labor and cost which have been expended on him (her).
>
> —Anna Julia Cooper

What is the appropriate context for examining the psychology of Afrikan American women? Is it the ghettoes in which thousands of Afrikan American women are trapped? Is it the boardrooms that a growing number of Afrikan American women occupy? Is it the plantations to which millions of us were relegated during the period of enslavement? Though each of these settings is instructive and can contribute, to some extent, to our understanding of the psychological experiences of Afrikan American women, none is sufficient. Unless we hone our lenses to include the ancient, precolonial Afrikan experiences from which Afrikan women emerged, the use of these oppressogenic settings will provide a distorted picture of Afrikan American women. In this chapter, I discuss the features of a model that examines Afrikan American women within an Afrikan-centered context.

In the absence of appropriate models for examining the lives of women of Afrikan ancestry, the color and character of the psychological experiences of Afrikan American women cannot be adequately understood. Thus, in order to fully appreciate women of Afrikan ancestry, we must construct models that use a lens with the power to shatter the narrow and constricting boundaries of the Western worldview paradigm. Models that reflect the culture, philosophy, history, and social–psychological needs of Afrikan American women are required for this task. In far too many instances, Afrikan American women have been defined by others; at best, this results in characterizations of Afrikan women that bear little resemblance or relevance to the lived experiences of women of Afrikan ancestry, and at worst, it results in characterizations that are actually harmful to and destructive of our physical and psychological well-being. The purpose of this chapter is to describe the dimensions of a culturally syntonic model of healthy identity for Afrikan American women. It suggests that the use of culturally appropriate models for examining the lives of women of Afrikan ancestry will generate valid and useful knowledge that will ultimately enhance the lives of Afrikan American women.

Characteristics of Culturally Syntonic Models

To be "culturally syntonic" is to exhibit congruence with the values, norms, beliefs, traditions, customs, and history of a particular group of people. According to Diop (1991), the cultural identity of an individual cannot be separated from the identity of their group. Further, he states that the identity of a group consists of an historical factor, a linguistic factor, and a psychological factor. Since time immemorial, oppressogenic systems such as colonization and enslavement have used the destruction of the historical conscience of the targeted group (Diop, 1991). The term that has been coined to delineate these ongoing historical traumas inflicted on Afrikan people is the *Maafa* (Ani, 1980). It is defined as "great disaster" and describes the procession of events that have ensued since the Eurasian cultural encroachment of Afrika (Kambon, 2012). Once a group of people has been conquered, one of the first efforts of the conquerors is to outlaw the indigenous or native language and require that the conquered people conduct their transactions in the language of the oppressor. It is through language that we retain our cultural memory; therefore, by disrupting the continuity facilitated by a shared language, the oppressogenic process can be expedited. The third factor identified by Diop (1991)—the psychological factor—consists of those aspects of the group's personality recognizable by everyone (e.g., being warriors, being traders, etc.). Under conditions of oppression, the cultural identity of the targeted group is grossly misrepresented and redefined, and myths and stereotypic images that denigrate the group are promulgated (Collins, 2000; Hine & Thompson, 1998).

Just as the weather, the quality of the soil, and other environmental conditions provide the ecological setting that enables certain plants, flowers, trees, birds, and animals to thrive, so too do various ethnic groups construct cultures that reflect their history, their values, and the beliefs that allow their members to develop. Amos N. Wilson (1998) defines culture as a design for living supported by ideas and values that guide its members, provide standards, and construct definitions, meanings, and purposes. Models that are culturally syntonic center culture and are grounded in the worldview of the referenced group—values, norms, beliefs, traditions, philosophy, and history. Culturally syntonic models are tied to the deep structural concepts that inform how reality is defined by the group and are not just superficially linked to the external aspects of culture.

Afrikans across the continent demonstrate certain consistencies in their view of the world. As noted by many scholars (Akbar, 1998; Ani, 1994; Grills, 2004; Kambon, 1998; Nobles, 2006), there is recognition of a sense of oneness/consubstantiation reflected in the appreciation of the interconnectedness of all life; emphasis on the collective; and acknowledgment of the sacredness of life and the spiritual essence of beingness. Humanity and Nature are seen as intricately interwoven; neither is superior or inferior. The discipline of physics confirms what ancient Afrikans knew—that nothing operates in isolation and everything is connected to something bigger (Bejan, 2012). From the perspective of Afrikan people, learning to live in harmony and balance with Nature rather than controlling or exploiting Nature is the mandate. Functioning in an environment in which all things are perceived to be connected and sacred—and, therefore, in which action in one area affects another—results in the structuring of societies where the group rather than the individual is central, and where Spirit is seen as the essence of all living things. The evidence of these values and this way of seeing the world is reflected in the multitude of Afrikan proverbs that speak to these themes (see Afrikan Proverbs About Values, later in this chapter). Thus, a culturally syntonic approach to understanding the identity of women of Afrikan ancestry must be grounded in the Afrikan worldview, which prioritizes spirituality in contrast to materialism; recognizes interconnectedness and interdependence in contrast to separateness and extreme independence; and honors collectiveness, cooperation, and harmony with the natural environment. The Maafa (Ani, 1980) was a major and catastrophic disruption that contributed to the shattering of our Afrikan lens and its replacement with, or at least contamination by, a Western Eurocentric worldview that denies the humanity of Afrikan people. The sense of who we are—our identity, the capacity to be our authentic selves, and the capacity to fulfill our purpose—have been deeply affected by the lingering and ongoing effects of the Maafa. A major project for Afrikan American women is, therefore, our healing, which is facilitated by the recovery of our true identities.

Afrikan Proverbs About Identity

What messages do these proverbs convey about the significance of one's identity?

> *An egg should not wrestle with a rock. (Wolof)*

> *What was hatched a hen must not try to be a rooster. (Grenada, Tobago)*

> *The strength of a fish is in the water. (Morocco)*

> *A log may stay in water for ten years but it will never become a crocodile. (Cameroon)*

> *A cat may go to the monastery but it will never become a monk.*

The Quest for an Authentic Identity

Franz Fanon (cited in Karenga, 1988) delineated three identity-related questions that people victimized by oppression must confront in their quest for liberation. The first question—Who am I? (Who are we?)—emphasizes the fundamental importance of knowing who we are. The second question—Am I really who I think I am? (Are we really who we think we are?)—focuses on the consideration of our authenticity, that is, our capacity to be who we are fully, genuinely, without "distortion, mutation, or imitation" (Grills, 2004). The third question—Am I all I ought to be? (Are we all we ought to be?)—challenges us to consider our purpose in life. Fela Sowande (n.d.), Yoruba ethnomusicologist, states that "the search for roots is the search for identity." He elaborates, suggesting that the quest for a meaningful life compels addressing the questions: "Who am I? Where am I? Why am I here? How can I derive maximum benefit from the fact that I AM NOW HERE?" Akbar (1998) asserts the primacy of the questions "Who am I?" and "What am I?" as fundamental to manifesting our true human nature. For Fanon, Sowande, Akbar, and many ancient philosophers, all knowledge begins with self-knowledge. In an oppressogenic environment, self-knowledge is essential in order for oppressed people to challenge, resist, and defy the images and messages projected by the oppressor. For Afrikan American women, our knowledge of self must not be locked in a 500-year room defined by our enslavement; instead, it must embrace the totality of our existence on this planet.

Table: Identity and Oppression

Critical Issues	Key Questions
Identity	Who am I?/Who are we? Whose am I?/Whose are we? Where am I?/Where are we?
Authenticity	Am I really who I think I am?/Are we really who we think we are? How have racism, classism, sexism, patriarchy, etc. affected my ability to be my true self?
Purpose	Am I all I ought to be?/Are we all we ought to be? Why am I here?/Why are we here?

An Afrikan-Centered Model of Identity

The Afrikan view of identity is extended (Nobles, 2006). Ogbonnaya (1994) provides a model in which he conceptualizes the extended self as composed of a community of selves that are connected to the past, present, and future; to the natural world; and to both the physical and metaphysical aspects of being. Grounded in the Afrikan worldview, a sense of oneness—interconnectedness, or what Nobles (2006) refers to as consubstantiation—is the hallmark of Afrikan identity. The sense of connectedness is expressed at the backward, lateral, forward (Jackson-Lowman, 1998; Taylor, 1994), and transcendental (Jackson-Lowman, 2010) levels.

In the "community of selves" model (Ogbonnaya, 1994), self is delineated as inclusive of the ancestral self, contemporary self, mischievous self, totem self, emergent self, not-yet self, and divine self. When Ogbonnaya's model is linked with the Bantu-Kongo concept of self, six of the seven aspects of identity described by Ogbonnaya may be categorized as the Been Self, the Being Self, and the Will-be Self (Nunley, 2020), encased by the Divine Self that Ogbonnaya (1994) identifies (see Figure 1.0.1).

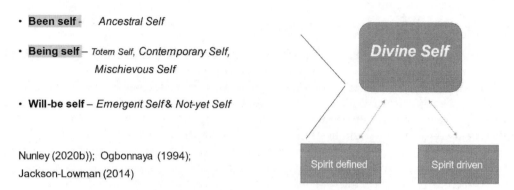

- **Been self** - *Ancestral Self*

- **Being self** – *Totem Self, Contemporary Self, Mischievous Self*

- **Will-be self** – *Emergent Self & Not-yet Self*

Nunley (2020b)); Ogbonnaya (1994); Jackson-Lowman (2014)

Figure 1.0.1. Extended Self/Community of Selves

The Been Self

However long the stream, it never forgets its source. (Yoruba Proverb)

The *Been Self*, or *ancestral self* as described by Ogbonnaya (1994), is the culmination of over 12 previous generations or 4,094 ancestors manifested in our current lived existence (Community Healing Network, n.d.). We are the continuation of a lineage that includes all of these genetically related ancestors. *Backward connectedness* represents the idea that we stand on the shoulders of our ancestors, both genetic and cultural. Symbolically, one of the representations of backward connectedness is the Akan symbol of a bird with its neck turned backwards—*Sankofa*—which beckons us to go back and retrieve that which we have lost (see Figures 2 and 3). Recent developments in the field of biogenetics have enabled us to trace our lineage through our DNA, thereby confirming this flow. Many Afrikan Americans have taken advantage of this opportunity, tracing their lineage to the Afrikan ethnic groups from which their families were separated. It is important to understand that what we inherit is not merely the physical attributes of our ancestors but also their cultural, socio-emotional, and behavioral legacies that have been transmitted from one generation to the next.

Evidence of the *ancestral self* is apparent in the latest research in the field of epigenetics (Kellermann, 2001), which documents the transgenerational transmission of trauma. At the genetic level, different genes may be turned on or off, thereby contributing to a variety of dysfunctions that are expressed in forthcoming generations who were not exposed to the original trauma. For example, amongst people of the Caribbean, Stromberg (2013) has noted an indelible record of their history, stretching back to the arrival of the Europeans, the decimation of the indigenous populations, and the Transatlantic trade of enslaved Afrikans. The genealogical exploration of our ancestry may facilitate healing and resolution of generational traumas that impact our lives. Retrieval of ancestral memories and knowledge through backward connectedness are essential components of a healthy, well-functioning sense of self. In traditional Afrikan societies, maintaining connections with one's ancestors was an integral part of life that occurred through naming practices, rituals and ceremonies, and a host of honored traditions. The critical nature of backward connectedness is expressed in a variety of Afrikan proverbs.

Cut your chains and you are free; cut your roots and you die.

A split tree still grows.

A tree cannot stand without roots.

No matter how high the house is built it has to stand on something.

Figure 1.0.2. Image of Sankofa Bird

Figure 1.0.3. Akan Adinkra Symbol of Sankofa

Each of these proverbs appreciates the importance of a being or an object paying homage to that which precedes its manifestation, whether it is seen or unseen. Each implies that one's present existence is sustained by the connection to this source of support. If we use these proverbs as metaphors to assist us in understanding the critical nature of backward connectedness, it becomes apparent that the reason why the stream identified in the proverb (*However long the stream, it never forgets its source*) continues to flow is that it retains its connection to its source, which sustains it. Similarly, a house is sturdy and secure in part because of the foundation on which it is built; without that foundation, its stability and survival are endangered. These proverbs suggest that the past serves as our foundation and, therefore, that connection to the past is an essential source of sustenance. The essentiality of ancestral veneration represents the fullest expression of this sense of connectedness displayed by Afrikan people. Thus, maintaining the linkage to the past is highly functional because our very survival depends upon it. From an Afrikan-centered perspective, what is true in Nature is also true for humanity since Nature and humanity are not separate, nor is humanity superior to Nature. Consequently, for Afrikan American women to fully know themselves, we must explore our past biogenetically and culturally and celebrate, honor, and nurture these aspects of who we are through ancestral veneration rituals and through study of the ancient history and culture that are our foundation. All groups of people pay homage to their ancestors through the holidays they celebrate, the monuments they construct, the names they give their children, and the places they occupy. Our ability to be whole and healthy is, in part, dependent upon the viability of our connection with our ancestors. As Sowande (n.d.) states:

> Only when a seed begins to sprout its roots does it begin to live. It must first have embraced Mother Earth before it can hope to catch a glimpse of the Sky. Only through those roots can it take what it needs from Mother Nature in order to grow and mature. Only then can it hope to realize its potentialities. The more deeply and powerfully entrenched its roots are in the soil native to it, the more able it is to weather all storms … . (p. 14)

Sowande (n.d.) suggests that augmented strength, endurance, and resistance are the by-products of backward connectedness. Achieving backward connectedness, however, requires clarification of what "the past" means for Afrikan American women; it requires debunking the myth that our existence began with our enslavement and replacing it with the acknowledgment of our primordial presence on the planet. As a part of this process, definitions of our ancestors as "slaves" must be discarded, for slaves have no history or culture, and such definitions promote self-objectification.

For women of Afrikan ancestry the past extends back to the beginning of humanity. Archaeological evidence indicates that the origins of modern man/woman occurred in Afrika 9–12 million years ago (King, 1990). In 1974, paleontologists identified fossil remains in Afrika of a woman they called "Lucy" who was estimated to be 3.8 million years old (Cookson, n.d.), providing further confirmation that an Afrikan woman was the mother of humanity, and therefore was the source of human existence. In light of the fact that humanity emerged from an ancient Afrikan woman, Afrikan American women are "first-degree relatives" of the mother of humanity. The question that surfaces is: As daughters of the mother of humanity, how did we come to be among the most maligned people on the planet? Furthermore, what are the implications for this reversal in affairs? Exploring our personal past as well as our cultural past is a crucial component of the task of gaining insight into who we are as women of Afrikan ancestry and claiming our appropriate place on the stage of humanity.

The Being Self

The cattle are as good as the pasture in which they graze. (Afrikan Proverb)

Using Ogbonnaya's (1994) model of identity, the Being self comprises the contemporary self, the mischievous self, and the totem self. The contemporary self may be described as the physical self which thrives through *lateral connectedness,* the bonds and relationships that we have with our family, community, society, and the natural environment. Lateral connectedness refers to our relationships with the ecological settings that Bronfenbrenner (as cited in Dalton et al., 2007) describes as consisting of the microsystem, mesosystem, exosystem, and macrosystem. The importance of these relationships is recognized in Western psychology and viewed as essential to the healthy development of the person (Dalton et al., 2007). Experiences of being protected, nurtured, and supported by family, friends, community, and society—in essence, of being connected to others—are viewed as necessary elements in the development of a secure sense of self (Grills, 2004); however, from an Afrikan perspective, lateral connectedness also includes our relationship with the natural world.

The *contemporary self* may be characterized as who we are from birth to death and all of the influences that contribute to shaping our identity. The underside of the contemporary self, the *mischievous self,* represents those aspects of self that may be hidden from public view—our weaknesses, or our Achilles' heel, which often contribute to missteps and difficulties in our lives. The mischievous self presents an opportunity for personal growth and transformation to occur, if it is acknowledged and integrated into one's personality. Knowledge of the mischievous self contributes to fully knowing who we are, not just as the ideal image that we prefer to project, but as persons who recognize the value of self-correction and strive to be "mo better" (Nobles, 1993).

The mischievous self reveals those attitudes, attributes, and behaviors that are dissonant with who we are, in order to foster harmony, balance, and alignment with our Divine self. For Afrikan American women— living in an oppressogenic environment and frequently being bereft of self-knowledge—adapting to the pressures of a racist, sexist, and classist society may appear to be the only viable option for survival. By exposing unhealthy adaptations to oppression (e.g., overeating, substance use), the mischievous self, when acknowledged, can enable us to confront harmful attitudes and behaviors and can facilitate engagement in a corrective and healing process. As Jiddu Krishnamurti insightfully states: *It is no measure of health to be well adjusted to a profoundly sick society.* Thus, it becomes essential that we investigate the extent to which we have adapted to unhealthy conditions—conditions that are unnatural and debilitating to our physical, psychological, social, and spiritual well-being. Some questions that we may pose as we examine the role that the mischievous self plays in our lives include: To what extent have we internalized the definitions, myths, and stereotypes of Black womanhood promulgated by those in positions of power and authority? What is the relationship between living under oppressive conditions and the high rates of intimate-partner violence, HIV/AIDS, infant mortality, breast cancer mortality, and numerous other afflictions plaguing Afrikan American women? How has our history of oppression affected our ability to have healthy connections with other women of Afrikan ancestry, with men of Afrikan ancestry, with our families, and with others?

Further understanding of the mischievous self may be garnered from the work of Melissa Harris-Perry (2011). Using the analogy of the crooked room from field-dependent studies, Harris-Perry (2011) describes the effects of Afrikan American women's efforts to confront *engendered racial myths and stereotypes* (Jackson-Lowman, 2007) that are designed to simultaneously degrade our race and gender, stating: "Bombarded with warped images of their humanity, some Black women tilt and bend themselves to fit the distortion" (p. 29). The capacity of Afrikan American women to enjoy fulfilling relationships with family, community, and society is impaired by the endemic presence of engendered racial myths and stereotypes that viciously distort who we are, resulting in *misrecognition.* In order to gain recognition, or in response to misrecognition, some Afrikan American women may engage in behaviors that do not represent who we are. According to Harris-Perry (2011), recognition is an unequivocal component of democratic societies, and to be democratic, societies must provide equal opportunities for recognition. Misrecognition occurs when a group is subjected to stereotypes and stigma that cloud clear vision of the group and prevent the stigmatized group from being acknowledged. By examining the features of Afrikan American women's environments, we can assess the extent to which Afrikan American women are recognized, and therefore protected, nurtured, and supported in knowing who they are and being who they are authentically. The mischievous self is instrumental in facilitating Afrikan American women's quests to be their authentic selves.

The *totem self* aspect of the Being Self reflects the interdependent relationship that exists between human beings and the natural world, and with each other (Jackson-Lowman, 2020). Human life cannot be sustained without the support of the natural environment, and for Afrikan people, gratitude and appreciation of that which sustains you is a cultural mandate. Mbiti's statement, "*I am because we are; since we are therefore I am*" (Mangena, 2016), is an acknowledgement of the inextricable connection that we have with each other and of our collective responsibility for members of the same clan or ethnic group. Many traditional Afrikan societies identified totems (plants or animals), whose qualities they admired (courage, perseverance, etc.) and strived to express, as symbols for their ethnic groups. Members of the group wore the symbol of the totem on clothing or in jewelry, which facilitated recognition when they traveled to places where they were not personally known and often resulted in their being welcomed and treated with great respect. Contemporary examples of totems can be observed in the symbols representing sororities—for example, the ivy is associated with Alpha Kappa Alpha sorority and the elephant identifies Delta Sigma Theta. Totems serve to unify us with members of our group and to remind us of our collective responsibility to each other and to our environment. As a result of the Maafa, the connection that Afrikan American women had with their ancestral ethnic groups has been disrupted and lost for the most part; however, the strong commitment that Afrikan American women display to their families and Afrikan people is highly visible in their communities. A growing body of research from various disciplines indicates that at the most fundamental levels, human beings are structured: to seek out and maintain connections with their families, their clans, and those with whom they share similarities; to defend them; and even to make sacrifices on their behalf (E. O. Wilson, 2012). It is through lateral connectedness that the linkages between the contemporary, mischievous, and totem selves occur and are brought into harmony and balance with each other, in concert with the connection to the ancestral self that is facilitated by backward connectedness.

The Will-Be Self

If you know the beginning well, the end will not trouble you. (Afrikan Proverb)

The *will-be self* is exemplified by Ogbonnaya's (1994) emergent and not-yet selves. The *emergent self* is the notion that we are constantly changing, and that who we are from moment to moment reflects this evolutionary process. The Yoruba proverb—*When evening comes, a different person enters the home than left in the morning*—is illustrative of this dynamic process (Crespi, n.d.). The *not-yet self* informs us that many possibilities and potentialities are within us; however, oftentimes we lack awareness of these latent capabilities. It is conceivable that we can be something tomorrow (metaphorically) that we have no visible evidence of today. In nature this transformational process may be observed in the evolution of the caterpillar into a butterfly. Examples of these changes may also be seen in the lives of Isabella Baumfree, who became Sojourner Truth in her forties, and Detroit Red, who through the guidance of the Black Muslims evolved from being a hardened criminal to being Malcolm X and later to being El Hajj Malik El-Shabazz, one of the most profound, inspirational, and spiritual leaders that the Afrikan American community has known. The not-yet self also serves as a link to future generations. Understanding our roles as co-creators of the world that prospective generations will inhabit emerges from an appreciation of *forward connectedness*. Certainly, enslaved Afrikans who struggled relentlessly for liberation from chattel slavery appreciated the importance of forward connectedness and sought emancipation not just for themselves but for the generations that would follow them. Forward connectedness reminds us of the role we play in shaping the futures that we and our progeny will experience. In the United States and throughout the world, the absence of lateral and forward connectedness has resulted in the destructive treatment of the planet's lakes, rivers, oceans, forests, air, animal life, and ocean life. When Afrikan women assimilate the Western/Eurocentric worldview and its values, there is a concomitant diminishment in our respect for Nature and a reduced awareness of our roles as co-creators of the world in which we live. Under these conditions, Self-Determination/*Kujichagulia*—the capacity to name ourselves, define ourselves, speak for ourselves, and create for ourselves (Karenga, 1988)—becomes deficient. Any study of the history of women of Afrikan ancestry in the United States as well as in Afrika and throughout the Diaspora reveals that Afrikan women understood the power of self-definition and self-determination, and that they exercised these qualities in their resistance to oppression, their activism, and their institution-building (Collins, 2000; Hine & Thompson, 1998; Schwarz-Bart, 2001). Forward connectedness is therefore an integral aspect of the identity of women of Afrikan ancestry; accompanied by backward and lateral connectedness, it is an essential component of health and wholeness.

The Divine Self

All human beings are children of God; no one is a child of the earth. (Afrikan Proverb)

Afrikan spiritual traditions and the various myths that explain the creation process suggest that we emerge from the spiritual realm and will return to the spiritual realm (Kambon, 2012). These issues, as Grills (2004) indicates, address the question of whose we are. Ogbonnaya (1994) identifies this aspect as the *Divine self*. The identification of the Divine self as the essence of who we are affirms our divinity and sacred nature (Akbar, 2003). In truth, we are "Spirit beings" rather than human beings (Nobles, 2006). As some would say, "We are all children of God." Extending this logic, if we are God's children, then we are also gods and goddesses. Maintaining and nurturing our connection to Spirit, or *transcendental connectedness*, becomes an essential component of a healthy and well-balanced sense of self for Afrikan American women. Without this connection, our mental and physical health is jeopardized.

Inherent in the notion of the Divine self is divine purpose, the unique contribution that we have each agreed to make to the world. Assuming a teleological universe, the Yoruba of southwestern Nigeria believe that before we are born we enter into an agreement with the Divine about the purpose of our life on Earth (Crespi, n.d.). During the birth process, we forget this agreement; thus, many Afrikan societies engage in divination and other rituals, such as naming ceremonies, to facilitate remembering the agreement that we made. Divine self suggests that the changes we undergo are intelligent and purposeful and lead to a specific, agreed-upon outcome, when we live in harmony and balance with our Divine self. Recognizing this aspect of who we are has important implications for how Afrikan American women perceive ourselves and interact with others, and for what we do, create, and build. Examples of disconnection in this area may be observed in the overemphasis on the physical and material aspects of being and in the internalization of engendered myths and stereotypes of Afrikan womanhood that mischaracterize us as mammies, Jezebels, Sapphires, and welfare queens. On the other hand, an overemphasis on transcendental connectedness, paired with dismissal of other aspects of self, also leads to imbalance and dis-ease.

Intersectionality and Black Female Identity

Black feminists have been very vocal and active in declaring the need for intersectional analysis of Black women's experiences (Cole & Guy-Sheftall, 2003; Collins, 2000; Crenshaw, 1991; hooks, 1981). *Intersectionality*, originally conceptualized by Kimberlé Crenshaw (1991), is defined as the recognition of the simultaneity of race and gender in the lives of Black women (Settles et al., 2006). It spotlights the multiplicative, debilitating effects of oppression on those having more than one marginalized identity. In the words of Crenshaw, "Intersectionality is about capturing dynamics and converging patterns of advantage and disadvantage" (Moffitt, 2021). Theories of intersectionality state that both race and gender significantly predict psychological outcomes for Black women. Settles et al. (2006) found that the Black women in their study assigned equal importance to their race and their gender, according greater importance to their identity as "Black women." Differential values were attached to identity as "Black" versus identity as a "woman." When one's "woman" identity interfered with their "Black" identity, this was related to lower self-esteem and higher levels of depression; however, the same was not true when one's "Black" identity interfered with their "woman" identity. Those women who acknowledged their identities as "Black women" were healthier than those who gave primacy to their identities as "women." While intersectional analysis has expanded our understanding of Black female identity, from the perspective of a culturally syntonic model of Black female identity, it is only one essential element of a healthy identity for Black women. Intersectionality is an acknowledgment of lateral connectedness and highlights the importance of all facets of the contemporary self—racial/ethnic, gender, class, and other identities—but the extended identity of women of Afrikan ancestry, the community of selves that exists within them, is not recognized.

Afrikan Proverbs About Values

Identify the values and principles that are reflected in these proverbs.

All wisdom comes from God.

One always learns from someone else.

When a fowl drinks water, it first takes it and shows it to the Supreme Being.

Virtue is better than wealth.

A community without elders does not prosper.

Knowledge is better than riches.

When a yam does not grow well, do not blame the yam; it is because of the soil.

Healthy Identity

This discussion raises issues critical to the psychological, physical, and spiritual health and wellness of Afrikan American women from an Africentric perspective. Although the discipline of psychology has placed greater emphasis on dis-ease and psychological disorder than it has on health, I discuss two approaches to psychological health in Afrikan Americans here, as offered by Ramseur (2004) and Kambon (1998, 2012).

Ramseur (2004) critiques the efficacy of "universal" models of psychological health for Afrikan Americans. His critique of dominant models of psychological health (Freud, Maslow, Jahoda, Erickson) focuses on the failure of these models to consider the unique sociocultural context of Afrikan Americans, the diversity of responses amongst Afrikan Americans to sociocultural contexts, and the pathology bias that pervades these models. He identifies six crucial issues for the psychological health of Afrikan American adults:

> (1) Maintaining a globally healthy self-conception; (2) maintaining a positive group identity (African American) and community connection; (3) maintaining an accurate perception of the social environment—including its racism; (4) effectively adapting to the social environment confronting an African American individual—coping with its stressors and adapting to both African American and White cultures; (5) developing and maintaining emotional intimacy with others; and (6) maintaining a sense of competence and the ability to work productively. (Ramseur, 2004, p. 448)

Kambon's (1998, 2012) seminal work on Afrikan personality provides an in-depth conceptualization of a healthy, well-functioning personality for Afrikan Americans. Rooted in the Afrikan worldview, Kambon delineates the traits of Afrikan personality, which consists of "beliefs, attitudes, and behaviors which naturally reflect, project, and reinforce African Spirituality" (p. 316). Two major constructs provide the foundation of Kambon's personality theory: (1) ASEO—African Self-Extension Orientation; and (2) ASC—African Self-Consciousness. ASEO connotes Afrikan Spirituality and reflects the striving for collective-communal relatedness, as expressed in a sense of wholeness and unity. ASC is characterized by four dimensions: (1) awareness of one's collective African identity; (2) prioritization of Afrikan survival, liberation, and positive development; (3) prioritization of self-knowledge as expressed through Africentric values, customs, and institutions; and (4) resistance and defense against anti-Afrikan/Black forces and threats. Health is expressed through the "continual striving for authentic African affirmation and self-determination" (p. 317). Harmony and balance—health—occur when ASEO and ASC operate as a "unified, undifferentiated system" (Kambon, 2012, p. 317).

Utilizing the proposed culturally syntonic model, what Ramseur (2004) identifies as healthy self-conception involves awareness of our collective Afrikan identity. Each aspect of our identity (ancestral, totem, etc.) requires acknowledgement and nurturance. Maintaining a globally healthy self-conception necessitates connectedness at the four levels of connectedness—backward, lateral, forward, and transcendental. In order for Afrikan American women to manifest our collective extended Afrikan identity, we must know who we are (backward connectedness); we must have the support of family and community to authentically display our true identities (lateral connectedness); we must make choices that facilitate our development and foster our ability to thrive (forward connectedness); and we must recognize the divinity within us and the unique destiny and purpose bestowed on us (transcendental connectedness).

The importance of manifesting a positive group identity is reflected in our totem self, which represents the connection to our clan/ethnic group, in collaboration with our ancestral and contemporary selves. It is through these connections at the backward and lateral levels that the history of who we are is revealed and that values, beliefs, traditions, and norms are transmitted. Kambon's (2012) third ASC factor emphasizes the prioritization of activities that affirm self-knowledge, as expressed in our values, customs, and institutions. Self-knowledge accrues through backward connectedness, which is displayed in our relationships with elders, and through ancestor veneration and the study of our history. It is nourished and sustained through lateral connectedness with family and community, and with the institutions created therein.

Additionally, the accurate perception of our environment also requires knowledge of our history, and connection to the family, community, and institutions that reflect the perspectives, values, and needs of Afrikan people; this is a combination of backward and lateral connectedness. Integral to this process is the recognition of those anti-Afrikan forces—actions, activities, practices, policies, laws, etc.—that maintain our oppression. By prioritizing Afrikan survival and liberation, we counter and neutralize anti-Afrikan forces; however, it is through the operation of backward, lateral, forward, and transcendental connectedness that we learn to operate in our best interests, garner the material/physical and spiritual/metaphysical support to do so, and recognize the significance of our actions for future generations. Our capacity to resist and defend ourselves against anti-Afrikan forces is facilitated by the ancestral self, which through backward connectedness provides us with a sense of who we really are, arms us with historical self-knowledge, and reminds us of our ability to successfully defy our oppressors (Akbar, 1998). The harmonious and balanced functioning of our community of selves enables us to minimize the effects of anti-Afrikan forces on us.

Ramseur (2004) suggests that health for Afrikan Americans also involves the capacity to adapt to and cope effectively with stressors, to exhibit emotional intimacy with others, and to display a sense of competence and work productivity. In Kambon's (2012) system, these qualities are expressed through an Afrikan lens that is aligned with the values, beliefs, customs, and needs of Afrikan people. The four aspects of connectedness offer a sense of directionality regarding how we cope, what we adapt to versus what we reject, the quality of our relationships, and what exemplifies competence and productivity.

In conclusion, drawing from our Afrikan past, it is possible to conceptualize a healthy identity for Afrikan American women. Four dimensions of connectedness must be engaged, as expressed through what Ogbonnaya (1994) calls the ancestral self, contemporary self, mischievous self, totem self, emergent self, not-yet self, and Divine self. Kambon (2012) articulates a Pan-Afrikan mission embedded in spiritness that provides directional context in the lives of Afrikan American women. The proposed culturally syntonic model suggests that the health of Afrikan American women is contingent upon engaging each dimension of who we are through values, relationships, activities, processes, rituals, and institutions that, together, regularly nurture each facet of our identity. The process of balancing and harmonizing each aspect of self is continuous and contiguous, and is one for which one level of connectedness has implications for other aspects of connectedness. In other words, interconnectedness is a fundamental characteristic of healthy functioning for Afrikan American women.

Journaling Activity

Using different adjectives and nouns as well as phrases, answer the question: Who am I?

After you have answered this question, review your responses. Identify aspects of the extended self that are represented in your responses. To what extent do they reflect a sense of backward connectedness, lateral connectedness, forward connectedness, and transcendental connectedness?

References

Akbar, N. (1998). *Know thy self.* Mind Productions & Associates.

Akbar, N. (2003). African roots of Black personality. In *Akbar papers in African psychology.* Mind Productions and Associates.

Ani, M. (aka Dona Marimba Richards). (1980). *Let the circle be unbroken: The implications of African spirituality in the diaspora.* The Red Sea Press.

Ani, M. (1994). *Yurugu: An African-centered critique of European cultural thought and behavior.* African World Press, Inc.

Bejan, A. (2012, March 23). *The case for a constructal law of design in nature* [Video]. YouTube. https://youtu.be/s9eB_i-hK94

Cole, J. B., & Guy-Sheftall, B. (2003). *Gender talk: The struggle for women's equality in African American communities*. The Ballantine Publishing Group.

Collins, P. H. (2000). *Black feminist thought: Knowledge, consciousness, and the politics of empowerment* (2nd ed.). Routledge.

Community Healing Network. (n.d.). Ancestral mathematics.

Cookson, C. (n.d.). Discovery of earliest *Homo sapien* skulls backs 'Out of Africa' theory. Retrieved February 29, 2012 from www.bradshawfoundation.com

Crenshaw, K. (1991). Mapping the margins: Intersectionality, identity politics, and violence against women of color. *Stanford Law Review*, *43*(6), 1241–1299. https://doi.org/10.2307/1229039

Crespi, J. A. J. (n.d.). The psychology and metaphysics of Ifa [Unpublished manuscript]. (Oluo Ifajoye Ojoawo, Trans.).

Dalton, J. H., Elias, M. J., & Wandersman, A. (2007). *Community psychology: Linking individuals and communities* (2nd ed.). Thomson Higher Education.

Diop, C. A. (1991). *Civilization or barbarism: An authentic anthropology.* Lawrence Hill Books.

Grills, C. T. (2004). African psychology. In R. L. Jones (Ed.), *Black psychology* (4th ed.). Cobb and Henry.

Harris-Perry, M. V. (2011). *Sister citizen: Shame, stereotypes, and Black women in America.* Yale University Press.

Hine, D. C., & Thompson, K. (1998). *A shining thread of hope: The history of Black women in America.* Broadway Books.

hooks, b. (1981). *Ain't I a woman: Black women and feminism.* South End.

Jackson-Lowman, H. (1998). Sankofa: A Black mental health imperative. In R. Jones (Ed.), *African American mental health.* Cobb & Henry.

Jackson-Lowman, H. (2007, August). *Preliminary research on engendered racial stereotypes: Focus on Afrikan American women* [Conference presentation]. Association of Black Psychologists Convention, Houston, TX.

Jackson-Lowman, H. (2010, January). *Reclaiming our traditional greatness: Identity, authenticity, and purpose and Afrikan American womanhood* [Conference presentation]. General Assembly Meeting of the Association of Black Psychologists, Los Angeles, CA.

Jackson-Lowman, H. (2020). Serial forced displacements and the decline of *Ubuntu* in Afrikan American communities. *Alteration*, *27*(1), 153–169.

Kambon, K. K. K. (2012). *African/Black psychology in the American context: An African-centered approach* (2nd ed.). Nubian Nation Publications.

Karenga, M. (1988). *The African American holiday of Kwanzaa: A celebration of family, community & culture.* University of Sankore Press.

Kellermann, N. P. F. (2001). Transmission of Holocaust trauma - An integrative view. *Psychiatry*, *64*(3), 256–267. https://doi.org/10.1521/psyc.64.3.256.18464

King, R. (1990). *African origin of biological psychiatry.* U.B. and U.S. Communications Systems, Inc.

Mangena, F. (2016). African ethos through Ubuntu: A post-modern exposition. *Africology: The Journal of Pan African Studies*, *9*(2), 66–79.

Moffitt, K. (2021, February 22). What does intersectionality mean in 2021? Kimberle Crenshaw's podcast is a must-listen way to learn. *Columbia News.* https://news.columbia.edu/news/what-does-intersectionality-mean-2021-kimberle-crenshaws-podcast-must-listen-way-learn

Nobles, W. W. (1993, April). [Speech]. "Family Affair" Conference, Pittsburgh, PA.

Nobles, W. W. (2006). *Seeking the Sakhu: Foundational writings for an African psychology*. Third World Press.

Nunley, P. (2020). Spirit molestation: Identity development abuse in Western early childhood education programmes serving Black African American students. *International Journal of African Renaissance Studies - Multi-, Inter- and Transdisciplinarity*, *15*(2), 30–49. https://doi.org/10.1080/18186874.2021.1884986

Ogbonnaya, A. O. (1994). Person as community: An African understanding of the person as an intrapsychic community. *Journal of Black Psychology*, *20*(1), 75–87.

Ramseur, H. P. (2004). Psychologically healthy African American adults. In R. L. Jones (Ed.), *Black psychology* (4th ed.). Cobb and Henry.

Schwarz-Bart, S. (2001). *In praise of Black women: Ancient African queens.* University of Wisconsin Press.

Settles, I., Navarrete, D., Pagano, S. J., Abdou, C. M., & Sidanius, J. (2006). Race identity and depression among African American women. *Cultural Diversity & Ethnic Minority Psychology*, *16*(2), 248–255.

Sowande, F. (n.d.). *The learning process* [unpublished manuscript].

Stromberg, J. (2013, November 15). A history of slavery and genocide in modern DNA. *Smithsonian.* https://www.smithsonianmag.com/science-nature/a-history-of-slavery-and-genocide-is-hidden-in-modern-dna-180947707/

Taylor, J. (1996). The Pittsburgh Project, part III: Toward a purposeful systems approach to parenting. In R. L. Jones (Ed.), *African American children, youth, and parenting.* Cobb and Henry.

Wilson, A. N. (1998). *Blueprint for Black power: A moral, political and economic imperative for the twenty-first century.* Afrikan World InfoSystems.

Wilson, E. O. (2012, April 9). What's your tribe? *Newsweek*, 42–46.

Reading 1.1. Ancient Models of Afrikan Womanhood

Challenging Contemporary Perceptions of Black Womanhood

Huberta Jackson-Lowman and Mawiyah Kambon

The prevalence of controlling images that present Afrikan American women as mammies, Jezebels, Sapphires/matriarchs, and welfare mothers (Collins, 2000) operates like a worldwide matrix controlled by the White male elite power structures. Supported by myths of non-femininity, inferiority, criminality, promiscuity, and unshakeability (Jones & Shorter-Gooden, 2003), these pejorative portrayals stand in sharp contrast to the lives of many ancient, pre-colonial Afrikan women. Unfortunately, though, most Afrikan Americans know little to nothing about ancient Afrikan civilizations, and even less about the roles of women within them. Having little to no knowledge about our history as Afrikan people and being systematically disconnected from our Afrikan past contributes to the maintenance of myths and stereotypes about Black womanhood. Knowing the truth and the reality of the lives of ancient Afrikan women can be the first crucial step in recognizing and ultimately destroying these myths and images in the psychology of Afrikan people. In this chapter, we evaluate the lives of 12 ancient Afrikan women whose courage, strength, perseverance against the odds, love for their people, and character challenge the veracity and preeminence of Western/Eurocentric notions of femininity and gender roles (Lips, 2006). The values that these women enacted are likened to the *Nguzo Saba* (Ani, 2011; Karenga, 1988), a value system drawn from observations of Afrikan cultural life across the continent. By lifting up these women, their values, and the characteristics they exhibited in significant aspects of their lives, we can begin to use them as models of womanhood for women of Afrikan ancestry and provide an alternative to the stereotypic images promoted by the media and other Eurocentric-controlled societal institutions that serve to maintain and reinforce the oppression of Black women.

Gender and Femininity

In many places throughout the world, being a woman and a leader is viewed as a contradiction. Women have been consistently perceived and portrayed as being too emotional and too weak to assume positions of leadership at the national, political, military, and business levels in particular, but also in most other sectors of many societies. In spite of the general acceptance of these provincial views of the capabilities and behaviors of women by many in the United States and throughout the world, social scientists declare that gender is a "socially constructed" notion (Lips, 2006). In essence, each society creates its own definition of what it means to be a woman or a man, delineates the roles and behaviors acceptable for each gender, and prescribes rules by which persons assigned to a particular gender should function. As Lindsay and Miescher (2003) suggest, gender roles can be flexibly or rigidly defined by different cultural groups. A number of Indigenous North American societies and some Polynesian ethnic groups identify more than two genders (Lips, 2006). Definitions of the other genders do not view them as admixtures of the other two; instead, they reflect a unique identity that is not associated with sexual orientation. And in still other cultures, such as the Yoruba of southwestern Nigeria, there are no gender distinctions made in the language (Lips, 2006). The fact that Western societies associate masculinity with men and femininity with women, and negatively characterize individuals who don't adhere to these boundaries, reflects the either–or kind of thinking that dominates the Eurocentric worldview (Collins, 2000).

17

The epitome of womanhood for U.S. European American women has historically been identified as the "cult of true womanhood" (Collins, 2000). Prescriptions of the cult of true womanhood suggest that women should exhibit the qualities of submissiveness, piety, purity, and domesticity, in order to be classified as "ladies" (Collins, 2000; Vaz, 1995). Typically, these qualities were considered unachievable for poor women and women of color. However, in spite of efforts by middle-class White women to disqualify Afrikan American women's claims of ladyhood, a primary focus of many Black women's clubs/organizations was achieving a sense of "respectability" as ladies. Thus, an important goal for the National Association of Colored Women (NACW), one of the foremost Black women's organizations in the late 19th century and early 20th century with a membership of some 50,000 at its height, concerned challenging the myths and stereotypes of Black womanhood (Giddings, 1984). It can be speculated that lack of knowledge of their ancient Afrikan past, which potentially could have provided alternative models of womanhood, was a contributing factor in their endorsement of the "cult of true womanhood" as a model of womanhood for Afrikan American women. Yet, in many ways, the lives of these 19th and early 20th century Afrikan American women stood in sharp contrast to the restrictions imposed by the cult of true womanhood, in much the same way that the lives of ancient Afrikan women often challenged the non-Afrikan cultural models of womanhood of their time (Diop, 1974; Van Sertima, 1984).

Backward Connectedness

How much do you know about ancient Afrikan women leaders? Identify those women whom you recognize below by placing an "X" next to their name.

Ahmose Nofretari	Ana de Sousa Nzinga
Beatrice Kimpa Vita	Yennenga
Mamochisane	Taitu Bethel
Queen Tiye	Yaa Asantewa
The Candaces	Hatshepsut
Queen Makeda	Sarraounia
Queen Heleni	Ranavalona III

The Nguzo Saba as a Strategy for Examining the Lives of Ancient Afrikan Women

Using the Nguzo Saba as a lens, this chapter examines the lives of Ahmose-Nofretari, Hatshepsut, Queen Makeda, The Candaces, Queen Tiye, Yennenga, Empress Heleni, Ana de Sousa Nzinga, Beatrice Kimpa Vita, Sarraounia, Taitu Bethel, and Yaa Asantewa, with the intent of identifying commonalities in the values and behaviors that characterize these women and distinguish them as ancient Afrikan models of womanhood for women of Afrikan heritage. This text does not intend to provide a comprehensive historical discussion or analysis of the lives of these women; for that, other sources are available (Schwarz-Bart, 2001; Sweetman, 1984; Van Sertima, 1984). Instead, the intent here is to illustrate how the history of women of Afrikan ancestry can be employed to provide a corrective for the nefarious images of Afrikan American women that are presented in contemporary Eurocentric American society, and to stress the importance of learning about this history.

The Nguzo Saba was offered by Maulana Karenga (19 88) both as a cultural strategy for strengthening connections between Afrikan Americans and as a pathway to cultural restoration. Karenga delineated the *Nguzo Saba*, a KiSwahili word that means seven principles, as the foundation of the Afrikan American cultural holiday called "Kwanzaa." For seven days from December 26th through January 1st, Afrikan Americans and Afrikans throughout the diaspora celebrate *Kwanzaa* (First Fruits). The seven principles on which Kwanzaa is based are drawn from the values and traditions of Afrikan people across the continent. They include *Umoja*/Unity, *Kujichagulia*/Self-Determination, *Ujima*/Collective Work and

Responsibility, *Ujamaa*/Cooperative Economics, *Nia*/Purpose, *Kuumba*/Creativity, and *Imani*/Faith. As a cultural holiday, Kwanzaa is designed to celebrate all that is good in the Afrikan American community and to promote the expression of these principles in the day-to-day lives of Afrikan Americans (see Figure 4 on Nguzo Saba). Marimba Ani (2011) has further elaborated on these principles, highlighting their PanAfrikan foundations. Many of the principles that Karenga has lifted from traditional Afrikan cultures can be observed in the lives of the women discussed in the following sections.

Ahmose-Nofretari

Ahmose-Nofretari is most acclaimed in the history of ancient Kemet/Egypt for being the only woman to achieve the status of goddess. Born at the end of the occupation of Kemet/Egypt by the Hyksos and described as having "beautiful black skin," she was the daughter of Queen Ahhotep and King Seqenenre Tao (Schwarz-Bart, 2001). When King Seqenenre is killed in a battle with the Hyksos, Ahmose-Nofretari's mother, Queen Ahhotep, assumes leadership of the troops and continues the pursuit of liberation for her country in her husband's name. At the Temple of Karnak, credit is given to her for reuniting Kemet/Egypt.

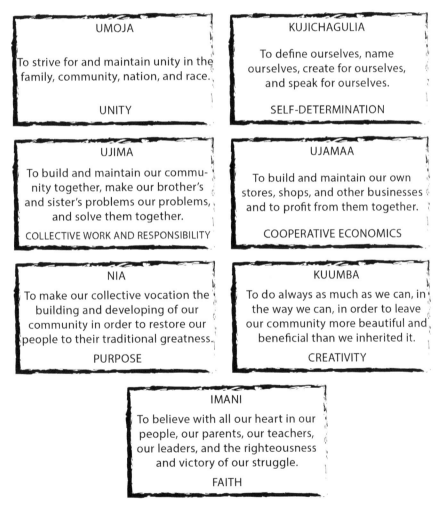

Figure 1.1.1. The Seven Principles of Kwanzaa

At the time of her father's death, Ahmose-Nofretari is very young. As is traditional in this patriarchal society, her brother assumes the title of Pharaoh of the Two Lands, the earthly representative of the god Amon. According to the story, side by side, the Pharaoh and Ahmose-Nofretari conquer the Hyksos, eventually chasing them out of the Sinai Desert. As royal custom prescribes, Ahmose-Nofretari marries her brother.

Figure 1.1.2. Queen Ahmose-Nofretari

Ahmose-Nofretari's many achievements included ensuring that the temples were raised again and restoring her people's customs. She was also known as a protector of the poor. Her duties included the enactment of the daily ritual of walking around the palace so that the sun could complete its circle in the sky, thus maintaining the cult of Amon. This ritual suggests a deeply spiritual and humble nature and the recognition of the importance of honoring Nature's role in the sustenance of life. With the death of her husband, Ahmose-Nofretari is charged with maintaining the material and spiritual life of the kingdom. She dons the headdress associated with the goddess Mut, Amon's wife in heaven, which consists of a helmet with two long feathers and a golden sun above surrounded by the horns of the god Sothis. It is said that as a priestess devoted to the worship of Amon, she can be seen singing hymns for Amon, dancing, playing a musical instrument called the sistrum, and hugging Amon as he holds the symbol of life, the "ankh."

Schwarz-Bart's (2001) portrayal of Ahmose-Nofretari reveals a woman who is comfortable with what would be defined, in Western terms, as both her feminine and masculine sides. On the one hand, she is capable of being very nurturing—as suggested by the reference to her as protector of the poor—while on the other hand, she is aggressive enough to join her brother on the battlefield in war against their enemies. Like generations of queens/co-regents before her, Queen Ahhotep continues this well-established tradition by astutely modeling these behaviors for her daughter. It can be conjectured that it is their ability to seamlessly transition between so-called gendered roles, assuming their presence, which enables them to save their country.

A passionate commitment to restoring their people to their traditional greatness—*Nia*—and uncompromising belief in the importance of self-definition—*Kujichagulia*—can be observed in the actions of both Queen Ahhotep and Ahmose-Nofretari. They set about the tasks of restoring and rebuilding their temples and revitalizing their customs, exemplifying *Kuumba* and *Nia*, once they had regained control of

Kemet. Restoring and rebuilding their temples was necessary because they provided a place for the worship of their deities and for conducting their rituals, a critical part of their identity. By prioritizing the restoration and rebuilding of their temples and reinstituting their customs, Queen Ahhotep and Ahmose-Nofretari demonstrated their recognition of the importance of maintaining their ancestral connections through continuing to adhere to their authentic spiritual system and customs—those things that defined who they were.

Queen Ahhotep's actions demonstrate the principles of *Umoja, Kujichagulia, Ujima, and Nia*. Karenga (1988) gives the principle of *Umoja* the lead position among the seven principles, suggesting that group members' connections to family, community, and nation are critical aspects of any group's identity, what Jackson-Lowman (1998) refers to as lateral and backward connectedness. Recognition of the importance of *Kujichagulia* is indicated by value placed upon national and cultural sovereignty. *Ujima* is expressed in the willingness exhibited by Queen Ahhotep to take on these national concerns, and it is carried out with a sense of purpose, *Nia*.

Finally, the principle of *Imani* is enacted through the daily ritual that Ahmose-Nofretari performs to honor the sun and worship the Creator God Amon. Her deep and abiding faith appears to be a critical dimension of the success of her rulership over her people after her husband's death. These actions support the salience of transcendental connectedness (Jackson-Lowman, 2013)—one's linkage to a higher power—as foundational in the life of Ahmose-Nofretari.

Hatshepsut

The rulership of Hatshepsut from 1490–1468 BC is considered the only time in the history of ancient Kemet when a woman rose to the position of pharaoh. Hatshepsut's ascent to the throne occurred after the death of her brother, Thutmose II, to whom she was married and with whom she shared joint rulership for eight years. As this was a patriarchal society, Thutmose III became the next pharaoh; however, because of his youth, Hatshepsut was the actual ruler, though in title she was the regent.

In ancient Kemet, women did not traditionally hold the highest position of power and authority, that of pharaoh. Nevertheless, their influence was significant in a variety of other ways. For example, a pharaoh's position could be fortified by marriage to a royal lady, a custom that was practiced when a new strong man took power from an old dynasty (Schwarz-Bart, 2001). Additionally, the new pharaoh often married one of the sisters of their new royal wife from the previous dynasty, to further solidify their power. Thus, women might be perceived as essential to the authorization and legitimization of the power that the male pharaohs were granted. From an Afrikan-centered perspective, this was not a subordinate role. Women also served in the capacity of regents when, as in the case of Thutmose III, the designated new ruler was not yet ready to assume leadership. Thus, though not acknowledged, women often were the actual leaders, in the case of a weak pharaoh or in the capacity of a regent. Co-regencies were a frequent occurrence throughout the history of Kemet, from its earliest dynasties onward (Wimby, 1984). Wimby notes that the names of the mothers of the kings were identified on the Palermo Stone,[2] acknowledging them as the foremothers of the dynasties. The names of their fathers were rarely mentioned. More telling is the fact that the mothers of the pharaohs were asserted to have experienced divine conception.

Hatshepsut is said to have married her daughter to Thutmose III; however, still dissatisfied with her designation as regent, in the following year she chose to send Thutmose III away and declared herself the Pharaoh of Kemet. To reinforce her claim to this position, she assumed a masculine appearance; wore a false beard, which is one of the symbols of Divine Kingship; and proclaimed herself "Her Majesty the King." Hatshepsut's bold and aggressive actions certainly differentiate her style from those characteristics associated with femininity in Western society. No doubt she encountered resistance—and would be deposed

---

[2] The **Palermo Stone** is a large fragment of a stele known as the Royal Annals of the Old Kingdom of Ancient Egypt. It contains records of the kings of Egypt from the first dynasty through the fifth dynasty.

by Thutmose III some 20 years later—but there is no historical documentation that the resistance she experienced was misogynistic in its tenor.

Hatshepsut was very strategic in her leadership of Kemet. Recognizing that she lacked experience as a warrior, she chose to focus her rulership on building and enhancing Kemet's stability. She organized an expedition to Punt (now Somalia) using large boats, rather than taking the voyage by land. The purpose of this journey was to obtain perfumes and incense needed for worship and for personal adornment. One of the greatest architectural sites in the world, the funeral temple at Dayr-al-Bahri (Deir-el-Bahri), which stands beside her tomb, was erected during her reign. She is also noted for commissioning mining expeditions to North Sinai for turquoise and to South Aswan for granite, resources used for the building of obelisks that served to document her legacy and the history of the country. Although she had no co-ruler, Senenmut—who is described as a "Black man," a high priest, steward of the royal house, architect of the Temple of Dayr-al-Bahri, scientist, and counselor—advised her and supported her throughout her reign. In all, over the course of her 20-year reign, Hatshepsut can be credited with stabilizing and enriching Kemet and maintaining peace (Schwarz-Bart, 2001; Van Sertima, 1984).

Hatshepsut's rulership was not constrained by the dictates prescribed by Kemet with regard to female leadership. Nor did she attempt to prove her worth by engaging in war and competing with previous rulers or aspiring ones. She implemented an agenda that prioritized the principles of *Umoja, Nia, Kuumba*, and *Imani*. As ruler, she ensured that Kemet retained its integrity by strengthening the foundation on which the nation stood. A sense of purpose—*Nia*—rooted in her recognition of the greatness of her people is indicated by her focus on building and enriching Kemet—*Kuumba*—and on acquiring the resources needed for the construction of the obelisks that were used to record their history, which is also an example of her awareness of the importance of forward connectedness (Jackson-Lowman, 2013). Commitment to her spiritual tradition—*Imani*, indicative of a sense of backward connectedness as well as transcendental connectedness—is suggested by the importance she assigned to procuring the incense needed for the worship of their deities. Incense was considered an essential element in their communication with their deities. Hatshepsut provides a model of strength, vision, purpose, courage, and devotion to uplifting her people and her nation, along with a deep sense of spirituality.

Queen Tiye of Kemet

Queen Tiye lived from 1398 BC to 1338 BC. Though not of royalty, Tiye's family served in prominent positions within the royal court. Queen Tiye's childhood years were rich with family love and guidance. She was nurtured and taught traditional spiritual systems by her parents. Her mother is known to have participated in and practiced several traditional systems. Later in life, Tiye married Amenhotep III, the renowned pharaoh of the 18th Dynasty. She became his Great Royal Wife, a special distinction from other of his wives. Her special position was commemorated by Amenhotep with the scarab he commissioned for her, commonly referred to as the "marriage scarab." Amenhotep lavished Queen Tiye with many gifts, including "buildings, shrines, a palace, and an artificial lake in her honor" (Lorenz, 2000). Together they brought forth six children. The most distinguished of them was the pharaoh Amenhotep IV (later called Akhenaten), father of Tutankamen (King Tut).

Queen Tiye is distinguished by her major influence on the throne. She had a strong personality and strong political and spiritual/religious views. She instructed her son to follow these spiritual teachings. His reign has become a significant part of Kemetic (Egyptian) history. As king, Akhenaten revolutionized religion in Kemet. During his reign and while she was still alive, Akhenaten raised his mother to the realm of a goddess, a deified queen. In many carvings Queen Tiye was depicted at the side of her husband, Amenhotep III. Theirs was a cooperative rule, though she instituted her own agenda.

Queen Tiye epitomizes several principles of the Nguzo Saba, including (1) *Umoja*: Her teachings sought to unite the people; (2) *Kujichagulia*: She did not ask permission to move forward her agenda for the family or the people, and took over major responsibilities; (3) *Ujima*: She shared the workload in the reign of two pharaohs; and (4) *Imani*: She believed in the wisdom and teachings of her parents and furthered their spiritual practices with the people. In turn, the people responded with respect, admiration, and cooperation. Queen Tiye illustrated the ability to exert profound influence that, though feminine in nature, did not deter or inhibit her unique leadership abilities.

Figure 1.1.3. Queen Tiye

Queen Makeda

Among Afrikan women leaders, perhaps the most widely acknowledged/publicized in Eurocentric historiographies is Queen Makeda. She is referred to as the Queen of Sheba and is referenced biblically in the second book of Chronicles and the first book of Kings. Though she is often recognized for her awesome beauty, her mind was equally acute. She is most recognized for undertaking a visit to Jerusalem to test the king of Solomon's wisdom. Smitten by her, King Solomon impregnated her, and from their union was born a child, the first Menelik in the long, almost uninterrupted Solomonic lineage that culminated with the deposition of Negus Haile Selassie in 1974 (Schwarz-Bart, 2001). When Queen Makeda's son grew up, she sent him to Jerusalem to meet his father. He was anointed king in the temple at Jerusalem and given the name Menelik I, becoming the first king of the dynasty of the Lions of Judah (Schwarz-Bart, 2001).

Makeda descended from a dynasty that began in Ethiopia in 1370 BC. She became the Queen of Ethiopia when her father, on his deathbed, selected her to be his successor. Some have said that her rulership extended beyond Ethiopia to Upper Egypt, "parts of Arabia, Syria, Armenia, India …" (Williams & Finch, 1984, p. 17). She is described as a just leader, a great builder, and an international stateswoman who astutely oversaw her nation and territories. Her skills as a leader and businesswoman were most observable in her shrewd organization of trade by land and sea, particularly in the areas of Damascus and the Gaza. Also attributed to her is the building of the capitol in the district of Azeba called Mount Makeda. It is speculated that her visit to King Solomon, during which he wined, dined, and wooed her, may have resulted in a trade agreement, diplomatic relations, and quite possibly a military alliance (Williams & Finch, 1984).

The most popular Eurocentric accounts of Makeda, Queen of Sheba, have reduced her legacy to her extended visit with King Solomon; however, it is apparent that she was King Solomon's equal and wielded as much or more power and influence. While she provides a distinctly feminine model of leadership, its breadth, depth, scope, impact, and effectiveness are at least comparable to those of her male counterparts. The principles of *Kujichagulia, Ujamaa*, and *Kuumba* are most visible in the quality of leadership that she provided. Her interactions with other world leaders appeared not to have threatened her capacity for holding true to those things that uniquely defined her people, nor did she shrink from ensuring the protection of her nation—*Kujichagulia*. Furthermore, she enhanced her nation through the building and development that she commissioned—*Kuumba*. Finally, she was extremely adept at managing her country's financial and business affairs and negotiated cooperative economic exchanges with other nations—*Ujamaa*.

The Candaces

Over a number of centuries, a series of independent women leaders known as the "Candaces" ruled the city of Meroe in Kush (now known as Ethiopia). The name "Candace" is actually the corruption of a Meroitic title, "kdke," used by all royal consorts ranging from kings' wives to queen mothers and ruling queens (Sweetman, 1984). Meroe, which became the center of power for this Nubian kingdom, is considered the second-greatest civilization in Afrika; however, because the language has not been deciphered and very little archeological research has been undertaken, little is known about the powerful women leaders known as the Candaces. Because women rulers were so typical in Nubia, people believed that no men ever ruled and deemed it "the land of powerful queens" (Sweetman, 1984). During this time, Meroe was considered a world power and engaged in those activities associated with nations of this status. Indications of the great power of the Candaces may be observed in such notable activities as having ambassadors and consulates all over the Roman Empire; dominating the trade in Afrika's luxury goods such as "gold, ivory, ebony, incense, rare oils, semi-precious stones, animal skins"; and maintaining diplomatic residencies all over the world (Williams & Finch, 1984, p.31).

It is believed that there were at minimum five Candaces, none of whom ruled consecutively. Because their influence was so great, even when a man was the ruler, references to Nubia suggested that it was under the rulership of a Candace. It is thought that the transfer of the capitol from Napata to Meroe, in 300 BC, was in some way brought about by royal women (Sweetman, 1984).

Of the first ruling queen, Queen Bartare, little is known. She was buried in a pyramid at Meroe and is estimated to have ruled circa 284–275 BC (Sweetman, 1984). She was the third ruler to be buried here rather than in the old capitol of Napata. Queen Shanakdakhete, who is said to be the first sole ruler of Kush, ruled from 170 to 160 BC (Williams & Finch, 1984). The available source evidence about the Candaces is both minimal and conflicting. Two other Candaces who are identified by Williams and Finch (1988) are Nawidemak and Maleqereabar.

The little historical information that can be gleaned about the Candaces reveals that some of them were fierce warriors. Queen Amanerinas is thought to have ruled circa 29–24 BC who possibly jointly ruled with her husband, Prince Akinidad. She led her Kushite army across the Egyptian border, confronting Augustus Caesar, attacking the Roman forces that were occupying Egypt/Kemet, sending them fleeing, and destroying statues of Caesar (Williams & Finch, 1984). Caesar's extremely violent response—destruction of towns and of the capitol at Napata—did not deter her; she simply retreated, reorganized, and launched another attack. Rome ultimately renounced the tribute it had imposed on the people of Lower Nubia. More is known about Queen Amanishakete, who is believed to have ruled from 26 to 20 BC, though these dates would have overlapped with the reign of Queen Amanerinas. Her reign was marked by great prosperity; numerous buildings were constructed, and pyramid tombs, usually reserved for kings and queens, were erected for wealthy nobles (Sweetman, 1984).

Queen Amanitere, another Candace, ruled from AD 25 to 41. She and her husband, King Natakamani, are recognized as the greatest builders of Meroe. Among their notable achievements were the restorations of the Temples of Amon at the old capitol, Napata, and at Meroe. The Lion Temple at Naqa outside Meroe, which features carved portraits of them at the entrance, is a great architectural monument that is also attributed to them. Queen Amanikhatashan, identified as the last of the Candaces, ruled from AD 83 to 115; however, it is believed that there was yet another Candace, whose identity remains unknown but who ruled circa AD 317.

The Candaces are considered among Afrika's greatest builders. Their legacy includes trade with the outside world, international intercourse via ambassadorships and diplomatic residencies, and defense and protection of their nation during war. In modern terms, they may be considered the embodiment of progressive women who, like the earlier women discussed, were not bound by constraints of gender. Their leadership embraced each of the seven principles, with a special emphasis on *Umoja, Kujichagulia, Ujamaa, Nia, Kuumba,* and *Imani.* These bold, visionary Afrikan women established Meroe as the center of the Nubian Kingdom (*Kujichagulia and Nia*), a place of cultural vitality (*Kuumba*), vibrant economic activity (*Ujamaa*), and commitment to their spiritual system (*Imani*). They fought their aggressors for centuries (*Umoja*) while also nurturing and promoting the prosperity of their people.

Yennenga

In the 11th century, one of the most ancient Afrikan kingdoms—one that, from that point forward, manifested a single hereditary chain with no missing links—began in an area north of Ghana: the Mossi kingdom (Schwarz-Bart, 2001). The first ruler of this kingdom was a man by the name of Ouedrago, which means "stallion," in honor of the horse that brought his mother, Yennenga, to her newly chosen life. Yennenga, a beautiful young woman praised for her warrior skills, was given a battalion at the age of 14 and put in charge of the royal guard by her father, King Madega. She engaged in war expeditions, rode on horseback, and brought back war loot. Because of her skills and appearance, she was compared to a lion. To honor Yennenga's memory, the Mossi people do not kill lions, even though they hunt other large animals such as buffalo and elephants (Schwarz-Bart, 2001).

The story of Yennenga pays homage to a woman whose courage and convictions led to the formation of a kingdom that managed to maintain its sovereignty through massive, unrelenting assaults from both Europeans and Arabs throughout the continent of Afrika. Yielding to her desire for marriage and children and facing the resistance of her father, who expressed dissatisfaction with all potential mates, Yennenga disguised herself as a man and fled from the kingdom. In the forest, she encountered a young man, Riale, who had also fled his kingdom after his father had been murdered. She took up residence with him. He soon discovered that she was a woman, and they became lovers. Eventually a son, Ouedrago, was born from their relationship. Yennenga did not return home; however, when her son reached his 17th birthday, she recognized the need for him to be connected to his grandfather, once again summoned up her courage, and took him to meet her father. Ouedrago remained with his grandfather until he was of age. His grandfather attempted to persuade him to assume leadership of the kingdom; however, he declined because he wanted to create his own kingdom. King Madega is said to have given Ouedrago 200 armed men who departed, first stopping to pay their respects to Yennenga and Riale and then continuing on to what is now known as the Mossi kingdom (Schwarz-Bart, 2001). To this day, Yennenga is known as the mother of the Mossi people.

The story of Yennenga reveals a woman equally in tune with the feminine and masculine aspects of her identity. In contrast to the women previously discussed, she defended her commitment to marriage and motherhood and demonstrated the strength and courage to pursue what she considered to be her most important aspiration. Her actions display the principles of *Kujichagulia* and *Nia.* She is insistent about the desire to give expression to the feminine dimensions of her identity (*Kujichagulia*) but exhibits no difficulty tapping into what may be viewed as masculine characteristics. She is intent on fulfilling her purpose (*Nia*), which is integrally connected to maintaining the legacy of her people; thus, she recognizes the importance of ensuring that her son has a connection with his grandfather, her father.

Empress Heleni

At the beginning of the 1400s, Afrika was under siege by European nations determined to colonize her and extract her resources for their benefit. Supported by a Papal Declaration asserting that Portugal could take possession of a significant part of Afrika—its people and resources—the nation of Portugal was intently carrying out this mission by enslaving Afrikan people, placing them in captivity, and transporting many of them to Portugal to provide a free labor force for the Portuguese. For centuries Afrika had contended with the Eurasian and Arab invaders, and now another set of Western European intruders had arrived. In spite of the intrusion of Arabs and the imposition of Islam on many Afrikan nations, the Ethiopians had managed to fight off their enemies and maintain their traditional, ancient Coptic Christian religion for approximately 1,200 years. But Ethiopia, which was under the rulership of Emperor Vayda Maryam, was now facing threats of Muslim invasion. Thus entered Queen Heleni, the wife of the Emperor, whose political savvy and strategic abilities provided the salve that enabled Ethiopia to maintain some semblance of its sovereignty.

An astute politician and the power behind the throne, Queen Heleni recognized her country's vulnerability and pursued an alliance with Portugal based on shared religion. Even though there were distinct differences between Coptic Christianity and Western European Christianity, she drew upon their similarities to negotiate a successful alliance with Portugal, to assist Ethiopia in resisting the Muslim invasion. As a result of these negotiations, Portugal sent troops to Ethiopia to help Queen Heleni fight off the Muslim attack.

Queen Heleni ruled Ethiopia for 50 years in the capacity of queen and regent. She was a multifaceted woman whose abilities included authoring two books and being a head of state, and she was characterized as a "mystic, pious, and smart politician" along with being a courageous warrior. She stands as another example of a great Afrikan woman leader who comfortably integrated the masculine and feminine aspects of her identity in her leadership. Her dedication to the maintenance of Ethiopia's religious sovereignty reveals the operation of the principles of *Umoja* and *Kujichagulia*. She used her well-developed negotiation skills to forge an alliance with an unlikely ally, Portugal, suggesting her willingness to do whatever it took to ensure the well-being of her people and her nation. Commitment to the principles of Ujima and Nia is also evident in her leadership. She recognized that the problems facing Ethiopia required her involvement (*Ujima*) and purposefully and strategically pursued the alliance with Portugal (*Nia*) to ensure the sovereignty of her people (*Kujichagulia*).

Ana de Sousa Nzinga

Born in 1581 in Kabasa, the capital of the Ndongo Kingdom, Ana de Sousa Nzinga's birth occurred in the midst of the Portuguese conquest of the Kongo (Schwarz-Bart, 2001). Her father, Ngola Kiluanji, who was the ruler of the Ndongo kingdom, initially tolerated the Portuguese and their enslavement of those from other ethnic groups. He even disposed of criminals, and others considered undesirable, through exchanges with the Portuguese. However, he strongly resisted their efforts to convert people to Christianity and warred against the Portuguese when they turned their attention toward his people.

The Mbundu people lived in what is today called Angola. The name "Angola" was erroneously interpreted by the Portuguese to be the name of the country, though it was actually the title of the rulers of the Ndongo people—*ngola* means "leader." Eventually Ngola Kiluanji was killed, and Nzinga's half-brother, Mbandi, seized control and made himself *ngola* (Sweetman, 1984). In an effort to quell any potential challenge to his leadership, Mbandi killed his younger brother, Nzinga's younger son, and some of the chiefs who had supported him.

After incurring several defeats at the hands of the Portuguese, Ngola Mbandi sought Nzinga's help. The Portuguese wanted to gain control over the silver mines and had become addicted to "black ivory"—a term that was used to refer to the Afrikans who were being enslaved. In spite of the injuries that Mbandi had inflicted on Nzinga, she set aside her personal wounds to defend her people. Thus, she accepted the monumental task of negotiating a treaty with the Portuguese. The most historic moment of her legacy is recounted in a picture that shows her seated on one of the women in her army who served as a "human seat." Nzinga's remarkable skills as a negotiator are revealed in her ability to extract an agreement from the Portuguese governor. When the governor attempted to secure her surrender, she responded with the statement: "I represent a sovereign country and I am ready to continue this conversation only on that basis" (Schwarz-Bart, 2001).

For years, Nzinga fought to maintain her people's land and to ensure the continuation of their sovereignty. Strategically, in order to protect her people, she formed alliances at various times with different enemies: the Portuguese; the Jagas, who were considered a cannibalistic ethnic group; and the Dutch. But she never lost her sense of focus on the ultimate goal—the freedom and independence of her people. Nzinga led a very complex life, in which she exhibited few commitments to gender restraints or cultural dictates; she dressed like a man when going into battle, required that her husbands dress like women, and insisted on being called "King." She converted to Catholicism and did whatever she thought would assist her in achieving her goals, ruling for 30 years. Although she did not achieve her ultimate goal, it is said is that she lost many battles but she never lost the war.

Nzinga's rulership reflects a woman whose life was wholly dedicated to defending her people and maintaining their national sovereignty—*Umoja* and *Kujichagulia*. Her actions relating to gender norms suggest an elasticity similar to that of the other female leaders we have discussed: she assumed traditionally masculine behaviors, both in her dress and in her interactions with others, in some instances (warfare, official duties, etc.), but she was also very charming and exhibited some aspects of traditional femininity in other activities (marriage, children, etc.). This implies that she resisted some of the gender norms of the day in order to carry out a very crucial mission—*Nia*. The preeminence of the principles of *Umoja*, *Kujichagulia*, *Ujima*, and *Nia* is manifested in her actions. She displayed unremitting persistence and fierce courage, and she exuded political craftiness.

Beatrice Kimpa Vita

In the late 1600s and early 1700s, the Kongo was already in the grip of the Portuguese. The Kongolese people had been forced to convert to Christianity and, subsequently, to relinquish their traditional dress and many of their customs. The king of the Kongo, who had become brainwashed to revere the White man's knowledge, pledged to give King Manuel I of Portugal all the gold in the kingdom in exchange for the Portuguese sharing their knowledge of carpentry, blacksmithing, coppersmithing, and other skills. Instead of the technical knowledge that he had sought, he was given the imposition of Christianity, whereby the Portuguese gained entry to the Kongo (Schwarz-Bart, 2001).

A young woman by the name of Beatrice Kimpa Vita, a priestess in the Marinda cult of noble birth and a prophetess who wore a crown of the musenda plant emblematic of her gifts, was extremely displeased with the state of affairs in the Kongo. Unhappy with the fact that the people had relinquished their customs and the king was controlled by the missionaries, Beatrice Kimpa Vita paid a visit to the king (Schwarz-Bart, 2001). It is said that she challenged the thoughtless adherence to customs such as marriage, baptism, and prayers, viewing them as worthwhile only if they were grounded in good intentions. Furthermore, she conveyed to the king her belief that there were Afrikan saints and that they were from the Kongo.

Kimpa Vita is credited with restoring the old, ruined sacred capitol after she visited the king and for Afrikanizing, to whatever extent possible, the Catholic religion imposed on the Kongo by the Portuguese. She recreated the story of the birth and baptism of Jesus, locating him, St. Francis, and other notable Biblical figures in the Kongo and tracing "our Lady of Madonna" to a Kongolese enslaved woman from Nzimba

Npanghi. Through her ministry she sought to increase her people's awareness of how the Portuguese had used their religion to conquer and oppress them. In an effort to restore cultural integrity to the Kongo, she encouraged her fellow countrymen and women to assume their traditional names, wear their traditional clothes, and return to polygamy—*Kujichagulia* and *Nia*. She sent her disciples out wearing their crowns of musenda to carry her message, which placed Afrikan people of the Kongo at the center of their new form of religious worship once again and emphasized the value of their being more of their authentic selves, rather than imitating the Portuguese. Ultimately she was arrested by the Portuguese and subsequently executed, with child in arms, after claiming that she had had a virgin birth. She thereby lost the favor of her people (Sweetman, 1984).

Beatrice Kimpa Vita is the epitome of an Afrikan woman of courage, strength, vision, and commitment to her people, her traditions, and the cultural integrity of the Kongolese people. Her wisdom is evident in her approach to fostering *Umoja* through Afrikanizing the religion that the Portuguese had imposed upon her people. She pursued *Kujichagulia* on behalf of her people by recontextualizing the foreign religion to reflect them and their needs, and by encouraging them to use their traditional names and wear their traditional clothing. When she recognized that the Kongolese people had the capacity to return to their traditional greatness by acknowledging their divinity and facilitated this by skillfully recasting the foreign religious story, she also exuded a deep sense of purpose and creativity—*Nia* and *Kuumba*. A priestess with profound spiritual gifts, she demonstrated her faith in her ancestors and their traditions through her actions—*Imani*.

Sarraounia

The story of Sarraounia's rise to queen of the Azna occurs amidst the European invasion of Afrikan territories and subsequent efforts to lay claim to those territories. Sarraounia, whose mother died during childbirth, is described as having "a pinched mouth, clenched fists, and shiny yellow eyes" that reminded her people of a leopard (Schwarz-Bart, 2001). The leopard, the totem of the Azna people, symbolizes their willingness to fight to the death. Symbols of the leopard were placed on the clothing of the Azna and over the doorways of their homes.

Sarraounia defies most modern conceptions of femininity. She exhibited exceptional skills as an archer, climbed trees, caught fish barehanded, and jumped rocks. She freely associated with men as she pleased, but did not desire children. She is described as a sorceress who disappeared for weeks at a time while she consorted with spirits and learned the secrets of herbs and plants. She assumed the throne at the age of 20, upon the death of her father, and in her hands lay the fate of her people (Schwarz-Bart, 2001).

Sarraounia's father fought the Tuaregs, who wanted to enslave the men and capture the beautiful Azna women, and the Muslim Marabous of Sokoto, who wanted to impose their faith on the Azna. When Sarraounia took the throne, her first challenge was to deal with two Frenchmen who had been ravaging the countryside—pillaging, killing, and burning—in an effort to become kings. She attempted to establish alliances with the Tuaregs and the Sokoto, to enhance the Azna's ability to resist their French attackers. Neither group accepted her proposal, so she built a wall around the Capitol at Lougou, smashed the granaries, and sent the women, children, and elders away to safety, in preparation for the coming war. Using her strategic skills as a warrior and her knowledge of sorcery, she equipped her men with weapons and with a mixture that would protect them from harm, and then launched an attack against the Frenchmen at night. This unexpected attack evoked confusion among the mercenaries. Although their efforts to defeat Sarraounia continued, she proved to be a formidable foe and eventually succeeded in killing the two Frenchmen who wanted to become kings and subduing their forces. After defeating these imposters she rebuilt the capitol. However, the Europeans eventually returned and defeated this fierce queen, who fought valiantly to maintain the sovereignty of her people.

Sarraounia provides another model of an Afrikan female leader who was extremely comfortable with her masculinity. She was dedicated to ensuring the sovereignty of her people through maintaining

Umoja, defending *Kujichagulia,* and operating from a sense of *Ujima.* Her clear sense of mission—*Nia*—appears to have left little time for social or cultural constraints related to gender norms/roles that might have deterred her efforts.

Taitu Bethel

Taitu Bethel was an Ethiopian woman born in 1853. Her story reflects the immense challenges that women in general, and Afrikan women leaders in specific, experienced if their lives failed to conform to the gender roles prescribed within their society. Made infertile as a result of a deflowering ritual, she is said to have had only two options available to her: to become a nun, or to become a prostitute. To her credit, she chose neither. After going through four husbands, who abandoned her upon discovering her inability to have children, she married Menelik II, *Negusa Negast,* "King of kings," at the age of 40 (Schwarz-Bart, 2001).

Taitu Bethel is said to have been a multitalented woman: a skilled chess player, a poet, and a musician who was able to read and write in Amharic and was also knowledgeable in the liturgical language Ge'ez. She used her strategic skills, knowledge, courage, and love for her people to protect them from a possible takeover by Italy. After building the Suez Canal, Europeans viewed Ethiopia as having a global strategic advantage; consequently, the European powers—France, England, and Italy—along with Russia agreed not to provide arms to Ethiopia because they feared her predatory abilities. Taitu, calling on her knowledge of strategy gained from chess, urged her husband to carry out an opening move and invite Italy to sign a treaty of perpetual friendship. On May 2, 1889, the Treaty of Wichale was signed with Italy. Ethiopia began stockpiling Italian arms and importing skilled Italian technicians, engineers, and teachers to assist Ethiopia with moving into the 20th century (Schwarz-Bart, 2001). The treaty with Ethiopia was threatened when, six months later, Italy published a map on which Ethiopia was depicted as an Italian protectorate. Immediately, Menelik II renounced the treaty, and the possibility of war with Italy arose. Daunted by this possibility, Menelik wavered in a meeting with the Italian diplomat. Taitu stepped up and declared, "You cannot threaten Ethiopia. Please take leave!" The diplomat ignored her demand, and she asserted even more sternly that he had better leave, or risk being thrown out like a bum (Schwarz-Bart, 2001).

Taitu's courage and boldness frightened her husband and the great council of Ethiopia. They therefore planned to issue an apology and to give Italy a piece of their territory on the Red Sea, in an effort to cajole Italy into accepting their apology. Once again, Taitu expressed her deep dissatisfaction with this approach, stating: "For what you give them today will be a ladder to scale the walls of your fortress, and tomorrow they will come into your house. If you must lose, let it be with weapon in your hand" (Schwarz-Bart, 2001). War ensued. Accompanying her husband Emperor Menelik II to war with 5,000 troops, Taitu issued the order to capture the Italian water reserves, thus defeating the Italians in this opening battle. In a subsequent battle at Adowa, when her troops froze in their tracks, she disembarked from her mule and marched toward the Italian troops. In response, the Ethiopian troops took action and defeated the Italians. The stunning defeat of Italy brought Ethiopia international acclaim, as it was the first time in 2,500 years (since Carthage) that an Afrikan nation had defeated a European nation (Schwarz-Bart, 2001). As a result of Ethiopia's victory over Italy, France and England signed treaties of friendship with Ethiopia, while other European nations and those of the Middle East established permanent diplomatic posts in Ethiopia. Many Afrikan American and Haitian intellectuals visited Ethiopia to share in their victorious experience of independence (Schwarz-Bart, 2001).

After the victory over Italy, Taitu returned to her poetry, cooking, chess, and theological debates. When her husband became gravely ill, she devoted herself to his care, while simultaneously overseeing the kingdom. After his death, she retired to a convent in grief (Schwarz-Bart, 2001).

The complexity, strength, and courage of Taitu Bethel reflect a truly phenomenal woman who was as comfortable with the display of power, toughness, and aggression as she was with nurturance and love. Her actions illustrate a strong commitment to the principles of *Umoja, Kujichagulia,* and *Ujima* on behalf of the Ethiopian people, along with a deep sense of purpose—*Nia*. She made it her priority to maintain the unity and cultural sovereignty of her people and her nation, and she never backed down, even against tremendous odds, from her principles and values.

Nana Yaa Asantewaa

Figure 4. Nana Yaa Asantewaa

Nana Yaa Asantewaa was born in 1855 at Besease in Edweso, Ghana, West Afrika. Yaa Asantewaa stands as a symbol of womanhood, in sharp contrast to traditional Eurocentric models of womanhood, and is still honored today in Ghana. Fierce, brave, and outspoken, she recognized the importance of her leadership at a critical time in the history of the Asante people. Though she was a royal of the Asona Clan of Edweso, her early childhood was similar to those of most young girls; she, like her peers, was responsible for fetching water and preparing food. While growing up she was exposed to the civil strife among the Asante people, particularly within her own region, Edweso, and Kumase. Her brother was the Edwesohene (King), Kwasi Afrane Okpese, known for his military might, wisdom, and courage. She watched the Edwesohene's rule while, at the same time, practicing her spiritual work as a priestess.

Upon the death of her brother the king, Yaa Asantewaa's grandson, Kofi Tene, assumed the stool. He appointed his grandmother to serve as the Queen Mother. Among the Asante, the Queen Mother has her own stool, thereby her own authority. As Queen Mother she consulted with the king regarding affairs of the state and had much power over social and political affairs. When Nana Kofi Tene, the Edwesohene, was captured by the British along with Asantehene Prempeh I and taken to Seychelles Island, Nana Yaa Asantewaa appointed herself Edwesohene.

In early 1900, Yaa Asantewaa met in council with the remaining Asante chiefs to prepare to address the British governor and demand the return of the rulers and others. At that meeting the governor insulted the Asante nation by demanding the Golden Stool, the seat of the Asante nation and a symbol of their cultural sovereignty. Nana Yaa Asantewaa lashed out at him for his actions; the governor left without the stool and without responding to the demands. Later that day she turned to her chiefs, chastising them for the lack of bravery they displayed in front of the governor. She challenged them, declaring that if they would not fight, she would organize the women to fight. Thus began the Yaa Asantewaa war on March 28, 1900. She led the mightiest campaign against the British but lost the war when betrayed by several conspirators.

Yaa Asantewaa's leadership exemplifies the principles of the Nguzo Saba. Her actions reflect *Umoja*, as indicated by her success in uniting her people to stand up and fight for the principles of the nation and the freedom of the captured rulers; *Kujichagulia*, as illustrated by her self-appointment as king, her efforts to ensure that the Asante people were the ones who directed their course as a people, and her commitment to maintaining the cultural sovereignty of the Asante; *Ujima*, as demonstrated by her resolve to do whatever she could to bring about the resolution of the problems faced by the Asante people; *Nia*, as exhibited by the consistency of her agenda with the highest good of the Asante people—the maintenance of their integrity, dignity, and autonomy; and *Imani*, as displayed by her fervent belief in the strength and bravery of the Asante nation and her reliance on traditional spiritual practices as her guide. Coming from a society that recognized the importance of male–female balance in leadership, Nana Yaa Asantewaa embodied leadership that was unrestrained by the limitations commonly erected in relation to gender in Western/Eurocentric societies.

Conclusion

Across these stories of some of Afrika's outstanding women leaders—known for their brilliance as political strategists and diplomats, their courage and abilities as warriors, their persistence in the face of great adversity, their selflessness, their awesome beauty, and their spirituality—several consistent themes and attitudes can be identified. Many of these women were of noble birth, although a few emerged from humble origins. No doubt, as Gladwell's (2008) analysis of factors contributing to success reveals, their successes were intimately tied to the privileges and opportunities they experienced in their upbringing. As a consequence of their birth, developmental circumstances, and subsequent life experiences, they learned not to allow their gender or the existing social norms to constrain their abilities to exercise their potentialities as great leaders, whether they were in the forefront or in the background. Their leadership was commonly expressed in their courageous, unrelenting defense of their communities/kingdoms/nations from external invaders and enslavers, as well as from internal detractors; in their capacities as mothers who influenced their daughters/sons and the destinies of their people; and/or in their protective and nurturing attitudes toward the development, restoration, and cultivation of their kingdoms/nations. In multifarious ways and to varying degrees, they were attached to a cultural legacy (Gladwell, 2008) that gave them a sense of purpose—*Nia*. They exhibited a deep sense of spirituality and a commitment to authenticity, and (to a greater or lesser extent) they emphasized the principles of *Umoja, Kujichagulia, Ujima, Ujamaa, Nia, Kuumba*, and *Imani* in their leadership. The freedom from gender restrictions that these women displayed can serve as a model for contemporary women of Afrikan ancestry and challenge the myths and images promulgated about Afrikan women.

The stories of these women therefore suggest that they possessed very healthy self-concepts. Strongly integrated within their families, ethnic groups, and nation states, they exhibited *backward connectedness*—reverence for their ancestors and commitment to sustaining their values, customs, and traditions; *lateral connectedness*—deep love and commitment to their people; *forward connectedness*—willingness to make those sacrifices that they believed essential to maintaining their integrity and sovereignty as a people; and *transcendental connectedness*—strong and unmitigated belief in spirit, as expressed through ritual, prayer, and religious involvement (Jackson-Lowman, 2013). These qualities, and their commitment to principles of *Umoja, Kujichagulia, Ujima, Ujamaa, Nia, Kuumba*, and *Imani*, enabled these women to effectively assume positions of leadership when their people were experiencing their most dire need.

There are many outstanding women of Afrikan ancestry—ancient and contemporary, continentally born and diasporan—whose exemplary lives provide potential models of leadership for modern-day women of Afrikan ancestry. However, they remain hidden from our view due to a combination of the severe lack of general knowledge of the history of Afrikan women, the abysmal failure of educational institutions to recognize phenomenal women of Afrikan ancestry in curricula and texts, and a lack of attention from the media. In order to tap into the deep reservoir of talents, abilities, and strengths that reside in Afrikan American women, with backgrounds that range from the most destitute conditions of poverty to the most fortunate, we must study the lives of both ordinary and extraordinary women of Afrikan ancestry who have overcome great odds as an essential beginning point. The lives of Afrikan women such as these, and many more, can provide an alternative to the nefarious depictions of women of Afrikan ancestry throughout the media, and serve to encourage and inspire future generations of Afrikan women to pursue their great human potential as local and global leaders committed to improving the overall quality of Afrikan life.

Excerpt of Presentation by Dr. Marimba Ani, Cultural Anthropologist

By Min. Mxolisi Ozo-Sowande.

In Visions & Victories:

The Kwanzaa/Nguzo Saba foundational symbol, the Mkeka/Straw Mat, calls us to realize and revere the immaculate interconnectedness of Creator and Creation, divinity and humanity, and the sacredness of all life. From that foundation the principle of Umoja/Unity arises, wherein we are inspired/required to know and revere that each of us (all of us) are sons and daughters of The Most High, worthy of the love, respect, compassion and fellowship that this reality commands, who will allow nothing (not age, gender, finances, nor tribal or denominational distinctions) to undermine this sacred reality! From that great foundation, we are called to go forward—honoring worthy Ancestors and invoking their presence; cultivating visions and avenues for the greatest good for the greatest numbers of our people; using every resource at our individual and collective command—mental, spiritual, financial, et al.—to produce, protect and perpetuate that greatest good; and always, always involving and teaching the children![3]

Activity

- Assign students to small groups.
- In each group, ask students to nominate one of the 12 women addressed in the chapter to be "Woman of the Millennium."
- Each group should explain why they selected the woman of their choice.
- Compile the data from all groups and identify the woman chosen by the class.
- What does the choice of the students suggest about their preferred model of womanhood and female leadership?

Assignment

- Identify one of the women covered in the chapter whom you most admire.
- Write a short paper and indicate the reasons why you chose the particular woman. Describe the qualities/behaviors/actions that you most admire in the selected woman.

Discussion Questions

- How does learning about these women affect your perceptions of Afrikan American women?
- How many of these women did you have previous knowledge of? If you lacked knowledge of most of them, then why do you think this is the case?
- How do you think that knowledge of these women would affect Afrikan American girls' self-perceptions? Afrikan American boys' perceptions of Afrikan American women? Other non-Afrikan groups' perceptions of Afrikan American women?

---

[3] From: Min. Mxolisi Ozo-Sowande, "In the Throes of Fag-End* Xmas Madness: 'We Need to Rebuild Our Cultural Immune System!!'" [Blog post]. *Visions and Victories*. https://hcvoice.wordpress.com/2011/12/15/in-the-throes-of-fag-end-xmas-madness-we-need-to-rebuild-our-cultural-immune-system/

References

Ani, M. (2011). Kwanzaa: An explanation by Mama Marimba Ani [Unpublished paper].

Collins, P. H. (2000). *Black feminist thought: Knowledge, consciousness, and the politics of empowerment* (2nd ed.). Routledge.

Diop, C. A. (1974). *The African origin of civilization: Myth or reality* (M. Cook, Trans., 1st ed.). [Translation of sections of *Antériorité des civilisations négres* and *Nations nègres et culture*]. Lawrence Hill.

Giddings, P. (1984). *When and where I enter: The impact of Black women on race and sex in America.* William Morrow.

Gladwell, M. (2008). *Outliers: The story of success.* Little, Brown and Company.

Jackson-Lowman, H. (1998). Sankofa: A Black mental health imperative. In R. Jones (Ed.), *African American mental health* (pp. 51–69). Cobb & Henry.

Jackson-Lowman, H. (2013). A culturally syntonic approach to the study of the lives of Black women in America. In H. Jackson-Lowman (Ed.), *Afrikan American women: Living at the crossroads of race, gender, class, and culture.* Cognella Academic.

Jones, C., & Shorter-Gooden, K. (2003). *Shifting: The double lives of Black women.* HarperCollins.

Karenga, M. (1988). *The African American holiday of Kwanzaa: A celebration of family, community & culture.* University of Sankore Press.

Lindsay, L. A., & Miescher, S. F. (2003). *Men and masculinities in modern Africa.* Heinemann.

Lips, H. M. (2006). *A new psychology of women: Gender, culture, and ethnicity* (3rd ed.). McGraw-Hill.

Lorenz, M. (2000). Queen Tiye: A biography. Heptune. http://www.heptune.com/Tiye.html

Schwarz-Bart, S. (2001). *In praise of Black women: Ancient African queens.* University of Wisconsin Press.

Sweetman, D. (1984). *Women leaders in African history.* Heinemann.

Van Sertima, I. (Ed.). (1984). *Black women in antiquity.* Transaction.

Vaz, K. (Ed.). (1995). *Black women in America.* Sage.

Williams, L., & Finch, C. S. (1984). The great queens of Ethiopia. In I. Van Sertima (Ed.), *Black women in antiquity* (pp. 12–35). Transaction.

Wimby, D. (1984). The female Horuses and great wives of Kemet. In I. Van Sertima (Ed.), *Black women in antiquity* (pp. 36–48). Transaction.

Reading 1.2. In the Tradition of Our Mothers

Meditations on Feminine Power and Agency in Yorùbá-Atlantic Religious Practice

Sheriden M. Booker

Introduction

The ancient, Òrìsà-based religious traditions of the Yorùbá people pivot on a profound philosophy and symbolism of the divine feminine. These provide a blueprint for a more African-centered womanhood and feminist praxis, as opposed to earlier womanist[4] theories rooted in a Christian experience and Abrahamic religious scriptures (Coleman, 2006, p. 89). However, incorporating these alternative feminist models within our lives requires that we unpack the meaning behind African indigenous concepts of feminine power and agency, which have often been erroneously interpreted and translated within post-colonial contexts. Through meditations on the divine feminine as conceived by the Yorùbá, and through deeper exploration of the social context, aesthetics, and ethics that have traditionally informed the deployment of this power, we can gain grounding and inspiration for conceptualizing what it means to live in the tradition of Our Mothers going forward.

A Black Woman's Place?

African-descendant women today are caught at the crossroads of myriad conversations around gender roles, feminism, African spirituality, and movements for racial justice in our communities. For many millennials, entry into these conversations has been fueled by digital pop celebrity content that circulates in and through social media. Beyoncé's *Lemonade* album, released in April 2016, incited an unprecedented wave of public debates about African spirituality and Black women's empowerment, as did her embrace of the word "feminist" (Gottesman, 2016) and her Instagram posts about the Yorùbá goddesses Yemoja and Òsun[5] (Idowu & Adegoke, 2017). In response, established thought leaders such as bell hooks also took to the internet to question who can serve as agents of a "just culture of optimal well being where black females can become fully self-actualized and be truly respected" (hooks, 2016).

The following year, Trinidadian-Dominican-American rapper Cardi B—a self-professed "former stripper and a one-time reality TV star"—subtly highlighted the intersection of race, class, and respectability politics at the heart of these burgeoning debates, declaring:

> being a feminist is such a great thing and some people feel like someone like me can't be
> as great as that, they think feminism is … only a woman that can speak properly, that has

---

[4] Womanism is a social theory based on the history and everyday experiences of women of color, especially Black women. Author and poet Alice Walker first used the term "womanist" in her short story "Coming Apart" in 1979, and again in her 1983 book In Search of Our Mother's Gardens. Both Black and Latina women came to embrace the term in contradistinction to White feminism, which they believed held no room for them because of classism and racial issues.

[5] Yemoja and Òsun are spelled Yemoja/Iemanjá and Oshun/Ochun/Oxum in various parts of the Diaspora, depending on local pronunciations and Spanish, Portuguese, and English spelling norms. Since it is impossible to accommodate all of these throughout the course of this chapter, I will try to stick to the Yorùbá spellings of religious words, as it often helps in breaking down the root meaning of concepts. Please see the Glossary for definitions.

a degree, who is a boss, a businessperson … but being a feminist is real simple; it's that a woman can do things the same as a man. I'm equal to a n****. (Collins, 2018)

A few months later, Cardi B collaborated with Puerto Rican rappers Fat Joe and Anuel to create a song and music video that opened with a chant and ritual to Yemoja at the sea and a sample of Hector Lavoe and Willie Colon's famous 1972 salsa tune "Aguanile," also dedicated to Yemoja. While controversial in its juxtaposition of religious symbolism and elements of stripper culture, it was yet another drop in the bucket indicating the emergent relevance of African spirituality within pop culture conversations. Fat Joe himself had just come off of filming the last season of Spike Lee's *She's Gotta Have It* Netflix series, in which the cast and crew travelled to Puerto Rico to film an episode laced with magical realism and references to Òṣun.

Likewise, in 2019, Nigerian-American hip-hop artist Jidenna promoted his new album *85 to Africa* on Power 105.1's *The Breakfast Club,* chiming in with metaphors of the earth and soil:

For men right now, in terms of women … you need to listen, and you need to get out of the way … a king looks at his ground as fertile. Which is a word that is usually associated with woman. But if you understand it as power, when it's fertile ground, people can grow. Then that's when you are truly a king … . [masculinity] is actually being strengthened by women being in power. (Breakfast Club, 2019a)

One month later, African American R&B singer Fantasia came on the same *Breakfast Club* show, asserting the need to return to male-led households by drawing on the oft-cited expression that women are the neck and men are the head: "You can't be the king in the house, fall back and let your man lead the way. You have to learn how to submit …" (Breakfast Club, 2019b). Rooted in her strong Christian faith, her comments sparked Instagram, YouTube, and Twitter conversations about Ephesians Chapter 5:23–27.[6] One woman commented, "Catch it. We were created to be help mates. Bring back old school love and respect. Y'all can keep this New Age mess."

The message is clear. Somehow our actions and behavior as Black women have a critical impact on the future of society. And somehow religion and spirituality are pivotal in justifying how we should act and be. Yet the message is confusing at the same time. Whose religion and what religion? Is talk of the earth and the ground just New Age mess? And how do we reconcile the ideas of stripper culture, "submitting" and "falling back," in the age of *Surviving R. Kelly* and Stand Your Ground, where we are haunted by images of not only dead Black men and boys, but also disappeared Black girls and crying, angry Black mothers? To paraphrase Tarana Burke, a sexual violence survivor and founder of the #MeToo movement,[7] who is coming to the defense of Black women and girls? For years, no one has spoken up (Bellis & Finnie, 2019).

The Òrìṣà Traditions and Alternative Models of Womanhood

Beyoncé, Cardi B, Fat Joe, and Spike Lee's nods to African spirituality are by no means isolated references. Their various odes to Òṣun and Yemoja are a direct reflection of the greater visibility African-based religions have achieved within American popular culture and within African American, African, Caribbean, and Latinx communities across the United States. Many youth of African descent are now leaving the church in large numbers, searching for alternative spiritual paths that resonate with their ancestry and their desire to connect with African roots (Adegoke, 2016; Chappel, 2014; Davis, 2016; Malbroux, 2017; Rutledge, 2017).

---

[6] "For the husband is the head of the wife as Christ is the head of the church, his body, of which he is the Savior. Now as the church submits to Christ, so also wives should submit to their husbands in everything. Husbands, love your wives, just as Christ loved the church and gave himself up for her to make her holy, cleansing her by the washing with water through the word."

[7] #MeToo is a movement against sexual harassment and sexual abuse in which people publicize their allegations of sex crimes, typically committed by powerful and/or prominent men. The objective is to empower women through empathy and strength in numbers, by visibly demonstrating how many women have survived sexual assault and harassment.

The most widely practiced of these African-derived traditions are those based on the worship of Òrìṣà (Orisha/Oricha/Orixa), deities who represent different forces of nature and whose worship originated amongst the Yorùbá people (and their neighbors) in West Africa. As one of the most numerically prominent ethnic groups forcibly brought to the Americas in the latter part of the Transatlantic Slave Trade,[8] the Yorùbá left an indelible impression on New World cultural life. They literally and figuratively sowed the seeds of their religious philosophy and practices in the soil of places such as Haiti, Cuba, Brazil, Trinidad, and, through later inter-Diasporic movement, the United States, Mexico, Jamaica, Puerto Rico, Colombia, and now even Europe, Canada, and Japan. Today, Òrìṣà are worshiped globally through intertwined networks of African Diasporic religious denominations such as the *Nago Nayson*, an order of Yorùbá-derived spirits or *lwa* worshiped within Haitian Vodou; *Lukumí/Regla de Ocha/Santería* (based on Cuban lineages); *Candomblé Ketu/Nago* (based on Brazilian lineages); *Shango/Shango Baptism* (based on Trinidadian lineages); and *Ìṣẹṣe Làgbà/ẹsìn Ibílẹ* (based on Nigerian lineages).[9]

Replete with influential female divinities and void of any concept of Original Sin,[10] Òrìṣà-based traditions have amplified contemporary conversations around gender roles and women's empowerment, providing new context for discussing African-inspired models of womanhood. With the exception of the Black Madonnas in Catholicism, for many African-descendant women, the female Òrìṣà are the first time we have even seen the divine, or aspects of what the Yorùbá call Olódùmarè (God), depicted in our image—God herself in the form of Òṣun, Yemọja, Ọyá, Yewa, Ọbà, and the list goes on. The possibility that we can then be initiated into the mysteries of these Great Mothers is a miracle that has given new meaning to Ntozake Shange's famous quote: "i found god in myself and i loved her, i loved her fiercely" (Shange, 1977, p. 63).

In Search of Tradition

Incorporating these notions of the divine feminine within our everyday lives, however, can be complicated and fraught with intercultural misinterpretations. Within the various Òrìṣà-based traditions, there are a variety of perspectives on women's roles and empowerment, all of which have been influenced by the complex cultural overlays of the diverse post-colonial societies in which we find ourselves living. Added to this, the Yorùbá religious community has never been a singular thing. In the United States, efforts to reclaim African-based religious traditions have always been cross-ethnic and transnational in nature, beginning even with the 1950s Òrìṣà Revivalist Movement, which was spearheaded by African Americans who went on to establish Oyotunji Village in South Carolina in the 1970s (Clarke, 2004). While the tendency has been to search for African roots, Òrìṣà-based religions as they exist today across major American metropoli—New York City, Atlanta, New Orleans, Chicago, Houston, Miami, Los Angeles, etc.—encompass a melange of African descendants from different national, linguistic, and ethnic backgrounds, contributing to the

---

[8] Due to internecine wars that led to the demise of the Old Ọyọ empire in the late 18th and 19th centuries, the Yorùbá were the most numerically prevalent ethnic groups sold into bondage during the latter part of the Transatlantic Slave Trade. While large Bantu populations had been sold to the Americas early on (and therefore made important contributions to the development of culture across the Diaspora), Yorùbá religion is most visible today because these populations were the last to arrive. Even in the United States, the last ship to arrive directly from Africa in 1860 carried 110 Yorùbá of Tapa origin who had been captured by the neighboring Kingdom of Dahomey and sold illegally through the port at Ouidah to a group of Alabama slaveholders, who were circumventing the 1807 Act Prohibiting Importation of Slaves (to the United States directly from Africa). For more on this specific incident, please see Sylviane Anna Diouf (2007), Dreams of Africa in Alabama: The Slave Ship Clotilda and the Story of the Last Africans Brought to America, Oxford University Press.

[9] Please note that I explicitly do not use the term Ifá to refer to Nigerian Òrìṣà-based practices. Orunmila is one Òrìṣà amongst others, and various Òrìṣà priesthoods maintain a complementary yet distinct existence from Ifá. Furthermore, while Orunmila is said to have been witness to creation and destiny, there are several oral texts that point to the fact that the secrets of divination were first owned by female Òrìṣà (see Abimbola, 2001) and activated through *meerindillogun*, the method of divination most commonly used by Ìyálòrìṣà and Bàbálòrìṣà. In Nigeria, priests of different Òrìṣà work closely with Babaláwo but often refer to themselves as "Iṣẹṣe people" or "traditionalists." Also, ẹsìn Ibílẹ is commonly used to refer to "native or indigenous worship/religion."

[10] Original Sin is an Augustine Christian doctrine that says that everyone is born sinful and with a built-in urge to do bad things and to disobey God, as a result of Adam and Eve having eaten the forbidden fruit in the Garden of Eden.

development of a dynamic, transnational religious culture that supersedes the borders of the United States and epitomizes the complex multiplicity of contemporary Blackness.

Spinning off Robert Farris Thompson's concept of the Black Atlantic first expounded in his 1984 text *Flash of the Spirit: African and Afro-American Art & Philosophy*, anthropologists and historians such as J. Lorand Matory, Andrew Apter, and Niyi Afolabi and Toyin Falola have popularized the term "Yorùbá-Atlantic" to label the massive, transnational cultural and religious complex that has emerged over the past three centuries (Afolabi & Falola, 2017; Apter, 2018; Matory, 2004). The "Yorùbá-Atlantic" term is also a springboard for recognizing the ways the Diaspora and those in Africa have participated in a coeval process of creation over the course of this period (Matory, 1999). The oral and written archives reveal that our roots do not lie in one single place of departure, but rather are the result of complex political and historical processes.

This chapter accordingly takes a pan-Diasporic approach, drawing on a multiplicity of written sources, lived experiences, and fieldwork conducted in Nigeria, Cuba, Brazil, and the United States, in order to present a set of meditations on feminine power and agency through the lens of the Yorùbá-Atlantic kaleidescope. Given the complexity of the Yorùbá-Atlantic formation and "the protean idiom of situational alliance making and resistance" that informs Òrìṣà practice (Apter, 2018; Matory, 2019), this chapter eschews a superficial and static appropriation of religious icons and concepts. I instead propose that engaging African ancestral ways requires we take a deeper look at the cosmology, aesthetics, and ethics that have traditionally informed the meaning and deployment of concepts of feminine power and agency within Yorùbá-Atlantic cultural and religious spheres. A complete and global analysis of these phenomena is beyond the scope of this chapter. But by beginning this process, we can at least arrive at a set of meditations that has the potential to catalyze our development of *imọ ijinlẹ̀*. Typically translated as "deep knowledge, "profundity," or "scientific knowledge" (Dictionary of the Yorùbá Language, 1913, p. 113), *imọ ijinlẹ̀* etymologically stems from *mọ* (to know), *jin* (to be deep), and *ilẹ̀* (the earth/the ground)—in other words, earth-deep knowledge. And as we will discover in the next section, the earth/ground is a recurring reference point within Yorùbá language and concepts of the divine feminine.

Witches and Brujas?: *Àjẹ́* in the Yorùbá Worldview

> *I'm that Black a-Rican bruja*
> *Straight out from the Yorùbá ...*
> *We is them ghetto witches*
> *Speaking in tongue b******
> *Fall on the floor*
> *Got sage on the door*

> —Princess Nokia (aka Destini Frasqueri, OniYemọja)

No discourse on feminine power and agency, nor any attempt to arrive at alternative models of womanhood inspired by a Yorùbá worldview, is complete without a discussion of the *àwọn Ìyá Wa*—Our Great Mothers—also referred to as *Àjẹ́, Ìyàmi, Ìyàmi Osoronga*, or simply the Elders of the Night. Traditions for honoring the Ìyàmi are integral to deeper aspects of religious practice in Yorùbáland and within Diasporic systems such as Lukumí and Candomblé. For instance, the annual *Festa das Ayabas* (Festival for the Queens) hosted within religious houses in Bahia, Brazil is an example of how reverence for the Great Mothers and the principal female Òrìṣà has been reproduced and enshrined in Diasporic practice. Yet little is known about The Mothers, as they have been intentionally shrouded behind layers of ritual secrecy. And at best, the archetypal divine feminine energy that they represent has been glossed in popular culture under the terms *witches* (Anglophone), *brujas* (Hispanophone), and *bruxas* (Lusophone).

But within Western societies, the concept of *witches* is saddled with a long history of abuse against women. In places such as the United States, Spanish-speaking America, Brazil, and even parts of Africa that have been colonized and Christianized, the words *witch/bruja/bruxa* have long invoked negative images of unattractive women who are the paradigmatic enemies of progress, science, reason, and organized religion. Indeed, part of the mission of modernization and Christianization in Western Europe was to contain, control, and eradicate indigenous forms of nature-based spiritual practices led by women. Historians estimate that during the transition to capitalism (1450–1750), at least 100,000 accused witches were burned at the stake in Western Europe. Additionally, the Catholic Inquisition of 1492 precipitated the expulsion to the Americas of thousands of accused witches. Meanwhile, as the emergent bourgeois class seized and enclosed common agricultural tracts and introduced wage labor across Western Europe, they forcibly and permanently divorced peasant populations from their traditional relationship to the land and the soil. The Salem Witch Trials. as well as the persecution of Native American and African women across the American colonies, were an extension of this war waged in Europe (Federici, 2004). However, in the colonies the war against alleged witches took on a distinctly racial tone, as non-European women were constantly accused of being innately licentious and prone to using witchcraft to sexually dominate European men, as part of their supposed ploy to undermine the colonial caste system and gender norms (Gutiérrez, 2007).

In more recent years, practitioners of African-based religions, such as hip-hop artist Princess Nokia, have sought to publicly reclaim the words *witch* and *bruja* to positively reference strong women who are aligned with indigenous spiritual practices. On the other hand, scholar-practitioners such as Teresa Washington have advocated that we stop using the word *witch* altogether and instead explore the terms *Ìyàmí* and *Àjẹ́,* as original Yorùbá terminology for women of great spiritual and mystical power. While it is likely that we will continue to see the usage of pro-*witch* and pro-*bruja* terminology in popular culture and social media, the exploration of original Yorùbá terminology can indeed be useful toward recovering a world of deeper sociocultural meaning and religious symbolism.

Washington (2005) argues that the *Ìyàmí* are viewed as the "architects of existence" in Yorùbá cosmology and that *Àjẹ́* in its most basic essence is divine feminine energy, a primordial force that gives efficacy to all things that exist in the universe. *Àjẹ́* possess the secret to life and longevity, as well as the wisdom and efficacy to enable the healthy reproduction of society. Similarly, Nigerian Babaláwo Adedayo Ologundudu asserts that "they are the strong energy of the strong mothers, who will go to any length to protect theirs … . A secret society of all women who, when they get together could make wonders" (Ologundudu, 2008, p. 113). The Mothers are most often depicted as birds who have the mystical power to fly between heaven and earth at night, while others are sleeping. *Àjẹ́* are thus sometimes referred to as *elẹyẹ*—the owner of birds—and are represented by bird motifs and bright red parrot feathers on Yorùbá crowns and other royal iconography (Washington, 2005, p. 22).

The bright red color of the feathers from the tail of the African Grey Parrot, which are used to represent the *Àjẹ́,* seems to reference *Àjẹ́*'s association with women's menstrual blood. In Yorùbá culture:

> the ability to pray effectively is called *ofo àṣẹ* [and] women have *ofo àṣẹ* as a consequence of menstruation. Men receive *ofo àṣẹ* as a consequence of initiation [into Òrìṣà priesthoods]. Because the power of the word is a natural birthright of women, this power has been erroneously associated with 'witchcraft' by those who have tried to give it a negative connotation. (Fatunmbi, 1991, p. 66)

Further, while all women are considered *Àjẹ́,* elderly women beyond menstruating years are especially revered for wielding *Àjẹ́,* precisely because "the blood of these females [is] no longer fertile and no longer flow[s]. It is believed that their barren wombs trap menstrual blood … turning them into vessels of concentrated *àṣẹ,* the vital force of ritual potency and effective verbal command" (Apter, 2018, p. 103). For this reason, the *Àjẹ́* are also referred to as "the one[s] with the vagina that turns upside down without pouring blood" (Drewal & Drewal, 1983, p. 75).

In contrast to women in Western societies, women in West Africa have not historically been relegated to the house. In fact, women are firmly planted at the center of the Yorùbá social, economic, and political universe through their association with the marketplace, the quintessential metaphor for life, as exemplified by the Yorùbá adage *Ayé lojà, Orunilé* —the world (the physical plane) is a marketplace, heaven is home. It is very typical to see women:

> occupy [market] stalls at the center of kingdoms and subordinate towns ... where the road[s] dividing chieftaincy jurisdictions converge, where town criers and king's messengers ma[k]e important announcements, and where the townspeople also mobilize against local and government figures, often led by the market women themselves. (Apter, 2018, p. 103)

The head of the market women is called the *Ìyálóde*—mother of the outside—and she is often a leader of the *Ẹgbẹ́ Àjẹ́*, a sacred society of empowered women who through their covenant with the *Ìyámi* are responsible for ensuring the healthy flow of goods and wealth throughout the community (Ologundudu, 2008, p. 113). While market women may be of all ages, the role of *Ìyálóde* is typically occupied by a post-menopausal woman after she has raised her children and has more time to dedicate to socio-economic affairs and leadership within the community. The fact that she no longer has her monthly menses makes her a "vessel of concentrated *àṣẹ*" and a paradigmatic representative of *Àjẹ́* on Earth.

Within Yorùbá thought, the power of *Àjẹ́* is also intrinsically linked to the actual Earth and to Odùduwà, the highly esoteric Earth goddess. In civil society, Odùduwà is regarded as the male progenitor of the Yorùbá people and the first king of the ancient Yorùbá town Ilé-Ifẹ̀. Yet within deep religious spaces, Odùduwà is regarded as a female Òrìsà, hinting that perhaps the first "king" of the Yorùbá may actually have been a woman. In the origin myths, Odùduwà—whose name means "she who emerged from the dark womb of existence" (Washington, 2005, p. 14)—is said to have descended from heaven and used a bird to scratch out land and life on Earth (Lawal, 2007, p. 24). She is praised as *Yewájobí*—"The Mother of All the Òrìsà and All Living Things"—and is the tutelary goddess and "embodiment of *Àjẹ́*," as it is believed she used divine feminine cosmic energy to create life (Washington, 2005, p. 14). Not surprisingly, amongst Odùduwà's ritual implements is a calabash with a bird inside, the same implement utilized by the *Ìyálóde* in town markets to symbolize the *Ẹgbẹ́ Àjẹ́* sacred sorority.

The calabash is a central icon threaded throughout Yorùbá culture and religion in both Africa and the Diaspora. It is said that Olódùmarè (God/the owner of the universe) gave this icon with the bird inside to the first woman on Earth as a means for her to counteract the muscular advantage of men, and to endow her with mystical powers and the ability to procreate (Lawal, 2007, p. 24). The round calabash itself is a metaphor for both a woman's womb and for the Earth, both of which the Yorùbá have always regarded as round, long before Amerigo Vespucci, Columbus, and the emergence of the modern gynecology. The bird inside the calabash is symbolic of the awesome mystery of creation and conception that occurs inside the womb. Likewise, *òdùmarè* (the universe) is likened to a large pot in which unfathomable and incomprehensible phenomena occur—*òdù* (large pot, cauldron) + *àrè* (unknown phenomenon) (Fakinlede, 2003, pp. 498, 697).

Àjẹ́, as the common thread that runs through this entire chain of symbolism—Odùduwà, the universe, the Earth, the womb, calabashes, and pots—firmly situates The Mothers and women within discourses of divine justice, prefiguring them as judges of human character and actions in relationship to cosmic and terrestrial laws. In Yorùbá society, it is widely believed that "the ground bears witness to everything we do on Earth ... if you hide and do evil, the ground you stand on is watching your actions." This is summarized in the Yorùbá maxim:

> Ogborile o je ku
> Ogbo ri ile oje ja
> To ba gbori ile to seke
> Àṣẹ d'owo ile taa jomu

You live on ile (the ground) and you eat the animals
You live on the ground and eat the fishes
If you live on the ground and betray awo (sacred wisdom, mysteries)
The power to take judgment is in the oath we swear on the ground.
(Ologundudu, 2008, p. 43)

Thus, if Odùduwà is the Earth goddess and Àjẹ́, symbolized by the bird, is the substance she used to create the ground we walk upon, Àjẹ́ play a fundamental role in checking unfettered power, ensuring balance on the Earth by opposing social hierarchies, oppression, and exploitation, and thereby contributing to a healthy and expansive society (Washington, 2005, p. 15).

Due to their association with divine justice, Àjẹ́ also figure prominently in the cosmography of Ògbóni, the ancient Yorùbá society dedicated to the worship of Mother Earth. Inside Ògbóni, Mother Earth is referred to as *Onílè/Onílé* (owner of the ground/owner of the house). In political terms, Ògbóni "is an all-purpose town council, serving as a court for civic and criminal cases as well as an electoral college for selecting a new king or dethroning a bad or unpopular one" (Lawal, 2007, p. 67). In more spiritual terms, the power to act in judgement of important political, criminal, and civic matters stems from Mother Earth, and the society itself revolves around the "veneration of Mother Earth so she can ensure the fertility, survival, happiness, and social stability of a community" (Lawal, 2007, p. 67). Members or initiates of the society refer to themselves as *Ọmọ Ìyá*—Children of the Great Mother.

By extension of their integral role in Ògbóni, Àjẹ́ are associated with the *Ọba's* (king's) authority to rule. As Babatunde Lawal notes, almost all Yorùbá crowns are stylistically adorned with a bird motif as well as parrot feathers, which has a three-fold meaning (Lawal, 2007, p. 24). One, it identifies the *Ọba* as a descendant of Odùduwà and the bird she used to create life on Earth. Two, the bird motif denotes the king as *èkéjì Òrìṣà* (second in command to Òrìṣà) and as an intermediary between heaven and Earth, much like the *Ìyàmi* who transform themselves into birds to fly between heaven and Earth at night. Lastly, it notifies the people that the King rules with the permission of the mystical Àjẹ́ and the archetypal female power (Abiodun, 2001, p. 19). In fact, in many Yorùbá towns it is the king's actual mother, *Ìyá Ọba*, who seats new kings on the throne, extending the idea that he is only able to rule with the support and permission of The Mothers and women more generally (Lawal, 2007, p. 24). Thus invested with the blessing of Àjẹ́, the king is responsible to rule for the benefit of all and to submit to cosmic retribution if he transgresses the natural laws of Our Mothers.

The Divine Feminine and Female Agency Within a Patrilineal Society

Given the lauded position and power wielded by Àjẹ́ within Yorùbá cosmology, it is easy to see why scholars, artists, and religious practitioners such as Princess Nokia and Teresa Washington pinpoint colonialism as pivotal in redefining African women's power and societal roles. This is a valid argument that begs us to continue to scrutinize how Western prejudices, colonial social structures, enslavement, and Christianization have served to undercut the authority and voices of women. At the same time, however, our analysis of feminine power and agency is not complete until we examine how this religious symbolism plays out in a patrilineal society such as the Yorùbá. While The Mothers are approached with awe and respect, they are also viewed with an ambivalent fear due to the raw, creative power that Àjẹ́ are said to possess. For if the Great Mothers are revered as the "architects of existence" and the sustainers of an equitable society, they are simultaneously dreaded as the "great destroyers."

Àjẹ́ and the cosmic energy that they represent are considered extremely dangerous, primarily because of their unpredictable potential to destroy and block all blessings. The word Àjẹ́ itself comes from the contraction of *Ìyá jẹ* (mother who eats,) and their capacity to devour is frequently referenced in Yorùbá oral poetry such as the following:

> Mother who kills without striking
> My mother who kills quickly without a cry
> Mother who kills her husband yet pities him
> (Abiodun, 2001, p. 25)

Babaláwo Ologundudu (2008), who one minute refers to *Àjẹ́* as "women who can accomplish wonders," comes back later to say, "everybody fears them. Babaláwos and Asawosìṣẹ̀gùn (herbalists) also respect them. They always appeal to them in prayers and when performing rituals" (p. 113).

This fear of *Àjẹ́* and women's womb-centered power and agency extends to everyday life, where females who possess *àṣẹ*—the ability to make things happen—are simultaneously regarded with "condemnation [and] admiration." And this is particularly true if their power is perceived as a potential threat to the hierarchical authority and reproduction of the patrilineal family compound. Karin Barber (1991) notes that command of witchcraft powers in Okuku, Ọ̀yọ́ State,[11] where she performed extensive field research during the 1980s, often resulted in women being "branded as a pariah, not fully human, and not fully integrated into the community" (p. 250). Whereas

> a big man's success depend[ed] on command of the social environment, including women, whose fertility must be harnessed to his project of social expansion … a woman who threaten[ed] to alienate her fertility to her own project of self-aggrandizement (through accumulation of wealth) [was] therefore a witch rather than merely a big woman in control of juju. (Barber, 1991, p. 250)

Apter (2018) cites a similar phenomenon, based on his research in the Ekiti region of Yorùbáland, also in the 1980s. Female traders who became too successful were viewed as a threat to their husband's project of social expansion, in that their sons might choose to abandon the patrilineage in order to inherit their mother's wealth. These women were often labeled witches and were believed to "subvert fertility by sabotaging, even cannibalizing, procreative vitality and by blocking the flow of money and commodities—hoarding, hiding, and accumulating profit by removing it from circulation" (Apter, 2018, p. 104). Cash Madams—labeled as such due to the huge wads of cash they stored in their bras and to the conspicuous wealth they had accumulated over the years—"may [have been] publicly praised, but privately … suspected of witchcraft" (Apter, 2018, p. 104).

Ultimately, accumulation and material success have traditionally resulted in women's near erasure from the social and historical record. Speaking of the few wealthy, self-made women that she knew in Okuku, Karin Barber (1991) proffers the insightful commentary that "Ayantayo, Omolola and Ìyá Keke had no *oríkì* about their achievements" (p. 251)—*oríkì* being praise songs used for "greeting the head" and telling the history of Òrìṣà, family lineages, and prominent social figures.

> In their careers, the cycle of self-aggrandizement suffered [a] crucial block. Any reputation at all was likely to turn to a reputation for evil … . Though there were and still are a number of successful and wealthy women in Okuku, they are not usually marked down in memory as people of great reputation. They are spoken of with reluctance, and with a mixture of disapproval and unwilling admiration by other women as well as by men. (Barber, 1991, p. 251)

This broader sociological analysis of feminine power and agency adds nuance to our understanding of the concept of *Àjẹ́*. In the above examples, the marketplace—the quintessential metaphor for life itself,

---

[11] Today, Okuku is now a part of Ọ̀ṣun State very close to the border of ọ̀yọ́ State, according to new state lines redrawn in 1991.

and the domain over which *Àjẹ́* are said to maintain control—appears to be turned against successful women precisely as a means of undercutting their power, where it is perceived as subverting the authority of men within the patrilineal family compound. While one could interpret this as a proof of ultimate patriarchal dominance and the silencing of women, it can also be read as an indicator of the way *Àjẹ́*, the marketplace, and women's wombs are actually *the* stopgap that mitigates against men's dominance over women within the domestic, marital, and political spaces. After all, the mythology states that the calabash with a bird inside was given by Olódùmarè to women precisely "to counteract the muscular advantage of men" (Lawal, 2007, p. 24).

Rather than overlook these contrasting conceptions of women's power and social roles, it is imperative that we lean into them, and that we explore the purposeful function of dualities and polarities in the Yorùbá worldview. The admixture of admiration and fear, of resentment and reverential respect for *Àjẹ́*—as well as the interplay of female and male domains (i.e., the marketplace versus the patrilineal compound)—are critical for understanding traditional *approaches to* and *interpretations of* feminine agency and power within Òrìṣà religious spheres. Even the apparent silencing of wealthy, successful women with no *oríkì* is an exposition on power itself, within the Yorùbá-Atlantic cultural matrix.

While it is clear that the concept of *Àjẹ́* is the cosmological axis upon which the Òrìṣà traditions spin, there are distinct ethical and aesthetic principles that inform the way this feminine power and agency is deployed and honored. For one, within Yorùbá culture, beauty is generally perceived in mediums and complementary dualities (Hallen, 2000). As Deidre Badejo (1998) notes, "African femininity complements African masculinity and defends both with the ferocity of a lioness while simultaneously seeking male defense of both as critical, demonstrable, and mutually obligatory" (p. 101). Likewise, "since African religions and men maintain an ancestral bond to women's reproductive ability, the total abnegation of women's power is tantamount to self-destruction" (Badejo, 1998, p. 101). This ethos of complementary dualities is reflected in the conception of "the cosmos as a delicate balance of opposites—the masculine and feminine, day and night, hot and cool, hard and soft" (Lawal, 2007, p. 68). These properties tend to be gendered within Yorùbá parlance—for instance, to be cool, dark, and soft is considered female; to be hard and hot is considered male. And the preference is for one to aspire to coolness and femaleness, as indicated by the typical Yorùbá new year greeting—*Ki ódún ó ya abo*—meaning, may the year turn out to be female, i.e., smooth and full of blessings (Lawal, 2007, p. 71). Art historian Robert Farris Thompson (1973) describes this aspiration to coolness as a "return to freshness [and] … to an immaculate concentration of the mind" (p. 41). Coolness is to have a composure and self-mastery that places one in closer proximity to the ancestors and enables one to transcend time so that one "can concentrate on truly important matters of social balance" and "stability in the context of the group" (Thompson, 1973, p. 41). Viewed through this lens, while *Àjẹ́* and femaleness are core principles that tether us, they have no ethical basis outside a context of purposeful balance polarities, as it is the interplay of these polarities and their continuous harmonization that constitute the totality of the universe and a healthy society.

Secondly, within Òrìṣà traditions, ritual power and authority is circumscribed by *èèwọ̀* (taboos) and oaths of silence, the maintenance of which is believed to abet one's accumulation of *àṣẹ* (the power to be and command). Even after initiation into one of the Òrìṣà priesthoods, there is a constant process of learning that leads to deeper levels of *imọ ijinlẹ̀* throughout one's life. A Yorùbá proverb asserts, *Awo j'awo lo, awo le gb'awo mi tori tori*—Secret surpasses secret, secret can swallow secret completely. Similarly, the concept of discretion and strategic silence is highly valued in the Diaspora. A common saying employed within the Cuban Lukumí/Santería tradition asserts: *Él que no sabe y no sabe que no sabe, húyelo. Él que sabe que no sabe, instrúyelo. Y él que sabe que sabe pero no hace alarde de lo que sabe, síguelo, es un sabio.*—The one who does not know and has no idea that he does not know anything, stay away from him. The one who knows that he does not know anything, instruct him. And the one who knows that he knows but does not flaunt what he knows, follow him. He is a wise man.

This aesthetic of silence and discretion can clash with outward-focused displays of power common in our social-media-driven Westernized societies, and in fact, it may be erroneously construed as a sign of disempowerment. But in a Yorùbá worldview, it is precisely the silent and pregnant threat of *Àjẹ́*'s potential power and their ability to destroy that endow women with *àṣẹ* and agency. As Apter (2018) notes, "if actual witches are feared and despised for their cannibalistic appetites and destructive agency, as *potential witches* Yorùbá women are honored and respected, for within their blood lies the secret of their power and value" (p. 105, my emphasis). Mother Earth and the principal female Òrìsà model this aesthetic of the cool, which carries with it an aesthetic of silence and discretion. In particular, Odùduwà—"she who emerged from the dark womb of existence"—the powerful Earth goddess who used *Àjẹ́* to create existence, is not called upon every day, nor are her ritual implements viewable by the uninitiated eye. Instead, she is empowered through strategic silence, "retired behind taboo … triumphant in being forgotten, well-loved, and faithfully served while hidden in the … Ògbóni society" (Wenger, 1983, p. 195). Interestingly, the Ọọni of Ifẹ̀ (the supreme king of the Yorùbá, who is said to be a direct descendant of Odùduwà) has traditionally never spoken in public. Until 1903, under increasing British colonial pressures, he never left his palace after ascending the throne. Ruling with the blessings and authority of *Àjẹ́* behind them, the Ọọnis of antiquity governed their people for thousands of years from the confines of their royal court, their faces covered with the beaded veil of their crown so that "no mortal, not even the representative of the English monarch could behold their face" (Omonhinmin, 2019).

Which Way From Here?

Ooh hey
I'm trying to decide
Which way to go
Think I made a wrong turn
Back there somewhere
Didn't cha know
Didn't cha know

—Erykah Badu, "Didn't Cha Know"

In her 1999 bestseller *When Chickenheads Come Home to Roost: My Life as A Hip Hop Feminist,* Jamaican-born, Bronx-bred hip-hop journalist and Yemọja priestess Joan Morgan famously argued that many of us who came of age after the Civil Rights generation vacillate between worlds of meaning and aspirations for female empowerment. On the one hand, we wonder if the distinct brand of Black feminism forged by that foundational generation and encapsulated by the heart-wrenching poems of great lyricists such as Ntozake Shange can really serve as a guide for our experience. And on the other, we love the hip-hop sounds that have come to punctuate the beat of our walk. Yet, 30 years into the rise of hip-hop as a global phenomenon, we carry guilt that we have been complicit in building an entire culture that can be misogynistic, dismissive of women's worth and power, and at times violent toward those who do not fit Euro-heteronormative standards. In a sort of ironic African cultural retention of *Àjẹ́*, Black women are glibly labeled "chickenheads" and "birds" in rap songs, but not the good kind.

Ni*** you know how it go
She deserved that, she a bird, it's a bird trap
You think if I didn't rap she would flirt back?

—J. Cole, "No Role Modelz"

The cultural debates discussed at the beginning of this chapter are a source of constant tension for many of us as we attempt to define what it means to be a Black feminist at this moment in time. Who has authority to claim these labels for us? What kinds of behaviors do Black feminists engage in? How do we position ourselves in relationship to heteronormative masculinity and patriarchal institutions, whilst also battling the institutionalized racism that impacts our families, our communities, our partners, and our spouses? For many years, meditations on these issues within scholarly circles have been rooted primarily in a Christian experience, informed by Abrahamic texts that define women as merely a rib of Adam.

Within this context, the concept of *Àjẹ́* offers us a profound alternative model of feminine power and agency that prefigures women as central to Creation and validates our direct connection to divinity as integral beings independent of, yet complementary to, men. The Yorùbá concept of the feminine divine opens space for us to meditate on the following ideas and principles:

- **The primacy of the womb**. The metaphorical womb of the universe, as well as the human womb out of which we are born and have capacity to birth things into the world, is sacred, as is menstrual blood. More than just an instrument of pleasure or reproduction in service of patriarchy, it is a seat of power and a microcosm of the potentiality of all life. These awesome regenerative powers give women authority as social agents. Embracing this is also key to understanding the deeper symbolism around the calabash of *Àjẹ́* and the use of pots that is threaded throughout Yorùbá-Atlantic religious practices.

- **The sovereignty of the ground we walk upon**. As the first emanation of *Àjẹ́* in this world, the ground is our source of truth, justice, and self-worth. While some may deign to seize, own, and horde land, no one can really own the Earth. By respecting, caring for, and rooting ourselves in the soil, we bring ourselves into alignment with laws of divine justice, which are the laws of the universe itself.

- **The centrality of women to the marketplace of.** Women and *Àjẹ́* are indispensable to economic life and to the circulation of money, supplies, food, and other goods. We also have a moral imperative to participate in political life and governance. In the market women of yore, we have a prototype for the underground railroad conductor, contemporary social justice organizer, public defender, filmmaker, news commentator, professor, city councilwoman, or any number of other social roles in which we have the capacity to shape public opinion and values and hold the powers-that-be accountable for maintaining a healthy, expansive society.

- **The complementarity of the feminine and masculine**. The totality of the universe is maintained through a cosmic interplay of male and female principles, and part of our purpose is to seek harmonization and balance between these polarities. Within a feminist praxis based on the concept of *Àjẹ́,* this means that the healing and empowerment of African-descendant women is tied to the healing and empowerment of men.

- **The power of cool silence**. Because we are born with God-given *ofo àṣẹ*, our words have the power to shape our social reality … as do our silence and the potentiality of things unsaid. An aesthetic of cool silence and discretion does not equal submission; rather, when strategically deployed, it is the paramount expression of transcendental power and aspiration to social balance.

These meditations are an invitation to further study, not solely in a book sense but also in the sense of studying the phenomenon within ourselves and within the world. The concept of *Àjẹ́* is both alluring and promising in terms of its ideation of women as vessels and agents of creative power. Yet there is a lot contained within this philosophy that may challenge some of our preconceived notions of leadership, authority, and power in Westernized cultural contexts. This will require us to think deeply about the social contours within which womb-centered power manifests itself today, and about where and how the aesthetic of the cool and strategic silence are wielded in relationship to outward-facing institutions of power and governance.

Ultimately, the Yorùbá concept of *Àjẹ́* offers a vision of women as powerful social agents with full rights to participation in the marketplace of life. We are not confined to being any one thing, and like the river, we must keep flowing. Our central role in the marketplace requires that we employ situational intelligence to construct balance in our own lives and in our communities. And this is perhaps where notions of womanhood rooted in the oral-based religious traditions of the Yorùbá Atlantic may depart from Abrahamic faiths rooted in the fixed written texts of the Bible and the Koran.

Renowned Yorùbá linguist Olabiyi Yai (1994) asserts that "we cannot hope to do justice to Yorùbá … history unless we are prepared to reexamine, question, even abandon certain attitudes, assumptions and concepts of our various disciplines" (p. 107). Delving deeper into the concept of tradition from a Yorùbá philosophical and linguistic perspective, he states:

"Tradition" in Yorùbá is *àṣà*. Innovation is implied in the idea of tradition. The verb *ṣà*, from which *àṣà* is derived, means to select, choose, discriminate, or discern. Something cannot qualify as *àṣà* which has not been the result of deliberate choice (*ṣà*) based on discernment and awareness of historical practices and processes (*ìtàn*) by individual or collective *orí*. And since choice presides over the birth of an *àṣà* (tradition), the latter is permanently liable to metamorphosis. (Yai, 1994, p. 114)

If tradition is constant metamorphosis, what are we looking for, then? Turning his attention to the Yorùbá art form of *oríkí,* Yai (1994) asserts, "by its nature, *oríkí* is an unfinished and generative art enterprise" (p. 114) as exemplified by the phrase "akiikitan" (the one whose praises are endless). Similarly, in her book *I Could Speak Until Tomorrow,* Karin Barber (1991) speaks about *oríkí* as an art form promulgated principally (but not exclusively) by women as a way of actively recounting the past *and* creating the future, breath after breath, line after line, word after word. In other words, *oríkí* is an attempt to "evoke and provoke" our existence with a cognizance that "Yorùbá aesthetics is an invitation to infinite metonymic difference and departure, and not a summation for sameness and imitation" (Yai, 1994, p. 113). In Yorùbá-Atlantic religious practice, we are charged with bringing forth our reality and invoking relevant histories in the present, much like the seasoned women sitting at the edge of Yorùbá towns using their *ofo àṣẹ*—power of words—to recite *oríkí* "until tomorrow."

But as Karin Barber (1991) notes, the best performers of *oríkí* have never been the ones who simply create their own verses and style. Like in hip-hop battles, where the best lyricists signify and riff off classic rhymes or respond to the lyrics of another MC, "the preferred [*oríkí*] style" amongst the Yorùbá has always been "somewhere between … where the performer's individual skill and creativity ha[s] scope for display but where *the inherited knowledge* [is] preserved, allowing multiple voices from the past to continue to speak in the present" (Barber, 1991, p. 160, my emphasis).

Within the Yorùbá-Atlantic, the canonic oral literatures (*oríkí, ìtàn, eṣe Ifá* and *pàtàkì*) about powerful female Òrìsà and The Great Mothers who wielded influence over the creation of the universe are the multiple voices which we have at our disposal to draw upon as paradigms of *feminine power and agency.* They provide direction for how to remain grounded in the primordial essence of the divine feminine. Additionally, the voices of our immediate elders and of the community, who initiate us into the mysteries of Òrìsà in the kitchen and the *igbodù*, are another set of voices who reach back like an unbroken chain of wisdom. Rather than offering a singular answer about a woman's role or a static concept of African-centered womanhood, they give us examples of power, purpose, and *àṣẹ*. They model the timeless, divine struggle to achieve balance between the masculine and the feminine; they exemplify the regal efficacy of cool, strategic silence; and they root us within the Earth, providing us with inspiration to stand *our* own ground.

Glossary

Àjẹ́—loosely translated as "witch" in English; Yorùbá term for women of extraordinary spiritual power and for the cosmic, divine feminine energy responsible for creation at the beginning of time. Contraction of *Ìyá* (mother who eats).

àṣà—literally Yorùbá for "tradition, culture," but etymologically breaks down to mean that which is the product of a process of collective informed selection and choice.

àṣẹ—the power to be and command; also a term used to conclude prayers in Yorùbá, as in "so it will be." In this sense, also translated as "Amen."

asawosiṣègùn—herbalists who have mastered the art of using herbs to heal; literally *asawo* (the one who deals in mysteries) + *iṣègùn* (the art and science of medicine).

àwọn Ìyá Wa—literally "Our Great Mothers"; another honorific title for *Àjẹ́*.

babaláwo—literally "the father of the mysteries"; high priest of Ifá, initiated to Orunmila, Òrìṣà of fate, destiny, and divination.

brujas—term for "witch" in Spanish; often used in the Hispanophone Daspora to refer to women who possess knowledge of the occult.

bruxas—term for "witch" in Portuguese; often used in the Lusophone Diaspora to refer to women who possess knowledge of the occult.

Candomblé Ketu/Nago—the largest and most influential branch (*nation*) of Candomblé, an African-based religion practiced in Brazil. Centered on the worship of Òrìṣà (Orixá), the word Candomblé means "ritual dancing or gathering in honor of the gods," and Ketu is the name of the Ketu region of Benin bordering present-day Nigeria, where this variant of Òrìṣà worship originated. Nago was a term applied to enslaved Africans exported from this region of West Africa.

èèwò—literally "taboo" or "sacred prohibition" in Yorùbá; by maintaining observance of taboos, one increases his or her *àṣẹ*.

ẹṣẹ Ifá—chapters of *Ifá* corpus; poetic incantations that correspond to the 256 Odù of the *Ifá* literary corpus (see next entry below). The ese contain prescriptions for ebo and moral lessons and reflect Yorùbá history, language, beliefs, cosmovision, and contemporary social issues.

Ifá—a system of divination that provides an avenue of communication to the spiritual realm and the intent of one's destiny. *Babaláwo* perform *Ifá* divination either using an *opele* (divining chain) or 16 *ikin* (palm nuts). The divination is organized around 16 "books" called Odù, which when combined (16 x 16) produce 256 letters that provide guidance to the client about her/his life. The Ifá proverbs, stories, and poetry attached to each of these 256 letters are orally passed down. In 2005, UNESCO added the Ifá divination system to its list of Masterpieces of the Oral and Intangible Heritage of Humanity.

Igbodù—igbó (bush) and Odù (wife of Ọrunmila) refers to the room or area where an initiation ceremony takes place, which also houses the altar or throne for the Òrìṣà.

Ìṣẹṣe Làgbà/ẹ̀sìn Ibílẹ̀—terms used to refer to Òrìṣà-based practices in Yorùbáland/Nigeria. *Ìṣẹṣe Làgbà* literally translates as "actions and deeds in the way of the elders from way back when." *ẹ̀sìn Ibílẹ̀* literally translates as "native or indigenous worship/religion."

ìtàn—literally "history" or "story."

Ìyámi or Ìyámi Osoronga—literally "my mother"; another appellative for the divine feminine energies known as *Àjẹ́*.

Lukumí/Regla de Ocha/Santería—terms used to refer to the system of Òrìṣà worship that developed in Cuba. *Santería* is a deeply cultural term specific to the Cuban social context. The term has become controversial in recent decades due to its association with the practice of using Catholic Saints to cover the Òrìṣà during the Colonial period and through the present. Nevertheless, many argue that the deeper one is initiated in Santería, the more apparent it becomes that the religion pivots on African-based practices rooted in Òrìṣà worship. Lukumí is also a colonial term, used by Spanish slaveholders to label enslaved Africans brought from the Yorùbá ethnic region of West Africa.

#MeToo Movement—a movement against sexual harassment and sexual abuse in which people publicize their allegations of sex crimes, typically committed by powerful and/or prominent men. The objective is to empower women through empathy and strength in numbers, by visibly demonstrating how many women have survived sexual assault and harassment.

Ọbà—Òrìṣà of the Ọbà River, whose source lies near the town of Igbon, where her worship originates. She is a female warrior and is generally considered the senior wife of Sàngó, the deified third king of the Yorùbá Ọ̀yọ́ Empire. Oba rules over stable relationships, marriage, and love, but conversely is also a protector of abused women and of those who have been neglected. Also spelled Obbá (Cuba) or Obá (Brazil) in the Diaspora.

Odùduwà—Òrìṣà of primordial creation and the Earth; the progenitor of the Yorùbá people.

ofo àṣẹ—words of power; the power to change things with words.

Ògbóni—a secret and ritually united corporation of political and religious leaders dedicated to worshiping Onílẹ̀ (Mother Earth) and to adjudicating social issues. They formed part of the checks-and-balances system of the Yorùbá kingdoms. They held the power to both seat and depose kings.

Olodùmarè—the Yorùbá concept of God; It is neither he nor she, but rather the totality of existence. Literally a contraction of *Oni* (owner) + *òdù* (large pot) + *àrè* (unknown phenomenon); translates as the "owner of the universe" (*òdùmarè* is also the Yorùbá word for Universe). This term for God plays off the metaphor of rounded containers and wombs that are a mysterious source of creation.

Onílẹ̀—Mother Earth, central Òrìṣà worshiped within the Ògbóni secret society. Literally "owner of the ground."

Onílé—another term for Mother Earth used within the Ògbóni temple. Literally "owner of the house."

Original Sin—an Augustine Christian doctrine that says that everyone is born sinful and with a built-in urge to do bad things and to disobey God, as a result of Adam and Eve having eaten the forbidden fruit in the Garden of Eden.

oríkí—literally "greetings for one's head"—*orí* (head, destiny) + *kí* (to greet); praise songs for Òrìṣà or prominent social figures. Also praise songs used within families to recount to members and individuals who they are, what their lineage is, and the great feats of their ancestors.

Òrìṣà (Orisha/Oricha)—loosely translated to mean "gods" and "goddesses." In actuality, Yorùbá religion is a monotheistic practice in which the Òrìṣà are not separate or distinct from God, but rather aspects or manifestations of the one supreme divinity Olodùmare. Òrìṣà are believed to have come to Earth to serve as guides for all creation and humanity in particular, on how to live in balance and be successful on *Ayé* (the physical realm/the world).

Ọ̀ṣun (Oshun/Ochun/Oxum)—a riverine Òrìṣà whose name means "the source." She is closely associated with fertility, the moment of conception, and the healing properties of water, the most indispensable element of all life. She is also associated with purity, love, sensuality, wealth, and diplomacy. The Ọ̀ṣun river bears her name in Southwest Nigeria. Also spelled Oshun (English), Ochun (Spanish), and Oxum (Portuguese) in the Diaspora.

Ọyá—Òrìṣà of the Niger River whose name means "the tearer." She wields the power winds, lightning, and violent storms, and rules over death and rebirth. She too is a female warrior and is married to Sàngó, the deified third king of the Yorùbá Ọ̀yọ́ Empire. In Brazil and Nigeria, she is sometimes referred to as Iyánsán—mother of nine. Also spelled Oiá or Iansã (Portuguese) in the Diaspora.

pàtàkì—literally "important matter"; often used in the Diaspora to refer to a story or parable about Òrìṣà that contains an ethical or moral lesson for practitioners.

Shango/Shango Baptism—In Trinidad, Òrìṣà worship is also called Shango, and the term "Shango Baptist" is sometimes used to describe worshipers who are involved with both Spiritual Baptism and Orisha/Shango. The term "Shango Baptist" has come to have negative connotations for some worshippers of both Spiritual

Baptism and Òrìṣà/Shango, who argue that those who say "Shango Baptist" conflate the two religions, when in fact they are separate.

Yemọja (Yemaya/Iemanjá)—Òrìṣà of maternity, motherhood, and the sea, salt waters, and Ogun River in Nigeria. Name literally means *Yèyé + ọmọ + ẹja*—Mother whose children are plentiful as fish. Also spelled Yemaya (Cuba) or Iemanjá (Brazil) in the Diaspora.

Yewa—Òrìṣà who resides in the graveyard and is responsible for the decomposition of bodies in the transition to the afterlife. Name literally means "mother of beautiful character." She is a mysterious and reclusive Òrìṣà who is associated with virginity. Her worship originated amongst the Egbado-Yorùbá along what is today the border of Benin and Nigeria.

Womanism—a social theory based on the history and everyday experiences of women of color, especially Black women. Author and poet Alice Walker first used the term "womanist" in her short story "Coming Apart" in 1979, and again in her 1983 book *In Search of Our Mother's Gardens*. Both Black and Latina women came to embrace the term in contradistinction to White feminism, which they believed held no room for them because of classism and racial issues.

References

Abimbola, W. (2001). The bag of wisdom: Ọ̀ṣun and the origins of the Ifá divination. In J. M. Murphy & M.-M. Sanford (Eds.), *Ọ̀ṣun across the waters: A Yorùbá goddess in Africa and the Americas*. Indiana University Press.

Abiodun, R. (2001). Hidden power: Ọ̀ṣun, the seventeenth Odu. In J. M. Murphy & M.-M. Sanford (Eds.), *Ọ̀ṣun across the waters: A Yorùbá goddess in Africa and the Americas*. Indiana University Press.

Adegoke, Y. (2016, September 13). 'Jesus hasn't saved us': The young Black women returning to ancestral religions. *Vice*. https://www.vice.com/en/article/bjgxx4/jesus-hasnt-saved-us-young-black-women-returning-ancestral-religions

Afolabi, N., & Falola, T. (2017). *The Yorùbá in Brazil, Brazilians in Yorùbáland: Cultural encounter, resilience, and hybridity in the Atlantic world*. Carolina Academic Press.

Apter, A. (2018). *Odùduwà's chain: Locations of culture in the Yorùbá-Atlantic*. University of Chicago Press.

Badejo, D. (1998). African feminism: Mythical and social power of women of African descent. *Research in African Literatures*, 29(2), 94–111.

Barber, K. (1991). *I could speak until tomorrow: Oríkí, women, and the past in a Yorùbá town*. Edinburgh University Press.

Bellis, N., & Finnie, A. (Directors). (2019). *Surviving R. Kelly* [Documentary series]. Lifetime Network.

Breakfast Club Power 105.1 FM. (2019a, August 20). *Jidenna talks new music, African history, polyamory + more*. YouTube. https://www.youtube.com/watch?v=J1so1OswmY4

Breakfast Club Power 105.1 FM. (2019b, September 16). *Fantasia on happiness, love and balance, new music + more*. YouTube. https://www.youtube.com/watch?v=cTk07kPS1-4

Chappel, E. (2014, November 13). More Blacks embrace African spirituality. *Indianapolis Recorder*. https://indianapolisrecorder.com/2493800a-6b5d-11e4-8903-9b9666b8bba3/

Clarke, K. M. (2004). *Mapping Yorùbá networks: Power and agency in the making of transnational communities*. Duke University Press.

Coleman, M. A. (2006). Must I be a womanist? *Journal of Feminist Studies in Religion, 22*(1), 85–96.

Collins, H. (2018, February 8). why the whole world is talking about cardi b. *i-D.* https://i-d.vice.com/en_us/article/vbpe33/cardi-b-interview-2018

Davis, S. (2016, December 14). Princess Nokia talks infusing santería in her music. *Vibe.* https://www.vibe.com/features/viva/princess-nokia-talks-santeria-473957/

Dictionary of the Yorùbá language. (1913). Lagos: Church Missionary Society Bookshop.

Drewal, H. (1983). *Gẹlẹdẹ: Art and female power among the Yorùbá*. Indiana University Press.

Fakinlede, K. J. (2003). *Yorùbá-English modern practical dictionary*. Hippocrene.

Fatunmbi, A. F. (1991). *Iwa-Pele: Ifa quest: The search for the source of Santeria and Lucumi*. Original Publications.

Federici, S. (2004). *Caliban and the witch: Women, the body, and primitive accumulation*. Autonomedia.

Gottesman, T. (2016, April 4). EXCLUSIVE: Beyoncé wants to change the conversation. *Elle.* https://www.elle.com/fashion/a35286/beyonce-elle-cover-photos/

Gutiérrez, R. A. (2007). Women on top: The love magic of Indian witches of New Mexico. *Journal of the History of Sexuality, 16*(3), 373–390.

Hallen, B. (2000). *The good, the bad, and the beautiful: Discourse about values in Yorùbá culture*. Indiana University Press.

hooks, b. (2016, May 9). Moving beyond pain [Blog post]. bell hooks Institute. http://www.bellhooksinstitute.com/blog/2016/5/9/moving-beyond-pain

Idowu, T., & Adegoke, Y. (2017, May 30). Five times Beyoncé was influenced by Nigerian culture. *CNN.* https://www.cnn.com/2017/05/29/africa/beyonce-nigerian-culture/index.html

Lawal, B. (2007). *Embodying the sacred in Yorùbá art: Featuring the Bernard and Patricia Wagner Collection*. High Museum of Art.

Malbroux, L. (2017, December 18). Why more young Black people are trading in church for African spirituality. *SplinterNews.com.* https://splinternews.com/why-more-young-black-people-are-trading-in-church-for-a-1821316608

Matory, J. L. (1999). The English professors of Brazil: On the diasporic roots of the Yorùbá nation. *Comparative Studies in Society and History, 41*(1), 72–103.

Matory, J. L. (2004). Gendered agendas: The secrets scholars keep about Yorùbá-Atlantic religion. *Gender & History, 15*(3), 409–439.

Matory, J. L. (2019). Oduduwa's chain: Locations of culture in the Yorùbá-Atlantic [Book review]. *African and Black Diaspora: An International Journal, 12*(1), 109–113.

Morgan, J. (1999). *When chickenheads come home to roost: My life as a hip hop feminist*. Simon & Schuster.

Ologundudu, A. (2008). *The cradle of Yorùbá culture*. Center for Spoken Words: Institute of Yorùbá Culture.

Omonhinmin, G. (2019, January 20). In the past, Ooni neither travelled nor spoke in public. *The Guardian: Sunday Magazine*. https://guardian.ng/sunday-magazine/in-the-past-ooni-neither-travelled-nor-spoke-in-public/

Rutledge, E. (2017, October 9). African spirituality and the power of religious reclamation. Black Perspectives (African American Intellectual History Society). https://www.aaihs.org/african-spirituality-and-the-power-of-religious-reclamation/

Shange, N. (1977). *for colored girls who have considered suicide / when the rainbow is enuf*. MacMillan Publishing.

Thompson, R. F. (1973, Autumn). An aesthetic of the cool. *African Arts*, *7*(1), 40–43, 64–67, 89–91.

Thompson, R. F. (1984). *Flash of the spirit: African and Afro-American art & philosophy*. Vintage Books.

Washington, T. (2005). *Our mothers, our powers, our texts: Manifestations of Àjẹ́ in Africana literature*. Indiana University Press.

Wenger, S. (1983). *A life with the gods in their Yorùbá homeland*. Austria: Perlinger Verlag.

Yai, O. (1994). In praise of metonymy: The concepts of tradition and creativity in the transmission of Yorùbá artistry over space and time. In R. Abiodun, H. J. Drewal, & J. Pemberton III (Eds.), *The Yorùbá artist: New theoretical perspectives on African arts*. Smithsonian Institution Press.

Reading 1.3. Black and Afrikan Feminisms

For the Liberation of Our People

Helen A. Neville and Nimot M. Ogunfemi

> *Nobody's free until everybody's free.*
>
> —Fannie Lou Hamer

> *I am a feminist because I want to live in a world that is more just.*
>
> —Chimamanda Ngozi Adichie

Women of Afrikan descent have struggled for liberation throughout the centuries. They have resisted multiple forms of oppression that challenged their individual ability and their community's ability to live a life of dignity and self-determination. We began the chapter with the words of Afrikan American civil rights activist Fannie Lou Hamer and Nigerian writer Chimamanda Ngozi Adichie to underscore the core concepts of freedom and justice in liberation struggles. Freedom fighters from anti-colonialist Afrikan warrior Queen Nzinga (1620s) to Alicia Garza (2000s), co-founder of the Black Lives Matter network and principal of the Black Futures Lab, all recognized that justice benefits everyone. And when Black women work for justice, it is often from a "feminist" lens, whether implicitly or explicitly. In this sense, Black women's approach to activism centers the voices and concerns of Black girls and women in the definition of, and agenda for, liberation. No matter where we are in the world, we fight against rape and other forms of violence directed against us, inside and outside of our homes. We demand better pay and working conditions for our labor. We raise questions about the rights of girls to receive an education. We struggle against colonialization and anti-Blackness in all of its forms. We refuse to be silent. We resist; we envision; we lead.

Although there are many strands of Black and Afrikan feminisms, new articulations of these approaches share at least three core principles. Girls, women, transgender, and gender non-conforming (GWTG) people of Afrikan descent:

- have the right to dignity, equity, and shared power;
- are impacted by multiple forms of oppressions; and
- name and resist oppression(s) and actively work toward liberation.

Each form of Black and Afrikan feminism, however, may differ in its emphasis on the core forms of oppression used to explain the lived experiences of GWTG people (e.g., capitalism, patriarchy, racism, white supremacy, [neo] colonialism, heterosexism, transphobia), in its conceptualization of liberation, and in its resultant type of justice activism. Queer, radical Black feminist activist Charlene Carruthers (2018) reminds us that liberation is a perpetual project involving multiple pathways. Thus, the degree to which gender is positioned varies across approaches. For example, some forms of feminism primarily focus on Black GWTG, others center national or racial liberation, and additional approaches center gender and consider the mainstream feminist movement their primary audience (e.g., Kendall, 2020). Across these varied approaches, activism efforts may vary in their emphasis on location (local or transnational), level of intervention (individual or group), or foci (ideological, institutional, or both).

In this chapter, we highlight four broad forms of Black and Afrikan feminisms: radical Black feminism, intersectionality, Afrikan feminism, and hip-hop feminism. The richness and the diversity of approaches to gender equity is expansive, and these broad categories may at times seem insufficient to capture these nuances. As a way to contextualize the pathways to liberation espoused by each broad category of feminism, we outline key questions that are addressed. Undergirding these questions are assumptions about the root causes of oppression and the parameters of activism. We highlight contemporary praxis within each section because so much of Black feminism involves both theory and practice. Diverse GWTG voices are unearthed to name, define, and analyze the social realities and collective struggles for liberation. These voices help to center the resistance of our foremothers and our ancestors, who paved the way for our freedom.

Radical Black Feminisms

*If Black women were free, it would mean that everyone else would have to be free
since our freedom would necessitate the destruction of all the systems of oppression.*

Combahee River Collective, 1977, p. 213

In 1974 a group of Afrikan American lesbian feminists formed the Combahee River Collective to provide a radical Black feminist analysis and revolutionary plan action for Black liberation. Riding on the coattails of the liberation struggles of the 1960s, the Collective penned a statement explicating a radical understanding of feminism. In this framework, ending capitalism is as essential to liberating Black women as is purging racial and gender oppressions. Thus, they adopted a socialist solution to liberation, arguing that "Black women will never be free within capitalism [as] it is a system dependent on racism, gender and sexual oppression, and sexism" (Taylor, 2019, p. 324). Activism—designed to eradicate sexual violence against Black women, increase Black women's access to a living wage, and end work and housing segregation among Black women—as a result must root out the very foundations of injustice (i.e., racial and gender oppressions under a system of capital accumulation). Black GWTG folx are at the helm of contemporary abolition efforts: abolition of capitalism, patriarchy, police, prisons, etc. Scholars and activists working within the Black radical feminist tradition seek to uncover the voices and perspectives that have been marginalized and/or erased through interlocking forms of oppression (Lindsey, 2015).

Drawing on insights from the Combahee River Collective's statement, Neville and Hamer (2001) outlined core tenets of revolutionary or radical Black feminism. First, while the core goals remain constant—transformation into a socialist society and the eradication of all forms of oppression—what constitutes a *revolutionary analysis is dynamic*; it changes over the course of time and geopolitical space. Discussions of defunding the police were revolutionary just weeks before George Floyd's murder by Minneapolis police officers on May 25, 2020. But, since the ensuing international uprisings against anti-Blackness in policing and all public life, even liberal organizations have considered policies to defund police and invest in social institutions to support Black survival and thriving.

Second, *racial, gender, and other forms of oppression are configured under periods of capitalism*. GWTG folx of Afrikan descent are suffering mightily under global (digital) capitalism. In the Democratic Republic of Congo (DRC), girls and women toiling in mines for coltan—the mineral used in most electronics, such as smartphones—face threats of sexual violence and economic exploitation, while the state accumulates capital to support wars in the region and multinational tech companies add to their bottom line. Black women in the United States are disproportionately impacted by the COVID-19 pandemic, in part because of segregation in housing and on jobs (Pirtle, 2020). Racial-gender oppression restricts job opportunities for Black women. Black women are segregated in low-wage service jobs that put them at increased risk for exposure to COVID-19 (Pirtle, 2020). The racial-gender wage gap further creates burdens for Black women during the pandemic, including housing instability (Greene & McCargo, 2020).

Third, the interdependent functionality of *structures of oppression and ideologies sustains the oppression of* GWTG folx of Afrikan descent. The policies and practices adopted by institutions, including admissions policies, hiring practices, laws, and legal decisions, influence key decisions that wittingly or unwittingly lock out and/or exploit *all* Black people. Ideologies or controlling images of GWTG people conspire to justify racial-gender inequity and exploitation. For example, the stereotype of Black women as sexually loose served to rationalize rape and forced reproduction during slavery so that enslavers could profit. The flawed logic asserted that if Black women were subhuman and always desirous of "sex," then they could not be violated (Neville & Hamer, 2001). More recently, the cosmetic industry has profited by fueling White supremacist notions of beauty and by exploiting colorism within communities. Skin-bleaching is a case in point. GWTG folx of Afrikan descent across the globe purchase lightening crèmes for themselves and their children. In a quest for "white beauty," some women argue they bleach their skin to attract a high-status romantic partner, a better job, and/or increased social standing (Hunter, 2011). While all genders practice skin-bleaching, women are particularly vulnerable to whitening their skin because society (via ideological messages) enforces standards of beauty and worth that often counter Black women's natural aesthetics. This form of racialized-gender oppression leads to harmful effects on one's self-esteem and physical health.

And, last, activists engage in *praxis* to create change. Reflecting on a critical understanding of the multiple and interlocking forms of oppression, radical Black feminists work with others to resist and to struggle for greater equity. For some, this work consists of mainly operating within Black organizations. Others work within predominantly women's or labor's circles. And still others, such as Barbara Smith (co-founder of the Combahee River Collective) and Francis Beal (co-founder of Third World Women's Alliance), carved out sacred spaces to practice Black women's liberation. Working from the assumptions that Black feminist, queer, and trans stories are embedded within the Black radical tradition, we outline two contemporary youth-based struggles: BYP 100, a U.S.-based Afrikan American organization, and FeesMustFall, a South Afrikan movement.

BYP100 emerges from the pain of a racial or soul wound. The acquittal of George Zimmerman for the murder of Trayvon Martin was rendered at the end the "Beyond November Movement Convening" in 2013. The youth gathering was the brainchild of radical Black feminist scholar-activist Cathy Cohen, as an offshoot of her Black Youth Project. A decade earlier, Cohen had created the internet-based research project to collect, archive, and curate data by and for Black millennials. The meeting in 2013 pulled together students, artists, service workers, and other Black folx under the age of 35. Fueled by sadness and rage, the youth in attendance resolved to create a community-based organization that over time grew into a national project.

Using a Black, queer, feminist lens, BYP100 "envisions a world where all Black people have economic, social, political, and educational freedom" (BYP100, n.d.). The dozen or so BYP100 chapters challenge state violence against Black youth and organize around abolition projects, reparations, and universal childcare. Their She Safe, We Safe campaign is designed to end gender-based violence against GWTG folks of Afrikan descent. Members of BYP100 center the voices of the most marginalized youth in their communities as they provide leadership to bring about justice and liberation, with an eye toward creating opportunities for young people to thrive. In her book, *Unapologetic,* BYP100 founding director Charlene Carruthers (2018) advances a mandate for radical movements. The call reminds us that "together we can imagine and move toward transformative change in our lifetimes and for future generations" (p. 137).

Two decades after becoming a democracy, South Africa erupted with student protests demanding free, quality, and decolonized higher education for all. In response to the 2015 announcement of a 10.5% student fee increase at the University of Witwatersrand (Wits), Black students mobilized (Fihlani, 2019). Challenging the broken promises of free education at the end of apartheid, students formed #FeesMustFall. Black- and often queer-led protests spread throughout the country over the subsequent months. Students were met with state-sanctioned violence as they raged against the vestiges of white supremacy and colonialism, burning down paintings and buildings. Marching under the slogan, "This revolution will be intersectional, or it will be bullshit," students demanded that universities attend to the needs of all students. This included potential students with limited access to higher education because of their class position, as well as women, queer, trans, and differently abled students, whose subjectivities are often violently erased from these educational spaces. As part of the decolonizing efforts, the related #RhodesMustFall campaign at the University of Cape Town (UCT) aimed to remove the statute of colonialist Cecil Rhodes as a symbol of racial terror. Although they were leading the movement, radical Black, queer, and non-binary activists' contributions are hidden and at times erased from the historical record (Ndelu et al., 2017; Xaba, 2018). These leaders not only shaped the strategies and tactics of the movement to liberate the educational system of the country, but also challenged multiple forms of oppression within the movement itself (e.g., sexual violence perpetrated by movement members, ableism, and trans-erasure).

In sum, both the BYP100 and the #FeesMustFall movements centered the liberation of all Black youth within their respective countries. These struggles used an intersectional, radical, Black, feminist, and queer analysis to inform their praxis. New technologies were used to help mobilize support for demonstrations, and as a form of activism in and of themselves. Consistent with Black radical feminist tradition, leaders called out the intersecting forms of oppression operating in society (BYP100) and within their own movement (#FeesMustFall).

Intersectionality Feminisms

An intersectional approach to our blackness takes into account that we are not only defined by our blackness, but that some of us are also defined by our gender, our sexuality, our able-bodiedness, our mental health, and our class, among other things. We all have certain oppressions and certain privileges, and this must inform our organising so that we do not silence groups among us, and so that no one should have to choose between their struggles. Our movement endeavours to make this a reality in our struggle for decolonisation.

—UCT Rhodes Must Fall, n.d.

The #RhodesMustFall campaign adopted a radical and intersectional lens to analyze and chart out a course of action to root out the dehumanization of Black people and decolonize the South Afrikan university. Intersectionality theory, originally conceived by Afrikan American legal scholar Kimberlé Crenshaw (1989), reshaped Black feminist struggles globally. The theory provides an explicit framework to name and conceptualize the lived experiences of women who experience multiple forms of oppression (based on gender, race, class, sexual orientation, ability). Although the application of an intersectional feminist approach during the 2015 South Afrikan student uprisings was radical in nature because the students sought to bring about societal transformation by embracing tenets of socialism (free education for all), intersectionality theory is not synonymous with radical Black feminism.

As originally conceived, intersectionality was designed to capture the unique experiences Black women face because the "intersection of racism and sexism factors into Black women's lives in ways that cannot be captured wholly by looking at the race or gender dimensions of those separately" (Crenshaw, 1991, p. 1244). Intersectionality builds on earlier Black feminist conceptualizations such as Frances Beal's (1969) double jeopardy and the writings of Barbara Smith, who was instrumental in the creation of Black Women's Studies. In her classic text *Home Girls,* Smith (1983) asserted that the "concept of the simultaneity of oppression is still the crux of a Black feminist understanding of political reality," arguing that it was in fact "one of the most significant ideological contributions of Black feminist thought" (p. xxxiv). The image that Crenshaw paints so well of a street intersection in which racial and gender oppressions collide to create harm is powerful. As such, intersectionality provides a helpful heuristic to consider the increasingly complex nature of human relations and multiple and interlocking systems of oppression.

Intersectionality has touched almost every aspect of scholarly writing on GWTG folx of Afrikan descent, and it has shaped the analysis of Black activism in the contemporary moment. Crenshaw's (1991) seminal work has received over 20,000 citations on Google Scholar, not to mention the other informal ways in which her "everyday" conceptualization has influenced the framing of research and practice with Black folx. Crenshaw and the African American Policy Forum (AAPF) provide an intersectional lens to their web-based movement-building activities. The #SayHerName campaign emerged in response to the police violence against Black girls and women and the erasure of this violence from public memory.

The AAPF honors the memories of Black girls and women like Sandra Bland and Natasha McKenna by creating videos and sponsoring educational forums, to share their stories and to encourage community to bear witness to the violence inflicted on them and their families. Drawing on its legal expertise, AAPF also advocates for institutional change to promote safety, justice, and health in Afrikan American communities, including ending no-knock polices, holding police accountable for violence directed toward Black girls and women, and terminating the use of Tasers and excessive force, particularly with children and pregnant women (AAPF, n.d.). During the global health pandemic, Crenshaw and her team created Under the Blacklight: The Intersectional Vulnerabilities that COVID Lays Bare, as part of her *Intersectionality Matters* podcast. This form of intersectional activism centers critical consciousness (i.e., ideological shifts) of multiple systems of oppression and how they have operated over time and space.

Scholar-activist Della Mosley (assistant professor) and Pearis Bellamy (graduate student) co-founded #Academics4BlackLives (#A4BL) to address anti-Black racism and healing in the academy. From an explicitly Black, intersectional, and queer lens, they created an international community of scholars committed to challenging and disrupting anti-Blackness (White and non-Black People of Color) and/or healing and wellness (Black folx). #A4BL emerged out of pain and hope—the pain from the disproportionate COVID-19-related deaths among Afrikan Americans as a result of a history of systemic oppressions, and the 8:46 minute torture of George Floyd by police officers. Captured on video by teenager Darnella Frazier and broadcasted on the internet, the murder of a human being killed by police was witnessed by the world. The anti-Blackness surrounding the Afrikan American deaths due to COVID-19, and due to police or mob violence (Breonna Taylor, Ahmaud Arbery, and George Floyd), became inescapable.

Black people in the academy were burdened with the emotional and physical toll of attending to institutional racism both inside and outside of the academy during a global pandemic. As a way to shift the burden, #A4BL emerged to hold White people accountable for anti-Blackness and for transforming the academy, while providing space for Black people to focus on healing and wellness. The first phase of the initiative included offering a week-long, intensive teach-in for non-Black people to understand the history of anti-Blackness, White supremacy, their role in colluding with the system, and their responsibility to serve as change agents. Black folx participated in alternative programming around healing and well-being, with sermons, discussions, and wellness classes (yoga, meditation, twerking, art, etc.) to rejuvenate the spirit and liberate the soul. The intersectional framework was integral throughout each activity and was seen in the purposive centering of Black feminist and Black queer voices as well as in the content (e.g., intersectional theory) and delivery of the material (e.g., all content was accessible, and there were sign language interpreters for each of the synchronous virtual events).

In sum, adopting some form of intersectional analysis has become the standard in contemporary research on, and activism around, issues related to Black women and to Black liberation more broadly. Although feminist movements inspired by intersectionality can operate from a radical lens—such as #FeesMustFall, which called for social and/or economic transformation—this is not necessary. Intersectionality activism can take up an explicitly Black GWTG cause (e.g., #SayHerName), or it can operate from within a larger Black liberation frame (e.g., #Academics4BlackLives).

Afrikan Feminisms

By naming ourselves as feminists we politicise the struggle for women's rights, we question the legitimacy of the structures that keep women subjugated, and we develop tools for transformatory analysis and action.

—African Feminist Forum, 2006, p. 3

In 2006, the African Feminist Forum convened a meeting in Accra, Ghana to draft a Charter of African Feminist Principles for African Feminists hosted by the African Women's Development Fund. The diverse working group members drew on their ancestors' wisdom as they drafted the document. The goal was to honor the women who paved the way for their increasing freedoms, by providing guidance and accountability for feminist organizing on the continent. At the root of their understanding of Afrikan women's liberation was freedom from patriarchy and its connection to "other systems of oppression and exploitation which frequently mutually support each other" (African Feminist Forum, 2006, p. 4). In this founding document, the women proposed individual ethics (e.g., universality of women's human rights, nurture and care, access to just livelihoods) and institutional ethics (e.g., supporting Afrikan women's labor rights and instituting accountable leadership).

As indicated in the charter, feminist thought and action in Africa has a long history. Everyday women have worked to improve the lives of their families for centuries. Additionally, African women have a legacy of leadership as warriors and spiritual guides. Feminist thought and action in Africa predate Western use of the term. In support of this, one can think of Mekatilili wa Menza (ca. 1860–1924) of Kenya, who fearlessly led her people in a rebellion against British colonization during the first World War. She often used her resources as a mother, community leader, and performer to mobilize others (Lihamba et al., 2007). Also, the Amazons of Dahomey, warrior women who played a noble role in several battle victories (Adeyinka, 1974), represent African feminist strength and ferocity. In addition to their military prowess, Indigenous African feminists utilized spiritual practices and knowledge to resist traditional and foreign patriarchies. For example, the Tumbuka women in Northern Malawi could express innermost critiques on male behavior through spirit possession (Lihamba et al., 2005).

The actual term "feminism" is a newer concept on the continent, taking hold in the 1980s. The growth of women in the development of legal programs and women's movements sweeping across various countries marks the emergence of feminism as a formal approach to gender equality. For example, women began demanding greater political representation leading up to the 1992 Kenyan elections, as did the African National Congress (ANC) Women's League during South Africa's transition to democracy (Mikell, 1995). Women scholars such as Nigerian/British Amina Mama (former director of the African Gender Institute), Ghanaian Ama Ata Aidoo (former Minister of Education), and Sierra Leonean Filomena Steady (founding member of the Association of African Women and Research Development) formally introduced the theory of feminism to various countries on the continent.

Many Afrikan women did not embrace the term feminism, as for some, the concept connoted women's rights over that of men. Through the lens of Afrikan feminisms, however, women are viewed first and foremost as human. Thus, *all* people struggle for freedom from oppression, based on the political, economic, and social manifestations of injustice (Steady, 1996). Afrikan feminists in the 1990s, such as Aidoo (1998), demystified the concept and helped Afrikan women and men make connections between feminism and human rights:

> When people ask me rather bluntly every now and then whether I am a feminist, I not only answer yes, but I go on to insist that every woman and every man should be a feminist— especially if they believe that Africans should take charge of African land, African wealth, African lives and the burden of African development. It is not possible to advocate independence for the African continent without also believing that African women must

CraftsMATERIAL — DO NOT DUPLICATE, DISTRIBUTE, OR POST

have the best that the environment can offer. For some of us, this is the crucial element in our feminism. (p. 39)

Afrikan feminism is as heterogenous as the continent; it bears the marks of having been forged in quite diverse indigenous and colonial contexts (e.g., Portuguese, Italian, Belgian, Spanish) and influenced by a multiplicity of religious cultures (e.g., Islam, Christianity, and Indigenous Religions) before being further shaped by an array of anti-colonial and nationalist movements (Mama, 2011). Many of the forms of Afrikan feminism identify patriarchy as a root cause of girls' and women's oppression while also working toward gender harmony. Although there is diversity on the continent, there are common worldview values including *ubuntu*, or the collective notion of "we-ness," and democracy. Afrikan feminists center *ubuntu* in which spirituality, interdependence, and the communal well-being are essential for gender equity (Ngunjiri, 2016).

Nego-feminism embraces *ubuntu* and consists of negotiation; the word stands for "no ego" feminism (Nnaemeka, 2004). These Afrikan feminists challenge patriarchy through negotiations that require a dismissal of the ego. On the continent, this is seen as a skill that requires great wisdom, power, and creativity. Through their negotiations, they balance conflict and compromise toward the aim of equity. Similarly focused on maintaining harmony between men and women is Ogundipe-Leslie's variant, Stiwanism. This term was introduced because she "wanted to stress the fact that what we want in Africa is social transformation. It is not about warring with men, the reversal of role, or doing to men whatever women think that men have been doing for centuries, but it is trying to build a harmonious society" (Ogundipe-Leslie, 1994, p. 1). Feminisms from these standpoints focus on harmony in the broadest sense.

Afrikan radical feminism pushes for gender expansion rather than for harmony per se. This form of radical feminism differs from its U.S. counterpart, which espouses focusing on capitalism and working toward socialist transformation. Afrikan radical feminism also centers critical thought around the gender binary and heteronormativity. Tamale (2006) asserts that:

> We should embrace radical strategies in our struggles. We must reject the arguments that Africa is not ready for radical feminism. What such arguments are saying in essence is that we are not ready. Radical Africanism raises issues around Africa heteronormativity and homophobia, for *transformation.* (p. 40)

The transformation from this vantage is the transformation of gender relations and traditional gender norms, especially around respectability. In 2017, Ugandan poet, educator, and radical feminist Stella Nyanzi was arrested for posting her poem about the president. Upon her arrest, she was quoted as saying, "send me to Luzira [maximum security prison]. I am proud [of what] I told a dirty, delinquent dictator … I want to embolden the young people … I want them to use their voices and speak whatever words they want to speak" (Mesigwa, 2019). In writing a poem that was considered vulgar by conservatives and liberals alike, Nyanzi used the literary technique of raunch to practice her artistic and political freedom. Through her art activism, she both challenged restrictive gender norms and liberated herself from them.

Pan-Afrikan or transnational feminists are also concerned with gender politics, but within the bounds of Afrikan liberation. Similar to U.S. radical Black feminists, they understand the connections between capitalism and other forms of oppression in the exploitation and misery of people of Afrikan descent. Uncovering women's contributions to pan-Afrikan struggles throughout history, transnational feminism arises from two basic assumptions: (a) working across borders and cultures is an essential feature of our contemporary world; and (b) specific locations and identities must be the bases of any analysis (Boyce Davies & Graves, 2014). Questions about women's paid and unpaid labor, and about who has access to power and resources, are concerns in any liberation struggle.

Indigenous feminism relies on the wisdom of the past to forge an Afrikan future. Afrikan feminists have documented these knowledges, using methods similar to those their feminist foremothers passed on to younger generations (Jagire, 2013). Indigenous Afrikan feminists recognize women's power in a context that celebrates motherhood, sisterhood, and friendship (Chilisa & Ntseane, 2010). Ecofeminism, for example, recognizes the Indigenous by honoring ancient sacred relationships between all aspects of nature. Women in Africa have remained engaged and resilient in the ecological war against capitalism. Afrikan ecofeminism focuses on humankind's responsibility for, and relation to, the natural world. Central to this strand is the necessity of engaging with capitalism, which is structured around a system that continues to kill life by conquering, occupying, and commodifying any manifestation of life for profit (Kaara, 2010).

The Greenbelt Movement is one of the most impactful indigenous feminist-led efforts. Kenyan-born Wangari Maathai received the Nobel Peace prize in 2004 for her activism to promote peace and a healthy ecology by planting trees. In response to deforestation in her home country and its environmental impact on the earth and livelihoods of communities, Maathai elicited local women to plant "seeds of hope." Through participation in the movement, which began in 1977, women learned forestry and related life skills as they planted millions of trees. But these advances came at a personal cost. Maathi (2006) documented the decades-long struggles she endured while challenging patriarchal norms about women's leadership roles and financial independence. She willingly accepted personal discomfort, social ostracization, and conflicts with authority, making these sacrifices for her vision. The Greenbelt Movement inspired similar movements across the globe, in part because of its community-based-education approach to activism. Drawing on Indigenous teachings, women learned about how sustainable and equitable management of natural resources are related to issues of governance and human rights (Lawrence, 2009). Movement participants accessed their power and their efficacy to make a difference as they became financially independent and ecologically minded (Florence, 2018).

Afrikan feminists work within and outside of movements to challenge patriarchal representations of women(hood). Art activism, for example, has gained increasing recognition over the years. Many Afrikan feminists are also poets, painters, singers, and directors who use their creativity to initiate conversations and action around gender inequality. Billie Zangewa, a Malawian/South Afrikan artist, weaves empowering stories of femininity and domesticity. Her choice of embroidery as her primary artistic mode reflects a radicality in her work and an awareness of the creative power of women (Kouoh, 2017). By depicting scenes of domesticity using a traditionally feminine medium, she enacts what she calls "daily feminisms." The feminist art collective IQuiya—whose name derives from a cloth Afrikan women use to cover their head while carrying water vessels—similarly uses art to celebrate Afrikan women's contributions to culture and society (Davies, 2017). Adopting an interdisciplinary approach, IQuiya Collective depicts the daily realities of Afrikan women. These Afrikan feminist forms of activism illustrate how the arts can be used as a tool to dismantle inequity through disrupting ideological representations of work and gender.

In sum, the tradition of Afrikan feminism is embedded into the histories and stories of the diverse nations on the continent. Contemporary and explicit expressions of feminism incorporate a range of perspectives, but at their core is an Afrikan worldview including *ubuntu*, respect for interdependence, the value of human life, and the desire to create harmonious societies that are equitable. Some Afrikan feminist movements work to transform oppressive forces in society (e.g., patriarchy and global capitalism), and others center ideological representations of gender in the Afrikan context.

Hip-Hop Feminism

Hip-hop feminism aims to dismantle gender inequity and to uplift women, using hip-hop as both the tool and the site for societal change (Durham et al., 2013). According to hip-hop feminist pioneer Joan Morgan (2017), "rap music is essential to the struggle against sexism because it takes us straight to the battlefield" (p. 72). Hip-hop as a genre extends beyond rap music to include art, fashion, and film. This form of feminism uses storytelling and creativity to name and heal from gender, race, class, and sexuality oppression.

Many believe hip-hop feminism as an art form emerged around the time that Roxanne Shante broke onto the scene at 14, demanding respect and equality (1985), or when Queen Latifah demanded, "Ladies First" (1989). As hip-hop culture continued to cement its place in music history in the mid-90s, Black women performers like Lil' Kim and Lauryn Hill revisited the cult of true womanhood, femininity, and respectability in their music. It was at this time that hip-hop superstars like Tupac Shakur, who represented a lineage of Black Liberation and radicalism, received critical acclaim for their art. Shakur, like a number of his contemporaries, was writing beautiful rhymes that uplifted Black women while living a life that reflected misogyny and sexism. These complexities are constant realities for Black women, who both love and value their whole community, yet dream of a more just future in which girls and women are respected.

Morgan (1995) created hip-hop feminism theory to explore the gray areas of both feminism and femininity. The birth of hip-hop feminism in print was a means to reconciliation and reclamation for Black women, creating a space where most first encountered a conscious naming and exploration of feminism, and of the maleness of the hip-hop culture that many grew up in (Peoples, 2008). Hip-hop feminist theory was developed with functionality in mind and is to be "as helpful to Shequanna on 142nd as it is to Samantha at Sarah Lawrence" (Morgan, 1995, p. 155). For Morgan, being immersed in hip-hop culture necessitated a feminism that would allow her to explore who women were as women, as opposed to victims; a feminism that was sensitive to the pain of Black men; and a feminism that recognized and embraced the potentials in the inherent complexities of being Black girls and being sistas of the post-civil-rights, post-soul, and post-hip-hop generation.

Political education is imperative to hip-hop feminism. Hip-hop as a curricular and academic resource is important because despite the race, class, religion, or gender of a student, hip-hop represents the ways in which the urban youth speak, think, create, move, and understand the world (Love, 2014). Hip-hop feminist political education takes place in and outside of the classroom, facilitated by a diverse group of institutional and community educators. When rapper and Chicago native Noname started Noname's Book Club, aimed at uplifting POC voices, she took on the dual role as emcee and community educator. In light of the recent murders of Black women, she holds Black men in the rap community accountable in her June 2020 response song, "Song 33." In both using her platform to address patriarchy inside and outside the Black community and utilizing her organizing skills for community education, Noname embodies the non-institutional approach.

Hip-hop feminists also re-examine Western respectability. Black women are often held to rigid standards of propriety, piety, and self-respect that glorify Western norms of behavior and demonize the indigenous and cultural mannerisms of the Global Majority. Nowhere is this more evident than in hip-hop, where Black GWTG are loudly, boldly, and unapologetically themselves, despite existing stereotypes (e.g., the mammy, Jezebel, and Sapphire) that work to silence and shame them. For example, Bettina Love uses the Black ratchet imagination to reclaim often-misunderstood aspects of Black queer hip-hop communities, like the New Orleans Bounce scene. In this context, being ratchet is about embracing vibrance and volume; it's about making room for Black people to explore and define their own femininity, outside of the soul-suffocating standards of white respectability. The Black ratchet imagination is a methodological lens that is deeply focused on gaining an in-depth understanding of Black queer youth's identity. This is accomplished through reflective research questions that are intersectional, that aim to understand youth's agency, and that reclaim space and create economic opportunities (Love, 2017). In their refusal to quiet their cultural and expressive spirits, hip-hop feminists demand the space to explore and define themselves outside of racial and gendered stereotypes.

Another core concept of hip-hop feminism is pleasure. As hip-hop feminists deconstructed respectability politics, they began to realize that European standards of propriety were suffocating not only their self-expression, but also their pursuit of pleasure. According to Morgan (2015), a politics of pleasure recognizes that feminist principles do not necessarily legislate desire and elevates the need for sexual autonomy and erotic agency without shame. Morgan uses her Jamaican lineage as a site to explore pleasure and a source to remind her of indigenous sexual expression. According to pleasure activist Adrienne Maree Brown (2019), pleasure is about autonomy and collectivity, about emotional expression, sex and sexuality, humor, performance, and health. Because they are often raised to put the needs of the family/community first, all Black women, but especially working-class and urban Black women, have to fight for the space and opportunity to feel and share pleasure. For hip-hop feminists, pleasure is political, in that it reminds us that we deserve more than just survival; we deserve to seek and find delight. It gives us the opportunity to envision a more just and equitable future by making us aware that the ultimate pleasure is freedom.

Ruth Nichole Brown's afterschool program, SOLHOT (Saving Our Lives Hear Our Truths), applies hip-hop feminist pedagogy to create a collective space that celebrates Black girlhood. SOLHOT uplifts Black girls' talents and ideas in developmentally and culturally embracing ways. Creating authentic, human relationships is a central element of the program. As Brown explains in an interview, "We approach each other as people first without having to fight all of the isolation and the complicity that the university sets up. We can just really ask each other questions and have a real learning experience" (Crunk Feminist Collective, 2012, para. 11). Her program shows an awareness that hip-hop necessitates intergenerational education and connection. By respecting the inputs and truths of youth participants, Brown creates a reciprocal learning and healing space.

Hip-hop feminists have used multiple forms of media to challenge misogynoir and the racial-gender oppression of Black GWTG. For example, Black women in the community are publicly calling for the accountability of well-known hip-hop executives, musicians, and producers. When the #MeToo movement began in October 2017, Black women were hidden from the discourse. This is surprising considering that Tarana Burke, a Black woman, created the social media trend. Against media marginalization, women in hip-hop made room for justice for themselves. Dream Hampton and Tamra Simmons were executive producers on the *Surviving R. Kelly* series, which documented the acclaimed singer's sexual violence against Black girls and women. *On the Record,* another documentary with the same tagline ("Believe Black Women"), chronicles the toll that disclosing sexual violence has taken on the lives of the women who shared their abuse stories about music mogul Russell Simmons. Although the directors and producers on this project were White, Black women boldly told their truth. Drew Dixon explained that she remained silent for 22 years about her abuse at the hands of Russell Simmons because she did not want to contribute to existing stereotypes of Black men as violent and sexually depraved. Like many Black women, she found that her love and loyalty for the Black community were also a source of her ongoing pain. Hip-hop feminism can be a site to process this pain by demanding justice for transgressions and by unveiling stigma around the disclosure of intra-racial abuse.

In sum, hip-hop feminists use art and political education to deconstruct gender representations, reclaim pleasure, and name and demand justice for the racial-gender violence directed against Black GWTG. Hip-hop feminism centers younger people's voices in the definition and identification of new possibilities. Artists name and redefine girlhood and womanhood, at times in direct opposition to Western notions of respectability. While challenging societal gender role expectations, hip-hop feminists also respond to questions of sexual violence within and outside of Black communities.

Recommendations for Our Collective Struggle for Liberation

Various forms of Black and Afrikan feminisms developed over time, to theorize about the lived experiences of GWTG of Afrikan descent and to inform collective action to improve the lives of *all* Black people. Black and Afrikan feminisms at this current moment are connected to liberation—our ability to live a life of dignity, justice, and harmony. We offer the below five considerations for setting a feminist agenda for GWTG of Afrikan descent. We encourage individual feminists and feminists' organizations/initiatives/movements to:

1. Clearly identify the core philosophical assumptions guiding the work. Questions to consider include: What are the root causes of the target focus? What are the short- and long-range goals of your activism in addressing these root causes? How do the specific actions align with the goals? In what ways does your activism promote liberation of girls, women, and all Black people? How will you evaluate your internal and external work?

2. Create opportunities to develop relationships and dialogue across national borders, to increase a sense of shared common fate among people on the continent and throughout the Afrikan diaspora. Through these relationships can emerge opportunities to identify the unique cultural context of our lived realities as well as the commonalities that unite our experiences. Our freedom and liberation are interconnected.

3. Adopt a future orientation in dreaming and taking action. Our ancestors paved the way for us; we must honor and return that gift by contributing to the well-being of future generations. Exploration of Afrofuturism may assist in these efforts. Afrofuturism requires the constant dialogue of past, present, and future, and the recognition that we need to simultaneously move forward while looking backward (or *Sankofa)*.

4. Prepare GWTG of Afrikan descent for liberation work through public education that operates from a stance of *ubuntu*, prioritizes relationships, promotes healing, respects multiple perspectives, develops a critical analysis, provides space to develop desired skills, and includes intergenerational learning opportunities.

5. Amplify the voices, writings, actions, and contributions of GWTG of Afrikan descent, especially of the most marginalized among us. Many times, Black GWTG folx are written out of the herstories of liberation struggles, or we are assigned to an historical footnote. We are living history, and we must begin to center the voices of everyday GWTG folks now, to ensure that our contributions are part of the written record and of public memory.

Conclusion

Women of Afrikan descent have a long tradition of fighting for justice inside and outside of our communities. Our foremothers sacrificed so that we could have the opportunities to visualize a better, more egalitarian world in which girls and women, on the continent and throughout the Diaspora, are treated with respect and dignity. Our struggle for liberation continues as we confront interlocking forms of oppression (e.g., global capitalism, patriarchy, anti-Black racism, [neo]colonialism, heterosexism, and transphobia). In this chapter, we discussed four broad branches of feminism—radical Black feminism, intersectional feminism, Afrikan feminism, and hip-hop feminism. Although each type of feminism engages in praxis (theory and action) designed to liberate girls and women, they differ in their level of emphasis on structural changes (e.g., transformation into socialism) and in the ideological representations (e.g., self-defined gender role expression) that are needed for personal and group liberation. Multiple modes of feminist action are taken up in liberation efforts including art, social media, public education, protest, and demonstration. We encourage contemporary Black and Afrikan feminists to continue the legacy of our foremothers by building efforts that nurture our development, build connections across borders, and adopt a clear analysis of contemporary social conditions. And, as feminists decades earlier informed us, until Black women are free, none of us will be truly liberated.

References

Adeyinka, A. A. (1974). King Gezo of Dahomey, 1818–1858: A reassessment of a West African monarch in the nineteenth century. *African Studies Review, 17*(3), 541–548.

African American Policy Forum. (n.d.). #SayHerName demands and policies. https://www.aapf.org/our-demands

African Feminist Forum. (2006). *Charter of African feminist principles for African feminists.* http://www.africanfeministforum.com/feminist-charter-introduction/

Aidoo, A. A. (1989). The African woman today. In O. Nnaemeka (Ed.), *Sisterhood, feminisms and power: From Africa to the diaspora* (pp. 39–50). Africa World Press.

Beal, F. M. (1969). *Black women's manifesto; Double jeopardy: To be Black and female.* Third World Women's Alliance. http://www.hartford-hwp.com/archives/45a/196.html

Boyce Davies, C., & Graves, A. A. (Eds.). (1986). *Ngambika: Studies of women in African literature.* Africa World Press.

Brown, A. M. (2019). *Pleasure activism: The politics of feeling good.* AK Press.

BYP100. (n.d.). About BYP100. https://www.byp100.org/about

Carruthers, C. A. (2018). *Unapologetic: A Black, queer, and feminist mandate for radical movements.* Beacon Press.

Chilisa, B., & Ntseane, G. (2010). Resisting dominant discourses: Implications of indigenous, African feminist theory and methods for gender and education research. *Gender and Education, 22*(6), 617–632.

Combahee River Collective. (1977). *The Combahee River collective statement.* https://www.blackpast.org/african-american-history/combahee-river-collective-statement-1977/

Crenshaw, K. (1989). Demarginalizing the intersection of race and sex: A Black feminist critique of antidiscrimination doctrine, feminist theory and antiracist politics. *University of Chicago Legal Forum, 1989*(1), Article 8, 139–167.

Crenshaw, K. (1991). Mapping the margins: Intersectionality, identity politics, and violence against women of color. *Stanford Law Review, 43*(6), 1241–1299. https://doi.org/10.2307/1229039

Crunk Feminist Collective. (2012, October). Learning community with Black girls. http://www.crunkfeministcollective.com/2012/10/17/learning-community-with-black-girls/

Davies, C. (2017, May 9). The 5 female art collectives you need to know. *Sleek.* https://www.sleek-mag.com/article/female-art-collectives/

Durham, A., Cooper, B. C., & Morris, S. M. (2013). The stage hip-hop feminism built: A new directions essay. *Signs: Journal of Women in Culture and Society, 38*(3), 721–737.

Fihlani, P. (2019, April 30). "We are students thanks to South Africa's #FeesMustFall protests." *BBC News*, Johannesburg. https://www.bbc.com/news/world-africa-47952787

Florence, N. (2018). Wangari Maathai the educator: Straddling tradition and modernity. *Journal of Global Education and Research, 1*(1), 48–67. https://www.doi.org/10.5038/2577-509X.1.1.1008

Greene, S., & McCargo, A. (2020). New data suggest COVID-19 widening housing disparities by race and income. *Urban Wire.* https://www.urban.org/urban-wire/new-data-suggest-covid-19-widening-housing-disparities-race-and-income

Hunter, M. L. (2011). Buying racial capital: Skin-bleaching and cosmetic surgery in a globalized world. *The Journal of Pan African Studies, 4*(4), 142–164.

Ivan, M. (n.d.). Profile: Who is Dr. Stella Nyanzi. *Watchdog.* https://www.watchdoguganda.com/news/20190804/73865/profile-who-is-dr-stella-nyanzi-2.html

Jagire, J. (2013). Indigenous African knowledges and African feminism: Resisting Eurocentric ways of knowing. In *Ruptures: Anti-colonial & anti-racist feminist theorizing* (pp. 77–89). Brill Sense.

Kaara, W. (2010). Reclaiming peoples' power in Copenhagen 2009: A victory for ecosocialist ecofeminism. *Capitalism Nature Socialism*, *21*(2), 107–111.

Kendall, M. (2020). *Hood feminism: Notes from the women that a movement forgot*. Viking Press.

Kouoh, K. (2017). Billie Zangewa: Embroidery for constructing collective identity. *Esse*, *90*, 60–63.

Lawrence, R. (2009). Proceedings of the 50th Annual Adult Education Research Conference. (2009). *Adult Education Research Conference Proceedings*. https://digitalcommons.nl.edu/ace_aerc/1

Lihamba, L. (Ed.). (2007*). Women writing Africa: The eastern region*. Feminist Press.

Lindsey, T. B. (2015). A love letter to Black feminism. *The Black Scholar*, *45*(4), 1–6.

Love, B. L. (2012). *Hip hop's li'l sistas speak: Negotiating hip hop identities and politics in the new South*. Peter Lang.

Love, B. L. (2014). Urban storytelling: How storyboarding, moviemaking, and hip-hop-based education can promote students' critical voice. *English Journal*, 53–58.

Maathi, W. (2006). *Unbowed: A memoir*. Knopf.

Mama, A. (2011). What does it mean to do feminist research in African contexts? *Feminist Review*, *98*(1_suppl), e4–e20.

McLean, N., & Mugo, T. K. (2015). The digital age: A feminist future for the queer African woman. *IDS Bulletin*, *46*(4), 97–100.

Mikell, G. (1995). African feminism: Toward a new politics of representation. *Feminist Studies*, *21*(2), 405–424.

Morgan, J. (1995). Fly-girls, bitches, and hoes: Notes of a hip-hop feminist. *Social Text*, *45*, 151–157.

Morgan, J. (2015). Why we get off: Moving towards a Black feminist politics of pleasure. *The Black Scholar*, *45*(4), 36–46.

Morgan, J. (2017). *When chickenheads come home to roost: A hip-hop feminist breaks it down*. Simon & Schuster.

Ndelu, S., Dlakavu, S., & Boswell, B. (2017). Womxn's and nonbinary activists' contribution to the RhodesMustFall and FeesMustFall student movements: 2015 and 2016. *Agenda, 31*, 1–4. https://doi.org/10.1080/10130950.2017.1394693

Neville, H. A., & Hamer, J. (2001). "We make freedom": An exploration of revolutionary Black feminism. *Journal of Black Studies*, *31*(4), 437–461.

Ngunjiri, F. W. (2016). "I am because we are": Exploring women's leadership under Ubuntu worldview. *Advances in Developing Human Resources*, *18*(2), 223–242.

Nnaemeka, O. (2004). Nego-feminism: Theorizing, practicing, and pruning Africa's way. *Signs: Journal of Women in Culture and Society*, *29*(2), 357–385.

Pirtle, W. (2020, July 1). Black women need to be free. *The Grio*. https://thegrio.com/2020/07/01/black-women-need-to-be-free/

Smith, B. (Ed.). (1983/2000). *Home girls: A Black feminist anthology*. Rutgers University Press.

Steady, F. C. (1981). *The Black woman cross-culturally*. Schenkman Publishing Company.

Tamale, S. (2006). African feminism: How should we change? *Development, 49*(1), 38–41.

Taylor, K. Y. (2019). The dialectic of radical Black feminism. In S. Y. Evans, A. D. Domingue, & T. D. Mitchell (Eds.), *Black women and social justice education: Legacies and lessons* (pp. 319–325). State University of New York Press.

UCT Rhodes Must Fall. (n.d.). Mission statement. http://jwtc.org.za/resources/docs/salon-volume-9/RMF_Combined.pdf

Xaba, W. (2017). Challenging Fanon: A Black radical feminist perspective on violence and the Fees Must Fall movement. *Agenda, 31*(3–4), 96–104. https://doi.org/10.1080/10130950.2017.1392786

Unit II. Seeking Authenticity at the Crossroads of Race, Gender, Class, and Culture: The Maafa and Self-Definition Among Afrikan American Women and Girls

Introduction: The Maafa and the Distortion of Black Female Authenticity

Huberta Jackson-Lowman

The territory of authenticity is rooted in the soil of identity. Both backward and lateral connectedness are essential aspects of authenticity. Thus, to be authentic, Afrikan American women (AAW) must be grounded in a thorough knowledge of who they are and must have the courage and *Kujichagulia*/Self-Determination to express it in their day-to-day lives. For AAW, what ordinarily was a natural process was disrupted by the trauma of the *Maafa o*r African Holocaust (Ani, 1980). The violent uprooting of Afrikan people from our native land, resulting in a loss of connectedness to our families, clans, tribes, and culture—traditions, values, languages, history, customs, rituals—followed by systematic and legally enforced strategies to repress and suppress our memories, and accompanied by ongoing physical and psychological terrorism, abuse, slaughter, and destruction heaped upon Afrikan Americans after the so-called Emancipation Proclamation, has ensured that being our authentic selves is a radical act of resistance. Consequently, Fanon's question of the oppressed—"Are we really who we think we are?"—assumes great significance. As educational psychologist and scholar Asa Hilliard once proclaimed at an annual convention of the Association of Black Psychologists, our charge is "to be Afrikan or not to be."

Afrikan proverbs capture the coupled nature of authenticity and identity quite beautifully and succinctly, while also being instructive. Proverbs such as *A log may stay in water for ten years but it will never become a crocodile* and *A cat may go to the monastery but it will never become a monk* suggest that one's experiences and/or location do not alter the core or essence of who one is. From the proverb *When a tree builds on its own roots, it will be healthy*, we are reminded that our health, our well-being, our longevity, and our future depend upon maintaining a strong connection to our ancestry. These proverbs, along with many others, provide the formula and ingredients for healing and recovery for AAW.

Gaining awareness of the historical and contemporary tragedies that have affected our ability to be authentic is an initial step toward our healing. Confronting these deeply rooted traumas is necessary to move toward more authentic expressions of who we are. Neither the spaces nor the resources for such healing work have been provided for AAW. Focused on the survival of our families, not enough of us have demanded it; however, the absence of any well-coordinated, national, private, or public restorative attempts directed at correcting the devastation that we experienced as a result of the ongoing drama of the Maafa rears its gruesomely ugly head in countless ways. Specifically, its effects may be counted in how we perceive and care for ourselves; how we interact with each other, our lovers, our spouses, our children, and our families; how we live, work, and carry out our lives; and how we are perceived and treated by others, intraracially and interracially. Fortunately, in cities and towns throughout the country, AAW in particular have recognized and continue to recognize the need for healing and are taking charge of their healing process for themselves and engaging in a variety of healing and uplifting activities. A few recent examples include the *Capitol City Natural Hair and Health Expo*, held in Tallahassee, Florida, which promotes natural hair care and artistry and integrates holistic health messages, while also encouraging women of Afrikan ancestry to appreciate their natural beauty. Podcasts such as Kimberlé Crenshaw's *Intersectionality Matters* and LaVerne Baker Hotep's *Black Girl Back Talk Podcast: Stories of Racial Bias From Girlhood to*

Womanhood, and online wellness initiatives, are becoming popular ways for women and girls of Afrikan ancestry to pursue healing. Targeting the entire Afrikan American population, The Community Healing Network, Inc. (CHN), a grassroots organization dedicated to the emotional emancipation of Afrikan people, has launched Community Healing Days, which are celebrated annually across the country during the third weekend of October. Activities that target the destruction of the myth of Black inferiority are implemented during these days. CHN and the Association of Black Psychologists have also developed a curriculum focused on overcoming the myth of Black inferiority and the lie of White superiority, specifically for people of Afrikan ancestry, that is being utilized throughout the country and in several international sites. The curriculum is implemented by trained facilitators, who establish Emotional Emancipation Circles (EEC). Other examples of activities designed to raise consciousness and promote healing include the increasing production of films and documentaries addressing historical, cultural, and social issues pertinent to Afrikan Americans. Films such as Haile Gerima's *Sankofa,* and documentaries such as *The Question of Color by* Kathe Sandler, *All of Us* by Emily Abt, and *Dark Girls* by Bill Duke, are intended to increase our awareness of the effects of the Maafa and to initiate critical thought and dialogue that can foster healing and self-acceptance. These are merely a few examples of many initiatives being undertaken in an effort to facilitate the restoration of the humanity and dignity of Afrikan people more generally, and of the authenticity of Black womanhood more specifically.

The chapters included in this unit directly and indirectly discuss the effects of the Maafa on AAW and represent our responses to it. They delineate the challenges that we have faced and still encounter, primarily as a result of racism, sexism, classism, attractional orientation, and lack of self-knowledge, and the ways that we have responded to these challenges in our efforts to be authentic, whole women. A decided core theme of many of the chapters is the role that engendered racial myths and stereotypes of Afrikan womanhood play in the adaptations that we have made. Through the imposition of a set of assumptions and beliefs about who Afrikan women are, responses to Black women have been manipulated and controlled, even within the group. Stepping out of this matrix of lies and deception requires self-knowledge and the awareness of how the oppressogenic process functions to maintain our status as inauthentic shadows of our true selves. In our efforts to claim our authenticity as women of Afrikan ancestry, there are several relevant questions:

1. What does it mean to be authentic?

2. What has been the impact of the Maafa—e.g., racism, sexism, classism, colorism, and lack of self-knowledge—on the choices, decisions, behaviors, and actions of women of Afrikan ancestry and their ability to be their authentic selves?

3. To what extent have AAW accommodated, adapted, and internalized the lies, misconceptions, myths, and stereotypes about who women of Afrikan ancestry are, and with what effects?

4. To what extent are demographic indicators, such as high rates of Black infant mortality and higher morbidity and mortality rates for Black women, a function of living in a society where racism, sexism, and classism continue to determine our life outcomes, and where Black women's lack of self-knowledge at the cultural and historical levels is the most common condition?

The articles in this unit center various aspects of issues emerging from the Maafa that affect the self-definition of Afrikan American women and girls (AAWG). In the opening chapter, Bentley-Edwards and Adams-Bass use an ecological lens to comprehensively examine the contemporary lives of AAWG from birth to senior years. They analyze the impact of the intersectional identities of AAWG on their developmental experiences and coping strategies, and address associated engendered racial myths and stereotypes across the life spectrum. In the subsequent chapter, Maxwell and colleagues provide an analysis of crucial socialization settings for Afrikan American girls (AAG) and discuss how adolescent girls negotiate the challenges of interlocking oppression and one of its byproducts—engendered racial myths and stereotypes. The authors provide guidelines for fostering the development of an Afrikan-centered identity in adolescent AAG, an approach that research suggests has protective functions. In the following chapter, using a psychohistorical lens, I discuss the history that surrounds one of the most devastating aspects of the oppressogenic process—the use of a Eurocentric yardstick in the evaluation of physical appearance. The role that colorism plays in undermining AAW's self-concept, self-confidence, relationships with each other and with Afrikan American men, and mental health and social outcomes, is examined as another example of the way that the Maafa has distorted our ability to be our authentic selves. Mbilishaka provides further insight into the discussion of the impact of Eurocentric concepts of beauty and suggests that women of Afrikan ancestry suffer from aesthetic trauma, as a result of their efforts to experience validation and affirmation in an anti-Afrikan society. Using the hair as an entry point for dealing with mental health issues among AAWG, she offers research and clinical strategies for dismantling aesthetic trauma. Townsend and Jones Thomas explore the effects of the Jezebel controlling image on young AAW and illustrate how this particular stereotype contributes to risky sexual behavior and to the sexual exploitation of AAWG. They evaluate the impact of intersectionality on the sexual decision making of AAG and discuss the sexual socialization practices their mothers utilize to prepare their daughters to deal with their sexuality. Interventions that contribute to the development of healthy sexuality among AAG are offered. Finally, the under-researched domain of Black lesbian relationships is discussed in the concluding chapter in this section. Robinson provides a compelling analysis of the experience of young AA women who are marginalized due to their attractional orientation.

References

Ani, M. (aka Dona Marimba Richards). (1980). *Let the circle be unbroken: The implications of African spirituality in the diaspora.* The Red Sea Press.

Reading 2.1. The Whole Picture

Examining Black Women Through the Lifespan

Keisha L. Bentley-Edwards and Valerie N. Adams-Bass

The Whole Picture: Examining Black Women Through the Lifespan

The nuanced lives of Black women are marked by challenges and triumphs that shape their transformation from childhood to adulthood. Research on Black women is often subsumed by research investigating Black males or women in general—neglecting the unique issues facing Black women throughout their lives (Hull et al., 1982). Recently, Black women have been at the forefront of movements (e.g., MeToo, Black Lives Matter, and Black Girl Magic) that generated support for research and activism elevating the experiences and needs of Black women, Black children, and their families. Scholarship has taken a more engaged approach that has led to policy initiatives like the Black Maternal Health Caucus in the U.S. Congress (Frazin, 2019) and to deeper examinations of the disparate school disciplinary practices for Black girls (Epstein et al., 2017). Using a developmental approach, this chapter will examine the supports and barriers that impact the normative tasks of Black women from the womb into old age.

In her challenge asking for a more disciplined approach to Black women's psychology, Thomas (2004) asserted that studying Black women without examining their contexts would lead to inadequate and inaccurate conclusions about their attitudes, behaviors, and motivations. Ecological approaches (Bronfenbrenner, 1993; Spencer, 1995) are particularly useful in understanding Black women, since they consider the interactions between contexts and their impact on both perceptions and outcomes. We will examine the lives of Black women through the lens of Spencer's Phenomenological Variant of Ecological Systems Theory (PVEST; Spencer, 1995, 1999; Spencer et al., 1997; Spencer et al., 2010; Velez & Spencer, 2018). Although PVEST has been used primarily to study youth, this cyclical and recursive model of resilience will be used in this chapter to carefully consider Black women from an individual and shared experience perspective that evaluates both supports and risks in determining the strengths and vulnerabilities that lead to healthy functioning. Our chapter utilizes an updated PVEST model (Figure 9.1) that considers the experiences of Black women and girls.

Figure 9.1 reveals the five components of Spencer's PVEST (Spencer et al., 2003; Spencer et al., 2010). The model begins with the *Net Risk/Vulnerability Level*, which are contextual factors that may provide support for or interfere with healthy functioning. The balance between risk contributors and protective factors is the *Net Stress Engagement Levels*, or what someone must deal with personally as they face the world. For example, even after a parent provides a safe home environment with appropriate supervision and affirmation of his/her child's whole self as valuable, a young girl may still have to deal with sexualized street harassment as she walks to school or withstand the ridicule of some peers about her natural hairstyle. The way the child responds to being repeatedly accosted is a result of her *Reactive Coping Strategies*, which may be positive/adaptive (becoming involved in extracurricular activities that emphasize academic achievement, rerouting her walk to school), or negative/maladaptive (engaging in premature sexual activities or withdrawing from interactions with peers as a buffer from the ridicule). After repeated responses to various contexts, the coping methods used transition from a reaction to a situation into an *Emergent Identity*, or an integral part of how that child sees herself or is perceived by others. This stable coping response is a function of actions merging into who the child is. In this case, the student may self-identify or be perceived by adults as a "good girl" or "*fast*."[12]

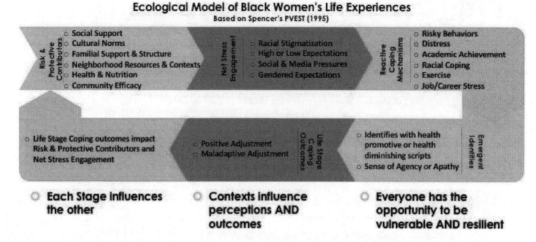

Figure 2.3.1. Black Women's Development From a PVEST Approach

The consequences of the reactive coping methods that are used, and the emergent identity that develops, put into motion *Life-Stage Specific Coping Outcomes*, which are either productive (e.g., excelling in school and extracurricular activities) or unfavorable (e.g., teen pregnancy, low self-esteem, or poor academic performance) (Spencer et al., 2003; Spencer et al., 2010). These Coping Outcomes in turn impact the Net Risk/Vulnerability levels for that girl [woman], and the cycle starts again. Spencer's PVEST focuses on interactions within and between processes that influence a woman's perceptions of self-efficacy, social challenges, and outcomes throughout each stage of her life. As we progress through the lifespan, we will use Spencer's PVEST (see Figure 9.1) as a guide for understanding how the interplay of supports and barriers, as well as coping responses, impacts Black girls' and women's outcomes.

The Womb Matters: Pregnancy and Infancy

Pregnancy is a unique period in that it simultaneously reflects the life experiences of the mother *and* lays the foundation for a new life. Black women are at greater risk than their White counterparts for adverse birth outcomes including gestational diabetes, low birth weight, and (pre)eclampsia as well as infant and maternal deaths (Petersen et al., 2019; Smith et al., 2018). Black–White racial disparities in the rates of maternal mortality (over three times higher for Black women) and infant mortality (double for Black babies) have presented calls for action to investigate the quality and consistency of perinatal care, as well as an examination of the lifelong physical and emotional health of Black women prior to pregnancy. Black women also face greater occurrences of gynecological health concerns—such as fibroids, endometriosis, and cysts—that can complicate pregnancy outcomes, but these do not adequately account for disparities in maternal and infant mortality (C. F. Collins, 2006).

Particularly for infant mortality, racial disparities were presumed to be based on socioeconomic status. Health initiatives were created that targeted low-income women, rather than Black women specifically. Although overall infant mortality rates have decreased, the disparity between Black and White women has remained stable for over 35 years (Smith et al., 2018). Shockingly high incidences of pre-term

---

[12] In African American culture, girls are given the label *fast* if they are perceived as sexually precocious (pre-pubescent) or promiscuous (in adolescence). Girls are condemned as *fast* if they are regarded as being too friendly with males, are early physical maturers, have sassy attitudes, and/or dress provocatively. The perception of a girl as *fast* is often used to excuse the inappropriate attention and behaviors of adult men (Cottom, 2018).

deliveries, low-birth-weight infants, maternal death, and infant mortality remain even after age, income, education, marriage, and health indicators have been controlled (Gaskin, 2008; Gennaro et al., 2008; Geronimus et al., 2006; Smith et al., 2018). Medical maltreatment is a problem that even elite athletes like Serena Williams and women with higher education levels encounter. Serena Williams detailed her near-death birthing experience (Haskell, 2018), and Shalon Irving, a CDC employee, died three weeks after birthing her daughter (Martin & Montagne, 2017). In both of these cases, the concerns expressed by these women about their well-being were diminished by medical staff. Black women are frequently admonished for their style of self-advocacy, which is often misunderstood as being disrespectful or incompetent—even when it concerns their own bodies (Cottom, 2018). These high-profile incidences have raised the alarm for providers to re-examine their perinatal care for Black women and to eliminate bias in their care as a whole (Rosser, 2019; Wheeler et al., 2018).

Health providers are now investigating social and psychological supports and barriers that, once understood, can be used to inform prevention strategies that increase healthy pregnancy and birth outcomes. Research has examined stressors such as neighborhood disorganization (Buka et al., 2003; Holland et al., 2009) and racism (Barnes, 2008; J. W. Collins et al., 2004; Hogue & Bremner, 2005) as contributors to adverse outcomes. Racism and community stressors impact both biological coping through neuroendocrine responses and autoimmune system suppression and psychological responses of depression and anxiety (Hogue & Bremner, 2005). It appears that these current and/or enduring stressors, whether direct or indirect, uniquely impact Black women who must also cope with the biological and social expectations of impending motherhood (Geronimus, 1992).

Social support from mothers and their partners has been revealed as a key protective contributor to prevent pre-term labor and low-birth-weight infants, particularly for Black mothers (Norbeck et al., 1996; Tach et al., 2010). The need for social support during pregnancy is in alignment with the Black cultural ethos of communalism and cannot be ignored. Unplanned pregnancies and troubled relationships with male partners can complicate the consistency of Black women's social support (Osborne & McLanahan, 2007; Tach et al., 2010). Promising interventions have found that researcher-imposed social support, in the form of regular phone calls and home visitations from nurses, significantly improved pregnancy outcomes for Black women (Lee et al., 2009; Norbeck et al., 1996). Culturally informed psychologists must be included in plans of care to treat perinatal depression, which is often under-diagnosed and under-treated in Black women (Field et al., 2009). Collaborations between psychologists, social workers, and health providers are necessary to make sure that Black mothers and their babies have the resources necessary to promote perinatal health and health throughout their lives. Black women have responded to these disparities by creating organizations such as Mama Toto's Village, Black Mamas Matter Alliance, and District Motherhued, which provide social support, resources, and advocacy for Black mothers.

Little Girls' School Life and Social Development

Early and middle childhood is marked by the onset of Black girls' academic life and the expansion of their social circles (Graham & Cohen, 1997). In essence, they are learning to read books and people simultaneously. Black girls' degree of preparedness and savvy, as well as their appearance, influence their peer and teacher interactions. Families, in their quest to raise strong and independent Black women, will encourage outspoken self-advocacy in their girls that is then often misinterpreted as defiant to their teachers (Adams-Bass & Bentley-Edwards, in press; Bentley et al., 2009; J. V. Ward, 2000). Whether it is rooted in gender-based societal pressures (L. M. Brown & Gilligan, 1991) or in defiance of stereotyping by authority figures, Black girls are often silenced just to get along (Fordham, 1993). Further, Black girls are regularly rewarded for demonstrating helpful behavior toward their teacher or for assisting classmates, more than for academic achievement. This phenomenon can be the result of a country that views service to White people as the most favorable position for Black women to be in. In the media this is reinforced by repeated images of "mammy" or caretaking figures. Girls who reject this pigeonholing may be susceptible to negative feedback and/or punishment from authority figures, and may be perceived as difficult (Morris, 2007; J. V. Ward, 2000). On the other hand, girls who do adopt stereotypic roles where they must give of themselves (to Whites, boys, family), with very little expected in return, suffer from decreased self-esteem (Thomas, Witherspoon, and Speight, 2004) that may impact their emotional development and their ability to maintain friendships later on in life.

Friendships

It is well known that at early ages, children will express same-race and -gender friendship preferences (Berndt, 1982; Evaldsson, 2005; Goodwin & Alim, 2010; Graham & Cohen, 1997; Quillian & Campbell, 2003; Scott, 2003, 2004). Even if they are unable to articulate it themselves, elementary-aged Black girls are able to understand that others react to them in ways that are specific to their ethnic and gender identities (McCombs, 1986). Both their self-perceptions and others' perceptions of them can determine the quantity and quality of their within- and out-group friendships, as well as their susceptibility to bullying.

Racial and gender stratifications in friendship building, in predominantly White school settings, can leave Black girls in a marginalized position. To protect themselves from social rejection at school, Black girls will often focus on friendships in neighborhood and religious settings, where they may find greater social acceptance (DuBois & Hirsch, 1990). Additionally, logistical, environmental, and financial factors may inhibit Black girls from interacting with their classmates outside of school (DuBois & Hirsch, 1993), where shared extracurricular or informal "hanging out" activities engender stronger social bonds. See the work of Kimberly Scott (2002, 2003, 2004) for in-depth understandings of the interpersonal relationships of Black girls.

Bullying

Black children, especially girls, are rarely examined as victims of bullying (Sawyer et al., 2008), even though research has revealed that they are bullied at similar or greater rates compared to children of other races (Centers for Disease Control and Prevention, 2016; Musu-Gillette et al., 2017). Several factors may cause Black girls to be absent in the bullying literature. First, Black girls are perceived as having thicker skin than other girls their age. These assumptions imply that even if Black girls are getting picked on, they are not as vulnerable to the negative outcomes associated with relational and physical bullying as their White counterparts. Secondly, Black girls (and boys) are studied for being aggressive (rarely as bullies), and for being victimized, but not in the context of being bullied. Thus, incidents that may be labeled as developmentally expected bullying or being bullied, when they are committed or experienced by children of other races, are designated as aggression or victimization when they are committed or experienced by Black children. These designations have deviant and/or criminal implications.

Researchers and practitioners must be careful in how they designate interpersonal conflict between Black children, so that it is addressed appropriately as a bullying incident. The ways that adults deal with relational and physical bullying set the stage for how children will respond to and perceive these incidents. This leads to the final reason for the lack of research on bullying for this group, which is that the Black girls themselves would not label themselves as a bully or as a victim of bullying. Sawyer and colleagues (2008) found no racial/ethnic differences when they simply asked children if they were being bullied. However, when they inquired about specific behaviors, Black elementary-school-aged girls were significantly more likely to experience both physical and relational bullying than their White male or female counterparts. The increased likelihood of victimization via physical bullying continued for Black girls in middle school as well (Sawyer et al., 2008). Little is known about the risks, protective factors, or outcomes related to Black girls and bullying.

The fact that being bullied does not become a part of Black girls' emergent identity may protect them from seeing themselves as bullied and from the negative outcomes related to that identification. On the other hand, because adults do not perceive Black girls as being bullied, opportunities for those adults to intervene, to shield those being bullied, and to promote conflict resolutions strategies are wasted. Perpetration and victimization may be different for Black girls, based on the content of relational bullying (e.g., colorism and exclusion) and on the context of physical bullying (e.g., neighborhood vs. school). Further, Black parents and family members may take a functional approach to bullying, and/or to racist encounters with peers, in which they encourage girls to stand up for themselves or fight back (before seeking teacher interventions) to deter future victimization (Coleman-King et al., under review). This strategy is complicated by the interplay between in-school bullying and cyberbullying, where conflicts at school often extend to social media and text messaging (Rose & Tynes, 2015).

With the surge of interest in preventing and protecting children from bullying, it is disheartening that Black girls are too often missing from the discourse. The suicide rate for Black elementary-aged children is on the rise, and peer relationship challenges have been cited as a common precursor (Bridge et al., 2015; Mueller et al., 2015; Sheftall et al., 2016). The dual minority status of Black girls, female and Black, makes examining bullying complex and requires a culturally responsive framework.Colorism—a preference for more Anglo-Saxon phenotypic features—as a mechanism for victimizing and isolation by Black and non-Black peers is just as relevant a form of bullying among this group as physical bullying and warrants examination. Researchers, practitioners, and educational stakeholders must take notice of this very real vulnerability faced by Black girls.

Adolescence

During adolescence, Black girls, like their peers, experience a surge in physical growth. Statistically, the onsets of breast development and menarche are earlier for Black girls than for their White counterparts (Herman-Giddens, 2006; Salsberry et al., 2009). However, these differences (earlier by seven months for breast development and 10 months for menarche) have greater meaning for pediatricians and endocrinologists than for the parents, teachers, and adults who encounter Black girls (Biro et al., 2013; Herman-Giddens, 2013). In reality, the difference is not really about the pace of Black girls' physical maturation, but about the nature and shape of their development. For many Black girls, the metamorphosis involves pronounced physical features—fuller hips, rounded breasts and buttocks, and increased height—that draw the attention of male peers and of some adult men. Further, teachers and adults cease to see Black girls as children and interpret their behaviors to have adult connotations, resulting in adult repercussions for those girls (Blake et al., 2011; Epstein et al., 2017). Still children, some adolescent girls are unable to manage, or uncertain about how to manage, the increased and different attention they are receiving.

Black teenaged girls need positive messages about sex and sexuality so that they can make healthy relationship choices and be able to seek help when they need it. Black girls who receive affirming racial socialization messages at home—messages that support academic performance and celebrate Black beauty—may be less likely to make decisions and engage in behaviors that negatively impact their futures.

Media Influences and Body Image

Contemporary media images include ratchet representations of Black women and White women who commodify aesthetics that are a norm in the Black community. Media presents an additional layer of messaging that Black girls must learn to navigate and interpret. These images are a challenge because Black girls encounter people who are exposed to this type of media content without cultural context, and who then endorse these images as representative of Black people (Adams-Bass & Henrici, 2019). Further, search engine results repeatedly display pornographic and racist images of Black women and girls (Noble, 2018). Black girls (and women) regularly use social media as a source for managing identities and stressful encounters (Adams-Bass & Bentley-Edwards, in press; Chapman-Hilliard et al., submitted for review).

Social media, specifically Black Twitter, serves as a source of support for managing in-person and virtual encounters (Adams-Bass, 2019). Black girls and women use these spaces for identity affirmations and social connections, and as a resource for activism (Adams-Bass & Bentley-Edwards, in press). Hashtags such as #BlackLivesMatter and #MeToo instigate movements and mobilize resources. Social media also provides a platform for expressing anxiety.

Peer Acceptance and Rejection

In spite of this, adolescence still spawns a change in peer relationships for Black female adolescents. For example, Black girls attending predominantly White institutions experience a decrease in invitations to social events such as sleepovers. Further, they have difficulty getting dates compared to their White counterparts and compared to Black adolescent males, who are easily able to secure interracial dates. In conjunction with the onset of pubescent changes, these social changes can have a damaging impact on Black girls' self-worth. Although affirmations of beauty from home may be a part of their experience, these messages contradict the beauty preferences of their peers.

Peer acceptance is an integral part of the adolescent identity process. Consistent parenting practices employed over time are likely to be absorbed and to have sustainable influence once children enter adolescence. During adolescence, youth are openly nursing an emergent identity, wrestling with contradictory messages, and shifting the priority of influential informants such as parents, peers, and siblings (Spencer & Markstrom-Adams, 1990; Spencer et al., 1991). African American adolescent girls do not consider their families as a primary source of support for stressful life events. They are more likely to rely on the advice and support of female peers than on that of their male counterparts or parents (Hammack, 2003; Saunders et al., 2004; Weist & Freedman, 1995). The coping mechanisms girls use to manage acceptance and/or rejection from peers has an impact on their emerging identities and on their lives as Black adult women.

Adulthood

Being a woman is hard work. Not without joy and even ecstasy, but still relentless, unending work.

(Angelou, 1994, p. 6)

Adulthood is a time of establishing independence as a productive adult and seeking long-term intimate relationships. Transitioning into adulthood, Black women often find themselves at war with conflicting expectations of independence and submission, audacity and reticence, and victim and combatant. The ways in which Black women cope with these expectations, which come from within as well as from others with varying intents, impact their emergent identities, health and life outcomes, and interpersonal relationships.

Black Women at Work

At the workplace, Black women's intersecting identities can leave them shunned when their assertiveness is mistaken for aggression (Hall et al., 2012). On the other hand, management may also see Black women as desirable diversity hires—as long as they appropriately fit in with the job culture. Stereotypes of Black women as angry, neck-rolling Sapphires can lead some women to feel that they need to code-switch—make adjustments to their appearance, tone of voice, and mannerisms—in order to establish themselves as appropriately qualified for their positions (Hall et al., 2012; Shorter-Gooden & Jones, 2003a, 2003b). When integrated into a strong racial identity, code-switching may be an effective reactive coping strategy for career success. However, code-switching based on internalized racism runs the risk of developing into assimilation, which leads to a devaluation of self and of racial membership (Constantine & Blackmon, 2002; Shorter-Gooden, 2004). Besides code-switching, Black women often deal with work-related stress by relying on avoidance or emotion-focused strategies (just letting it go), prayer, and the social support of family and intimate partners (Hall et al., 2012). According to a report from the Federal Reserve Bank of Kansas City (Gines, 2018), Black women are increasingly taking a solution-focused approach to work-based racial microaggressions by starting their own businesses. As a result, between 2007 and 2018, the number of businesses owned by Black women grew three times faster than for women overall, and Black women have greater rates of business ownership than Black men (Gines, 2018).

Relationships and Family

Many of the challenges that Black women face in the workplace, such as stereotyped beliefs and the need to code-switch, transfer into interpersonal relationships and home life. To protect girls from heartbreak and disappointment in relationships, mothers in particular may socialize their daughters to be strong, and to not count on men for financial or emotional sustenance. These messages may protect girls from predatory relationships, but may also result in an inability to build trusting relationships in adulthood. Cautioning girls and young women against becoming dependent on unhealthy relationships is important. However, recognizing and maintaining healthy relationships warrants equal attention.

In her qualitative research on the desired relationship characteristics of young Black women, Tyson (2011) found that the participants felt there was no intimacy without sexual behaviors. However, they felt that emotional connections better described their concept of close, trusted interactions both in and out of the bedroom. Further, the young women desired relationships that included commitment and stability, communication, trust, and respect, but felt uncomfortable with allowing themselves to be vulnerable enough to let these qualities flourish. They also wanted a true partnership that offered protection from social and societal hostilities. Like many Black women, the participants felt that many of the relationship qualities they were seeking were easier to achieve for White women (Tyson, 2011).

Black women are also hearing repeated messages that they need to seek interracial relationships in order to attain marital satisfaction (Banks, 2011). The statistics and alarm tactics used by the media about the Black male–female ratio imbalance, although anxiety-provoking, do not diminish Black women's desire and ability to have healthy relationships and families. Practitioners must help women be open to honest communication and healthy functioning with their partners and families.

Black families are often considered matriarchal because of the high prevalence of single-mother-headed households. However, *matrifocal* is a better descriptor of single motherhood, as it asserts a phenomenon "in which women are salient and men are unpredictable" (Quinlan, 2006, p. 464). By contrast, *matriarchal* families are defined as those in which women dominate and have total authority over their children and their men (Dietrich, 1975). The absence of social and economic power that most female-headed Black families exhibit suggests that the use of the term *matriarchal* to refer to them is inaccurate. It should be noted that social constraints placed on Black men have prevented them from securing employment and serving as primary income providers for their families, resulting in a redistribution of gender roles for African Americans as mothers have progressively become the main source of financial support for many families (Sanders & Bradley, 2005).

It is often argued that Black women's independence and control issues do not leave room for men to establish themselves in traditional male roles (Harvey, 2009). This rationale furthers the longstanding tradition of blaming Black women for familial and social problems (Moynihan, 1965) and fails to recognize the egalitarian nature of most Black relationships (Gray-Little, 1982) or the fact that single Black mothers often rely on boyfriends and male family members for feedback, guidance, and support—particularly when raising sons alone (Yancey, 1972). More empirical research is needed to decipher contemporary ideas of power and balance in Black relationships. Kinship support in the Black family was never meant to diminish familial roles, but to supplement emotional and caregiving resources in the face of hard economic times and oppression.

The New Grandmother

Black families have always relied on extended kinship networks to assist with childrearing. Recent trends indicate an increase in the number of grandmothers who serve as primary guardian for their grandchildren, particularly in the African American community (Kelch-Oliver, 2011). Grandmothers often become the custodial or primary caregiver when parents are deceased or too sick, poor, young, or high to care for their children (Kelch-Oliver, 2011; Murphy, 2008; See et al., 1998). With teenaged motherhood, sometimes intergenerational, women are becoming grandmothers before they are developmentally ready to take on that role (See et al., 1998). Most women in their 30s and early 40s feel inadequate to provide the stability, structure, and socialization that are expected of the archetypal Black grandmother. Further, these women may feel that they have just started a new round of parenting, possibly with a new partner, as their teenaged daughters become mothers. Thus, young grandmothers may be raising their teenaged and toddler children while simultaneously raising their infant grandchildren.

Traditional-aged grandmothers sometimes feel overwhelmed and under-resourced with the responsibilities of raising grandchildren, particularly if those children have experienced prior trauma (Carr, 2006; Simpson & Lawrence-Webb, 2009). Social service agencies may inaccurately assume that grandmothers have adequate emotional and financial resources to care for grandchildren, because they are considered kinship placements (Simpson & Lawrence-Webb, 2009). Health issues and widowhood can exacerbate these stressors.

Late Adulthood

Research on Black women in late adulthood has focused on physical health status. The life expectancy for Black women has extended into their 70s, and many have health complications that are common within the Black community, particularly cardiovascular disease risk factors and, more recently, Alzheimer's Disease.

Life expectancy in the United States is declining overall—except among Black women, whose 78-year life expectancy has remained stable (Milloy, 2016; Xu et al., 2016). Despite facing greater health burdens and social barriers throughout their lives, Black people tend to be more optimistic than other racial groups, and Black women are no exception. Research has found that this positive outlook is related to healthy aging in women (James et al., 2019). For many Black women, optimism and faith in a better tomorrow may be attributed to their higher levels of spirituality and religious involvement (Mattis et al., 2004). These and other social supports must be examined to further promote the resiliency of Black women in their later years.

Elderly Black Women and Religiosity

Black women in late adulthood rely heavily on prayer and the church to assist with life's problems. Whether through grandparent support groups, meals, or spiritual guidance, Black elderly women use the resources available at places of worship for reinforcement (E. Brown et al., 2008). Respect for elders and communalism are aspects of Black cultural ethos that are represented in Black churches. Whereas Black elderly women may feel invisible in their everyday lives, on Sunday they are the Church Mothers[13] who sit in the front pews and receive long hugs from fellow congregants (A. L. Brown, 1994; Mattis & Jagers, 2001). Research on elderly Black women focuses on their use of prayer or their reliance on religious figures as sources for coping, without adequately recognizing their specific and honored status in churches that reinforce religiosity and extend Black cultural norms to younger people (Black, 1999; Daniels, 2004; Musick, 1996).

Sex, HIV, and Mature Women

With the growth of senior residential communities, and with extended life expectancies, Black women are facing an imbalance of opportunities for social outlets and intimacy. Limited studies on the sexual health and behavior of Black women exist; however, Laganá and colleagues' 2013 review suggests that more senior women encounter many of the same issues that younger Black women do: health complications, limited

---

[13] *Church Mothers*, or *Mothers of the Church*, serve as the socializing and corrective agents in many traditional Black churches. These women are usually over the age of 70, are chosen for their spiritual commitment, and wield substantial influence in maintaining cultural norms and standards in a church.

partner options, and traumatic experiences. Black women have a longer life expectancy than Black men and may have difficulty partnering with a similarly aged peer for heterosexual companionship and sexual intimacy. Contrary to popular discourse, the desire for sexual intimacy does not disappear with age (Laganá et al., 2013); thus, lack of sexual activity may be attributed to another health issue or to experiences of unspoken sexual trauma. Laganá et al. speculate that older Black women's reluctance to discuss their sexual health with health professionals may be attributed to the persistent hyper-sexualized stereotype of Black women. Even as seniors, Black women must contend with Eurocentric standards of beauty, which often place them at the lower end of the racial spectrum for desirability. Menopausal hormonal changes impact sexual arousal and desire and contribute to a lack of sexual satisfaction. Laganá and colleagues (2013) conducted a mixed-method study with Black women aged 57–82. Participants were heterosexual and homosexual. All but one participant noted a decrease in sexual desire attributed to age and/or health. Over half of the participants indicated no sexual activity because of a deceased spouse. One participant noted, "I have no sexual problems. My only problem is trying to find someone to have sex and to be intimate with."

The lack of similarly aged partners also influences relationships with younger sexual partners. Older Black women, traditionally thought to be a low-risk HIV/AIDS group, have been contracting HIV. Ivy et al. (2014) found that women in their study over 35 were significantly more likely to be HIV unaware. Although their sample was not exclusively older Black women, 24% of their sample reported younger sexual partners.

Conclusion

Research on Black women is heavily concentrated on their childbearing years (adolescence and young adulthood), leaving early childhood and late adulthood severely under-studied in a number of areas. Black girls in early childhood are examined primarily for problems with obesity (Kaplowitz et al., 2001; Talpade, 2006) and classroom behavior management (Dobbs et al., 2004), both of which are important issues. Early childhood studies often focus on cognitive functioning or child socio-emotional well-being. Cognitive studies involve measuring normative child development. Parenting practice studies are often cited and are linked to early childhood socio-emotional outcomes, such as adjustment to school (making friends and responding to authority), sibling relationships, and the development of gender identity. Academic achievement is rarely studied with rigor among young children, especially Black children. The complexity of identity development for Black girls and the parenting strategies that Black parents employ with their female children, to prepare them for managing life as both a woman and a Black American (Anglin and Whaley, 2006; Anthis, Dunkel, and Anderson, 2004; Buckley and Carter, 2005; Hill, 2001, 2002; Stephens and Phillips, 2005), suggest that researchers should design studies that allow us to elucidate the impact of parent racial socialization and gender socialization practices on the socio-emotional well-being and academic performance of Black girls in early childhood.

The explosion of relatively inexpensive technological platforms (e.g., mobile phones, hand-held video games, tablets, lap-tops, etc.) has increased the number of studies concerned with how exposure to media impacts the well-being of children, yet much of this research does not specify the impact on Black girls and boys (Adams & Stevenson, 2012). When race is considered, most often, only basic race and socio-economic results are reported (Adams, 2011). Contemporary studies that include cultural nuances—e.g., viewing preferences—impacting media consumption among young Black children are scarce. Although redefined to include web-based streaming services such as Hulu and Netflix, television remains the media platform of choice for Black children and youth (Berry, 1998; Watkins, 2005); surely, increased exposure to media imagery via in-school instruction, web-based learning tools, and multiple TV-like platforms is worth investigating.

Today's generation of children is exposed to very high levels of media images. Unfortunately, Black media images are too often negative. While studies with adolescents are beginning to investigate media's impact on Black youth (Adams-Bass et al., 2014; Gordon, 2008; L. M. Ward, 2004), very few studies examine the impact of media on young children. Future studies should include young children, and these overlooked variables, to ascertain if there is an impact on development.

Elderly and Black women in late adulthood are researched primarily in the context of how their spirituality serves as a coping mechanism against isolation and ill health. Although Black women over the age of 65 are more likely to live alone than members of any other racial or gender group (U.S. Census Bureau, 2008), some women may experience this time as an opportunity to revel in their newly acquired independence from marriage and parenting. Research is needed to understand how Black women use technology and social networking to maintain current relationships and build new ones. Further, the dating and sexual behaviors of Black women need to be explored in this stage. This is particularly important in terms of encouraging safe-sex practices in the face of greater HIV/AIDS prevalence for African Americans in all age groups, including the elderly (Centers for Disease Control and Prevention, 2007). Overall, more research is needed that looks at how healthy Black women in late adulthood live vibrant, well-adjusted lives, in our efforts to promote resiliency among those who are struggling with psychosocial issues.

Although this chapter provides a comprehensive look at Black women's lives, it cannot be considered exhaustive of all the issues that Black women face. Finally, new measurement and assessments that reflect the interpretations and cultural values of Black women are imperative to providing Black women the exemplary treatment and resources they deserve.

References

Adams-Bass, V. N. (2019, February). Algorithms of oppression: How search engines reinforce racism [Book review]. *Teachers College Record*. http://www.tcrecord.org/Content.asp?ContentId=22663

Adams-Bass, V. N., & Bentley-Edwards, K. L. (2021). The problem with "Black girl magic" for Black girls. In D. Apugo, L. Mahwhinney, & A. M. Mblishaka (Eds.), *Strong Black girls: Patchwork stories of remembrance, resistance, and resilience*. New York, NY: Teachers College Press.

Adams-Bass, V. N., & Henrici, E. (2019). Hardly ever … I don't see it: Black youth speak about positive media images of Black men. In O. Banjo (Ed.), *African Diasporic media, content, consumers, and global influence*. Routledge.

Adams-Bass, V. N., Stevenson, H. C., & Kotzin, D. S. (2014). Measuring the meaning of Black media stereotypes and their relationship to the racial identity, Black history knowledge, and racial socialization of African American youth. *Journal of Black Studies*, *45*(5), 367–395. https://doi.org/10.1177/0021934714530396

Angelou, M. (1994). In all ways a woman. In M. Angelou (Ed.), *Wouldn't take nothing for my journey now* (p. 162). Virago.

Banks, R. R. (2011). *Is marriage for White people? How the African American marriage decline affects everyone*. Dutton Adult.

Barnes, G. L. (2008). Perspectives of African-American women on infant mortality. *Social Work in Health Care, 47*(3), 293–305. https://doi.org/10.1080/00981380801985457

Bentley, K. L., Adams, V. N., & Stevenson, H. C. (2009). Racial socialization: Roots, processes, and outcomes. In H. A. Neville, B. M. Tynes, & S. O. Utsey (Eds.), *Handbook of African American psychology* (pp. 255–267). Sage.

Berndt, T. J. (1982). The features and effects of friendship in early adolescence. *Child Development*, *53*(6), 1447–1460. https://doi.org/10.2307/1130071

Berry, G. L. (1998). Black family life on television and the socialization of the African American child: Images of marginality. *Journal of Comparative Family Studies, 29*, 233–242.

Biro, F. M., Greenspan, L. C., Galvez, M. P., Pinney, S. M., Teitelbaum, S., Windham, G. C., Deardorff, J., Herrick, R. L., Succop, P. A., Hiatt, R. A., Kushi, L. H., & Wolff, M. S. (2013). Onset of breast development in a longitudinal cohort. *Pediatrics, 132*(6), 1019–1027. https://doi.org/10.1542/peds.2012-3773

Black, H. K. (1999). Life as gift: Spiritual narratives of elderly African-American women living in poverty. *Journal of Aging Studies, 13*(4), 441–455. https://doi.org/10.1016/S0890-4065(99)00020-1

Blake, J. J., Butler, B. R., Lewis, C. W., & Darensbourg, A. (2011). Unmasking the inequitable discipline experiences of urban Black girls: Implications for urban educational stakeholders. *The Urban Review, 43*(1), 90–106. https://doi.org/10.1007/s11256-009-0148-8

Bridge, J. A., Asti, L., Horowitz, L. M., Greenhouse, J. B., Fontanella, C., Sheftall, A., Kelleher, K. J., & Campo, J. V. (2015). Suicide trends among elementary school-aged children in the United States from 1993 to 2012. *JAMA Pediatrics, 169*(7), 673–677. https://doi.org/10.1001/jamapediatrics.2015.0465

Bronfenbrenner, U. (1993). The ecology of cognitive development: Research models and fugitive findings. In R. H. Wozniak & K. W. Fischer (Eds.), *Development in context: Acting and thinking in specific environments* (pp. 3–44). Lawrence Erlbaum Associates.

Brown, A. L. (1994). Afro-Baptist women's church and family roles: Transmitting Afrocentric cultural values. *Anthropological Quarterly, 67*(4), 173–186.

Brown, E., Caldwell, C. H., & Antonucci, T. C. (2008). Religiosity as a moderator of family conflict and depressive symptoms among African American and White young grandmothers. *Journal of Human Behavior in the Social Environment, 18*(4), 397–413. https://doi.org/10.1080/10911350802486718

Brown, L. M., & Gilligan, C. (1991). Listening for voice in narratives of relationship. In M. B. Tappan & M. J. Packer (Eds.), *Narrative and storytelling: Implications for understanding moral development* (pp. 43–62). Jossey-Bass.

Buka, S. L., Brennan, R. T., Rich-Edwards, J. W., Raudenbush, S. W., & Earls, F. (2003). Neighborhood support and the birth weight of urban infants. *American Journal of Epidemiology, 157*(1), 1–8. https://doi.org/10.1093/aje/kwf170

Carr, G. F. (2006). Vulnerability: A conceptual model for African American grandmother caregivers. *Journal of Theory Construction & Testing, 10*(1), 11–14.

Centers for Disease Control and Prevention. (2007). Racial/ethnic disparities in diagnoses of HIV/AIDS—33 states, 2001–2005. *MMWR Morb Mortal Weekly Report 2007, 56*, 189–193. U.S. Department of Health and Human Services.

Centers for Disease Control and Prevention. (2016). Youth risk behavior surveillance 2015. In *Surveillance summaries* (p. 180). Centers for Disease Control and Prevention.

Chapman-Hilliard, C., Hunter, E., Adams-Bass, V., Mbilishaka, A., Jones, B., Holmes, E., et al. (2020, 6/25) The roles of racial identity and Blacks' historical narratives in predicting civic engagement among Black emerging adults. *Journal of Diversity in Higher Education.* 10.1037/dhe0000251

Coleman-King, C., Adams-Bass, V. N., Bentley-Edwards, K. L., Thomas, D. E., Thompson, C. I., Miller, G., et al. (under review). Got skillz? Recasting and negotiating racial tension in teacher-student relationships.

Collins, C. F. (2006). *African American women's health and social issues* (2nd ed.). Praeger.

Collins, J. W., Jr., David, R. J., Handler, A., Wall, S., & Andes, S. (2004). Very low birthweight in African American infants: The role of maternal exposure to interpersonal racial discrimination. *American Journal of Public Health*, *94*(12), 2132–2138.

Constantine, M. G., & Blackmon, S. K. M. (2002). Black adolescents' racial socialization experiences: Their relations to home, school, and peer self-esteem. *Journal of Black Studies*, *32*(3), 322–335.

Cottom, T. M. (2018). *Thick: And other essays*. The New Press.

Daniels, J. E. (2004). Biographical sketches of elderly African-American women in later life. *Journal of Women & Aging*, *16*(3–4), 169–178. https://doi.org/10.1300/J074v16n03

Dietrich, K. T. (1975). A reexamination of the myth of Black matriarchy. *Journal of Marriage & Family*, *37*(2), 367–374.

Dobbs, J., Arnold, D. H., & Doctoroff, G. L. (2004). Attention in the preschool classroom: The relationships among child gender, child misbehavior, and types of teacher attention. *Early Child Development & Care*, *174*(3), 281–295. https://doi.org/10.1080/0300443032000153598

DuBois, D. L., & Hirsch, B. J. (1990). School and neighborhood friendship patterns of Blacks and Whites in early adolescence. *Child Development*, *61*(2), 524–536. https://doi.org/10.2307/1131112

DuBois, D. L., & Hirsch, B. J. (1993). School/nonschool friendship patterns in early adolescence. *The Journal of Early Adolescence*, *13*(1), 102–122. https://doi.org/10.1177/0272431693013001006

Epstein, R., Blake, J. J., & González, T. (2017). Girlhood interrupted: The erasure of Black girls' childhood. Center on Poverty & Inequality at the Georgetown University Law Center.

Evaldsson, A.-C. (2005). Staging insults and mobilizing categorizations in a multiethnic peer group. *Discourse and Society*, *16*(6), 763–786. https://doi.org/10.1177/0957926505056663

Field, T., Diego, M., Hernandez-Reif, M., Deeds, O., Holder, V., Schanberg, S., & Kuhn, C. (2009). Depressed pregnant black women have a greater incidence of prematurity and low birthweight outcomes. *Infant Behavior and Development*, *32*(1), 10–16. https://doi.org/10.1016/j.infbeh.2008.09.005

Fordham, S. (1993). "Those loud Black girls": (Black) women, silence, and gender "passing" in the academy. *Anthropology & Education Quarterly*, *24*(1), 3–32.

Frazin, R. (2019, April 9). Dem lawmakers form Black Maternal Health Caucus. *The Hill*. https://thehill.com/homenews/house/438004-dem-reps-form-black-maternal-health-caucus

Gaskin, I. M. (2008). Maternal death in the United States: A problem solved or a problem ignored? *The Journal of Perinatal Education*, *17*(2), 9–13. https://doi.org/105812408X298336

Gennaro, S., Shults, J., & Garry, D. J. (2008). Stress and preterm labor and birth in Black women. *Journal of Obstetric, Gynecologic, & Neonatal Nursing: Clinical Scholarship for the Care of Women, Childbearing Families, & Newborns*, *37*(5), 538–545. https://doi.org/10.1111/j.1552-6909.2008.00278.x

Geronimus, A. T. (1992). The weathering hypothesis and the health of African-American women and infants: Evidence and speculations. *Ethnicity & Disease*, *2*(3), 207–221.

Geronimus, A. T., Hicken, M., Keene, D., & Bound, J. (2006). "Weathering" and age patterns of allostatic load scores among Blacks and Whites in the United States. *American Journal of Public Health*, *96*(5), 826–83

Gines, D. (2018). Black women business startups.The Federal Reserve Bank of Kansas City.

Goodwin, M. H., & Alim, H. S. (2010). "Whatever (neck roll, eye roll, teeth suck)": The situated coproduction of social categories and identities through stancetaking and transmodal stylization. *Journal of Linguistic Anthropology*, *20*(1), 179–194. https://doi.org/10.1111/j.1548-1395.2010.01056.x

Gordon, M. K. (2008). Media contributions to African American girls' focus on beauty and appearance: Exploring the consequences of sexual objectification. *Psychology of Women Quarterly*, *32*(3), 245–256. https://doi.org/10.1111/j.1471-6402.2008.00433.x

Graham, J. A., & Cohen, R. (1997). Race and sex as factors in children's sociometric ratings and friendship choices. *Social Development*, *6*(3), 355–372. https://doi.org/10.1111/j.1467-9507.1997.tb00111.x

Hall, J. C., Everett, J. E., & Hamilton-Mason, J. (2012). Black women talk about workplace stress and how they cope. *Journal of Black Studies*, *43*(2), 207–226. https://doi.org/10.1177/0021934711413272

Hammack, P. L. (2003). Toward a unified theory of depression among urban African American youth integrating socioecologic, cognitive, family stress, and biopsychosocial perspectives. *Journal of Black Psychology*, *29*(2), 197–209.

Harvey, S. (2009). *Act like a lady, think like a man: What men really think about love, relationships, intimacy, and commitment*. Amistad.

Haskell, R. (2018, January 10). Serena Williams on motherhood, marriage, and making her comeback. *Vogue*. https://www.vogue.com/article/serena-williams-vogue-cover-interview-february-2018

Herman-Giddens, M. E. (2006). Recent data on pubertal milestones in United States children: The secular trend toward earlier development. *International Journal of Andrology*, *29*(1), 241–246.

Herman-Giddens, M. E. (2013). The enigmatic pursuit of puberty in girls. *Pediatrics*, *132*(6), 1125–1126. https://doi.org/10.1542/peds.2013-3058

Hogue, C. J. R., & Bremner, J. D. (2005). Stress model for research into preterm delivery among Black women. *American Journal of Obstetrics & Gynecology*, *192*(5), S47–55.

Holland, M. L., Kitzman, H., & Veazie, P. (2009). The effects of stress on birth weight in low-income, unmarried Black women. *Women's Health Issues*, *19*(6), 390–397. https://doi.org/10.1016/j.whi.2009.07.005

Hull, A. G., Bell-Scott, P., & Smith, B. (1982). *All the women are White, all the Blacks are men, but some of us are brave: Black women's studies*. Feminist Press.

Ivy, W., Miles, I., Le, B., & Paz-Bailey, G. (2014). Correlates of HIV infection among African American women from 20 cities in the United States. *AIDS and* Behavior, *18*(S3), 266–275. https://doi.org/10.1007/s10461-013-0614-x

James, P., Kim, E. S., Kubzansky, L. D., Zevon, E. S., Trudel-Fitzgerald, C., & Grodstein, F. (2019). Optimism and healthy aging in women. *American Journal of Preventive Medicine*, *56*(1), 116–124. https://doi.org/10.1016/j.amepre.2018.07.037

Kaplowitz, P. B., Slora, E. J., Wasserman, R. C., Pedlow, S. E., & Herman-Giddens, M. E. (2001). Earlier onset of puberty in girls: Relation to increased body mass index and race. *Pediatrics*, *108*(2), 347–353.

Kelch-Oliver, K. (2011). The experiences of African American grandmothers in grandparent-headed families. *Family Journal, 19*(1), 73–82. https://doi.org/10.1177/1066480710388730

Laganá, L., White, T., Bruzzone, D. E., & Bruzzone, C. E. (2013). Exploring the sexuality of African American older women. *British Journal of Medicine and Medical Research, 4*(5), 1129–1148. https://doi.org/10.9734/bjmmr/2014/5491

Lee, E., Mitchell-Herzfeld, S. D., Lowenfels, A. A., Greene, R., Dorabawila, V., & DuMont, K. A. (2009). Reducing low birth weight through home visitation: A randomized controlled trial. *American Journal of Preventive Medicine, 36*(2), 154–160. https://doi.org/10.1016/j.amepre.2008.09.029

Martin, N., & Montagne, R. (2017). Black mothers keep dying after giving birth. Shalon Irving's story explains why. *NPR*. https://www.npr.org/2017/12/07/568948782/black-mothers-keep-dying-after-giving-birth-shalon-irvings-story-explains-why

Mattis, J. S., Fontenot, D. L., Hatcher-Kay, C. A., Grayman, N. A., & Beale, R. L. (2004). Religiosity, optimism, and pessimism among African Americans. *Journal of Black Psychology, 30*(2), 187–207. https://doi.org/10.1177/0095798403260730

Mattis, J. S., & Jagers, R. J. (2001). A relational framework for the study of religiosity and spirituality in the lives of African Americans. *Journal of Community Psychology, 29*(5), 519–539. https://doi.org/10.1002/jcop.1034

McCombs, H. G. (1986). The application of an individual/collective model to the psychology of Black women. *Women & Therapy, 5*(2–3), 67–80. https://doi.org/10.1300/J015V05N02_06

Milloy, C. (2016, December 13). Black women defy trend of declining life expectancies. What explains this miracle? *The Washington Post*. https://www.washingtonpost.com/local/black-women-defy-trend-of-declining-life-expectancies-what-explains-this-miracle/2016/12/13/5f09a876-c165-11e6-8422-eac61c0ef74d_story.html

Morris, E. W. (2007). "Ladies" or "loudies"?: Perceptions and experiences of Black girls in classrooms. *Youth & Society, 38*(4), 490–515. https://doi.org/10.1177/0044118X06296778

Moynihan, D. P. (1965). *The Negro family: The case for national action*. U.S. Department of Labor, Office of Policy Planning and Research.

Mueller, A. S., James, W., Abrutyn, S., & Levin, M. L. (2015). Suicide ideation and bullying among US adolescents: Examining the intersections of sexual orientation, gender, and race/ethnicity. *American Journal of Public Health, 105*(5), 980–985. https://doi.org/10.2105/AJPH.2014.302391

Murphy, S. Y. (2008). Voices of African American grandmothers raising grandchildren: Informing child welfare kinship care policy-practice. *Journal of Intergenerational Relationships, 6*(1), 25–39. https://doi.org/10.1300/J194v06n01_03

Musick, M. A. (1996). Religion and subjective health among Black and White elders. *Journal of Health and Social Behavior, 37*(3), 221–237. https://pubmed.ncbi.nlm.nih.gov/8898494/

Musu-Gillette, L., Zhange, A., Wang, K., Zhang, J., & Oudekerk, B. (2017). *Indicators of school crime and safety, 2016* (NCES 2017064/NCJ 250650). National Center for Education Statistics, U.S. Department of Education & Bureau of Justice Statistics, U.S. Department of Justice.

Noble, S. U. (2018). *Algorithms of oppression: How search engines reinforce racism*. New York University Press.

Norbeck, J. S., DeJoseph, J. F., & Smith, R. e. T. (1996). A randomized trial of an empirically-derived social support intervention to prevent low birthweight among African American women. *Social Science & Medicine*, *43*(6), 947–954. https://doi.org/10.1016/0277-9536(96)00003-2

Osborne, C., & McLanahan, S. (2007). Partnership instability and child well-being. *Journal of Marriage and Family*, *69*(4), 1065–1083. https://doi.org/10.1111/j.1741-3737.2007.00431.x

Petersen, E. E., Davis, N. L., Goodman, D., Cox, S., Mayes, N., Johnston, E., Syverson, C., Seed, K., Shapiro-Mendoza, C. K., Callaghan, W. M., & Barfield, W. (2019). Vital signs: Pregnancy-related deaths, United States, 2011–2015, and strategies for prevention, 13 States, 2013–2017. *Morbidity and Mortality Weekly Report* (MMWR), *68*(18), 423–429. Centers for Disease Control and Prevention.

Quillian, L., & Campbell, M. E. (2003). Beyond Black and White: The present and future of multiracial friendship segregation. *American Sociological Review*, *68*(4), 540–566.

Quinlan, R. J. (2006). Gender and risk in a matrifocal Caribbean community: A view from behavioral ecology. *American Anthropologist*, *108*(3), 464–479.

Rose, C. A., & Tynes, B. M. (2015). Longitudinal associations between cybervictimization and mental health among U.S. adolescents. *Journal of Adolescent Health*, *57*(3), 305–312. https://doi.org/https://doi.org/10.1016/j.jadohealth.2015.05.002

Rosser, M. L. (2019). At the heart of maternal mortality. *Obstetrics & Gynecology*, *134*(3), 437–439.

Salsberry, P. J., Reagan, P. B., & Pajer, K. (2009). Growth differences by age of menarche in African American and White girls. *Nursing Research*, *58*(6), 382–390.

Sanders, J.-A. L., & Bradley, C. (2005). Multiple-lens paradigm: Evaluating African American girls and their development. *Journal of Counseling & Development*, *83*(3), 299–304. https://doi.org/10.1002/j.1556-6678.2005.tb00347.x

Saunders, J., Davis, L., Williams, T., & Williams, J. H. (2004). Gender differences in self-perceptions and academic outcomes: A study of African American high school students. *Journal of Youth and Adolescence*, *33*, 81–91. https://link.springer.com/article/10.1023/A:1027390531768

Sawyer, A. L., Bradshaw, C. P., & O'Brennan, L. M. (2008). Examining ethnic, gender, and developmental differences in the way children report being a victim of 'bullying' on self-report measures. *Journal of Adolescent Health*, *43*(2), 106–114. https://doi.org/10.1016/j.jadohealth.2007.12.011

Scott, K. A. (2002). 'You want to be a girl and not my friend': African-American/Black girls' play activities with and without boys. *Childhood: A Global Journal of Child Research*, *9*(4), 397–414. https://doi.org/10.1177/0907568202009004003

Scott, K. A. (2003). In girls, out girls, and always Black: African-American girls' friendships. In K. B. Rosier & D. A. Kinney (Eds.), *Sociological studies of children and youth: Vol 9* (pp. 179–207). Elsevier Science.

Scott, K. A. (2004). V. African-American–White girls' friendships. *Feminism & Psychology*, *14*(3), 383–388.

See, L. A., Bowles, D., & Darlington, M. (1998). Young African American grandmothers: A missed developmental stage. *Journal of Human Behavior in the Social Environment*, *1*(2–3), 281–303.

Sheftall, A. H., Asti, L., Horowitz, L. M., Felts, A., Fontanella, C. A., Campo, J. V., & Bridge, J. A. (2016). Suicide in elementary school-aged children and early adolescents. *Pediatrics*, *138*(4), e20160436. https://doi.org/10.1542/peds.2016-0436

Shorter-Gooden, K. (2004). Multiple resistance strategies: How African American women cope with racism and sexism. *Journal of Black Psychology*, *30*(3), 406–425.

Shorter-Gooden, K., & Jones, C. (2003a). The roots of shifting. In *Shifting: The double lives of Black women in America* (pp. 1–36). Harper Collins.

Shorter-Gooden, K., & Jones, C. (2003b). *Shifting: The double lives of Black women in America*. Harper Collins.

Simpson, G. M., & Lawrence-Webb, C. (2009). Responsibility without community resources: Informal kinship care among low-income, African American grandmother caregivers. *Journal of Black Studies*, *39*(6), 825–847.

Smith, I. Z., Bentley-Edwards, K. L., El-Amin, S., & Darity, W. Jr. (2018). *Fighting at birth: Eradicating the Black-White infant mortality gap*. Duke University's Samuel DuBois Cook Center on Social Equity and Insight Center on Community Economic Development.

Spencer, M. B. (1995). Old issues and new theorizing about African American youth: A phenomenological variant of ecological systems theory. In R. L. Taylor (Ed.), *African American youth: Their social and economic status in the United States* (pp. 37–69). Praeger.

Spencer, M. B. (1999). Social and cultural influences on school adjustment: The application of an identity-focused cultural ecological perspective. *Educational Psychologist*, *34*(1), 43–57.

Spencer, M. B., Dupree, D., & Hartmann, T. (1997). A phenomenological variant of ecological systems theory (PVEST): A self-organization perspective in context. *Development and Psychopathology*, *9*(4), 817–833.

Spencer, M. B., Fegley, S. G., & Harpalani, V. (2003). A theoretical and empirical examination of identity as coping: Linking coping resources to the self processes of African American youth. *Applied Developmental Science*, *7*(3), 181–188.

Spencer, M. B., & Markstrom-Adams, C. (1990). Identity processes among racial and ethnic minority children in America. *Child Development, 61*(2), 290–310.

Spencer, M. B., Swanson, D. P., & Cunningham, M. (1991). Ethnicity, ethnic identity, and competence formation: Adolescent transition and cultural transformation. *The Journal of Negro Education*, *60*(3), 366–387.

Spencer, M. B., Swanson, D. P., & Edwards, M. C. (2010). Sociopolitical contexts of development. In D. P. Swanson, M. C. Edwards, & M. B. Spencer (Eds.), *Adolescence: Development during a global era* (pp. 1–27). Academic Press.

Tach, L., Mincy, R., & Edin, K. (2010). Parenting as a "package deal": Relationships, fertility, and nonresident father involvement among unmarried parents. *Demography*, *47*(1), 181–204. https://doi.org/10.1353/dem.0.0096

Talpade, M. (2006). African American child-women: Nutrition theory revisited. *Adolescence*, *41*(161), 91–102.

Thomas, V. G. (2004). The psychology of Black women: Studying women's lives in context. *Journal of Black Psychology*, *30*(3), 286–306. https://doi.org/10.1177/0095798404266044

Thomas, A.J., Witherspoon, K.M., & Speight, S.L. (2004). Toward the development of the Stereotypic Roles for Black women Scale. *Journal of Black Psychology, 30*(3), 426-442. doi:10.1177/0095798404266061

Tyson, S. Y. (2011). Developmental and ethnic issues experienced by emerging adult African American women related to developing a mature love relationship. *Issues in Mental Health Nursing*, *33*(1), 39–51. https://doi.org/10.3109/01612840.2011.620681

U.S. Census Bureau. (2008). *Current population survey, annual social & economic supplement, 2008.* Washington, DC.

Velez, G., & Spencer, M. B. (2018). Phenomenology and intersectionality: Using PVEST as a frame for adolescent identity formation amid intersecting ecological systems of inequality. *New Directions for Child and Adolescent Development, 2018*(161), 75–90. https://doi.org/10.1002/cad.20247

Ward, J. V. (2000). Raising resisters: The role of truth telling in the psychological development of African American girls. In L. Weis & M. Fine (Eds.), *Construction sites: Excavating race, class, and gender among urban youth* (pp. 50–64). Teachers College Press.

Ward, L. M. (2004). Wading through the stereotypes: Positive and negative associations between media use and Black adolescents' conceptions of self. *Developmental Psychology*, *40*(2), 284–294.

Watkins, S. C. (2005). Black youth and mass media: Current research and emerging questions. *African American Research Perspectives*, *6.* https://www.semanticscholar.org/paper/Black-Youth-and-Mass-Media%3A-Current-Research-and-Watkins/3679706f93569f76af255a3acac4ebe13611a46f

Weist, M. D., & Freedman, A. H. (1995). Urban youth under stress: Empirical identification of protective factors. *Journal of Youth and Adolescence*, *24*(6), 705–717.

Wheeler, S., Truong, T., & Brown, H. L. (2018). Provider comfort with teaching patients and learns about racial and ethnic disparities in Ob/Gyn outcomes [8I]. *Obstetrics & Gynecology*, *131 Supplement*(1), 99S.

Xu, J., Murphey, S. L., Kochanek, K. D., & Arias, E. (2016). Mortality in the United States. *2015 NCHS Data Brief*, *2017 Dec*(293), 1–8. Centers for Disease Control and Prevention, National Center for Health Statistics.

Yancey, W. L. (1972). Going down home: Family structure and the urban trap. *Social Science Quarterly*, *52*(4), 893–906.

Reading 2.2. Black Female Adolescents

Defying the Odds

Morgan Maxwell, Jasmine Abrams, Michell Pope, Faye Belgrave, Huberta Jackson-Lowman, and Moesha Ciceron

To truly understand the Black woman, we must first address her beginnings. Who she is and how she has come to be are firmly rooted in her adolescent development. The tools and coping mechanisms Black women employ to negotiate historical oppression and social challenges all begin to take form in adolescence. While adulthood offers the opportunity for identity solidification and ideological modifications, her well-being is hinged on the intersectionality of growing up Black and female. The strategies Black adolescent girls use to successfully navigate their surroundings, define their identities, and resist cultural imperialism carry into adulthood. In this sense, an exploration of Black female adolescent development is critical to gaining a complete and contextual understanding of women of African ancestry.

In this chapter we examine Black female adolescent development in the United States across several domains. In framing the chapter, we focus on the process of socialization and the ways in which parental/kin influences and media influences guide the behavior and perceptions of Black female adolescents. How Black girls are socialized in areas such as self-identity, gender roles, racial and ethnic identity, body image, skin color, and hair has significant bearing on their development into women. To begin, the chapter reviews two primary modes of socialization: familial and media influences. The subsequent sections further explore the impact of these influences as they relate to the previously mentioned domains. Finally, the chapter closes with a discussion of promoting an African- and female-centered identity.

Who Are Black Girls?

Black girls comprise a unique and diverse group. Although they share certain traits and characteristics with other girls and with African American boys, Black girls find that growing up Black and female constructs a social context of racism and sexism unique to their experience. There are notable problems such as teen pregnancy, chronic health conditions (e.g., obesity, cardiovascular disease, diabetes, asthma, etc.), and school failure that can stifle positive Black female adolescent development (National Center for Health Statistics, 2011; Wood et al., 2007). However, in spite of these potential obstacles, through resiliency, Black girls find a way to defy the odds and surpass even their own expectations. For example, in comparison to African American boys, African American girls finish high school and graduate from college at higher rates (Hechman & LaFontaine, 2007). They are more likely to have higher life and vocational expectations, and contrary to popular belief, Black girls are more assertive than girls from other ethnic groups (Hellenga et al., 2002). Across various areas of importance, there are examples of Black girls excelling beyond their circumstances.

The socio-environmental contexts within which Black girls operate have a powerful impact on their overall development as Black women. In the United States, a majority of Black girls live in urban neighborhoods with highly concentrated populations. However, this does not mean that the experiences of Black girls are homogenous. They are members of families of varying socioeconomic backgrounds, they live in both rural and suburban communities, and they are a part of extended and intergenerational families. In varied parts of the country, the responsibilities, stresses, and personalities of Black girls differ; however, notwithstanding their diversified experiences, during the developmental stage of adolescence, every Black girl will encounter biological, social, and psychological transitions that will shape the trajectory of her life.

Socially, she will search for an identity outside of the home. She will exhibit an increased desire to reason independently and develop an interest in exploring her sexual identity. More importantly, she will become subject to various social influences that will socialize her and affect her perceptions of herself and the world.

Socialization of Black Girls

Socialization, according to the symbolic interaction theory, is a fluid, never-ending process in which an individual's behavior, personality, attitudes, and perceptions are shaped by social interactions (Denzin, 1977; Hill, 1999). It is through socialization that individuals develop social identities as well as visual, audio, and mental interpretations of the world. Various influences facilitate the process of socialization. However, in this chapter, we will focus on family and media, as research has revealed these two sources to be significantly influential on the lives, behavior, and perceptions of Black girls.

Familial Influence

Exploring the role of families in the process of socialization is critical to understanding how and why Black girls behave and think as they do. Of particular importance are parents. As primary socializing agents, African American parents are instrumental in helping girls to manage essential developmental tasks and negotiate social challenges (Aquilino & Supple, 2001; Parker et al., 1995). From style of dress and choices in food to communication skills and musical preferences, parents, unknowingly and consciously, mold their daughters into images of themselves. The relationship a Black girl has with her parents is vital to her development of self-attributes (i.e., self-esteem, self-worth), her personality, and her resilience.

Various studies have shed light on the ability of family members to affect the cognitive, behavioral, and social development of Black girls. For example, in their exploration of childhood obesity and the eating practices of African American families, Ritchie and colleagues (2011) supported previous literature and found healthy family food habits to be significantly related to decreased child intake of total high caloric foods and discretionary fat (Golan et al., 1998; Reimer et al., 2004). The influence of family has also been documented in risky adolescent behavior. Positive family relationships have been shown to deter Black girls from engaging in drug use as well as early sexual encounters (T. Clark et al., 2008; McBride et al., 2003). Teen pregnancy is also less prevalent when Black girls feel connected to their parents and extended families (South & Baumer, 2000).

In addition to parents, extended family members/kin (e.g., grandmothers, aunts, and uncles) and fictive kin (e.g., neighbors, coaches, and church members) are also agents of socialization for young Black girls (Harris & Skyles, 2008; Hirsch et al., 2000). Kin networks consisting of maternal caregivers such as grandmothers and aunts serve as key sources of information, knowledge, and support—especially for single parents (Perry, 2009). Through behavior modeling and the endorsement of ideologies, these individuals can play an integral part in socializing the perceptions and actions of Black girls. In a study of academic achievement and family/fictive kin, Wood and colleagues (2007) found parents and teachers to have significantly higher vocational and educational expectations for Blacks girls than for Black boys. As Black girls *are* more likely to attend college and have higher rates of academic achievement, perhaps these expectations also translate into greater support and/or elevated self-efficacy.

Studies on Black female adolescent development reveal immediate and extended family members to be very influential. However, there is also evidence to suggest that outside sources, such as the media, can equally affect Black girls' psychological and social functioning.

Media Influences

For Black girls, the mainstream media is a major purveyor of societal norms and behavioral expectations. With seemingly unlimited access to traditional media (i.e., television, movies, and magazines) and newer media outlets (i.e., the internet and social networking sites), adolescents have at their disposal a number of tools from which to seek out and gain information on a variety of topics including sex, health, beauty, style/clothing, dating, and relationships. Like never before, the media has become a powerful socio-cultural influence in the lives of adolescents (Brown & Bobkowski, 2011; Stice, 2002; Ward, 1996). This is especially true for Black adolescents, who are exposed to more media images and messages than any other racial/ethnic group. In fact, compared to their White counterparts, Black youth consume nearly 4.5 more hours of media daily (Rideout et al., 2010).

This pattern of media consumption among Black adolescents is concerning, given research linking high levels of media exposure with a number of negative health outcomes including increased substance use (alcohol and tobacco), sexual risk-taking behaviors, lowered self-esteem, lower academic performance, obesity, and negative body image (L. Clark & Tiggemann, 2006; P. H. Collins, 2004; Grabe et al., 2008; Strasburger, 2009). For instance, one study found that when Black girls watch more hours of rap music videos, they are more likely to engage in binge drinking, marijuana use, and risky sexual behaviors (e.g., having multiple sexual partners and exhibiting greater negative body image) (Peterson et al., 2007). Gordon (2008) found that the more girls identified with television characters and objectified female artists, the more they internalized media messages and endorsed the importance of attractiveness and appearance.

The risks associated with extensive media exposure have been well documented; however, there is emerging research suggesting that media can also have positive and/or educational benefits on adolescent girls' outcomes. For example, a recent study revealed that reality television showcasing teen parents (e.g., MTV's 16 and Pregnant, Teen Mom) have increased adolescent awareness of the negative consequences and challenges associated with teen pregnancy and adolescent parenthood (Suellentrop et al., 2010). L. Collins et al. (2003) similarly found that Black adolescents exposed to frequent sexual content on television reportedly learned how to be more confident and efficacious when negotiating condom use and communicating with their partners. Popular public service announcements (e.g., Be Safe, Rap It Up, and Know Your Status) have also successfully raised STI and HIV/AIDS awareness and promoted the importance of testing and condom use among teens.

Research on family and media has revealed both to be highly influential agents of socialization. By way of modeling and reinforcing particular ideals, parents and extended family, fictive kin, music, television, and movies can significantly guide how Black girls behave and engage their environments. The process of socialization is intricately linked to adolescent development. Through social influences, Black girls develop their sense of self-worth and identity.

Self-Identity

Identity development is one of the most central processes of adolescence. Through observations, life experiences, and social teachings, adolescents define who they are and what they will become. More specifically, adolescents begin to develop feelings and beliefs about their "selves." The self is complex. It consists of such attributes as self-esteem, sexual identity, racial and ethnic identity, self-concept, and self-worth. In this section we focus on self-worth and its importance to positive adolescent development. We will return and explore other self attributes later in the chapter.

What Is Self-Worth?

Self-worth (also referred to as self-esteem) is defined as one's affective or emotional reaction toward oneself (Rosenberg & Simmons, 1971). Self-esteem is a buffer against negative influences and a major predictor of developmental outcomes (Mann et al., 2004). High levels of self-esteem have been linked to well-being, the development of social relationships, academic achievement, and greater congruence between self-perceptions and behaviors (Impett et al., 2008; Ward, 1996). For example, girls with higher levels of self-esteem engage in less risky sexual behavior (DiClemente & Wingood, 2000), are less likely to use drugs (T. Clark et al., 2008), and are more protected against teen pregnancy (Freeman & Rickels, 1993).

How Do Families Influence Black Girls' Self-Worth?

In their development of self-worth, Black girls are highly influenced by their parents. While fathers are important in shaping Black girls' self-concept and promoting positive self-perceptions, mothers teach their daughters about other aspects of life such as sex and sexuality, education/career opportunities, ethnic/racial identity, motherhood, and health (Bean et al., 2003; Belgrave, 2009; C. Jackson et al., 1994; Prevatt, 2003). Although both parents share in this responsibility, the mother-daughter relationship is particularly vital to girls' development. In fact, several studies have found that positive mother-daughter relationships serve as a protective factor against sexual risk-taking behaviors (e.g., risky behaviors regarding condom use and number of sexual partners), lowered self-esteem, depression and negative body image, and other unhealthy behaviors (Belgrave, 2009; Donenberg et al., 2011; Stice & Bearman, 2001). Overall, positive relationships with family members heighten the self-esteem of Black girls.

How Does the Media Shape Self-Worth?

Much has been written about the impact of media on the self-worth and self-concept of Black Americans. This has primarily been a result of the negative and stereotypical images that inundate media outlets. While Black women and men alike have been visually misrepresented in the media, it has been argued that Black females are victims of the most egregious and extensive portrayals (P. H. Collins, 2004). The tragic mulatto, the welfare mother, the mammy, the gangsta girl, the dyke, and the loud diva are among the negative images the media offers to represent women of African ancestry (Stephens & Few, 2007). As Black girls are often exposed to these stigmatizing visuals, it is important to consider how these depictions of Black females influence the way that they feel about themselves. There has been little research examining the cognitive processes that Black female adolescents employ to interpret media images (Adams-Bass et al., 2014).

For example, if continuously bombarded with images of Black women as servants, as in the popular film *The Help*, or obese and poor, as in the movie *Precious*, or loud and obnoxious, like the women on Basketball Wives, Black girls may feel relegated to these identities. Crafting a self-concept or self-worth void of these influences is difficult, but not impossible. Fortunately, there remain a few exceptional images of successful Black women (e.g., Oprah, Michelle Obama, and Beyoncé) who offer hope and the existence of non-stereotypical lifestyles. However, as such images are few and far between, some argue that such little representation reinforces the idea that these Black women are rare and distinct from the majority.

The high amounts of media to which Black girls are exposed can have both negative and positive effects on their development. While the stereotypical portrayals of Black females can give the impression of limited identities, safe-sex messages can raise social and health awareness. Each year, the reach of the media continues to grow; social networks expand, and the Internet becomes increasingly accessible. #BlackGirlMagic has provided a radical platform which encourages Black girls to recognize their feminine power and appreciate their unique gifts (C. J.-M. Jackson, 2020). Given this expansion, examining how Black girls develop self-worth within this context is critical to understanding their sense of self. In the next sections, we will further explore the identities that Black girls assume, beginning with gender, which is arguably one of the most socially defining and potentially stigmatized aspects of Black female adolescent identity.

Why Is Gender Important?

Gender role socialization begins as early as birth and influences a wide range of life experiences. Gender roles can determine how one can be influenced as well as how one influences others (Carli, 2001). Gender role beliefs affect identity development, how individuals interact with their environment (Noppe, 2009), mental health (Broman, 1991), self-concept (Frome et al., 2006), sexual behaviors and attitudes (Amaro et al., 2001), and coping behaviors (Friedman & Silver, 2007). In this sense, how Black girls are socialized to assume either feminine or masculine beliefs is meaningful to their development and well-being.

Becoming a Phenomenal Woman

When parents buy dolls with bottles, encourage emotional release, reward autonomous behaviors, and don't allow daughters to play games their brothers play, they send distinct messages to young girls about what roles they should embrace as they grow older. Compared to females in other ethnic groups, Black girls tend to identify more with androgynous gender identities, having high belief in both feminine and masculine gender roles (Boyd et al., 2004). Research has also found that Black girls with androgynous gender identities engage in less risky behaviors, have better psychological functioning, and have higher levels of ethnic identity, self-worth, and confidence (Buckley & Carter, 2005; Rose & Montemayor, 1994).

During their childhoods, Black girls are socialized to be strong and independent and are raised to be able to take on an extensive array of roles and meet an endless list of expectations (Beauboeuf-Lafontant, 2007, Thomas & King, 2007). When asked about what it means to be a woman, Black female adolescents describe Black womanhood as: being economically productive, being independent, being emotionally strong, and being a caretaker (Kerrigan et al., 2007).

The ability to hold the weight of the world with the grace of a woman is a prominent characteristic of the "Superwoman" or "Strong Black Woman (SBW)" schema (Woods-Giscombé, 2010). This schema, which many Black women embrace, can have varied social and health outcomes. On one hand, being a SBW is associated with depression and anxiety; on the other, it can translate into survival and resiliency—motivating women to overcome adversities and preserve themselves, their families, and their communities (Beauboeuf-Lafontant, 2003, 2007; Woods-Giscombé, 2010). The endorsement of the SBW schema has significant implications for adolescent development. For many girls, strong Black women are models—idolized for their abilities to maintain strength while managing caretaking, financial independence, and leadership roles (Kerrigan et al., 2007). Similar to SBW, Black girls can see themselves as combinations of identities: a daughter, a friend, a student, a church member, an athlete, a choir singer, a member of an extended family, or a community agent.

This assumption of multiple identities and seeing oneself as having more than one aspect of one's life, is referred to as self-complexity (Linville, 1987). Overall, high self-complexity (having multiple roles) is positive and in many ways protective. If a person is not performing particularly well in one area, success in another can create balance, which may facilitate adaptations to new experiences and effective coping with hardships. High self-complexity can, however, be problematic as well. Inconsistent or competing roles and responsibilities can be stressful and/or emotionally and physically taxing. For example, if a Black girl has to sacrifice extracurricular activities to assume after-school care for her siblings, she may become resentful, feel unfulfilled, and potentially miss the opportunity to develop her passion. To this end, while the construction of multiple identities can lead to successes in varied arenas, conflicting responsibilities and roles can also stymie Black girls' development.

The degree to which a Black girl internalizes feminine or masculine qualities or the SBW schema can significantly affect how she negotiates her surroundings. Just being female alone requires one to hurdle obstacles derived from male chauvinism and misogynistic beliefs. However,, when being female is paired with being a member of a racial minority group, the intersection renders Black females subject to both racial and gender discrimination. In this sense, gender and racial identity can both define and construct an oppressive environment. The intersection of gender and racial identity has become increasingly challenging for Black girls in the school setting and has resulted in disproportionate rates of suspension. In the next section, we discuss its impact on the criminalization of Black girls.

The Criminalization of Black Girls in the Public Schools

Across the country, a trend of disparate rates of suspension of Black girls is occurring (Crenshaw et al., 2015; Watson, 2016). The U.S. Department of Education Office for Civil Rights (2014) reported that Black girls are suspended at higher rates (12%) than girls of other racial/ethnic groups and most boys. Although

Black girls make up only 16% of the school population nationwide, they account for one out of three of the school-related arrests (Morris, 2016). School policies and practices, including zero tolerance, the presence of law enforcement officials in schools, and the use of metal detectors, create a hostile and threatening environment that problematizes Black girls, whose behaviors are often misunderstood (Epstein et al., n.d.; Morris, 2016). In comparison with Black boys and White girls, Black girls face harsher and more punitive disciplinary practices (Crenshaw et al., 2015). Monique Morris (2016) suggests that the end of de jure segregation (*Brown v. Board of Education*, 1954) resulted in Black girls being subjected to the denigrating stereotypes of Black femininity emerging from the enslavement of Afrikan people and evident in desegregated public-school settings. Contemporary public-school education is now dominated by the presence of White female teachers who, consistent with societal norms, view White femininity as the standard for all girls and women and lack understanding and appreciation of Black femininity, which assumes a devalued status (Morris, 2016).

Wrestling with their historically oppressed status due to their race, gender, and class, Black girls are often characterized as attitudinal, defiant, loud, sassy, flamboyant, aggressive, and hypersexual (Epstein et al., n.d.; Morris, 2016). They are perceived as "bad girls" who defy the traditional standards of femininity. Their efforts to resist the stultifying treatment of teachers who ignore them, stereotype them, and hold low expectations for them are erroneously interpreted, and thus, a vicious cycle of exclusion and disciplinary actions often occurs. Their loudness is frequently a tactic designed to gain visibility; their defiance, an effort to resist mistreatment; their aggressiveness, a protective maneuver; and their flamboyance, an attempt to reinvent themselves. However, these behaviors, when viewed through the Western Eurocentric lens of femininity, are considered undesirable and inappropriate for girls. In many instances, Black girls are adultified—held to standards more appropriate for women than for girls—and denied the same grace granted to their peers of other race/ethnicities when they err (Epstein et al., n.d.; Morris, 2016). When girls are adultified, it is assumed that they require less nurturance, protection, and support. The experience of adultification is also associated with reduced leadership and mentorship opportunities within the schools for Black girls (Epstein et al., n.d.).

The struggles of Black girls to assert their humanity and to demand recognition and visibility, in environments in which they lack protection, contribute to their vulnerability and place them at risk for critical scrutiny by those in positions of power. Unfortunately, the structural inequities that characterize many of the environments in which Black girls are schooled and the prevailing consciousness of Black feminine inferiority lead some Black girls to internalize their oppression and to assume greater responsibility for their difficulties than is warranted. Under these conditions, their ability to develop a healthy identity may be greatly compromised. In the next section we examine what is required to develop a healthy racial/ethnic identity.

Am I Black and Proud?

Racial identity is defined as the significance and meaning that individuals ascribe to being a member of their racial group (Sellers et al., 1998). Ethnic identity, on the other hand, refers not only to the extent to which an individual identifies with a racial group, but also to how they identify with the group's social and cultural perceptions (Phinney & Rotheram-Borus, 1987). In this chapter, the term "ethnic identity" will be used most often.

The construct of ethnic identity—especially within the African American community—and its relation to other variables have been examined extensively. Researchers have found ethnic identity to be a protective factor against varied risk behaviors (Brook & Pahl, 2005; Caldwell et al., 2004). Most African Americans function along a continuum of low-to-high ethnic identity. Those operating high in ethnic identity feel good about being of African ancestry, desire to be with other African Americans, and engage in behavior that reinforces these feelings and desires.

Among Black girls, high ethnic identity translates into positive behavior and favorable outcomes (Corneille & Belgrave, 2007; Thomas et la., 2003). Some of these outcomes include less drug use, better academic performance and school bonding (Dotterer et al., 2009), delayed initiation of first sexual encounter, engaging in safer sexual practices, and more positive social interactions with peers (Belgrave et al., 2000; Burlew et al., 2000).

In a recent study of gendered experiences with ethnic identity, ethnic identity became more salient for Black girls as they grew older than it did for Black boys (Smith et al., 2009). Such differences may be attributed to the fact that Black girls experience dual forms of discrimination. Encounters with gender exclusion could heighten awareness of other identities—especially those that may be judged or evaluated unfairly. Ergo, being female appears to bring into focus the import and social implications of being of African ancestry. Ethnic identity is also a byproduct of socialization.

How Do Black Girls Learn About Race and Ethnicity?

Racial socialization is defined as the developmental processes by which children both acquire the behaviors, perceptions, values, and attitudes of an ethnic group and come to see themselves and others as members of the group (Stevenson, 1994). For girls, racial socialization involves receiving messages that help prepare them to be women. The racial socialization process of Black girls is distinct due to the combination of racism and sexism experienced by this group. Black girls tend to be aware of their double minority status and to acknowledge the difficulties associated with being Black and female (Thomas & King, 2007; Thomas et al., 2011). Black parents face the challenge of encouraging their daughters to be proud of their gender, racial, and ethnic background while simultaneously recognizing their marginalized status in larger society. In a study about the gendered racial socialization of African American girls, Thomas and King (2007) found that daughters received messages from their mothers about self-pride, self-determination, assertiveness, spirituality, racial pride, and the value of education. Proactive racial socialization ensures that Black girls develop a healthy suspiciousness about racial encounters and bolsters their esteem by affirming ethnic standards of beauty (Adams-Bass et al., 2014).

Black girls reared to possess high levels of ethnic identity are better equipped to withstand those socioenvironmental contexts that breed both gendered and racial discrimination. Navigating a world that historically supported the oppression of those of African ancestry and the denigration of Black females can be mentally and physically trying. Yet, through familial teachings, guidance, and encouragement, Black girls learn how to harness the resiliency of their ancestors and develop an ethnic identity capable of buffering the impact of social restraints. And while these social restraints are largely driven by racist and sexist ideologies, they reflect cultural perceptions of the body as well. In addition to their racial and gender identities, Blacks girls are also defined by the shape and weight of their bodies.

Drive for Thinness or Chasing the Curves?

Body image is a major component of Black girls' self-concept. Body image is broadly defined as the perceptions, attitudes, evaluations, thoughts, and/or behaviors that girls hold regarding their body, which encompasses weight, shape, size, hair, skin color, and facial features (Bartlett & Harris, 2008; Cash & Szymanski, 1995; Gillen et al., 2006). Girls who exhibit a positive body image (i.e., body satisfaction) are more confident and realistic about their own bodies and more apt to challenge media messages emphasizing White cultural body ideals.

Overall, research findings indicate that Black girls are more confident about their appearance and exhibit higher levels of body satisfaction than girls of any other race or ethnicity (Milkie, 1999; Nishina et al., 2006; Roberts et al., 2006). Within the Black community, a "thicker," larger body size and curvier body shape are preferred over a thinner, straighter body shape or size. In fact, studies have found that both male and female adolescents tend to describe fuller-figured, more voluptuous females as healthier, more attractive, and more socially acceptable than those with a smaller, thinner frame (Parker et al., 1995).

Messages Black girls receive from their external environment (i.e., parents, media, peers, and partners) influence how they define physical attractiveness and contribute to their body image. Black girls are taught to be more accepting and flexible in terms of beauty ideals and to place more emphasis on "making what you've got work" (Parker et al., 1995, p. 110). Moreover, instead of adhering to the standards set by Western ideals, Black girls learn to focus on and evaluate their self-worth using factors that are not typically associated with physical beauty, such as personality, fashion/style, and character (Hesse-Biber et al., 2004; Parker et al., 1995; Rubin et al., 2003). For this reason, it is not surprising that Black girls report lower prevalence rates of body dissatisfaction, dieting, extreme exercising, and eating disorders than their peers (White et al., 2003).

Although Black girls may not desire the idealized body images portrayed in Western culture, they do report relying upon other Black females as frames of reference when evaluating their own physical appearance (Schooler et al., 2004). Many emulate the Black female images and characters depicted in the media (e.g., actors, musicians, and athletes). For example, Frisby (2004) found that Black females experienced more body dissatisfaction when viewing media images of other Black females than when viewing images of White females (Frisby, 2004). Therefore, girls who perceive themselves as possessing characteristics similar to those being portrayed may experience body image concerns.

Even though Black girls are less likely than their peers to experience poor body image, they are not immune to the adverse effects of messages promoting thin beauty ideals. In fact, several studies have revealed that differences among racial/ethnic groups are relatively small and/or diminishing, with African American girls becoming increasingly vulnerable to body image problems and eating disorders (e.g., bulimia) (Roberts et al., 2006; Shaw et al., 2004). In exploring the decline in body satisfaction among Black girls, researchers have begun to take a closer look at specific non-weight-related aspects of appearance, such as hair and skin color, and their influence on how Black adolescent girls perceive and evaluate their bodies.

Red Bones and Dark Girls

Skin color has been recognized as an important physical attribute for people of African ancestry. Skin color guides not only how individuals feel about themselves, but also how they evaluate other intragroup members (Wilder, 2010). Due to White supremacist ideologies, there is evidence that Black females with lighter skin—commonly labeled as "red bones" as a result of their red undertones—are considered to be more attractive and appealing than their darker contemporaries (Hall, 1995; Hill, 2002). This system of skin tone preferences is referred to as colorism and can significantly affect the perceptions and development of Black female adolescents (Herring, 2004; Hunter, 2005; Russell et al., 1992; Wilder, 2010).

Colorism is defined as an interracial and intraracial system of inequality based on skin color, hair texture, and facial features (Wilder, 2010). Moreover, within the Black community, colorism fosters an environment in which Eurocentric physical attributes (i.e., light skin, narrower nose, and straight hair) are preferred to more Afrocentric attributes (i.e., dark skin, wider nose, and kinky textured hair) (Maddox & Chase, 2004). When Black girls are subjected to Eurocentric standards of beauty, not possessing such attributes can lower their self-worth, and escaping such color-conscious messages can be difficult. Although at times inconspicuous, messages conveying a preference for light skin can be found embedded within families and the most popularized forms of media.

Where Do Black Girls Get Colorist Messages?

Recent examinations of color-conscious messages indicate that the media and family are largely responsible for socializing Black girls to perceive certain skin tones as preferable and others as undesirable. After conducting focus groups with African American women, Wilder and Cain's (2011) research revealed maternal figures, such as grandmothers, aunts, and mothers, as the primary disseminators of messages espousing skin-tone biases. From these individuals, participants learned as young girls to associate blackness with negativity and lightness with ideal beauty (Wilder & Cain, 2011). Such teachings of skin-tone biases are further reinforced in music. Stephens and Few (2007) found the sexualized scripts of women in rap culture to significantly influence how Black boys and girls viewed skin tone. After being exposed to visual representations of eight sexualized scripts, participants reported the Diva, characterized by her light skin, to be the preferred mate, while the Earth Mother, said to have dark skin, was perceived as unattractive (Stephens & Few, 2007).

Skin tone and its stereotypical portrayals in music and familial teachings can significantly inform how Black girls feel about themselves. And as they develop into women, such sentiments may continue. The manifestations of colorism, as seen through preferential treatment of light skin and/or disdain of dark skin, influence the social interactions and intragroup perceptions of Black girls and women. However, it is important to recognize that the discrimination of dark skin is but one of the ways in which African features are socially appraised as less appealing. Evaluations of hair texture are also subject to Eurocentric influences.

Am I Not My Hair?

Whether it's relaxed, straightened, locked, picked out, braided, twisted, sculpted, curled, dyed, sewn in, glued in, or weaved in, hair, like skin color, carries with it social, emotional, and cultural significance for Black girls and women. Research suggests that Black women with long straight hair are considered more desirable and attractive than those with kinky or tightly coiled hair (Russell et al., 1992). In the Black community, girls learn early on what it means to have "good hair" or "bad hair." Part of a lyric by singer-songwriter India.Arie explains that, "Good hair means perms and waves/ Bad hair means you look like a slave" (Simpson et al., 2001). Black women and girls are taught that naturally curly or kinky hair is not appealing, not beautiful, and certainly not manageable (Radtke, 2007). In American culture, physical attributes associated with being Black (e.g., darker skin tone, coiled hair texture, Afrikan facial features, voluptuous body shapes, etc.) have often functioned as the antithesis to feminine attractiveness, which is typically defined by Eurocentric features (Grayson, 1995). The desire to be beautiful and attractive often leads Black women to a hair crossroads for themselves and their daughters—to straighten or not to straighten.

The Natural Dilemma

Black girls are generally socialized by their parents and by mass media to achieve an American ideal standard of beauty, leading Black mothers to relax, straighten, and/or supplement their daughters' hair with extensions, to reinvent their hair texture to match idealized long, flowing, straight tresses (Grayson, 1995; Johnson, 2011; Radtke, 2007). The constant restructuring of Black hair has led to many Black adolescents having no remembrance of their natural hair texture, due to early and frequent applications of chemical relaxers and heat-straightening techniques. For example, a recent study of hair-care practices among African American girls ages 1 to 15 found that 46% of Black girls receive their first relaxer between the ages of 4 and 8, and 80% of girls have their hair straightened with heat, with nearly half starting as early as age 4 (Wright et al., 2011). Embracing Eurocentric ideals of beauty and shunning African features can have important implications for the psychological well-being of Black girls. For example, it is possible that girls who idealize Eurocentric features but do not possess such features may have lowered self-worth, a factor associated with risky and negative behaviors (Belgrave & Allison, 2010). On the other hand, girls who accept a Black standard of beauty (e.g., preferring natural hair over straight hair) report lower levels of risky behaviors such as substance abuse (Wallace et al., 2011).

As time has progressed, the import of skin color and hair to the lives of women and girls of African ancestry has become clearer. As seen in growing bodies of academic and popular literature, the extent to which African features such as dark skin and kinky hair are either degraded or praised has a significant effect on the ways in which Black women and girls evaluate themselves and other group members. This influence also extends into their development of self-worth and engagement in positive behavior. Acceptance and appreciation for one's ethnicity, and for those associated features, is a critical component to positive cognitive, behavioral, and social development. Moreover, it is important to note that such appreciation is largely achieved through the development of an African-centered identity.

Developing an African-Centered Identity

African-centered identities have been shown to protect against negative influences and promote well-being (Thomas et al., 2003). For a Black girl, the development of an African-centered identity is, in many ways, dependent on how she is socialized. Discussions of gendered and racial experiences will buffer her and prepare her for likely encounters, especially as she grows older. Since parental and media socialization contribute much to her sense of self and identity, we believe that defying the odds can be achieved in part through examining how and where to intervene in these socialization agents.

In the book African American Girls, Belgrave (2009) provides several suggestions and recommendations of ways in which parents can socialize their daughters to promote positive well-being and an African-centered identity. Because of space limitations, we can highlight only a few suggestions and refer the reader to Belgrave for more details.

One primary suggestion is that parents socialize their daughters about what it means to be Black and female in this country. These messages may convey the historical and contemporary challenges Black women have faced and also reveal how they have overcome these challenges. Providing concrete examples of these women can help strengthen this concept. In conjunction with Black girls' own relatives, such as grandparents, aunts, and cousins, parents should reference historical and contemporary figures as well.

Parents should also seek out products and services from businesses owned by Black females and introduce their daughters to Black women who exemplify quality womanhood. While it is important to expose a girl to women with high professional achievements (e.g., physicians, professors, lawyers, engineers), it is equally important to expose her to character role models who live in her community. These role models might in fact be more effective than those outside her community because they can show her possibilities. This might be the woman who runs the food bank, the woman who has a successful day care business in her home, or the woman with four children who have all attended college. It is also important to introduce her to, and to seek services and products from, Black-women-owned businesses because they show that Black women can create and sustain their livelihood and that of others.

Research indicates that Black girls are more likely to be androgynous than girls from other racial and ethnic groups and that androgynous gender-role beliefs should continue to be promoted since they are beneficial. Thus, parents may choose to teach their daughters how to change a car tire and cook a meal, how to mow the lawn and take care of a younger sibling, and how to speak assertively when in disagreement while considering the wishes and opinions of others.

Similarly, parents should promote racial and ethnic identity by exposing girls to African-centered activities, places, and people. Suggestions include celebration of Kwanzaa, visiting a historically Black college or university, and participating in a club or activity group with other Black girls. It is also important for parents to discuss historical and contemporary biases based on skin color and hair texture and to explore the girl's feelings about her own skin color and hair as well as her body type. Messages that girls receive from family members should never suggest the superiority of light skin and straight hair. Here it is important that parents monitor their own behavior and that of other family members and be aware of their own potential biases and how these messages might be subtly communicated (e.g., when dark-skinned Blacks are never seen as attractive and light-skinned girls are always seen as such).

It is also crucial to recognize that the media exerts a tremendous influence on the self-esteem and identity of Black girls. Therefore, parents should make it a priority to discuss these images with their daughters. In attending to her questions or comments, parents can help their daughter better understand the differences between reality and depictions and remind her that not every Black woman is reflected in the media. Parents can also clarify that she is, in no way, relegated to a certain identity. Like her ancestors and others before her, she is powerful enough to construct her own path in life and completely deviate from that which she sees. To impart this guidance, it is critical that parents familiarize themselves with the images their daughters may witness and potentially internalize.

For example, although it may be uncomfortable, parents may consider watching misogynistic videos and movies with their daughters—perhaps the controversial "Tip Drill" video, in which rapper Nelly slides a credit card down the buttocks of a Black female dancer. Having an open dialogue about how that woman is portrayed and how the video makes their daughter think and feel could allow parents the opportunity to counter these negative images and to reaffirm that she does not have to conduct herself in that manner. This could also be achieved by watching videos with positive messages, such as Common's "The Light," 2Pac's "Keep Ya Head Up," and India.Arie's "Video." Introducing young Black girls to videos in which Black women are portrayed as queens, ladies, and career women can elucidate what the media attempts to obscure: that Black women are varied and come in beautiful shapes and sizes. They are a myriad of identities and cannot, nor should they, be boxed into one.

Conclusion

Growing up Black and female carries significant implications for cognitive, behavioral, and social adolescent development. Due to racist and sexist ideologies, Black girls are required to navigate socioenvironmental contexts often characterized by negative and stereotypical portrayals in the media, disproportionate health disparities, harsh and punitive school policies and practices, and unequal socioeconomic mobility. Yet, in spite of these obstacles, many Blacks girls are able to excel. They perform well academically, establish strong bonds within their families and communities, and develop self-efficacious attitudes. Much of Black girls' resiliency and development can be attributed to the way in which family members/fictive kin and media outlets socialize them along various areas of importance. Through modeling and reinforcing societal norms and cultural beliefs, these influences guide and inform how Black girls define their racial and gender identities, construct perceptions of their skin color and hair, and evaluate the biological changes in their bodies. As we have reviewed, the developmental changes Black girls experience during adolescence have considerable bearing on their transitions into adulthood, for it is who they are and what they deem important that will serve as the basis for the growth of resilient and thriving Black women.

References

Adams-Bass, V., Stevenson, H., & Kotzin, D. (2014). Measuring the meaning of Black media stereotypes and their relationship to the racial identity, Black history knowledge, and racial socialization of African American youth. Journal of Black Studies, 45(5), 367–395.

Amaro, H., Raj, A., and Reed, E. (2001). Women's sexual health: The need for feminist analyses in public health in the decade of behavior. Psychology of Women Quarterly, 25(4), 324–334.

Aquilino, W. S., & Supple, A. J. (2001). Long-term effects of parenting practices during adolescence on well-being outcomes in young adulthood. Journal of Family Issues, 22, 289–308.

Arie, I. (2001). Acoustic soul [Album]. Motown Records.

Barlett, C., & Harris, R. (2008). The impact of body emphasizing video games on body image concerns in men and women. Sex Roles, 59, 7–8.

Beauboeuf-Lafontant, T. (2003). Strong and large Black women? Exploring relationships between deviant womanhood and weight. Gender and Society, 17(1), 111–121.

Beauboeuf-Lafontant, T. (2007). You have to show strength: An exploration of gender, race, and depression. Gender and Society, 21(1), 28–51.

Belgrave, F. Z. (2009). African American girls: *Reframing perceptions and changing experiences.* Springer Science + Business Media. https://doi.org/10.1007/978-1-4419-0090-6

Belgrave, F. Z., & Allison, K. W. (2006). African American psychology: From Africa to America. Sage.

Belgrave, F. Z., Van Oss Marin, B., & Chambers, D. B. (2000). Cultural, contextual, and intrapersonal predictors of risky sexual attitudes among urban African American girls in early adolescence. Cultural Diversity & Ethnic Minority Psychology, 6(3), 309–322.

Boyd, K., Ashcraft, A., & Belgrave, F. (2006). The impact of mother-daughter and father-daughter relationships on drug refusal self-efficacy among African American adolescent girls in urban communities. Journal of Black Psychology, 32(1), 29–42.

Broman, C. L. (1991). Gender, work-family roles, and psychological well-being of Blacks. Journal of Marriage and Family, 53(2), 509–520.

Brook, J. S., & Pahl, K. (2005, January 1). The protective role of ethnic and racial identity and aspects of an Africentric orientation against drug use among African American young adults. The Journal of Genetic Psychology, 166(3), 329–345.

Brown, J. D., & Bobkowski, P. S. (2011). Older and newer media: Patterns of use and effects on adolescents' health and well-being. Journal of Research on Adolescent Adolescence, 21(1), 95–113.

Brown v. Board of Education, 347 U.S. 483 (1954).

Buckley, T., & Carter, R. (2005). Black adolescent girls: Do gender role and racial identity impact their self-esteem? Sex Roles, 53, 9–10.

Burlew, K., Neely, D. K., Johnson, C., Hucks, T., Purnell, B., Butler, J., Lovett, M., & Burlew, R. (2000). Drug attitudes, racial identity, and alcohol use among African American adolescents. Journal of Black Psychology, 26(4), 402–420.

Caldwell, C. H., Kohn-Wood, L. P., Schmeelk-Cone, K. H., Chavous, T. M., & Zimmerman, M. A. (2004). Racial discrimination and racial identity as risk or protective factors for violent behaviors in African American young adults. American Journal of Community Psychology, 33, 1–2.

Carli, L. L. (2001). Gender and social influence. Journal of Social Issues, 57, 725–741.

Cash, T. F., & Szymanski, M. L. (1995). The development and validation of the body-image ideals questionnaire. Journal of Personality Assessment, 64, 466–477.

Clark, L., & Tiggemann, M. (2006). Appearance culture in nine- to 12-year-old girls: Media and peer influences on body dissatisfaction. Social Development, 15(4), 628–643.

Clark, T., Belgrave, F., & Nasim, A. (2008). Risk and protective factors for substance use among urban African American adolescents considered high-risk. Journal of Ethnicity in Substance Abuse, 7(3), 292–303.

Collins, P. H. (2004). Black sexual politics: African Americans, gender, and the new racism. Routledge.

Collins, R. L., Elliott, M. N., Berry, S. H., Kanouse, D. E., & Hunter, S. B. (2003). Entertainment television as a healthy sex educator: The impact of condom-efficacy information in an episode of *Friends*. Pediatrics, 112, 1115–1121.

Corneille, M. A., & Belgrave, F. Z. (2007). Ethnic identity, neighborhood risk, and adolescent drug and sex attitudes and refusal efficacy: The urban African American girls' experience. Journal of Drug Education, 37(2), 177–190.

Crenshaw, K., Ocen, P., & Nanda, J. (2015). *Black girls matter: Pushed out, overpoliced, and underprotected.* African American Policy Forum and Center for Intersectionality and Social Policy Studies. http://static1.squarespace.com/static/53f20d90e4b0b80451158d8c/t/54dcc1ece4b001c03e323448/1423753708557/AAPF_BlackGirlsMatterReport.pdf

Denzin, N. K. (1977). Childhood socialization. Jossey-Bass Publishers.

DiClemente, R. J., & Wingood, G. M. (2000). Expanding the scope of HIV prevention for adolescents: Beyond individual-level interventions. The Journal of Adolescent Health: Official Publication of the Society for Adolescent Medicine, 26(6), 377–378.

Donenberg, G. R., Emerson, E., & MacKesy-Amiti, M. E. (2011). Sexual risk among African American girls: Psychopathology and mother-daughter relationships. Journal of Consulting and Clinical Psychology, 79(2), 153–158.

Dotterer, A. M., McHale, S. M., & Crouter, A. C. (2009). Sociocultural factors and school engagement among African American youth: The roles of racial discrimination, racial socialization, and ethnic identity. Applied Developmental Science, 13(2,) 61–73.

Epstein, R., Blake, J. J., & Gonzalez, T. (n.d.). Girlhood interrupted: The erasure of Black girls' childhood. Georgetown Law Center on Poverty and Inequality.

Freeman, E., & Rickels, K. (1993). Early childbearing: Perspectives of Black adolescents on pregnancy, abortion and contraception. Sage.

Friedman, H. S., & Silver, R. C. (2007). Foundations of health psychology. Oxford Press.

Frisby, C. M. (2004). Does race matter? Effects of idealized images on African American women's perceptions of body esteem. Journal of Black Studies, 34, 323–347.

Frome, P. M., Alfeld, C. J., Eccles, J. S., & Barber, B. L. (2006). Why don't they want a male-dominated job? An investigation of young women who changed their occupational aspirations. Educational Research and Evaluation, 12(4), 359–372.

Gillen, M., Lefkowitz, E., & Shearer, C. (2006). Does body image play a role in risky sexual behavior and attitudes? Journal of Youth and Adolescence, 35(2), 230–242.

Golan, M., Fainaru, M., & Weizman, A. (1998). Role of behaviour modification in the treatment of childhood obesity with the parents as the exclusive agents of change. International Journal of Obesity and Related Metabolic Disorders: Journal of the International Association for the Study of Obesity, 22(12), 1217–1224.

Gordon, M. K. (2008). Media contributions to African American girls' focus on beauty and appearance: Exploring the consequences of sexual objectification. *Psychology of Women Quarterly, 32*(3), 245–256. https://doi.org/10.1111/j.1471-6402.2008.00433.x

Grabe, S., Ward, L. M., & Hyde, J. (2008). The role of the media in body image concerns among women: A meta-analysis of experimental and correlational studies. Psychological Bulletin, 134, 460–476.

Grayson, D. R. (1995). Black women, spectatorship and visual culture. Indiana University Press.

Hall, R. (1995). The bleaching syndrome: African Americans' response to cultural domination vis-à-vis skin color. Journal of Black Studies, 26(2), 172–184.

Harris, M., & Skyles, A. (2008, January 1). Kinship care for African American children. Journal of Family Issues, 29(8), 1013–1030.

Hellenga, K., Aber, M. S., & Rhodes, J. E. (2002). African American adolescent mothers' vocational aspiration-expectation gap: Individual, social and environmental influences. Psychology of Women Quarterly, 26(3), 200–212.

Herring, C. (2004). Skin deep: Race and complexion in the "color-blind" era. In C. Herring, V. Keith, & H. D. Horton (Eds.), Skin deep: How race and complexion matter in the "color-blind" era (pp. 1–22). University of Illinois Press.

Hesse-Biber, S. N., Howling, S. A., Leavy, P., & Lovejoy, M. (2004). Racial identity and the development of body image issues among African American adolescent girls. The Qualitative Report, 9, 49–79.

Hill, S. A. (1999). African American children: Socialization and development in families. Sage.

Hill, S. A. (2002). Teaching and doing gender in African American families. Sex Roles: A Journal of Research, *47*, 493–506.

Hirsch, B. J., Roffman, J. G., Deutsch, N. L., Flynn, C. A., Loder, T. L., & Pagano, M. E. (2000). Inner-city youth development organizations: Strengthening programs for adolescent girls. Journal of Early Adolescence, 20*(2)*, 210–230. https://doi.org/10.1177/0272431600020002005

Hunter, M. L. (2005). Race, gender, and the politics of skin tone. Routledge.

Impett, E. A., Sorsoli, L., Schooler, D., Henson, J. M., & Tolman, D. L. (2008). Girls' relationship authenticity and self-esteem across adolescence. Developmental Psychology, 44(3), 722–733.

Jackson, C. J.-M. (2020). Hashtags and hallelujahs: The roles of #BlackGirlMagic performance and social media in spiritual #Formation. Fire!!!, 6(1), 98–131. https://www.jstor.org/stable/10.5323/48581555

Jackson, C., Bee-Gates, D. J., & Henriksen, L. (1994). Authoritative parenting, child competencies and initiation of cigarette smoking. Health Education Quarterly, 21, 103–116.

Kerrigan, D., Andrinopoulos, K., Johnson, R., Parham, P., Thomas, T., & Ellen, J. M. (2007). Staying strong: Gender ideologies among African-American adolescents and the implications for HIV/STI prevention. Journal of Sex Research, 44(2), 172–180.

Linville, P. W. (1987). Self-complexity as a cognitive buffer against stress-related illness and depression. Journal of Personality and Social Psychology, 52(4), 663–676.

Maddox, K. B., & Chase, S. G. (2004). Manipulating subcategory salience: Exploring the link between skin tone and social perception of Blacks. European Journal of Social Psychology, 34(5), 533.

Mann, M. M., Hosman, C. M. H., Schaalma, H. P., & de Vries, N. K. (2004). Self-esteem in a broad-spectrum approach for mental health promotion. Health Education Research, 19(4), 357–372.

McBride, C. K., Paikoff, R. L., & Holmbeck, G. N. (2003). Individual and familial influences on the onset of sexual intercourse among urban African American adolescents. Journal of Consulting and Clinical Psychology, 71(1), 159–167.

Morris, M. W. (2016). Pushout: The criminalization of Black girls in schools. The New Press.

National Center for Health Statistics. (2011). Health, United States, 2011: With special feature on socioeconomic status and health. U.S. Department of Health and Human Services, Centers for Disease Control and Prevention. http://www.cdc.gov/nchs/data/hus/hus11.pdf

Nishina, A., Ammon, N. Y., Bellmore, A. D., & Graham, S. (2006). Body dissatisfaction and physical development among ethnic minority adolescents. Journal of Youth and Adolescence, 35, 189–201.

Noppe, I. C. (2009). *Gender-role development—The development of sex and gender*. http://social.jrank.org/pages/272/Gender-Role-Development.html

Parker, S., Nichter, M., Nichter, M., Vuckovik, N., Sims, C., & Ritenbaugh, C. (1995). Body image and weight concerns among African-American and White adolescent females: Differences that make a difference. Human Organization, 54, 103–114.

Perry, A. (2009). The influence of the extended family on the involvement of nonresident African American fathers. Journal of Family Social Work, 12(3), 211–226.

Peterson, S. H., Wingood, G. M., Diclemente, R. J., Harrington, K., & Davies, S. (2007). Images of sexual stereotypes in rap videos and the health of African American female adolescents. Journal of Women's Health, 16, 1157–1164.

Phinney, J. S., & Rotheram-Borus, M. J. (1987). Children's ethnic socialization: Pluralism and development. Sage.

Prevatt, F. (2003). The contribution of parenting practices in a risk and resiliency model of children's adjustment. British Journal of Developmental Psychology, 21(4), 469–480.

Radtke, S. (2007). African American hair and its role in advertising, Black women's careers, and consumption behavior. GRIN Verlag GmbH.

Reimer, K., Smith, C., Reicks, M., Henry, H., Thomas, R., and Atwell, J. (2004). Child-feeding strategies of African American women according to stage of change for fruit and vegetable consumption. Public Health Nutrition, 7(4), 505–512.

Rideout, V. J., Foehr, U. G., & Roberts, D. F. (2010, January). Generation M2: Media in the lives of 8- to 18-year-olds [Report]. Kaiser Family Foundation. https://www.kff.org/wp-content/uploads/2013/04/8010.pdf

Ritchie, L. D., Raman, A., Sharma, S., Fitch, M. D., & Fleming, S. E. (2011). Dietary intakes of urban, high Body Mass Index, African American children: Family and child dietary attributes predict child intakes. Journal of Nutrition Education and Behavior, 43(4), 236–243.

Roberts, A., Cash, T., Feingold, A., & Johnson, B. T. (2006). Are Black-White differences in females' body dissatisfaction decreasing? A meta-analytic review. Journal of Consulting and Clinical Psychology, 74, 1121–1131.

Rose, A. J., & Montemayor, R. (1994). The relationship between gender role orientation and perceived self-competency in male and female adolescents. Sex Roles, 31, 579.

Rosenberg, M., & Simmons, R. G. (1971). Black and White self-esteem: The urban school child. American Sociological Association.

Rubin, L. R., Fitts, M. L., & Becker, A. E. (2003). "Whatever feels good in my soul": Body ethics and aesthetics among African American and Latina women. Culture, Medicine and Psychiatry, 27(1), 49–75.

Russell, K., Wilson, M., & Hall, R. E. (1992). The color complex: The politics of skin color among African Americans. Harcourt Brace Jovanovich.

Schooler, D., Impett, E., Hirschman, C., & Bonem, L. (2008). A mixed-method exploration of body image and sexual health among adolescent boys. American Journal of Men's Health, 2(4), 322–339.

Sellers, R. M., Smith, M. A., Shelton, J. N., Rowley, S. A. J., & Chavous, T. M. (1998). Multidimensional model of racial identity: A reconceptualization of African American racial identity. Personality and Social Psychology Review, 2(1), 18–39.

Shaw, H., Ramirez, L., Trost, A., Randall, P., & Stice, E. (2004). Body image and eating disturbances across ethnic groups: More similarities than differences. Psychology of Addictive Behaviors, 18, 12–18.

Simpson, I. A., Sanders, S., Ramsey, D., & Thiam, A. (2006). I am not my hair. On India.Arie, Testimony: Vol. 1 [Album]. Motown Records.

Smith, C. O., Levine, D. W., Smith, E. P., Dumas, J., & Prinz, R. J. (2009). A developmental perspective of the relationship of racial–ethnic identity to self-construct, achievement, and behavior in African American children. Cultural Diversity and Ethnic Minority Psychology, 15(2), 145–157.

South, S. J., & Baumer, E. P. (2000). Deciphering community and race effects on adolescent premarital childbearing. Social Forces, 78(4), 1379–1407.

Stephens, D., & Few, A. (2007). The effects of images of African American women in hip hop on early adolescents' attitudes toward physical attractiveness and interpersonal relationships. Sex Roles, 56, 3–4.

Stevenson, H. C. J. (1994). Validation of the scale of racial socialization for African American adolescents: Steps toward multidimensionality. Journal of Black Psychology, 20(4), 445–468.

Stice, E. (2002). Risk and maintenance factors for eating pathology: A meta-analytic review. Psychological Bulletin, 128, 825–848.

Stice, E., & Bearman, S. K. (2001). Body image and eating disturbances prospectively predict growth in depressive symptoms in adolescent girls: A growth curve analysis. Developmental Psychology, 37, 597–607.

Strasburger, V. C. (2009). Why do adolescent health researchers ignore the impact of the media? Journal of Adolescent Health, 44(2009), 203–205.

Suellentrop, K., Brown, J., & Ortiz, R. (2010, October). Evaluating the impact of MTV's *16 and Pregnant* on teen viewers' attitudes about teen pregnancy. Science Says, 45, 1–5. *The National Campaign to Prevent Teen and Unplanned Pregnancy.* https://powertodecide.org/sites/default/files/resources/primary-download/science-says-45-evaluating-the-impact-of-mtvs-16-and-pregnant-on-teens-attitudes-about-teen-pregnancy.pdf

Thomas, A. J., Hoxha, D., & Hacker, J. (2011). Gendered racial identity development of African American girls. Sex Roles, 64, 530–542.

Thomas, A. J., & King, C. (2007). Gendered racial socialization of African American mothers and daughters. The Family Journal, 15(2), 137–142.

Thomas, D. E., Townsend, T. G., & Belgrave, F. Z. (2003). The influence of cultural and racial identification on the psychosocial adjustment of inner-city African American children in school. American Journal of Community Psychology, 32, 3–4.

Wallace, S. A., Townsend, T. G., Glasgow, Y. M., & Ojie, M. J. (2011). Gold diggers, video vixens, and Jezebels: Stereotype images and substance use among urban African American girls. Journal of Women's Health, 20(9), 1315–1324.

Ward, J. V. (1996). Raising resisters: The role of truth telling in the psychological development of African American girls. In B. J. R. Leadbeater and N. Way (Eds.), Urban girls: Resisting stereotypes, creating identities (pp. 86–116). New York University Press.

White, M. A., Kohlmaier, J. R., Varnado-Sullivan, P., & Williamson, D. A. (2003). Racial/ethnic differences in weight concerns: Protective and risk factors for the development of eating disorders and obesity among adolescent females. Eating and Weight Disorders, 8(1), 20–25.

Wilder, J. (2010). Revisiting "color names and color notions": A contemporary examination of the language and attitudes of skin color among young Black women. Journal of Black Studies, 41(1), 184–206.

Wilder, J., & Cain, C. (2011). Teaching and learning color consciousness in Black families: Exploring family processes and women's experiences with colorism. Journal of Family Issues, 32(5), 577–604.

Wood, D., Kaplan, R., & McLoyd, V. C. (2007). Gender differences in the educational expectations of urban, low-income African American youth: The role of parents and the school. Journal of Youth Adolescence, 36, 417–427.

Woods-Giscombe, C. L. (2010). Superwoman schema: African American women's views on stress, strength, and health. Qualitative Health Research, 20(5), 668–683.

Wright, D. R., Gathers, R., Kapke, A., Johnson, D., & Joseph, C. L. M. (2011). Hair care practices and their association with scalp and hair disorders in African American girls. Journal of the American Academy of Dermatology, 64(2), 253–262.

Reading 2.3. An Analysis of the Impact of Eurocentric Concepts of Beauty on the Lives of Afrikan American Women

Huberta Jackson-Lowman and Kristina Jean-Baptiste

> *... the capture of the mind and body both is a slavery far more lasting, far more severe than conquest of bodies alone ...*
>
> —Ayi Kwei Armah, *Two Thousand Seasons*

Introduction

Standards of beauty serve as the lens through which the attractiveness, desirability, and worth of women in American society are evaluated. Within the United States, this lens is shaped by the history of European racial domination and oppression of the Indigenous populations of America and formerly enslaved Afrikans. One of the most insidious effects of European racial domination, terrorism, and oppression (aka "White supremacy racism") has been its impact on the self-perceptions of people of color. Throughout the world, the globalization of Eurocentric standards of beauty, what Menakem (2017) refers to as "white body supremacy"' has resulted in the development of industries that support it, the marketing of images that reify it, the structuring of policies that reward it, and the enactment of interpersonal and personal behavioral routines that emulate it. Menakem (2017) defines "white-body supremacy" as "seeing white as the norm or standard for human, and people of color as a deviation from that norm" (p. xix). White-body supremacy is a characteristic of White supremacy, which is a "political-economic social system of domination" (Menakem, 2017, p. xviii). In this chapter we evaluate the influence of White body supremacy, expressed as colorism, on attitudes, values, and beliefs about beauty globally, and specifically with regard to Afrikan American women. The infusion of White body supremacy into the culture, systems, institutions, businesses, organizations, communities, and families of people throughout the world has created an environment in which the bodies of women of color, and particularly those of Black women, are devalued, inferiorized, and deformed. We examine the history of colorism in Afrikan American communities, its manifestations in our institutions, organizations, families, and relationships, and its psychosocial effects. Finally, we address the role of activism and policy initiatives in combating White body supremacy and strategies for expelling and eradicating the injurious presence of internalized racism.

Globalizing White Supremacy

Over the past five centuries, White supremacy racism has steadily eroded the cultures, values, and standards of people throughout the world, and created a color caste system that is cloaked by the emphasis on race (Wilkerson, 2020). Since the middle of the 15th century, when the Portuguese began abducting Afrikans, the notion of White supremacy has continually evolved (R. E. Hall, 2018). Before European intrusions into Afrika, race order did not exist, nor did the idea of racial inferiority. The idea of a racial hierarchy based on phenotypic characteristics was conceived to consolidate European power. It has been forced upon individuals, embodied in systematic practices, and upheld through social structures. The imposition of a racial hierarchy based on skin color facilitated the hegemonic enterprise of colonialism and the enslavement of Afrikan people, and has resulted in the globalization and normalization of White body supremacy. This process has been slow and gradual, sometimes intentional and sometimes unintentional, and more recently, as the result of technology, rapidly expedited. The effects of this globalization are most notable throughout the continent of Afrika, where European invasions beginning in the 1400s brought turmoil, chaos, and destruction, which persists today in the 21st century in many Afrikan nations. Although not the focus of this chapter, the effects of Arab intrusions on Afrika must be acknowledged as well and perhaps can be seen as setting the stage for the later European conquests. The complexity of the interaction of these external forces, plus the internal dynamics of Afrika, often epitomized by ethnic warfare, have been discussed in depth by scholars such as Chancellor Williams, Ben Jochannan, John Jackson, and John Henrik Clarke (Kambon, 2012) and must be understood as critical features that have facilitated White supremacy racism's intrepid domination in Afrika and throughout the world.

The globalization of Eurocentric standards of beauty assumes many forms. The manufacture and distribution of products designed to lighten the skin is one of many glaring examples of White body supremacy. The release of an expensive skin lightening cream in the Nigerian market known as "Diamond Illuminating & Brightening Cream" is one of the latest examples of the impact of White body supremacy. Created and popularized by American model and influencer Blac Chyna, it was advertised as an illumination cream that brightened and lightened skin and was marketed as a luxury item (Muzenda, 2018). Similarly, in India, a product called "Clean and Dry" was purported to lighten dark vaginas and increase the sexual appeal of Indian women (Pal, 2012). These products continue to be sought after by women in the Caribbean, Africa, and the United States in spite of the devastating effects that skin bleaching has on the skin. The harmful consequences of skin bleaching can be seen in the faces of women whose skin, though lighter, exhibits thinning, and who are requiring dermatological treatment to deal with the destructive health effects of skin bleaching (Saint Louis, 2010.).

In the United States, internalized European standards of beauty are most evident in the Black community and have their greatest impact on the outcomes of Afrikan American women in every realm of our lives: education, occupation, income, family relationships, male-female relationships, female-female relationships, mate selection processes, mental health, physical health, and self-esteem. One of the most debilitating aspects of the globalization of White supremacy has been the resulting conflation of power with what is defined as beautiful. Those who are deemed most powerful are often emulated in terms of their physical appearance, their behavior, their standards, and their values. Furthermore, those in power project themselves as the ideal physically, mentally, and spiritually and construct reality to support their beliefs. Thus, policies that reward those who look like them and punish those who least resemble them are put in place, from the type of clothing that one must wear to the language that one must speak. The least powerful, in their attempts to survive their oppression, often reorganize themselves and reconfigure their lives and bodies in order to benefit from the reward structure created by their oppressors. White supremacy suggests that to be human, one needs to be White, or to adopt Nordic standards of beauty; this creates dissonance in the least powerful and forces them to adopt harmful practices to assimilate (Nogueira, 2013). Dehumanizing practices (e.g., cosmetic surgery, skin bleaching, etc.) are a form of social control which maintains White supremacy racism. This process does not occur without resistance, both formally and informally organized; however, through tactics such as "divide and conquer," oppressive forces have often been able to marginalize their resisters within their own communities. Numerous authors have discussed these dynamics in detail and should be consulted for more elaboration of the history of this globalization process and its effects (Ani, 1994; Rodney, 1982). For the purposes of this discussion, it is important to understand the scope of White supremacy and to recognize that the negative effects that result from it in the Afrikan American community have not solely affected Afrikan Americans but have been reinforced by worldwide imposition. Again, this has not occurred without resistance, but it has nevertheless been sustained through the use of industries, technology, and the media. Thus, skin color discrimination, obsession with Nordic facial features, preoccupation with body image and youthfulness, and the desire for straight blonde hair have affected conceptions of beauty more or less globally. Most decidedly, they have impacted the self-perceptions of Afrikan women, whose physical appearance is most distant from that of Europeans.

Measuring Colorism Globally

The pervasiveness of a pro-light-skin mentality is apparent across multiple countries and races. The Implicit Association Test (IAT), developed by a Harvard research team, has been utilized to assess the presence of colorism globally. Specifically, the Race IAT examines racial biases by comparing response times to positive and negative concepts and images associated with photos of Black and White individuals. For example, "bad" words include "annoy, evil, abuse," and "good" words include "lovely, friend, glorious." To test the presence of implicit biases, researchers measured how fast individuals pressed the key associated with the "good" valence when presented with a White image vs. how fast they pressed the "good" valence when presented with a Black image. Additionally, they assessed how often individuals associated "bad" with Black and "bad" with White. Based on these reaction times, the researchers were able to calculate pro-White or pro-Black biases within the participants. The results of the IAT across multiple races, ethnicities, and nationalities supported the presence of a favorable stance towards Whites or a pro-White mentality. While 88% of the IAT test-takers came from the United States, the other 22% came from 146 different countries. The results revealed a pro-White mentality ranging from a low of 6% in Ghana to 69% in Singapore (Coutts, 2020). In the United States these statistics were much higher, with a little over 70% portraying a pro-White mentality and less than 20% portraying a pro-Black mentality. The IAT results provide evidence of the prevalence of colorism throughout the world. Understanding why these results have occurred requires recognition of the Eurocentric worldview as the fundamental cosmology undergirding White supremacy racism.

Eurocentric Worldview

Colorism is an integral component of the Eurocentric worldview. Worldview refers to the lens through which we engage the world. Typically, this lens is invisible, is applied unconsciously, and goes unrecognized by its users, yet it influences everything that we observe and interact with. It carries with it certain assumptions and values that shape how we view reality. In the case of the Eurocentric worldview, these assumptions include: emphasis on control and mastery over nature, survival of the fittest, either/or thinking, competition, and aggression; focus on individual rights and on the material/physical aspects of life in contrast to the spiritual; and belief in the supremacy of Europeans over other groups of people, including the patriarchal domination of men over women (Kambon, 2012). These beliefs manifest themselves in every area of human functioning including economics, politics, the military, religion, education, science, technology, sex, family, and the media.

Eurocentric assumptions and beliefs permeate conceptions of what is beautiful. The operation of a single standard of beauty, which ascribes physical beauty to certain European characteristics—e.g., very fair skin, straight blonde hair, blue eyes, Nordic facial features, and thin bodies—and ranks the beauty of other racial/ethnic groups against this standard, reflects the belief in the superiority of Europeans. The belief that "white" represents purity, goodness, cleanliness, beauty, and power, while "black" represents that which is evil, dirty, ugly, and inferior, is a reflection of either/or thinking. The possibility that both whiteness and blackness can exhibit any of these characteristics is not acknowledged within this context.

Eurocentric standards of beauty also reflect the operation of patriarchal domination over women. Men determine what is "beautiful" and reward and punish women based upon these standards. The emphasis on the physical aspects of one's appearance leads to the objectification of women. As objectified bodies whose main purpose is the satisfaction of the sexual appetites of men, women of all races and ethnicities are subjected to this single standard of beauty, which is utilized to assess their worth and value. Once Afrikan Americans adopt the Eurocentric worldview, they are set up to denigrate all things Afrikan in themselves and in other people of Afrikan ancestry. Thereby, we become the arbiters of our own oppression.

The Male Gaze

The male gaze is an example of patriarchal privilege and an influencer of women's perceptions of their beauty and desirability. It is a further extension of the impact of the Eurocentric worldview on standards of beauty. The pervasiveness of Eurocentric ideals of beauty has negatively affected Black men's perceptions of Black women, as well as their treatment of them. Often, Afrikan women experience the harshness of the Black male gaze, which has been modified by the internalization of European standards of beauty. A further complication thrust on Black women who are desirous of affirmation from Black men involves the perpetuation of the myth of Black female sexual promiscuity (Roberts, 2017). Black men's emphasis on certain body characteristics (e.g., large hips and breasts), juxtaposed against the oversexualization of Black women's bodies and prevailing Eurocentric beauty standards, creates a confusing and dangerous environment for Black women who are desirous of Black male attention. In such an environment, Black women may internalize pejorative stereotypes about themselves (cultural misorientation) (Kambon, 2012), leading to the belief that their worth and desirability are reflected in their bodies. Thus, their efforts to attract Black men may lead to an exaggerated emphasis on their physical bodies as a measure of their beauty and worth. Consistent with the norm of White-body supremacy, people in the music industry, particularly Black male rap artists, are incentivized to exploit and objectify the Black female body, with an emphasis on lighter-complexioned Black women (Reid-Brinkley, 2007).

The Roots of Colorism

Colorism involves the preference for and privileging of lighter-complexioned persons in contrast to darker-complexioned persons amongst groups of people. It manifests as "interracial and intra-racial mistreatment of people based on skin color pigmentation" (Mbilishaka, 2020, p. 63). For Afrikan people, it is a manifestation of cultural misorientation—or the internalization of the European worldview (Kambon, 2003)—and a byproduct of oppression. The tentacles of oppression take root in the consciousness of the oppressed as well as the oppressor. It is an unfortunate reality that the victims of oppression often reenact their oppressive experiences. Sadly, the emancipation of enslaved Afrikans did not eradicate the system that had been created by White enslavers to ensure their power and control over their victims. A system of privilege and division, based on a color caste system and supported by a host of laws, had been instituted; with little or no support and no intervention to rectify the wrongs that enslaved Afrikans had endured, the same system was recreated in the communities of freed Afrikan Americans. A complex and often contradictory history ensured the color caste system's persistence in the Afrikan American community.

Miscegenation Laws

To enforce the color caste system, as early as 1622, the first miscegenation law sprung up in Virginia (Russell et al., 1992). This law was created because of the race-mixing that had begun between Afrikans and Europeans. Race mixing threatened the developing institution of slavery and was troubling to European men, in part because of the scarcity of European women. Efforts by White men to exert control over relationships between enslaved Afrikans and Europeans took many forms. In Maryland, sex between enslaved Afrikan men and White female servants could result in a life sentence for the woman; however, as a means of increasing their enslaved population, some White enslavers encouraged the rape of these women by enslaved Afrikan men (Russell et al., 1992).

Another law passed in 1662 in Virginia declared that mixed children born to enslaved Afrikan women would share their mother's legal status. This law stood in stark contrast to traditional English law, which mandated that children take their fathers' status. White enslavers were able to benefit from these laws and increase their enslaved populations. In essence, the miscegenation laws contributed to complicated, sexually exploitative relationships between Whites and Blacks and between men and women. The development of miscegenation laws occurred in parallel with the presence of free mulattoes who were not enslaved. Other laws were instituted to ensure the marginalization of communities of free mulattoes. Laws were passed forbidding property ownership, voting rights, and the seeking of political office, to ensure the separation of these mixed-blood Afrikans. Later, the "one drop rule" would be instituted in the upper South, including Virginia and Maryland, proclaiming that any amount of Afrikan blood resulted in one being labeled "Black." Simultaneously, another reality was also taking shape that further complicated racial relationships.

Because of the scarcity of European American women, many European American men had sexual and emotional relationships with enslaved Afrikan women. The mulatto children they produced were freed in some instances; sometimes, these mulatto children were granted the same privileges as their White peers or siblings—they were given other enslaved Afrikans as property and were assisted with launching businesses or farming. Thus, a new class of "Coloreds" was created. In colonies such as South Carolina, mulattoes were able to apply for status as "Whites," and in other cases, they simply passed. These developments and events led to the formation of a three-tiered color caste system composed of Whites, Coloreds, and pure Afrikans. The Coloreds served as a buffer class between Europeans and Afrikans. Whites conducted business with the Coloreds, and the Coloreds were used to minimize tensions between the groups (Russell et al., 1992).

The Formation of Mulatto Communities

The Revolutionary War led to the darkening of mulatto communities. Enslaved Afrikans who joined the British army were granted their freedom after the war (Russell et al., 1992). Additionally, enslaved Afrikans, who sometimes substituted for their enslavers in the Colonial Army, frequently took advantage of the opportunity to escape to freedom. Further, in the spirit of celebration, a few enslavers liberated their enslaved populations when the colonies declared their independence from England (Russell et al., 1992). As these newly freed Afrikans entered mulatto communities, concerns emerged amongst mulattoes about losing their privileged status as buffers. In an effort to protect their status, mulatto communities sought to distinguish themselves from their pure Afrikan counterparts. They established color-based distinctions and discouraged intermarrying and interacting across color lines.

The arrival of Creoles from the West Indies in the late 17th and early 18th centuries added another troublesome dimension to the already challenging intra-group rivalries developing within the Afrikan American community (Russell et al., 1992). Settling in the Charleston and New Orleans areas, the Creoles brought deeply embedded attitudes about skin color from their relationships with the French. Once in the United States, they separated themselves from other Afrikans and only married within their group. Prior to the Civil War, the majority of free Afrikans were mulattoes (Hughes & Hertel, 1990); however, most mulattoes were enslaved. Their experiences of privilege in slavery contributed to the ever-widening wedge between darker- and lighter-skinned Afrikans. In reality, their privileges did not come without substantial physical and emotional costs. They were often granted preferred positions as artisans, craftsmen, valets, housekeepers, and cooks. At the same time, their darker-skinned peers were consigned to toiling in the fields. The proximity of many lighter-complexioned but enslaved Afrikans to their enslavers led to abuse, including rape, physical attacks, and beatings on many occasions. Mulatto children and their enslaved Afrikan mothers often evoked the jealousy of their White mistresses, who could see the resemblance between these children and their husbands but blamed Afrikan women for these transgressions, frequently attacking them and their children in extremely sadistic ways.

On the other hand, sexual relationships did also occur between White mistresses, as well as their daughters, and enslaved Afrikan men. Sometimes these relationships resulted in pregnancies with highly disruptive consequences, such as divorce and evacuation of the pregnant girls, many of whom took refuge in the Black community. Afrikan men caught up in these relationships risked castration, severe beatings, and death.

Another macabre feature of the color caste system was the commodification of mulatto women. The commodification of Afrikans was an integral component of slavery; however, because mulatto women were viewed as "more attractive and desirable," they experienced some unique consequences. At auctions of enslaved Afrikans, they brought higher prices than their darker-skinned sisters and were often purchased specifically for the purposes of sexual exploitation and increased economic benefit. Of course, all Afrikan women were potential victims of sexual molestation, and it was rare for any to reach the age of 16 without having been molested by their White enslavers or their sons. However, there were formalized processes of sexual exploitation that emerged regarding mulatto women. In New Orleans and Charleston, Quadroon balls served as sites for which mulatto women were specifically bred, creating Quadroons (one fourth Black) and Octoroons (one eighth Black) for purchase by White men (Russell et al., 1992). These women were auctioned off to the highest bidder at these balls, becoming mistresses to White men, who would simply cast them off and purchase another if they lost interest in them. For some, though, these were lifelong relationships that offered them certain privileges not granted to other women of Afrikan ancestry.

Institutionalization of Color Divisions in the Black Community

After the Civil War, mulattoes created institutions and organizations designed to maintain the color divisions within the Afrikan American community. The Bon Ton Society of Washington, DC and the Blue Veins of Nashville were social clubs that applied strict color standards for admission (Russell et al., 1992). Though less characteristic today, Jack and Jill and the Links also maintained color barriers in their clubs. Neighborhoods composed primarily of lighter-skinned Afrikan Americans arose in many large cities, e.g., Chicago, Philadelphia, and New York. Even churches designated specifically for lighter-skinned Afrikan Americans sprung up. The splitting off of the Colored Methodist Episcopal Church (C. M. E.) in 1870 from the African Methodist Episcopal Church (A. M. E.) was based on skin color issues. The 20th century saw the emergence of the "paper bag test" and the "comb test," used by color-conscious churches and some social organizations to maintain their lighter-skinned membership. The paper bag test required potential members to place their arm in a paper bag. Those who were lighter than the paper bag could gain admission, while being darker than the paper bag resulted in rejection. Some churches painted their doors light brown, communicating to those who were darker than the door that they were not welcome. Still other churches hung a comb at their doors, signaling that only those with hair textures more like Whites should enter. Black preparatory schools and historically Black colleges and universities such as Wilberforce, Howard, Fisk, Atlanta University, Morgan, Hampton, and Spelman were known to discriminate against darker-skinned Afrikan Americans (Russell et al., 1992). The use of color tests occurred at some schools. Selection of homecoming queens on Black campuses was typically limited to the very light-complexioned coeds, even when darker-skinned students were present. In 1964 Howard University selected its first brown-skinned homecoming queen. This history of privilege based upon skin color has led to the solidification of an elite group of mulattoes and lighter-skinned Afrikan Americans who have served as the intellectual and political leaders of the Afrikan American community (Hughes & Hertel, 1990). Certainly, darker-skinned Afrikan Americans have risen to positions of leadership, but the preponderance of the leadership in the Black community has reflected the favoritism based upon color that has existed since slavery. The 1960s, with the emergence of the Black Consciousness "Black is Beautiful" Movement, represented a temporary reprieve from these dynamics; however, by the 1980s the benefits of this movement had significantly waned. The effects of this long, complicated history of privilege and discrimination based upon skin color persist and may be observed in Black women's self-perceptions, relationships with other Black women and Black men, mate selection, family dynamics, educational and occupational outcomes, income levels, and mental and physical health.

Discussion and Dialogue Activity

1. As women, what messages have you received about your skin color, hair, features, body, and its attractiveness and desirability?

2. As men, what messages have you given women (e.g., sisters, girlfriends, etc.) about their physical appearance and beauty?

Black Women and Concepts of Beauty

Because it is with our bodies that we meet the world, the issue of physical appearance has been and continues to be a source of great ambivalence, despair, and sometimes shame and pain for many women of Afrikan ancestry. Beliefs about the desirability of our skin color, hair texture, and facial features are imposed on us from birth and used to evaluate our worth and value. Whether subtly or directly communicated, these messages begin to shape our self-perceptions. The messages come to us through all forms of the media— both print and electronic—and through our interactions with family and friends, at school, and in employment settings; they consistently inform us that the more closely our physical appearance resembles that of Caucasian women, the more attractive, desirable, and acceptable we are. In the Black community, certain sayings and proverbs have been passed down that reflect our experiences around skin color discrimination and our attitudes about beauty (see Figure X). Yet, even when we grow up in families that exude Afrikan consciousness and appreciation of beauty from an Afrikan-centered perspective, it is extremely difficult to escape the critical gaze of a society that depreciates those whose appearance differs from the projected standards of beauty.

Afrikan Americans' torrential historical experiences have contributed to a diverse range of complexions within the Black community. The greatest amount of hostility, jealousy, resentment, rejection, disdain, and malfeasance is directed at the extremes of this continuum—the very light and the very dark. For Afrikan American women, the intensity of the critical gaze on our physical appearance is magnified by the prevailing presence of controlling images of Black womanhood. Images of Black women as mammies, Jezebels, Sapphires, matriarchs, and welfare mothers interact with Eurocentric beauty standards, pressing us into two-dimensional figures, distorting our relationships, often severely limiting our choices, and constricting opportunities (Collins, 2000; Hunter, 2005). Very light-skinned Afrikan American women are both privileged and cursed as a result of their skin color. Viewed as more attractive, these women are sought after by Black men, often envied and taunted by their darker skinned sisters, and challenged to prove their blackness, while also receiving preferential treatment in the education, business, and employment sectors, and in the print, TV, and film industries (Hunter, 2005).

On the other hand, the image of the Jezebel, with its oversexualized depiction of Afrikan women, has had detrimental effects on their very dark-skinned sisters, who are frequently the victims of even more hostile rejection, vicious teasing, and taunting—often within their families (Boyd-Franklin, 1989), from the Afrikan American community, and from institutions in the larger society (Hunter, 2005). For them there is no salve of privilege to help them tolerate the pain and suffering they regularly experience at the hands of their families and communities as well as the larger society. Black women fiction writers such as Toni Morrison (*The Bluest Eye*), Zora Neale Hurston (*Their Eyes Were Watching God*), Mary Helen Washington (*Maud Martha*), April Sinclair (*Coffee Will Make You Black*), and countless others have poignantly depicted the brutally destructive and psychologically undermining consequences of this internalized racism on the lives of Black girls and women.

Afrikan American Proverbs and Aphorisms on Beauty

What do these proverbs and aphorisms mean? What values do they reflect?

- The Blacker the berry, the sweeter the juice.
- Beauty's only skin deep, but love/ugly is to the bone.
- Beauty is as beauty does.
- If you're white, you're all right; if you're yellow, you're mellow; if you're brown, stick around; but if you're black, oh brother, get back, get back, get back!

Doll Studies

The deleterious effects of living in a society with deeply rooted color biases manifest early in its citizens' lives. The ground-breaking doll studies implemented by Kenneth Clark and Mamie Clark in the 1930s and 1940s revealed that Afrikan American children, when given a choice of a Black or a White doll, exhibited preferences for the White doll, who they identified as "nicer" and "prettier." Replications of the Clark doll study (Michael Barnes in the 1980s; Darlene Powell-Hopson & Derek Hopson in the 1980s, as cited in Russell et al., 1992) have yielded similar findings. To gain a better understanding of the dynamics that influenced Black children's preferences for the White doll, Powell-Hopson and Hopson (1988) carried out an intervention with Black and White preschoolers. Following the dolls' initial presentation to the children, praise was offered to those who selected the Black doll, and they were allowed to sit in the front with the researchers, while those who had selected the White doll were sent to the back of the room. Retesting, 15 minutes later, demonstrated that the intervention significantly affected the children's subsequent choices of the dolls. A shift from 35% to 71% preference for the Black doll by Black children occurred post-intervention (Powell-Hopson & Hopson, 1988).

Furthermore, the responses of the White children also showed significant increases in preference for the Black doll, though not as great as those of the Black children. Powell-Hopson and Hopson's (1988) research illustrated the importance of social learning in shaping the children's responses and indicated that these responses were malleable, at least temporarily. Unfortunately, more recent studies using convenience samples continue to reveal preferences for White images by children, both Black and White (birgitvanhout, 2007; CNN, 2010). All of these studies suggest that awareness of the color hierarchy within the United States occurs very early in life and that Afrikan American and Caucasian children recognize that on this hierarchy, darker skin occupies the lowest rung. This message continues to be reinforced in every arena of American society. As Powell-Hopson and Hopson's (1988) research indicated, only when there is systematic enculturation that acknowledges the beauty of blackness are Black children able to overcome this conditioning.

Use of Color Names

JeffriAnne Wilder's (2010) qualitative research study of 40 Afrikan American women with varying skin tones revealed that the color names of the 19th century still persist. In her research a three-tiered color hierarchy was identified, ranging from light to medium brown to dark. While color names were associated with the extremes of the continuum, very few names were attributed to those in the middle. The women in her sample described internalized scripts that they attributed to Afrikan American women with lighter versus darker skin tones. More positive qualities were used to describe women with lighter complexions— "trustworthy, amiable, nonthreatening, beautiful, pretty," while darker-complexioned women were stereotypically labeled as "ghetto, loud, unattractive, nonintelligent, intimidating, suspicious, and violent." Having skin tones in the medium range was somewhat protective for Afrikan American women. These women escaped much of the hostility, jealousy, and rejection often experienced by their lighter and darker sisters. Focus group members affirmed the felt privilege of lighter-skinned Afrikan American women in the areas of employment, interracial friendships, and relationships. While dark-skinned women vigorously defended themselves against the onslaught of engendered racial myths and stereotypes, light-complexioned women indicated that they had to defend their Blackness regularly. The presence of a three-tiered color hierarchy was further confirmed by the responses of those women classified as "medium brown." Some of these women distanced themselves from being identified as "dark" and acknowledged the feeling that they had a competitive edge over their darker-skinned sisters. Wilder's (2010) study provides further evidence of colorism's continued presence in contemporary Afrikan American communities, albeit expressed more subtly than in the past.

Body Image and Beauty

Public attacks on the physical appearance of Afrikan American women continue to occur. In 2011, accusations of "peddling racist psuedo-science" were lodged against *Psychology Today* by the Association of Black Psychologists and other individuals across the United States after it published derogatory claims about the physical appearance of Black women in a blog by controversial evolutionary psychologist Satoshi Kanazawa (May 15, 2011). Kanazawa stated that "BLACK women are less attractive than white, Asian and Native American Women. And there's scientific proof." The blog post, "Why are Black women rated less physically attractive than other women, but Black men are rated better looking than other men?" (Kanazawa, 2011) created a nationwide stir in the Black community and among some feminists. Yet this attack on the physical appearance of Black women is only the most recent of many. One of the earliest attacks on the image of Afrikan women is recounted in the tragic story of Sara Baartman, also pejoratively known as the "Hottentot Venus" (Baker, 1981). Baartman's misadventure begins in 1814 when she is persuaded by an Englishman to travel to Europe where, he promises, she will be able to earn money exhibiting herself. Instead, when she reaches Paris, she is abandoned to an animal exhibitor and exhibited under the name of "La Venus hottentote." On exhibit throughout England, she is persuaded to remove her clothing, and paintings of her naked image are thereby obtained. Her near-nude body was exposed to the gawking gazes of European men, women, and children who threw money at her, and who were both fascinated and titillated by the size of her buttocks, which they likened to animalistic qualities. By the end of the year she died, supposedly succumbing to an undescribed inflammatory disease; however, her early demise, estimated to be around 26 years of age, was likely precipitated by the inhumane treatment she received. Her abuse continued after her death, at which point she was dissected and her genitalia were placed on display in France. In 1817, Cuvier made a presentation focusing on her anatomy, displaying her genitalia to the audience and exposing her enlarged labia minora. Her genitalia remained a part of an exhibit in France until 1985 (Maseko, n.d.). Baartman has been cast as a symbol of the savage sexuality and racial inferiority of women of Afrikan heritage. Rap videos are saturated with images that associate Black women with savage sexuality, which is a continuation of the objectification of Black women noted in Sarah Baartman's tragic story.

SAARTJEE, THE HOTTENTOT VENUS.
Now Exhibiting in London.
Drawn from Life

Figure 2.1.1. Sarah "Saartjie" Baartman (also *spelled Bartman, Bartmann, Baartmen*) was born before 1790 and died 29 December 1815. She was the most famous of at least two Khoikhoi women who were exhibited as freak show attractions in 19th-century Europe under the name *Hottentot Venus*—"Hottentot" as the then-current name for the Khoi people, now considered an offensive term, and "Venus" in reference to the Roman goddess of love.

In spite of the saturation of negative images of Afrikan American women as "mammies, Jezebels, and Sapphires" in the media, for the most part Black women have been able to maintain relatively positive views of our bodies. Our ability to resist the dominant emphasis on thinness may be attributed to the fact that Afrikan American men are attracted to the "thick" bodies of Afrikan American women. Full hips and curved bodies have evoked the praise and admiration of Black men. "Big is beautiful" is a resounding echo heard in the Black community, accentuated through such references as "phat, big boned, healthy, thick, and brick house," which idealize the body types of large Afrikan American women (Alleyne, 2004, p.348). Black female comedians, like MoNique, have normalized "big-is-beautiful" in the attempt to empower overweight and obese women; however, simultaneously, this cultural preference minimizes the health risks associated with obesity, which is a significant problem for Afrikan American women. Alleyne (2004) suggests that the social tolerance of obesity in the Afrikan American community may be an influential factor in its acceptance by Afrikan American adolescent girls. National Health and Nutrition Examination Surveys conducted in 1976–1980, 1988–1994, and 1999–2000 revealed obesity prevalence rates of 31.0%, 39.1%, and 50.8% respectively, for adult Black females over the age of 20 (Alleyne, 2004).

For complex reasons, many of them related to ecological factors such as living in food deserts, Afrikan American women wrestle with issues of being overweight and obese. Our relationship with food and the environment has made Afrikan women more susceptible to body-image-related disorders, such as Binge Eating Disorder or bulimia. These larger implications of our diet affect our self-perception, as well as the treatment of our bodies. Our body image has consistently been a double-edged sword. On the one hand, Afrikan American men praise us for it, but they also collude with White men in our objectification, dissecting us into parts much like Sarah Baartman. On the other hand, though the majority of Afrikan American women reject the thinness ideal presented by larger society, being overweight or obese frequently leads to chronic physical health conditions and sometimes reflects unresolved psychological issues that need our urgent attention. Beyond our physical health, the salience of Eurocentric standards of beauty also has other implications for the lives of Afrikan American women.

Effects of Colorism on Afrikan American Women's Outcomes

Research examining relationships between skin color and educational attainment, employment, income, and dating and marriage consistently demonstrates the built-in advantage accorded to Afrikan American women of lighter complexions (C. C. I. Hall, 1995; Hunter, 2005). These findings emerge from Hunter's analysis of a data set of 1,310 Afrikan American women taken from the National Survey of Black Americans:

- Skin color is a statistically significant predictor of education for Afrikan American women. A one-year difference in educational levels of lighter- vs. darker-skinned Afrikan American women who shared similar characteristics was found, with lighter-complexioned women advantaged.

- There were significant differences in income for very light vs. very dark Afrikan American women. A difference of $2,600 in the annual income of light brown vs. dark brown Afrikan American women with similar credentials was obtained, with lighter-complexioned women favored.

- There were no differences in marriage rates across skin color; however, significant differences in the spousal education of light- vs. dark-complexioned Afrikan American women were observed. On average, Afrikan American women selected husbands who had .58 years less education than they had; however, with each gradation in skin color from dark to light, there was a .28 increase in the years of schooling completed by the spouse. Thus, having a lighter complexion enabled Afrikan American women to secure husbands with more education.

The above findings provide compelling support of the operation of White-body supremacy within larger American society and of its endorsement within the Afrikan American community. Further, this data offers evidence of the effects of living in a dissonant environmental context, defined by Rosenberg (1975, as cited in Keith & Thompson, 2003) as one in which the individual's salient characteristics differ from the majority of those in the setting: "… for darker-skinned African Americans a dissonant social context might be one in which both the culture and the majority of people support the belief that lighter skin tone is preferred and held in high social esteem whereas darker skin tones carry low social esteem" (Keith & Thompson, 2003, p. 119). In a patriarchal and capitalistic society dominated by the Eurocentric worldview, which elevates the physical over the spiritual and objectifies women, beauty becomes the most important form of social capital that women possess (Hunter, 2005). Within this environmental context, the narrative of whiteness, which ascribes qualities of cleanliness, purity, beauty, intelligence, and desirability to "white" skin tones, while defining blackness as its polar opposite—dirty, evil, ugly, unintelligent, and wholly undesirable—is dominant. Thus, in the beauty queue, White women are privileged because of skin color, and lighter-skinned Afrikan American women are privileged over their darker-skinned sisters in both White and Black communities. These patterns are so regularly modeled and rewarded that the connection becomes unconscious for most citizens, and behaviors that support these pronouncements are enacted unquestioningly, with the resultant negative outcomes for darker-complexioned Afrikan American women.

Skin Color and Self-Esteem

Thompson and Keith (2001), in their analyses of data from the National Survey of Black Americans, found a direct and negative relationship between skin tone and self-esteem for Afrikan American women. As skin tone became darker, self-worth declined, even after sociodemographic and socioeconomic variables were considered and body image and racial context were assessed. The importance of childhood interracial contact for Afrikan American women's self-esteem was also indicated in this research. For Afrikan American women who attended majority White grade schools, self-esteem was lower. This finding is consistent with Rosenberg's (1975, as cited in Keith & Thompson, 2003) research indicating that dissonant environments have harmful effects on self-esteem; however, the effects of these dissonant settings were not differentiated by skin tone. Regardless of skin tone, Afrikan American women's feelings of self-worth were diminished when they attended predominantly White elementary schools. The benefits of privilege typically accorded to lighter-skinned Afrikan American women were not evident in these majority White settings. The researchers suggest that racism functions as an "equal opportunity operator," exerting, with equivalence, its deleterious impact on lighter- as well as darker-complexioned Afrikan American women. The most troubling finding that emerges from this study (Thompson & Keith, 2001) concerns the interaction of class and color. The combination of low socioeconomic status and dark complexion was particularly lethal, resulting in significantly lowered self-esteem for darker-complexioned Afrikan American women. The convergence of four forms of low status in the United States, or quadruple jeopardy—race, class, gender, and color—takes its toll on the self-esteem of Afrikan American women of darker complexions. However, a more complex picture of how issues of skin color affect outcomes surfaces when physical attractiveness is considered. While lighter complexions privileged Afrikan American women who were considered unattractive, being "attractive" appeared to neutralize the disadvantages associated with darker skin tone. There were observable salutary effects on the self-esteem of women deemed "unattractive" with increases in the lightness of their skin tones. It is interesting to note that with regard to self-efficacy—"the belief that one can influence events in their life or master situations" (Bandura, 1977, 1982, as cited in Keith & Thompson, 2003)—neither skin color nor attractiveness was of import. Rather, educational attainment and income were predictors of Black women's sense of self efficacy, suggesting that these strategies have been utilized to confront the barriers posed by colorism, particularly for Afrikan American women with darker skin tones. Not surprisingly, the struggles that Afrikan American women and girls experience with regard to skin color are replicated with regard to hair.

Attitudes About Hair Texture

For many Afrikan American women, the fact that their hair is "kinky" adds insult to injury. Since hair grooming is usually a daily activity, we are constantly reminded that our hair, in many instances, does not conform to prevailing standards of what is considered "beautiful" hair projected in the media and, more often than not, what is valued by our peers and families. Like lighter skin color, hair texture that more closely resembles the hair texture of most Caucasians—straight—is prized by many Afrikan Americans and considered "good" hair. In contrast, the more Afrikan in texture our hair is, the more it is judged as "bad." These evaluations are often internalized by Afrikan American girls and women, influencing self-worth as well as feelings of attractiveness. Statements like those of Don Imus in 2007, referencing the Afrikan American young women competing for the national championship on Rutgers's basketball team as "nappy-headed hos," are multi-purpose "zingers." These preconceptions have had negative implications for young women in multiple environments, with the creation of appearance policies that work against Afrikan women by deeming their natural hair "unprofessional" (Opie, 2018). The intention of these comments and policies is to inferiorize Black women so that even when we are displaying excellence, we are castigated, prevented from fully enjoying our success, and collectively given the message that we are unacceptable images of women.

The Hair and Beauty Industry

Every year Afrikan American women give billions of dollars to a hair care and beauty industry which, for the most part, is now no longer owned by people of Afrikan ancestry. We buy straight, often Indian or Asian, hair for the purposes of weave and extensions, and purchase wigs and hair care products primarily made by non-Afrikan people. Our obsession with our hair has literally made the owners of these industries rich. In order for these industries to continue to thrive, it is essential that women of Afrikan ancestry be thoroughly indoctrinated with the myth of the inferiority of our hair. We must be made to believe that our hair in its natural state is inadequate, unattractive, and stylistically limited. We must be shielded from the negative repercussions of using certain hair products, lest we begin to reconsider our investment. We must be bombarded with images of both Black and White women with long, flowing hair. We must be reminded and sometimes taunted by our peers and family members about the undesirability of our hair in its natural state. Print and electronic media are highly complicit in the dissemination of these messages, including the few media sources that are Black-owned. Control of the Black hair care and beauty industry has shifted from the hands of Afrikan Americans to the hands of Europeans and Asians. The current predominantly non-Black ownership of the Black hair-care industry stands in stark contrast to its early beginnings.

Although the acclaim of being the first woman millionaire in the United States has been accorded to Madame C. J. Walker, in actuality she shares this recognition with Annie Malone (Powers, 2019). Possessing a net worth of $14 million in 1924, Annie Malone employed 75,000 sales agents around the world and established 32 beauty schools (Powers, 2019). Her beauty school, Poro University (name based on a West Afrikan word for spiritual and physical growth), covered an entire block in St. Louis, Missouri and included a dining room, chapel, roof garden, gym, and space for community gatherings. She is also noted for her philanthropy, her commitment to the uplift of the Black community, and her entrepreneurial acumen. Similarly, Madame C. J .Walker, who was one of Malone's sales agents before separating from her, accrued her fortune through the development, marketing, and sale of hair, scalp, and skin aids which targeted Black women's concerns about their hair and skin coloration. While Ms. Walker is often accused of capitalizing on the insecurities that Black women held about their physical appearance, she states that she was merely offering Black women products that would enhance their natural beauty. In her lifetime, Madame C. J. Walker employed thousands of Afrikan American women and generously supported self-advancement within the Afrikan community through her philanthropy (Dwojeski et al., 2007).

Black Hair Care and Health

Understanding the motivations of Afrikan American women who perm their hair, and/or wear weaves, extensions, and wigs, is fraught with difficulty. On the one hand, arguments can be made that they have internalized society's attitudes, which denigrate natural Afrikan textured hair; on the other hand, there are many personal, political, social, and economic factors that impinge on the decisions Afrikan American women make about their hairstyles. Some of these factors include perceived ease of care, work demands, desire for variety, and desire to please those closest to us (Okazawa-Rey et al., 1987). For the sake of our health—both physical and emotional—disentangling these motivating factors is essential. More and more evidence is amassing that reveals the harmful effects of the use of certain chemicals to relax and perm our hair. When we make decisions to relax and perm our hair in the face of this evidence, are we trading our physical health for social acceptability? Are we attempting to manage feelings of shame while simultaneously risking our physical well-being? Are we buying into a racially gendered view of what beauty is and reinforcing the existing Eurocentric standards of beauty? And what of the economically debilitating effects that this behavior has on the Black community? By pouring billions of dollars into the hair and beauty product industry, again most of which is not owned by people of Afrikan ancestry, are we stripping the Black community of resources needed for its stability and progress?

Afrikan Cultural Identity and Attitudes About Beauty

Adopting an Afrikan-centered concept of beauty may provide a corrective to the damaging effects that internalization of Eurocentric values and standards of beauty have exerted on Afrikan American women. Within an Afrikan cultural context, character plays a prominent role in the assessment of beauty. As one Afrikan American proverb suggests: "Beauty is as beauty does." Utilizing the Afrikan worldview, which stresses a diunital approach (both/and), a single monolithic standard of beauty is untenable. Nature, with its phenomenal diversity, provides a model of the range and variety that beauty may assume. Thus, a lily is no more beautiful than a rose; an oak tree no more beautiful than a palm tree; and an opal no more beautiful than a pearl. Each is beautiful in its own right, and each has unique value and plays a special role in nature. For Afrikan people, particularly prior to colonization, beauty had no meaning outside of the group. Comparisons across groups were therefore meaningless, and beauty was aligned with a sense of harmony with one's community and environment (Ibanga, 2017). "Beauty of a person or thing should be participatory and interconnective rather than individualistic; and should be meaningful only in the context of the acceptable standards of the community" (p. 255). Thus, from a traditional Afrikan perspective, no one is inherently beautiful because beauty is dynamic and contextual. Worth and value are assessed on the basis of one's character and contribution to the community, not their physical appearance. When Afrikan American women succumb to Eurocentric standards of beauty, it results in denying our unique essence, our value, and our authenticity as Afrikan women and, perforce, indicates the acceptance of an inferior status. By showing appreciation for our Afrikan features, we resist oppression and challenge the status quo.

Several research studies support the benefits of African self-consciousness (ASC), a concept developed by Kambon (1998, 2012) that measures the extent to which people of Afrikan ancestry exhibit a positive orientation toward their identity as Afrikans. ASC has been found to correlate with a number of prosocial and healthy outcomes among Afrikan Americans (Kambon, 2012). In a study of skin color attributions, Chambers and cplleaagues (1994) found that those individuals demonstrating high ASC associated significantly more positive attributes to faces with Afrikan features than those with medium or low ASC. On the other hand, individuals with high ASC did not make negative attributions to faces with few Afrikan features. Azibo's (1983) research revealed a relationship between strong Black personality scores and preferences for Black photos. Falconer and Neville's (2000) study of 124 Afrikan American women attending an Historically Black College or University indicated that ASC, skin color satisfaction, and body mass significantly predicted appearance evaluation. This study noted a positive correlation between ASC and Afrikan American women's perceptions of their bodies. Although more research is needed, these studies provide supportive evidence of the relationship between an Afrikan-centered orientation and positive self-evaluations by Afrikan Americans.

Black Beauty, Activism, Advocacy, and Policy

Recently, with the rise of movements such as Black Lives Matter (BLM), we are witnessing a revitalization of "Black is Beautiful" declarations. Large corporations have taken note of these movements and appear to be monetizing the emerging changes in consciousness within the Black community. One example is Procter & Gamble, which has developed multiple initiatives that support Black creators, debunked negative stereotypes, and brought awareness to issues affecting the Black community (My Black is Beautiful, 2020).

In conjunction with the development of advocacy programs, there has also been a surge in films and productions addressing concepts of beauty. In 2013, the film *Imagine the Future* was released. Companies including Sundance and BET debuted this documentary examining Black girls' issues pertaining to beauty and self-esteem (Cortes & Lynch, 2013). Documentaries (Stilson, 2009) similar to this one provide a counter-narrative to Eurocentric standards of beauty for young women of color. Later films, such as the short film *Hair Tales* (Cherry, 2019) and the feature film *Nappily Ever After* (al-Mansour, 2018), have expanded this message and have provided essential representations of Black beauty and Black hair. Music is also an essential form of expression that has allowed for Black beauty to shine. Songs such as *Whip My Hair* by Willow Smith and *I Am Not My Hair* by India.Arie provide positive representations of Black hair in a multi-media format. These important inclusions of Black representation in the media portray a new form of media activism.

Social media has also become a vibrant and dynamic platform for activism. Networks such as Instagram, Twitter, Facebook, TikTok, and others have created new opportunities for individuals to participate in activism. Hashtag activist movements such as #BlackOutTuesday, a hashtag of a black screen posted in solidarity with those lost due to police brutality, have stimulated similar forms of hashtag activism pertaining to Black beauty. Black women have created hashtags such as #BlackIsBeautiful and, more recently, #PullUpOrShutUp, calling for beauty industries to reveal the number of women of color working for them. These forms of activism have led to changes in the beauty industry and legislation.

As discussed previously in this chapter, skin lightening has been a deleterious issue affecting Afrikan communities. However, with the rise in social movements such as Black Lives Matter (BLM) and #BlackIsBeautiful, some industries are taking note. Major companies in the skin lightening industry, such as Unilever and L'Oréal, have noted these shifts in attitudes. In response, they have decided to change the names and terminology used in their most popular brands. Unilever's popular skin lightening brand, "Fair & Lovely," developed to lighten darker skin, will become "Glow & Lovely" by the end of 2020 (Frayer, 2020). Another large skincare brand, L'Oréal, will remove the terms bleaching, whitening, fair, fairness, and lightening from all of their products (Frayer, 2020). Unfortunately, these changes appear to be clever and disguised modifications designed to maintain their customer base and ensure the maintenance of their profit margins, since no changes in the chemical content and purpose of these products have been indicated. Certainly, these changes demonstrate the power of activism; however, it is important that activists and community leaders are not seduced by superficial alterations.

Of historical significance is the enactment of policies in seven states that prohibit discrimination against Afrikan hair. The 2019 CROWN (Create a Respectful and Open World for Natural Hair) Act (SB 188) is a recently instituted policy that prohibits discrimination against race-based hair textures and protective styles (e.g., braids, weaves, cornrows, etc.) in multiple sites including housing, workplace, and educational settings (The CROWN Act, n.d.). Created by the CROWN Coalition and skincare company Dove, The CROWN Act has now been passed in California, Washington, Colorado, Virginia, Maryland, and New York (The CROWN Act, n.d.). With legislation enactments such as The CROWN Act, it is clear that efforts to redefine beauty and acknowledge the limitations of Eurocentric standards of beauty are finally beginning to shift the landscape. Concomitantly, it is equally important that shifts in the consciousness of the Black community also occur.

Overcoming Internalized Racist Attitudes About Beauty

Just as Powell-Hopson and Hopson's (1988) study revealed, it is possible to modify attitudes about our physical appearance by changing the reward structures and by modeling positive responses to Afrikanity.

To do this, we must begin to implement all or some of the following steps:

- Significantly reduce the amount of time spent viewing television, particularly shows which reinforce Eurocentric notions of what is beautiful.

- Never say, "She's pretty to be so dark." Such remarks are not only uncomplimentary, but they also reinforce the idea that being dark-skinned is unattractive.

- Never put anyone down or tease them about their skin color.

- Cease using color names such as "redbone," and referring to people as "black and ugly," as if being "black" automatically indicates that one is also "ugly" and these two attributes are inseparable.

- Surround yourself with images of Afrikan people—on the walls at home, in your workplace, etc.

- Buy magazines that present positive images of people of Afrikan heritage.

- Read books and stories about the significant contributions that people of Afrikan heritage have made to children.

- Stop saying, "S/he has good/bad hair." Recognize that all hair that grows on your head is good.

- Say complimentary things to darker-skinned women and girls about their physical appearance.

- Challenge friends and family members who make negative remarks about other people of Afrikan ancestry based on skin color, hair texture, or the presence of Afrikan physical features.

- Insist that educational curricula, at the elementary, middle, and secondary as well as the college levels, include courses on Afrikan/ Afrikan American history and literature and the contributions of ancient Afrikans to science and math, and demand that these courses occupy the same status as courses with a Eurocentric focus.

Okazawa-Rey and colleagues (1987) suggest that "nothing short of structural change will permanently alter our social relations in this society" (p. 101). These researchers suggest that Afrikan American women must actively challenge the social foundations of White supremacy racism in this society. To do this, they indicate, requires a positive view of ourselves, an appreciation of the diversity amongst us, and a recognition of the history that brought us to this place.

References

Alleyne, S. & LaPoint, V. (2004). Obesity among Black adolescent girls: Genetic, psychosocial, and cultural influences. *Journal of Black Psychology*, *30*, 344–365.

al-Mansour, H. (Director). (2018). *Nappily ever after* [Film]. Netflix.

Ani, M. (1994). *Yurugu: An African-centered critique of European cultural thought & behavior.* Africa World Press, Inc.

Azibo, D. A. (1983). Perceived attractiveness and the Black personality. *Western Journal of Black Studies*, *7*, 229–238.

Baker, J. R. (1981). The 'Hotentot Venus.' In *Race* (pp. 313–319). Foundation for Human Understanding.

birgitvanhout. (2007, August 13). Black doll White doll [Video]. *YouTube.* https://www.youtube.com/watch?v=ybDa0gSuAcg

Chambers, J. W., Clark, T., Dantzler, L., & Baldwin, J. A. (1994). Perceived attractiveness, facial features, and African self-consciousness. *Journal of Black Psychology*, *20*, 305–324.

Chambers, J. W., Kambon, K., Birdsong, B. D., Brown, J., Dixon, P., & Robbins-Brinson, L. (1998). Africentric cultural identity and the stress experience of African American college students. *Journal of Black Psychology*, *24*(3), 368–396. https://doi.org/10.1177/00957984980243007

Cherry, M. (Director). (2019). *Hair tales* [Film]. Sony Pictures Animation.

CNN. (2010, May 14). Study: White and Black children biased toward lighter skin. http://www.cnn.com/2010/US/05/13/doll.study/index.html

Collins, P. H. (2000). *Black feminist thought: Knowledge, consciousness, and the politics of empowerment* (2nd ed.). Routledge.

Cortes, L., & Lynch, S. (Directors). (2013). *Imagine a future* [Film]. P & G Entertainment.

Coutts, A. (2020, June 24). Racial bias around the world. osf.io/39svq

The CROWN Act. (n.d.). About. https://www.thecrownact.com/about

Dwojeski, A. E., Grundy, W., Helms, E., Miller, K., & Koehn, N. F. (2007, March). *Madam C. J. Walker: Entrepreneur, leader, and philanthropist.* Harvard Business School Case 807-145. https://store.hbr.org/product/madam-c-j-walker-entrepreneur-leader-and-philanthropist/807145?sku=807145-PDF-ENG

Falconer, J. W., & Neville, H. A. (2000). African American college women's body image: An examination of body mass, African self-consciousness, and skin color satisfaction. *Psychology of Women Quarterly, 24*, 236–243.

Frayer, L. (2020, September 7). NPR choice page. *NPR.* https://choice.npr.org/index.html?origin=https://www.npr.org/sections/goatsandsoda/2020/07/09/860912124/black-lives-matter-gets-indians-talking-about-skin-lightening-and-colorism

Hall, C. C. I. (1995). Beauty is in the soul of the beholder: Psychological implications of beauty & African American women. *Cultural Diversity & Mental Health, 1*(2), 125–137.

Hall, R. E. (2018). The globalization of light skin colorism: From critical race to critical skin theory. *American Behavioral Scientist, 62*(14), 2133–2145. https://doi.org/10.1177/0002764218810755

Hughes, M., & Hertel, B. R. (1990). The significance of color remains: A study of life chances, mate selection, and ethnic consciousness among Black Americans. *Social Forces, 68*(4), 1105–1120.

Hunter, M. H. (2005). *Race, gender, and the politics of skin tone.* Routledge.

Ibanga, D-A. (2017). The concept of beauty in African philosophy. *Africology: Journal of Pan African Studies, 10*(7), 249-260.

Johnson, M. S. (2013). Strength and respectability. *Gender & Society, 27*(6), 889–912. https://doi.org/10.1177/0891243213494263

Kambon, K. K. K. (1998). *African/Black psychology in the American context: An African-centered approach* (1st ed.). Nubian Nation Publications.

Kambon, K. K. K. (2003). *Cultural misorientation: The greatest threat to the survival of the Black race in the 21st century.* Nubian Nation Publications.

Kambon, K. K. K. (2012). *African/Black psychology in the American context: An African-centered approach* (2nd ed.). Nubian Nation Publications.

Keith, V. M., & Thompson, M. S. (2003). Color matters: The importance of skin tone for African American women's self-concept in Black and White America. In D. R. Brown & V. M. Keith (Eds.), *In & out of our right minds*. Columbia University Press.

Maseko, Z. (2011). *The life and times of Sara Baartman: The "Hottentot Venus."* Icarus Films. http://icarusfilms.com/new99/hottento.html

Mbilishaka, A. M. (2020). Throwin' shade: Disrupting the aesthetic trauma of colorism and hair bias in the lives of Black women. In H. Jackson-Lowman (Ed.), *Afrikan American women: Living at the crossroads of race, gender, class, and culture* (Custom preliminary 2nd ed.). Cognella Academic Publishing.

Menakem, R. (2017). *My grandmother's hands: Racialized trauma and the pathway to mending our hearts and bodies*. Central Recovery Press.

Muzenda, M. (2018, November 30). Blac Chyna came to Nigeria to launch a skin-lightening cream at $250 a jar. *NPR*. https://www.npr.org/sections/goatsandsoda/2018/11/30/671879261/blac-chyna-came-to-nigeria-to-launch-a-skin-lightening-cream-at-250-a-jar4

My Black is Beautiful. (2020). *Hair care & beauty products for natural hair*. https://www.mbib.com/en-us

Nogueira, S. (2013). Ideology of White racial supremacy: Colonization and decolonization processes. *Psicologia & Sociedade, 25*, 23–32.

Okazawa-Rey, M., Robinson, T., & Ward, J. V. (1987). Black women and the politics of skin color and hair. *Women & Therapy, 6*(1), 89–102. http://search.proquest.com/docview/216253869?accountid=10913.

Opie, T. (2018). Let my hair be me: An investigation of employee authenticity and organizational appearance policies through the lens of Black women's hair. *Fashion Studies, 1*(1), 1–28. https://doi.org/10.38055/fs010111

Powell-Hopson, D., & Hopson, D. (1988). Implications of doll color preferences among Black preschool children and White preschool children. *Journal of Black Psychology, 14*(2), 57–63.

Powers, A. (2019). The first self-made female millionaire built a business empire in cosmetics in the 1900s by pioneering a sales strategy still in use today. *Forbes*. https://www.forbes.com/sites/annapowers/2019/11/30/the-first-self-made-female-millionaire-built-a-business-empire-in-cosmetics-in-1900s-by-pioneering-a-sales-strategy-still-in-use-today/?sh=63f8b4681690

Reid-Brinkley, S. R. (2007). The essence of res(ex)pectability: Black women's negotiation of Black femininity in rap music and music video. *Meridians: Feminism, Race, Transnationalism, 8*(1), 236–260. https://doi.org/10.2979/mer.2007.8.1.236

Roberts, D. (2017). *Killing the Black body: Race, reproduction, and the meaning of liberty*. Vintage Books.

Rodney, W. (1982). *How Europe underdeveloped Africa*. Howard University Press.

Rosenberg, C. (1975). The female world of love and ritual: Relations between women in nineteenth century America. *Signs: Journal of Women in Culture and Society, 1*(1), 1–29. https://doi.org/10.1086/493203

Russell, K., Wilson, M., & Hall, R. (1992). *The color complex: The politics of skin color among African Americans*. Harcourt Brace Jovanovich.

Saint Louis, C. (2010, Jan. 15). Creams offering lighter skin may bring risks. *New York Times.* https://www.nytimes.com/2010/01/16/health/16skin.html

Stilson, J. (Director). (2009). *Good hair* [Film]. HBO Films.

Thompson, M.S. & Keith, V.M. (2001). The blacker the berry: Gender, skin tone, self-esteem, and self-efficacy. *Gender & Society, 15*(3), 336-357. doi:10.1177/089124301015003002

Wilder, J. (2010). Revisiting "color names and color notions": A contemporary examination of the language and attitudes of skin color among young Black women. *Journal of Black Studies, 41*(1), 184–206.

Wilkerson, I. (2020). *Caste: The origins of discontent.* Random House.

Resources

Podcasts/Audios

164: Body image for women of color (w/ dr. nikki coleman). (2019, December 31). Living Corporate. https://www.living-corporate.com/2019/12/31/164-body-image-for-women-of-color-w-dr-nikki-coleman/

A discussion on body image and the misconceptions surrounding body image for women of color.

Bradford, J. H. (2020, January 9). *Session 74: Body image & Black women athletes.* Therapy for Black Girls. https://therapyforblackgirls.com/2020/01/09/session-74-body-image-black-women-athletes/

A discussion on body image in Black female athletes, such as Serena Williams, and their relationships with their bodies.

Roundtable: Black Women and Body Image. (2005, June 9). NPR.org. https://www.npr.org/templates/story/story.php?storyId=4696065

Podcast discussing the misconceptions surrounding Black Women and body image as well as the factors affecting it.

Short Videos

Cherry, M., Downing, F., & Smith, B. W. (Directors). (2019). *Hair Love.* United States: Lion Forge Animation.

Short film that explores the relationship between Zuri and her dad as he attempts to style her natural hair.

CNBC. (2018). *The Business Of Black Hair.* YouTube. https://youtu.be/mo1EHYkFP8I

Data and statistics on the cost of Black beauty are discussed. Testimonials by women are given to further examine our economic relationship with beauty products.

OWN. (2019). *Beauty: Are you judged by your hair? | black women own the conversation | Oprah Winfrey network.* YouTube. https://youtu.be/Vr14-23FxLk

Women in the audience discuss their feelings and thoughts on Black hair.

Tedx Talks. (2017, December 19). *No. You Cannot Touch My Hair! | Mena Fombo | TEDxBristol*. YouTube. https://youtu.be/OLQzz75yE5A

> Presentation on the uncomfortableness surrounding the touching of Black hair. Discusses how our hair is seen as different and is often violated.

The Guardian. (2017). *Eating disorders are black women's issues too' | young minds*. YouTube. https://youtu.be/YVqCZCf7Xnc

> Combats the stereotypes of eating disorders only affecting one group. Provides data and testimonials of the effects of eating disorders on Black women.

Documentaries/ Full-Length Films

Channsin Berry, D., & Duke, B. (Directors). (2011). *Dark Girls*.

> An exploration of deep-seat ed bias rooted in Black culture against those with dark skin.

Effiong, D. (Director). (2019). *Skin*. Netflix.

> Film that explores that effects of colorism in host Beverly Naya's country of Nigeria.

Kimbell, R. & Bluemke, J. (Directors). (2010). *My Nappy Roots: A Journey through Black Hair-itage*. United States: Virgin Moon Entertainment.

> "My Nappy Roots" explores the politics, culture, and history of African American hair. It seeks to answer questions such as, is there such a thing as "Good and Bad" hair, and how has the Eurocentric ideal of beauty influenced Black hair throughout history?

Scott-Ward, G. (Director). *Back to Natural: A Documentary Film*. (2019). United States: Sound View Media Partners.

> This film explores the new age natural hair movement. Examining the policies surrounding natural hair and the connections between hair, politics, and racial identity.

Valerius, D. (Director). (2008, December 1). *The souls of Black girls*.

> Documentary surrounding media's effects of the self-esteem of Black girls.

Children's Books

Nancy Amanda Redd, & Nneka Myers. (2020). *Bedtime bonnet*. Random House.

> Children's book highlighting the young Black girl's hair nighttime routine.

Nyong'o, L., & Harrison, V. (2019). *Sulwe*. Simon & Schuster Books for Young Readers.

> Young children's book outlining themes of colorism, self-esteem, and self-worth.

Perry, L. M., & Jackson, B. (2015). *Hair like mine*. G Publishing LLC.

> Children's book outlining the journey of hair acceptance and feelings surrounding having hair that is different than others'.

Websites and Documents

Black Impact: Consumer Categories Where African Americans Move Markets. (2018, February 15). Nielsen.com. https://www.nielsen.com/us/en/insights/article/2018/black-impact-consumer-categories-where-african-americans-move-markets/

Website article outlining the economic spending power of Black individuals.

Eating Disorders in Women of Color: Explanations and Implications Background. (2012). https://www.nationaleatingdisorders.org/sites/default/files/ResourceHandouts/EatingDisordersinWomenofColor.pdf

PDF document outline explanations, research bias, and implications of negative body image.

People of color and eating disorders. (2018, February 18). National Eating Disorders Association. https://www.nationaleatingdisorders.org/people-color-and-eating-disorders

Statistics outlining eating disorders and race.

Noël, R. (2014). Income and spending patterns among Black households. In *bls.gov*. https://www.bls.gov/opub/btn/volume-3/pdf/income-and-spending-patterns-among-black-households.pdf

Document outlining prices and spending patterns amongst Black households.

The "good hair" study appendix. (2016). https://perception.org/wp-content/uploads/2020/06/Good-Hair-Study-Appendix.pdf

PDF document outlining results of a study regarding good hair and perceptions of natural hair conducted by the Perception Institute.

Reading 2.4. Throwin' Shade

Disrupting the Aesthetic Trauma of Colorism and Hair Bias in the Lives of Black Women

Afiya M. Mbilishaka

Introduction

African people have long utilized their physical appearances to communicate the exquisiteness of their beauty, the complexity of their identity, and to affirm ancestral pride to the physical and spiritual worlds (Byrd & Tharps, 2014; Morrow, 1990; Sherrow, 2006). Due to the intricate grooming practices that uphold an African aesthetic, our ancestors could spend hours to days preparing the physical body for a spiritual ceremony (Beckwith & Fisher, 1999). Physical beauty was grounded in healing rituals and spiritual sciences that helped our ancestors establish order and structure within the community (Beckwith & Fisher, 1999; Byrd & Tharps, 2014). Unfortunately, the consciousness and grooming behaviors of Black women in modern history have been manipulated through a cultural–historical system of racism that treasures Eurocentric aesthetics (T. A. Johnson & Bankhead, 2014; Lewis, 1999). Light skin, long straight hair, and thin lips/noses serve to symbolize and reinforce systems of White supremacy and anti-Blackness at individual and institutional levels of American society (Capodilupo, 2015). Black women particularly fall prey to the aesthetic criteria of White beauty standards due to the intersection of race and gender, where Black female bodies are largely classified as property to be owned and controlled (DeGruy, 2005).

What is worse, Black people have been both the victims and the perpetrators of reinforcing systems of oppression based on Eurocentric aesthetics, specifically those related to skin color variation and hair traits. Colorism, the interracial and intra-racial mistreatment of people based on skin color pigmentation, can dictate the daily interactions and oppression of people of color based on a skin color hierarchy in American society (Monk, 2014). Colorism ranks lighter-skinned people as "better" than darker-skinned people. With Black communities, skin color can predict income (Keith & Herring, 1991), educational attainment (Keith & Herring, 1991), rate of employment (J. H. Johnson et al., 1998), marital status (Keith & Herring, 1991), and even health outcomes like blood pressure (Krieger et al., 1998). Similarly, differences in the appearance of hair have been associated with discriminatory behaviors on multiple levels. Hair bias includes mistreatment due to hair texture, length, color, or density (Mbilishaka, 2018a Mbilishaka & Apugo, 2020). Black hair is an entry point into the deeper understanding of economics, education, entertainment, health labor, law, politics, sex, religion, and war (see Mbilishaka, 2018a, 2018b, 2018c; Wilson et al., 2018). As evidenced by Neil and Mbilishaka (2019, p. 162), "Black women with tightly coiled hair often face more discriminatory actions in the workplace, by family members, and in mate selection." As soon as they exit the womb, some Black people experience mistreatment from their own mothers based on the texture of their hair (Lewis, 1999). These early experiences can have a lifetime of impact on a Black woman, as reconstructed in her most intimate memories (Wilson et al., 2018).

Black women may experience significant emotional pain as a result of individual and institutionally reinforced criticism of their aesthetics; this is the concept of aesthetic trauma. Aesthetic trauma can best be defined as a deeply distressing or disturbing experience concerning beauty (see Mbilishaka & Haileab, 2017). Similar to racial microaggressions, aesthetic trauma can be understood as the psychological bite resulting from verbal and non-verbal, intersectional, cumulative attacks on phenotype (see Pérez Huber & Solorzano, 2015). This form of trauma can consist of isolated incidents but tends to play on repeat within the life experiences of Black women (see Mbilishaka & Apugo, in press). These aesthetic traumas are cumulative, often occurring within a certain time window, setting, and relational dynamic. As a result, some may have intrusive thoughts, anxiety, and further stress in navigating this appearance-based society. Aesthetic trauma interferes with life areas of economics, entertainment, education, health, labor, law, politics, sex, religion, and war. The perpetuators of aesthetic trauma can engage in intentional abuse or may act on a subconscious level because they may have experienced the social- and emotional-based aesthetic trauma themselves. Aesthetic trauma, therefore, exists within systems of history, politics, and social relationships, and within a cultural space.

Therefore, to deepen the discussion around the psychology of Black women, this chapter aims to: 1) affirm the cultural beauty of African phenotypes, while unpacking colorism and hair bias; 2) glorify narrative methodology in racial and aesthetics research; and 3) and summarize existing techniques to dismantle the structures that support aesthetic trauma. The historical context for African aesthetics must be clearly understood, by researcher and clinician, as it establishes the infrastructure of modern-day belief systems and beauty rituals. The historical timeline of our aesthetics is an admixture of politics, culture, spirituality, and health practices. Therefore, this chapter aspires to take readers on a journey on which to build the awareness, knowledge, and skills to disrupt the aesthetic trauma that we have collectively faced.

Historical Elements of African Aesthetics

African Proverb

No matter how far the river travels it will never forget its source.

Face Value

To outline the rich history of African beauty and meanings, study must begin with the face. Evolutionary psychology and medicine teach us that the human face could indicate partner and mating preferences because the face easily communicates the health of the full body (Afrika, 2013). Ancient African cultural systems implemented makeup as a tool of communication for spiritual rites and ceremonies (Beckwith & Fisher, 1999). Cultural anthropologists found that cultures in the Ancient Nile Valley civilization viewed the addition of pigmentation to the face, in the form of makeup, to be both protective and healing (Lucas, 1930). Both men and women used makeup in ancient times, as an appeal to their attractiveness. For example, our Ancient Egyptian ancestors choose black paint for the eyes, which was produced using kohl, as a way to enhance the beauty of the eyes and protect the eyes from the intensity of the sun's rays (Lucas, 1930). Even green was used to shadow the eyes of men and women, to make the eyes present as larger and to channel the energy and healing protection of the sky god, Horus (Lucas, 1930). Further, the use of red paints on the face, especially around the mouth, represented increased fertility and ovulation periods for African women (Graham & Kligman, 1985). These rich colors could attract mates by enhancing the existing beauty of facial features.

Within a psychology of color, the interpretation of African skin color and the texture of faces were shaped by cultural value systems (Graham & Kligman, 1985). Each appendage of the face espoused cultural nuance to attract potential mates, signify social status, and carry out ritual (Graham & Kligman, 1985). This meant that African people across the continent engaged in cultural practices of scarification, inserting holes into the ears and lips, neck stretching, and nose flattening (Beckwith & Fisher, 1999). These practices can represent a form of body modification that expresses economic status, age, and spiritual initiation (Beckwith & Fisher, 1999). During these rituals of facial modification in particular, various medicines are rubbed in the face to enhance the spiritual potency of the overall body (Beckwith & Fisher, 1999). Scarification is commonly practiced in African cultures because the deep melanin concentration would not reveal tattoos

(Garve et al., 2017). The lack of scars on the face was often considered a taboo and was seen as unattractive in most West African countries (Brooks, 2017). These (voluntary or forced) scars could even protect various African ethnic groups during times of war, as a means to identify in- and out-group membership, as individuals wore their identification on their faces, and could also indicate royal status (Garve et al., 2017). These scars often had to be earned through rites of passage, the birth of a child, secret society membership, warriorhood, or hunting ability, and could indicate grief (Garve et al., 2017). "Scarification is achieved through cuts of the skin, removal of skin parts, burns and branding, chemical imprinting, skin laceration and a variety of other techniques" (Garve et al., 2017, p. 709). The patterns of the scars on the face could come in a variety of forms, like a fishbone, birds, or crocodiles; these patterns would result from highly melanated skin's ability to keloid and from extending the length of time of healing through the application of medicinal tinctures (Garve et al., 2017). Here, we see an African aesthetic of scars on the face, and the body, being interpreted with value. The head, and specifically the hair, held even more significance and power within this cultural context.

Love on Top

Black women's beautiful hair has been archived through permanent residence on the pyramid walls that date back thousands of years in Africa. The impenetrable hair follicles of our ancient African queens still exist from this time, too, with the preserved mummified bodies that still display the most ornate braided styles of royalty (Walker, 2011). Through the images etched into the walls and from the physical remnants of Black bodies from millennia ago, we see that African people engaged in calculated rituals to honor the beauty of hair. In these ancient societies, hair was a symbol of both royal status and initiation into priesthood (Byrd & Tharps, 2014). Therefore, only royal family members could have their hair groomed by individuals who reached an elevated level of consciousness and spirituality. Special combs were blessed in ceremonies, and the scalps would be anointed with specific herbs and oils for medicinal purposes (Byrd & Tharps, 2014). To amplify the position of beauty in royalty, special wigs were prepared by craftsmen that were uniquely fitted to the head and social roles of the royal family (Walker, 2011). For example, pharaohs were assigned elongated beard hair to represent their rulership (Walker, 2011). Therefore, Queen Hatshepsut, who attained the status of pharaoh and was the longest-reigning female pharaoh, also decided to adorn her face with the hair of pharaohs by wearing a braided beard! Since she had the option to curate her own image, she chose to embed herself into history with braids ascending from both her scalp and her chin. Another highly recognized female leader, Queen Tiye, the grandmother of King Tut, archived her personal image with a full, blown-out Afro. Her position in history included expanding the political territory of Ancient Egypt and co-ruling with her spouse for almost 50 years (Walker, 2011). Queen Tiye's image of herself with a large Afro supported the belief that hair growing towards the heavens reflected someone's spiritual connection and power (see Byrd & Tharps, 2014). It was a belief at this time, and through modern-day cosmology, that spirit can enter the body through hair and enhance physical power (Byrd & Tharps, 2014).

In traditional African society, hair was employed as a tool to enrich dimensions of spirituality through ritual (see Mbilishaka, 2018a). Ritual can best be defined as techniques to prepare the mind, body, and spirit to receive blessings (Some, 1997). Hair rituals are embedded in rituals from birth to death in traditional African societies. For example, the Maasai of today's Kenya and Tanzania are quite inclusive of hair in their rites of passage across the lifespan. Within 10 days of a newborn baby's birth, the baby must have his or her hair shaved as part of the rites of passage of the naming ceremony (Beckwith & Fisher, 1999). In this ritual, the entire community gathers, and a practitioner of the African spiritual science shaves the hair of the baby and the mother, as an offering to the spiritual world and as a form of gratitude for the safe birth of the baby. The baby's name is selected with the intent of evoking life purpose and is agreed upon by the entire community, as in most traditional African naming ceremonies (Some, 1997). Later in life, if this baby is selected to participate in the warrior class as an adolescent, he must begin a process of growing locs, as only warriors are permitted to grow their hair long in Maasai culture (Beckwith & Fisher, 1999). These locs are dyed a deep red, as a methodological approach to evoking warrior deities within this culture (Beckwith & Fisher, 1999). Upon the warrior's safe return after battle, their mother or other female village elder is permitted to shave the hair of their warrior sons and then engage in a cleansing ritual with the hair at the waterfront (Beckwith & Fisher, 1999).

Beauty rituals related to women's hair are most pronounced in marriage rituals in African cultures. Further, the brides of the Maasai must shave their hair on their wedding day, as another offering to the spiritual world and as an indication to the community that this woman is no longer available for courtship (Beckwith & Fisher, 1999). For the women of the Mauretania desert, the guests at the wedding ceremony braid the hair of the bride as a part of the ritual, each guest selecting a special pendant to braid into the hair as a method of wishing wealth or fertility for the couple (Beckwith & Fisher, 1999). Similarly, for the Tuareg women of today's Mali and Niger, the bride engages in a community-based ceremony to shine and braid her hair. The bride's hair is rubbed with medicinal oils and fine black sand before the blacksmith's wife braids her hair, as a signifier of the heat and power of metal workers (Beckwith & Fisher, 1999). The adornments of hair for African women are significant, as the placement and density of the objects offer a sophisticated language to communicate with the physical and spiritual world (Byrd & Tharps, 2014).

Social Seats of Stylists

In traditional African society, professional styling and grooming was an ordained position. To become a hair care professional, women would need to study for years to develop mastery of the skills for caring for the spiritual head and physical body. For the Mende people, the extension of an invitation to groom someone's hair is an official offer to become close friends (Byrd & Tharps, 2014). Within Wolof cultures in Senegal, women inherit their hairdresser from their mothers, as this individual is the griot of family history due to the intimacy of discussion during the hair care process (Byrd & Tharps, 2014). In the Yorùbá tradition, hairstylists are considered priestesses because of their impact on the spiritual health of the spiritual head (Sherrow, 2006). All Yorùbá girls are taught how to braid hair, but any girl who exhibits particular strengths and creativity in hair care techniques is selected to become a hair care professional and is beholden to care for the hair of her entire family and community (Byrd & Tharps, 2014). Hairstylists pledge to engage in purification rituals as a means to cleanse and feed the head, the spiritual center of the body (Olugbemi, 2004). Yorùbá hairstylists shave the scalps of new babies for spiritual ceremonies, and then use that same hair to evoke protection. That hair may be utilized for medicines later on in life for that same individual (Sherrow, 2006). In many African cultures the work of a hair care professional is complex and is deeply rooted in a cultural value system that emphasizes spirituality.

Further, there are rules that govern the behaviors of individuals involved in beautification. For the Yorùbá, there are taboos—a system of values and penalties—that come from appropriate or inappropriate conduct between hair care professional and client. In practice, Yorùbá hairstylists are not encouraged to wash their hair minutes after styling someone's hair because it is thought that this behavior could result in the loss of positive energy (Olugbemi, 2004). It is also suggested that clients should not bargain with payments for hair care, as the hairstylist could discount the client's personal destiny (Olugbemi, 2004). From a Yorùbá perspective, according to Parham (2002), these taboos have particular relevance for one's mental health since personal destiny is centralized in the spiritual head. The *Yoruba* term *ori ire* best translates to mean the alignment of one's consciousness with one's destiny and is associated with the maintenance of mental health (Parham, 2002). Here, we see that hairstylists are responsible not only for beauty, but also for recognizing spiritual essence and collective support (Mbilishaka, 2018). Grooming within a cultural framework is of critical importance for African women and is a strategy for the maintenance of spiritual and mental health (Mbilishaka, 2018).

Aesthetic Trauma as a Context for Black Female Identity

Trauma is subjective, exists on a spectrum, and is culturally embedded because life experiences shape our interpretation of threat and harm (Van der Kolk, 2015). Therefore, research scientists and clinicians need to amplify the nuances of trauma for Black women. Trauma work is typically centered on extremely harmful and dangerous experiences, like sexual or physical assault, the death of a loved one, accidents, and injuries (see Van der Kolk, 2015). While trauma is typically conceptualized as the emotional reaction that an individual can have to a negative lived experience, appearance is not centralized in the conversation of navigating pain in Black communities. We must see the roots of modern traumas in enslavement and the Jim Crow era to address the psychological complexities of Black womanhood.

Enslavement of African people through chattel slavery required a redefinition of beauty and politics for Black women. Through the dismissal and degradation of African aesthetics, European slave catchers and masters began the dehumanization process of African people (DeGruy, 2005). With the development of a Manichean psychology (Harrell, 1999), anything that was labeled as Black became ugly and evil, including Black people, which shaped interactions with Black people in the Americas. This Manichean psychology enforced in Eurocentric spaces was a requirement to form whiteness and undergirds concepts of White terrorism and domination (DeGruy, 2005). Historians noted that one of the first things European slave catchers did on the shores of West Africa was to publicly shave the ornate hairstyles of African women (Byrd & Tharps, 2014). This technique was considered sacrilegious to African people because hair was considered the spiritual center of the physical body. The conditions on the ships would often result in scalp diseases and lice problems because of harsh conditions for human life in filth. Upon arrival to the plantations in the Americas, enslaved people encountered living conditions that were sub-human, causing further issues of hair loss and shaming. Black people did not have access to their medical tinctures, oils, and blessed combs and were forced to groom themselves by utilizing materials found in the plantation life that were made for animals. Enslaved Africans were forced to groom themselves with horse brushes and to use sheep fleece carding tools for their hair (Morrow, 1990). In the Americas, African hair was labeled as "wool" or "fur" in attempts to further dehumanize African people through their phenotypic expressions of strong thick hair (Byrd & Tharps, 2014).

Skin color and hair textures were methods for institutionalizing mistreatment in plantation life for Black women (DeGruy, 2005). Yes, Black people of all skin colors were terribly oppressed during the hundreds of years of chattel slavery in the Americas. However, Black women with lighter skin, and with hair with looser curl patterns, were delegated tasks in the home, including cooking and cleaning for the family of the slave master. Black women with darker skin and tightly coiled hair were considered less feminine and were forced to do manual labor outside in the fields, such as harvesting crops (DeGruy, 2005). These distinctions were sometimes enforced through the rape culture in which the lighter-skinned Black people were the biological offspring of the slave master (DeGruy, 2005). The hierarchy of phenotypic variation of Black people in the Americas during these time periods of enslavement were brutally enforced, and clear benefits could be observed in a skin-color-based caste system in plantation life. Therefore, Black women who could manipulate their physical appearance to look closer to a white aesthetic were reinforced with additional social privileges of "better" clothes, access to particular foods, and protection from harsh environmental elements (Byrd & Tharps, 2014; Morrow, 1990). Black women began techniques of hair straightening through the use of axle grease from farm tools and ironed their own hair during domestic duties (Morrow, 1990). Additionally, many free Blacks in America during the time of institutional slavery wore their hair in straightened styles, and straight hair became associated with being free (Byrd & Tharps, 2014). Some enslaved Africans would go to the lengths of shaving off their own hair, if they were very light-skinned, as a means of "passing" as White, because hair often would be an indication of race since there were so many variations of skin color on American plantations (DeGruy, 2005).

American laws dictated the grooming practices of Africans in America. For example, the Tignon Laws of Louisiana argued that Black women could not expose their hair follicles in public. Black women were forced to cover their hair with scarves and wraps a means to neither offend Whites nor disrupt the politics of appearance during that time and space (see Mbilishaka, 2018a). However, Black women who were skilled in the manipulation of textiles, scarves, and fashion created gravity-defying head pieces to cover their hair, which positioned White women as inferior in beauty. This artistry of ostentatious beauty of African women in Louisiana then also became outlawed because of its ability to outshine whiteness (see Mbilishaka, 2018a). In these instances, Black aesthetics were consistently under attack by the law.

Black Americans began to reinforce these systems of African aesthetic oppression after the end of institutionalized enslavement. Black organizations such as sororities and churches denied or offered entrance by assessing likeness to whiteness, measuring skin color against brown paper bags or determining hair texture by using a thin-toothed comb to measure the ease of the comb sliding through the hair (Byrd & Tharps, 2005). Systems of European beauty standards have been enforced by the political climate across American history. Black aesthetics were used as scare tactics to continue the cultural enslavement of African people and used as justification for the mistreatment of Black communities. Poster images of Black women with dark skin, big lips and noses, big buttocks, and tightly coiled hair were used to illustrate their inferior status in American society (Rooks, 1996). After the emancipation of enslaved Africans, there were still politically based strategies to control acceptable images. And yet there was resistance in the 1960s, and most recently for the Black is Beautiful movement, where a range of Black phenotypes was praised. Further methods are needed to see how the aesthetics are carried out in modern lived experiences of race.

Narrative Methodology in Racial and Aesthetics Research

Guided Race Autobiography

Race adds an additional layer to the structure of Black women's personalities, and this race meaning can be processed narratively (Winston et al., 2004). There are few psychological methods that elicit rich stories about race and racism within lives. The Guided Race Autobiography (GRA) is a narrative personality tool focused on externalizing stories about the lived experiences of race. This tool, developed by Burford and Winston (2005), is a semi-structured research instrument that has adjusted the language of McAdams's (1997) Guided Autobiography and that requires deep reflection about various life episodes. Participants are expected to tell a variety of stories. The GRA includes the following seven episodes that each participant is required to describe: 1) "race earliest memory"; 2) "race childhood memory"; 3) "race adolescent memory"; 4) "race peak memory"; 5) "race nadir memory"; 6) "race turning point memory"; and 7) "race continuity memory." For example of direct quote of the instrument (Burford &Winston, 2005, p. 4), the prompt for the childhood memory is:

> Describe a childhood (age 12 or younger) memory related to your life experiences related to race: 1. That stands out as a particularly prominent or significant personal experience related to race; 2. And for which you are able to identify what happened, who was involved, and what you were thinking and feeling. Provide your best guess at your age at the time of the event. The event may be positive or negative, important or seemingly trivial. The point here is that this is a memory that stands out—it is something that you recall clearly and something that, when you think about your past, seems to have a certain prominence. Make sure that this is a particular and specific incident and not a general "time" or "period" in your life. Make sure your narrative includes a description of the following: exactly what happened, when it happened, who was involved, what you were thinking and feeling, why this event is significant, and what this event says about you and your personality.

Below, the narratives represent the lived experiences of Black women attending a historically Black college in the northeastern United States. All participants participated in a study through the institutional review board and consented to anonymous sharing of their stories. Here, we get an intimate look into the minds of Black women experiencing aesthetic trauma and how they respond to the psychological bite of an anti-Black society. Here, Effie describes her internalized aesthetic trauma from her childhood memory of race:

> Mostly from childhood I remember being ashamed of my race because I didn't know many black people other than myself and was raised by fair skinned Puerto Rican women. I thought I was ugly and begged my mother to straighten my hair while I practiced tucking my lower lip in so that it was thinner. I especially hated my nose and thought I would get a nose job when I was older because it

was too big. Race was always on my mind and I constantly thought I was sticking out compared to the others in my school and in my family. I couldn't read books about slavery or race because I was embarrassed and ashamed, and I really just wished I looked more like my mother and more like the white girls at school. I couldn't understand why I had to look so different and often times felt very alone, like no one could or would understand.

This narrative sample highlights the emotional toll of feeling "different" and attributing life dissatisfaction to skin color, hair texture, and facial features. This narrative sample emphasizes the shame related to race-based appearance. Effie does not identify a particular person who teased her about her appearance but explains that she did not have the emotional threshold to tolerate the social politics associated with the appearance of Blackness. It is clear that she felt isolated and unlike her peers, and even unlike her own family. She expressed an intense feeling of self-hate because of the historical trauma of Black people, including the processes of enslavement.

Other narratives do identify a particular perpetrator of the offense. Deanna describes her childhood experience of traveling for a school trip with her White female classmates:

I would have to say that a low personal experience would be when I was in 5th grade and my class had traveled to Washington DC. During the trip I had to share a hotel room with 4 other girls who were all white. Each night I had to roll my hair and grease, the normal things for a Black girl. Well, obviously they saw me doing this. Well one day when we were touring a site, we all decided to go to the bathroom together. While we were in there I started primping in the mirror and my friend Abby came up beside me and I asked her if I could use her comb for a second. She turns to me with a disgusted look on her face and goes "Didn't you put that stuff in your hair?" At this point I felt really bad because she made me feel like I was disgusting and that because I didn't have hair like her that I was "bad." I felt even worse afterward because I didn't tell her how much it hurt me and how mean her comment was.

This story illustrates feelings of shame and disgust as the result of a White person questioning and invalidating the participant's hair. Deanna discloses how terrible she felt to be put into that position and feel pain because of her physical appearance as a Black person. Not only did she feel bad about how her hair and hair products were talked about, but she also articulates how silenced she felt in the aftermath of a critical comment about her Black hair product.

And yet, these aesthetic traumas do not need to be lasting. Laurel described an experience of an aesthetic trauma, followed by the necessary processing of the experience to access a deeper healing dynamic coming from racial socialization:

I was nine years old. I grew up in a predominantly white neighborhood and went to a predominantly white school. Up until that point I had no real knowledge of being black. I knew I was, but it never truly occurred to me that I was different. It didn't hit me until Spring of my third-grade year when I was invited to a friend's birthday party (she was white). It was supposed to be a sleep over and we were supposed to dress up and do each other's hair and make-up and have a fun time. She told everyone on the invitations to bring supplies like brushes and barrettes in order for us to do each other's hair. I went to the party, but my hair was done up in plaits and I did not bring anything to do my hair because my mother would not let me take my hair out. When I got to the party my friend became very mad because she specifically told everyone to come to the party prepared to have their hair played with. She didn't understand that my hair was different, and it wasn't meant for little girls just to be playing in. I didn't understand why my hair was different either. All of the others girl's hair was smooth and silky and straight. My hair was kinky and greasy and stiff. I remember going home that day crying, taking out all of my plaits and combing my hair over and over again until it would lay flat like the other girls' hair. But it never did. My mother finally explained to me that my hair was different and that it wasn't going to be like the other girls' hair. This event started my long journey dealing with issues of hair. Looking back on it now, I've done everything EVER to try and ameliorate this issue I have with my natural hair. No one around me knew how to work with natural curls and they definitely didn't appreciate natural curls. In the south a person must perm, press, or braid his or her hair. It was not until I came to Howard that I really figured out that the standard of beauty that was being sold to me for so long was not mine. I wish I had had the foresight to appreciate my natural hair before. I never would have gone through bouts of sadness, despair, and eventually traction alopecia from all of the stress on my hair if I had known the information and learned to appreciate my race's standard of beauty from the very beginning. I have now taken control and ownership of my natural curls and wear them proudly. I know in the future that I will always teach my little girls to appreciate their own natural hair and beauty.

Laurel expressed deep and penetrating inner turmoil due to feeling very different from her peers, because of her hair texture and her hair maintenance practices. She expressed significant dissatisfaction with her "kinky and greasy and stiff" hair. She could not see her own beauty. Laurel's mother had to redirect her from obsessing over hair dissatisfaction. She even highlights her health consequence of traction alopecia, from excessive hair grooming to get a desired smooth appearance of her hair. After being exposed to African standards of beauty, she began to reject this Eurocentric conception of beauty and to exhibit a sense of pride in her natural hair. Not only is she proud now, in her adulthood, but she is also committed to socializing other Black girls about the importance of self-acceptance and love.

Black women also identify stages during which they viewed lighter skin and straighter hair as "good." Magic shared memories of her observations about the differences in treatment that Black women of various complexions received while she was growing up:

As I grew up, I remember always seeing females with a caramel skin tone and long wavy hair. I remember when I was about 8, I heard someone call this long wavy hair "good hair" as in "O GIRL YOU GOT SOME GOOD HAIR!" I also remember the same person I heard those words come out of tell me that the caramel colored girls were considered better and prettier than us brown skin girls. I thought to myself, "This girl is trippin!" However, after she said that, I began to notice that I did see a lot more caramel girls on the TV screen than brown skin girls. Then I became jealous, I blamed everything that went wrong on the fact that I had brown skin. Soon thereafter, I developed a light skin complex and began to think that they thought that they were better than us and "HOW DARE THEY!?" I mean, this was all in the course of a month, a summer month at that, so it didn't last long. It got nipped in the bud when I realized that my mother has light skin and neither she nor any other female with a caramel complexion has ever said or done anything to me that would in the least bit validate my light skin complex. I actually had to laugh at myself. As I got older and became more religious, I realized (after learning it in bible study) that God made us all the same and we are all a part of him. I realized that if I don't appreciate what God gave me, then that's an insult on Their parts. I would never want to insult Them, so from then on I saw myself as a beautiful creation of the love that God has for me. I haven't had the thought to complain ever since then.

This narrative illustrates how Black women organize the social order of their environments and respond emotionally when they do not fit into the upper class of the caste system based on Eurocentric standards of beauty. Magic rationalized the behavioral differences as a result of phenotype and expressed her anger about these rules. She identified the intra-racial conflicts based on skin and hair within Black communities. Magic used her spiritual beliefs to disrupt the psychological toll on her by seeing herself connected to a greater sense of creation. Through her spirituality, she shifted her vision of herself to be beautiful with her darker skin tone and textured hair.

Guided Hair Autobiography

The Guided Hair Autobiography (GHA; Mbilishaka, 2014) was developed to centralize hair in the lived experience of race. Here, there are less narrative prompts, but the purpose of the GHA is still to get participants to reflect on their experiences of hair that shape their identity. The prompts from this instrument include the earliest memory of hair, a nadir (low point) related to hair, and a turning point in how one thinks of hair. This is the language of the prompt for the earliest memory of hair:

> Every story begins somewhere and stories about your hair are no exception. Your earliest memory might be considered the beginning of your hair story. This may be an experience involving a family member doing your hair, your first trip to a salon or barbershop, or even being teased about your hair at school. Please think as far back in your life as you can. Choose from your distant memory what you consider to be your earliest childhood memory involving hair for which you are able to identify: what happened, who was involved, what you were thinking, and what you were feeling. Give us your best guess of your age at the time of the event. In addition, please speculate as to why this event is significant in your hair story and how it shaped you as an individual.

These narratives included a range of lived experiences related to hair. However, for the purposes of explaining aesthetic trauma, emotional experiences are included to provide evidence of the phenomenon.

> Some of the narratives were focused on the physical trauma of grooming Black hair:

> When I was about 7 or 8, my grandmother did my hair for the first time and it was TERRIBLE, she was really aggressive. I never allowed her to do my hair again. Every time I went around her my hair was already done so she wouldn't try to do it.

> It was not unusual to get a "smack" from the brush if you did not sit still.

> Getting burned with a hot comb by my mom and grandmother.

> Using the hot comb and having to hold your ear so it would not get burned and hearing the sizzle of the "grease" used to get the shine (along with the smell of the burning hair as the hot comb was placed back on the fire) are also part of my early memories.

> I remember always being afraid to get my hair wet when I was younger because I would get in trouble.

Other narratives included more of emotional pain related to hair.

> My mother had pressed (stretching hair in a combing motion with high heat) my hair for school but by the time recess was over it began to return to is natural state. As we were lining up to return into the school building, I reached the line before one of my male classmates who was upset that I got there before he did. In his anger he pushed me and called me a "nappy-headed little girl." I felt embarrassed, began to cry silently and wanted to die right then. This event served as another reinforcer for the idea that my hair was bad and that I had to make sure no matter what, that I keep it straight even if it meant destroying my hair and scalp.

> I was in high school. I was attempting not to straighten my hair as often, so I began to let my hair air dry in braid to achieve a wavy look. One night, I suppose that the braids were not fully dry, so the waves may have been a bit frizzy. I went to school with my hair half up- half down. One of my friends came up to me and said, "Okay we get it, you're black" and another said, "yes, your hair is looking a little nappy today." I remember being so embarrassed. It took so much effort to achieve that look and to be insulted in such a way where I was made to feel embarrassed about my natural curls prevented me from truly feeling comfortable in my own skin for a long time. I think that even today that statement affects me where I do not like to leave my apartment looking unkempt in any way.

And yet, some narratives indicated that through knowledge of the African Diaspora, it was possible to take a different stance regarding the acceptability of natural hair.

I went to Spelman. I took a class on the African Diaspora and decided to research and write a paper on the politics of black hair. After seeing ads for years telling black women that they owed it to themselves not have ugly nappy hair, and men tell women that their hair was their crown and glory. I felt like I didn't have to listen to the lies. I decided to take out my weave and cut off all my hair, which was processed.

Aesthetic Trauma Fueled Interventions

Mental health professionals and hair care professionals can code the thematic content and emotional tone of the hair narratives from a healing justice framework. Hair stories are internalized and may unconsciously be triggered in deciding how to interact with other Black people in daily life. In compliance with Eurocentric femininity and beauty standards of hair, about 70% of Black women chemically straighten their curly or tightly coiled natural hair textures or add false hair to the scalp to produce an appearance of a straight hair texture (Davis-Sivasthothy, 2011). This process can cause "hair stress," the psychological and physiological consequences of altering hair from its authentic state to one that is compliant with Eurocentric standards and anti-Black appearance (Winfield, 2008).

PsychoHairapy (Mbilishaka, 2018a) is a community-based therapeutic intervention to address the mental health needs of Black communities through hair care. There are several interventions included in this concept, such as training hair care professionals in basic counseling techniques, hosting workshops in the hair care space, facilitating group therapy in the hair care space, and providing psychoeducational materials in this setting. The narrative data about texturism can extend the scope of PsychoHairapy to be inclusive of techniques that focus on coping with discriminatory behaviors and prejudicial beliefs about Black women with tightly coiled hair.

Narrative therapy and group process (Mbilishaka, 2018b) are embedded within the code of using hair as an entry point into mental health services. The GHA can be used as a tool to elicit traumatic experiences from Black women that deserved to be verbalized and processed with a mental health professional. Black women have internalized evolving narratives of hair that can be further unpacked in a group space, where other women may have had the same experiences. Instead of infusing the self-concept with shame, the group processing of these hair stories of texturism may encourage critical analysis of a social system that would make these injustices so pervasive. It is unfortunate that it has become a statistical norm for Black women to be devalued by their hair texture, but systems of White supremacy and anti-Black racism must be attacked as a method to cope with the racial traumas (see DeGruy, 2005). Trained mental health professionals can use narrative therapy techniques of writing, externalizing, and re-authoring the story of racism within the hair care space (Mbilishaka, 2018b).

Hair stylists can be trained to collaborate with mental health professionals for interventions for Black girls and women (Ashley & Brown, 2015). Ashley and Brown (2015) identified the positive outcomes of talking during the professional hair care experience for Black female samples, where the physical touch and shift in appearance encouraged emotional release of past traumas. The hair care process that integrates mental health and hair grooming increases the feelings of attachment to other Black women (Ashley & Brown, 2015). This may also be the case when explicitly discussing experiences of texturism. Hair stylists who have expertise in working with tightly coiled hair can provide advice and support as women learn about and embrace their own hair textures. This forum may serve to effectively recapitulate the origin stories of texturism for these women.

The internet has been crucial in assisting Black women to cope with the challenges of wearing natural hair. Research scholars and educators have identified YouTube as a source of hair education for Black women (Alston & Ellis-Hervey, 2014). Black women intentionally flock to various websites and YouTube videos of Black women who also share their hair stories. These YouTube vlogs not only engage social cognitive learning and observational learning, but also provide detailed information on how to have healthy, tightly coiled hair through self-care techniques (Neil & Mbilishaka, in press).

This chapter framed hair narratives as a tool to process and heal from internalized racism, as manifested through texturism within Black communities. Further studies can enhance and inform techniques and strategies of healing from aesthetic trauma through hair care. Black women must continue to maintain their strong roots.

References

Afrika, L. (2013). *The complete textbook of holistic self diagnosis*. Holistic Therapies and Education Center.

Alston, G., & Ellis-Hervey, N. (2014). Exploring public pedagogy and the non-formal adult educator in 21st century contexts using qualitative video data analysis techniques. *Learning Media and Technology, 40*, 502–513. doi:10.1080/17439884. 2014.968168

Ashley, W., & Brown, J. (2015). Attachment tHAIRapy: A culturally relevant treatment paradigm for African American foster youth. *Journal of Black Studies, 46*(6), 587–604. https://doi.org/10.1177/0021934715590406

Beckwith, C., & Fisher, A. (1999). *African ceremonies*. Harry Abrams.

Burford, T., & Winston, C. (2005). The guided race autobiography. Washington, DC: The Identity and Success Research Lab, Howard University. [Data collection instrument]

Brooks, K. (2017, December 6). This is the last generation of scarification in Africa. *Huffington Post*. https://www.huffpost.com/entry/scarification_n_5850882

Byrd, A., & Tharps, L. (2014). *Hair story: Untangling the roots of Black hair in America*. St. Martin's Press.

Capodilupo, C. M. (2015). One size does not fit all: Using variables other than the thin ideal to understand Black women's body image. *Cultural Diversity and Ethnic Minority Psychology, 21*, 268–278.

DeGruy, J. (2005). *Post Traumatic Slave Syndrome: America's legacy of enduring injury and healing*. Joy DeGruy Publications.

Garve, R., Garve, M., Turp, J., Fobil, J., & Meyes, C. (2017). Scarification in sub-Saharan Africa: Social skin, remedy and medical import. *A European Journal of Tropical Medicine & International Health, 22*(6), 708–715.

Graham, J., & Kligman, A. (1985). *The psychology of cosmetic treatments*. ABC-CLIO.

Johnson, J. H., Jr., Farrell, W. C., Jr., & Stoloff, J. A. (1998). The declining social and economic fortunes of African American males: A critical assessment of four perspectives. *Review of Black Political Economy, 25*(4), 17–40.

Johnson, T. A., & Bankhead, T. (2014). Hair it is: Examining the experiences of Black women with natural hair. *Open Journal of Social Sciences, 2*, 86–100.

Keith, V., & Herring, C. (1991). Skin tone and stratification in the Black community. *American Journal of Sociology, 97*(3), 760–778.

Krieger, N., Sidney, S., & Coakley, E. (1998). Racial discrimination and skin color in the CARDIA Study: Implications for public health research. *American Journal of Public Health, 88*(9), 1308–1313.

Lewis, M. L. (1999). Hair combing interactions: A new paradigm for research with African American mothers. *American Journal of Orthopsychiatry, 69*, 504–514.

Lucas, A. (1930). Cosmetics, perfumes and incense in Ancient Egypt. *The Journal of Egyptian Archaeology, 16*(1/2), 41–53. https://www.jstor.org/stable/3854332

Magubane, Z. (2007, April 12). Why 'nappy' is offensive. *The Boston Globe.* https://www.commondreams.org/views/2007/04/12/why-nappy-offensive

Mangum, A. M., & Woods, A. (2011). "Psychohairapy": Integrating psychology, public health, and beauty shop talk [Presentation]. 43rd Annual Association of Black Psychologists Convention, Crystal City, VA.

Mbilishaka, A. M. (2014). *The guided hair autobiography* [Data collection instrument]. PsychoHairapy Research Lab, Department of Psychology, Howard University.

Mbilishaka, A. M. (2018a). PsychoHairapy: Using hair as an entry point into Black women's spiritual and mental health. *Meridians: Feminism, Race & Transnationalism, 16*(2), 382–392.

Mbilishaka, A. M. (2018b). Black Lives (and stories) Matter: Race narrative therapy in Black hair care spaces. *Community Psychology in Global Perspective, 4*(2), 22–33.

Mbilishaka, A. (2018c). Strands of Intimacy: Black Women's Narratives of Hair and Intimate Relationships with Men. *Journal of Black Sexuality and Relationships*, 5(1), 43-61.

Mbilishaka, A., & Apugo, D. (2020). Brushed aside: African American women's narratives of hair bias in school. *Race, Ethnicity and Education, 23*, 634–653. http://dx.doi.org/10.1080/13613324.2020.1718075

Mbilishaka, A. M. & Haileab, L. (February 2017). Aesthetic Trauma: Narrating Beauty Myths Within the Lives of Black Women. Presented at the Winter Roundtable on Cultural Psychology. New York, NY.

McAdams, D. P. (1997). The guided autobiography. [Data collection instrument]. Evanston, IL: Foley Center for the Study of Lives, School of Education and Social Policy, Northwestern University.

McGill Johnson, A., Godsil, R. D., MacFarlane, J., Tropp, L. R., & Atiba Goff, P. (2017). *The "Good Hair" Study: Explicit and implicit attitudes toward Black women's hair.* The Perception Institute. https://perception.org/wp-content/uploads/2017/01/TheGood-HairStudyFindingsReport.pdf

Monk, E. P. (2014). Skin tone stratification among Black Americans, 2001–2003. *Social Forces, 92*(4), 1313–1337. https://doi.org/10.1093/sf/sou007

Morrow, W. (1990). *400 years without a comb.* Black Publishers of San Diego.

Neil, L. & Mbilishaka, A. (2019). "Hey Curlfriends!": Hair Care and Self-Care Messaging on YouTube by Black Women Natural Hair Vloggers. *Journal of Black Studies*, 50 (2), 156–177.

Rooks, N. (1996). *Hair raising: Beauty, culture and African American women.* Rutgers University Press.

Rosette, A. S., & Dumas, T. L. (2007). The hair dilemma: Conform to mainstream expectations or emphasize racial identity. *Duke Journal of Gender Law & Policy, 14*(1), 407–421.

Sherrow, V. (2006). *Encyclopedia of hair: A cultural history.* Greenwood Press.

Some, M. (1997). *Ritual: Power, healing and community.* Penguin Putnam.

Van der Kolk, B. A. (2015). The body keeps the score: brain, mind, and body in the healing of trauma. New York, New York: Penguin Books.Walker, R. (2011). When we ruled: The ancient and medieaval history of Black civilisations. Black Classic Press.

Wilson, I., Mbilishaka, A., & Lewis, M. (2018). "White folks ain't got hair like us": African American Mother-Daughter Hair Stories and Racial Socialization. *Women, Gender, and Families of Color*, 6(2), 226–248.

Winston, C .E., Rice, D. W., Bradshaw, B. J., Lloyd, D., Harris, L. T., Burford, T. I., Clodimir, G., Kizzie, K., Carothers, K. J., McClair, V., & Burrell, J. (2004). Science success, narrative theories of personality, and race self complexity: Is race represented in the identity construction of African American adolescents? *New Directions for Child and Adolescent Development, 106*, 55–77.

Reading 2.5. Jezebel's Legacy

The Development of African American Heterosexual Girls' Emerging Sexuality in the Context of Oppressive Images and the Armoring Influence of Mother–Daughter Relationships

Tiffany G. Townsend and Anita Jones Thomas

Following the historic election of Madame Vice President Kamala Harris, America's first African American, first Asian American, and first woman of any race/ethnicity to the nation's second highest seat in the land, America continues to struggle with the remnants of slavery manifested through an intersecting system of oppression, including but not limited to racial subjugation and sexual discrimination. It is within this societal structure that African American girls must develop a healthy view of themselves as women, even when prevailing images of Black women in mainstream culture are negative (Jones & Shorter-Gooden, 2003; Ward, 2002). Some scholars have suggested that these negative, frequently hypersexual images of African American girls/women not only may influence the way in which African American girls view themselves but also may shape the way others value and appreciate their sexuality (Stephens & Phillips, 2003). In other words, the objectification of African American girls and women as purely sexual beings may encourage others to exploit them merely for the purpose of gratifying their sexual desires, creating an environment in which sexual coercion and rape are much more likely to occur.

According to the Centers for Disease Control and Prevention (CDC, 2006a), African American adolescent girls report higher rates of involuntary first intercourse than their European American and Latina counterparts. In a study of African American girls ages 14–17, Teitelman et al. (2011) found that 59% of these girls reported having experienced some form of sexual abuse in their lives. The reported abuse included threats, verbal coercion, condom coercion, and physical violence. In fact, Teitelman and her colleagues (2011) suggest it is this environment of coercion and abuse that is contributing to the alarmingly high rates of STIs among this population.

In 2004, African American adolescent girls ages 10–14 and 15–19 were more likely to be infected with chlamydia and gonorrhea than their White counterparts (CDC, 2005a). In 2009, African American adolescents accounted for 65% of newly diagnosed cases of HIV infection among the 13–24 age group (CDC, 2011), while African American adolescent girls and young women ages 15–24 accounted for 70% of the HIV diagnoses among girls and women in this age group (CDC, 2006b). Importantly, the increase in HIV infection among African American women and girls can largely be attributed to heterosexual contact (CDC, 2005b). These statistics suggest that the sexual development and subsequent heterosexual behavior of African American girls can pose a serious threat to their health and overall well-being. It therefore becomes increasingly important to understand the factors that influence the sexual development of this population.

Using a framework of intersectionality and Black feminist thought, this chapter explores some of the experiences and contextual influences that help to shape the ways in which heterosexual African American girls view themselves and come to understand their emerging sexuality. Special attention is given to the sexual socialization process that occurs between African American girls and their mothers, as mothers have been identified as one of the chief sexual socialization agents of their daughters. In addition, the chapter concludes with a discussion of critical interventions recommended to foster the development of healthy sexuality among African American girls. Although this chapter focuses on the influence of stereotypes and emphasizes the role that mothers play in helping to protect African American girls against this form of societal denigration, this analysis is not intended to imply that societal stereotypes and negative images are the only, or even most important, contextual factor that affects African American girls' developing sexuality. Instead, it is intended to highlight one way in which the intersection of racism, sexism, and frequently classism is manifested and experienced in the lives of many inner-city heterosexual African American girls as they are developing into sexual beings.

Intersectionality as a Framework for the Developing Sexuality of African American Girls

Examinations of the social experiences of any oppressed group, particularly groups with multiple social identities (e.g., inner-city, heterosexual African American girls), have a tendency to compartmentalize their experiences into discrete categories (e.g., racism vs. sexism vs. classism). This can lead to sweeping generalizations and/ or essentialism, in which certain characteristics are thought to be inherently race-, class-, or gender-based (Stewart & McDermott, 2004; Williams, 2005). Additionally, essentialist approaches often produce limited views of social groups that do not reflect the diversity within groups or the complexities of real life. In reality, lived experiences are much richer than a one-dimensional category can capture. As a response to the distortions that can result from this approach, feminist theorists have proposed an alternative framework: intersectionality (Collins, 1996, 2000; Guy-Sheftall, 1995; Harvey, 2005; Simien & Clawson, 2004). These theorists assert that we must analyze the social structure in which experience takes place (Collins, 2000; Stewart & McDermott, 2004). The framework of intersectionality maintains that social experiences are shaped by the intersection of multiple systems of oppression, organized along axes of race, class, gender, sexuality, ethnicity, nation, and age (Collins, 1998, 2000). The interplay of these systems creates a distinct standpoint unduplicated by any other group.

The Collective Standpoint of Oppression and the Legacy of Slavery

For African American women and girls, the legacy of slavery and their unique experience of oppression in this country have produced stereotypes and images that negatively impact the ways in which African American girls/women are viewed and valued by others (Stephens & Phillips, 2005). Jezebel, one of the most overtly sexual images of Black women that have emerged, is perceived as seductive, manipulative, and unable to control her sex drive (Mitchell & Herring, 1998; West, 1995). Jezebel's legacy includes the current images of the "welfare queen" who is promiscuous, loose, immoral, and lacking in sexual restraint; her many children are a physical manifestation of her inability to control her sexual behaviors (Bell, 1992; Collins, 2000; Daniel, 2000; Greene, 1994, 1997). In direct opposition to the highly sexual Jezebel image is the image of the asexual mammy who worked in the master's house, often serving as nanny, housekeeper, and cook (Mitchell & Herring, 1998; West, 1995), and was forced to provide custodial and sometimes emotional care for her oppressors. Mark Anthony Neal (2009), a professor of African and African American Studies at Duke University, identifies Oprah Winfrey as a post-modern permutation of the mammy image, catering to her primarily White middle-class audience in the same way that mammies were made to care for and serve White families. Finally, the Sapphire image—based on a character named Sapphire from the *Amos 'n' Andy* radio and television show in the 1940s and 1950s—portrayed a woman who took pleasure in emasculating men. Instead of representing the passive, supportive image that described femininity and feminine sexuality at the time, Sapphire was seen as loud, crude, callous, argumentative, and full of verbal assaults (Mitchell & Herring, 1998; West, 1995). Sapphire's sexual power seemed to come from emasculating men, again in direct opposition to the supportive feminine ideal of the time. Interestingly, African American women continue to be bound by the chains of Sapphire's image, as Black women are constantly depicted in the media as "angry." Even America's former First Lady Michelle Obama has occasionally fallen victim to the "angry Black woman" stereotype in mainstream media, particularly as she was portrayed in Kantor's (2012) book, *The Obamas*.

Although more positive images and role models for African American women are beginning to emerge, the stereotypes described above simply mutate with the time, creating modern versions that are hard for African American girls/women to escape (Collins, 1991). Many of the contemporary images that resonate with African American girls and young women are influenced by hip-hop culture and often have a very strong sexual connotation (Stephens & Few, 2007). Townsend et al. (2010) found that historical images of African American women were perceived differently by African American adolescent girls. Using the Black Girl Perception Scale (BGPS), a modified version of the Stereotypic Roles of Black Women Scale (Thomas et al., 2004), Townsend and her colleagues conducted a factor analysis, which revealed a one-factor structure. The factor, which they termed "Modern Jezebel," was internally consistent, suggesting that the scale measured a reliable construct that seems to be most relevant to this age group.

The construct tapped aspects of both the Jezebel and Sapphire stereotypes. Girls who endorsed the Modern Jezebel stereotype believed that Black girls are highly sexual, while also being quite aggressive and even combative. In other words, endorsers of the Modern Jezebel subscale believed that Black girls used sex and a combative, controlling attitude to get their needs met. In addition, endorsement of this stereotype was found to be associated with attitudes tolerant of risky sexual behaviors among African America girls (Townsend et al., 2010). Although there is not a one-to-one association, this Modern Jezebel image closely aligns with the "Freak" and "Gangster Bitch" stereotypes, as outlined by Stephens and Phillips (2003). The Freak is a sexually aggressive woman who gets enjoyment out of sex, and can have sex (often high-risk sex) without any emotional attachment. The Gangster Bitch may also be sexual, but her most defining characteristics are her aggression and survival attitude. She is seen as tough, cold-blooded, and willing to fight to the death if necessary, especially in support of her "man."

Given the strong connection between sexual desire and physical appearance, it is not surprising that many of the stereotypic images of African American women not only have strong sexual connotations, but also often present physical depictions, which provide implicit messages about the characteristics that are considered desirable. For instance, Jezebel, similar to Stephens and Phillips's (2003) Diva, is often depicted as a "mulatto" woman, with light skin, a slim build, and long hair (Collins, 1998), in contrast to Mammy, an obese, dark-skinned woman with broad features (Mitchell and Herring, 1998; West, 1995). The implicit message is the light-skinned Jezebel (or Diva) is considered sexually desirable, while the dark-skinned Mammy is not. Skin-color stratification, in which African Americans who are aesthetically closer to White are considered more desirable, has been termed "colorism" (Okazawa-Rey et al., 1987). As appearance often plays a central role in the evaluation of women, the effect of colorism on self-esteem and well-being is stronger for African American girls and women than for their male counterparts (Thompson & Keith, 2001). Societal messages and media images that emphasize the appearance of women and girls are thought to foster self-objectification among adolescent girls and women (Gordon, 2008). This could lead girls to believe that their value and self-worth is a function of their appearance and sex appeal (Gordon, 2008). For African American girls, self-objectification may be manifested in a preference for physical characteristics that they believe will be judged more favorably (e.g., lighter skin, longer hair, keen features, fine hair texture, etc.). This preference may pose a particular risk for African American girls who may not conform to this standard. For instance, Wingood et al. (2002) found that African American girls who judged their physical appearance negatively felt they had less personal control regarding condom use and choice of sexual partners. Thus, African American girls who adopt standards consistent with "colorism" may judge their physical appearance too harshly and may adopt risky behaviors to be seen as sexually attractive/desirable.

Stereotypic Images and African American Girls' Emerging Sexuality

According to Sinclair et al. (2006), continual exposure to stereotypes may influence a person's self-evaluation and ultimately her behavior. In other words, a phenomenon referred to as self-stereotyping can occur, in which a person can begin to behave in ways consistent with stereotypes judged to be most salient to her social identity. Since the sexuality of African American girls may be influenced by media depictions of African American women, the sexual identity of African American girls may include vestiges of negative stereotypes, which can devalue their aesthetic beauty and their sexual power (Stephens & Phillips, 2003). For African American girls, images that portray Black women as sexually promiscuous, amoral, and overbearing can foster the development of negative self-schemas and risky sexual scripts (Stephens & Phillips, 2003).

Scripts are a type of schema, used to help construct meaning out of behavior, responses, and emotions. In the sexual domain, the scripts provide a guide for sexual behavior, including how to appropriately interpret and respond to sexual cues (Wiederman, 2005). When individuals feel anxious and uncomfortable, or lack confidence and efficacy in their ability, the reliance on scripts to help direct behavior is high (Weiderman, 2005). Consequently, adolescents, who are just beginning to experiment with sexual behavior and develop a sexual identity, rely heavily on sexual scripts. Accordingly, images that stem from an intersecting system of oppression (Collins, 2000) send messages to African American girls about how they should look and behave in order to be deemed desirable in sexual situations, and as girls progress toward womanhood, being seen as sexually desirable is extremely important for their identity development. In truth, it is difficult for most African American girls to conform to the narrowly defined standard of beauty that has emerged from "colorism" in the Black community, and the images of African American girls/women perpetuated in society present gender roles that are confining. Those girls who endorse stereotypic roles may be more likely to report attitudes and behaviors in the sexual domain that are consistent with those stereotypes.

In the most extreme cases, Black women [Black girls] who don't feel good about themselves, who feel pressure to fulfill traditional gender roles by being passive and submissive, or who feel that they must give up parts of themselves in order to secure and keep a male partner may put themselves at risk for emotional abuse, violence, and even HIV infection. (Jones & Shorter-Gooden, 2003, p. 9)

Clearly, the ways in which African American girls view themselves, their sexuality, and their role as emerging women have definite behavioral implications.

Equally powerful in shaping African American girls' sexual scripts are societal images of African American men, who have also been portrayed as animalistic and highly sexual, as well as lazy, irresponsible, abusive, inherently criminal, and sexist (Smith, 2001). After years of exposure to negative images, many African American women and men may begin to believe these stereotypes and to incorporate the myths into their opinions of each other, without understanding the racist structure that these stereotypes were developed to support (Boyd-Franklin, 2006; Smith, 2001). For instance, African American men can start to believe that African American women are domineering, sexually demanding, and competitive, while African American women can begin to believe that African American men are undependable, chauvinistic, and abusive, creating mutual distrust and divisiveness between the sexes. Instead of viewing each other as allies, African American women and men can begin to perceive each other as adversaries (Boyd-Franklin, 2006), causing some African American women to feel that they must confront negative images not only from external society but also from within their own romantic relationships.

Is There Truth in the Stereotype? The Use of Stereotypic Behaviors as a Coping Strategy

In response, many African American girls/women feel that they must appear strong, tough, resilient, and self-sufficient (Shorter-Gooden & Jackson, 2000) in order to withstand these racist and sexist forces. However, due to the Sapphire or "angry Black woman" stereotype, others may misinterpret African American girls'/women's strength and fortitude as aggression and hostility, or misinterpret their self-sufficiency as emotional distance. Accordingly, girls who internalize Sapphire may develop into women who have difficulty expressing their needs or displaying anger comfortably. They may believe that being loud, aggressive, or full of rage is the only way to be heard or taken seriously (Mitchell & Herring, 1998; West, 1995), so they may use anger and other externalizing behaviors (such as sexual acting out) to cope when problems arise (West, 1995). In a similar vein, African American girls' internalization of the Jezebel stereotype may lead them to become women who perceive sexuality as one of their few assets (West, 1995). In an attempt to have more control, some girls may decide to use their sexuality as a means to get their needs met. In fact, some female performers in the hip-hop industry have suggested that profiting from their sexuality can be empowering. Instead of allowing their sexuality to be exploited by men, these women are finding power in using their sexuality to control men (Steffans, 2005). In reality, this professed control is tenuous, and it only further supports the perception that African American women are sexually demanding, overbearing, and manipulative.

In these instances, African American girls may develop behaviors consistent with certain stereotypes, as a defense and in an attempt to protect their emotional well-being from potentially damaging societal effects. However, coping strategies that result from these stereotypes frequently foster maladaptive behaviors (e.g., risky sexual behavior, interpersonal conflicts, etc.) and may place these girls at risk for other problems down the road. Yet many African American girls are exposed to these stereotypical images/messages and never develop maladaptive behaviors in response, likely due to protective influences in their environment.

Armoring: The Protective Influence of African American Mothers

Since the African American mother is often the primary parental figure in the home, she frequently has been cited as the most important person to assist her daughter in facing adulthood (Stevens, 2002) and coping with the negative messages often directed at African American girls (Turnage, 2004). Indeed, many African American mothers devote a considerable amount of energy attempting to buffer, defend, and fortify their girls against external societal assaults in addition to within-group prejudices, even while struggling against these forces themselves (Jones & Shorter-Gooden, 2003). In other words, African American mothers are attempting to "armor" their daughters against racial and sexual oppression (Edmondson Bell & Nkomoa, 1998), thereby helping to reduce the negative consequences of this oppression on their girls.

Armoring is a socialization process through which African American mothers teach their daughters psychological resistance to racism and sexism (Greene, 1990). African American mothers assume a defensive stance when socializing their daughters, as the socialization process serves a necessary protective function for African American girls. In addition to learning self-esteem-protecting strategies, African American girls become aware of their mother's attitudes and beliefs concerning sexuality. It is through the armoring process that African American girls begin to learn how to view themselves not only as women but also as Black women in the context of romantic, familial, communal, and societal relationships.

Social learning theory asserts that girls receive implicit and explicit messages concerning gender roles and get the most rewarding incentives for imitating their mothers' gendered behavior (Reid & Bing, 2000). In other words, mothers influence their children's internalization of values and behaviors directly through instruction and indirectly through modeling (Tinsely et al., 2004). The process of gendered socialization begins long before adolescence (Fox, 1980). Among African American families, mothers train their daughters toward independence, self-sufficiency, and survival by assigning household chores and caretaking responsibilities for younger siblings at a fairly early age (Hill, 2002). In addition, through exposure to mothers, grandmothers, and other female relatives who are often the sole provider for the family, African American adolescent girls learn implicitly that survival of the family is often the responsibility of women. So while African American mothers fully expect that their daughters will develop romantic relationships with African American men, they socialize their daughters through implicit and explicit messages that they should not be dependent on African American men for survival (Joseph & Lewis, 1981).

Regarding sexual socialization, researchers have found that African American mothers who openly discuss sexual issues with their daughters often use storytelling as a means to communicate about sexuality and to facilitate armoring (Nwoga, 2000; Pluhar & Kuriloff, 2004). While direct instruction and explicit socialization messages are important, the indirect means of transmitting values often receive less attention.

By employing esteem-enhancing strategies in their own lives (i.e., setting and achieving goals, treating themselves lovingly, refusing to own unhealthy images of womanhood), African American mothers can help their daughters develop a stronger sense of self and a healthier view of Black women (Turnage, 2004). Similarly, African American girls who witness their mothers in a loving, egalitarian relationship develop a schema for healthy romantic relationships in their own lives (Jones & Shorter-Gooden, 2003). Through observations of their mothers' behavior in romantic relationships, girls learn how to interact with and relate to their own partners. This also suggests that mothers who struggle with self-efficacy and poor communication in their own partner relationships will have daughters who are less effective in negotiating sexual situations with their partners. By modeling healthy behavior in romantic relationships, mothers may help girls adopt positive tools for practicing safe sex, establishing healthy relationships, and communicating with their partners (Brakefield et al., 2012).

Armoring in Context: African American Mother–Daughter Relationships

It is important to note that the relationship between African American mothers and daughters is complex and can be quite intense (Collins, 1991). It is normal for adolescents to struggle with the development of independence from parents during these years, and African American adolescent girls are no different. According to a qualitative study of African American early adolescents, Stevens (1997) indicated that most girls found maternal monitoring and supervision unnecessary. Instead, they would have preferred their mothers to recognize their developmental changes and acknowledge their entrance into womanhood with increased independence. Unfortunately, the living conditions of many of these families prompted fear in the mothers for their daughters' safety. Unsure of the fate that could befall their daughters in neighborhoods that were fraught with crime, community violence, and drug use, many mothers responded with increased monitoring and strict supervision (Stevens, 1997). Thus, given the living conditions of many inner-city communities, some African American girls may be given double messages. On one hand, they are socialized to be responsible and self-sufficient in order to fight the oppressive conditions of being a Black woman in America. On the other hand, their mothers often feel the need to be overly protective in order to shield these girls from the crime, violence, and other dangers that often develop in oppressed communities (Collins, 1989). This can result in a fairly tense relationship. The focus on survival means that some African American mothers may make protection more critical than affection. Their mothering can be perceived as harsh, resulting in a mother–daughter relationship that can seem antagonistic and emotionally intense. As cited in Collins (1991), feminist scholar Rosalie Troester eloquently describes the complexity and sometimes intensity of the Black mother–daughter relationship in her article "Turbulence and Tenderness":

> Black mothers, particularly those with strong ties to their community, sometimes build high banks around their young daughters, isolating them from the dangers of the larger world until they are old and strong enough to function as autonomous women. Often these dikes are religious, but sometimes they are built with education, family or the restrictions of a close knit and homogenous community. … This isolation causes the currents between Black mothers and daughters to run deep and the relationship to be fraught with an emotional intensity often missing from the lives of women with more freedom. (Collins, 1991, p. 55)

The protective or defensive stance assumed by African American mothers in the armoring process, particularly in the sexual domain, may create a schism in the mother–daughter relationship, and may foster feelings of shame and secrecy among adolescent girls regarding sexual issues. In an effort to prevent the sexual victimization of their daughters, some African American mothers may explicitly or implicitly relay the message that their daughters should not discuss issues that will call attention to their sexuality (Warren-Jeanpiere, 2006). So, while adolescent girls may be engaging in age-appropriate sexual experimentation, they may also receive a contradictory message that sex is not worthy of discussion. As a result, they may not develop a healthy appreciation for their sexuality, or learn to honor their beauty as sexual beings (Kelly, 2001). Instead, they may learn avoidance as a strategy for dealing with their emerging sexuality, resulting in critical sexual health issues receiving limited discussion or consideration. In the midst of so many competing and often damaging sexual messages, those girls who have limited sexual knowledge or who lack the ability to critically analyze information in the sexual health arena are left vulnerable to sexual risks.

Based on the aforementioned literature, it is clear that mother–daughter relationships and the armoring process play a significant role in the development of African American girls. However, the quality of the mother–daughter relationship has significant implications regarding the effectiveness of this socialization process. Although some degree of conflict is normative, frequent conflicts that contribute to a pervasive climate of hostility and mutual distrust in the mother–daughter relationship can significantly increase a girl's risk, particularly if they contribute to the girl's alienation from the family and increase her affiliation with deviant peers (Dishion et al., 1995). The emotional complexity experienced in the relationship between some African American daughters and their biological mothers highlights the importance of what Collins (1997) has termed the community "othermother."

Community Armoring: The Influence of Othermothers

Historically, the experience of slavery and later economic limitations required that African American women share their mothering responsibilities with other women in the family, neighborhood, or community. As a result, the role of community othermother is central to African American motherhood, and othermothers are often as important to the socialization of African American girls as biological or "bloodmothers" (Collins, 1997). Because they are not directly responsible for the survival of the adolescent girl, these othermothers are available to offset the emotional intensity, and sometimes provide the affection or open communication, that may be lacking in the bloodmother–daughter relationship (Collins, 1991).

Sister circles that include othermothers, among other networks of women, offer a "safe space" for African American women to freely express their thoughts and feelings, while providing a vehicle for women to mentor the younger generation (Collins, 2000). According to Collins (1998), knowledge and critical lessons learned from the collective experience of oppression are often shared among African American women through their relationships with each other, frequently in these protective circles or networks. For African American women, relationships that develop out of shared experiences, mutual empathy, and supportive listening are very therapeutic and quite powerful (Jenkins, 1996). In the past, these circles emerged naturally and often informally, but urbanization and the internalization of mainstream values such as individualism among the African American community have limited the use of this very effective socialization tool. For girls who may not have a healthy relationship with their bloodmother for various reasons (e.g., mother is physically unavailable due to incarceration or social service intervention, or emotionally unavailable due to mental illness, substance use, or neglect, etc.), these circles are critical.

It is important to acknowledge that not all circles of women are therapeutic. The internalization of society's negative images of African American women and men has introduced a divisive element into the African American community. African American girls/women who internalize these stereotypes can become suspicious, mistrustful, and competitive with each other, creating an atmosphere that is less than therapeutic, and sometimes even destructive. But, in the safest of these sister circles, African American women can let down their guard and not feel it necessary to defend their blackness or their womanhood, fostering an environment in which mutual healing can occur. In this way, othermothers and concomitant sister circles can provide the emotional seal to the armoring process, facilitating the healthy development of African American girls' emerging sexuality.

Fostering Healthy Sexual Identity Among African American Girls: Conclusions and Implications

Scholars who examine sexuality and corresponding sexual behavior among African American girls have found evidence that African American girls not only are aware of stereotypic images of African American girls/women in the media (Stephens & Phillips, 2003; Stephens & Few, 2007) but also may be negatively influenced by these images (Townsend et al., 2010). In fact, there is evidence that some populations of African American girls/women may actually use these images and their associated behaviors as a protective strategy to cope with societal denigration. Stephens and Phillips (2003) contend that the over-sexualized stereotypes of African American girls/women propagated in broader society have helped to shape the perception of African American girls' sexuality. These images influence the ways in which African American girls view themselves as well as the ways in which others appreciate and interact with them, possibly contributing to the negative sexual health statistics and the high rates of sexual victimization experienced among this population (Stephens & Phillips, 2005).

While an obvious solution would be for society to produce less-stereotypical images for adolescent girls' consumption, this is probably not a realistic solution given the enormous economic gain that results from the production of these images. Instead, interventions aimed at reducing sexual risk and promoting healthy sexual development among African American girls should address the influence and impact of stereotypes and colorism. An intervention that can help a girl understand the influence of environmental factors (e.g., discrimination, racially charged gendered stereotypes, colorism, etc.), while enhancing her self-esteem and cultural appreciation, will likely provide a strong foundation for the development and maintenance of healthy sexual behaviors and responsible sexual decisions. In addition, the buffering effects of families and communities must be incorporated as well.

The armoring process of African American mothers has been identified as a critical factor in the healthy functioning (Jones & Shorter-Gooden, 2003) and sexual development of African American girls. For the most part, armoring serves a protective function. But because African American mothers are often dealing with their own struggles, it is not uncommon for stereotypes and negative images to seep through and permeate this process, highlighting the importance of othermothers and female relatives to the armoring process. Thus, interventions that include aspects of the armoring process may be most beneficial for African American girls. Although every aspect of the process may not be positive, there are several factors identified in this chapter that can and should be included in risk-prevention interventions. Specifically, the creation of sister circles or safe spaces for African American mothers and daughters to share their experiences, particularly in relation to sexual issues, should be encouraged in African American communities. It may also help to increase their relevance and subsequent effectiveness if these interventions incorporate mothers and their culturally specific socialization methods, such as encouraging balanced gender roles among girls and fostering the use of oral tradition and storytelling in communication about sexual issues. For example, Nwoga (2000) found that mothers who relayed sexual education through age-appropriate stories about their own sexual experiences were able to engage and effectively communicate with their daughters concerning sex and safer-sex practices. This culturally congruent storytelling strategy can be incorporated into an intervention and taught to participating mothers. In addition, interventions that include African American mothers should be mindful of the defensive stance used in the armoring process and its historical and protective significance. Programs that help African American mothers achieve open communication about sexuality with their daughters while maintaining their protective stance may be most successful at keeping mothers engaged and involved.

Finally, an important implication of this analysis is that intervention programs should begin incorporating mothers into programs at several different levels. In addition to acting as sex educators, as mothers are beginning to do in some programs, we contend that mothers should also serve as program participants, receiving developmentally appropriate and culturally congruent esteem- and skill-building strategies similar in content and purpose to the information their daughters receive. As previously mentioned, mothers who are struggling with low self-esteem, overly restricted gender roles, and an inability to exert personal control in their romantic relationships are likely to socialize their daughters to evidence similar difficulties. Therefore, it would be important for participating mothers to evidence a healthy appreciation for their own sexuality in order to serve as models for their girls' sexual development.

References

Bell, E. L. (1992). Myths, stereotypes, and realities of Black women: A personal reflection. *Journal of Applied Behavioral Science*, *28*, 363–376.

Boyd-Franklin, N. (2006). *Black families in therapy: Understanding the African American experience.* Guilford.

Brakefield, T., Wilson, H., & Donenberg, G. (2012). Maternal models of risk: Links between substance use and risky sexual behavior in African American female caregivers and daughters. *Journal of Adolescence*, *35*(4), 959–968.

Centers for Disease Control and Prevention. (2005a). *Sexually transmitted disease surveillance, 2004*. U.S. Department of Health and Human Services. https://www.cdc.gov/std/stats/archive/2004SurveillanceAll.pdf

Centers for Disease Control and Prevention. (2005b). *HIV/AIDS surveillance in women* [Slide series]. Retrieved July 3, 2006, from http://www.cdc.gov/hiv/topics/surveillance/resources/slides/women/index.htm

Centers for Disease Control and Prevention. (2006a). Youth risk behavior surveillance—United States 2005. Surveillance Summaries. *MMWR*, *55*(SS05), 1–108. https://www.cdc.gov/mmwr/preview/mmwrhtml/ss5505a1.htm

Centers for Disease Control and Prevention. (2006b). Racial/ethnic disparities in diagnoses of HIV/AIDS—33 states, 2001–2004. *MMWR*, *55*(5), 121–125. https://pubmed.ncbi.nlm.nih.gov/16467777/

Centers for Disease Control and Prevention. (2011). *HIV among youth.* National Center for HIV/AIDS, Viral Hepatitis, STD, and TB Prevention: Division of HIV/AIDS Prevention. Retrieved September 12, 2012, from http://www.cdc.gov/hiv/youth/index.htm

Collins, P. H. (1989). The social construction of Black feminist thought. *Sign*, *14*(4), 745–773.

Collins, P. H. (1991). The meaning of motherhood in Black culture and Black mother/daughter relationships. In P. Bell Scott et. al. (Eds.), *Double stitch: Black women write about mothers and daughters* (pp. 42–60). Beacon Press.

Collins, P. H. (1997). The meaning of motherhood in Black culture and Black mother/daughter relationships. In M. M. Gergen & S. N. Davis (Eds.), *Toward a new psychology of gender* (pp. 325–340). Routledge.

Collins, P. H. (1998). Intersections of race, class, gender, and nation: Some implications for Black family studies. *Journal of Comparative Family Studies*, *29*(1), 27–36.

Collins, P. H. (2000). *Black feminist thought: Knowledge, consciousness, and the politics of empowerment* (2nd ed.). Routledge.Daniel, J. H. (2000). The courage to hear: African American women's memories of racial trauma. In L. C. Jackson & B. Greene (Eds.), *Psychotherapy with African American women: Innovations in psychodynamic perspectives* (pp. 126–144). Guilford.

Dishion, T. J., French, D. C., & Patterson, G. R. (1995). The development and ecology of antisocial behavior. In D. Cicchetti & D. J. Cohen (Eds.), *Developmental psychopathology* (pp. 421–471). John Wiley & Sons.

Edmondson Bell, E. L., & Nkomoa, S. M. (1998). Armoring: Learning to withstand racial oppression. *Journal of Comparative Family Studies*, *29*(2), 285–295.

Fox, G. L. (1980). The mother-adolescent daughter relationship as a sexual socialization structure: A research review. *Family Relations*, *29*(1), 21–28.

Gordon, M. K. (2008). Media contributions to African American girls' focus on beauty and appearance: Exploring the consequences of sexual objectification. *Psychology of Women Quarterly*, *32*(3), 245–256. https://doi.org/10.1111/j.1471-6402.2008.00433.x

Greene, B. A. (1990). What has gone before: The legacy of racism and sexism in the lives of Black mothers and daughters. *Women & Therapy*, *9*(1–2), 207–230.

Greene, B. (1994). African American women. In L. Comas-Diaz and B. Greene (Eds.), *Women of color: Integrating ethnic and gender identities in psychotherapy* (pp. 10–29). Guilford.

Greene, B. (1997). Psychotherapy with African American women: Integrating feminist and psychodynamic models. *Smith College Studies in Social Work*, *67*, 299–322.

Guy-Sheftall, B. (1995). *Words of fire.* New York Press.

Harvey, A. M. (2005). Becoming entrepreneurs: Intersections of race, class, and gender at the Black Beauty Salon. *Gender & Society*, *19*(6), 789–808.

Hill, S. A. (2002). Teaching and doing gender in African American families. *Sex Roles: A Journal of Research*, *47*, 493–506.

Jenkins, S. Y. (1996). Psychotherapy and Black female identity conflicts. *Women and Therapy*, *18*, 59–74.

Jones, C., & Shorter-Gooden, K. (2003). *Shifting: The double lives of Black women*. HarperCollins.

Joseph, G.I. & Lewis, J. (1981). Common Differences: Conflicts in Black and White Feminist *Perspectives*. Doubleday & Co., Anchor Press.

Kelly, E. M. (2001). Female, young, African American and low income: What's feminism got to do with her? *Feminism & Psychology*, *11*(2), 152–156.

Mitchell, A., & Herring, K. (1998). *What the blues is: Black women overcoming stress and depression.* Perigee.

Neal, M. A. (2009). Post modern mammy? *The New Black Magazine.* http://www.thenewblackmagazine.com/view.aspx?index=2175

Nwoga, I. A. (2000). African American mothers use stories for family sexuality education. *American Journal of Maternal Child Nursing*, *25*, 31–36.

Okazawa-Rey, M., Robinson, T., & Ward, J. V. (1987). Black women and the politics of skin color and hair. *Women & Therapy*, *6*(1), 89–102. http://search.proquest.com/docview/216253869?accountid=10913.

Pluhar, E. I., & Kuriloff, P. (2004). What really matters in family communication about sexuality? A qualitative analysis of affect and style among African American mothers and adolescent daughters. *Sex Education, 4*(3), 303–321.

Reid, P. T., & Bing, V. M. (2000). Sexual roles of girls and women: An ethnocultural lifespan perspective. In C. B. Travis & J. W. White (Eds.), *Sexuality, society, and feminism* (pp. 141–166). American Psychological Association.

Shorter-Gooden, K., & Jackson, L. C. (2000). The interweaving of cultural and intrapsychic issues in the therapeutic relationship. In L. C. Jackson & B. Greene (Eds.), *Psychotherapy with African American women: Innovations in psychodynamic perspectives* (pp. 15–32). Guilford.

Simien, E. M., & Clawson, R. A. (2004). The intersection of race and gender: An examination of Black feminist consciousness, race consciousness, and policy attitudes. *Social Science Quarterly*, *83*(3), 793–811.

Sinclair, S., Hardin, C. D., & Lowery, B. S. (2006). Self-stereotyping in the context of multiple social identities. *Journal of Personality and Social Psychology*, *90*(4), 529–542.

Smith, G. E. (2001). *Walking proud: Black men living beyond the stereotypes*. Kensington.

Steffans, K. (2005). *Confessions of a video vixen*. HarperCollins.

Stephens, D. P., & Few, A. L. (2007). The effects of images of African American women in hip hop on early adolescents' attitudes toward physical attractiveness and interpersonal relationships. *Sex Roles*, *56*, 251–264.

Stephens, D. P., & Phillips, L. D. (2003). Freaks, gold diggers, divas, and dykes: The sociohistorical development of adolescent African American women's sexual scripts. *Sexuality & Culture*, *7*, 3–47.

Stephens, D. P., & Phillips, L. (2005). Integrating Black feminist thought into conceptual frameworks of African American adolescent women's sexual scripting processes. *Sexualities, Evolution, and Gender*, *7*(1), 37–55.

Stevens, J. W. (2002). *Smart and sassy: The strengths of inner-city Black girls.* Oxford University.

Stevens, J. W. (1997). African American female adolescent identity development: A three dimensional perspective. *Child Welfare*, *126*, 145–172.

Stewart, A. J., & McDermott, C. (2004). Gender in psychology. *Annual Review of Psychology*, *55*, 519–534.

Teitelman, A. M., Tennille, J., Bohinski, J. M., Jemmott, L. S., & Jemmott, J. B. (2011). Unwanted, unprotected sex: Condom coercion by male partners and self-silencing of condom negotiation among adolescent girls. *Advances in Nursing Science, 34*(3), 243–259.

Thomas, A. J., Witherspoon, K. M., & Speight, S. L. (2004). Toward the development of the Stereotypic Roles for Black Women Scale. *Journal of Black Psychology*, *30*, 426–442.

Thompson, M. S., & Keith, V. M. (2001). The blacker the berry: Gender, skin tone, self-esteem, and self-efficacy. *Gender & Society, 15*, 336–357.

Tinsely, B. J., Lee, N. B., & Sumartojo, E. (2004). Child and adolescent HIV risk: Familial and cultural perspectives. *Journal of Family Psychology*, *18*(1), 208–224.

Townsend, T. G., Thomas, A. J., Neilands, T. B., & Jackson, T. R. (2010). 'I'm no Jezebel, I'm young, gifted and Black': Identity, sexuality and Black girls. *Psychology of Women Quarterly*, *34*, 273–285.

Turnage, B. F. (2004). African American mother-daughter relationships mediating daughter's self-esteem. *Child and Adolescent Social Work Journal*, *21*(2), 155–172.

Ward, J. (2002). *The skin we're in: Teaching our teens to be emotionally strong, socially smart, and spiritually connected.* Free Press.

Warren-Jeanpiere, L. (2006). From mothers to daughters: A qualitative examination of the reproductive health seeking behaviour of African American women. *Women's Health and Urban Life: An International and Interdisciplinary Journal, 5*(2), 42–61.

West, C. M. (1995). Mammy, Sapphire, and Jezebel: Historical images of Black women and their implications for psychotherapy. *Psychotherapy, 32*, 458–466.

Wiederman, M. W. (2005). The gendered nature of sexual scripts. *The Family Journal, 13*, 496–502.

Williams, C. B. (2005). Counseling African American women: Multiple identities—Multiple constraints. *Journal of Counseling and Development, 83*, 278–283.

Wingood, G. M., DiClemente, R. J., Harrington, K., & Davies, S. L. (2002). Body image and African American females' sexual health. *Journal of Women's Health & Gender-Based Medicine, 11*(5), 443–449.

Reading 2.6. Black Lesbian Youth

Living Their Truths and Breaking Through the Margins

Amorie Robinson

> It's a struggle but that's why we exist, so that another generation of Lesbians of color will not
> have to invent themselves, or their history, all over again.
>
> (Lorde, 1985)

Introduction

Today's Black lesbian youth[14] are "coming out" earlier and more frequently, redefining and self-validating, and speaking their own truths with a pride and confidence unseen in decades past, yet they are in critical need of supportive services and resources. This chapter focuses on promoting optimal health and well-being for Black lesbian youth in America. It provides an overview of insights into some of the psychological experiences, health data, and adaptive coping strategies of this population. It also summarizes recommendations for mental health providers, systems of care, educators, family, and community.

Black Lesbian Youth in Need of More Attention

Black lesbian youth have always existed and have participated in the social justice and liberation movements of oppressed, marginalized peoples. They have been fiercely profound, outspoken leaders demonstrating incredible endurance (Lorde, 1985; Smith, 1998). Black Lives Matter, Black Girls Matter, #BlackGirlMagic, Black Girls Rock, #SayHerName, #NoMore, and #MeToo movements include the activism of today's Black lesbian youth. They are among the survivors of sexual harassment and assault, police brutality, racial profiling, and intimate partner violence (Gillem, 2017; Hill et al., 2012; Robinson, 2002). Tragically, their suffering and endurance go unnoticed, leaving these and other health matters of Black lesbian youth unattended, as they are an understudied group.

Studies that "center" the psychological experiences of Black lesbian youth are virtually nonexistent, despite increases in research among LGBT youth (Follins, 2011; Robinson, 2008). Findings on LGBT youth, Black youth, and Black lesbian adults may not always apply to Black lesbian youth, although there may be overlapping experiences. Psychologists have opportunities to include their voices and create meaningful supportive services (Harley et al., 2014)—for example, by discovering how Black lesbian youth master racial identity development while developing a healthy attractional orientation. Meanwhile, limited but

---

[14] This chapter defines *lesbian* as: a cisgender girl or woman who is socially, romantically, emotionally, physically, and sexually attracted to girls/women. This description does not presume that she is sexually active; sexual attraction can be a feeling without requiring a physical sexual encounter. Youth (defined here as ages 12–18) who are lesbians may not necessarily be sexually active, but this applies to adults as well. Similarly, lesbians may not necessarily be cisgender, and some lesbians are transwomen. Finally, some who meet the description of lesbian above may identify otherwise. However, the author's scope of expertise, clinical experience, and available research are limited to cisgender girls/women who identify as lesbian. More research is needed that includes transgender lesbians and other sexual minorities who identify within LGBTQIA+.

155

meaningful inferences from studies of LGBT youth, youth of color, and Black lesbian adults can guide service providers in a forward direction when serving Black lesbian youth.

Most essential to finding out about their lives is engaging Black lesbian youth and listening to their stories. Black lesbian teens in Detroit, Michigan, and New York City revealed their feelings of invisibility and their complex struggles with balancing each of their identities, simultaneously being Black, female, and lesbian (Follins, 2011; Robinson, 2008, 2010). Both qualitative studies had subjects complete a questionnaire and undergo a semi-structured interview. As a diverse, multi-dimensional group, Black lesbian youth undergo certain types of minority stress as they encounter biases, assaults, and invisibility at school, at home, and within systems of care. More research is needed to examine how Black lesbian youth cope with configurations of multiple systemic oppression such as racism, sexism, and heterosexism (Follins, 2011; Maxwell et al., 2014; Robinson, 2008, 2010).

Black Lesbian Adolescent Identity Development

Developmental issues for Black lesbian youth should be viewed through an intersectional lens, taking into account race, gender, attractional orientation, gender expression, socioeconomic status, age, and generational origin. Adolescence is a period in which girls begin to acquire their sense of self and their sense of group identities. For Black girls, this includes the path toward a healthy sense of themselves as racial beings and of their Blackness, within a toxic sociopolitical landscape, while they are striving for a positive developmental trajectory (Grills et al., 2016; Helms, 1990). Simultaneously layering the developments of Black identity with gender identity can present complex challenges for Black girls (Maxwell et al., 2014). For a Black girl discovering her same-gender attraction, the experience of growing up becomes even more multifaceted.

As girls grow up, they discover the sources of their attractions while forming their own personal, social, and cultural identities. Girlhood crushes are common and are typically reinforced heterocentrically. Such early socialization is impactful and normalized. Yet for girls who are not heteroattractional, negative consequences may result, with pressure to conform and an urgency to re-route one's attractions towards heteroattractionality. Conversion therapy has been used for such purposes, as have threats and abuse (Mallory et al., 2019; Ryan et al., 2020). Caregivers and youth-centered agencies should be aware of these possibilities and act responsibly.

Narratives by Black lesbian youth describe the joys of living out their authentic lives during routine adolescent development, as well as the difficulties of feeling misunderstood, marginalized, and invisible (Follins, 2011; Robinson, 2008, 2010). Although Black communities have increasingly become more openly accepting of their LGBT family members, the stigma of being a lesbian still exists. For Black lesbian youth, peer acceptance and rejection are especially impactful for identity formation (Bentley-Edwards & Adams-Bass, 2014). The need to belong is heightened, and the fear of rejection is anxiety-provoking and isolating. Many Black lesbian youth independently learn how to confront stigma, prejudice, and discrimination, while striving to form positive self-identities, with very few accessible roadmaps or role models. The chances of developing a healthy Black lesbian identity can be compromised without needed supports and safety nets, which are not necessarily guaranteed for them. When a Black girl comes out as a lesbian, her family can help her prepare for and navigate societal racism, but might not be able to provide her with experience-based insights on how to figure out the world as an out lesbian. Recognizing and understanding some of the developmental crossroads for Black lesbian youth can highlight why specialized resources are needed to provide support for optimal well-being.

Adolescent development requires the formation and maintenance of healthy friendships and romantic relationships, regardless of which gender(s) adolescents are attracted to. Black lesbian youth need dating advice and access to positive role modeling for romantic bonding, such as adult lesbian couples in healthy relationships. Depending on the era, one's childhood journey can be anxiety-provoking, isolating, traumatic, and depressing, requiring coping strategies for maintaining a sense of security (Robinson, 2010).

When Black lesbian youth come out within the context of a Black community setting, it can pose additional complications that can delay the formation of a positive Black lesbian identity (Greene, 2000). Being "out" while being Black has its challenges; not being out also has its own set of challenges.

Black lesbian youth report experiencing minority stress through gendered racism (Follins, 2011; Robinson, 2008, 2010). Research on gendered racism confirms the existence of intersecting forms of subtle acts of oppression that can be sources of psychological stress for Black women (Lewis et al., 2013). Black lesbian youth endure moments of uncertainty regarding which of their identities is being targeted—race, gender, attractional orientation, gender expression, or a combination. The effects of gendered racism, racist homophobia, and homophobic sexism, along with other psychosocial and systemic stressors, have been identified and discussed within Black lesbian communities and documented by researchers and writers (Bowleg, 2008; Greene, 2000; Lorde, 1985; L. Moore, 1997; Smith, 1998). Youth who are vulnerable to internalizing racism, sexism, and homophobia could benefit from therapeutic and other types of supports in order to work past and counteract their effects (Robinson, 2008). More investigation of these experiences among Black lesbian youth is needed.

Even so, Black lesbian youth have shown the ability to thrive and to develop the capacity to overcome societal and interpersonal barriers that stem from bias, prejudice, and systemic oppression (Follins, 2011; Follins et al., 2014; Robinson, 2008). Not all Black lesbian youth face formidable challenges during their identity development. Support and acceptance from loved ones and community, accessible resources and opportunities, and the coping skills to integrate and manage their multiple identities serve as protective factors to help buffer vulnerabilities, create a sense of security, and mitigate barriers to wellness and healthy identity formation (Follins, 2011; Robinson, 2008, 2010). Another level of stress is experienced by Black lesbian youth who are gender variant, requiring specialized supports which will be discussed in the next section.

Considerations of Masculine Gender Expression Among Black Lesbian Youth

Oftentimes, the gender and femininity of Black lesbian youth are questioned and scrutinized. Those having a gender expression that does not conform to "traditional" gender expectations are especially targeted for social disapproval, discipline, and punishment, resulting in negative mental health outcomes such as depression and anxiety (Robinson, 2010). People who have never had their gender questioned or scrutinized, or who have never been misgendered,[15] may not be privy to the concept of "gender expression" or may confuse it with attractional orientation. Gender expression is one's outward presentation, typically expressed through behavior and styles which may or may not align with socially defined behaviors and characteristics typically associated with binary notions of masculinity or femininity. Black lesbian youth may express their gender through clothing and other physical markers like hairstyles, mannerisms, and other self-expressions (M. Moore, 2011). Some examples are a girl wearing a tie and suspenders and playing football. Knowledge of this type of diversity can be useful to schools and youth-serving professionals.

Girls presenting as masculine have been targeted for harassment and assaults. The case of Sakia Gunn provides an example of a young person who was targeted for being both a lesbian and a masculine-presenting woman (Wright, 2019). As one Black lesbian client remarked in a therapy session, "Some of us look like Trayvon Martin and it's scary" (Personal communication, May 3, 2019). Being mistaken for a Black male is not the same as being a Black male, yet others' misperceptions can still cause potential risks to Black lesbian youth who are visibly masculine or androgynous (gender nonconforming). The findings of a few studies show that gender-nonconforming adolescents were more than twice as likely to have experienced severe psychological distress compared to gender-conforming youth, and that high levels of

---

[15] To *misgender* is to refer to someone using a word, especially a pronoun or form of address, that does not correctly reflect the gender with which they identify (Lexico, 2019).

parental pressure to change an adolescent's gender expression to enforce gender conformity are related to high levels of depression and suicide (D'Augelli et al., 2006; Wilson, Choi, et al., 2017). Although Black lesbian youth may not have been represented in their sample, these findings provide evidence that affirming mental health care and other supports that educate parents, schools, and communities on the mental health needs of gender-nonconforming youth are needed (Wilson, Choi, et al., 2017). They also clearly demonstrate the urgency of reducing known risk factors for Black lesbian gender-nonconforming youth, such as harassment, ridicule, and bias. Schools can provide safer environments by adopting anti-harassment policies and procedures, mandating training for staff, creating non-gendered spaces such as restrooms, and establishing inclusive practices regarding school uniforms (Toomey et al., 2013). Common knowledge equates masculinity to maleness, without considering a womanist-centered female masculinity (Adoma, 2016; Halberstam, 2018). An anthology of narratives by Black and Brown masculine-identified lesbian youth offers insights (Willis, 2016). It is also just as important to consider the stressors affecting Black lesbian youth who, by society's standards, meet the gender status quo of being feminine. Femme lesbians may encounter a different set of challenges than their more masculine counterparts do.

Promoting Health and Psychological Well-Being for Black Lesbian Youth

While most LGBT youth are resilient, healthy, happy, and well-adjusted (Lassiter, 2017; Russell, 2005), they are disproportionately at an increased risk of stress-related mental and physical health problems. The most notable risks are depression, anxiety, suicidality, post-traumatic stress, substance abuse, positive HIV status, cardiovascular diseases, obesity, and teen pregnancy (Dragowski et al., 2011; Hafeez et al., 2017; Saewyc, 2014). LGB youth seriously contemplate suicide at approximately three times the rate of heteroattractional youth and are almost five times as likely to have attempted suicide. Body dissatisfaction and eating disorders are prevalent among LGBT youth and can be indicators of underlying emotional issues related to societal pressure (McClain & Peebles, 2016).

Black lesbian youth are vulnerable to mental health risks that can lead to suicidal ideation without adequate support systems (Human Rights Campaign, 2018; Johns, 2019). National Strategy for Black Gay Youth in America's 2012 survey indicates that 43% of Black gay youth have thought about or attempted suicide as a result of issues related to their attractionality. Just over half reported they had experienced, or believed they would experience, family disownment for coming out. Twenty-two percent indicated they experienced mental abuse, and 10% reported physical abuse as a result of their attractionality (Sosin, 2012). Interviewing Black lesbian youth who never contemplated suicide can be key to learning about protective factors. Black lesbian youth may hesitate to contact a mental health provider, fearing that their search for help could reveal their identities to unsupportive family members or that the professional is not lesbian-friendly (Chollar, 2013; Hafeez, et al., 2017; Koh, 2010; Lorde-Rollins, 2012; Mahza & Krehely, 2010; Mays & Cochran, 2001). A 16-year-old Black lesbian client disclosed in a therapy session that when she told her doctor she was experiencing anxiety, the doctor told her it was because she is a lesbian and is going to hell (personal communication, January, 2019). The doctor's conduct of shaming the client was harmful abuse, warranting a mandated reporter follow-up. Black lesbian youth can benefit from health and mental health care providers who are educated, trained, receptive of consultation, and experienced in serving marginalized communities. For a more inclusive list of health disparities for LGBT youth and recommendations, refer to the Human Rights Campaign LGBTQ Youth Report (2018) and to the Williams Institute.

School Experiences

School systems determined to enhance the success of Black lesbian youth should be privy to risk factors that thwart their optimal learning, and protective factors that promote their learning process and social development. These are students who could be vulnerable to the vicious school-to-prison pipeline found among Black girls in America, resulting in school disengagement and significant mental health issues

(Crenshaw et al., 2015; Morris, 2012). Black lesbian youth have spoken of encountering racial, gender, and anti-lesbian bullying, harassment, discrimination, and unfair punishment at school, making it difficult for them to make friends and feel safe (Moodie-Mills, 2011; Robinson, 2010; Truong et al., 2020).

To endure these challenges without adults intervening, and to concentrate on academic goals, Black lesbian youth can benefit from programs like Gay Straight Alliance (GSA), an after-school club that provides safe haven and buffering from anti-LGBT stress (Moodie-Mills, 2011; Truong et al., 2020). Educators need to invest in GSAs in light of the latest study by the Gay and Lesbian Straight Education Network (GLSEN), which found that with the mere presence of a GSA in the school, Black LGBTQ students were less likely to miss school due to safety concerns and felt more connected to their school community. Unfortunately, Black lesbian youth are not likely attending schools that offer GSAs (Truong et al., 2020). However, it is clear that such purposeful support within their schools contributes to reducing risk factors such as depression, isolation, and behaviors leading to system involvement.

GLSEN's (Kosciw et al., 2019) recommendations for schools include the provision of multi-faceted resources, realistic representations of Black LGBT people throughout the curriculum, books reflecting various family configurations, and confidential ways to report victimization (Truong et al., 2020). Health and sex education classes should include reproductive health information aimed at Black lesbian students. All school personnel should receive professional development training on best practices, ethics, and legal responsibilities. Schools should establish policies, guidelines, and procedures for responding to racist, sexist, and anti-LGBT behavior, and should be held accountable for enforcement. Black lesbian youth would benefit from messages of Black lesbian excellence highlighting movers and shakers such as Chicago mayor Lori Lightfoot and political analyst Karine Jean-Pierre. These suggestions are key to creating safe and inclusive school environments for Black lesbian youth to be successful.

Black Lesbian Youth in Foster Care and Juvenile Systems

LGBTQ youth are grossly overrepresented in the foster care and juvenile justice systems (Conron & Wilson, 2019; Fish et al., 2019; Hunt & Moodie-Mills, 2012; Irvine & Canfield, 2016; Mallon & Woronoff, 2006; Singh, S. & Durso, L.E., 2017). Although the school-to-prison pipeline contributes to these disparities, the numbers are mainly a result of family rejection, which often leads to homelessness, a major pathway into foster care and juvenile justice systems (Mallon & Woronoff, 2006; Ray & Berger, 2007). Homelessness also leads to higher risks of sex trafficking and "survival sex" for Black lesbian youth (Choi et al., 2015).

Approximately 90% of incarcerated LGBT youth are of color (Center for American Progress, 2016; Movement Advancement Project et al., 2017) and are therefore most vulnerable to mistreatment and discrimination in juvenile detention (Robinson, 2017). Black girls are 25% more likely to be detained in juvenile detention (Cancio et al., 2019; Crenshaw et al., 2015), and 40% of girls in the system are attractional and gender-nonconforming minorities (Irvine & Canfield, 2016; Movement Advancement Project et al., 2017). Black lesbian youth in juvenile detention are likely to experience mental, emotional, sexual, and physical harassment; abuse, hate, violence, and threats targeted at their minority attractional orientation or gender expression; conversion therapy, unnecessary solitary confinement, and discrimination disguised as punishment; and harsh discipline by peers and staff (Reck, 2009; Redman, 2010). Since detention facilities are gendered spaces of heteronormativity and femininity, Black gender-nonconforming lesbian youth tend to be perceived as "other" and are subject to hostile, scrutinizing punishment and inequitable treatment (Holsinger & Hodge, 2016; Wilkinson, 2008; Wilson, Jordan, et al., 2017).

These data strongly suggest that reforms within the system are necessary and that Black lesbian youth are in need of humane care. It is incumbent upon systems of care to institute and enforce policies and procedures that enhance resiliency, prevent homelessness and court-involvement, and develop trauma-focused standards of care (Robinson, 2017). Guidelines that youth-serving professionals can use to support

Black lesbian youth are provided by the Massachusetts Department of Children and Families (2015) and the PREA Resource Center.

Parents and Families of Black Lesbian Youth

For Black lesbian youth, the path to wholeness and authenticity begins at home. Feeling love and protection by family fundamentally contributes to developing a healthy sense of self-identity, Black identity, overall well-being, and self-worth (Belgrave, 2009). Close kinship ties within Black families have provided a secure refuge and buffer from the impacts of racial oppression (Brown, 2008). For Black lesbian youth, the risk of losing such security and care can be devastating (LaSala, 2010). The 2012 survey by the National Strategy for Black Gay Youth in America found that 90% of Black gay youth listed family acceptance as the top choice that would make life more bearable (Sosin, 2012). In sharing their stories, Black lesbian youth express relief and joy when they come out to parents who respond with unconditional acceptance, instilling a sense of security, motivation, and confidence to focus on school and build beneficial peer relationships (Robinson, 2008, 2010).

Nevertheless, for too many Black lesbian youth, this is not always the case. Some youth may experience verbal and physical abuse, hostile threats, and disownment from their family due to rejection of their attractional orientation and/or nonconforming gender behavior, resulting in poor health outcomes including suicide, depression, and substance abuse (Ryan et al., 2010). Given that accepting families are protective factors for Black lesbian youth, improved family relationships are needed to help reduce homelessness and other risk components. It is the responsibility of parents/guardians to provide their best care, which could mean allowing the child or adolescent room to explore her feelings, attractions, and gender expressions. Families can receive accurate information, resources, and support from informed health providers. Culturally affirming peer support groups are available for Black parents who may not understand the "coming out" process or the potential health risks. Recommended resources are the Human Rights Campaign's 2019 report *Black and African American LGBTQ Youth*, the Family Acceptance Project, and the Ruth Ellis Center.

The Role of Spirituality in the Lives of Black Lesbian Youth

Living on the margins as a Black lesbian youth can be tense and isolating without external or internal resources and supports. Religion and spirituality have played a significant role for Black lesbian youth in managing adversity, or maintaining a sense of groundedness and inspiration (Brooks, 2017; Follins et al., 2014; Lewis & Marshall, 2012; Robinson, 2010). Black churches and mosques have served as the backbone of Black liberation and civil rights movements and are foundational for family and community bonding. However, many "out" Black lesbian youth have been rejected and abandoned by their faith communities, causing irreparable scars. Black lesbian adults recall leaving their childhood faith communities feeling wounded and angry. Attending places of worship can be particularly stressful and discomforting for Black lesbian gender-nonconforming youth who are pressured or forced by their caregivers to conform to feminine gender behavior and appearance. The film *Pariah* illustrates this tension, as 17-year-old Alike is ordered by her mother to change clothes before going to church with the family (Rees, 2011). For decades, Black lesbian youth have mentally and spiritually survived through involvement with affirming faith communities, such as the national Unity Fellowship Church Movement, where they can receive messages of validation and worthiness (Robinson, 2008).

Courage, Strengths, and Resiliencies

Black lesbian youth are remarkably courageous, capable, and resilient (Follins & Lassiter, 2017; Follins et al., 2014; Nicolas et al., 2008). To place these young women in an historical context, Black lesbian youth come from a long legacy of survival and triumph against the odds, utilizing the same tools and strategies to resist heterosexism that have historically been used by their ancestors to counteract racism and sexism. They are the descendants of those Black women who fearlessly faced adversities from being othered, and they stand on the shoulders of Black lesbian freedom fighters such as Audre Lorde, Pat Parker, Barbara Smith, Angela Davis, and others. This new generation of Black lesbian youth have become assertive about being true to self, in their own way, allowing themselves to be authentically "real" with no apologies and no need to justify who they are.

Having a Black lesbian identity in America requires radical intentional stress management and social support. Black lesbian youth have shown a great deal of stamina, endurance, creativity, and persistence, demonstrating that they can survive and thrive with appropriate conditions in place.

Black lesbian youth are coming into their own sense of powerfulness and fierceness while enduring and resisting efforts to marginalize them, even as lesbian spaces across America are diminishing. As survivors, Black lesbian youth have naturally and creatively relied on families of their own making, whenever they have been painfully alienated from their families of origin (Reed & Valenti, 2012). These nonbiological kinship connections have served as humanitarian spaces for them to receive unconditional love, acceptance, comfort, safety, support, care, and validation (Follins et al., 2014; Maxwell et al., 2014; Weston, 1991). Black lesbian youth can also find affirming homes within faith-based communities as part of their self-care, and have found healthy social connections on the internet.

Black lesbian youth must be able to depend on their schools, health providers, and systems of care and trust that they have done their work to implement the necessary in-house training and education, and policy and practice adjustments, while ethically applying an intersectional lens. Efforts to improve conditions for Black lesbian youth must come from the adults in their lives. Understanding that Black lesbian youth have endured and withstood challenges that can potentially create barriers to liberating their mind and illuminating their spirit, family and community members are accountable for forming and preserving healthy bonds of love, acceptance, and protection, regardless of a child's attractionality or gender expression. This may require having open conversations, educating oneself about attractional orientation, joining a parent support group, and referring the adolescent to trusted resources, such as mentors/elders with lived experience of being a Black lesbian. Culturally appropriate medical, mental health, and academic services, family preservation programs, and family counseling are also available in most cities (see the Ruth Ellis Center).

A Final Wake-Up Call for Ujima: Collective Work and Responsibility

Fifteen-year-old Sakia Gunn's untimely death in 2003 from a brutal homophobic attack in New Jersey, a story that failed to receive the same national attention that the hate crime against Matthew Shepherd did, is an example of the urgent need for adult protection of Black lesbian youth. Caring for the most vulnerable in a community is caring for the entire community (Ubuntu). In Sakia Gunn's memory, an LGBT community center was created in the city of Newark, a reminder of precious lives that can be enriched by safety, acceptance, validation, and visibility (Wright, 2019).

Black men[16] who accept their role in Black communities as the protectors of women and children are especially needed. They can reach out to each other as a group of men committed to defending all youth, especially those most vulnerable. Black lesbian youth are our daughters, sisters, nieces, granddaughters, and neighbors. Black women are especially called upon to ensure that these girls and young women are nurtured within their families and respected throughout the community. One of Ma'at's Divine Principles is, "I have not closed my ears to truth." The future of Black people is returning to more African ways of being where each member is valued, embracing the children and elders within the village. As such consciousness grows

---

[16] Black men across all attractionalities and gender identities.

over time, and as Black lesbian youth find their voices, their mental, physical, and spiritual well-being will be fully realized.

References

Adoma, K. (2016). Women who dare to be themselves: The creation of the Jerry Palmer Group of Detroit. In M. W. Willis (Ed.), *Outside the XY: Queer Black and brown masculinity* (pp. 113–121). Riverdale Avenue Books.

Belgrave, F. Z. (2009). *African American girls: Reframing perceptions and changing experiences.* Springer Science + Business Media. https://doi.org/10.1007/978-1-4419-0090-6

Bentley-Edwards, K., & Adams-Bass, V. N. (2014). The whole picture: Examining Black women through the lifespan. In H. Jackson-Lowman (Ed.), *Afrikan American women: Living at the crossroads of race, gender, class, and culture* (pp. 189–202). Cognella Academic Publishing.

Bowleg, L. (2008). When Black + lesbian + woman ≠ Black lesbian woman: The methodological challenges of qualitative and quantitative intersectionality research. *Sex Roles, 59*(5–6), 312–325.

Brooks, S. (2017). Balancing act: Identity management and mental health among LBT women. In L. Follins & J. Lassiter (Eds.), *Black LGBT health in the United States: The intersection of race, gender, and sexual orientation* (pp. ix–xiii). Lexington Books.

Brown, D. L. (2008). African American resiliency: Examining racial socialization and social support as protective factors. *Journal of Black Psychology, 34*(1), 32–48. https://doi.org/10.1177/0095798407310538

Cancio, R., Grills, C. T., & Garcia, J. (2019). The color of justice: The landscape of traumatic justice: Youth of color in conflict with the law. The Alliance of National Psychological Associations for Racial and Ethnic Equity. https://www.researchgate.net/publication/333149484_THE_COLOR_OF_JUSTICE_The_Landscape_of_Traumatic_Justice_Youth_of_Color_in_Conflict_with_the_Law

Choi, S. K., Wilson, B. D. M., Shelton, J., & Gates, G. (2015). *Serving our youth 2015: The needs and experiences of lesbian, gay, bisexual, transgender, and questioning youth experiencing homelessness.* The Williams Institute with True Colors Fund.

Chollar, R. (2013). Ten physical and emotional concerns of LGBTQ students. Campus Pride. https://www.campuspride.org/resources/10-physical-and-emotional-health-concerns-of-lgbt-students/

Conron, K. J., & Wilson, B. D. M. (Eds.). (2019). *A research agenda to reduce system involvement and promote positive outcomes with LGBTQ youth of color impacted by the child welfare and juvenile justice systems.* The Williams Institute.

Crenshaw, K. (1989). Demarginalizing the intersection of race and sex: A Black feminist critique of antidiscrimination doctrine, feminist theory and antiracist politics. *University of Chicago Legal Forum, 1989*(1), Article 8, 139–167.

Crenshaw, K., Ocen, P., & Nanda, J. (2015). *Black girls matter: Pushed out, overpoliced, and underprotected.* African American Policy Forum and Center for Intersectionality and Social Policy Studies. http://static1.squarespace.com/static/53f20d90e4b0b80451158d8c/t/54dcc1ece4b001c03e323448/1423753708557/AAPF_BlackGirlsMatterReport.pdf

D'Augelli, A. R., Grossman, A. H., & Starks, M. T. (2006). Childhood gender atypicality, victimization, and PTSD among lesbian, gay, and bisexual youth. *Journal of Interpersonal Violence*, *21*(11), 1462–1482. https://doi.org/10.1177/0886260506293482

Dragowski, E. A., Halkitis, P. N., Grossman, A. H., & D'Augelli, A. R. (2011). Sexual orientation victimization and posttraumatic stress symptoms among lesbian, gay, and bisexual youth. *Journal of Gay & Lesbian Social Services*, *23*(2), 226–249. https://doi.org/10.1080/10538720.2010.541028

Fish, J. N., Baams, L., Wojciak, A. S., & Russell, S. T. (2019). Are sexual minority youth overrepresented in foster care, child welfare, and out-of-home placement? Findings from nationally representative data. *Child Abuse Neglect*, *89*, 203–2011.

Follins, L. (2011). Identity development of young Black lesbians in New York City: An exploratory study. *Journal of Gay and Lesbian Mental Health*, *15*(4), 368–381.

Follins, L., & Lassiter, J. (Eds.). (2017). *Black LGBT health in the United States: The intersection of race, gender, and sexual orientation*. Lexington Books.

Follins, L. D., Walker, J. N. J., & Lewis, M. K. (2014). Resilience in Black lesbian, gay, bisexual, and transgender individuals: A critical review of the literature. *Journal of Gay & Lesbian Mental Health*, *18*(2), 190–212.

Gillem, T. (2017). Adolescent dating violence experiences among sexual minority youth and implications for subsequent relationship quality. *Journal of Child and Adolescent Social Work*, *34*(2), 137–145.

Greene, B. (2000). African American lesbian and bisexual women. *Journal of Social Issues*, *56*(2), 239–249.

Grills, C., Cooke, D., Douglas, J., Subica, A., Villanueva, S., & Hudson, B. (2016). Culture, racial socialization, and positive African American youth development. *Journal of Black Psychology*, *42*(4), 343–373.

Hafeez, H., Zeshan, M., Tahir, M. A., Jahan, N., & Naveed, S. (2017). Health care disparities among lesbian, gay, bisexual, and transgender youth: A literature review. *Cureus*, *9*(4).

Halberstam, J. (2018). *Female masculinity*. Duke University Press.

Harley, D. A., Stansbury, K. L., & Nelson, M. (2014). Sisters gone missing: The lack of focus on African American lesbians in mental health counseling and research. In H. Jackson-Lowman (Ed.), *Afrikan American women: Living at the crossroads of race, gender, class, and culture* (pp. 287–304). Cognella Academic Publishing.

Helms, J. (Ed.). (1990). *Black & white racial identity: Theory, research, & practice*. Greenwood Press.

Hill, N. A., Woodson, K. M., Ferguson, A. D., & Parks, C. W. (2012). Intimate partner abuse among African American lesbians: Prevalence, risk factors, theory, and resilience. *Journal of Family Violence*, *27*(5), 401–413.

Holsinger, K., & Hodge, J. P. (2016). The experiences of lesbian, gay, bisexual, and transgender girls in juvenile justice systems. *Feminist Criminology*, *11*(1), 23–47.

Human Rights Campaign. (2019). *Black and African American youth report*. https://www.hrc.org/resources/black-and-african-american-lgbtq-youth-report

Hunt, J., & Moodie-Mills, A. (2012, June 29). The unfair criminalization of gay and transgender youth. http://www.americanprogress.org/issues/lgbt/report/2012/06/29

Irvine, A., & Canfield, A. (2016). The overrepresentation of lesbian, gay, bisexual, questioning, gender nonconforming and transgender youth within the child welfare to juvenile justice crossover population. *Journal of Gender, Social Policy & the Law, 24*(2), Article 2, 243–261. http://digitalcommons.wcl.american.edu/jgspl/vol24/iss2/2

Johns, D. (2019). We failed them, Black kids deserve to grow up too. National Black Justice Coalition. http://www.nbjc.org/blog/we-failed-them-black-kids-deserve-grow-too

Kosciw, J.G., Clark, C.M., Truong, N.L., & Zongrone, A.D. (2019). *The 2019 National School Climate Survey: The experiences of lesbian, gab bisexual, transgender, and queer youth in our nation's schools.* GLSEN.

Lasala, M. (2010, October 21). African American gay and lesbian youth and their parents. *Psychology Today.* https://www.psychologytoday.com/us/blog/gay-and-lesbian-well-being/201010/african-american-gay-and-lesbian-youth-and-their-parents

Lassiter, J. (2017). For us, by us: A manifesto of Black SGL and trans health. In L. Follins & J. Lassiter (Eds.), *Black LGBT health in the United States: The intersection of race, gender, and sexual orientation* (pp. 1–10). Lexington Books.

Lewis, M., & Marshall, I. (2012). *LGBT psychology: Research perspectives and African descent.* Springer.

Lewis, J., Mendenhall, R., Harwood, S., & Browne Huntt, M. (2013). Coping with gendered racial microaggressions among Black women college students. *Journal of African American Studies, 17*(1), 51–73. https://doi.org/10.1007/s12111-012-9219-0

Lexico. (2019). Misgender. *Lexico English dictionary.* https://www.lexico.com/en/definition/misgender

Lorde, A. (1985). *I am your sister: Black women organizing across sexualities* (Vol. 3). Kitchen Table/Women of Color Press.

Lorde-Rollins, E. (2012). "Just ask me." Clinical care for lesbian adolescents. In S. L. Dibble & P. A. Robertson (Eds.), *Lesbian health 101: A clinician's guide* (pp. 23–53). UCSF Nursing Press.

Mallon, G. P., & Woronoff, R. (2006). Busting out of the child welfare closet: Lesbian, gay, bisexual, and transgender-affirming approaches to child welfare. *Child Welfare, 85*(2), 115.

Mallory, C., Brown, T. N. T., & Conron, K. J. (2019, June). *Conversion therapy and LGBT youth update.* The Williams Institute.

Maxwell, M., Abrams, J., Pope, M., & Belgrave, F. (2014). Black female adolescents: Defying the odds. In H. Jackson-Lowman (Ed.), *Afrikan American women: Living at the crossroads of race, gender, class, and culture* (p. 204). Cognella Academic Publishing.

Mays, V., & Cochran, S. (2001). Mental health correlates of perceived discrimination among lesbian, gay, and bisexual adults in the United States. *American Journal of Public Health, 91*(11), 1869–1876. http://www.midus.wisc.edu/findings/pdfs/212.pdf

McClain, Z., & Peebles, R. (2016). Body image and eating disorders among lesbian, gay, bisexual, and transgender youth. *Pediatric Clinics of North America, 63*(6), 1079–1090.

Moodie-Mills, D. (2011, September 8). The kids are not alright: The plight of African American LGBT youth in America's schools. Center for American Progress. https://www.americanprogress.org/issues/lgbt/news/2011/09/08/10362/the-kids-are-not-alright/

Moore, L. (Ed.). (1997). *Does your mama know?* RedBone Press.

Moore, M. (2011). Gender presentation in Black lesbian communities. In M. Moore (Ed.), *Invisible families: Gay identities, relationships, and motherhood among Black women* (pp. 65–91). University of California Press.

Morris, M. W. (2012). *Race, gender, and the school-to-prison pipeline: Expanding our discussion to include Black girls*. African American Policy Forum & Columbia Law School Center for Intersectionality and Social Policy Studies. https://static1.squarespace.com/static/53f20d90e4b0b80451158d8c/t/5422efe3e4b040cd1f255c1a/1411575779338/Morris-Race-Gender-and-the-School-to-Prison-Pipeline+FINAL.pdf

Movement Advancement Project, Center for American Progress, & Youth First. (2017, June). Unjust: LGBTQ youth incarcerated in the juvenile justice system. http://www.lgbtmap.org/

Nicolas, G., Helms, J. E., Jernigan, M. M., Sass, T., Skrzypek, A., & DeSilva, A. M. (2008). A conceptual framework for understanding the strengths of Black youths. *Journal of Black Psychology*, *34*(3), 261–280. https://doi.org/10.1177/0095798408316794

Ray, N., & Berger, C. (2007). *Lesbian, gay, bisexual and transgender youth: An epidemic of homelessness*. National Gay and Lesbian Task Force Policy Institute. http://www.thetaskforce.org/static_html/downloads/HomelessYouth.pdf

Reck, J. (2009). Homeless gay and transgender youth of color in San Francisco: "No one likes street kids"—Even in the Castro. *Journal of LGBT Youth*, *6*(2–3), 223–242.

Redman, D. (2010). I was scared to sleep: LGBT youth face violence behind bars. https://www.thenation.com/article/i-was-scared-sleep-lgbt-youth-face-violence-behind-bars/

Reed, S. J., & Valenti, M. T. (2012). "It ain't all as bad as it may seem": Young Black lesbians' responses to sexual prejudice. *Journal of Homosexuality*, *59*(5), 703–720.

Rees, D. (Director). (2011). *Pariah* [Film]. Focus Features.

Robinson, A. (2002). There's a stranger in this house: African American lesbians and domestic violence. *Women & Therapy*, *25*(3–4), 125–132. https://doi.org/10.1300/J015v25n03_09

Robinson, A. (2008). Misunderstood, misled, and misfit: The marginalization experiences of African American lesbian youth. In *Benefiting by Design: Women of Color in Feminist Psychological Research*, *90*(103), 90–103. Cambridge Scholars Publishing in association with GSE Research.

Robinson, A. (2010). Living for the city: Voices of Black lesbian youth in Detroit. *Journal of Lesbian Studies*, *14*(1), 61–70.

Robinson, A. (2017). The forgotten intersection: Black LGBTQ and gender nonconforming youth in juvenile detention in the United States. In L. Follins & J. Lassiter (Eds.), *Black LGBT health in the United States: The intersection of race, gender, and sexual orientation* (pp. 11–23). Lexington Books.

Ryan, C., Russell, S. T., Huebner, D., Diaz, R., & Sanchez, J. (2010). Family acceptance in adolescence and the health of LGBT young adults. *Journal of Child Adolescent Psychiatry Nursing*, *23*(4), 205–213.

Ryan, C., Toomey, R. B., Diaz, R. M., & Russell, S. T. (2020). Parent-initiated sexual orientation change efforts with LGBT adolescents: Implications for young adult mental health and adjustment. *Journal of Homosexuality*, 67(2), 159–173.

Saewyc, E. M. (2014). Adolescent pregnancy among lesbian, gay, and bisexual teens. In A. Cherry & M. Dillon (Eds.), *International handbook of adolescent pregnancy*. Springer.

Singh, S. & Durso, L.E. (2017). Widespread discrimination continues to shape LGBT people's lives in subtle and significant ways. Center for American Progress.

Smith, B. (1998). *The truth that never hurts: Writings on race, gender, and freedom*. Rutgers University Press.

Sosin, K. (2012, May 23). YPS releases stunning results of Black gay youth survey. *Windy City Times*. http://www.windycitymediagroup.com/lgbt/YPS-releases-stunning-results-of-Black-gay-youth-survey/37805.html

Toomey, R. B., Ryan, C., Diaz, R. M., Card, N. A., & Russell, S. T. (2013). Gender-nonconforming lesbian, gay, bisexual, and transgender youth: School victimization young adult psychosocial adjustment. *Psychology of Sexual Orientation and Gender Diversity*, 1(S), 71–80.

Truong, N. L., Zongrone, A. D., & Kosciw, J. G. (2020). *Erasure and resilience: The experiences of LGBTQ students of color: Black LGBTQ youth in U.S. Schools*. GLSEN. https://www.glsen.org/sites/default/files/2020-06/Erasure-and-Resilience-Black-2020.pdf

Wilkinson, W. W. (2008). Threatening the patriarchy: Testing an explanatory paradigm of anti-lesbian attitudes. *Sex Roles*, 59(7–8), 512–520.

Willis, M. W. (Ed.). (2016). *Outside the XY: Queer Black and brown masculinity*. Riverdale Avenue Books.

Wilson, B. D. M, Choi, S. K., Herman, J., Becker, T., & Conron, K. (2017). *Characteristics and mental health of gender nonconforming adolescents in California: Findings from the 2015–2016 California Health Interview Survey*. Williams Institute and UCLA Center for Health Policy Research.

Wilson, B. D. M., Jordan, S. P., Meyer, I. H., Flores, A. R., Stemple, L., & Herman, J. L. (2017). Disproportionality and disparities among sexual minority youth in custody. *Journal of Youth and Adolescence*, 46(7), 1547–1561. https://doi.org/10.1007/s10964-017-0632-5

Wright, G. P. (2019). Remembering the murder of Sakia Gunn, and Newark's lost opportunity—Opinion. New Jersey Voices. https://www.nj.com/njv_guest_blog/2013/05/remembering_the_murder_of_saki.html

Resources

Affinity https://affinity95.org/acscontent/

Black Lesbians United (BLU) mentorships for youth http://blacklesbiansunited.org

CWLA Best Practice Guidelines: Serving LGBT Youth in Out-of-Home Care. Washington, DC: Child Welfare League of America.

Family Acceptance Project https://familyproject.sfsu.edu/training

Gay and Lesbian Straight Education Network (GLSEN) https://www.glsen.org

Gay Straight Alliances: GSA Network https://gsanetwork.org/

Human Rights Campaign Black and African American LGBT Youth Report
https://www.hrc.org/resources/black-and-african-american-lgbtq-youth-report

Human Rights Campaign LGBTQ Youth Report (2018)

Massachusetts Department of Children and Families (2015). LGBTQ: A Guide for Working with Youth
and Families. www.mass.gov/dcf

Miss UnderSTUD Video of voices of intergenerational masculine-identified lesbians
https://www.youtube.com/watch?v=mcuNaNSyozc&feature=youtu.be

National PREA Resource Center Guidelines for safety and respect for LGBT youth in confinement
http://www.preasourcecenter.org

Parents and Families of Lesbians and Gays (PFLAG) http://www.pflag.org

SAMSHA (Substance Abuse and Mental Health Services Administration) Conversion therapy information
https://store.samhsa.gov/product/Ending-Conversion-Therapy-Supporting-and-Affirming-LGBTQ-
Youth/SMA15-4928?referer=from_search_result

The Ruth Ellis Center http://www.ruthelliscenter.org/

The National Black Justice Coalition http://nbjc.org

The Trevor Project: Suicide among LGBT youth https://www.thetrevorproject.org/resources/

Unity Fellowship of Christ Church https://ufcmlife.org/

Williams Institute (research on sexual orientation and gender identity law and policy)
https://williamsinstitute.law.ucla.edu/

Unit III. Seeking Authenticity at The Crossroads of Race, Gender, Class, And Culture: Impact of the Maafa on the Lived Experiences of Afrikan American Women

Introduction: Impact of the Maafa on the Lived Experiences of Afrikan American Women

Huberta Jackson-Lowman

In this unit, several critical issues that affect Afrikan American women and girls' (AAWG) ability to be their authentic selves are explored. Collins's classic work on love relationships examines the vicissitudes and intricacies of interpersonal love relationships and the role that the sexual politics of Black womanhood plays in these relationships. By elucidating the dynamics of these relationships, she strives to liberate women of Afrikan ancestry from the system of domination imposed on us since slavery. Thomas and Fletcher examine the paradoxical relationship between young AAW's perceptions of themselves as strong Black women and their endorsement of traditional Western views of femininity in their relationships with men. Hitchens and Payne explore Black single motherhood from an adaptive perspective, giving readers an opportunity to walk in the shoes of mothers whose choices and decisions are influenced by their impoverished conditions. Using an historical lens, Bogan offers a unique analysis of how colonial history and myths have contributed to the minimization of sexual assault of AAWG. Haile focuses on the HIV/AIDS crisis in the Black community and dissects the role that oppression plays in feeding these disturbing statistics among AAWG. Applying an historical perspective, Haile weaves together social, economic, and cultural factors, emphasizing the importance of social justice and gender equity in winning the battle against HIV/AIDS. Finally, this unit concludes with an investigation of the effects of the myth of the Strong Black Woman. Woods-Giscombé's qualitative research suggests that AAW endorse aspects of the Superwoman schema while also recognizing its liabilities and impact on our physical and mental health and our relationships.

The adaptations that AAW have made to the unrelenting assaults associated with the Maafa must be identified and acknowledged before healing can occur, and before we are able to fully assert our authenticity. If we are to embrace our authenticity and be who we really are, we must understand the past that colors the landscape of the present and that, if not effectively addressed, will continue to shape our futures. The issues discussed in these readings delineate crucial aspects of what a healing agenda for Black women must include as we strive to manifest authenticity and *Kujichagulia*/Self-Determination.

Reading 3.1. Black Women's Love Relationships

Patricia Hill Collins

In Toni Morrison's Beloved (1987), Sethe tells her friend Paul D how she felt after escaping from slavery:

> It was a kind of selfishness I never knew nothing about before. It felt good. Good and right. I was big, Paul D, and deep and wide and when I stretched out my arms all my children could get in between. I was that wide. Look like I loved em more after I got here. Or maybe I couldn't love em proper in Kentucky because they wasn't mine to love. But when I got here, when I jumped down off that wagon—there wasn't nobody in the world I couldn't love if I wanted to. You know what I mean? (Morrison 1987, 162)

By distorting Sethe's ability to love her children "proper," slavery annexed Sethe's power as energy for its own ends. Her words touch a deep chord in Paul D, for he too remembers how slavery felt. His unspoken response to Sethe expresses the mechanisms used by systems of domination such as slavery in harnessing potential sources of power in a subordinated group:

> So you protected yourself and loved small. Picked the tiniest stars out of the sky to own; lay down with head twisted in order to see the loved one over the rim of the trench before you slept. Stole shy glances at her between the trees at chain-up. Grass blades, salamanders, spiders, woodpeckers, beetles, a kingdom of ants. Anything bigger wouldn't do. A woman, a child, a brother—a big love like that would split you wide open in Alfred, Georgia. He knew exactly what she meant: to get to a place where you could love anything you chose—not to need permission for desire—well, now, *that* was freedom. (Morrison 1987, 162)

Sethe and Paul D's words suggest that in order to perpetuate itself, slavery corrupts and distorts those sources of power within oppressed groups that provide energy for change. To them, freedom from slavery meant not only the absence of capricious masters and endless work but regaining the power to "love anything you chose." Both Sethe and Paul D understood how slavery inhibited their ability to have "a big love," whether for children, for friends, for each other, or for principles such as justice. Both saw that systems of oppression often succeed because they control the "permission for desire"—in other words, they harness the power of deep feelings to the exigencies of domination.

This type of power that flows from "a big love" flies in the face of Western epistemologies that often see emotions and rationality as different and competing concerns (Collins 1998a, 243–245). Described by Black feminist poet Audre Lorde (1984) as the power of the erotic, deep feelings that arouse people to action constitute an important source of power. In her groundbreaking essay, "Uses of the Erotic: The Erotic as Power," Audre Lorde explores this fundamental link between deep feelings and power and provides a road map for an oppositional sexual politics:

> There are many kinds of power, used and unused, acknowledged or otherwise. The erotic is a resource within each of us that lies in a deeply female and spiritual plane, firmly rooted in the power of our unexpressed or unrecognized feeling. In order to perpetuate itself, every oppression must corrupt or distort those various sources of power within the culture of the oppressed that can provide energy for change. For women, this has meant a suppression of the erotic as a considered source of power and information in our lives. (Lorde 1984, 53)

For Lorde sexuality is a component of the erotic as a source of power in women. Lorde's notion is one of power as energy, as something people possess that must be annexed in order for larger systems of oppression to function.

Lorde suggests that this erotic power resides in women, but men too can experience these deep feelings. Divergent expressions of deep feelings may lie less in biologically based gender differences than in social structures that associate this type of passion with femininity and weakness. Sadly, within capitalist marketplace relations, this erotic power is so often sexualized that not only is it routinely misunderstood, but the strength of deeply felt love is even feared.

African-American women's experiences with pornography, prostitution, and rape demonstrate how erotic power becomes commodified and exploited by social institutions. Equally important is how Black women hold fast to this source of individual empowerment and use it in crafting fully human love relationships. When people "protect themselves and love small" by seeing certain groups of people as worthy of love and deeming others less deserving, potential sources of power as energy that can flow from love relationships are attenuated. But when people reject the world offered by intersecting oppressions, the power as energy that can flow from a range of love relationships becomes possible.

All love relationships potentially tap the energy associated with deep feelings, but not all love relationships are the same. Such relationships can be arranged on a continuum from caring yet asexual love relationships, to sexualized love relationships—those where deep feelings find sexual expression—to those that reflect the "just sex" commodity relations of the capitalist marketplace.

This chapter examines selected Black women's love relationships that tap deep feelings, whether or not they find sexual expression. The deep love that African-American women feel for our parents, children, and siblings constitutes spiritual, deeply felt love relationships that are not considered sexual. Conversely, love relationships that encompass sexual expression constitute sexualized love relationships. Loving friendships of all sorts remain arrayed in between, with some of the most contested relationships occurring when people do not know where to draw the sexual line. In some cases, sexuality itself clouds the boundaries. For example, for many heterosexual Black men and Black women, dominant constructions of Black male and Black female sexuality often limit the ability to form nonsexualized, loving friendships. In other cases, loving a forbidden other becomes the source of contention. Love across the color line, where individuals of different "races" fall in love, or across social class categories muddy the waters between asexual friendships and sexualized love relationships. In still other cases, the fear lies in loving too deeply elements of oneself found in the other. As Black lesbians point out, much homophobia expressed by heterosexual African-American women stems from the fear that their love of Black women might find sexual expression.

The intersecting oppressions that produce systems of domination such as slavery aim to thwart the power as energy available to subordinate groups. The sexual politics that constrains Black womanhood constitutes an effective system of domination because it intrudes on people's daily lives at the point of consciousness. Exactly how do the sexual politics of Black womanhood influence Black women's interpersonal love relationships? More important, how might an increased understanding of these relationships enable African-American women to tap sources of power as energy and thus become more empowered?

Black Women, Black Men, and The Love and Trouble Tradition

In her groundbreaking essay, "On the Issue of Roles," Toni Cade Bambara remarks, "Now it doesn't take any particular expertise to observe that one of the most characteristic features of our community is the antagonism between our men and our women" (Bambara 1970a, 106). Exploring the tensions between African-American men and women has been a long-standing theme in U.S. Black feminist thought. In an

1833 speech, Maria Stewart boldly challenged what she saw as Black men's lackluster response to racism: "Talk, without effort, is nothing; you are abundantly capable, gentlemen, of making yourselves men of distinction; and this gross neglect, on your part, causes my blood to boil within me" (Richardson 1987, 58). Ma Rainey, Bessie Smith, and other classic Black women blues singers offer rich advice to Black women on how to deal with unfaithful and unreliable men (Harrison 1978, 1988; Russell 1982; Davis 1998). More recently, Black women's troubles with Black men have generated anger and, from that anger, self-reflection: "We have been and are angry sometimes," suggests Bonnie Daniels, "not for what men have done, but for what we've allowed ourselves to become, again and again in my past, in my mother's past, in my centuries of womanhood passed over, for the 'sake' of men, whose manhood we've helped undermine" (1979, 62).

Juxtaposed against this tradition of trouble is another long-standing theme—namely, the great love Black women feel for Black men. African-American slave narratives contain countless examples of newly emancipated Black women who spent years trying to locate their lost children, spouses, fathers, and other male loved ones (Gutman 1976). Black women writers express love for their sons and fears about their futures (Angelou 1969; Golden 1995). Love poems written to Black men permeate Black women's poetry. Black women's music is similarly replete with songs about sexualized love. Whether the playful voice of Alberta Hunter proclaiming that her "man is a handy man," the mournful cries of Billie Holiday singing "My Man," the sadness Nina Simone evokes in "I Loves You Porgy" at being forced to leave her man, or the powerful voice of Jennifer Holliday, who cries out, "You're gonna love me," Black vocalists identify Black women's relationships with Black men as a source of strength, support, and sustenance (Harrison 1978, 1988; Russell 1982). As U.S. Black feminists point out, many Black women reject feminism because they see it as being anti-family and against Black men.

They do not want to give up men—they want Black men to change. Black activist Fannie Lou Hamer succinctly captures what a good love relationship between a Black woman and man can be: "You know, I'm not hung up on this about liberating myself from the black man, I'm not going to try that thing. I got a black husband, six feet three, two hundred and forty pounds, with a 14 shoe, that I don't want to be liberated from" (Lerner 1972, 612).

African-American women have long commented on this "love and trouble" tradition in Black women's relationships with Black men. Novelist Gayl Jones explains: "The relationships between the men and the women I'm dealing with are blues relationships. So they're out of a tradition of 'love and trouble.' … Blues talks about the simultaneity of good and bad, as feeling, as something felt. … Blues acknowledges all different kinds of feelings at once" (Harper 1979, 360). Both the tensions between African-American women and men and the strong attachment that we feel for one another represent a rejection of binary thinking and an acceptance of the both/and conceptual stance in Black feminist thought.

Understanding this love and trouble tradition requires assessing the influence of heterosexist, Eurocentric gender ideology—particularly, ideas about men and women advanced by the traditional family ideal—on African-American women and men. Definitions of appropriate gender behavior for Black women, Black men, and members of other racial/ethnic groups not only affect social institutions such as schools and labor markets, they also shape daily interactions. Analyses claiming that African-Americans would be just like Whites if offered comparable opportunities implicitly support prevailing sexual politics. Such thinking offers hegemonic gender ideologies of White masculinity and White femininity as models for African-Americans to emulate. Similarly, those proclaiming that Black men experience a more severe form of racial oppression than Black women routinely counsel African-American women to subjugate our needs to those of Black men (see, e.g., Staples 1979). However, advising Black women to unquestioningly support sexual harassment, domestic violence, and other forms of sexism done by U.S. Black men buttresses a form of sexual politics that differently controls everyone. As Audre Lorde queries, "If society ascribes roles to black men which they are not allowed to fulfill, is it black women who must bend and alter our lives to compensate, or is it society that needs changing?" (1984, 61). Bonnie Daniels provides an answer: "I've learned … that being less than what I am capable of being to boost someone else's ego *does not help either of* us for real" (1979, 61).

Black women intellectuals directly challenge not only the derogation of African-American women within prevailing sexual politics—for example, the controlling images of mammy, the matriarch, the welfare mother, and the jezebel—but often base this rejection on a more general critique of Eurocentric heterosexism itself. Sojourner Truth's 1851 query, "I could work as much and eat as much as a man—when I could get it—and bear the lash as well! And ain't I a woman?" confronts the premises of the cult of true womanhood that "real" women were fragile and ornamental. Toni Cade Bambara contends that Eurocentric understandings of gender derived from White, middle-class experience are not only troublesome for African-Americans but damaging: "I have always, I think, opposed the stereotypical definitions of 'masculine' and 'feminine,' … because I always found the either/or implicit in those definitions antithetical to what I was all about—and what revolution for self is all about—the whole person" (Bambara 1970a, 101).

As many U.S. Black feminist activists point out, the sexual politics of Black womanhood limits the development of transformative social justice projects within Black civil society. Black activist Frances Beale identifies the negative effects that sexism within the Black community had on Black political activism in the 1960s:

> Unfortunately, there seems to be some confusion in the Movement today as to who has been oppressing whom. Since the advent of Black power, the Black male has exerted a more prominent leadership role in our struggle for justice in this country. He sees the system for what it really is for the most part, but where he rejects its values and mores on many issues, when it comes to women, he seems to take his guidelines from the pages of the *Ladies' Home Journal.* (Beale 1970, 92)

Mainstream social science also seems overly preoccupied with Black men's issues. Sociologist William Julius Wilson's (1987, 1996) groundbreaking work on joblessness and poverty among U.S. Blacks pays more attention to men's issues than women's. From Black conservatism to Black nationalism, regardless of Black political perspective, an implicit male bias persists. The inordinate emphasis placed on providing more Black male role models for Black boys in contemporary Black political theory and practice often occurs by neglecting the needs of girls. This masculinist bias spurred two Black feminist thinkers to observe: "The struggle is defined as one to reclaim and redefine Black manhood. Ironically, this is also the point at which the politics and positions of some cultural nationalists, liberals and right-wing conservatives seem to converge" (Ransby and Matthews 1993, 60).

While some African-American women criticize the sexual politics that accompanies intersecting oppressions, even fewer have directly challenged Black men who accept prevailing notions of both Black and White masculinity (Wallace 1978). Until the watershed event of Anita Hill's 1992 public testimony against Clarence Thomas, the blues tradition provided the most consistent and long-standing text of Black women who demand that Black men "change their ways." Both then and now, songs often encourage Black men to define new types of relationships. In "Do Right Woman—Do Right Man," when Aretha Franklin (1967) sings that a woman is only human and is not a plaything but is flesh and blood just like a man, she echoes Sojourner Truth's claim that women and men are equally human. Aretha sings about knowing that she's living in a "man's world" but she encourages her man not to "prove" that he's a man by using or abusing her. As long as she and her man are together, she wants him to show some "respect" for her. Her position is clear—if he wants a "do right, all night woman," he's got to be a "do right, all night man." Aretha challenges African-American men to reject the prevailing sexual politics that posit "it's a man's world" in order to be a "do right man." By showing Black women respect and being an "all night" man—one who is faithful, financially reliable, and sexually expressive—Black men can have a relationship with a "do right woman."

Within the corpus of their works, some Black women hip-hop artists echo Aretha's challenge. In her song "U.N.I.T.Y.," Queen Latifah asks for a man who knows how to respect a woman. For those who need more details, Salt-n-Pepa's anthem "Whatta Man" on *Very Necessary* (1993) identifies the qualities of a "mighty good man." Recognizing that "good men are hard to find," the song aspires to "give respect to the men who made a difference." The list of qualities is clear. A good man is one who makes a woman laugh, does not run around with other women, has a good body, is a good lover, can hold a decent conversation, and "spends time with his kids when he can." He always has his woman's "back" when she needs him, and he's "never disrespectful 'cause his momma taught him that."

Many Black men have not taken kindly to these requests. Black men's response to the publications of Black women writers illustrate these reactions. Apparently forgetting the norms of racial solidarity that they long expected Black women to show for Black men's achievements, many men resented the success of Black women writers. Explaining this situation, Black literary critic Calvin Hernton describes how this antagonistic posture stems from Black men's acceptance of prevailing sexual politics:

> Too often Black men have a philosophy of manhood that relegates women to the back burner. Therefore, it is perceived as an offense for black women to struggle on their own, let alone achieve something independently. Thus, no matter how original, beautiful, and formidable the works of black women writers might be, black men become "offended" if such works bear the slightest criticism of them, or if the women receive recognition from other women, especially from the white literary establishment. They do not behave as though something of value has been added to the annals of black literature. Rather, they behave as though something has been subtracted, not only from the literature, but from the entire race, and specifically, from *them*. (Hernton 1985, 6)

Whereas some men merely grumble at no longer having their perceived needs always come first, other men interpret Black women's success as a direct attack on them. If the sexual politics that foster these reactions remain unexamined, as Lisa Jones succinctly states, the potential damage done to both Black women and Black men is great: "Between rappers turning 'ho' into a national chant and [the movie *Waiting to*] *Exhale* telling African Americans that our real problem is the shortage of brothers who are both well hung and well paid, I'm getting to think that all we can offer each other as black women and men is genitalia and the paycheck" (Jones 1994, 267).

Avoiding being reduced to the "genitalia and the paycheck" requires developing a comprehensive analysis of how prevailing sexual politics influences Black heterosexual love relationships. In developing this analysis, however, it is equally important to keep in mind the analytical distinction between the interpersonal domain of power where men and women as individuals interact, and how broader overarching structures of power operate to encourage these individual outcomes. For example, womanist thinker Geneva Smitherman maintains this distinction when pressed to describe some Black men's treatment of Black women. In responding to claims that Black men are sexist, she contends, "This is not to argue that Black men don't display sexist attitudes. Of course. Such attitudes are in the very fiber of American society; they have infected us all—including women. However, the practice of patriarchy, the subordination of women— and men—requires power, on a grand scale, and control over the nation's institutions. Sorry, but the Brothers ain't there" (Smitherman 1996, 105). Black men may not be in corporate boardrooms, and thus cannot be blamed for actions aimed at protecting the privileges associated with White masculinity (Ferber 1998). But at the same time the "Brothers" most certainly are in Black women's homes. They can be held accountable, no matter how badly treated they may be under racial oppression, for how they treat Black women, children, and each other.

The antagonism that many African-American women and men feel and express toward one another reflects the contradictions characterizing Black masculinity and Black femininity within prevailing U.S. sexual politics. Racialized heterosexism objectifies both Black men and Black women. Thus, when African-American men see Black women as little more than mammies, matriarchs, or "hoochies," or even if they insist on placing African-American women on the same queenly pedestal reserved for White women, they objectify not only Black women but themselves (Gardner 1980). Conversely, when Black women demand of their partners, "Show me the money," they not only reduce Black men to a measure of their financial worth, but reinscribe controlling images of themselves as materialistic "bitches." The challenge lies in disrupting Eurocentric scripts of Black masculinity and Black femininity, not just to receive better treatment for oneself, but to undermine and change prevailing sexual politics.

In her article "Sensuous Sapphires: A Study of the Social Construction of Black Female Sexuality," Annecka Marshall (1994) explores how Black women perceived the controlling images applied to them and how they negotiated those images in shaping their sexual selves. The women in her study saw the limitations of Eurocentric scripts of Black femininity concerning sexuality, and reported diverse strategies in dealing with them. While some women reject all of the stereotypes, they see no way of avoiding them. Some feel that they must choose between being seen as asexual mothers or hypersexual whores. Others recognize the power that being seen as "sensuous sapphires" has in how others see them, and try to exempt themselves from the category. By claiming that it's the other Black women who are "sapphires," not them, they may receive individual relief, but they leave the images themselves intact. Marshall also reports a range of coping strategies where women aim to challenge the very foundations of the images themselves.

Until recently, many heterosexual Black men have remained either unable to challenge controlling images of Black masculinity or have been unwilling to try. Sadly, believing in dominant notions of Black masculinity and Black femininity, they engage in controlling behaviors that often go unrecognized as such. U.S. Black men encounter contradictory expectations concerning Black manhood. On the one hand, Black men have been constructed as sexually violent rapists, as brutes, and as irresponsible boys who fail to marry the mothers of their children and financially support their children. Whereas Black men under slavery knew that they were not these things, their powerlessness denied them the trappings of manhood as defined by White propertied men. Emancipation brought with it Black male outrage at the treatment of Black women under slavery. A good deal of Black male energy went into protecting Black women from both economic and sexual exploitation. Given this history, efforts by Black men to protect Black women become valued. Many Black women want protection. Sonsyrea Tate, who was raised within the Nation of Islam, ultimately rejected the strict gender norms that routinely elevated boys above girls. But Tate also describes how protected she felt within the Nation: "While I was growing up, the Fruit of Islam, the security unit of the Nation of Islam, had made me, a small black child, feel safer than I felt at any other time in America" (Tate 1997, 4–5).

Barbara Omolade argues that "protecting black women was the most significant measure of black manhood and the central aspect of black male patriarchy" (1994, 13). If Omolade is correct, then this important choice to protect Black women, for many men, became harnessed to ideologies of Black masculinity in such a way that Black manhood became dependent on Black women's willingness to accept protection. Within this version of masculinity, a slippery slope emerges between *protecting* Black women and *controlling* them. This control is often masked, all in defense of widespread beliefs that Black men must be in charge in order to regain their lost manhood. As Paula Giddings points out, "It is men, not women, who control the sociosexual and professional relationships in the black community. Among other notions that must be dispensed with is the weak male/strong female patriarchal paradigm that clouds so much of our thinking about ourselves" (Giddings 1992, 463).

This general climate fosters a situation where some Black women feel that they must subordinate their needs to those of Black men in order to help Black men regain and retain their manhood. Yet at the same time, Black women's daily struggles for survival encourage patterns of self-reliance and self-valuation that benefit not just Black women, but men and children as well. As Barbara Omolade points out, "A black woman could not be completely controlled and defined by her own men, for she had already learned to manage and resist the advances of white men" (1994, 16). Tensions characterizing Black women's necessary self-reliance joined with our bona fide need for protection, as well as those characterizing Black men's desire to protect Black women juxtaposed to their admiration and resentment of Black women's assertiveness and independence, result in a complicated love and trouble tradition.

Failure to challenge an overall climate that not only defines Black masculinity in terms of Black men's ability to "own" and "control" their women, and Black femininity in terms of Black women's ability to help U.S. Black men feel like men, can foster African-American women's abuse. Black men who feel that they cannot be men unless they are in charge can be highly threatened by assertive Black women, especially those in their own households. In *The Color Purple*, Alice Walker's portrayal of Mister, a Black man who abuses his wife, Celie, explores the coexistence of love and trouble in African-American communities generally, and in Black men specifically:

> At the root of the denial of easily observable and heavily documented sexist brutality in the black community—the assertion that black men don't act like Mister, and if they do, they're justified by the pressure they're under as black men in a white society—is our deep, painful refusal to accept the fact that we are not only descendants of slaves, but we are also the descendants of slave *owners*. And that just as we have had to struggle to rid ourselves of slavish behaviors we must as ruthlessly eradicate any desire to be mistress or "master." (1989, 80)

Those Black men who wish to become "master" by fulfilling traditional definitions of masculinity—White, prosperous, and in charge—and who are blocked from doing so can become dangerous to those closest to them (Asbury 1987).

Rethinking relationships such as these has garnered increasing attention in Black feminist thought (E. White 1985). Refusing to reduce Black men's abuse to individualistic, psychological flaws, Black feminist analyses are characterized by careful attention to how intersecting oppressions of race, gender, class, and sexuality provide the backdrop for Black heterosexual love relationships (White 1985). Angela Davis contends, "We cannot grasp the true nature of sexual assault without situating it within its larger sociopolitical context" (1989, 3 7). Author Gayl Jones concurs: "It's important for me to clarify ... relationships in *situation*, rather than to have some theory of the way men are with women" (Harper 1979, 356). In Toni Morrison's *The Bluest Eye* (1970), Pecola Breedlove is a study in emotional abuse. Morrison portrays the internalized oppression that can affect a child who experiences daily assaults on her sense of self. Pecola's family is the immediate source of her pain, but Morrison also exposes the role of the larger community in condoning Pecola's victimization. In her choreopoem, *For Colored* Girls *Who Have Considered Suicide*, Ntozake Shange (1975) creates the character Beau Willie Brown, a man who abuses his lover, Crystal, and who kills their two young children. Rather than blaming Beau Willie Brown as the source of Crystal's oppression, Shange considers how the situation of "no air"—in this case, the lack of opportunities for both individuals—stifles the humanity of both Crystal and Beau Willie Brown.

Investigating the problems caused by abusive Black men often exposes Black women intellectuals to criticism. Alice Walker's treatment of male violence in works such as *The Third Life of Grange Copeland* (1970) and *The Color Purple* (1982) attracted censure. Even though Ntozake Shange's choreopoem is about Black women, one criticism leveled at her work is its purportedly negative portrayal of Black men (Staples 1979). Particularly troubling to some critics is the depiction of Beau Willie Brown. In an interview, Claudia Tate asked Ntozake Shange, "Why did you have to tell about Beau Willie Brown?" In this question Tate invokes the bond of family secrecy that often pervades dysfunctional families because she wants to know why Shange violated the African-American community's collective family "secret." Shange's answer is revealing: "I refuse to be a part of this conspiracy of silence. I will not do it. So that's why I wrote about Beau Willie Brown. I'm tired of living lies" (Tate 1983, 158–59).

This "conspiracy of silence" about Black men's physical and emotional abuse of Black women parallels Black women's silences about the politics of sexuality in general. Both silences stem from a larger system of legitimated, routinized violence targeted toward Black women and, via silence, both work to reinscribe social hierarchies (Richie 1996; Collins 1998d). Because hegemonic ideologies make everyday violence against Black women appear so routine, some women perceive neither themselves nor those around them as victims. Sara Brook's husband first assaulted her when she was pregnant, once threw her out of a window, and often called her his "Goddam knock box." Despite his excessive violence, she considered his behavior routine: "If I tried to talk to him he'd hit me so hard with his hands till I'd see stars. Slap me, and what he slap me for, I don't know. ... My husband would slap me and then go off to his woman's house. That's the way life was" (Simonsen 1986, 162). Ostensibly positive images of Black women make some women more likely to accept domestic violence as routine (E. White 1985). Many African-American women have had to exhibit independence and self-reliance to ensure their own survival and that of their loved ones.

But this image of the self-reliant Black woman can be troublesome for women in violent relationships. When an abused woman like Sara Brooks believes that "strength and independence are expected of her, she may be more reluctant to call attention to her situation, feeling that she should be able to handle it on her own; she may deny the seriousness of her situation" (Asbury 1987, 101).

Abused women, particularly those bearing the invisible scars of emotional abuse, are often silenced by the image of the "superstrong" Black woman (Richie 1996). But according to Audre Lorde, sexual violence against Black women is "a disease striking the heart of Black nationhood, and silence will not make it disappear" (1984, 120). To Lorde, such violence is exacerbated by racism and powerlessness such that "violence against Black women and children often becomes a standard within our communities, one by which manliness can be measured. But these woman-hating acts are rarely discussed as crimes against Black women" (p. 120). By making visible the pain the survivors feel, Black feminist intellectuals like Alice Walker, Audre Lorde, and Ntozake Shange challenge the alleged "rationality" of this particular system of control and rearticulate it as violence.

One of the best Black feminist analyses of domestic violence is found in Zora Neale Hurston's *Their Eyes Were Watching God* (1937). In the following passage, Hurston recounts how Tea Cake responded to a threat that another man would win the affections of Janie:

> Before the week was over he had whipped Janie. Not because her behavior justified his jealousy, but it relieved that awful fear inside him. Being able to whip her reassured him in possession. "Tea Cake, you sho is a lucky man," Sop-de-Bottom told him. "Uh person can see every place you hit her. Ah bet she never raised her hand tuh hit yuh back, neither. Take some uh dese ol' rusty black women and dey would fight yuh all night long and next day nobody couldn't tell you ever hit 'em. … Lawd! wouldn't Ah love tuh whip uh tender woman lak Janie! Ah bet she don't even holler. She jus' cries, eh Tea Cake?" (Hurston 1937, 121)

Hurston's work can be read as a Black feminist analysis of the sexualized violence that many Black women encounter in their deepest love relationships. Tea Cake and Sop-de-Bottom see women as commodities, property that they can whip to "reassure their possession." Janie is not a person; she is objectified as something owned by Tea Cake. Even if a man loves a woman, as is clearly the case of Tea Cake and Janie, the threat of competition from another male is enough to develop an "awful fear" that Janie will choose another man and thus deem him less manly than his competitors. Whipping Janie reassured Tea Cake that she was his. The conversation between the two men is also revealing. Images of color and beauty pervade their conversation. Sop-de-Bottom is envious because he can "see every place" that Tea Cake hit her and that she was passive and did not resist like the rest of the "rusty black women." Tea Cake and Sop-de-Bottom have accepted Eurocentric gender ideology concerning masculinity and femininity and have used force to maintain it. Furthermore, Janie's transgression was the potential to become unfaithful, the possibility to be sexually promiscuous, to become a whore. Finally, the violence occurs in an intimate relationship where love is present. This incident shows the process by which power as domination—in this case gender oppression structured through Eurocentric gender ideology and class oppression reflected in the objectification and commodification of Janie—has managed to annex the basic power of the erotic in Janie and Tea Cake's relationship. Tea Cake does not want to beat Janie, but he does because he *feels,* not thinks, he must. Their relationship represents the linking of sexuality and power, the potential for domination within sexualized love relationships, and the potential for using the erotic, their love for each other, as a catalyst for change.

Black Women Alone

Many Black women want loving sexual relationships with Black men, but instead end up alone. Black men may be the closest to Black women, and thus receive the lion's share of the blame for all the daily ways that Black women are caused to feel less worthy, yet this societal judgment and rejection of Black women permeates the entire culture. As Karla Holloway points out, "the tragic loneliness black women consistently face as we stand before judgmental others—sometimes white, but sometimes black; sometimes male, but sometimes female—demands that we have some wisdom, experience, and some passion with which to combat this abuse" (1995, 38). For African-American women, rejection by Whites is one thing—rejection by Black men is entirely another. In coping with the loneliness of not finding Black male partners, "wisdom, experience, and some passion" become important weapons.

This aloneness, the sense that one is at the bottom of the scale of desirability, fosters divergent reactions among African-American women. Many continue to express hope that one day they will be married to a good Black man and go on with their lives. Some pour their energies into Black motherhood, a respected and important part of Black civil society. Black single mothers are not as looked down upon in Black civil society, because most African-American women know that Black men are hard to find. The intensity of their ties with their children meshes with long-standing belief systems that value motherhood. However, despite the importance of this choice, for many, it can substitute for the lack of steady, sexualized love relationships in their lives. The character of Gloria in Terry McMillan's *Waiting to Exhale* (1992) typifies this choice of giving up hope that one will ever be lovable enough to find Salt-n-Pepa's (1993) "mighty good man." Gloria pours all of her energies into raising her son. She cooks for him, gains weight, and never dates for fear of compromising the respectability she has carved out within the stigma attached to unmarried Black mothers. Yet Gloria confronts a crisis when her son becomes sexually active and is old enough to leave home. He is becoming a man and can no longer be "her man." MacMillan provides a storybook resolution to Gloria's situation. A widower moves in across the street, becomes captivated with Gloria, and helps her learn to love herself as a sexual being. Real life is rarely this forgiving.

Dealing with the reality that Black men reject them leads other Black women to become devoted to careers. Eventually, these women become the middle-class, respectable, often childless Black ladies that Wahneema Lubiano (1992) argues Anita Hill symbolizes. Despite the often remarkable achievement of middle-class Black women, the pain many experience on the way to middle-class respectability, while masked by achievement, is no less real. Gloria Wade-Gayles describes the anger and frustration of the Black women college students in her classes when they realize the breadth of rejection. Many of her students spend all four years of their college lives without a single romantic relationship, Wade-Gayles observes. Conversations about this loneliness reveal the anger, sadness, and sorrow that many young Black women feel when living through rejection of this magnitude. In a nutshell, Black men pick non-Black women over them, and for many, it hurts.

Wade-Gayles reaches back into her own experiences to try to understand this situation: "The pain we experience as black teenagers follows many of us into adulthood, and, if we are professional black women, it follows with a vengeance. As a colleague in an eastern school explained our situation, 'Black men don't want us as mates because we are independent; white men, because we are black'" (Wade-Gayles 1996, 106)

In this context, heterosexual Black women become competitors, most searching for the elusive Black male, with many resenting the White women who naively claim them. These efforts to grapple with societal rejection that emerge from these sexual politics cut across age and class. As Wade-Gayles points out, "Teenagers know about athletes and entertainers; we know about politicians and scholars. Teenagers see faces; we see symbols that, in our opinion, spin the image of white women to the rhythm of symphonic chords" (Wade-Gayles 1996, 106–107).

In this context of what is perceived as widespread rejection by Black men, often in favor of White women, African-American women's relationships with Whites take on a certain intensity. On the one hand, antagonism can characterize relationships between Black and White women, especially those who appear blissfully unaware of the sexual politics that privileges White skin. Despite claims of shared sisterhood, heterosexual women remain competitors in a competition that many White women do not even know they have entered. "White men use different forms of enforcing oppression of white women and of women of Color," argues Chicana scholar Aida Hurtado. "As a consequence, these groups of women have different political responses and skills, and at times these differences cause the two groups to clash" (1989, 843). On the other hand, given the culpability of White men in creating and maintaining these sexual politics, Black women remain reluctant to love White men. Constrained by social norms that deem us unworthy of White men and norms of Black civil society that identify Black women who cross the color line as traitors to the race, many Black women remain alone.

This speaks to the double standard within Black civil society concerning interracial, heterosexual love relationships. For Black women, the historical relationship with White men has been one of legal but not sexual rejection: Propertied White men have exploited, objectified, and refused to marry African-American women and have held out trappings of power to their poorer brothers who endorse this ideology. The relationships between Black women and White men have long been constrained by the legacy of Black women's sexual abuse by White men and the unresolved tensions this creates. Traditionally, freedom for Black women has meant freedom *from* White men, not the freedom to choose White men as lovers and friends. Black women who have willingly chosen White male friends and lovers have been severely chastised in African-American communities for selling out the "race." Or they are accused of being like prostitutes, demeaning themselves by willingly using White men for their own financial or social gain.

Given the history of sexual abuse of Black women by White men, individual Black women who choose White partners become reminders of a difficult history for Black women as a collectivity. Such individual liaisons aggravate a collective sore spot because they recall historical master/slave relationships. Any sexual encounters between two parties where one has so much control over the other could never be fully consensual, even if the slave appeared to agree. Structural power differences of this magnitude limit the subordinate's power to give free consent or refusal. Controlling images such as jezebel are created to mask just this power differential and provide the illusion of consent. At the same time, even under slavery, to characterize interracial sex purely in terms of the victimization of Black women would be a distortion, because such depictions strip Black women of agency. Many Black women successfully resisted sexual assault while others cut bargains with their masters. More difficult to deal with, however, is the fact that even within these power differentials, genuine affection characterized some sexual relationships between Black women and White men (d'Emilio and Freedman 1988, 100–104).

This history of sexual abuse contributes to a contemporary double standard where Black women who date and marry White men are often accused of losing their Black identity. Within this context, Black women who do engage in relationships with White men encounter Black community norms that question their commitment to Blackness. A 20-year-old student participant in Annecka Marshall's (1994) study of how British Black women construct sexuality describes her own experiences with "mixed race" relationships as positive. But she also recognizes the double standard that is often applied to crossing the color line: "It's more acceptable in the Black community for Black men to go out with white women than for Black women to go out with white men. It's all about control and power. A Black man is seen as the one who controls the relationship and so his 'race' isn't being downtrodden and trampled. But if a Black woman does the same thing she is being submissive" (p. 119).

Relationships among U.S. Black women and U.S. White women demonstrate a similar complexity. Because White men have not married Black women, in large part due to laws against miscegenation designed to render the children of unions between White men and Black women propertyless (d'Emilio and Freedman 1988, 106), few delusions of enjoying the privileges attached to White male power have existed among Black women. In contrast, White women have been offered a share of White male power, but at the cost of participating in their own subordination. "Sometimes I really feel more sorrier for the white woman than I feel for ourselves because she been caught up in this thing, caught up feeling very special," observes Fannie Lou Hamer (Lerner 1972, 610). Thus even though "white women, as a group, are subordinated through seduction, women of Color, as a group, through rejection" (Hurtado 1989, 844), many White women appear unwilling to relinquish the benefits they accrue. This is the view of Tina, a Black woman in Minneapolis, whose White coworker routinely shared the details of her many sexual liaisons with Black men. Unconvinced that her coworker could be so ignorant of Black women's issues in finding men to date and marry, Tina rejected the view that White women are "racial innocents." She asked, "What stake would she have in dismantling a pecking order of femininity that puts her at the top?" (Jones 1994, 255).

This historical legacy of rejection and seduction frames relationships between Black and White women. Black women often express anger and bitterness against White women for their history of excusing the transgressions of their sons, husbands, and fathers. In her diary, a slaveholder described White women's widespread predilection to ignore White men's actions:

> Under slavery, we live surrounded by prostitutes. … Who thinks any worse of a negro or mulatto woman for being a thing we can't name? God forgive us, but ours is a monstrous system. … Like the patriarchs of old, our men live all in one house with their wives and their concubines; and the mulattoes one sees in every family partly resemble the white children. Any lady is ready to tell you who is the father of all the mulatto children in everybody's household but her own. Those, she seems to think drop from the clouds. (Lerner 1972, 51)

If White women under slavery could ignore transgressions of this magnitude, contemporary White women can more easily do the same.

For many African-American women, far too few White women are willing to acknowledge—let alone challenge—the actions of White men because they have benefited from them. Fannie Lou Hamer analyzes White women's culpability in Black women's subordination: "You've been caught up in this thing because, you know, you worked my grandmother, and after that you worked my mother, and then finally you got hold of me. And you really thought … you thought that you was *more* because you was a woman, and especially a white woman, you had this kind of angel feeling that you were untouchable" (Lerner 1972, 610). White women's inability to acknowledge how racism privileges them reflects the relationship that they have to White male power. "I think whites are carefully taught not to recognize white privilege," argues feminist scholar Peggy McIntosh, "just as males are taught not to recognize male privilege" (1988, 1). McIntosh describes her own struggles with learning to see how she had been privileged: "I have come to see white privilege as an invisible package of unearned assets which I can count on cashing in each day, but about which I was 'meant' to remain oblivious" (p. 1).

One manifestation of White women's privilege is the seeming naiveté many heterosexual White women have concerning how Black women perceive White women's sexualized love relationships with Black men. In *Dessa Rose*, Nathan, a Black slave, and Rufel, a White women on whose land they both live, have sexual relations. Even though Dessa, a Black woman, is not romantically attracted to Nathan, she deeply resents his behavior:

> White folks had taken everything in the world from me except my baby and my life and they had tried to take them. And to see him, who had helped to save me, had friended with me through so much of it, laying up, wallowing in what had hurt me so—I didn't feel that nothing I could say would tell him what that pain was like. And I didn't feel like it was on me to splain why he shouldn't be messing with no white woman; I thought it was on him to say why he was doing it. (Williams 1986, 186)

Like many African-American women, Dessa sees Black male admiration for White women as a rejection of her. She asks, "Had he really wanted me to be like Mistress, I wondered, like Miz Ruint, that doughy skin and slippery hair? Was that what they wanted?" (Williams 1986, 199).

The numbers of U.S. Black men who "want" White women has risen since the 1960s, in the context of two developments. For one, the elimination of de jure (but not de facto) racial segregation has brought Blacks and Whites in close contact in schools and job sites, often as equals. In particular, the laws against miscegenation that forbade interracial marriage passed by Southern states during the 1860s were abolished. When it comes to Black men and White women, legally at least, the *Driving Miss Daisy* days are done. At the same time, changes in sexual attitudes challenged long-standing arrangements where, according to Paula

Giddings, "sex was the principle around which wholesale segregation and discrimination was organized with the ultimate objective of preventing intermarriage. The sexual revolution … separated sexuality from reproduction, and so diluted the ideas about purity—moral, racial, and physical" (Giddings 1995, 424). These changing social conditions allowed Black male desire for White women as well as White female desire for Black men to be expressed without the censure afforded Nathan and Rufel's relationship.

The birth of biracial or mixed-race children speaks to the reality of these sexualized love relationships between Black men and White women. Historically, mixed-race children were accepted into a segregated Black civil society because everyone knew that such children should not be held accountable for the circumstances of their conception and birth. More often though, biracial and mixed-race children were the offspring of Black mothers and, as such, participated in Black civil society much as their mothers did. Currently, however, the birth of biracial and mixed-race children to so many White mothers raises new questions for African-American women. Even in the face of rejection by Black men that leaves so many without partners, ironically, Black women remain called upon to accept and love the mixed-race children born to their brothers, friends, and relatives. By being the Black mothers that these children do not have, these women are expected to help raise biracial children who at the same time often represent tangible reminders of their own rejection.

Currently, much more is known about how White women negotiate these new relationships with their biracial children than we do about either Black men's participation in being a parent to these children or the Black women who are so often called upon to help White mothers raise them. What does appear in accounts of children are reports of how important their Black relatives can be in helping them understand and cope with racism (see, e.g., Jones 1994).

Biracial Black women who recognize these contradictions struggle with this situation. On the one hand, the biracial girlchild's White mother positions her closer to Whiteness, and this physical beauty often makes her more attractive to many Black men. But on the other, she joins the ranks of Black women and thus inherits the history of rejection. In her essay titled "Mamas White," Lisa Jones describes her reactions to seeing White female and Black male couples and thus taps some of the complexities that accompany these new relationships: "Clearly I was saying that these duos tangle up my emotions; I look at them as a child of an interracial marriage, but also as a black woman who has witnessed the market value put on white femininity" (Jones 1994, 30). Rejecting yet another form of seduction, the seeming benefits of a mixed-race identity as a haven within a society that derogates Blackness, Jones recognizes the difficulties if not impossibility of stepping outside racial categories by pretending that they simply don't apply. Putting brackets around the term "Black woman" and pointing out its socially constructed nature does not erase the fact of living as a Black woman and all that entails. By simultaneously problematizing and accepting these relationships, Jones points the way toward a new analysis.

No matter how much in love Black men and White women may be, such couples will continue to attract Black women's attention. Gloria Wade-Gayles describes the power that the reality of these couples has for many African-American women:

> We see them, and we feel abandoned. We feel abandoned because we have been abandoned in so many ways, by so many people, and for so many centuries. We are the group of women furthest removed from the concept of beauty and femininity which invades every spot on the planet, and, as a result, we are taught not to like ourselves, or, as my student said, not to believe that we can ever do enough or be enough to be loved and desired. The truth is we experience a pain unique to us as a group when black men marry white women and even when they don't. It is a pain our mothers knew and their mothers before them. A pain passed on from generation to generation because the circumstances that create the pain have remained unchanged. (Wade-Gayles 1996, 110)

Moving through this pain requires more than blaming White women for allegedly taking Black men, or Black men for rejecting us. It demands changing the "circumstances that create the pain."

Black Women and Erotic Autonomy

Changing the circumstances that create the pain requires developing an analysis of Black women's deep love relationships of all sorts. As Evelynn Hammonds points out, "mirroring as a way of negating a legacy of silence needs to be explored in much greater depth than it has been to date by black feminist theorists" (1997, 179). Karla Holloway suggests that one important first step occurs at an "essential moment when black women must acknowledge the powerful impact of our physical appearance. How we look is a factor in what happens to us" (1995, 36). Holloway argues that via constructions of Black women's sexuality, systems of oppression hold up distorted mirrors of a "public image" through which Black women learn to view ourselves. Holloway counsels Black women to disable "mirrored reflection of a prejudicial gaze" via a "reflexive, self-mediated vision of our bodies" (p. 45). When Black women learn to hold up new "mirrors" to one another that enable us to see and love one another for who we really are, new possibilities for empowerment via deep love can emerge.

Theoretically, this sounds good, but practically, Black women learning to provide mirrors for one another that enable us to love one another comes face to face with the possible eroticization of such love. When it comes to issues of sexuality, mirroring reveals how the sharing required to support and love one another can find erotic expression. If sexuality constitutes a dimension of expressed love, then, for many Black women, loving Black women means loving them sexually. This recognition that loving oneself and loving Black women may find erotic or sexual expression can be threatening. The stigmatization of lesbian relationships seems designed to contain this threat.

In this sense, Black lesbian relationships are not only threatening to intersecting systems of oppression, they can be highly threatening to heterosexual African-American women's already assaulted sense of self. Certainly the homophobia expressed by many Black heterosexual women is influenced, in part, by accepting societal beliefs about lesbians. For Black women who have already been labeled the Other by virtue of race and gender, the threat of being labeled a lesbian can have a chilling effect on Black women's ideas and on our relationships with one another. In speculating about why so many competent Black women writers and reviewers have avoided examining lesbianism, Ann Allen Shockley suggests that "the fear of being labeled a Lesbian, whether they were one or not" (1983, 84), has been a major deterrent.

The issues, however, may go much deeper. "I think the reason that Black women are so homophobic," suggests Barbara Smith, "is that attraction–repulsion thing. They have to speak out vociferously against lesbianism because if they don't, they may have to deal with their own deep feelings for women" (Smith and Smith 1981, 124). Shockley agrees: "Most black women feared and abhorred Lesbians more than rape—perhaps because of the fear bred from their deep inward potentiality for Lesbianism" (1974, 31–32). In the same sense that men who accept Eurocentric notions of masculinity fear and deny the dimensions of themselves that they associate with femininity—for example, interpreting male expressiveness as being weak and unmanly (Hoch 1979)—avowedly heterosexual Black women may suppress their own strong feelings for other Black women for fear of being stigmatized as lesbians. Similarly, in the way that male domination of women embodies men's fears about their own masculinity, Black heterosexual women's treatment of Black lesbians reflects fears that all African-American women are essentially the same. Yet, as Audre Lorde points out, "in the same way that the existence of the self-defined Black woman is no threat to the self-defined Black man, the Black lesbian is an emotional threat only to those Black women whose feelings of kinship and love for other Black women are problematic in some way" (1984, 49).

Black lesbian relationships pose little threat to "self-defined" Black men and women secure in their sexualities. But loving relationships among Black women do pose a tremendous threat to systems of intersecting oppressions. How dare these women love one another in a context that deems Black women as a collectivity so unlovable and devalued? The treatment of Black lesbians reveals how the sexual expression of all Black women becomes regulated within intersecting systems of oppression. As a specific site of intersectionality, Black lesbian relationships constitute relationships among the ultimate Other. Black lesbians are not White, male, or heterosexual and generally are not affluent. As such, they represent the antithesis of Audre Lorde's "mythical norm" and become the standard by which other groups measure their own so-called normality and self-worth. Sexual politics functions smoothly only if sexual nonconformity is kept invisible or is punished if it becomes visible. "By being sexually independent of men, lesbians, by their very existence, call into question society's definition of woman at its deepest level," observes Barbara Christian (1985, 199). Visible Black lesbians challenge the mythical norm that the best people are White, male, rich, and heterosexual. In doing so, lesbians generate anxiety, discomfort, and a challenge to the dominant group's control of power and sexuality on the interpersonal level (Vance 1984).

For African-American women, taking seriously the idea of generating loving "mirrors" for one another requires taking on all of the "isms" that keep Black women down, including heterosexism. It means moving beyond the stigmatization of Black heterosexual women as jezebels—the sexual deviants inside an assumed heterosexuality—and of Black lesbians, whose homosexuality labels them sexual deviants *outside* heterosexuality. In crafting such an argument, Evelynn Hammonds is one of many who argues for a "different level of engagement between black heterosexual and black lesbian women as the basis for the development of a black feminist praxis that articulates the ways in which invisibility, otherness, and stigma are produced and re-produced on black women's bodies" (Hammonds 1997, 181–82). Examining these connections in order to explore what M. Jacqui Alexander (1997) describes as *erotic autonomy* may provide space to think and do something new.

Alexander suggests that women's sexual agency or erotic autonomy has been threatening to a series of social institutions. In particular, the prostitute and the lesbian have historically functioned as the major symbols of threat. Both sets of women reject the heterosexual nuclear family upon which so many social institutions rely for meaning. As a result, "the categories lesbian and prostitute now function together … as outlaw, operating outside the boundaries of law and, therefore, poised to be disciplined and punished within it" (Alexander 1997, 65). Alexander examines how this erotic autonomy becomes suppressed within the Bahamian state. Yet her arguments contain important insights for U.S. Black women where the need exists to develop an erotic autonomy that does three things.

First, it must help U.S. Black women reject the dual stigma applied to Black heterosexual women as "hoochies" and to Black lesbians as sexual deviants. Recognizing how heterosexual and lesbian sexualities are both stigmatized within an overarching heterosexism and how this dual stigmatization has long been important in shoring up intersecting oppressions should help identify practices within Black civil society that are harmful to Black women as a collectivity. Evelynn Hammonds suggests that within the historical legacy of silences concerning Black women's sexuality, certain expressions of Black female sexuality will be rendered as dangerous, for individuals and for the group. Within this logic, a culture of dissemblance that counsels a self-imposed silence concerning Black women's sexuality makes it acceptable for some heterosexual Black women to cast both openly sensual heterosexual Black women and Black lesbians as "traitors" to the race. This censure operates in much the same way as Anita Hill's testimony against Clarence Thomas did. The continuation of a culture of dissemblance explains why Black heterosexual women who take control of their sexuality in public are often censured. When they sing of Black women's sensuality and erotic desires in public, the Black blues women of the 1920s and hip-hop group Salt-n-Pepa's music both become cast as inappropriate public expressions of Black female sexuality. This culture of dissemblance might also explain why Black lesbians, "whose 'deviant' sexuality is framed within an already existing deviant sexuality—have been wary of embracing the status of 'traitor,' and the potential loss of community such an embrace engenders" (Hammonds 1997, 181).

A second component of moving toward erotic autonomy involves redefining beauty in ways that include Black women. New understandings of beauty would necessarily alter the types of mirrors held up to Black women to judge Black women's beauty. Redefining beauty requires learning to see African-American women who have Black African features as being capable of beauty. Proclaiming Black women "beautiful" and White women "ugly" merely replaces one set of controlling images with another and fails to challenge Eurocentric masculinist aesthetics. This is simply binary thinking in reverse: In order for one individual to be judged beautiful, another individual—the Other—must be deemed ugly. Dessa Rose's view of Miz Ruint as having "doughy skin and slippery hair" illustrates one Black woman's attempt to protect herself from a derogated Blackness by reversing the categories of beauty. Creating an alternative Black feminist aesthetic involves, instead, rejecting binary thinking altogether.

In this endeavor, African-American women can draw on African-derived aesthetics (Gayle 1971; Walton 1971) that potentially free women from standards of ornamental beauty.[4] Though such aesthetics are present in music (Sidran 1971; Cone 1972), dance (Asante 1990), and language (Smitherman 1977; Kochman 1981), quilt making offers a suggestive model for a Black feminist aesthetic that might move Black women and others toward erotic autonomy. African-American women quilt makers do not seem interested in a uniform color scheme but use several methods of playing with colors to create unpredictability and movement (Wahlman and Scully 1983 in Brown 1989, 922). For example, a strong color may be juxtaposed with another strong color, or with a weak one. Contrast is used to structure or organize. Overall, the symmetry in African-American quilts does not come from uniformity as it does in Euro-American quilts. Rather, symmetry comes through diversity. Nikki Giovanni points out that quilts are traditionally formed from scraps. "Quilters teach there is no such thing as waste," she observes, "only that for which we currently see no purpose" (1988, 89).

This dual emphasis on beauty occurring via individual uniqueness juxtaposed in a community setting and on the importance of creating functional beauty from the scraps of everyday life offers a powerful alternative to Eurocentric aesthetics. African-derived notions of diversity in community and functional beauty potentially heal many of the binaries that underlie Western social thought. From African-influenced perspectives, women's beauty is not based solely on physical criteria because mind, spirit, and body are not conceptualized as separate, oppositional spheres. Instead, all are central in aesthetic assessments of individuals and their creations. Beauty is functional in that it has no meaning independent of the group. Deviating from the group "norm" is not rewarded as "beauty." Instead, participating in the group and being a functioning individual who strives for harmony is key to assessing an individual's beauty (Asante 1987). Moreover, participation is not based on conformity but instead is seen as individual uniqueness that enhances the overall "beauty" of the group. With such criteria, no individual is inherently beautiful because beauty is not a state of being. Instead beauty is a state of becoming. Just as all African-American women as well as all humans become capable of beauty, all can move toward erotic autonomy.

A final component of developing African-American women's erotic autonomy requires finding ways to stress that African-American women learn to see expressing love for one another as fundamental to resisting oppression. This component politicizes love and reclaims it from the individualized and trivialized place that it now occupies. Self-defined and publicly expressed Black women's love relationships, whether such relationships find sexual expression or not, constitute resistance. If members of the group on the bottom love one another and affirm one another's worth, then the entire system that assigns that group to the bottom becomes suspect.

Many Black women understand the power that maternal love has had in empowering them as individuals. Yet this power of deep love remains circumscribed in biological motherhood, biological sisterhood, sorority ties, and other similar socially approved relationships. As the next two chapters explore, this legitimated maternal love has spurred many Black women into more activist arenas and can be seen as an important dimension of U.S. Black feminism. Broadening the spectrum of Black women's loving relationships with one another, including those that find sexual expression, may move Black womanhood closer to reclaiming the power of deep love.

Love and Empowerment

"In order to perpetuate itself, every oppression must corrupt or distort those various sources of power within the culture of the oppressed that can provide energy for change" (Lorde 1984, 53). The ability of social practices such as pornography, prostitution, and rape to distort the private domain of Black women's love relationships with Black men, with Whites, and with one another typifies this process. The parallels between distortions of deep human feelings in racial oppression and of the distortions of the erotic in sexual oppression are striking. Analysts of the interpersonal dynamics of racism point out that Whites fear in Blacks those qualities they project onto Blacks that they most fear in themselves. By labeling Blacks as sexually animalistic and by dominating Blacks, Whites aim to repress these dimensions of their own inner being. When men dominate women and accuse them of being sexually passive, the act of domination, from pressured sexual intercourse to rape, reduces male anxiety about male impotence, the ultimate sexual passivity (Hoch 1979). Similarly, the suppression of gays and lesbians symbolizes the repression of strong feelings for members of one's own gender, feelings U.S. culture has sexualized and stigmatized within heterosexism. All of these emotions—the fact that Whites know that Blacks are human, the fact that men love women, and the fact that women have deep feelings for one another—must be distorted on the emotional level of the erotic in order for oppressive systems to endure. Sexuality in the individual, interpersonal domain of power becomes annexed by intersecting oppressions in the structural domain of power in order to ensure the smooth operation of domination.

Recognizing that corrupting and distorting basic feelings human beings have for one another lies at the heart of multiple systems of oppression opens up new possibilities for transformation and change. June Jordan (1981) explores this connection between embracing feeling and human empowerment: "As I think about anyone or any thing—whether history or literature or my father or political organizations or a poem or a film—as I seek to evaluate the potentiality, the life-supportive commitment/possibilities of anyone or any thing, the decisive question is, always, *where is the love?"* (p. 141).

Jordan's question touches a deep nerve in African-American social and ethical thought. In her work *Black Womanist Ethics,* Katie G. Cannon (1988) suggests that love, community, and justice are deeply intertwined in African-American ethics. Cannon examines the work of two prominent Black male theorists—Howard Thurman and Martin Luther King, Jr.—and concludes that their ideas represent core values from which Black women draw strength. According to Thurman, love is the basis of community, and community is the arena for moral agency. Only love of self, love between individuals, and love of God can shape, empower, and sustain social change. Martin Luther King, Jr., gives greater significance in his ethics to the relationship of love and justice, suggesting that love is active, dynamic, and determined, and generates the motive and drive for justice. For both Thurman and King, everything moves toward community and the expression of love within the context of community. It is this version of love and community, argues Cannon, that stimulates a distinctive Black womanist ethics.

For June Jordan, love begins with self-love and self-respect, actions that propel African-American women toward the self-determination and political activism essential for social justice. By grappling with this simple yet profound question, "Where is the love?" Black women resist multiple types of oppression. This question encourages all groups embedded in systems of domination to move toward a place where, as Toni Morrison's Paul D expresses it, "You could love anything you chose—not to need permission for desire—well, now, that was freedom" (1987, 162).

Reading 3.2. Strong but Submissive

How African American Women Negotiate Traditional Feminine Roles and Strong Black Women Ideology in Early Romantic Relationships

Khia A. Thomas and Kyla Day Fletcher

Introduction

Across their formative years, African American women are exposed to a variety of gendered messages from parents, peers, media, and religious institutions, which shape understandings of womanhood. These gendered messages incorporate elements of traditional feminine ideology, as articulated by mainstream White America, and are enacted along appearance, behavioral, cognition, and affective domains (Bay-Cheung et al., 2002; Mahalik et al., 2005). As a unique developmental challenge, young Black women must reconcile these notions alongside equally informative and influential culture-specific notions of femininity.

Among the prominent gendered racial socialization messages that young African American women receive is the importance of self-determination, assertiveness, and strength (Hill, 2002; Thomas & King, 2007; Thomas & Speight, 1999). These traits are mirrored in the Strong Black Woman image (Abrams et al., 2014; Beauboeuf-Lafontant, 2007, 2014; Wyatt, 2008). Beauboeuf-Lafontant (2014) describes the Strong Black Woman as "exhibit(ing) formidable self-reliance, emotional and physical resilience, race loyalty, and an infinite ability to care for others." Other scholars have situated the Strong Black Woman image as self-sacrificial, prioritizing the needs of family and community above self and at all costs (West et al., 2016).

Among the growing body of literature that addresses how African American women conceptualize and engage with femininity, few studies explore the overlapping behavioral dictates of traditional feminine ideology, as articulated through mainstream American norms, and Strong Black Woman ideology. Traditional feminine role ideology centers being affectionate, cheerful, eager to soothe hurt feelings, sensitive to the needs of others, soft-spoken, and understanding (Bem, 1974). Recent feminine ideology models, normed using multicultural samples, characterize feminine roles as: being relationally connected to others, being sweet and nice, being thin, putting others first, looking young, being sexy, being modest, being domestic, caring for children, prioritizing romantic relationships, maintaining sexual fidelity, and investing in personal appearance (Mahalik et al., 2005). Evidence has emerged that African American girls, in particular, may hold alternate notions of femininity, despite expectations to conform to mainstream feminine ideals (Morris, 2007; Sanders & Bradley, 2005).

Strong Black Woman ideology centers diametrically opposed traits as prototypical of African American women. These characteristics include independence, assertiveness, self-sufficiency, stoic emotionality where crying is a form of weakness, and near-infinite reserves of emotional and psychological resilience (Beauboeuf-Lafontant, 2003, 2007; Romero, 2002). Despite remarkable divergence from traditional feminine ideology, the Strong Black Woman image overlaps in describing Black women as nurturers and caretakers (Abrams et al., 2014).

A review of the literature reveals a burgeoning understanding of how African American women conceptualize womanhood in light of the diverging models highlighted above. It is often overlooked that Black women may simultaneously endorse and embody gendered expectations in the intersection of mainstream and culturally specific models of womanhood. When they describe what it means to be a woman, there may be a complex interplay of traditional feminine ideals and those reminiscent of Strong Black Woman ideology—and potentially, some of these roles may be at odds with each other. These inherently opposing expectations are, at best, challenges to reconcile; at worst, they pose a threat to psychological well-being.

Becoming Strong Black Women

Strong Black Woman ideology has been described as ubiquitous within the African American community (Nelson et al., 2016; Parks, 2010). However, there are gaps in the developmental literature, which lacks specific examinations of how gendered expectations socialized to Black youth are then endorsed and embodied. In particular, we know very little about how these ideals are conceptualized across different age groups. A review of over two decades of research reveals that very few studies address gender role endorsement among African American female youth (Jones et al., 2018). Among the few studies that employ a developmental framework, there are distinctions in how Strong Black Woman ideology is conceptualized—as a positive element that bolsters well-being, or as a negative element that sets the stage for physical, emotional, and psychological difficulties (Ford, 2006; Shorter-Gooden & Washington, 1996).

African American girls may begin incorporating notions of strength into self-conceptualizations as early as adolescence. Black adolescent girls highlighted being tough, determined, and able to overcome adversity, as well as possessing a strong sense of self, as positive qualities (Shorter-Gooden & Washington, 1996). These girls also described themselves as embodying these characteristics, working to develop them, or admiring them in other Black women (Shorter-Gooden & Washington, 1996). Across cultural groups, adolescence is thought to be a developmental period characterized by a central task of identity development (Erikson, 1980); as such, this racialized concept of gender may be a distinguishing quality of identity development for African American girls.

Other studies using samples of emerging adult Black women have described Strong Black Woman ideology in a less than positive light. Ford (2006) noted that college-aged Black women associated the Strong Black Woman image with femininity, with some negative connotations. They described these women as defeminized, headstrong, emotionally tough, loud, domineering, rude, or pushy. Analyses even went so far as to equate the Strong Black Woman to an "emasculating Black bitch" (Ford, 2006). This may suggest a move toward a more nuanced set of gender role beliefs as African American girls move from adolescence to adulthood. Indeed, in the more prevalent studies of racialized gender role beliefs in adulthood, evidence points to increasingly conflictual attitudes among Black women. Some women invest in these gendered behaviors while some are ambivalent and attempt to resist, whereas other women outright reject them (Dow, 2015).

Although the field has made long strides towards understanding the Strong Black Woman image, most researchers have done so from the developmental frame of reference of older African American women—those already juggling multiple roles and responsibilities with children, family, career, and relationships. Here, there is growing evidence that "being strong" may place Black women at risk for health challenges and psychological difficulties (Beauboeuf-Lafontant, 2003, 2014; Settles et al., 2008; West et al., 2016). We argue for broadening the scope of research, as it is necessary to understand how endorsement and embodiment of gender ideology affects African American women across different life stages and social contexts.

Strong Black Woman Ideology and Gender Role Conflict in Romantic Relationships

It seems clear that Black women are expected to embody a complicated scope of gendered traits; however, these expectations do not solely impact Black women. Indeed, men may endorse similarly complex expectations of Black women's roles. Some have characterized Strong Black Women as unfeminine, or serving to emasculate or displace Black men in the "natural order" according to patriarchal norms (Lawrence-Webb et al., 2004). Previous studies suggest a degree of conflict between Black women and men when it comes to the occupation of so-called traditional gender roles, especially in the context of romantic relationships (Lawrence-Webb et al., 2004). Haynes's (2000) qualitative study of middle-class Black men and women found a complex mix of traditional and egalitarian gender roles relating to marital expectations. Men were expected to assume the role of the financial provider to bolster their sense of masculinity and self-worth, whereas women were expected to serve as nurturers, taking care of children and the home, regardless of competing work demands. Analyses pointed out gender role tension, citing the clashing of Black women's and men's roles (Haynes, 2000). In this regard, one of the men in the study says:

> My definition of femininity is a woman who is strong but feminine … . I want a woman who is sensitive, who is caring … . That's fine for you to be corporate-tycoon type [of a woman], [but] you [have to] control it when you're in the house. (Haynes, 2000, p. 820)

Black women may be expected to negotiate a precarious position of being strong and independent in some contexts, while being dependent and being emotional centers of the family in other contexts. The lines between these contexts may not always be clear, and the code-switching necessary for smooth transition from one context to the other may take a high toll. Certainly Black men and women differ in the extent to which they experience the stress of straddling traditional feminine and Strong Black Woman ideology; much of the burden of navigating and reconciling these complexities may fall on Black women.

Previous research has considered the impact of racialized gender role norms on romantic relationships between Black women and men. Key (2004) examined psychological well-being among college-educated African American women between the ages of 35–50 years. Interestingly, one of the women in this study cited maintaining a certain level of strength or assertiveness, but learning how to express certain sentiments in a less overt manner to prevent conflict in romantic relationships (Key, 2004). Studies suggest that African American adolescent girls may have a rudimentary understanding that healthy romantic relationships involve interpersonal communication abilities and compromise (Debnam et al., 2014). However, at this age, they may also have a limited understanding of how to reconcile their own burgeoning role expectations with those of a partner.

Our Current Study

What is lacking in the present literature is an understanding of how African American women engage with and negotiate between divergent understandings of femininity, as articulated through so-called traditional feminine ideology, and culture-specific messages outlined by Strong Black Woman ideology. How are these ideologies woven into a complex, nuanced understanding of womanhood? Even fewer studies couch these negotiations within the years of emerging adulthood. According to current developmental models, women between the ages of 18–25 years will have achieved a more secure identity and will gradually adopt adult roles and responsibilities (Arnett, 1998). At the same time, limited socialization about navigating the conflicting expectations of Strong Black Woman and traditional ideologies may ill-prepare Black women in emerging adulthood to reconcile gendered expectations with real-life dating experiences, as expectations and realities may not align.

Each model of femininity articulates its own version of what women are or what women should be. Engaging with this content may be particularly challenging for young African American women, as they pull from a wide variety of gendered notions while learning how to navigate independently as emerging adults. A more complex investigation into this process is necessary. The current study aims to address these gaps by employing a series of semi-structured interviews. Specifically, the study is guided by the following questions:

To what extent do African American emerging adult women reference the behavioral dictates of traditional feminine ideology and Strong Black Woman ideology as central to the navigation of this developmental period?

What are the perceived challenges, difficulties, and benefits of navigating the conflicting behavioral demands of both articulations of womanhood, as seen in dating experiences or romantic relationships in emerging adulthood?

Method

Participants

Participants were 13 African American emerging adult women, aged 18–22 years, attending a large, predominantly White Midwestern university. This group represents a subsample of a larger study on gender and sexual socialization. Participants were asked to complete an additional form to be contacted for an interview study, and were selected by demographic information provided, such as age, sexual orientation, and level of dating experience. All identifying information has been changed, including names and references to specific identifying locations or organizations, in order to preserve confidentiality.

Participants were contacted by a Black female researcher and scheduled to meet in a private room to conduct interviews. All interviews were tape-recorded and later transcribed to identify emergent themes from the narratives. At the conclusion of the interview, participants were thanked for their time and paid $20 for participation.

Procedure

A semi-structured interview format was used for this study. The interviewer asked a series of questions about what it means to be a woman and what it means to be a Black woman, and, if it had not been previously mentioned, further probed to describe the participant's level of identification with the Strong Black Woman image. Participants were asked a series of questions about their attitudes and experiences with dating and romantic relationships. Transcribed narratives were coded, according to a grounded theory approach, to identify emergent themes. The data presented reflects analyses and interpretations made significant by the researchers.

The central goal of this research was to integrate multiple perspectives from emergent adult African American women. Specifically, this study details and describes diverse experiences and interpretations among African American women of the same age group and the shared social context of a collegiate environment. A series of field notes was created to highlight central issues brought up by the women, and to propose how different variables fit together to produce these experiences, grounded in the developmental context of emerging adulthood.

Results

Split Between the Two: Engaging Two Models of Womanhood

One of the major emergent themes is the extent to which the Strong Black Woman ideal is a central element of femininity. Among the 13 women interviewed, all but one spontaneously generated the word "strong" when asked to describe what it means to be a woman. Nearly all respondents reinforced characteristics of strength, independence, willfulness, and emotional power. The importance of being strong received further emphasis when participants were asked to reflect on what it means to be a Black woman. Brandy (age 19) shares: "Yeah, like I want to say strong, but not strong, it's more than that, like you can get through things … being opinionated … I think you should be able to form your own opinions. Confident." Another participant, Christina (age 22), details: "In some ways they've been looked down upon, kind of like they have too much mouth or nasty or things like that, but I feel Black women are positive and strong." Interviewees continued to detail examples of African American women—mostly older family members or historical figures—and emphasized Strong Black Woman ideology as a celebrated element of their femininity. They saw themselves sharing and participating in historical continuity with past generations of Black women.

Nearly all participants agreed with the importance of being strong and described ways in which they prized these characteristics or ways in which they had embodied Strong Black Woman ideology in their daily lives. Participants invoked Strong Black Woman ideology as they described navigating through an academically rigorous, predominantly White university to succeed in obtaining their degrees. They detailed discriminatory experiences in which they had been underestimated, or someone had insinuated that they did not belong, because of their race, gender, or some combination of both.

Ebony (age 19) opines: "Being in college, going to a predominantly White college, I think you have to be a survivor to maintain yourself." Another participant, Tina (age 19), shared an anecdote about a school counselor discouraging her from attending her university. She was told that her chances of admission were slim and that she was unlikely to succeed on the pre-medical track. Tina's response: "It took all the strength I had not to cuss them out … I just bit my tongue and didn't let it bother me, even though it did." Whereas some women related utilizing these negative perceptions or discriminatory experiences as a "fuel" to succeed, others adopted a more passive approach. Tina describes "moving on" from the negative situation, to ultimately prove the counselor wrong. She also juxtaposed her response with a typical feminine response of crying or becoming emotional.

Whether choosing to fight against negative perceptions or "just move on," participants shared many stories of invoking Strong Black Woman ideology to overcome adverse and discriminatory experiences, associating the Strong Black Woman image with feelings of positivity and empowerment. At this age, the most relevant examples took place within an academic or collegiate context; however, these feelings did not necessarily carry over outside of this context. Interestingly, participants voiced expectations of traditional feminine roles in romantic relationships. While navigating current dating and romantic experiences, they experienced difficulty in striking a balance between those traditional feminine roles and the Strong Black Woman messages they had received.

"I Still Haven't Found That Balance Yet": Being Strong and Traditional

A large focus of the interview addressed the extent to which traditional and Strong Black Woman ideologies are mirrored in dating and romantic relationships. Emerging adults are very likely to be single, unmarried, exploring romantic relationships with different partners, or engaging in their first serious relationships. Do they engage with divergent gendered expectations in this social context? If so, how does negotiating alternate gender ideologies affect romantic experiences?

Some women shared positive outcomes associated with being strong in the context of romantic relationships. They highlighted personal benefits realized from maintaining a strong sense of self. Lena, age 18, said, "If you're not strong when you're in a relationship, then a lot of people will take advantage of you. You can act out of character, do things you wouldn't regularly do." Lena went on to assert the importance of women defining their personal values and making decisions accordingly—rather than going against their own judgment or automatically deferring to a partner. She alluded to a danger inherent in losing a sense of self and associated this with vulnerability to manipulation and harmful outcomes. In this way, being "strong" emerged as an asset for women as they begin to explore and navigate through relationships as young adults. However, other participants, including Lena herself later in the interview, detailed challenges they faced as they navigated between being the strong woman they were raised to be and being the traditional woman they felt they ought to be within relationships. Praised characteristics of Strong Black Woman ideology were often seen to conflict with men's traditional gender roles; these traits and behaviors would need to be "checked," or guarded against, to ensure that the relationship continued.

Tina (age 19) shared difficulties inherent in navigating differing models of femininity. Earlier in the interview, she defined Strong Black Woman characteristics as being akin to an inherited legacy of African American women. However, in romantic relationships, she tossed away this "birthright" in favor of being more traditional. She said of relationships: "There would be times where you would have to kind of take a more passive role even though that's definitely going against what you believe in, just in order to prevent conflict." She articulated an idea of adhering to mainstream feminine ideals, including being passive, as a standard of "correct" behavior in relationships.

When asked directly about how to deal with expectations of being both traditional and strong, Lena (age 18) stated:

> I think relationship-wise there are some ways that you have to be traditional, but still strong, because the male is always supposed to open the door for the lady, take the lady out, spend his money on her. It's been some times where I was in a relationship and the guy wants to do stuff for me and I'm like, 'No, I got it. I got it,' because I'm independent.

In this quote, Lena carefully articulates traditional male norms dictating "appropriate" dating behaviors, such as opening car doors and spending money on dates, and suggests that women should oblige. She also positions being independent as a transgression against traditional notions. She later reflects on being raised and socialized by her family to be independent and to do things for herself, and then having to learn to allow a male partner to perform those traditional male norms. She explains:

> I've been in a relationship for two years now and I still haven't got the hang of it. Opening the car door for me? I can do that myself, you know? So it's been some times when I've had to let go, and it's like OK, he has to do this for you.

A common chord across interviews was a perception that within the realm of relationships, "traditional" is right and "strong" is wrong. Embodying traditional feminine roles was described as: giving "space" for men to rightfully occupy traditional male roles, preventing gender role conflict, and engendering relationship harmony and longer-lasting relationships. Strong Black Woman ideological characteristics, which women prized and embodied, were also described as characteristics they needed to monitor, in order to align with mainstream traditional notions of feminine behavior.

Some women recounted stories of losing relationships due to being perceived as too strong-willed, assertive, or outspoken. For example, Brandi (age 18) described arguing with a suitor about coming over to "chill" on study night. The suitor tried to convince her to push her work aside, but she ultimately declined. She said about such experiences:

> They try to get mad at me just because I'm a strong-willed person. My academics come first and that's it. They might get mad at me and maybe choose not to talk to me anymore. That's perfectly

fine because I have my priorities. It might have hurt our relationship, but at the same time, I don't really care. If they want to act like that, then I guess it wasn't meant to be anyway.

Brandi describes being strong-willed and resolute, even being willing to sacrifice a potential relationship, as a necessity to achieve her educational goals.

By contrast, other participants state that for long-term relationships, for those seeking marriage, being "strong" is an asset. Maya (age 18) says: "If you want to go as far as marriage, that's going to be important in terms of having a family and stuff like that." She suggests not only that marriage-minded men seek out strength in mates, but also that such a strategy is in the best interests of the family unit.

Nicole (age 20) shares a similar perspective, pointing out how emotional resilience can be advantageous within long-term romantic relationships. She says:

If they're looking for a monogamous relationship, I think [men] really want support, they want you to be the womanly type, like nurturing, considerate to their needs. I think they want you to be a strong woman, like not crying all the time, not being able to handle situations. Just like you need them to be a strong tower, they need you to be a strong tower sometimes.

Here, Nicole describes strength and resilience as a means of supporting her partner's emotional needs. She alludes to flexibility, rather than a rigid separation of gender roles between Black men and women, particularly when she emphasizes reciprocity in sometimes needing to be "the strong one" in a relationship.

Although some women noted difficulty in negotiating between traditional and Strong Black Woman ideologies and/or described favoring traditional feminine norms in romantic relationships, there were voices of dissension as well. One participant disagreed that challenges existed in adhering to both models of femininity. Maya (age 18) stated: "I think it's definitely possible to be both … traditionally female if you choose to be and also strong at the same time." When probed further, she was unable to offer any concrete examples. Her lack of dating and relationship experience likely contributed to the lack of examples, as she cited "not being interested in relationships" in favor of concentrating solely on her studies.

A diversity of perspectives highlights differences in how young African American women engage with, negotiate, and enact behavioral dictates associated with traditional gender roles and Strong Black Woman ideology. On one hand, embodiment of Strong Black Woman characteristics is described as contributing to relationship discord. Many participants report learning to "dial down" Strong Black Woman characteristics as needed within their relationships. This appears to be an experientially based process of learning how to balance the traditional with being strong. However, the exact developmental process of how Black women learn to balance these competing notions, particularly as relationship goals shift toward long-term commitment and marriage, remains largely unknown.

Although some participants described relationship loss as a result of Strong Black Woman embodiment, others perceived these characteristics as prized, to the extent that Black men are seeking marriage and family-building. In emerging adulthood, young men are also examining and consolidating issues of identity, trying on relationships and exploring partners, and to the extent that they prioritize education as an overarching goal, they may not yet be interested in seeking out Strong Black Women as relationship partners.

Discussion

A primary goal of this study was to examine how African American women connect with the Strong Black Woman notion in emerging adulthood. Much of the literature portrays the Strong Black Woman image as articulated by women well into adulthood or approaching middle age. What significance do emerging adult women attach to the Strong Black Woman image, and in what social contexts are its behavioral dictates invoked?

A number of scholars have positioned the Strong Black Woman as an affirming symbol and a double-edged sword. It is a means of defining femininity independent of mainstream America, imbuing Black women with positive depictions of womanhood; however, many have questioned whether Strong Black Woman embodiment manifests in self-sacrifice, lack of self-care, and a mythical "superwoman-ism" that leaves little room for human frailty or emotional vulnerability (Beauboeuf-Lafontant, 2003, 2007; Dow, 2015; Nelson et al., 2016). Emerging research also links Strong Black Woman ideology with a host of physical health problems and adverse mental health outcomes (Beauboeuf-Lafontant, 2014; Stanton et al., 2017; Watson-Singleton, 2017; West et al., 2016).

Our study finds that African American women in emerging adulthood conceptualize Strong Black Women ideology in terms of a positive affirmation of Black womanhood and activate its behavioral traits as a means of coping and striving for success in a challenging environment. Strong Black Woman ideology allows these women to refute, and provides counterevidence against, negative perceptions in an attempt to preserve self-esteem. Scholars suggest that an additional developmental task faced by African Americans in emerging adulthood is reconciling negative societal stereotypes and undesirable perceptions and creating one's own healthy self-concept (Arnett & Brody, 2008). Strong Black Woman ideology may help in achieving this developmental task. Indeed, the emerging adults in this study seemed to be leveraging Strong Black Woman ideology in achieving secure identities.

A second goal was to explore whether emerging adult women perceived gender role conflict within heterosexual romantic relationships. If raised with a familiarity toward Strong Black Woman ideology, do young African American women feel that they must enact traditional feminine gender roles as well? Our study shows evidence that these women negotiate between two distinct feminine ideologies within romantic relationships. Strong Black Woman ideology was depicted as an advantageous factor in navigating through college; however, participants actively sought to embody traditional feminine characteristics and roles in their relationships with men. Among women actively participating in dating and romantic relationships, difficulties were expressed in meeting traditional gender role expectations. Indeed, participants dichotomized "natural" tendencies for Black women to be strong, independent, and assertive with expectations of being more "traditionally feminine" in romantic relationships.

Strength invoked in one social context may be downplayed in others, such that Black women desire to be perceived as ladylike and agreeable, and to empower men as dominant, active agents in romantic relationships. Studies have found that Black women voice overall support of traditional gender roles in which men ought to be breadwinners or maintain authority over certain aspects of relationships. On the other hand, women's roles include sustaining the relationship, and even tolerating undesirable behaviors for the sake of continuing the relationship (Bowleg et al., 2004).

Scholars have also suggested that Black women are especially sensitive to the "invisibility," lack of dominance, or lack of power that Black men may experience, which they may attempt to compensate for in other social contexts, including relationships, home, and family life (Cowdery et al., 2009). Other work has highlighted the impact of American patriarchy, suggesting that although Black women and men exhibit less strict adherence to traditional gender ideology, they may still cleave to pervasive societal ideals that subordinate women (Lawrence-Webb et al., 2004). So as not to appear "too strong," overbearing, or unfeminine, Black women may enact traditional feminine behaviors within opposite-sex relationships.

Our participants imply that embodiment of Strong Black Woman ideology may hinder the development of long-lasting, successful romantic relationships with men. Instead, women discuss masking perceived in-born independent tendencies, allowing male partners to uphold traditional roles, or self-silencing, in order to sustain relationships. These behavioral patterns are mirrored in prior studies in which women are observed justifying undesirable behaviors, acquiescing, or refusing to protest in order to preserve a male partner's self-worth or sense of masculinity (Bowleg et al., 2004; Haynes, 2000).

However, there were voices of dissension in this study, advocating that it is possible to be strong, be traditional, and have successful romantic relationships. These women stated that being strong is important for the Black family unit. They spoke of Black men valuing notions of strength and seeking out these qualities in marriage partners. However, emerging adult women conceded that men their age are not necessarily looking for long-term relationships. They suggested that these characteristics will increase in importance as interest grows in marrying and establishing families.

Overall, our study finds evidence that young African American women engage with multiple models of femininity. Given a historical continuity of negative racial stereotypes that portray Black women as angry, sexually aggressive, or other pejorative descriptions (Jerald et al., 2016), it seems plausible that Black women may feel driven to "prove" that they are indeed as feminine as other women by adhering to traditional feminine ideology. There is some evidence that this occurs in studies on beauty, where Black women rate the importance of feminine appearance and behaviors, such as wearing attractive clothing, more highly than White women do (Cole & Zucker, 2007). This is a provocative finding given that Black women experience marginalization from mainstream American beauty standards, yet more strongly aspire to be perceived as feminine by others.

This study asserts context-specific ways in which African American emerging adult women engage behavioral norms of femininity—with romantic relationships being a prime context for enacting traditional feminine norms. This effect is likely to extend to other contexts, such as in college, career, and other achievement-oriented environments. Cowdery and colleagues (2009) suggest that African American women aspire to traditional roles in romantic relationships as a marker of middle-class status. Embodiment of traditional roles exists as a relationship ideal, such that sociocultural, economic, and historical factors (e.g., wage and hiring discrimination and higher unemployment rates) may preclude its realization for many Black families (Collins, 2000). For example, in the historical past, when traditional gender ideologies were exercised in the form of the male breadwinner/stay-at-home wife dynamic, this option was typically available only to Black women of middle-to-upper class socioeconomic standing. Over recent decades, scholars have pointed out that educational and career opportunities engendering middle-class status may be more accessible to Black women than to Black men (Lawrence-Webb et al., 2004). As such, educated African American women may reify the concept of "creating space" for Black men to assert traditional masculine roles within relationships, home, and family life.

Limitations and Future Directions for Research

One of the study limitations was the use of a collegiate sample. African American women of diverse backgrounds and social settings may attach different meanings and significances to these gendered notions. This sample was drawn from a predominantly White college environment, which influences experiences referred to in the narratives. Additionally, when the semi-structured interview guide was constructed, there was not an integration of notions of social class or upward mobility. Future studies should consider nuances of socioeconomic experience by collecting a fuller set of demographic information to explore differences in how feminine conceptions are classed.

Although this interview addressed feminine ideals and behaviors, many participants were unable to reflect deeply on how these notions interacted in romantic relationships due to relative lack of experience. Lastly, there was variation within the sample as to whether the women interviewed fit the classic definition of emerging adulthood; a few participants were married, engaged, or had children of their own. It is likely that their perspectives and experiences are different than those of women of the same age without such roles and responsibilities. Caution is directed toward extending these findings to Black women in other contexts. Even within the ages of 18–24 years, Black women not enrolled in college may engage with feminine ideology in different ways than our sample did.

Although largely exploratory in examining the interplay of different models of femininity, this study contributes to the literature by grounding gendered ideological characteristics within the lived experiences of Black women at the cusp of adulthood. When embodying their own unique sense of womanhood, young women are drawing from early socialization messages, greater awareness of how mainstream society perceives Black women, and their own observations and lived experiences as they learn to negotiate gendered roles and behaviors within romantic relationships. Making sense of and "balancing" the dictates of traditional feminine ideology and Strong Black Woman ideology presents a challenging issue, perhaps paving the road for emotional and psychological difficulties—not only for emerging adults, but also for older women (Dow, 2015; Jones & Shorter-Gooden, 2003; Romero, 2002). Additional studies are needed to explore associated mental health outcomes among women who internalize Strong Black Woman ideology and embody its behavioral characteristics, as well as the potential for role conflict and the impact of gender role negotiations on relationship quality and satisfaction for Black women and men.

References

Abrams, J. A., Maxwell, M., Pope, M., & Belgrave, F. Z. (2014). Carrying the world with the grace of a lady and the grit of a warrior: Deepening our understanding of the "Strong Black Woman" schema. *Psychology of Women Quarterly, 38*, 503–518.

Arnett, J. J. (1998). Learning to stand alone: The contemporary American transition to adulthood in cultural and historical context. *Human Development, 41*(5–6), 295–315.

Arnett, J. J., & Brody, G. H. (2008). A fraught passage: The identity challenges of African American emergent adults. *Human Development, 51*, 291–293.

Bay-Cheung, L. Y., Zucker, A. N., Stewart, A. J., & Pomerlau, C. S. (2002). Linking femininity, weight concern, and mental health among Latina, Black, and White women. *Psychology of Women Quarterly, 26*, 36–44.

Beauboeuf-Lafontant, T. (2003). Strong and large Black women? Exploring relationships between deviant womanhood and weight. *Gender and Society, 17*(1), 111–121.

Beauboeuf-Lafontant, T. (2007). You have to show strength: An exploration of gender, race, and depression. *Gender and Society, 21*(1), 28–51.

Beauboeuf-Lafontant, T. (2014). The Strong Black Woman: A half-told tale of race, gender, and the body. In H. Jackson-Lowman (Ed.), *Afrikan American women: Living at the crossroads of race, gender, class, and culture.* Cognella Academic Publishing.

Bem, S. L. (1974). The measurement of psychological androgyny. *Journal of Counseling and Clinical Psychology, 42*, 155–162.

Bowleg, L., Lucas, K. J., & Tschann, J. M. (2004). "The ball was always in his court": An exploratory analysis of relationship scripts, sexual scripts, and condom use among African American women. *Psychology of Women Quarterly, 28*, 70–82.

Cole, E. R., & Zucker, A. N. (2007). Black and White women's perspectives on femininity. *Cultural Diversity and Ethnic Minority Psychology, 13*, 1–9.

Collins, P. H. (2000). *Black feminist thought: Knowledge, consciousness, and the politics of empowerment* (2nd ed.). Routledge.

Cowdery, R. S., Scarborough, N., Knudson-Martin, C., Seshadri, G., Lewis, M. E., & Mahoney, A. R. (2009). Gendered power in cultural contexts: Part II. Middle class African American heterosexual couples with young children. *Family Process, 48*, 25–39.

Debnam, K. J., Howard, D. E., & Garza, M. A. (2014). "If you don't have honesty in a relationship, then there is no relationship": African American girls' characterization of healthy dating relationships, A qualitative study. *The Journal of Primary Prevention, 35*(6), 397–407.

Dow, D. M. (2015). Negotiating "The Welfare Queen" and "The Strong Black Woman": African American middle-class mothers' work and family perspectives. *Sociological Perspectives, 58*, 36–55.

Erikson, E. (1980). *Identity and the life cycle*. W. W. Norton.

Ford, K. A. (2006). Masculinity, femininity, appearance ideals, and the Black body: Developing a positive raced and gendered bodily sense of self [Unpublished doctoral dissertation]. University of Michigan.

Haynes, F. E. (2000). Gender and family ideals: An exploratory study of Black middle-class Americans. *Journal of Family Issues, 21*, 811–837.

Hill, S. A. (2002). Teaching and doing gender in African American families. *Sex Roles: A Journal of Research, 47*, 493–506.

Jerald, M. C., Ward, L. M., Moss, L., Thomas, K. A., & Fletcher, K. D. (2016). Subordinates, sex objects, or sapphires? Investigating contributions of media use to Black students' feminine ideologies and stereotypes about Black women. *Journal of Black Psychology, 43*, 608–635.

Jones, M. K., Buque, M., & Miville, M. L. African American gender roles: A content analysis of empirical research from 1981 to 2017. *Journal of Black Psychology, 44*, 450–486.

Jones, C., & Shorter-Gooden, K. (2003). *Shifting: The double lives of Black women in America*. HarperCollins.

Lawrence-Webb, C., Littlefield, M., & Okundaye, J. N. (2004). African American intergender relationships: A theoretical exploration of roles, patriarchy, and love. *Journal of Black Studies, 34*, 623–639.

Mahalik, J. R., Morray, E. B., Coonerty-Femiano, A., Ludlow, L. H., Slattery, S. M., & Smiler, A. (2005). Development of the conformity to feminine norms inventory. *Sex Roles, 52*, 417–435.

Morris, E. W. (2007). "Ladies" or "loudies"?: Perceptions and experiences of Black girls in classrooms. *Youth & Society, 38*(4), 490–515. https://doi.org/10.1177/0044118X06296778

Nelson, T., Cardemil, E. V., & Adeoye, C. T. (2016). Rethinking strength: Black women's perception of the "Strong Black Woman" role. *Psychology of Women Quarterly, 40*, 1–13.

Parks, S. (2010). *Fierce angels: The strong Black woman in American life and culture*. One World/Ballantine Books.

Romero, R. E. (2002). The icon of the strong black woman: The paradox of strength. In L. Green & B. Greene (Eds.), *Psychotherapy with African American women: Innovations in psychodynamic perspectives and practice*. Guilford Press.

Sanders, J. L., & Bradley, C. (2005). Multiple-lens paradigm: Evaluating African American girls and their development. *Journal of Counseling and Development, 83*, 299–304.

Settles, I. H., Pratt-Hyatt, J. S., & Buchanan, N. T. (2008). Through the lens of race: Black and White women's perceptions of womanhood. *Psychology of Women Quarterly, 32*, 454–468.

Stanton, A. G., Jerald, M. C., Ward, L. M., & Avery, L. M. (2017). Social media contributions to Strong Black Woman ideal endorsement and Black women's mental health. *Psychology of Women Quarterly*, *41*, 465–478.

Thomas, A. J., & King, C. (2007). Gendered racial socialization of African American mothers and daughters. *The Family Journal: Counseling and Therapy for Couples and Families*, *15*(2), 137–142.

Thomas, A. J., & Speight, S. L. (1999). Racial identity and racial socialization attitudes of African American parents. *Journal of Black Psychology*, *25*, 152–170.

Watson-Singleton, N. N. (2017). Strong Black Woman schema and psychological distress: The mediating role of perceived emotional support. *Journal of Black Psychology*, *43*, 778–788.

West, L. M., Donovan, R. A., & Daniel, A. R. (2016). The price of strength: Black college women's perspectives on the Strong Black Woman stereotype. *Women & Therapy*, *39*, 390–412.

Wyatt, J. (2008). Patricia Hill Collins' Black sexual politics and the genealogy of the Strong Black Woman. *Studies in Gender and Sexuality*, *9*, 52–67.

Reading 3.3. Revisiting Brenda's Got a Baby

Black Motherhood, Families, and Structural Violence in the Streets

Brooklynn K. Hitchens and Yasser A. Payne

> I wanna be known for being a good mother and doing what I have to do. Knowing that I'm motivated to get up every day and I'm able to walk out that door and go to school, and go to work and take care of my child.
>
> —Toni (18), Black single mother in Wilmington, Delaware

> What is surprising is that so many women continue to be good mothers: women who continue to sacrifice their own lives' ends, spend their last dollar unselfishly on their children, live in desperation, and remain in violent homes because they refuse to give up being a mother. The astonishing aspect of many mothers' lives is the battle they fight for their children against sickness, poverty, war, and violence.
>
> (D. E. Roberts, 1995, p. 101)

Introduction

Analyses of Black single motherhood in urban communities often frame such motherhood as a contemporary phenomenon, one ravaged by urban poverty, welfare dependency, and absent fathers (Anderson, 1999; Burton & Tucker, 2009; Cherlin et al., 2008; Haney et al., 1974; Moynihan, 1965; Nadasen, 2007). Seldom do social scientists contextualize the phenomenological experiences of low-income, street life-oriented Black women. Instead, much of this research focuses on the supposed "deviance" and cultural "pathology" of Black motherhood (Anderson, 1999; Cherlin et al., 2008; Moynihan, 1965; Rowley, 2002; Sharp & Ispa, 2009), or solely on the experiences of middle-class, low-income, or non-street-identified Black women (Cole & Guy-Sheftall, 2003; Collins, 1990; Giddings, 1984; Mullings, 1997). Research on low-income Black mothers, particularly those with justice contact, typically ignores how institutional harms or violent, structural inequities are instrumental in creating the conditions for street life and reinforcing the permanence of Black single motherhood. This study provides an alternative framing of street-identified Black women and joins family composition and criminal record or street activity as predictive of shaping experiences of single motherhood within the Black community. Ruptured homes lead to high drop-out rates, unemployment, and criminal involvement among Black street-identified women. Using mixed methods, I examine these women's phenomenological experiences with "fatherless" homes in both childhood and adulthood, and the impact of such family dynamics on the lives of the women and their children. The present community-based phenomenological study elucidates the experiences of low-income, urban, street-identified Black women from Wilmington, Delaware, with a particular focus on these women's experiences with motherhood. This analysis is guided by the following question: How do family composition and criminal record or street activity influence notions of Black single motherhood?

Demographic Profile

Poverty and violence go hand-in-hand. If you're poor, you're seeking to do something (in order) to not be that way…and it's crazy because that's when the crime comes in. It's like you're trapping an animal in a corner. Eventually the animal (is) gonna come out fighting, doing whatever it needs to do to get where it needs to be.

—Basheera (46), Black single mother who has lost a son to homicide

Poverty and Economic Deprivation

Wilmington is a small U.S. city in Delaware that has a population of approximately 71,000 residents—58% of whom are Black (U.S. Census Bureau, 2017). Home to President Joseph R. Biden, Wilmington is a tale of two cities that is both *highly distressed* with concentrations of extreme economic deprivation and *highly prosperous* with sections of concentrated wealth. Given Delaware's unique domestic and foreign tax loophole, Wilmington is a corporate haven for national and international businesses, who are able to filter millions of dollars through the city without investing in its most vulnerable residents (Wayne, 2012; Wink, 2014). Wealthy, mostly White residents benefit from the city's downtown financial district and gentrifying communities, many of which sit adjacent to some of the poorest Black neighborhoods in the state. Black women make up 11.7% of Delaware's population and about 16% of Wilmington's population (National Coalition of 100 Black Women Inc., Delaware Chapter, 2018). Blacks are almost four times as likely as Whites to live in poverty in the city (Center for Community Research and Service, 2015; Prosperity Now, 2019). One in three children and one in five older Wilmington residents live in poverty, with some rates reaching 69% in Wilmington's poorest Black neighborhoods (Armbrister, 2003; Center for Community Research and Service, 2015).

In the Eastside and Southbridge neighborhoods, poor Blacks can actually sit on their front porches and gaze up at luxury corporate and residential buildings—while 60% of Black residents earn less than $25,000 per year (Fishman & Jedra, 2016; U.S. Census Bureau, 2010). The Black median income in Wilmington is $30,034, in comparison to the White median income of $60,772 (Prosperity Now, 2019). Black women make $38,000 per year on average in Delaware (National Coalition, 2018), and less than $20,000 per year on average in the Eastside and Southbridge neighborhoods. Urban street corners are littered with predatory lending companies, check-cashing stores, liquor stores, and pawn shops; the Black unemployment rate (21.8%) in Wilmington is five times higher than that of Whites (City of Wilmington, 2010; U.S. Census Bureau, 2010).

Over 40% of Black residents in Wilmington are homeowners, but a third have "zero net worth" (Center for Community Research and Service, 2015; Prosperity Now, 2019). Sixty percent of Black Wilmingtonians are "cost-burdened renters" who spend more than 30% of their income on rent (Prosperity Now, 2019). Nearly 25% of homes in the city of Wilmington are female headed (Shattuck & Kreider, 2011). However, in the two Wilmington neighborhoods under study, Eastside and Southbridge, 70% of homes in Eastside are female headed, and 74% of homes in Southbridge are female headed (Garrison & Kervick, 2005).

Motherhood

There are over two million more adult Black women than men in Black communities (Alexander, 2010; U.S. Census Bureau, 2017). These data are particularly relevant for Black women who seek to marry and bear children with heterosexual Black men. In fact, 47% of Black women have never been married (as compared with 28% of Caucasian women), and 70% of professional Black women are also unmarried (Alexander, 2010; S. Roberts, 2007). One in three Black households are female headed, and almost three quarters of all births to Black women occur outside of marriage (Child Trends Data Bank, 2015; U.S. Census Bureau, 2012). Nearly half of Black female-headed homes with children are living in poverty (Entmacher et al., 2013). Still, despite the disparities Black women face, more White women have nonmarital births and receive food stamps and public assistance than Black women (Gray, 2014; Shattuck & Kreider, 2011).

Local data on Black women in Wilmington elucidate how structural inequities shape differential lived experiences, and how Black mothers fare in comparison to other mothers in the city and state. Black women in Delaware are highly represented in the labor force and are often the family breadwinners, yet are more likely to live in poverty than other women (National Coalition, 2018). Poverty influences their ability to access quality medical care and treatment. While 27.5% of births in Delaware are to Black mothers, over 50% of births in Wilmington are to single Black mothers (Delaware Health Statistics Center, 2017). Almost three quarters of unmarried Black mothers are Medicaid recipients in Wilmington, and these mothers are twice as likely to have babies born with low birth weight than White women (Delaware Health Statistics Center, 2017). These women have an infant mortality rate of 12.5 per 1,000, 2.5 times that of White women (Delaware Health Statistics Center, 2017). Since 1998, infants of Black women have represented almost half of all fetal deaths in Delaware and over 76% of all fetal deaths in Wilmington (Delaware Health Statistics Center, 2017). Black women also have a higher rate of mortality than White women, and the life expectancy of Blacks in Delaware is three years less than that of Whites (Delaware Health Statistics Center, 2017). In pockets of neighborhoods in Wilmington, this Black–White disparity in life expectancy reaches 16 years (Delaware Health Statistics Center, 2017).

Street Life and Criminal Justice System

As mothers, partners, and residents, low-income Black women in Wilmington juggle the pressures of urban living, which compounds their struggles with violence, crime, and the criminal justice system. It is no surprise, then, that according to the U.S. Census, Wilmington is one of *the* hardest places to achieve social mobility in the United States (Bies, 2018; Stebbins & Comen, 2018). The small city has one of the highest per capita homicide rates in the United States (FBI Uniform Crime Reports, 2017). Labelled "MurderTown USA" by *Newsweek* and "Killington" more colloquially for its elevated rates of violent crime, Wilmington broke its first homicide record in 2010 and then again in 2017, with over 44 homicides per 100,000 residents (FBI Uniform Crime Reports, 2017) A. Jones, 2014; Wilmington Shootings, 2017). Ranked nine times higher than the national rate, in 2015, Wilmington was the fourth most violent city of its size (Center for Drug and Health Studies, 2016; Centers for Disease Control and Prevention [CDC], 2015). In fact, recent Gun Violence Archival data find that Wilmington leads the country in teen shootings, and 12- to 17-year-old youth are more likely to be shot in the city than elsewhere in the United States (Linderman et al., 2017).

Black mothers in Wilmington are tasked with the challenge of raising children under war-like conditions. They are not only disproportionately exposed to community violence; they also experience the strain of raising children in distressed neighborhoods and struggle to keep them safe. Yet far too often, they are forced to succumb to traumatic grief when their children are murdered at the hands of police or community residents. In 2015, Phyllis McDole's son, paraplegic Jeremy "Bam Bam" McDole, was shot and killed by the Wilmington Police Department while sitting in his wheelchair. Rodriguez (2016) and Smith (2016) call this "mothering while Black" beneath oppressive, violent conditions, a feature of a "global gendered necropolitics," where Black mothers all over the Diaspora suffer a physical and slow death as unprotected enemies of the state.

Black women and mothers feel the immense toll of mass incarceration when their loved ones are sentenced to prison, but also as direct victims of a racially biased criminal justice system. This inequality exacerbates conditions in urban Black communities and can facilitate street lifestyles that ultimately lead to incarceration. Black women comprise only about 14% of the general population of females in the United States, but they are disproportionately under the control of the criminal justice system relative to other women. Forty four percent of incarcerated women are Black (Hinton et al., 2018), and nearly two thirds of women in prison are mothers (Bronson & Carson, 2019; Sentencing Project, 2018; Sufrin et al., 2019). While the incarceration of women in the United States grew by 400% between 1986 and the early 2000s, the incarceration of women of color grew by 800% (DuMonthier et al., 2017; Honderich, 2003). The exponential growth in the number of incarcerated Black women can be traced to racialized and draconian drug policies during Reagan's administration: between 1989 and 1994, Black women experienced the greatest increase in criminal justice supervision of *all* demographic groups (Mauer & Huling, 1995). Black and Latina women are more often arrested and incarcerated for drug-related crimes than White women, though data indicate that women use and sell drugs at comparable rates (Alexander, 2010; DuMonthier et al. 2017; Szalavitz, 2011). Of those who have ever tried drugs, Black girls are more likely to have used marijuana than White girls, but they are less likely to have used harder drugs like cocaine, MDMA, or hallucinogenic drugs than White girls (Kann et al., 2018).

Coinciding with the shifts in incarceration rates for Blacks and Whites, the Black female imprisonment rate has been declining since 2000—down over 50% in the last two decades (Sentencing Project, 2018). Yet Black women continue to be imprisoned at twice the rate of White women and 1.3 times the rate of Latina women (Bronson & Carson, 2019; Sentencing Project, 2018). In 2017, the imprisonment rate for Black women was 92 per 100,000, while the rates for White and Latina women were 49 and 66 per 100,000, respectively (Bronson & Carson, 2019). Black women are largely imprisoned for nonviolent, drug-related offenses (Mauer, 2013; Sabol et al., 2008) while Black girls are disproportionately incarcerated for low-level status offenses such as running away, truancy, and curfew violations (Sentencing Project, 2018).

Black female incarceration in Delaware reflects the disproportionate national rates, as local Black men and women fare the worst within the criminal justice system. Although Delaware is the second smallest state, it has one of the highest rates of incarceration in the nation (Eichler, 2004). Delaware incarcerates 756 per 100,000 residents, compared to the national average of 698 per 100,000 residents (Wagner & Sawyer, 2018). Forty-one per 100,000 women in Delaware are imprisoned (Sentencing Project, 2018). Black women in the state are imprisoned at a rate of 168.07 per 100,000, which is more than twice the rate of White women (Delaware Department of Correction, 2019). In addition, the vast majority of those under correctional supervision in Delaware are on probation, but Black women are sentenced to probation at almost three times the rate of White women (Delaware Department of Correction, 2019).

This article grapples with street life-oriented Black women's involvement in street activity and how such activity can inform their notions of single motherhood.

Conceptual Framework

Black people are the magical faces at the bottom of society's well. … Over time, many reach out, but most simply watch, mesmerized into maintaining their unspoken commitment to keeping us where we are, at whatever cost to them or to us.

—Derrick Bell, 1993, forward

Street-identified Black women and girls are often victims of *structural violence*, or the invisible, disproportionate, and excessive death and disability of the poor as a function of their disadvantage (Farmer, 2005; Gilligan, 1996). Coined by Galtung (1969, 1971), structural violence as a theoretical framework describes how structural institutions and systems actively prevent individuals, groups, and communities from meeting their basic needs through policies, laws, and other forms of regulations. Blacks are especially vulnerable to structural violence in that they suffer from poverty and concentrated disadvantage at vastly higher rates than Whites, including unequal access to healthcare, and societal stressors caused by racial discrimination, adverse treatment, and blocked opportunity (Gilligan, 1996). In fact, Gilligan (1996) argues that poverty is the "deadliest form of violence" (p. 191) and that social actors directly and indirectly have a "vested interest" (p. 199) in the subjugation and discrimination of Blacks by preventing them from "realizing their potentialities" through policies, laws, and other forms of inequality (see also Galtung, 1969). Not only are poverty and blocked opportunity avoidable, but the *maintenance* of this inequality is also a symbolic example of structural violence and social injustice (Galtung, 1969). Institutions operate continuously to perpetuate racial and economic inequities through "social racism," or ubiquitous racism that is first legitimized by the government and then socially approved and internalized by the wider public to produce structural violence (Gržinić & Tatlić, 2014). Poor Black communities have been ravaged by structural violence for centuries, and the infusion of such violence permeates the lived experiences of Black men and women—which inevitably yields the development of a street identity. Street life then emerges as a site of resilience, based on both racial-ethnic and socio-cultural factors, in response to a persistent context of structural violence.

Sites of resilience theory provides an alternative framing of resilience and resiliency by conceptualizing a street identity in terms of (a) phenomenology, (b) relational coping, (c) historical patterns/trends, (d) structural systems, and (e) incidents of social injustice (Payne, 2001, 2011, 2013). This study applies sites of resilience and structural violence theories to better understand how street-identified Black women frame their experiences with motherhood in relation to the individual and structural conditions that shape their lives.

Street life or a street identity is a phenomenological concept viewed as an ideology centered on personal, social, and economic survival (Payne, 2008, 2011). We frame these notions of survival as a "site of resilience" and examine street identity through the racial, sociocultural, gendered, developmental, and classed lens of low-income urban Black girls and women who "come of age in the same distressed neighborhoods as those of [their] male counterparts" (N. Jones, 2010, p. 20). Epistemologically, we argue that centering Black women's experiences in the streets requires an understanding of how the intersectionality of race, gender, and class creates marginalized and exclusionary conditions for women of color, and shapes their social world and identities (Collins, 2000; Crenshaw, 1991; Mullings, 1997; Richie, 2012). Urban Black women and girls craft street identities that are developed in response to structural violence and institutional harms that are embedded in their social milieu. Attitudinal and behavioral characteristics of these women's street identities ultimately reflect how they "organize meaning around feeling well, satisfied, or accomplished and how [the women] choose to survive in relation to adverse structural conditions" (Payne, 2011, p. 429). As hustlers, mothers, and matriarchs, street-identified Black women are the glue that hold together their families. Juggling struggle and triumph, they achieve family cohesion, at least in part by hitting the streets, despite the risk of incarceration or demise. Illegal activities for street-identified Black women are generally employed to confront the effects of economic poverty and include interpersonal violence, prostitution, preparing drugs for sale, selling or holding drugs or drug money for others, robbery, gambling, and bookkeeping (Brunson & Stewart, 2006; Bush-Baskette, 2010; N. Jones, 2010).

In the streets, Black women find psychological and physical spaces of resilience that operate concurrently to produce sites of strength at the individual, group, and community levels (Hitchens & Payne, 2017; Payne, 2011; Payne et al., in press). Street-identified Black women buffer the sting of structural violence through bonding activities such as attending parties or bars, participating in social clubs such as motorcycle or car clubs, "hanging on the block" or street corner, and attending group gatherings with friends. They cultivate joy in times of sorrow by developing support groups for other women when tragedies like gun violence hit their communities, caring for the children of mothers who fall on hard times, and organizing social activities like barbecues, bookbag drives, and rent parties.

Street life is also passed on through intergenerational transmission, in which attitudes, behaviors, and cultural practices are transmitted from older to younger street generations and regulated through the "code of the streets" (Anderson, 1999; Hitchens & Payne, 2017; Payne, 2011). Intergenerational patterns of single motherhood and a street-life orientation have been found in generations of low-income Black women, largely in response to the systematic oppression of the Black family. Butterfield (1995) asserts that 25% to 40% of temperament can be passed on to subsequent generations, especially when the living environment and conditions remain the same across generations. Low-income Black mothers, in particular, face a unique challenge of raising their children in the same or similar conditions as their mothers and grandmothers, because they are trapped in a cycle in which structural inequality, violence, and crime play a significant role in their lives (McLanahan & Percheski, 2008). Thus, many of these women have been socialized to accept and even expect single motherhood, because of their experiences in childhood (Edin & Lein, 1997). These experiences and conditions facilitate street lifestyles and are influential in shaping single motherhood throughout low-income Black communities.

Literature Review

Black women living in conditions of imposed marginality bear the disproportionate brunt of…political and economic processes … Increasing social inequality is inflected by and in turn influences how race, gender, and social class are experienced in everyday struggles. … we often overlook how women of color are deeply affected by, challenge, and successfully resist—at least temporarily—how unemployment, mass incarceration, and state disinvestment (in the areas of health, child care, education, and job training, for example) impact their communities.

—Joao Costa Vargas, 2006, p. 85

The State of Black Families: Family Composition

Given the trauma of the Maafa, single motherhood is an enduring legacy of how Black families were ravaged by American slavery and how Black women continue to be oppressed through "Jane Crow" policies that disrupt their ability to mother under the carceral state (Battle, 2016; C. A. Jones & Seabrook, 2017). This assault on Black motherhood extends to social science literature, which has historically used "controlling images" and stereotypical conceptualizations to frame Black women, families, and mothering practices (Collins, 1990). Most of this literature ignores or misrepresents the phenomenological experiences of street-identified Black women and mothers. The Moynihan Report (1965) was instrumental in shaping the public imagination about the supposed "pathology" of Black motherhood—reifying cultural images of Black "fatherless" homes where children run amok and women raise children without a significant male partner or biological father (Alexander, 2010; Barras, 2002; Orleck, 2005). The "Black single mother" and "urban teen mother" are crippling social stigmas, especially for women living in street life-oriented environments where resources for upward mobility are limited (Jordan-Zachery, 2014). Stereotypes abound about a dependent, inept, and uneducated Black woman or "welfare queen" who greedily lives in public housing and abuses governmental assistance. Couched in racial rhetoric that codes "welfare" for race and therefore anti-Blackness, this perception of "economic dependency" wherein Black women recreate cycles of poverty through personal fault, and would rather rely on welfare funds than to "get a good job," has been utilized in the political and social assault of these women for decades (Iversen & Farber, 1996; D. E. Roberts, 1996). This rhetoric legitimizes the "criminalization of poverty" for poor Black women who interface with the criminal justice system, and singularly holds them responsible for their socioeconomic conditions, their criminal experiences, and the absence of a father figure for their children (Chunn & Gavigan, 2004; Richie, 2012).

Despite these stereotypes, Black mothers manage to nurture children and cultivate community while maintaining higher participation in the labor market than other mothers (McLoyd & Enchautegui-de-Jesús, 2005). The U.S. Bureau of Labor Statistics (2019) consistently finds that Black women ages 16 and older outpace White, Hispanic, and Asian women as members of the workforce—an empirical finding that helps to debunk the myth of the lazy "welfare queen." Mustering grit and perseverance, Black women maintain individual and collective resiliency, even while they experience family provider role strain disproportionate to other women (Mendenhall et al., 2013).

The truth is that the Black family is more complex and dynamic than is often captured in academic literature. Some scholars continue to elucidate the intricacies of mothering in Black families, and to examine how parenting is a collective feature of the Black community (Gurusami, 2018; Hunter, 1997; Letiecq & Koblisky, 2004). If children are not raised in a traditional two-parent household, they are instead often raised in an extended family network of support in which kin and "fictive kin" help in child rearing (Collins, 1987). More often than not, Black women raise children with a grandmother, aunt, close family friend, or another familial member present in the home. In addition, male figures often help raise Black women's children inside the home. Male cohabitation, coresidence, or "kinship networks" (Collins, 1990; Edin & Lein, 1997) in which other male family members (grandfather, uncles, older brothers, or cousins) or family friends live in the household need to be considered in analysis of family dynamics. Like Black mothers, Black men often step up to nurture and care for children with whom they may or may not have biological ties.

Black fatherhood continues to be central to the lived experiences of many Black children. Far too many studies focus on the *absence* of Black biological fathers from the home, rather than the *bond* between child and father outside of the home. Black fathers are more active in their children's lives than ever before, despite the loom of the criminal justice system and other destructive institutions (Coles & Green, 2010; Connor & White, 2006; Edin & Kefalas, 2011; Edin & Nelson, 2013; Livingston & Parker, 2011). A 2013 CDC report found that Black fathers are the *most involved* with their children compared to any other group of fathers—a finding that directly challenges the notion that Black men do not love or care about their children (J. Jones & Mosher, 2013). Among nonresidential fathers, Black fathers are far more likely than White or Hispanic fathers to talk with their children several times a week about their day (Livingston & Parker, 2011). In addition, a higher percentage of Black fathers (27%) take their children to and from daily activities than White fathers (20%), and more Black fathers (41%) help their coresidential children with their homework every day, in comparison to only 28% of White fathers (J. Jones & Mosher, 2013). Black fathers deeply value "imparting love, maintaining a clear channel of communication, and spending quality time" (Edin & Nelson, 2013, p. 2) with their children. Literature and theoretical arguments about Black families must contend with the varied family composition and complex social network of support that surround Black children and their mothers.

Black Women and Motherhood in the Streets

Street-identified Black women and mothers are often raised in interrupted family dynamics wherein street life becomes a method of coping with the stressors of urban living. Poverty and structural violence are integral in the maintenance of Black female-headed homes and the shaping of women's involvement in street life and carceral institutions. Black girls and women are disproportionately represented in the criminal justice system, and some utilize crime or violence to cope with structural inequality and negative lived experiences—such as growing up without a father in the home (Chesney-Lind, 2012; N. Jones, 2010; Payne, 2011; Steffensmeier & Haynie, 2000). Black mothers who are involved in the streets balance competing roles as both matriarchs and hustlers—they are often the breadwinners of their families who are tasked with providing for and protecting their children in an unjust society. Fagan (1994) argues that some Black women who live below the poverty line face a desperation that makes "participation in the growing informal economy … a part of the diverse network of income sources for poor women" (p. 180). Gurusami (2018) found that poor, formerly incarcerated Black mothers engage in collective, hypervigilant, and crisis motherwork strategies to anticipate, react to, and cope with state surveillance under post-release supervision and child welfare services. These mothers often struggle to maintain the boundaries of state intervention, but upon release, usually reenter communities where inadequate social and economic conditions remain. At its core, street life develops as an outgrowth of economic deprivation and manifests in the lives of street-identified Black men and women who seek to alleviate the sting of poverty (Payne, 2008, 2011).

For Black women, street life becomes a fluid ideological code and behavior that is shaped by their social locations at different points in their lives. Their roles and behaviors in the streets are a reflection of how they embody a street identity and their adherence to the "code of the streets" that organizes low-income Black communities (Anderson, 1999). Street-identified Black mothers can simultaneously sell drugs, or engage in prostitution, or participate in fights—and still fiercely love their children and view themselves as "good mothers." In many ways, they are no different than other individuals who hold conflicting or competing identities, perspectives, and behaviors that shift based on context. Street-identified Black mothers reconcile their involvement in the streets as a "means to an end," or a way to achieve opportunity, upward mobility, and well-being for themselves and their families.

This study demonstrates how family composition, criminal record, and street activity shape the mothering practices of street-identified Black women, particularly from the worldview of single Black mothers.

Method

A secondary analysis was conducted on data from "The People's Report," a street participatory action research (PAR) project organized in Wilmington, Delaware. PAR includes members of the population under study on the research team and gives members the opportunity to participate in all phases of the research (Payne, 2008). Also, PAR projects require a social-justice-based analysis to be organized in response to the data collected by the study. Street PAR explicitly organizes active and formerly active street-identified persons of color to document the lived experiences of others involved with the streets and/or the criminal justice system (Payne, 2013). The People's Report is a pilot study that examined physical violence, by organizing 15 individuals formerly involved with the streets and/or the criminal justice system to study street-identified Black men and women aged 18 to 35 years from the Eastside and Southbridge neighborhoods of Wilmington, Delaware. Mixed methods were employed to collect data in the form of (a) 520 surveys, (b) 23 individual interviews, (c) 3 dual interviews, (d) 3 group interviews, and (e) extensive ethnographic field observations. Also, a fourth group interview, not initially proposed or planned, was conducted with a group of mostly older men (ages 41–53 years) who were formerly involved with the streets and/or the criminal justice system. All data were collected on the streets of Wilmington, Delaware (e.g., street corners, local parks, barbershops, local record/DVD stores, etc.).

This secondary analysis solely examines street-identified Black women aged 18 to 35 years from the larger study. The analysis drew from 310 female surveys (N = 310), 6 female individual interviews (N = 6), 3 dual interviews (N = 6), 2 female group interviews (N = 5), and extensive field observations.

Sample

Survey Subsample. A total of 310 females completed surveys, which encompass 59.6% of the total survey sample (N = 520). Ninety-eight females were aged 18 to 21 years (or 31.6%); 122 females were aged 22 to 29 years (or 39.4%); and 90 females were aged 30 to 35 years (or 29%). The survey sample for men and women was a quota sample based on census data for the Eastside and Southbridge sections of Wilmington, Delaware. Sixty-three percent of the women reported currently living in Eastside, and nearly 25% of the women reported living in Southbridge. Approximately 12% of the women reported living outside of these two neighborhoods but reported visiting these two neighborhoods on a regular basis.

Individual Interview Subsample. Individual interviews were used to explore intimate subjects. A total of six female participants completed an individual interview, or 35% of the interview sample (N = 17). The average age for this subsample was 26.3 years, while ages ranged from 18 to 35 years.

Dual Interview Subsample. Dual interviews were conducted with two participants. A total of six female participants completed dual interviews, or 35% of the interview sample (N = 17). These women were scheduled for individual interviews but decided they would be more comfortable conducting their interview with a friend. The average age for this subsample was 31.2 years, while ages ranged from 27 to 35 years.

Group Interview Subsample. Group interviews are the least intimate and offer a group analysis. A total of two group interviews were conducted with both street life-oriented men and women living in the Southbridge section of Wilmington, Delaware. One group interview had three female participants aged 27 to 29 years, and one group interview had two female participants and one male participant. The females in the second group interview were aged 28 to 30 years, and the male in the second group interview was 29 years. The average age for this subsample was 28.6 years.

Instrumentation

Survey Design. Street PAR members codesigned the survey and interview protocols for the study with the principal investigator and graduate students. The survey consisted of 251 items covering attitudes toward and experiences with (a) psychological well-being, (b) social cohesion, (c) employment, (d) education, (e) overall crime, (f) physical violence, (g) prison reentry, (h) interactions with law enforcement, and (i) a demographic inventory. Descriptive analysis was used to examine survey data for this article.

Interview Protocol Design. Semi-structured interviews were conducted predominantly in the Hope Zone Center in Southbridge, Wilmington. All interviewees completed a brief demographic inventory or questionnaire. Each participant also completed an interview protocol, which included (a) demographic information, (b) attitudes toward community violence, (c) attitudes toward education, (d) attitudes toward employment, (e) attitudes toward their community, (f) attitudes toward civic and political leadership, (g) attitudes toward law enforcement, and (h) a debriefing section completed after interviews.

Procedure

Organizing the Wilmington Street Participatory Action Research Team. The Wilmington Street Participatory Action Research (WSPAR) team is made up of 15 Wilmington residents, formerly involved with the streets and/or the criminal justice system, who are aged 20 to 48 years. Twelve of the Street PAR members are male and three are female. The 15-member Street PAR team was joined by a robust institutional partnership that included (a) three academic project partners (University of Delaware, Delaware State University, and Wilmington University) and (b) four nonprofit project partners (Wilmington HOPE Commission, Christina Cultural Arts Center, Metropolitan Wilmington Urban League, and United Way of Delaware). The WSPAR members were selected through a citywide search, completed internal review board training, and, subsequently, were rigorously trained in all phases of research for a 2-month period. They met 3 to 4 times per week for 3 to 5 hours per session and completed 18 research method workshops in total. Research methods training centered on research theory, method, analysis, and social activism. On successful completion of the training, responsibilities for the research team included (a) literature reviews, (b) data collection, (c) qualitative and quantitative analysis, (d) written contributions, and (e) professional presentations. All street PAR researchers were monetarily compensated for all time contributed and received a formal certificate of completion of research methods training.

The research team then mapped out street communities and sites of interest into street locales classified as (a) "cool" sites—low street activity, (b) "warm" sites—moderate street activity, and (c) "hot" sites—high street activity. In each location, the research team identified "street allies," gatekeepers, or leaders in these street communities in order to gain permission to collect data in the street community. The team then collected surveys from various sites including street corners, barbershops, parks, and record stores and conducted most interviews in the Hope Zone located in the Southbridge section of Wilmington, Delaware. Surveys took about 30 to 45 minutes to complete, whereas interviews lasted between 1 to 2 hours. Participants received $5 for completing a survey and $10 for completing an interview. In addition, participants received a consent form as well as a resource package with information about employment, educational opportunities, counseling, and social programs.

Qualitative Data Coding Process. Content analysis was used to generate codes for this study. The coding session was centered on the frameworks of sites of resilience (Payne, 2011) and grounded theory (Glaser & Strauss, 1967); subsequently, transcripts of qualitative interviews were coded in relation to these theories.

"Family" was coded as the broad domain for both core codes: (a) Childhood Home Experiences with Nonresidential Biological Fathers and (b) Present Home Experiences with Non-Residential Biological Fathers of Children. Four subcodes informed the qualitative coding process: (a) Substance Abuse and

Use/Sale of Drugs, (b) Incarceration, (c) Entrenched Anger, and (d) Attitudes toward the Personal Safety of their Children (see Table 2.6.1 for Qualitative Coding Scheme).

Interrater Reliability. Four people were selected to be raters: three individuals and one professor, including one graduate student well versed in PAR, interrater reliability, and the experiences of Black women in the streets, and one undergraduate student with formal experience with PAR, interrater reliability, and the experiences of Black women. Raters convened in a conference room and were each given nine transcripts ranging between four and five pages. Raters were instructed to highlight all passages perceived to be congruent with codes presented and defined for the raters. Raters' transcripts were averaged out against a master copy (see Table 2.6.1).

Table 2.6.1. Qualitative Coding Scheme: Data Analysis Process

1st Phase of Qualitative Coding	2nd Phase of Qualitative Coding	Interrater	3rd Phase of Qualitative Coding	Interrater
Broad Domain	Core Code	Coding Alpha	Subcodes	Coding Alpha
Family	Childhood Home Experiences (Non-residential Biological Fathers of Women)	0.93	Substance Abuse Sales and Use	.75
			Incarceration	1.0
			Anger	.93
Family	Present Home Experiences (Non-residential Biological Fathers of Children)	0.72	Substance Abuse Sales and Use	.72
			Incarceration	.66
			Anger	.83
			Personal safety of child	.88

Results

To What Extent Do Family Composition and Criminal Record or Street Activity Influence Notions of Black Single Motherhood?

Data reveal varied perspectives on notions of "fatherless" homes and single motherhood in street communities as related to family composition and criminal record or street activity. Street-identified Black women hold both positive and negative attitudes toward their biological fathers and the biological fathers of their children. In addition, these women reveal similar experiences in both childhood and adulthood with female-headed homes. Content analysis and descriptive survey analysis were conducted to examine women's childhood and present home experiences. Results suggest that, to a larger extent, family composition and criminal record or street activity influence notions of single motherhood in this sample.

Childhood Home Experiences. In both survey and interview data, women report that they grew up around violence and criminal activity in their neighborhood as children. Almost 75% of women surveyed claim that street activity was widespread where they grew up (N = 310). Interview responses indicate that 12 out of the 17 women in the sample grew up without a biological father in the home. Women hold both positive and negative attitudes toward their fathers and toward the relationship between their biological parents in the home.

Brandy (29) lost her mother to complications from HIV and dropped out in the ninth grade due to her embarrassment about her mother's condition. Her father was in prison for the majority of her life. Although he kept in contact with her as a child, Brandy now refuses to keep in contact or financially support him because of the entrenched anger, bitterness, or resentment she still holds. Brandy says her father was unable to contribute primarily because he was incarcerated for most of her life. Nonetheless, she loves her father, although she never received child support from him, which was compounded by the fact that her mother was a single parent on welfare.

> Brandy (29): My dad went to jail when I was five years old, got 25 years [in prison]. [He] came home when I was 25. I'm 29 now. He got out [of prison] when I was 25, he went back when I was 27 and got life [in prison]… So basically, I know his first and last name. (Dual interview participant)

Gloria (35) also grew up without a father consistently in the home and was raised largely by her mother. Neither of her parents got along with each other, and she maintained a volatile relationship with both parents as a result.

> Gloria (35): I loved my father and I can honestly say now that I love my father more because he was an absent parent and my mother was discipline … but as I'm growing up, I'm like "My dad wasn't there for me," and I hated him for it for a very long time. … I had to come to grip with that … (Dual interview participant)

Several women in the interviews express an entrenched level of anger toward their nonresidential biological fathers, and over half of the women interviewed hold negative attitudes toward their biological father (N =11). These negative attitudes vary in severity, but many of the women reflect on growing up in female-headed homes with little or no financial support from their biological fathers. This anger can be contextualized as stemming from hurtful childhood experiences due to a lack of a father figure and the yearning for stability from both the absent parent and the biological mother. As demonstrated later, this anger influences their notions of motherhood, as several women who were embittered by their father's absence also became embittered as mothers toward the fathers of their children.

Some of the women interviewed grew up without a biological mother consistently in the home. In some cases, women were raised solely by their biological father, and in other cases, a grandparent raised them as children.

> Michelle (31): My mom left when I was two. … She didn't want nothing to do with me and my brother. So, my dad … took on what he had to do. So, from then on, it's been me, my dad and my brother. My dad raised me from age two and that's it … (Dual interview participant)

Michelle's (31) story sheds light on the complexities that often emerge in low-income, distressed households. She was raised with her biological father as a child, and her biological mother was largely absent due to drug addiction. Thus, she holds negative attitudes toward her mother for her absence but holds positive attitudes toward her father for raising her and her brother. Michelle's (31) interview suggests that some children in similar neighborhoods are in fact raised by Black single-parent fathers.

Several women maintained positive relationships with their fathers as children, although the majority of the women in the qualitative subsample report that their father was not in the home. Women provide examples of being able to communicate with and receive advice from their fathers, spend time outside of the home with their fathers, and feel a level of connectedness with their fathers, even while their fathers are outside the mother's home. These experiences provide an interesting commentary on the presence of fathers in the home and the relationship between the father and the child. Black men outside of the home can provide both emotional and financial support, as well as be positive role models for their children.

Tisha (27): Me and my father's relationship is fair, you know? He was always around as far as somebody to talk to. You feel me? Me and my dad got ... more like a brother and sister bond. We can laugh, we can talk about whatever ... he always made it clear to me ... "I'm the only man that's going to love you unconditionally, so you can come to me with whatever." (Group interview participant)

Kenyette (34): My father was the leader or head person inside the household. (Dual interview participant)

Erica (22): ... my dad put his kids before anything. (Dual interview participant)

Why Weren't Their Biological Fathers in the Home?

Substance Abuse and Incarceration. Several women interviewed report not having a biological father or parent living in the home as a child due to substance abuse, which includes both use and sale of narcotics and excessive use of alcohol.

Yasser: What were some of the reasons why [your mother] didn't want to be a part of your life?

Michelle (31): She chose drugs over us. My dad gave her an ultimatum, and she chose drugs. (Dual interview participant)

Yasser: What prevented you from being with [your parents]?

Dionne (29): Um, my mom was on drugs and my dad was an alcoholic. (Individual interview participant)

Lanise (34): My father was a Vietnam vet. ... He ended up being on drugs [and became] an alcoholic. (Individual interview participant)

The women reflect on the volatile relationship between their parents as a result of such substance abuse, and the way drug and alcohol use pushed fathers and mothers out of the home. Also, women reported that substance abuse and incarceration worked in tandem to remove their fathers from the home. For example, a father might use and sell drugs and become incarcerated due to his involvement with illicit substances. Biological fathers were incarcerated for extended periods of time due to crimes such as armed robbery or use/ sale of narcotics. Women reflected on unstable relationships with fathers due to recidivism and repeat encounters with law enforcement.

Dionne (29): [My relationship with my father] has always been the same. ... Just in and out. ... [I see] him sometimes. He stays in and out of jail. He's still in jail. So ... he would get out of jail, [and] my grandmom would give him a chance, [and] he would come back [home] ... [but] he kept coming home drunk, and grandmom [would] say, "The next time you come home drunk, you're not coming back." ... And that's how it's always been. (Individual interview participant)

Approximately 76% of the women surveyed agree that parents returning home from prison find it challenging to emotionally reconnect with their children (N = 306). Over 82% of the women surveyed agree that it is difficult for fathers, returning home from prison, to provide for their children (N = 308). Interviewed women also recognize the economic and emotional strain that incarceration has on family composition and share similar attitudes about their relationships with their incarcerated parent. Overall, the incarceration of their fathers during childhood has influenced their perceptions of fatherhood and relationships with men in their present adulthood.

Present Home Experiences. Approximately 88% of women surveyed currently live in either Southbridge or Eastside (N = 281), and almost all of the women interviewed currently live in either Southbridge or the Eastside. Most women interviewed reside in low-income housing. At least 65% of the women surveyed report residing in low-income housing, and 15% note living in middle-income apartment complexes (N = 310).

Nexus of Education and Economic Opportunity. High drop-out rates due to pregnancy result in large numbers of teenage mothers and young women raising children without a father. Although most women share positive attitudes about their own children's education, women in both the survey and interview data have struggled with school in their own lives. Interestingly, almost three quarters of the women surveyed said that they cared a lot about their grades in high school. However, survey responses reveal that only half of the women obtained at least a high school diploma, and only 5.5% have obtained some college or a college BA (N = 310). About a quarter of women interviewed received a high school diploma, and a third obtained a GED. Educational level and employment opportunities affect and stifle women's abilities to maintain economic self-sufficiency as single mothers. Nearly two thirds of women in the survey data (N = 303), and more than half of women interviewed, report being unemployed but actively looking for work. Most women in the study struggle to provide for their children without a father in home, which makes it difficult to break the cycle of single motherhood in their own children's lives.

Street or Criminal Activity. Most women in both qualitative and quantitative data were presently or formerly street-identified. A number of women interviewed report having criminal charges, and 34% of the women surveyed (N = 209) report being incarcerated. According to survey results, of those incarcerated, about 55% report selling drugs/narcotics as their primary hustle before being incarcerated. Other street activities included prostitution, theft, and robbery.

> Yasser: What drew you to the streets?
>
> Camille (24): … I was always enticed by the streets, you know, just because … of who I am, of who I grew up around, where I came from. (Dual interview participant)
>
> Chantel (30): [I've sold] the drugs, I done the charges, I done did the jail time and did all that. So of course, I'm gonna tell [my son] that's not the right thing to do. (Group interview participant)

Personal, social, and economic survival led these women to becoming street-identified. Many of them grew up around criminal activity in their homes and communities, and participated in such activity in their youth and adult lives. Street life influenced these women's notions of motherhood, as some of the women tried drugs to cope with being single mothers during distressed economic periods, and some women sold drugs to help feed their children. Although criminal activity is traditionally contextualized as "social deviance," this study argues that welfare, crime, and/or a street identity are, in fact, adaptive—as most participants regarded the streets as a "means to an end."

Interpersonal Violence. Survey and interview data reveal that only some women experienced physical violence. Over 15% of women surveyed have been attacked or stabbed with a knife at least once (N = 308). Almost 12% of the women surveyed have been chased by gangs or individuals at some point (N = 307). According to the survey data, 35% of women have been threatened with serious physical harm by someone (N = 309), and over 40% of women surveyed said that they have been slapped, punched, or hit by someone at least once (N = 308).

> Toni (18): [Before my son, I was] wild, didn't care. Fought anybody, I've been arrested, I have charges, [I] just didn't care.
>
> Yasser: Arrested for what?
>
> Toni (18): Assault. (Individual interview participant)

> Camille (24): … it used to be unheard … of a girl like slicing people up, you know, cutting people up … [now] it's like that … you got the girls that just go hard (fight aggressively) like [boys]. … They don't know what their place is. Like they don't know what [being] a lady is about. (Dual interview participant)

Both Toni (18) and Camille (24) separately discuss inner-city violence as both participants and witnesses of violence against women. Such violence can be understood in terms of the way street-identified Black women negotiate maintaining personal safety, and deal with economic poverty and community tension, due to poor living conditions. Rightly or wrongly, street-identified Black women often participate in interpersonal violence as a method of coping and survival. These women were also found to speak about physical violence in relation to motherhood and/or raising their children in potentially violent communities.

> Aneshia (29): Now you scared to let your child be born … it's a strain on your youth, and when your child goes outside. It's a shame … that they can't walk outside because you're afraid. When we first moved [to Southbridge] it was the Wild-Wild West … I mean, the movie scene, they were ducking on the basketball courts, and it was like a war zone. Like they were literally shooting in broad daylight. … I thought I was on TV. (Group interview participant)

The women struggle with issues of physical violence and safety for themselves and their children. They fear losing their sons to gun violence or losing their daughters to prostitution or drug use. These fears are echoed in the literature on Black women and community violence (Jarrett & Jefferson, 2004; Jenkins, 2002). Over 53% of women surveyed had a relative who had been shot and killed by a gun, most of whom were male figures. Yadira (31), a Southbridge single mother of three, lost her 17-year-old son, Dayveair, as a result of gun violence. She fears losing her other children to violence and feels the need to be more protective of them.

Many of these women are single and live in homes without a male figure present. In fact, almost 53% of the women surveyed are single without significant partners, and only 2.9% of the women are legally married (N = 300). In addition, none of the women interviewed are married, and only a few have significant partners. Also, nearly two thirds of women surveyed have children (N = 300), and all women interviewed have children. The issue of teen motherhood echoed through the interviews. Nearly half of women interviewed (N = 8) had their first child before the age of 18 years, some as young as 14 years (N = 3). Subsequently, these same teen mothers became single mothers without a consistent father figure in the home for their children. Camille (24) never met her biological father, and her stepfather left the home when she was 12 years old. Although she was an honor roll student, she had her first child at 14 years and dropped out of school in 10th grade.

> Camille (24): … I've been through my things, my issues. I had my first child when I was 14 years old … leaving school early … not having nothing to do, sitting around all day [watching] the good shows on TV … you know, not wanting to go to school. (Dual interview participant)

Although Camille's (24) response reflects a stereotypical depiction of Black youth and their supposed disinterest in school, it is important for her response to be contextualized. Camille (24) experienced not only a fatherless home but also a detachment from her birth father and neglect from her stepfather. Adverse home conditions played a significant role in Camille's attitude toward not only parenting and motherhood but also education and graduating from school. Camille experienced neglect and a lack of male support throughout her life, and these experiences influenced her distrust in men's ability to be "good fathers," and demotivated her interest in school success.

Most women interviewed were raising children without their children's father present in the home (N = 13). These women hold both positive and negative attitudes toward their children's fathers and reflect on the struggle of single motherhood in their communities.

Leslie (31): It makes me feel bad because there's no, it's like, hard raising 'em all by myself with no help. (Individual interview participant)

Tisha (27): It's hard to be a single mother out trying to raise your kids on your own. So the best thing you can do is just hold them tight and let them know everything's gonna be alright … you know, don't run to the streets. (Group interview participant)

Aneshia (29) is the mother of six children and two grandchildren. Her father was inconsistent in her life as a child, and none of the fathers of her children are actively in their lives. Aneshia would rather raise her children alone and rejects forcing Black men to support their children through "White men" or state child support agencies.

Aneshia (29): … If the White man (state child support agencies) gotta make you take care of my child, then we don't need you … it made me really dislike men too. 'Cause it started with my dad. … Yeah, I'm a male basher. … Like I was hurt by a man, really badly, deeply-rooted hurt by a man so that [has] a great impact on me to this day. (Group interview participant)

Aneshia's (29) anger toward her biological father and the fathers of her children reveals the effect of growing up without a father and how this shaped her notions of single motherhood as an adult.

Why Aren't the Fathers of Their Children in the Home?

Substance Abuse. Several women interviewed attribute their own nonresidential, fatherless homes to substance abuse, which includes the use and sale of narcotics. Nearly a quarter of women interviewed report the fathers of their children sell or sold drugs, and a smaller but critical mass of women report that their fathers use drugs.

Brandy (29): My children's father is not around, not in the household, sells drugs every day …. Like you live about a 20-minute walk from Southbridge, and it's been months since you looked my kids in their face … So no … I don't believe you love them. (Group interview participant)

Brandy (29) is very angry with her children's father and attributes his not visiting his children more regularly to his sales of narcotics. This anger deeply informs Brandy's social identity as a Black single mother and reverberates more strongly when she reflects on how she is forced to raise her children alone without male support. Anger and negative relationships toward the fathers of their children echoed through women's interviews. Several women believe that if the father is not currently involved emotionally or intimately with the mother, then the father will not provide for, or be present in the lives of, his children: "Some fathers feel like these days, if they're not with … the mother of their child then they don't want nothing to do with the child."

Incarceration. "Fatherless" homes as a function of incarceration are also apparent in women's present home experiences, as many of their children's biological fathers are removed from the home due to incarceration. Over 75% of women surveyed believe fathers sometimes leave the home when they are unable to provide for their families (N = 309), which results in unstable relationships between fathers and their children due to this removal.

Tasha (29): … [My children's] father is out-of-state, incarcerated … in and out of their lives. But it's … a shame 'cause us as mothers know that we have to be the mother and the father … We don't even look forward to the father no more. (Dual interview participant)

Yadira (31): … my oldest son, the one who was murdered, his father was incarcerated … all his life basically. And then when he got out, my son was already a teenager and [didn't want] to hear anything [his father] had to say … (Dual interview participant)

Tasha (29) discusses her lack of hope for father involvement in the home and how such lack shapes her conceptions of single motherhood, and Yadira (31) discusses the contentious relationship between her son and his father due to his father's incarceration. "Fatherless" homes are created as a function of incarceration of Black men, and almost two thirds of women surveyed believe that having a mother and father in the home would help reduce rates of incarceration (N = 271).

Discussion

You always was a black queen, mama.
I finally understand, for a woman it ain't easy tryna raise a man.
You always was committed:
A poor, single mother on welfare—tell me how ya did it?
There's no way I can pay you back,
But the plan is to show you that I understand:
You are appreciated.

—Tupac Shakur, "Dear Mama," 1995, *Me Against the World*

Family composition and criminal record or street activity were found to greatly shape experiences of Black single motherhood. Survey and interview data reveal varied perspectives on "fatherless" homes in street communities, as participants' childhood and present home experiences influence these women's interpretations of motherhood and relationships with men. Also, findings suggest evidence of social reproduction of attitudes toward single motherhood, as most women in the sample who grew up without their father in the home are now raising their own "fatherless" children. Nonetheless, as demonstrated in our findings, female-headed homes are created and perpetuated by violent, structural forces of inequality that remove low-income Black men from the home and make heterosexual marriage seem unobtainable for most low-income Black women.

Structural violence was found to ravage poor Black families, particularly through incarceration, substance abuse and addiction, and familial struggles. Use and sale of narcotics influenced the presence of "fatherless" homes in women's childhood and present home experiences, particularly because of the negative effect substance abuse had on family composition. Many women interviewed reflected on how their fathers were incarcerated due to substance abuse and, in turn, their children's father was also incarcerated due to substance abuse. Furthermore, issues of recidivism exacerbated the family and household instability as well.

Nevertheless, a smaller critical mass of Black women expressed positive attitudes toward their fathers and their children's fathers, despite the problem of "fatherless" homes, primarily due to the obvious injustices that deeply pervade their communities. We include these positive experiences to reframe popular conceptualizations about the Black family unit and to provide nuance about the relationships held between low-income Black fathers and their daughters. Black men outside of the home can and have been found, in many instances, to provide emotional and financial support, as well as advice and guidance for their children. This study seeks to provide a balanced perspective of Black men as fathers rather than continuing the demonization of the men as inadequate "deadbeats." This demonization only exacerbates sociocultural conditions faced by Black men, and distracts us from having critical, progressive, and frank conversations about race relations and inequality in America.

Implications

Black single motherhood in street life-oriented communities moves through spaces of structural and social inequalities that influence the lives of mothers and their children. Thus, it is imperative to reshape the framework on relevant notions of resilience, to more deeply address the complex developmental process of unwed, street-identified Black women with children. It is important to analyze these women in the context of their social phenomena and the societal forces that negatively affect their social well-being and mobility. Structural issues such as the mass incarceration of Black men, welfare policies that make it financially beneficial for Black women to remain single and reside in low-income conditions, and high-crime environments all make single motherhood normative for many Black women. Social and governmental policy must be remedied before there can be a decrease in female-headed homes. Most importantly, subsequent discourse on Black single mothers should not merely add to the literary dialogue without action. Instead, discourse should advocate for social change and advancement for these women and their families, including the men.

Funding

The authors disclosed receipt of the following financial support for the research, authorship, and/or publication of this article: This work was supported by the American Recovery Reinvestment Act, United Way of Delaware, and the University of Delaware.

References

Alexander, M. (2010). *The new Jim Crow: Mass incarceration in the age of colorblindness*. The New Press.

Anderson, E. (1999). *Code of the streets: Decency, violence and the moral life of the inner city*. W. W. Norton.

Armbrister, C. (2003). The concentration of poverty: Wilmington, Delaware. *The Realities of Poverty in Delaware, 2003–2004*, 39–42.

Barras, J. R. (2002). *Whatever happened to Daddy's little girl? The impact of fatherlessness on Black women*. One World/Ballantine.

Battle, N. T. (2016). From slavery to Jane Crow to Say Her Name: An intersectional examination of Black women and punishment. *Meridians, 15*(1), 109–136.

Bies, J. (2018, October 3). Wilmington: One of the hardest places to achieve the American dream. *The News Journal*. https://www.delawareonline.com/story/news/2018/10/03/wilmington-one-hardest-places-achieve-american-dream-united-states/1490481002/

Bronson, J., & Carson, E. A. (2019). *Prisoners in 2017* (NCJ 252156). Bureau of Justice Statistics. https://www.bjs.gov/content/pub/pdf/p17.pdf

Brunson, R. K., & Stewart, E. (2006). Young African American women, the street code, and violence: An exploratory analysis. *Journal of Crime and Justice, 29*, 1–19.

Burton, L. M., & Tucker, M. B. (2009). Romantic unions in an era of uncertainty: A post Moynihan perspective on African American women and marriage. *Annals of the American Academy of Political and Social Science, 621*, 132–148.

Bush-Baskette, S. (2010). *Misguided justice: The War on Drugs and the incarceration of Black women*. iUniverse.

Butterfield, F. (1995). *All God's children: The Bosket family and the American tradition of violence.* Harper Perennial.

Center for Community Research and Service. (2015). *An overview of poverty in Delaware.* https://courts.delaware.gov/supreme/docs/Peuquet-OverviewPovertyInDelawareBrief-10-2015.pdf

Center for Drug and Health Studies. (2016). *Cease violence Wilmington.* Newark: Center for Drug and Health Studies, University of Delaware.

Centers for Disease Control and Prevention. (2015). *Elevated rates of urban firearm violence and opportunities for prevention—Wilmington, Delaware.* https://dhss.delaware.gov/dhss/dms/files/cdcgunviolencereport10315.pdf

Cherlin, A., Cross-Barnet, C., Burton, L. M., & Garrett-Peters, R. (2008). Promises they can keep: Low-income women's attitudes toward motherhood, marriage, and divorce. *Journal of Marriage and Family, 70,* 919–933.

Chesney-Lind, M. (2012). *The female offender: Girls, women, and crime.* Sage.

Child Trends Data Bank. (2015, March). *Births to unmarried women.* http://www.childtrends.org/wp-content/uploads/2015/03/75_Births_to_Unmarried_Women.pdf

Chunn, D. E., & Gavigan, S. A. (2004). Welfare law, welfare fraud, and the moral regulation of the "never deserving" poor. *Social & Legal Studies, 13,* 219–243.

City of Wilmington. (2010). *Population & demographics: City of Wilmington Census 2010 data.*

https://www.wilmingtonde.gov/about-us/about-the-city-of-wilmington/Population-demographics.

Cole, J. B., & Guy-Sheftall, B. (2003). *Gender talk: The struggle for women's equality in African American communities.* One World/Ballantine Books.

Coles, R. L., & Green, C. S. C. (2010). *The myth of the missing Black father.* Columbia University Press.

Collins, P. H. (1987). The meaning of motherhood in Black culture and Black mother/daughter relationships. *Sage: A Scholarly Journal on Black Women, 4*(2), 3–10.

Collins, P. H. (1990). *Black feminist thought: Knowledge, consciousness, and the politics of empowerment* (1st ed.). Unwin Hyman.

Collins, P. H. (2000). Gender, Black feminism, and Black political economy. *Annals of the American Academy of Political Science, 548,* 41–53.

Connor, M. E., & White, J. (2006). *Black fathers: An invisible presence in America.* Routledge.

Crenshaw, K. (1991). Mapping the margins: Intersectionality, identity politics, and violence against women of color. *Stanford Law Review, 43*(6), 1241–1299. https://doi.org/10.2307/1229039

Delaware Department of Correction. (2019). *Inmate population.* Delaware Open Data. https://data.delaware.gov/Public-Safety/Inmate-Population/vnau-c4rn

Delaware Health Statistics Center. (2017). *Delaware vital statistics: Annual report 2017.* https://dhss.delaware.gov/dhss/dph/hp/files/ar2017_net.pdf

DuMonthier, A., Childers, C., & Milli, J. (2017). *The status of Black women in the United States*. Institute for Women's Policy Research (IWPR). https://iwpr.org/wp-content/uploads/2020/08/The-Status-of-Black-Women-6.26.17.pdf

Edin, K., & Kefalas, M. (2011). *Promises I can keep: Why poor women put motherhood before marriage*. University of California Press.

Edin, K., & Lein, L. (1997). *Making ends meet: How single mothers survive welfare and low-wage work*. Russell Sage Foundation.

Edin, K., & Nelson, T. (2013). Understanding the "new father" model in the inner city. *Spotlight on Poverty and Opportunity*, 1–2.

Eichler, T. P. (2004). *Race and incarceration in Delaware: A preliminary consideration* (Report). Delaware Center for Justice and Metropolitan Wilmington Urban League. https://static.prisonpolicy.org/scans/RaceIncarceration.pdf

Entmacher, J., Robbins, K. G., Vogtman, J., & Frohlich, L. (2013). *Insecure & unequal: Poverty and income among women and families 2000–2013*. National Women's Law Center. https://www.nwlc.org/sites/default/files/pdfs/final_2014_nwlc_poverty_report.pdf

Fagan, J. (1994). Women and drugs revisited: Female participation in the cocaine economy. *Journal of Drug Issues*, *24*, 179–225.

Farmer, P. (2005). Suffering and structural violence. In P. S Rothenberg (Ed.), *Beyond borders: Thinking critically about global issues* (pp. 368–384). W. H. Freeman.

Federal Bureau of Investigation (FBI) Uniform Crime Report. 2017. Table 6: Crime in the United States by Metropolitan Statistical Area, 2017." Crime in the United States. Retrieved May 1, 2020. https://ucr.fbi.gov/crime-in-the-u.s/2017/crime-in-the-u.s.-2017/topic-pages/tables/table-6

Fishman, M., & Jedra, C. (2016, October 28). Purzycki's business ties: Asset or liability? *Delaware Online*. http://www.delawareonline.com/story/news/2016/10/28/purzyckis-business-ties-asset-liability/92464820/

Galtung, J. (1969). Violence, peace, and peace research. *Journal of Peace Research*, *6*(3), 167–191.

Galtung, J. (1971). A structural theory of imperialism. *Journal of Peace Research*, *8*(2), 81–117.

Garrison, A., & Kervick, C. (2005). *Analysis of City of Wilmington violence and social/economic data* [Presentation]. Criminal Justice Council. http://wilmhope.org/wp-content/uploads/2012/01/Preliminary-Research-and-Data-Analysis.pdf

Giddings, P. (1984). *When and where I enter: The impact of Black women on race and sex in America*. William Morrow.

Gilligan, J. (1996). *Violence*. Vintage Book Edition.

Glaser, B. G., & Strauss, A. L. (1967). *The discovery of grounded theory: Strategies for qualitative research*. Aldine.

Gray, K. F. (2014, December). *Characteristics of Supplemental Nutrition Assistance Program households: Fiscal year 2013* (Report No. SNAP-14-CHAR). http://www.mathematica-mpr.com/~/media/publications/pdfs/nutrition/characteristics2013.pdf

Gržinić, M., & Tatlić, Š. (2014). *Necropolitics, racialization, and global capitalism: Historicization of biopolitics and forensics of politics, art, and life*. Lexington Books.

Gurusami, S. (2018). Motherwork under the state: The maternal labor of formerly incarcerated Black women. *Social Problems*, *66*(1), 128–143.

Haney, C. A., Michielutte, R., Vincent, C. E., & Cochrane, C. M. (1974). Factors associated with the poverty of Black women. *Sociology and Social Research*, *59*, 40–49.

Hinton, E., Henderson, L., & Reed, C. (2018). *An unjust burden: The disparate treatment of Black Americans in the criminal justice system*. Vera Institute of Justice. https://www.vera.org/downloads/publications/for-the-record-unjust-burden-racial-disparities.pdf

Hitchens, B. K., & Payne, Y. A. (2017). Brenda's got a baby: Black single motherhood and street life as a site of resilience in Wilmington, Delaware. *Journal of Black Psychology*, *43*(1): 50–76.

Honderich, K. (2003). *The real cost of prisons for women and their children*. The Real Cost of Prisons Project. http://realcostofprisons.org/materials/rcpp_background_women.pdf

Hunter, A. G. (1997). Counting on grandmothers: Black mothers' and fathers' reliance on grandmothers for parenting support. *Journal of Family Issues*, *18*(3), 251–269.

Iversen, R. R., & Farber, N. (1996). Transmission of family values, work, and welfare among poor urban Black women. *Work and Occupations*, *23*, 437–460.

Jarrett, R. L., & Jefferson, S. M. (2004). Women's danger management strategies in an inner-city housing project. *Family Relations*, *53*, 138–147.

Jenkins, E. J. (2002). Black women and community violence: Trauma, grief, and coping. *Women & Therapy*, *25*(3–4), 29–44.

Jones, A. (2014, December 9). Murder town USA (aka Wilmington, Delaware). *Newsweek*. http://www.newsweek.com/2014/12/19/wilmington-delaware-murder-crime-290232.html

Jones, C. A., & Seabrook, R. L. (2017). The new Jane Crow: Mass incarceration and the denied maternity of Black women. In M. Deflem (Ed.), *Sociology of crime, law and deviance*, *22*, 135–154. Emerald Publishing.

Jones, J., & Mosher, W. D. (2013). Fathers' involvement with their children: United States, 2006–2010. *National Health Statistics Reports*, *71*, 1–22.

Jones, N. (2010). Between good and ghetto: African American girls and inner-city violence. Rutgers University Press.

Jordan-Zachery, J. S. (2014). Mythical illusions: Cultural images and Black womanhood. In H. Jackson-Lowman (Ed.), *Afrikan American women: Living at the crossroads of race, gender, class, and culture* (pp. 137–154). Cognella Academic Publishing.

Kann, L., McManus, T., Harris, W.A., Shanklin, S. L., Flint, K. H., Queen, B., Lowry, R., Chyen, D., Whittle, L., Thornton, J., Lim, C., Bradford, D., Yamakawa, Y., Leon, M., Brener, N., & Ethier, K. A. (2018). Youth risk behavior surveillance — United States, 2017. *MMWR Surveillance Summaries*, *67*(8), 1–114. https://doi.org/10.15585/mmwr.ss6708a1

Letiecq, B. L., & Koblinsky, S. A. (2004). Parenting in violent neighborhoods: African American fathers share strategies for keeping children safe." *Journal of Family Issues*, *25*(6), 715–734.

Linderman, J., Horn, B., Parra, E., & Fenn, L. (2017, September 9). Smaller US cities struggle with high teen gun violence rates. *US News & World Report*. https://www.usnews.com/news/best-states/delaware/articles/2017-09-08/delaware-city-struggles-as-a-gun-plague-afflicts-its-youth

Livingston, G., & Parker, K. (2011, June 15). *A tale of two fathers: More are active, but more are absent.* Pew Research Center. https://www.pewresearch.org/social-trends/2011/06/15/a-tale-of-two-fathers/

Mauer, M. (2013). *The changing racial dynamics of women's incarceration.* The Sentencing Project.

Mauer, M., & Huling, T. (1995). *Young Black Americans and the criminal justice system: Five years later* [Report].

McLanahan, S., & Percheski, C. (2008). Family structure and the reproduction of inequalities. *Annual Review of Sociology, 34,* 257–276.

McLoyd, V. C., & Enchautegui-de-Jesús, N. (2005). Work and African American family life. In V. C. McLoyd, K. Dodge, & N. Hill (Eds.), *African-American family life: Ecological and cultural diversity* (pp. 135–165). Guilford Press.

Moynihan, D. P. (1965). *The Negro family: The case for national action.* U.S. Department of Labor, Office of Policy Planning and Research.

Mullings, L. (1997). *On our own terms: Race, class, and gender in the lives of African American women.* Routledge.

Nadasen, P. (2007). From widow to "welfare queen": Welfare and the politics of race. *Black Women, Gender and Families, 1,* 52–77.

National Coalition of 100 Black Women Inc., Delaware Chapter. (2018). *The state of our union: Black women and girls in Delaware.* https://73d149e1-f7cd-418e-93ea-7063a393d80f.filesusr.com/ugd/426915_5af07df1b02747789315518532e5b576.pdf

Orleck, A. (2005). *Storming Caesars Palace: How Black mothers fought their own war on poverty.* Beacon Press.

Payne, Y. A. (2001). Black men and street life as a site of resiliency: A counter story for Black scholars. *International Journal of Critical Psychology, 4,* 103–122.

Payne, Y. A. (2008). "Street life" as a site of resiliency: How street life–oriented U.S. born African men frame opportunity in the United States. *Journal of Black Psychology, 34*(1), 3–31.

Payne, Y. A. (2011). Site of resilience: A reconceptualization of resiliency and resilience in street life–oriented Black men. *Journal of Black Psychology, 37*(4), 426–451.

Payne, Y. A. (2013). *The people's report: The link between structural violence and crime in Wilmington, Delaware* (Formal Report). Wilmington HOPE Commission and University of Delaware, Wilmington.

Payne, Y. A., Chambers, D. L., & Hitchens, B. K. (In press). *Murder town, USA: Homicide, structural violence, and activism.* Rutgers University Press.

Prosperity Now. (2019). *Racial wealth divide in Wilmington* [Report]. https://prosperitynow.org/sites/default/files/resources/RWD_Profile_Wilmington.pdf

Richie, B. (2012). *Arrested justice: Black women, violence, and America's prison nation.* New York University Press.

Roberts, D. E. (1995). Motherhood and crime. *Social Text, 42,* 99–123.

Roberts, D. E. (1996). Welfare and the problem of Black citizenship. *Yale Law Journal, 105*(6), 1563–1602.

Roberts, S. (2007, January 16). 51% of women are now living without spouse. *The New York Times*, A1. https://www.nytimes.com/2007/01/16/us/16census.html

Rodriguez, C. (2016). Mothering while Black: Feminist thought on maternal loss, mourning and agency in the African Diaspora. *Transforming Anthropology, 24*(1), 61–69.

Rowley, C. T. (2002). The maternal socialization of Black adolescent mothers. *Race, Gender & Class, 9*, 168–182.

Sabol, W. J., West, H. C., & Cooper, M. (2008). *Prisoners in 2008*. U.S. Department of Justice, Bureau of Justice Statistics. http://www.bjs.gov/content/pub/pdf/p08.pdf

Sentencing Project. (2018). *Fact sheet: Incarcerated women and girls, 1980–2016*. https://www.sentencingproject.org/wp-content/uploads/2016/02/Incarcerated-Women-and-Girls.pdf

Sharp, E. A., & Ispa, J. (2009). Inner-city single Black mothers' gender-related childrearing expectations and goals. *Sex Roles, 60*, 656–668.

Shattuck, R. M., & Kreider, R. M. (2011). *Social and economic characteristics of currently unmarried women with a recent birth: 2011*. American Community Survey Reports, 1–10. U.S. Census Bureau. https://www2.census.gov/library/publications/2013/acs/acs-21.pdf

Smith, C. A. (2016). Facing the dragon: Black mothering, sequelae, and gendered necropolitics in the Americas. *Transforming Anthropology, 24*(1), 31–48.

Stebbins, S., & Comen, E. (2018, June). Are these the worst cities to live in? Study looks at quality of life across the U.S. *USA Today*. https://www.usatoday.com/story/money/economy/2018/06/13/50-worst-cities-to-live-in/35909271/

Steffensmeier, D., & Haynie, D. (2000). Gender, structural disadvantage, and urban crime: Do macrosocial variables also explain female offending rates? *Criminology, 38*, 403–438.

Sufrin, C., Beal, L., Clarke, J., Jones, R., & Mosher, W. D. (2019). Pregnancy outcomes in US Prisons, 2016–2017. *American Journal of Public Health, 109*(5), 799–805.

Szalavitz, M. (2011, November). Study: Whites more likely to abuse drugs than Blacks. *Time Magazine*. http://healthland.time.com/2011/11/07/study-whites-more-likely-to-abuse-drugs-than-blacks/

U.S. Bureau of Labor Statistics. (2019). *Women in the labor force: A databook* (No. 1084). https://www.bls.gov/opub/reports/womens-databook/2019/home.htm

U.S. Census Bureau. (2010). *2009–2013 ACS 5-year estimates*. U.S. Census Bureau's American Community Survey Office. http://www.census.gov/acs/www/data/data-tables-and-tools/easystats

U.S. Census Bureau. (2012, April). *Households and families: 2010*. https://www.census.gov/prod/cen2010/briefs/c2010br-14.pdf

U.S. Census Bureau. (2017). *2013–2017 ACS 5-year estimates*. U.S. Census Bureau's American Community Survey Office. https://factfinder.census.gov/bkmk/table/1.0/en/ACS/17_5YR/DP05/1600000US1077580

Vargas, J. H. C. (2006). *Catching hell in the city of angels: Life and meanings of blackness in South Central Los Angeles*. University of Minnesota Press.

Wagner, P., & Sawyer, W. (2018). *States of incarceration: The global context 2018*. Prison Policy Initiative. https://www.prisonpolicy.org/global/2018.html

Wayne, L. (2012, June 1). How Delaware thrives as a corporate tax haven. *New York Times*. https://www.nytimes.com/2012/07/01/business/how-delaware-thrives-as-a-corporate-tax-haven.html

Wilmington shootings: A research database of shootings in Wilmington. (2017). Retrieved April 9, 2017 from http://data.delawareonline.com/webapps/crime/

Wink, C. (2014, September 23). 64% of Fortune 500 firms are Delaware incorporations: Here's why. *Technical.ly*. http://technical.ly/delaware/2014/09/23/why-delaware-incorporation/

Reading 3.4. An Examination of Sexual Assault of African Women and Girls in Colonial America

History, Myths, and the Impact of Minimization of Sexual Assault

Yolanda K. H. Bogan

Since colonial America, African women and girls have had to endure double marginalization as women and Africans (Truth, 1851). The feminist movement's myopic view, which sidelined the concerns of non-White women at its 1848 Seneca Falls Convention, led to womanism, a phrase coined by Alice Walker more than a century later in 1979. Other scholars have also focused on the dual status and unique experiences of African women and girls. More recent writings of the experiences of African women and girls has led to the development of intersectionality (Crenshaw, 1989, 1991), a perceptual framework that acknowledges a gestalt of African identity and female identity.

In this chapter I examine the sexual assault of experiences of African women and girls in colonial America and how these experiences laid the foundation for current issues that impact African American women and girls. Given that most Africans came to America enslaved, deprived of their humanity and lacking agency over their bodies, the sexual assault of African women and girls is not a surprise. This paper argues that centuries of sexual abuse of African American women and girls laid the foundation for minimizing sexual assault and its consequences in the current era.

As part of any discussion regarding racial disparities, comparisons, or equality, the myth of a whitewashed slavery and its generational consequences for African Americans and non-African Americans is necessary to understand. Analyses of racial disparities related to economics, education, or health rarely include the historical context of the issue of focus. This chapter seeks to fill this gap in the literature by examining the historical context of sexual assault of African women and girls in America from the colonial period.

History of American Slavery

Those who read first-person accounts of slavery understand that it was a brutal, torturous business. In schools across America, the enslavement of people in American history is glossed over, if mentioned at all, with the implication that Africans had no history, culture, families, or structure prior to being enslaved and brought to America. In textbooks, Africans are presented as "workers" who came to America (Dart, 2015; Isensee, 2015), who were happy (E. Ball, 2015) in their roles as slaves, and who were virtual members of the family (Elison, 2019). These myths are portrayed in movies such as *Gone With the Wind* and *Birth of a Nation*, in which the humanity and perspective of the White characters are always in focus and African American characters are either minimized or demonized.

A great deal of attention was paid to the date of August 2019 for commemorating 400 years of slavery in America. Most noticeably, the *New York Times Magazine* launched "The 1619 Project" to examine how the legacy of slavery continues to shape and define life in America (The New York Times,

225

2019). A closer look at colonial America uncovers an even earlier date for examining the history of slavery and sexual assault of African women. Through LaFlorida: the Interactive Digital Archive of the Americas, researchers at the University of South Florida have revealed that the enslaved were part of every Spanish expedition to Florida dating back to 1528 (Francis et al., 2019). Records reveal that as early as September 1565, enslaved African women served in a variety of capacities in the daily life of the settled town, including as forced concubines. Slavery has been practiced in many cultures, including on the African content (Hurston, 2018), and has been referenced in ancient sacred texts. As long as there are enslaved women, sexual exploitation is a predictable aspect of this status.

This paper seeks to highlight how sexual assault in colonial America laid the groundwork for disparate treatment and sexual perceptions of African American women that continue to impact the lived experience of African American women and girls over a century after the 13th Amendment was passed. By examining the historical factors that gave rise to myths that impact our families and our communities, this paper explores how minimization of the pain of African American people is part of the institutionalization of racism and gender inequity, as evidenced by political and social movements in the early 21st century.

In her book, *They Were Her Property: White Women as Slave Owners in the American South*, Stephanie Jones-Rogers (2019) provides a detailed analysis of how White women, especially married White women, owned and managed the enslaved, tortured and exploited the enslaved, and defended the institution of slavery, both for pecuniary gain and as a way of establishing and maintaining their identity, power, and wealth, even in states that recognized coverture.

The instructional process of inter-relating with the enslaved and slave-owning itself took place throughout one's development, for both Whites and the enslaved. Whether or not she owned slaves herself, a White girl decided how she would engage with the enslaved based on the models in the environment, her personal preferences and disposition, and periodicals such as the *Rose Bud/Southern Rose* that included such instructional articles. Thus, White females (i.e., girls and women) exerted power over Africans as a part of their self-identity.

Enslaved African women and girls were the first type of property that White women owned in the United States. Property rights for the enslaved became more popular in the 1840s (Lewis, 2019). James Redman, a noted *New York Tribune* journalist, advanced the idea that although their fathers, brothers, or husbands may have owned the enslaved, White women were shielded from the atrocities and practices of slavery (Jones-Rogers, 2019). The false idea that White women were not involved in slave ownership may also be related to the institution of coverture. *Coverture* was an English legal concept which asserted that a newly married woman no longer needed an independent identity because her groom offered her cover. As such, a White woman's identity, her being, and her property (e.g., the enslaved), would be subsumed under the man's domination. However, Jones-Rogers (2019) revealed that the practice and the policy did not always coincide, using diaries and court documents.

Trauma of Sexual Assault

The researchers who identified the traumagenic dynamics of sexual assault in the late 20th century could have used the African woman or girl as their ideal prototype to identify the factors of betrayal, stigma, powerlessness, and traumatic sexualization (Browne & Finkelhor, 1986). Sexual assault in America, in the context of the institution of slavery, accorded no expected allegiance or humanitarian treatment. To maintain the system of slavery, the enslaved were taught to understand that they could be treated any way that Whites deemed appropriate. Thus, the kinship ties, feelings, identities, development, health status, and any other human characteristics of Africans were secondary to the commerce of slavery.

The slave trade and the laws that institutionalized its practices, such as the Fugitive Slave Acts of 1793 and 1850, must have taught the enslaved that their relationship with Whites was primarily about the financial profit and comfort of Whites, including the sexual pleasure of Whites. Betrayal means that there is an implicit or explicit violation of the trust that is necessary for the integrity of the relationship. Slavery afforded no trust. Thus, minimization of the effect of sexual trauma committed against African women and girls was likely both a psychologically necessary coping mechanism by the enslaved and a useful justification by Whites to perpetuate their dehumanizing behavior towards the Africans whom they enslaved.

The stigma associated with sexual assault was an additional burden for the enslaved African woman and girl. Her skin tone, her body structure, and her hair texture acted singularly or in concert to alert non-Africans that this female could be treated as a sex object at any time and place, with the approval of the slaveowner. The powerlessness ascribed to the enslaved was not specific to women; it also included men who would dare to protect their families and themselves. Moreover, the powerlessness of Africans was systematized and institutionalized, legally enforced, and barbarically administered should enslaved persons dare to protect themselves or their loved ones. Betrayal, stigma, and powerlessness were all part of the sexual assault process, within a system designed to dehumanize and to ignore any differences between genders.

Sexual Assault of Enslaved African Women and Girls

To understand American slavery is to accept that African men and women were not just considered property; they were brutalized. That is, Africans were deprived of positive human qualities and routinely subjected to indignities that served to strengthen the power divide between Whites and Africans and to justify the development and maintenance of the peculiar institution (Kolchin, 1993). The process of dehumanization was barbaric and violent and served as a constant reminder of the supposed inferiority of the enslaved. Rape and other types of sexual assault were a constant reminder to all parties of the bifurcation of physical, social, and emotional power. DNA provides evidence of the abuse of African women and girls. According to Bryc et al. (2010), the median proportion of European ancestry in African Americans is nearly 20%.

Sexual Assault for Others' Benefit

Several historical documents point to the sexual assault of African women and girls in colonial America. John Blassingame's *Slave Testimony* (1977) offers firsthand accounts of the torturous conditions of slavery and the barbaric and abusive methods used to incite fear, prevent resistance, and punish fugitives. In this book, as part of an interview with J. W. Lindsay, a former enslaved male recounts a slaveholder's maltreatment of women. "She had a husband too, but that made no difference; he used her whenever he saw fit. He generally carried a white oak cane … if the women did not submit, he would make nothing of knocking them right down" (Blassingame, 1977, p. 400).

In another interview, a formerly enslaved female responded to a question regarding her master harming her. "… Dat's my child by him. I had five, but dat de only one livin' now. I didn't want him, but I couldn't do nothin'. I uster say, 'What do yer want of a woman all cut ter pieces like I is?' But 'twant no use" (Blassingame, 1977, p. 540). Here, the woman is referring to her powerlessness in resisting the slavemaster's abuse of her, in spite of the hundreds of lashes she had suffered as punishment from running away from several cruel masters.

African women and girls were also abused as a means for White men to display their anger. Referring to the end of the Civil War which brought freedom for the enslaved, a formerly enslaved male recounts, "When that gran' ole freedom bell rung I see the niggers goin' to the city; yes, an' I see the white folks cut off women's breasts. They were mad, 'jes' mad" (Blassingame, 1977, p. 535).

During the Jim Crow period, Ida B. Wells-Barnett discussed the inconsistency of White men's treatment of White and African women. In discussing the reasons that White mobs lynch Black men, Wells-Barnett (1895) offers the following analysis of White men's behavior, implicating sexual assault during that period:

To justify their own barbarism they assume a chivalry which they do not possess. True chivalry respects all womanhood, and no one who reads the record, as it is written in the faces of the million mulattoes in the South, will for a minute conceive that the southern white man had a very chivalrous regard for the honor due the women of his own race or respect for the womanhood which circumstances placed in his power. That chivalry which is "most sensitive concerning the honor of women" can hope for but little respect from the civilized world, when it confines itself entirely to the women who happen to be white. Virtue knows no color line, and the chivalry which depends upon complexion of skin and texture of hair can command no honest respect.

Sexual Assault for Pecuniary Gain

Regarding the sexual assault of the enslaved, White women were as guilty of this offense as White men were. As a sign of their womanhood, and to maintain independence and establish wealth, White women were often gifted with enslaved women or girls at marriage. Specifically, African women or girls (not men or boys) were often used as gifts, so that the White husband would not use the African woman for his labor and thereby exploit the wife's gifts for his use. In addition, African women were preferred over men as gifts because they provided the means of increasing wealth through childbirth, given that children assumed the status of the mother.

As such, White women might arrange for the sexual assault of African enslaved women—to incite pregnancy, so that they could profit from the "natural increase" (Jones-Rogers, 2019, p. 22) of slave ownership and/or so that they could ensure a wet nurse for their own child. The perpetrator of the arranged sexual assault could be another slave or the White woman's husband. Either way, as the owner of an African woman, the White woman would profit from the development of a healthy child. Keeping women of childbearing age pregnant, by any means necessary, was a likely method of building wealth for Whites, especially after the passage of the Act to Prohibit the Importation of Slaves in 1807.

Like the African men, African women were at the mercy of White women's whims. The Africans could find themselves greatly suffering at the recommendation of White females (Blassingame, 1977). On the other hand, Africans who were pregnant may have been provided with special care and attention. Enslaved children may have been more likely to be fed a decent meal or to engage in play or exercise, with modified discipline— not out of care for their humanity, but for the sake of protecting the financial investment of White women (Jones-Rogers, 2019).

Like that of White men, White women's American identity was shaped by their perceived and institutionalized status in relation to enslaved women and their ability to exploit enslaved people for pecuniary gain. Thus, this perspective provides greater context for the feminist movement in which White women focused on White female equality with White men, specific to gender, as opposed to fighting for equality for all.

Sexual Assault for Scientific Gain

While sexual assault is often defined as sexual exposure, fondling, or intercourse, definitions of sexual assault (determined by the state) may also include nonconsensual touching, use of an instrument, and penetration. The definition of sexual assault may also list "physician" among categories of people who are in a "position of trust." A definition of sexual assault that includes the perpetrator's motivation minimizes the experience of the victim, whose feelings of shame and stigma are not likely altered because of the perpetrator's various motivations.

The scientific experimentation on enslaved Africans was the precursor to more recent nonconsensual medical experiments such as the Tuskegee study, the theft of cells from Henrietta Lacks, and the CDC measles study (Chisolm-Straker & Straker, 2017; West & Irvine, 2015). Marion James Sims was a physician who practiced in colonial America and who used enslaved African women and girls for gynecological experiments (Ojanuga, 1993). Through his experimentation, he invented the vaginal speculum, the Sims test, the Sims position, and other gynecological procedures. Commonly lauded as the father of gynecology (Ojanuga, 1993; M. J. West et al., 2015), Sims is also credited with authoring the first gynecological textbook.

Straughn et al. (2012) herald Dr. James Marion Sims as an exemplary ethical model, for characteristics such as professionalism and interpersonal relations. These authors indicate that medical students should aspire to be like Sims because he "cared for the indigent, hearthless, indentured and disenfranchised" (p. 193). With this description, the authors misrepresent, ignore, and minimize the socio-political context of Sims's work, the ethical issues associated with informed consent in medical practice, and the African women's nonconsensual status. Moreover, the invasiveness of the procedures perpetrated on these women, and the lack of anesthesia, made these experimentations excruciatingly painful. The fact that he invited others to watch while he performed his experiments had to greatly contribute to these women feeling degraded and humiliated (Ojanuga, 1993).

Trawalter and Hoffman (2015) report that during the pre-colonial period, many assumed that Africans had a higher threshold for pain or felt less pain than Whites. This attitude of racial bias may or may not have contributed to Sims's abuse of these women's sexual organs to satisfy his scientific curiosity. Unfortunately, the scientific literature reveals that the phenomenon of minimizing the physical pain of African Americans still continues through the present day (Chisolm-Straker & Straker, 2017; Washington, 2006).

Minimization of Sexual Assault of African Women and Girls

In their studies of perceived pain, Hoffman et al. (2016) found that laypersons, and half of the medical students who participated in the study, ascribed less pain to African Americans. These researchers point to a body of research indicating that Black patients are less likely than White patients to be medically treated for pain. Moreover, as one cause for this disparity, the researchers cite a body of literature indicating that people assume that Blacks feel less pain.

I posit that the misconception that Black people are able to withstand more pain was borne out of the dehumanization of chattel slavery in the United States and the resilience of African people. Further, this researcher theorizes that the process of ascribing less pain to Blacks is not circumscribed to physical pain, but is applied to emotional pain as well. African Americans, breathing the atmospheric lies advanced by institutionalized racism, often do not learn to recognize our emotional pain. Left untreated, emotional pain turns into depression (Williams, 2006) and other psychological illnesses while negatively impacting our familial, social, and occupational functioning.

Mental Pain of Rape

According to Thornhill and Thornhill (1991), rape does indeed lead to mental pain. As an evolutionary function, psychological pain functions to prompt the victim to consider the circumstances that led to the cause of the pain, and subsequently make efforts to avoid the situation. In this sense mental pain is adaptive, helping to protect the victim, just as physical pain can be adaptive as a self-preservation tool. In their study of rape victims of pre-reproductive age, productive age, and post-reproductive age, Thornhill and Thornhill (2015) found that rape leads to psychological pain. In addition, women who were mated or who experienced less violent rapes experienced more mental pain. Mated victims may have experienced more psychological trauma because the rape caused disruption in the couple's relationship and opened questions including the paternity of subsequent offspring. This fact is significant because rape prevents women from choosing the parentage of their offspring. Typically, men care more about their own genetic offspring than they do about other children (Daly & Wilson, 1983). Understanding this latter point in the context of slavery, enslaved females may have hoped that masters would free their genetic offspring from slavery. However, the offspring of rapes could just as easily be sold away, without being provided any advantage, or they could be punished more because of their status. What is clear is that the laws created no responsibility for men who impregnated enslaved women or girls.

Researchers also found that rape prevents women from choosing the timing and circumstances for reproduction. Women with less violent rapes experience more psychological trauma because victims are less likely to be believed and to gain the necessary emotional support from others (Thornhill & Thornhill, 2015). Thus, rape can also be socially isolating, adding to the trauma of this experience. Within the context of slavery, women were forced to endure all manner of treatment, and it may have been likely for others to have less empathy for victims whose experience of assault was on the less violent end of the assault continuum. Even when women have a recourse to report current sexual assaults, they often question whether their rape fits specific criteria in ascribing its legitimacy (Du Mont et al., 2003). Thus, if gaining present-day support is challenging, one can only imagine the mental and physical anguish of enslaved women.

Rape is a violation against the victim which leads to her psychological trauma. Rape also has reverberating effects on family relationships, female agency, and female relationships. In normal circumstances, the victim's psychological pain would lead her to the adaptive activity of avoiding the circumstances of the pain. Avoidance is the common symptom of the anxiety disorders which include Acute Stress Disorder and Post-traumatic Stress Disorder (American Psychiatric Association, 2013). Slavery prevented this adaptive avoidance, subjecting women and girls to a life of unavoidable sexual assault and Post-traumatic Stress Disorder.

Institutional Minimization of Sexual Assault1

I am of the opinion, as I have always been, and have very serious doubt as to whether the crime of rape can be committed upon a negro.

—Cole Blease, governor of South Carolina, 1910–1914

Blease's quote, in which he states that he does not know if it is possible to rape a Negro, is from an official pardoning statement more than 40 years after emancipation. His sentiments encapsulate the idea that African American women and girls are always available for sexual release, regardless of consent. The quote promotes a dehumanizing myth of permissiveness and one that is based on centuries of the institutionalized practice of using African women and girls as sexual objects.

Blease's position, as the elected governor, represented the highest level of the executive branch of the state government. At this level, the governor leads his or her elected and appointed cabinet in carrying out the governor's policies. Thus, not only do upper and lower level members of the executive branch pay attention to the ideology of the leadership, but citizens and all others are also informed and mindful of this ideology and experience its impact on their daily lives.

Blease's record of pardoning both Black and White men who had been convicted of attacking African women and girls sends a strong message to men and women alike. The fact that Blease pardoned both White men and Black men was not likely focused on social equality between these two groups, but was aimed at nullifying the idea of a perpetrator of aggression against African women and girls. Thus, Blease represents an example of the use of the institution of government to dehumanize African women and girls, justifying a terror of attacks against this most vulnerable group. The message to African women and girls is clearest: the pain of African women and girls is inconsequential to the sexual whims of men.

Myths That Promote Minimization of Sexual Assault

It is widely known that lynching was often used to terrorize Blacks, particularly during the Jim Crow era (Dray, 2010; Gates, 2019; Gunning, 1996), the period from the end of the Reconstruction period to the Civil Rights movement. During this dark period in American history, laws were passed to reinforce segregation and promote social, economic, and political disenfranchisement of African Americans, particularly in the South. For example, the intermarriage of Whites and Blacks was illegal in many parts of the United States, especially in the South, where most African Americans lived prior to the Great Migration. Lynching of Blacks was a reflection of the lack of due process and fairness in the criminal justice for Blacks. No longer of material value to Whites, Blacks were often perceived as the cause of White men's problems rather than the recipients or victims of their racial discriminatory behavior. As one result, lynching was an all too common practice in the Jim Crow era.

Many Blacks escaped the racial terror of the South and moved north or west during this period. In 1900, nine out of 10 Blacks lived in the South, and 75% lived on farms. After the Great Migration ended in 1970, fewer than half of all African Americans lived in the South, with 25% living on farms (Wilkerson, 2010). While there is a National Memorial of Peace and Justice in Montgomery, Alabama to highlight the racial terror of the Jim Crow era and of lynching in particular, little attention is given to the centuries of sexual assault that women have endured since America was founded (Gunning, 1996).

As Gunning (1996) points out, during the Jim Crow Era there was a need to advance mythology about the looseness of Black women, in order to avenge and justify White masculinity and passive White feminism. This mythology created a racially based triad of sexual deception that promoted White male sexual dominance over both White women and Black women. This triad of sexual deception ascribed unwanted and unjustified roles to women. As Wells-Barnett (1895) indicated, the honor of African American women and girls was never an issue for the chivalrous White male.

Wells-Barnett's analysis clearly conveys her belief in the equality of all women and reveals the illogical nature of White men's explanation for their mob lynching and terrorist behavior towards Black men and their families. Indeed, all women are worthy of chivalry; neither the Black woman, the Northern White woman, nor the Southern White woman was ever in need of protection from African men that would justify the illegal and unchecked behavior of White men, who routinely lynched Black men and assaulted African American women and girls.

In *Stolen Women*, Gail Wyatt (1998) provides a summary of the emotional, social, and physical anguish that accompanied the sexual violations of slavery. In western Africa, there were cultural practices that oriented men, women, boys, and girls to appropriate courtship behaviors for various stages of development (Hurston, 2018). Enslavement disrupted these practices.

Wyatt (1998) identifies several myths of African women and girls that grew out of systemic and institutionalized sexual assault in early America. These myths were passed down through institutions of art, literature, music, laws, policies, and practices. The permissive stereotype, the mammy, and the workhorse types are described below.

The Permissive Type

The "permissive" type myth is born out of the perpetrator projecting his salacious desire onto the victim, thereby making himself appear to be powerless, in a system in which he holds the power and accords power only to others like himself who are White and male. When White males generated this myth, they implied that Black women were unable to control their impulses and could not be trusted to be left alone (Wyatt, 1998).

Simultaneously, the permissive myth dehumanizes Black women as homogeneous sex objects, and minimizes individual characteristics that define a woman's humanity. The way a woman thinks, feels, and behaves defines her individuality and how she engages with people, the world, and ideas. The permissive stereotype implies that individual characteristics are of no consequence to African women's ever-present desire for sexual activity. Thus, when an African American woman is described primarily by characteristics associated with sexuality or physicality, the extent to which the permissive myth is being applied reflects the internalization of this myth.

While the permissive type was promoted during the antebellum period to justify enslavement, the historical consequence of the permissive type that was promoted beyond the Reconstruction period was the she-devil. Women who assume this character have internalized the permissive myth and capitalized on it to advance their personal agenda. This character appears to use, entrap, or exploit men by any method possible as she allows them to use her sexually. A discussion of the differences of opinion that the feminist and the womanist may have about the dress, speech, and behavior of the she-devil is beyond the focus of this chapter. The she-devil's use of sex to advance her cause historically made her a less than respected character who rarely demonstrated or received empathy.

The Mammy Type

Loyal to the racial status quo is the "mammy" character. Unlike the permissive type, the mammy is an asexual being whose fierce loyalty to the White family she serves makes her an acceptable character. She is typically not depicted with a husband or children; physically, she usually appears as very obese with dark complexion, and as uninterested in her appearance. This myth was portrayed by Hattie McDaniel, who played the role of "Mammy" in *Gone With the Wind*. The mammy mythical type is morally upright and religious, with no discontent aside from barriers that prevent her from serving White people. Thus, she does not appear to have hopes or dreams that promote her personal advancement either physically, emotionally, financially, or psychologically. One might assume that she is excluded from sexual assault; however, sexual assault is about power and control (Domestic Abuse Intervention Project, n.d.) and not sexual desire. For a review of workplace sexual harassment, see the review by McDonald (2011).

The Work-Horse Type

Finally, the relationship of the "work-horse" to sexual assault is that she is the superwoman (Wallace, 1978) who is able to be physical or sexually abused or neglected and still excel. Her work ethic and accomplishments define her, and she responds to hurt and rejection unemotionally and with a greater resolve to shine. A number of books have been written to shatter this myth and decloak the superwoman image, including *Black Macho and the Myth of the Superwoman* by Michele Wallace (1978), *Too Heavy a Yoke: Black Women and the Burden of Strength* by Chanequa Walker-Barnes (2014), and *Violence in the Lives of Black Women: Battered, Black and Blue* by Carolyn West (2002). African American women experience hurt and pain through an entrenched system of oppression whose tentacles are deep and far-reaching for the individual, the family, and the community.

Based in the chattel slavery of colonial America, these stereotypes of African American women are perpetuated in written and visual media and commercialism. These portrayals advance an oxymoron, that African American women and girls are willing participants in their own victimization. Just as African American men are perceived as creatures with larger-than-life strength and violence that need to be tightly controlled, the African American female is viewed as a super-sexed, charged being who is eager to engage in sexual activity whenever she is physically accessible (such as in her place of employment) and is unfazed by any challenges she may face. Such myths only serve to block legal recourse, minimize the impact of sexual assault of African women and girls, and question the validity and seriousness of our sexual victimization.

Current Implications and Recommendations

Sexual assault of women is a widespread problem in the United States. For African American women, sexual assault is of particular concern. According to the Maryland Coalition Against Sexual Assault (n.d.), African American women and girls over the age of 12 experienced higher rates of sexual violence than Asians, Whites, or Latinos from 2005–2010. Forty percent of African American women have experienced coercive sexual assault by the age of 18 and have been subjected to intimate partner violence during their lifetimes. In addition, 40% of confirmed sex traffic victims in the United States are African American women (Banks

& Kyckelhahn, 2011). Nearly half of African American women are at significant risk of some type of sexual assault. Given that most sexual assaults are perpetrated by someone known to the victim, the traumagenic dynamics of trust, betrayal, stigmatization, and disrupted sexual identity—compounded with epigenetic trauma (Yehuda & Bierer, 2009) and lived experiences—are of particular concern for African American women and girls. Any type of intervention should bear all of these dynamics in mind.

The historic experiences of African American women provide us with a perspective that appears to yield distinct present-day outcomes. A glaring example is found in the 2016 United States presidential election. African American women perceived a significant difference between the White male presidential candidate—who had no political experience, openly admitted to sexism, and supported White nationalism—and the White female candidate, who was portrayed as dishonest or disingenuous at worst, highly qualified at best. Only 4% of African American women voters endorsed Donald Trump, while 94% endorsed Hillary Clinton (M. Ball, 2018). Women of other races voted for Trump in much higher numbers. The blatant sexist and racist comments of Trump prior to the election were clear red flags to African American women to rely on our shared lived experience and trust our communal instincts of self-preservation. This significant voting difference may signify how the duality of race and gender of African American women merged to reflect an overwhelmingly different perspective from non-African American women, many of whom may have taken comfort in their race as the most protective factor from the sexist and racist rhetoric espoused by the winning candidate, similar to their colonial forbears.

The relatively recent enslavement of our ancestors, likely makes African American women more keenly aware of the threats to agency over our bodies. While a comprehensive review of abortion rights and Black women is beyond the scope of this chapter, according to Dorothy Height, former president of the National Council of Negro Women, African American women will have the most to lose if *Roe v. Wade* is curtailed (Marshall, 1989). The average cost of raising a child in the United States in 2015 was $233,610, with childcare costs sometimes being more expensive than housing (Steinour, 2018). Meanwhile, Black women's median salary is only 65.3% of White men's earnings (Hegewisch & Hartmann, 2018). Even if abortion is lawful in only a few states, the demographic of women who will be able to travel to these states for the procedure excludes poor African American women. Thus, the perception that abortion laws have racist undertones that serve to further marginalize the social and economic concerns of African American women is noted.

Black Women for America surveyed 600 multigenerational African American women who were registered as Democrats or independent voters to identify the major concerns for the 2020 United States presidential campaign. Black Women for America survey results indicated that healthcare was a major concern for the 2020 elections. Specifically, abortion rights were a major concern for African American women (Cision PR Web, 2019). African American women are mindful of the politics that impact their bodies and their families.

Feminists have long understood that most African American women are pro-choice. With the need to build a larger coalition of women to help advance this agenda, they have tried for decades to expand their network of supporters by aligning with Black women ("A Black Woman Responds," 1971; Fulwood, 1989). However, familial and religious concerns have contributed to African American women's discomfort with being vocal about this issue (Jones, 2019). Lack of trust in the feminist movement as representative of the views of African American women has been at issue since its inception. The womanist philosophy provides clarity regarding the differences between the two perspectives. According to Alice Walker (1983), womanist is to feminist as purple is to lavender.

The African American founder of the #metoo movement, Tarana Burke, created the movement for Black and brown girls to give them a safe and dedicated space to be heard (Burke, 2017). However, Burke acknowledges that the #metoo movement has gotten little attention or support from the feminist movement, except when the victims who come forward are celebrities or are White. The #metoo movement moniker is now primarily used to address the issues of sexual assault victimization of mainstream victims. That is, the original intent of the #metoo movement has been lost or co-opted by others to advance a different cause, as may have been done by the Women's Liberation Movement ("A Black Woman Responds," 1971). This shift in attention away from the needs of African American women and girls, in a movement that was founded for and by an African American woman, highlights the multiple oppressions that African American women and girls face as they relate to sexual assault. Moreover, the change in capitalization of the movement from #metoo to #MeToo also reflects how the original presentation of the movement has been repackaged and marketed to a different audience.

Some would argue that the lack of unity among all victims of sexual assault retards the collective progress in adopting an intersectional and multidimensional objective lens (Onwuachi-Willig, 2018) that works for all victims, especially those whose voices are least likely to be heard. On the other hand, as this chapter indicates, African American women and girls have a collective history that recognizes that our pleas for help from others may be sidelined or given less priority. Meanwhile, our needs for safety and protection persist.

Although we are constantly subjected to its consequences, institutionalized racism through the promotion of negative stereotypes and discrimination in health and criminal justice is not an issue that African Americans can solve. African Americans must maintain awareness and do our best to equip our children, families, and communities to overcome these multiple incidents through continuous education, strong family and community attachments, and high expectations of academic and social engagement. The vigilance of African American women is required to identify and address the gaps in individual, family, and community needs that impact sexual assault and its various consequences in our community.

To address sexual assault, African American women must be willing to maintain awareness of the issue, face our individual pain related to racism, sexism, and sexual assault, and help protect and educate our children. We must also be willing to work together to supervise and share parenting responsibilities for our children (Bogan, 2004) and to actively create villages of protection that support safety and protection for their members. In so doing, we focus on self-reliance and self-respect, based on the model of our ancestors whose energies were focused on African American liberation from within (Christian, 2008; Welsing, 1991; "Women's Lib and the Black Woman," 1971).

The need to maintain control over our bodies must be contextualized in ways that are inclusive of the sexual assault of African women and girls in colonial America. Within this context, African American women's challenge is to continue to build resilience and optimize family and community networks for increased wellness and self-sufficiency. This author offers recommendations for developing and maintaining safer African American families and communities. Through increased respect of women and girls, healthy relationship modeling, and problem-solving strategies, the community becomes safer and healthier, the healing process is facilitated, and we can meet the potential we were divinely created to reach.

Regarding sexual assault, several recommendations are provided that help to address prevention, response and treatment interventions:

1. Learn African American history, and focus on educational pursuits that lead to increased confidence and positive self-identities.

2. Educate and model for our sons how to reject the patriarchal messages that disrespect women, and embrace egalitarian practices that support healthier families and communities through practicing flexible gender roles.

3. Educate and model for our daughters how to support other women who are victims of sexual assault, and reject victim-blaming (Basile et al., 2016).

4. Educate our sons and daughters to understand the continuum of gender-based violence in settings where children and youth assemble (Basile et al., 2016).

5. Embrace community-based parenting (Bogan, 2004) that offers increased social support and child supervision.

6. Facilitate teaching the physical and emotional aspects of sexual development and the laws that inform appropriate interactions with others.

7. Develop and publish African-centered sexual assault intervention strategies related to sexual assault that recognize the whole person and her ascribed social and cultural appraisal of her experience (Bogan et al, in press).

8. Be aware of local resources to understand how to connect victims to systems of care that support cultural strategies in the recovery process.

References

(n.d.) African-American Women and Sexual Assault Fact Sheet. Maryland Coalition Against Sexual Assault. Retrieved November 2021 from https://mcasa.org/assets/files/African-American-Women-and-Sexual-Assault1.pdf

American Psychiatric Association. (2013). *Diagnostic and statistical manual of mental disorders* (5th ed.). American Psychiatric Association.

Ball, E. (2015, November). Retracing slavery's trail of tears. *Smithsonian Magazine.* https://www.smithsonianmag.com/history/slavery-trail-of-tears-180956968/

Ball, M. (2018, October 18). Donald Trump didn't really win 52% of the white women in 2016. *Time.* https://time.com/5422644/trump-white-women-2016/

Banks, D., & Kyckelhahn, T. (2011). *Characteristics of suspected human trafficking incidents, 2008–2010* (NCJ 233732). Bureau of Justice Statistics. https://bjs.ojp.gov/content/pub/pdf/cshti0810.pdf

Basile, K. C., DeGue, S., Jones, K., Freire, K., Dills, J., Smith, S. G., & Raiford, J. L. (2016). STOP SV: A technical package to prevent sexual violence. Division of Violence Prevention, National Center for Injury Prevention and Control, Centers for Disease Control and Prevention. https://www.cdc.gov/violenceprevention/pdf/sv-prevention-technical-package.pdf

A Black woman responds to women's liberation. (1971, April 15). *Off Our Backs*, *1*(18), 18–19. https://www.jstor.org/stable/25783156

Bogan, Y. K. H. (2004). Parenting in the 21st century: A return to community. *Negro Educational Review*, *55*(2).

Bogan, Y. K. H., Porter, R., Henderson, C. & Wells-Wilbon, R. (In press). Sexual assault Interventions: Inclusion of African-centered intervention strategies for sexual assault survivors. In R. Wells-Wilbon & A. Estreet (Eds.), *Trauma and mental health social work with urban populations: African-centered clinical interventions.* Taylor & Francis.

Browne, A., & Finkelhor, D. (1986). The impact of child sexual abuse: A review of the research. *Psychological Bulletin, 99*(1), 66–77. https://doi.org/10.1037/0033-2909.99.1.66

Bryc, K., Auton, A., Nelson, M. R., Oksenberg, J. R., Hauser, S. L., Williams, S., Froment, A., Bodo, J., Wambebe, C., Tishkoff, S. A., & Bustamante, C. D. (2010). Genome-wide patterns of population structure and admixture in West Africans and African Americans. Proceedings of the National Academy of Sciences, 107(2), 786-791. DOI:10.1073/pnas.0909559107

Burke, T. (2017, November 9). #MeToo was started for Black and brown women and girls. They're still being ignored. *Washington Post*. https://www.washingtonpost.com/news/post-nation/wp/2017/11/09/the-waitress-who-works-in-the-diner-needs-to-know-that-the-issue-of-sexual-harassment-is-about-her-too/

Chisolm-Straker, M., & Straker, H. O. (2017). Implicit bias in US medicine: Complex findings and incomplete conclusions. *International Journal of Human Rights in Healthcare*, *10*(1), 43–55. http://dx.doi.org/10.1108/IJHRH-11-2015-0038

Christian, M. (2008). Marcus Garvey and African unity: Lessons for the future from the past. *Journal of Black Studies*, *39*(2), 316–331. http://www.jstor.org/stable/40282562

Cision PR Web. (2019, August 22). New report: "Black Women for America" identifies key issues and top presidential candidates. Black Women for America.

Crenshaw, K. (1989). Demarginalizing the intersection of race and sex: A Black feminist critique of antidiscrimination doctrine, feminist theory and antiracist politics. *University of Chicago Legal Forum*, *1989*(1), Article 8, 139–167.

Crenshaw, K. (1991). Mapping the margins: Intersectionality, identity politics, and violence against women of color. *Stanford Law Review*, *43*(6), 1241–1299. https://doi.org/10.2307/1229039

Daly, M., & Wilson, M. (1983). *Sex, evolution and behavior* (2nd ed.). Willard Grant Press.

Dart, T. (2015, October 5). Textbook passage referring to slaves as 'workers' prompts outcry. *The Guardian*. https://www.theguardian.com/education/2015/oct/05/mcgraw-hill-textbook-slaves-workers-texas

Domestic Abuse Intervention Project. (n.d.). Power and control wheel. National Center on Domestic and Sexual Violence.

Dray, P. (2002). *At the hands of persons unknown: The lynching of Black America*. Random House.

Du Mont, J., Miller, K. L., & Myhr, T. L. (2003). The role of "real rape" and "real victim" stereotypes in the police reporting practices of sexually assaulted women. *Violence Against Women*, *9*(4), 466–486. https://doi.org/10.1177/1077801202250960

Elison, M. (2018, February 19). How I bought into *Gone With the Wind*'s mythology of whiteness. *Electric Literature*. https://electricliterature.com/how-i-bought-into-gone-with-the-winds-mythology-of-whiteness/

Francis, M., Mormino, G., & Sanderson, R. (2019, August 29

Slavery took hold in Florida under the Spanish in the 'forgotten century' of 1492–1619. *Tampa Bay Times*. https://www.tampabay.com/opinion/2019/08/29/before-1619-africans-and-the-early-history-of-spanish-colonial-florida-and-america-column/

Fulwood, S., III. (1989, November 27). Black women reluctant to join pro-choice forces. *Los Angeles Times*. https://www.latimes.com/archives/la-xpm-1989-11-27-mn-92-story.html

Gates, H. L. (2019). *Stony the road we trod: Reconstruction, white supremacy and the rise of Jim Crow*. Penguin Press.

Gunning, S. (1996). *Race, rape, and lynching: The red record of American literature, 1890–1912*. Oxford.

Hegewisch, A., & Hartmann, H. (2019, March). *The gender wage gap: 2018* [Fact sheet]. Institute for Women's Policy Research. https://iwpr.org/wp-content/uploads/2020/08/C478_Gender-Wage-Gap-in-2018.pdf

Hoffman, K. M., Trawalter, S., Axt, J. R., & Oliver, N. (2016). Racial bias in pain assessment. *Proceedings of the National Academy of Sciences*, *113*(16), 4296–4301. https://doi.org/10.1073/pnas.1516047113

Hurston, Z. N. (2018). *Barracoon: The story of the last "black cargo."* Amistad.

Isensee, L. (2015, October 23). Why calling slaves 'workers' is more than an editing error. *National Public Radio*. https://www.npr.org/sections/ed/2015/10/23/450826208/why-calling-slaves-workers-is-more-than-an-editing-error

Jones, J. (2019, July 11). For black women with means, money isn't the only barrier to abortion access. *Huffington Post*. https://www.huffpost.com/entry/black-women-abortion-coverage-shaming_n_5d2397c3e4b0cf2ac68b7ac6

Jones-Rogers, S. (2019). *They were her property: White women as slave owners in the American South*. Yale University Press.

Kolchin, P. (1993). *American slavery: 1619–1877*. Hill and Wang.

Lewis, J. J. (2019, August 27). A short history of women's property rights in the United States. *ThoughtCo*. https://www.thoughtco.com/property-rights-of-women-3529578

Marshall, S. (1989, September 13). Coalition of Black women to fight for abortion rights. *USA Today*, 03A.

McDonald, P. (2011). Workplace sexual harassment 30 years on: A review of the literature. *International Journal of Management Reviews*, *14*(1). https://doi.org/10.1111/j.1468-2370.2011.00300.x

The New York Times. (2019, August 13). *The New York Times Magazine presents the 1619 project*. Live Events. https://timesevents.nytimes.com/1619NYC

Ojanuga, D. (1993). The medical ethics of the 'father of gynaecology', Dr J Marion Sims. *Journal of Medical Ethics*, *19*(1), 28–31.

Onwuachi-Willig, A. (2018). What about #UsToo?: The invisibility of race in the #MeToo movement. *Yale Law Journal Forum*, *128*, 105–120. https://www.yalelawjournal.org/forum/what-about-ustoo.

Steinour, H. (2018, March 28). Baby bust: 5 charts show how expensive it is to have kids in the US today. *The Conversation*. https://theconversation.com/baby-bust-5-charts-show-how-expensive-it-is-to-have-kids-in-the-us-today-91532

Straughn, J. M., Gandy, R. E., & Rodning, C. B. (2012). The core competencies of James Marion Sims, MD. *Annals of Surgery*, *256*(1), 193–202. https://doi.org/10.1097/SLA.0b013e318249ce3b. PMID: 22514000

Thornhill, N. W., & Thornhill, R. (1991). An evolutionary analysis of psychological pain following human (homo sapiens) rape: The effect of the nature of the sexual assault. *Journal of Comparative Psychology*, *105*(3), 243–252.

Trawalter, S., & Hoffman, K. M. (2015). Got pain? Racial bias in perceptions of pain. *Social and Personality Psychological Compass*, *9*(3), 146–157.

Truth, S. (1851). Ain't I a Woman? [Speech delivered at the Women's Convention in Akron, OH]. Lit2Go. https://etc.usf.edu/lit2go/185/civil-rights-and-conflict-in-the-united-states-selected-speeches/3089/aint-i-a-woman/

Walker, A. (1983). In search of our mothers' gardens: Womanist prose. Phoenix.

Walker-Barnes, C. (2014). *Too heavy a yoke: Black women and the burden of strength*. Cascade Books.

Wallace, M. (1978). *Black macho and the myth of the superwoman*. Verso.

Washington, H. A. (2006). *Medical apartheid: The dark history of medical experimentation on Black Americans from colonial times to the present* (1st ed.). Doubleday.

Wells-Barnett, I. B. (1895). *The red record: Tabulated statistics and alleged causes of lynching in the United States*.

Welsing, F. C. (1991). *The Isis papers: Keys to the colors*. Third World Press.

West, C. (2002). *Violence in the lives of black women: Battered, black and blue*. Routledge.

West, M. J., & Irvine, L. M. (2015). The eponymous Dr James Marion Sims MD, LLD (1813–1883). *Journal of Medical Biography*, *23*(1), 35–45. https://doi.org/10.1177/0967772013480604

Wilkerson, I. (2010). *The warmth of other suns: The epic story of America's great migration*. Random House.

Williams, T. M. (2008). *Black pain: It just looks like we're not hurting*. Scribner.

"Women's lib and the Black woman." (1971, May 13). *Sacramento Observer* (1968–1975), B-1.

Wyatt, G. E. (1998). *Stolen women: Reclaiming our sexuality, taking back our lives*. Wiley.

Yehuda, R., & Bierer, L. M. (2009). The relevance of epigenetics to PTSD: Implications for the DSM-V. *Journal of Traumatic Stress*, *22*, 427–434. https://doi.org/10.1002/jts.20448

Reading 3.5. A Different Look Through the Lens of Oppression

African American Women and HIV/AIDS

Barbara J. Haile

This chapter will examine the crisis of HIV/AIDS in African American women as a result of the legacy of racial, gender, and economic oppression in our society. African American men are also impacted by HIV/AIDS in a disproportionate way, and have suffered racial and economic violence. The struggle of women, however, is unique. African American women endure racial oppression, along with Black men, at the hands of the White population—male and female— plus gender oppression at the hands of men, both Black and White. Because of the negative stereotypes inflicted upon them throughout history, African American women might experience gender oppression differently from their White counterparts (Haile & Johnson, 1989). While negative stereotypes certainly exist about African American men and other groups victimized by oppression, the focus of this chapter is to examine how the *unique* history of Black women in America has placed them in "triple jeopardy": discrimination based on race, gender, and economic status. I contend that the intersectionality of these three factors, in turn, places many African American women at risk for HIV/AIDS.

The next section of the chapter will present statistics on HIV/AIDS for African American women and identify factors that have contributed to these alarming numbers.

The Transmission of HIV/AIDS

Statistics from the Centers for Disease Control and Prevention (CDC) show that African American men and women are disproportionately affected by HIV/AIDS. While African Americans comprise approximately 13% of the U.S. population, they accounted for approximately 3% of all new HIV infections and 42% of people living with HIV in 2017 (CDC, 2017). In that same year, women made up 51% of the nation's population and 19% of individuals newly infected with HIV. Of the latter percentage of women, 59% were African American, 20% were White, and 16% were Hispanic/Latina. Despite the 25% decrease in new HIV diagnoses betweeen 2010 and 2016, the rate of new HIV infections among Black women in 2016 was still 15 times that of White women, and 5 times that of Hispanic/Latina women (CDC, 2017). Black men accounted for 75% of new infections among African Americans in 2016, and 80% of these were among gay and bisexual men (CDC, 2016). These numbers are not confined to new infections alone. Data show that African Americans represent a higher proportion of HIV infections at all stages of disease, from new infections to deaths (CDC, 2017). Between 2010 and 2016, however, HIV diagnoses decreased: by 26% among Black heterosexual men; and by 5% among young Black gay and bisexual men, aged 13 to 24 (CDC, 2017). Despite the promising results, in 2016, HIV was the sixth leading cause of death for Black men ages 25–34, and the fifth cause of death for Black women ages 35–44, ranking higher than it did for their counterparts in any other racial or ethnic group (Henry J. Kaiser Family Foundation, 2019). Hence, the African American community is still under assault from HIV/AIDS and must continue its efforts and commitment to fight this threat to survival.

Why are there such disparities between African American women and other women? Why are African American women at such high risk for HIV/AIDS? A number of reasons for these numbers have been suggested in the literature. They may be social/cultural, biological, and economic. First, a majority of African

American women with HIV (89% of new diagnoses) acquired it through heterosexual sex, usually with partners of the same race. Because the rate of infection is high in African American men, there is a greater risk of infection with each unprotected sexual encounter. Second, women may be unaware of their partner's risk behaviors (including intravenous drug use) or their own vulnerability to HIV transmission. Third, because of biology, women are more susceptible to HIV transmission than men. Women are exposed to semen for a longer period of time than men are exposed to vaginal fluid, and the concentration of HIV is much higher in semen than in vaginal fluid. Additionally, abrasions or tears in the vaginal lining can facilitate the transmission of the virus (van Dyk, 2008). While one may get HIV at any age, women over 50 may find themselves at increased risk for such cuts and tears due to decreases in hormone levels that result in vaginal dryness (Mouzon, 2013). Fourth, women who have experienced sexual abuse or intimate partner violence may be at greater risk for HIV transmission because they fear asking, or demanding when necessary, that their partners use a condom. Fifth, data show that women of color, including African American women, have higher rates of other sexually transmitted infections (STIs), such as gonorrhea and syphilis, compared to White women; these and other STIs can increase the likelihood of acquiring or transmitting HIV (CDC, 2017).

A sixth reason for the increased risk of HIV/AIDS among African American women is low income. Socioeconomic issues related to poverty can increase high-risk sexual behaviors, as women may exchange unprotected sex for money to pay bills, buy food, or meet other essential needs. Seventh, women engaging in high-risk behaviors may be very reluctant to go for HIV testing and counseling, due to stigma and fear of rejection if they are found to be HIV-positive. Therefore, stigma can result in late diagnoses of HIV, and the CDC has reported that the sooner an individual is diagnosed and treated for HIV, the better the outcome (CDC, 2016).

An eighth reason for the increased risk of HIV/AIDS among African American women stems from high incarceration rates of Black men, leaving few men in the community with whom women can establish stable relationships. With disparate ratios of women to men, the latter may have sexual relationships with multiple female partners at one time. The fear of rejection and of being alone may make women reluctant to initiate discussions about a partner's HIV status or risky behaviors, or to insist on the use of a condom. In her research, Wyatt et al. (2000) found that the perception of Black mate unavailability resulted in Black women being reluctant to challenge a partner about using condoms. Incarceration also has other consequences for African American men and women. While in prison, men may become sexually involved with one another, but view this as a "temporary" situation. Upon their return to the community, they resume having sexual relationships with women, thereby increasing the risk for spreading HIV. The CDC has estimated that HIV infection prevalence is about five times higher in those who are incarcerated than in the general U.S. population. Similarly, research conducted by Westergaard et al. (2013) found that the prevalence of HIV infection is high in correctional facilities. The lack of knowledge about HIV and its transmission and prevention is the ninth reason why African American women are at increased risk. Lack of knowledge is a particularly challenging issue in working with older women (aged 50 and over). Focus group research was conducted with 35 older Black women to determine their HIV knowledge and experiences. Participants were asked what they knew about HIV, and if they thought that older women were at risk for HIV. The findings revealed that participants "had experiential, cursory, and no or inaccurate knowledge about HIV. Additionally, women reported a great deal of stigma attached to HIV" (Belgrave et al., 2018, p. 662). The stigma of HIV and AIDS is a real barrier to being tested, disclosing one's status to significant others, and seeking appropriate treatment and care (CDC, 2016). Interestingly, one of the subthemes that emerged from the aforementioned research was the belief of some women that HIV or AIDS was an infection/disease that impacted primarily "homosexuals" or "men on the down low" (Belgrave et al., 2018).

Another study also examined the knowledge of HIV and AIDS in older African American women. Three convenience samples of older women were administered the Cary & Schroder (2002) questionnaire designed to assess knowledge of HIV and AIDS. Participants ranged in age from 50 to 80-plus. Following the collection of responses, research facilitators then conducted discussions about items on the questionnaire. Discussions revealed that inaccurate information about the transmission of HIV existed. For example, one participant did not believe that a woman of 66 (her age) could get HIV; others thought that those who contracted HIV were women who had multiple sexual partners, not those with a single partner. Additionally, it was found that women who were younger, more educated, married, and sexually active, as well as women with higher incomes, had more accurate knowledge of HIV transmission. What is most interesting is that participants were so energized by the discussions, that they asked for the discussions to continue in the future, and that they were eager to share the information they had gained with their adult children and grandchildren (Haile & Chambers, 2012; Haile et al., 2014). Both of the studies cited suggest implications for changes in the strategies that are utilized in educating older African American women and families about HIV.

The final reason to be considered here, for the spread of HIV/AIDS among African American women, is African American men who are on the "down low," who have sex with men and women. The "down-low" phenomenon gained widespread recognition in 2004 with the publication of a book by J. L. King depicting his experiences as a married man who slept with other men. Interestingly enough, he considered himself to be "heterosexual" (Payne, 2008). While scientific data do not directly link the incarceration theory or down-low theory to HIV/AIDS in Black women, it is recognized that both of these explanations have some merit, that they are plausible ideas (Payne, 2008).

As we review many of these factors that contribute to HIV/AIDS in African American women, one theme emerges as paramount—the intersection of race, gender, and economic status.

Economic Status of African American Women

African American women are said to suffer from triple jeopardy because they are Black, poor, and female. This statement is supported by recent data from the U.S. Bureau of Labor Statistics (BLS) for the first quarter of 2019. In that period, the median weekly earnings for African American women working at full-time jobs was $709 ($36,868 annually), compared to $826 ($42,952 annually) for White women, $772 ($40,144 annually) for Black men, and $1,033 ($53,716 annually) for White men (BLS, 2019). While the unemployment rate for African American men was higher than that for African American women (7.2% and 6.5%, respectively), men still averaged higher earnings than women. In 2016, the poverty rate among African American women was 21.4 %, compared to 9.7% for White, non-Hispanic women. Women in all racial and ethnic groups had higher poverty rates than White, non-Hispanic men, whose poverty rate was 7% (National Women's Law Center, 2017).

These data assume even greater significance when we see that poverty for African American female-headed households was 8.6 percentage points higher (38.8%) in 2016 than in White non-Hispanic female-headed households (30.2%). Married couple families, by comparison, were less likely to live in poverty: 6.8% for Black married couple families and 3.5% for White married couple families (BLS, 2018).

For individuals 65 and over, the poverty rate for African American females was 20.6%, compared to White females at 8.2%. For males 65 and over, the poverty rate for African Americans was 16.2%, compared to 5.8% for White males (National Women's Law Center, 2017).

For married African American women, the high rates of unemployment and underemployment for African American men result in women contributing more to the family income. Consequently, this income is critical in providing for the welfare of their families. When divorced, African American women, like other women, may receive little in child support payments. Perhaps due to selective social conditions discussed previously—i.e., inequities in numbers of available or marriageable men to women—African American women remain unmarried for longer periods of time than White women do (Jewell, 1993; Mouzon, 2013; Reeves & Guyot, 2017). Therefore, it has been argued that "African American divorced women are likely to experience a depressed economic status for a longer period of time than their White counterparts" (Jewell, 1993, p. 155).

While Current Population Survey data show that education is the key to higher earnings, they also reveal the disparities that exist according to race. In 2017, African American women with advanced degrees (master's, doctorate, and first professional degrees) earned a median weekly income of $1,133 ($58,916 annually) compared to $1,306 ($67,912 annually) for White women (American Association of University Women, 2018). Black women with advanced degrees earned nearly $9,000 less per year than White women with the same degrees.

African American women trapped at the lower ends of the economic spectrum, primarily in service jobs, must struggle for survival. They are often at minimum-wage jobs with few, if any, benefits or opportunities for upward mobility. Those who are single heads of households with children bear an additional burden. As pointed out earlier, such conditions may place women at risk for the transmission of HIV, as they may provide sexual favors in exchange for additional income from male partners, with few questions asked.

Gender Oppression by the Dominant Society

African American women have endured many *trials*. They were subjected, like African American men, to capture in their homelands, horrific conditions of the Middle Passage, and unthinkable forms of oppression in their "new home." Being torn away from their culture, Africans experienced multiple losses that would impact their lives for many centuries to come. Freeman and Logan (2004) portray their situation well: "They suffered countless deaths, loss of family and community, loss of their native language, and above all, loss of their rights to be free human beings. Life was not about living, but about existing and surviving" (pp. 185–186).

Under conditions of enslavement, African women could be physically and sexually abused, killed, disrespected, and/or sold on the auction block, all at the will or whim of the master. After Emancipation, there were the Black Codes, Jim Crow laws, and racially structured inequalities that circumscribed the social and economic circumstances of their lives and would go on to have long-term implications. And yet, they endured. They survived.

One of the most powerful weapons of oppression used by the dominant society against African American women has been the negative images perpetrated about them. Developed under slavery and continued following Emancipation, these images aimed to dehumanize, demoralize, and control Black women. The classic images promoted include: *Mammy, Amazon, Jezebel*, and *Sapphire*. Social changes in contemporary society added other images to the classic ones, further demeaning the value of Black womanhood. Mammy was depicted as a nurturer to White children and families, even when she did not have enough time to care for her own family. Since she worked in the house of the master, it was essential that White women feel comfortable with her. Therefore, she was portrayed as being plainly dressed, asexual, and non-threatening (N. Cole, 2011). With very large breasts and buttocks, she was also thought to be unfeminine. In her interactions with the master, Mammy was submissive and seemed "happy" most of the time, but could become more verbally aggressive in exchanges with other Africans, particularly men (Jewell, 1993).

During enslavement, African women often performed the same manual labor tasks in the fields that were assigned to men. In addition, they survived childbearing, and having children, family, and friends sold away from them. Because of their resiliency in facing such life crises, they were labeled *Amazons*—strong and super-human, the masculinized version of a woman (Haile & Johnson, 1989). During the 1960s, Aid to Families with Dependent Children (AFDC) policies created conditions (i.e., man-in-the-house-rules and "midnight raids") that forced many Black men to leave their families so that the latter could receive the meager assistance that welfare provided. As a result, there was an increase in the number of Black female-headed households. Such households were then said to be headed by *matriarchs*, whom Daniel Patrick Moynihan contended were primarily responsible for the emasculation of African American men. Moynihan further stated that children who grow up in matriarchal households develop a distorted view of the world, particularly of sex roles (Moynihan, 1967). The adverse social and economic conditions that Black families often experienced, then, were blamed on the cultural attributes of African American women, rather than on socially structured inequalities. The matriarch stereotype then evolved into the more modern one of *superwoman.* Like the matriarch, the superwoman is also domineering, fiercely independent, and aggressive; she down-plays femininity and emasculates African American men (N. Cole, 2011).

Slave masters felt that they could control the bodies and lives of African American women and men, and that enslaved Africans had no rights they had to recognize and honor. Although African women were sexually exploited by White men during enslavement and in the decades that followed, the women were portrayed as being lustful, morally loose, and sexually insatiable, which are the attributes of *Jezebel,* the *bad girl.* For this reason, men could not be blamed or held accountable for their aggressive actions. After all, Black women really desired this sexual "attention," and were really victimizers rather than victims (Beauboeuf-Lafontant, 2009). In agreement with a number of other feminist writers, Beauboeuf-Lafontant asserts that "references to Black women as categorically whorish by nature, then provided White men with an innocence and unquestionable authority with regard to their power over and abuse of Black women" (2009, p. 28). Unfortunately, this image led to many decades of Black female exploitation and harassment, wherever women lived, worked, attended school, or participated in social activities. One variant on the image of Jezebel is that of the Welfare Mother, who, according to the myth, is also lustful, bears many children by different fathers, and prefers to "get over on the government" rather than seek gainful employment and assume responsibility for herself and her family. A more contemporary image is the *Baby Mama,* which evolved from the welfare mother. The Baby Mama has been described as a variant of Jezebel, bearing multiple children as a result of her irresponsible sexual encounters (N. Cole, 2011).

Through movies and music, the media have reinforced these stereotypes, which undermine the integrity and character of Black women. For example, Halle Berry won the 2001 Academy Award for Best Actress in the film *Monster's Ball.* Enacting a version of the Jezebel image, Berry plays the role of a disturbed woman involved in a sexual liaison with a White police officer who had participated in the execution of her imprisoned Black husband. Some of the scenes could be described as sexually explicit and sexually "raw" (N. Cole, 2011).

In music, hip-hop stands out among other forms of music in deprecating Black women. Hip-hop often refers to women as "hos" and "bitches" and describes relationships between Black men and women in sexually explicit and derogatory terms. In describing the role of hip-hop music, Michael Eric Dyson (2001) states:

> Hip-hop reflects the intent of the entire culture: to reduce black female sexuality to its crudest, most stereotypical, common denominator … . If hip-hop has any virtue in this regard, it is that it uncovers what the larger culture attempts to mask. The bitch-ho nexus in hip-hop is but the visible extension of mainstream society's complicated, and often troubling gender beliefs. (Michael Eric Dyson, 2001, as cited in J. B. Cole & Guy-Sheftall, 2003, p. 182)

Of hip-hop music, bell hooks notes that "the messages of the Hip-Hop culture do not promote healthy intimate interactions" (hooks, as cited in Stephens and Few, p. 259). And hip-hop feminist Tara Roberts asserts: "If you are a woman in Hip-Hop, you are either a hard bitch who will kill for her man, or you're a fly bitch who can sex up her man, or you're a - - - - - d-up lesbian." (as cited in Roberts & Ulen, 2000, p. 7.

It must be noted here that the early history of hip-hop (early 1970s) suggests a more positive theme: that lyrics were directed against gang violence and gang behavior. And the way in which records were played represented a "new" cultural art form that would redirect the energies of inner city youths at risk. However, the commercial success of some rap artists also attracted the attention of record companies (J. B. Cole & Guy-Sheftall, 2003), hip-hop's themes changed, and the rest is history.

Behavioral scientists and social critics understand the significant impact that images have on individual and group behavior. As a result, some scholars have raised concerns about the influence of negative images projected in hip-hop culture on the interpersonal relationships between Black adolescent males and females. On the role of sexual images, Stephens and Few (2007) state, "Sexual images not only provide individuals with appropriate frameworks for their own behaviors and how to respond to them, but also inform them about others' behaviors and how to respond to them" (p. 259). So the question is, what types of messages are being communicated to adolescents through this music, concerning behavioral expectations for themselves and others? In response to this question, Stephens and Few (2007) make the following very poignant observation: "These current culture frameworks of African American women's sexuality do not project women as empowered beings with identities outside of male-defined desires. Instead, there is a focus on utilizing interpersonal relationships for achieving material gain and social success" (p. 259).

If African American women are portrayed as being disempowered, as being incapable of defining who they are and setting their own expectations for themselves rather than being defined by males, how do we expect them to become assertive in their negotiations with men around practicing safe sex?

While most of hip-hop's lyrics have been written and performed by African American men, the owners and producers in the music industry are not African American (Woodward & Mastin, 2005). In reality, these moguls control the messages and images that reach viewing and listening audiences, who are inundated with historical stereotypes of Black women as being immoral, sexually provocative, and unworthy of respect. Such messages are reinforced throughout contemporary majority culture as well as the African American community (Bell, 2004). In turn, these messages have a profound effect on the ways in which Black women, *collectively*, are viewed, and on their relationships with and to institutions and groups within society.

The *Sapphire* image portrays African American women as nagging, loud, outspoken, sassy, and aggressive. According to N. Cole (2011), her mannerisms include "neck and eye rolling, a hand on her hip and a bad attitude" (p. 13). She emasculates the male with her constant string of put-downs. This image was made popular in the 1950s, with the portrayal of Sapphire by Ernestine Ward as the long-suffering but nagging wife of Kingfish (played by Tim Moore) on the *Amos 'n' Andy Show*. What is interesting about the Sapphire image, and what is different from the other stereotypes, is that it is not effective without the presence of a male, who represents "the point of contention." A more contemporary representation of Sapphire is the African American woman who "knows everything" (a know-it-all), is "always running her mouth," and is never taken seriously (Jewell, 1993).

There are, undoubtedly, African American women who have some of the attributes described in the stereotypes, but they do not represent a majority of the Black female population. In fact, African American women differ, sometimes markedly, in their beliefs, attitudes, values, and behaviors, but this is not taken into account when stereotyped images and messages are disseminated and promoted in the culture. Why is diversity among Black women not reflected more in mainstream media programming? Because the beneficiaries of power and privilege are those who ultimately decide which images will be promoted, and such decisions are made according to their social and political agendas.

And how have these images impacted African American women? One way in which they have been affected is in their relationships with health care providers during the assessment, diagnosis, and treatment/intervention processes. If, for example, providers think that they are working with an Amazon, a Matriarch, or a Superwoman, they may expect the individual not to complain, and to just "suck it up." As a result, African American women's symptoms may be taken less seriously than they should be, with physicians and/or nurses not providing the information or follow-up necessary for effective treatment. And if health providers perceive a woman as Mammy, they may expect for her to behave in very compliant ways and not question them concerning any treatment intervention decisions that are being made (Beauboeuf-Lafontant, 2003). After all, in this perception, Mammy values the opinions of White people, particularly those in authority (i.e., the Master), more than the opinions of anyone else.

There is another way in which stereotypes adversely impact African American women. Negative images portrayed through the mainstream media have been "accepted" by too many in the Black community, even by women themselves. Acceptance can lead to internalized racism. Internalized racism exists when those being oppressed endorse the images and stereotypes perpetrated by oppressors (N. Cole, 2011).

Women who believe these images and internalize them may devalue themselves and their self-worth, and that of other Black women. At the same time, they may overestimate the value of the opinions of men in their lives. Or, because of feelings of low self-worth and "unlovability," they may decide that their survival depends upon manipulating relationships with male partners. Therefore, they may spend their time on tactics aimed at "getting over." Such vulnerable social and psychological states can lead to developing sexual liaisons with male partners that place women at risk for the transmission of HIV.

Some feminist writers have been critical of the image of the superwoman or the Strong Black Woman (Beauboeuf-Lafontant, 2009; Wallace, 1979) because it encourages women to endure physical and mental distress and disappointments, and places the interest of others (even family members) above their own, all in the name of being "strong." They may assume that "this is just the way life is," and that not much can be done about it. As a result, women may engage in social and economic "foreclosure" (settling in an unsatisfying, unfulfilling marriage or accepting a "dead-end job") without first having explored their life options. In response, some women may become depressed, alcoholic, or overweight, as they see their youth slipping away without ever having exercised any real control over their lives (Wallace, 1979). Wallace states that "such abuses and limitations are routinely suffered by Black girls and women but are also consistently minimized by appeals to their strength, their presumed power to defy victimization" (Wallace, 1979, pp. 105–106). Under the label of strength, are women expected to make choices that limit life expectations, and then "suffer in silence"? How does this influence the behaviors of women in violent relationships with men? The "silencing of women's voices" is an issue that will be discussed in the next section of the chapter as we examine gender politics between African American women and men, particularly gender oppression by Black men.

Gender Oppression by African American Men

When we study the history of African women in America, we find a documented list of outstanding accomplishments that exemplify resilience, as women raised their voices against the forces of oppression. For example, we see the thrust for racial liberation in the work of Harriet Tubman, with the underground railroad; Ida B. Wells, with the anti-lynching campaign; and Sojourner Truth, in her call for women's suffrage. Her famous "Ain't I a Woman?" speech is still cited as a high point in the 1851 Women's Convention in Akron, Ohio, and became one of the most well-known and frequently quoted slogans of the 19th-century women's movement (Davis, 1983). Undoubtedly, Sojourner's speech had a profound impact on that hostile audience of men. Davis (1983) states that:

> Sojourner single-handedly rescued the Akron women's meeting from the disruptive jeers of hostile men. Of all the women attending the gathering, she alone was able to answer aggressively the male supremacist arguments of the boisterous provocateurs. Possessing an undeniable charisma and powerful oratorical abilities, Sojourner Truth tore down the claims that female weakness was incompatible with suffrage—and she did that with irrefutable logic. (pp. 60-61)

While White women burst with pride at Truth's effectiveness, it was forgotten that just a few minutes earlier, some of them had advocated that a Black woman *not be allowed* to speak at *their* convention (Davis, 1983). Interestingly, although the 19th century witnessed African American men and women struggling together against slavery in order to establish a more just society, there were Black men of the era who envisioned a woman's role as being more traditional, as wife and mother, and encouraged women to assume a more subservient role (Freeman & Logan, 2004). While sexual equality between Black men and women did not always prevail, there were male activists (in the abolitionist movement)—e.g., Robert Purvis and James Forten, Sr.—who believed in the fundamental equality of the sexes (Giddings, 1984). In fact, Robert Purvis stated that "The relationship is perfectly reciprocal. God has given to both man and woman the same intellectual capacities, and made them subject to the same moral arguments" (Nell, 1968, p. 179).

The moral/ political position of Purvis and others, however, was not widely reflected in the gender dynamics of the Civil Rights Movement of the 1950s and 1960s; African American leaders did not raise questions about the inequalities of sexism. In fact, some Black male activists openly asserted that African American women should remain in the background, maintain traditional roles, take care of household tasks, and bear children who would serve as "warriors" for the revolution (Freeman & Logan, 2004). While some resisted, most African American women acquiesced (Alexander, 2001). According to bell hooks (as cited in Freeman & Logan, 2004, p. 192), "black women, perhaps like no other group in America, have had their identity socialized out of existence."

Failure to recognize the oppression of African American women and the suffering that results from it has had a number of dire consequences. It should come as no surprise that Black women are at a disproportionately high risk for depressive symptoms and clinical depression. They often put aside their talents and strengths in order to accommodate others or to support Black men. When discriminated against in the workplace or forced to endure childhood sexual abuse while growing up, they remain silent (Jones & Shorter-Gooden, 2003). As a result, they have obesity, high blood pressure, and eating disorders (Beauboeuf-Lafontant, 2009). The one place of "refuge," of "safety," that many African American women find is the church; yet they are often excluded from assuming leadership roles here as well. Feminist scholars Jones and Shorter-Gooden (2003) have portrayed their situation in the church as follows:

> Even though it is clearly women who form the church's backbone—filling the pews, organizing the fundraisers, cooking the dinners, and teaching Sunday School—in a large number of churches across the country, women are barred from standing in the pulpit and attaining other positions of leadership. Still, they do not often complain, hesitant to disrupt the one place that has traditionally been a safe harbor for Black women, their refuge from racial cruelty, and the one institution where Black men have been consistently empowered and affirmed. (p. 41)

Neither the church nor other institutions in the African American community seem to recognize the parallel between their discriminatory behaviors based on gender and those of White institutions based on race. On this issue, a noted male scholar observes:

> Is our attainment of patriarchal power through the oppression of women any less insidious than White people's perpetuation of a system of racial oppression to dehumanize us? Many of us have become so obsessed in fighting racism as a battle for the right to be patriarchal men that we have been willing to deploy the same strategies to disempower black women as White supremacists have employed to institutionalize racism. (Lemons, 1998, p. 45)

There seems to be widespread agreement in the Black community that Black-on-Black gender discrimination should not be recognized. Black women who raise the specter of such could face being marginalized, ostracized, or labeled "women's libbers." It is speculated that perhaps African American men really do identify with White men's views on patriarchy, forgetting the intersection between patriarchy and racism. Or, perhaps Black men believe that feminist views of Black women are not worthy of debate—that this is "just the way it is." Regardless, this silencing of Black women's voices has resulted in discussions of racism that focus primarily on African American men as an "endangered species," and discussions of sexism that focus on discrimination against White women. Hence, the 1982 title of the book edited by Hull, Scott, and Smith remains relevant: *All the Women Are White, All the Blacks Are Men, But Some of Us Are Brave.*

Collins (2004) contends that when the African American community fails to question repressive Black gender ideology, it is then replicated throughout the culture with special negative consequences, as in the case of HIV/AIDS. She states that:

> Black men who confuse masculinity with dominance and take these beliefs into their romantic relationships place their partners at risk. Whether gay, straight, or bisexual, Black men who make "booty calls" without condoms foster the spread of HIV. Black women

who confuse femininity with submission and weakness, fare no better. When partnered with these same men heterosexual African American women who try to be the "strong" Black woman can end up being sexually exploited, economically used, and abandoned when they can no longer compete sexually in the marketplace. (p. 281).

Similar circumstances may befall African American women who receive monetary assistance in exchange for sexual favors, or those who fear being alone because of disparities in the ratio of Black males to females. When women do not feel "free" to speak—or "safe" to assert their voices—where do they find the self-confidence and self-efficacy to communicate and negotiate safer sex practices with men? Therefore, the silencing of women's voices through negative stereotypes and lack of support within the Black community, in effect, contribute to the transmission of HIV/AIDS.

In summary, this chapter pointed out that the transmission of HIV is intricately related to issues of race, gender, and economic status among African American women. Images of African American women that developed during slavery and post-slavery have been continually reinforced through the culture, particularly the media, in shaping the dominant society's views of women. Through internalized oppression, African American women and men value patriarchy, and perpetuate the objectification and disempowerment of women, and these images shape both Black men's views of Black women and Black women's views of themselves. When stereotypes are internalized and acted on, African American men and women engage in risky sexual behaviors that fuel the transmission of HIV. If Black women are empowered economically, politically, and socially in their relationships with institutions both within and outside of the Black community, we may be able to stem the tide of this crisis. But the empowerment of African American women means that they must be encouraged and supported in "finding their voices." And African American men must also be committed to participating in the discourse. Collins (2004) says it well in the following quote: "In a context in which HIV/AIDS is killing Black people, standing by and refusing to speak out about gender and sexuality in African American communities contributes to the problem" (pp. 281–282).

What Do We Do Next?

In order for Black women's lives to change, according to J. B. Cole and Guy-Sheftall (2003), transformations must occur at two levels: the *individual* and the *systemic*. As individuals, African American women must become more aware of the inequities that exist in the home, school, church, and other segments of the community—inequities that breed rape, incest, sexual abuse, homicide, domestic violence, and HIV/AIDS. Once aware, they should be committed to sensitizing other women and men by speaking out against such abuses. These authors further suggest that when African American women see or experience sexism, they need to "call it out" for what it is; teach children of both genders to regard one another as equals, rather than allowing the subordination of one by the other; and teach children that Blacks are not the stereotyped labels (i.e., "hos," "bitches," or "dawgs") that are presented through some hip-hop music and other media forms (J. B. Cole & Guy-Sheftall, 2003). Further, Black women must refuse to assume or play roles that reinforce negative images (e.g., *Monster's Ball*) even when they promise commercial success. In addition, we should use our positions to practice gender equity in classrooms and in organizational, religious, workplace, and community settings. Black women are members of multiple and diverse organizations, including sororities, professional and civic groups, churches, social clubs, and civil rights organizations. Through these organizations, they can continue to monitor and disseminate information about pay and promotional inequities that keep Black women at the lower rungs of the opportunity ladder. Women must advocate on their own behalf. Despite anticipated resistance from the "powers that be," such action could lead to changes at the systemic level.

African American men can also take initiatives at the *individual* and *systemic* levels to challenge gender inequity. They can model non-sexist behaviors and serve as role models in their homes, workplaces, communities, and churches. Men can also examine and dislodge their own attitudes, values, and behaviors that support male dominance over women. This may be a challenging task for some Black men, since historically, they have also been the victims of negative images that may have resulted in internalized racist and/or sexist feelings toward Black women (Prather et al., 2018). Remember, enslavement happened to **both** Black men and Black women. How does the community begin to address this phenomenon? One strategy may be for men who are more progressive-minded on gender issues to challenge other Black men who exhibit sexism in language and other behaviors; this may help in constructing healthier, more humane definitions of manhood and womanhood than those projected historically, which influence the present culture. Men can also seek opportunities to interface with the media, provide more positive images of African American women, and demonstrate their support for Black women in the quest for liberation (J. B. Cole & Guy-Sheftall, 2003). It is interesting to note that as this chapter was being finalized for the first edition of this book, an article was published in the well-known magazine *Diverse Issues in Higher Education* (March, 2012) entitled: "The Black Woman's Burden: Images and Perceptions of Black Women from the White House to the Academy." So the plight of African American women is still a pressing issue that must be addressed.

African American women have become the "face" of HIV/AIDS, and perhaps the battle against this epidemic will not be won until women assume their rightful place, both in society and the African American community relative to race, gender, and economics. The question of *equity* is paramount and must become inculcated in all of our institutions: family, education, religion, health care, employment, and entrepreneurship. This paradigm shift would result in a restructuring of relationships of Black women to both the dominant society and the Black community. And Black men must come to accept Black women as equal partners in all facets of African American life. If the African American community is to heal and rid itself of the myriad issues that beset it, such as the mental and physical health problems that were noted in this chapter, it must work toward the liberation of all sectors of the community—most notably, Black women. Attempts at changing sexual behaviors without changing underlying inequities in gender relationships will not be successful. Hence, the empowerment of Black women is *essential* to the liberation of the entire Black community. And it must include men, particularly Black men who, in the tradition of Frederick Douglass, Robert Purvis, and James Forten, Sr., are willing to raise their voices in support of justice for women. Just as Black men and women walked hand in hand during the Abolitionist Movement, they must now walk hand in hand *in equity* for the liberation of African American women, and ultimately for the defeat of HIV/AIDS. One cannot happen without the other.

References

Alexander, A. (2001). *Fifty Black women who changed America*. Citadel Press.

American Association of University Women. (2018, Fall). *The simple truth about the gender pay gap*. https://www.aauw.org/resources/research/simple-truth/

Beauboeuf-Lafontant, T. (2009). *Behind the mask of the strong Black woman: Voice and the embodiment of a costly performance*. Temple University Press.

Belgrave, F. Z., Javier, S. J., Butler, D., Dunn, C., Richardson, J., & Bryant, L. (2018). "I don't know and I don't want to know": A qualitative examination of older African American women's knowledge and experiences with HIV. *The Journal of Black Psychology*, 44(7), 644–666.

Bell, E. L. (2004). Myths, stereotypes, and realities of Black women: A personal reflection. *The Journal of Applied Behavioral Science*, 40(2), 146–159.

Cary, M. P., & Schroder, K. E. (2002). Development and psychometric evaluation of the brief HIV Knowledge Questionnaire (HIV-KQ-18). *AIDS Education and Prevention*, 14, 174–184.

Centers for Disease Control and Prevention. (2016). *HIV among African Americans* [CDC Fact Sheet]. https://www.cdc.gov/nchhstp/newsroom/docs/factsheets/cdc-hiv-aa-508.pdf

Centers for Disease Control and Prevention. (2017). *HIV surveillance report: Diagnoses of HIV infections in the United States and dependent areas, 2017* (Vol. 29). National Center for HIV/AIDS, Viral Hepatitis, STD, and TB Prevention. https://www.cdc.gov/hiv/pdf/library/reports/surveillance/cdc-hiv-surveillance-report-2017-vol. 29.pdf

Cole, J. B., & Guy-Sheftall, B. (2003). *Gender talk: The struggle for women's equality in African American communities.* One World Ballantine Books.

Cole, N. (2011). *Engendered racial myth and stereotype endorsement and African self-consciousness among African American female college students* [Unpublished Master's thesis]. Department of Psychology, Florida A&M University, Tallahassee, FL.

Collins, P. H. (2004). *Black sexual politics: African Americans, gender, and the new racism.* Routledge.

Davis, A. (1983). *Women, race and class.* Vintage Books.

Dyson, M. E. (2001). *Holler if you hear me: Searching for Tupac Shakur.* Basic Civitas Books.

Freeman, E. M., & Logan, S. L. (2004). *Reconceptualizing the strengths and common heritage of Black families.* Charles C. Thomas.

Haile, B. J., & Chambers, J. W. (2012, February 17). Knowledge of HIV transmission in older African American women [Poster presentation]. National Association of African American Studies, Baton Rouge, LA.

Haile, B. J., Chambers, J. W., & Soto, M. (2014, June 14). Triple jeopardy: Impact of race, gender, and economics on HIV/AIDS in African American women [Presentation]. Black Women's Health Conference, Tulane University, New Orleans, LA.

Haile, B. J., & Johnson, A. E. (1989). Teaching and learning about Black women: The anatomy of a course. *SAGE: A Scholarly Journal on Black Women, 6*(1), 69–73.

Henry J. Kaiser Family Foundation. (2019, February 7). Black Americans and HIV/AIDS: The basics. https://www.kff.org/hivaids/fact-sheet/black-americans-and-hivaids-the-basics

hooks, b. (1981). *Ain't I a woman: Black women and feminism.* South End.

Jewell, K. S. (1993). *From Mammy to Miss America and beyond: Cultural images and the shaping of U.S. social policy.* Routledge.

Jones, C., & Shorter-Gooden, K. (2003). *Shifting: The double lives of Black women in America.* Harper Collins.

Lemons, G. (1998). To be Black, male, feminist: Making womanist space for Black men on the eve of a new millennium. In S. P. Schacht & D. W. Ewing (Eds.), *Feminism and men: Reconstructing gender relations* (pp. 43–66). New York University.

Mouzon, D. (2013, October 26). Why has marriage declined among Black Americans? Scholars Strategy Network. https://scholars.org/brief/why-has-marriage-declined-among-black-americans

Moynihan, D. P. (1967). *The Negro family: The case for national action.* U.S. Government Printing Office.

National Women's Law Center. (2017, September). *National snapshot: Poverty among women & families, 2016.* https://nwlc.org/wp-content/uploads/2017/09/Poverty-Snapshot-Factsheet-2017.pdf

Nell, W. C. (1968). *The colored patriots of the American Revolution*. Arno Press.

Payne, J. W. (2008, September 12). Black women's burden: An epidemic of HIV. *U.S. News and World Report*. http://health.usnews.com/health-news/articles/2008/09/12/black-womens-burden-an-epidemic-of-hiv

Prather, C., Fuller, T. R., Jeffries, W. L., Marshall, K. J., Howell, A. V., Belyue-Umole, A., & King, W. (2018). Racism, African American women, and their sexual and reproductive health: A review of historical and contemporary evidence and implications for health equity. *Health Equity*, *2*(1), 249–259. https://www.ncbi.nim.hih.gov/pmc/articles/PMC6167003/pdf/heq.2017.0045.pdf

Reeves, R. V., & Guyot, K. (2017, December 4). Black women are earning more college degrees, but that alone won't close race gaps. Brookings. https://www.brookings.edu/blog/social-mobility-memos/2017

Roberts, T., & Ulen, E. N. (2000, February/March). Sisters spin the talk on hip hop: Can the music be saved? *Ms. Magazine*, *10*, 69–74.

Stephens, D. P., & Few, A. L. (2007). The effects of images of African American women in hip hop on early adolescents' attitudes toward physical attractiveness and interpersonal relationships. *Sex Roles*, *56*(3–4), 251–264.

U. S. Bureau of Labor Statistics. (2018, August). Labor force characteristics by race and ethnicity, 2017 (Report 1076). *BLS Reports*. https://www.bls.gov/opub/reports/race-and-ethnicity/2017/home.htm#table

U. S. Bureau of Labor Statistics. (2019, April 22). Median weekly earnings were $806 for women, $1,004 for men, in first quarter 2019. *TED: The Economics Daily*. https://www.bls.gov/opub/ted/2019/median-weekly-earnings-were-806-for-women-1004-for-men-in-first-quarter-2019.htm

van Dyk, A. C. (2008). *HIV AIDS care and counselling: A multidisciplinary approach* (4th ed.). Pearson Education South Africa.

Wallace, M. (1979). *Black macho and the myth of the superwoman*. Dial.

Westergaard, R. P., Spaulding, A. C., & Flanigan, T. P. (2013). HIV among persons incarcerated in the US: A review of evolving concepts in testing, treatment, and linkage to community care. *Current Opinions in Infectious Disease, 26*(1), 10–16.

Woodward, J. B., & Mastin, T. (2005). Black womanhood: *Essence* and its treatment of stereotyped images of Black women. *Journal of Black Studies*, *36*(2), 264–281.

Wyatt, G. E., Vargas, C., Loeb, T. B., Guthrie, D., Chin, D., & Gordon, G. (2000). Factors affecting HIV contraceptive decision-making among women. *Sex Roles*, *42*(7/8), 495–521.

Reading 3.6. Superwoman Schema

African American Women's Views on Stress, Strength, and Health

Cheryl L. Woods-Giscombé

African American women experience disproportionately high rates of adverse health conditions, including cardiovascular disease (Thom et al., 2006), obesity (Wang & Beydoun, 2007), lupus (Pons-Estel, Alarcon, Scofield, Reinlib, & Cooper, 2009), adverse birth outcomes (Hamilton, Martin, & Ventura, 2009), and untreated or mistreated psychological conditions (Substance Abuse and Mental Health Services Administration, 2009). These disparities in health might relate to how African American women experience and cope with stress (Giscombé & Lobel, 2005; Kwate, Valdimarsdottir, Guevarra, & Bovbjerg, 2003; Nyamathi, Wayment, & Dunkel-Schetter, 1993). The relationship between stress and health in African American women is not understood fully, in part because of limited information about African American women's experiences of stress and their stress-related coping strategies.

Issues related to both gender and race influence the stress experiences of African American women (Woods-Giscombé & Lobel, 2008). Furthermore, for African American women, stress appraisal and coping responses exist within a unique sociocultural and historical context (Collins, 2000) that, according to conceptual frameworks such as "weathering" (Geronimus, 2001; Geronimus, Hicken, Keene, & Bound, 2006) and allostatic load (McEwen, 1998), greatly influence how stress impacts health outcomes in this population. In the weathering framework, Geronimus (2001) and Geronimus et al. (2006) suggested that life experiences of African American women historically have included an accumulation of racial inequality; social, political, and economic exclusion; and medical underservice. These inequities decrease access to resources and heighten susceptibility to psychological stress and premature stress-related illness (Geronimus, 2001). According to the weathering conceptual framework, these societal factors provide explanation for the disparities between the health of African American women and European American women (Geronimus, 2001). Similarly, in the theory of allostatic load, McEwen (1998) suggested that chronic exposure to psychological stress leads to cumulative risk and physiological dysregulation (e.g., impaired cardiovascular, metabolic, immune, and neuroendocrine functioning), yielding chronic illness and premature mortality. Authors of the allostatic load and weathering frameworks emphasized the importance of identifying and examining multiple stress-related factors that might increase overall health risks. One factor related to stress and coping among African American women that might be valuable to explore is the Strong Black Woman role, also referred to in the literature and the current study as the Superwoman role (e.g., Beauboeuf-LaFontant, 2009; Black, 2008; Hamilton-Mason, Hall, & Everette, 2009; Mullings, 2006; Romero, 2000; Thomas, Witherspoon, & Speight, 2004; Wallace, 1990).

Writers grounded in Black feminist theory have provided groundbreaking critical examinations of the development of this role among contemporary African American women. In the seminal work, *Black Macho and the Myth of the Superwoman,* originally published in 1978 and revised in 1990, Wallace attracted a great deal of attention to this topic and illuminated the potential detrimental effects of this image. In other significant works, including *Black Feminist Thought* (Collins, 2000), *Sisters of the Yam* (hooks, 1993), and Gillespie's discussion in *The Myth of the Strong Black Woman* (1984), the authors provided rich discourse about the potentially negative impact of the Super-woman ideal on the interpersonal, social, and emotional well-being of African American women. More recently, in *Sinners and Saints: Strong Black Women in*

African American Literature, Harris (2001) examined the perpetuation of this image in popular literary works, and in *Behind the Mask of the Strong Black Woman: Voice and the Embodiment of a Costly Performance,* Beauboeuf-Lafontant (2009) explored the sociocultural mystique of the phenomenon of strength.

The concept of Superwoman developed partially as a result of African American women's efforts to counteract negative societal characterizations (such as *Mammy, Jezebel,* and *Welfare Queen)* of African American womanhood, and to highlight unsung attributes that developed and continue to exist despite oppression and adversity (Beauboeuf-Lafontant, 2003; Harris-Lacewell, 2001). In this concept, the sociopolitical context of African American women's lives, specifically the climate of racism, race- and gender-based oppression, disenfranchisement, and limited resources—during and after legalized slavery in the United States—forced African American women to take on the roles of mother, nurturer, and breadwinner out of economic and social necessity. In other words, being a Superwoman has been a necessity for survival (Mullings, 2006). This was related partially to the compromised and disenfranchised position of African American men that limited their ability to provide the financial and emotional support to their partners and families (Harris-Lacewell, 2001; Mullings, 2006).

It is reasonable to examine how the role of Super-woman might be a double-edged sword for the health of this group—an asset and a vulnerability. African American women have been acclaimed for their strength (vis-a-vis resilience, fortitude, and perseverance) in the face of societal and personal challenges (Banerjee & Pyles, 2004; Cutrona, Russell, Hessling, Brown, & Murry, 2000; Davis, 1998). This has been viewed as a positive character trait or asset that has contributed to survival among the African American population (Angelou, 1978; Giovanni, 1996). It stands to reason that without this survival mechanism, African Americans might not have endured tremendous historical hardships. Nevertheless, Romero has stated that "an overused asset that develops uncritically without ongoing evaluation and attention to changing needs and demands runs the risk of becoming a liability" (2000, p. 225). Perhaps there is a price to the Superwoman role. The legacy of strength in the face of stress among African American women might have something to do with the current health disparities that African American women face.

Despite the growing discourse on the Superwoman role, there is a surprising dearth of published empirical or data-based research designed to examine and conceptualize this phenomenon and how it might contribute to the current health status of African American women. With rare exceptions (e.g., Beauboeuf-Lafontant, 2007; Edge & Rogers, 2005), most of the discourse on this topic comes from popular and clinical literature (e.g., Black, 2008; Morrison, 2006; Romero, 2000; Thompkins, 2005; Wallace, 1990). Other researchers (Amankwaa, 2003; Edge & Rogers, 2005) have not focused on the concept of strength, but obtained insight on the topic in the process of investigating other psychological or health-related phenomena. Although this growing body of literature has resulted in increased awareness of the Superwoman role, the potential impact on stress-related health outcomes, and the general well-being of African American women, more work could be done to explore the characteristics of this phenomenon, identify the contributing contextual factors, and examine the potential benefits and liabilities to the health and general well-being of African American women. A formal descriptive framework or operationalization of the Superwoman role could enhance understanding of this phenomenon and guide future empirical research to identify the mechanisms or pathways between stress and health in this population.

The Current Study

Stress and coping strategies have been found to be significant factors explaining health disparities in African American women. However, to examine how stress contributes to adverse health outcomes, the operationalization and measurement of stress must be culturally relevant, taking into consideration the context of African American women's lives. The Superwoman role has been highlighted as a phenomenon influencing the ways that African American women experience and report stress. Although descriptive information has been provided in previous research about the phenomenon of strength, limited empirical research has been published exploring women's perspectives on stress, the Superwoman role, and health.

The current research presented is part of a larger study designed to develop a framework (Superwoman Schema) to operationalize the Superwoman role and to develop an instrument to measure this phenomenon to facilitate empirical examination of the impact on health.

Presented here are perspectives from a demographically diverse sample of 48 African American women who participated in eight qualitative focus groups. The goal of the focus groups was to learn about how women characterize the Superwoman role, what they believe to be the contributing contextual factors, and what women describe as the benefits and liabilities of this role in relation to their general well-being.

Methods

Eight focus groups were conducted between December 2006 and June 2007. The design of the focus groups was guided by the work of Kitzinger and Barbour (1999) and Morgan and Krueger (1998). This methodology provided an opportunity to identify the various dimensions of the Superwoman role in African American women and to identify relevant contextual factors. Additionally, the focus groups provided a supportive environment for women to discuss sensitive issues related to experiencing and coping with stress (Jarrett, 1993). The institutional review board (IRB) of the sponsoring university approved the study methodology.

Sample and Setting

A community-based sample of African American women was recruited in a large metropolitan area in the southeastern region of the United States. Purposive sampling was used to obtain a sample of women who were diverse in age and educational levels. Each scheduled group was designed to be homogeneous in age and educational background, to bring individuals together who have shared life experiences (Kitzinger & Barbour, 1999). Eight focus groups were conducted to identify the critical components and important contextual elements (e.g., sociocultural, historical, economic) of the phenomenon based on the experiences and voices of the African American informants.

Six out of the eight focus groups were composed of 5 to 6 participants. One focus group had only 2 participants, because several of those scheduled did not attend. To capture the experiences of women from that demographic group, an eighth focus group was scheduled, which resulted in 12 additional participants, for a total of 48 women.

Flyers were distributed strategically at locations including a historically Black university campus, a community college, a women's health clinic, several government agencies (e.g., local health department), hair salons, local libraries, African American women's civic organization meetings, and a local recreation center and local cultural center (both of which served the local African American community). Interested persons were instructed on the flyers to contact, via telephone or email, the principal investigator (PI) to learn more about the study. Prospective participants were informed that the study objective was to learn more about how African American women experience and cope with stress; individuals were told that participation would include a 2-hour focus group and brief follow-up contact, and that participants would receive $30 as compensation for their time. After a telephone-based informed consent process, participants completed a screening questionnaire to determine eligibility and to obtain demographic information for the purposive sampling. If a woman chose to participate in the study, she was informed that research personnel would contact her to schedule a date, time, and location.

Focus groups were held in private rooms located in public facilities with adequate parking and accommodations to make the participants feel safe and comfortable. One focus group was held at a local university; the remaining seven focus groups were held at a local library located in an African American community. Participants were reminded of the purpose of the study and completed two copies of IRB-approved consent forms (one copy was retained by the participant). The moderator emphasized the topic of confidentiality.

Procedure

Each focus group lasted between 2 and 2.5 hours, and refreshments were served at each session. After a brief icebreaker activity, the moderator (an African American woman in her 30s), who is also the author and PI, used a topical outline of broad key questions to guide the discussion and to generate interaction among the participants (Farquhar & Das, 1999; Kitzinger & Barbour, 1999). Focus group discussions included the following questions: (a) When I say the word *stress,* what does it mean for you? (b) What causes stress in your life? (c) How do you cope with stress? (d) How did you see the women (mothers, grandmothers) in your life cope with stress? (e) Have you ever heard the term *Strong Black Woman/Black Superwoman*? (f) What is a Strong Black Woman/Black Superwoman? (g) What are her characteristics? (h) How did they develop? (i) Is being a Strong Black Woman/ Black Superwoman a good thing? (j) Is there anything bad about being a Strong Black Woman/Black Superwoman? The moderator guided the focus groups (e.g., kept the conversation focused, encouraged participation, prevented any one participant from dominating the discussion). However, the discussions followed the lead of the women (e.g., they were allowed to discuss issues related to stress and coping that were important to them). With the exception of one group (age 18 to 24 years, college-educated), participants brought up the topics of Superwoman, Strong Black Woman, or strength before the group moderator introduced them.

Strategies and techniques were used to facilitate an effective group process (Farquhar & Das, 1999). Because spatial arrangements influence discussion, focus group participants sat in a circular pattern (Merton, Fiske, & Kendall, 1990) to promote group interaction and intimacy. Participants were encouraged to be respectful of their fellow group members by listening without interrupting. They were invited to set additional ground rules so they could be active participants in the creation of safety within the group (Farquhar & Das, 1999). Techniques such as reflection (e.g., "Let me repeat what I have heard") were used to clarify statements and to help participants feel affirmed and valued in the group. All participants were given an opportunity to speak. Less vocal participants were encouraged to share comments, but were not pressured or called on individually. At the end of each focus group discussion, participants completed a brief demographic information questionnaire (devoid of names, including only a participant ID number) to obtain background information. A research assistant (an African American woman in her 20s) was present to distribute consent forms and questionnaires and to take careful notes during the focus group discussion.

Data Analysis

All focus groups were audiotaped and professionally transcribed. The author and research assistant then compared the transcript to the audiotaped data to confirm accuracy. Data analysis was begun after the first focus group was completed and continued throughout the duration of the study. Each group represented a case or unit of analysis (Frankland & Bloor, 1999). Transcripts were analyzed using analytic induction methods as described by Frankland and Bloor (1999). These methods were advantageous because they involve a prescribed process for systematic analysis of the data. Data indexing was conducted to facilitate comparative analysis by categorically grouping data on a specific topic heading or index code related to the content of the data. This step helped to make the large amount of data gathered from the focus groups more manageable. During the indexing stage, a nonexclusive approach was used. The index code categories were broad and general, and pieces of data were appropriate for more than one topic heading or index code. The emphasis at this stage was on including all potentially relevant material, to avoid selective attention to data.

Once all of the data had been indexed, systematic comparisons of all of the items of data within each index code category were conducted to determine which data pieces were most relevant to the topic or index code. Data indexing was cyclical. As more data was collected and transcribed, new index codes were identified and subcategories were created. The data that appeared to contradict the existing index code categories were embraced, not excluded universally. Deviant cases were used to understand when or under what circumstances African American women display characteristics such as strength or emotional suppression. For instance, some African American women reported that they suppress negative emotion to meet perceived expectations to be strong by society only when they are in professional settings. From these results, thematic categories were finalized to begin the development of a theoretical framework.

Several techniques were implemented to increase the scientific rigor of this qualitative focus group study. Field log notes and memos were maintained to enhance audit-ability of the study (Sandelowski, 1986). Debriefing with the study participants, which included a review of prominent topics that were raised by the participants, was conducted at the end of each focus group session to enhance accuracy. The moderator asked questions such as, "Is there anything I didn't ask that I should have?" and "What was it like being in the group?" Extensive quotations were used in data analysis. Finally, corroboration with experts in the field and the study participants was used to enhance credibility and validity (Sandelowski, 1986). The major thematic categories were shared in writing with the focus group participants, and they were invited to communicate feedback to the research team through written or verbal correspondence (Kitzinger & Barbour, 1999).

Results

The demographically diverse sample of African American women reported that the Superwoman role is multifaceted; women discussed how they characterized the Superwoman role, contributing contextual factors, perceived benefits, and perceived liabilities. These findings resulted in the preliminary development of the Superwoman Schema Conceptual Framework (see Figure 1).

Participants

Ages ranged from 19 to 72 years; the median age was 29 years and the average age was 34 years. Participants came from a range of educational (from less than 12 years of education to terminal degrees such as PhD and JD) and professional backgrounds (e.g., unemployed, law school faculty). Regarding education, 18% did not complete high school; 10% completed high school only; 17% completed trade school, technical school, or an associate's degree; 18.8% attended college but did not graduate; 17.4% graduated from a 4-year university; and 14.6% obtained a master's or terminal professional degree. Most (64%) were employed; 40% were current students; 35% were not working. Sixty percent were single; 10% were married; 15% were in a committed relationship; and 15% were divorced, separated, or widowed. A majority (65%) were mothers. The median annual household income was between $26,000 and $50,000 (34% of the sample), and 41% of the sample earned less than $15,000 per year.

Characterization of the Superwoman Role

Participants' characterizations of the Superwoman role were grouped into five major topic areas: obligation to manifest strength, obligation to suppress emotions, resistance to being vulnerable or dependent, determination to succeed despite limited resources, and obligation to help others.

Obligation to manifest strength. In each of the eight focus groups, women discussed issues related to feeling obliged to manifest strength. This topic was particularly relevant for the group of women who were more than 45 years old and had some years of college education. Many expressed a need to present an image of strength for the sake of their children, parents, other family members, and friends. Some reported being perceived as "the strong one" by others and that they were expected to be the strength of their families. When asked how they defined *strength, Strong Black Woman,* or *Superwoman,* a participant responded in the following way:

> I guess, being a strong Black woman is doing what you have to do like handling your business, taking care of yourself, taking care of what you have to get taken care of without, you don't really complain about it.

Some women felt they needed to present an image of strength because there were others (e.g., mothers, grandmothers, esteemed Black women in the media) who had gone through many more challenges than they were facing. Women also stated that they were expected to be strong even when they didn't feel like doing so. Others stated that they only felt obliged to present an image of strength at work. Some reported that presenting an image of strength was just part of a woman's life and, more specifically, an African American woman's life. Some women spoke with a sense of pride about manifesting an image of strength, but nevertheless seemed distressed by feeling obligated to do so most of the time. One participant from the group of women between the ages of 25 and 45 who were not college educated stated,

> You have to be strong. … Society makes you have to be a strong woman. People in relationships make you have to be a strong woman. Our past makes us have to be a strong woman and it's really annoying as hell.

Obligation to suppress emotions. Women indicated a perceived obligation to suppress emotions. They voiced concern that no one would understand what they were going through and that they felt difficulty "letting people in." Many women discussed that they had a lot of feelings inside that needed to be released. Some described that these feelings and emotions were "hidden from others," "internalized," "bottled up inside of me," kept in "my heart," and only displayed in privacy or demonstrated in the presence of God. For some, displaying emotions publicly was considered a "sign of weakness." Others were concerned that people would "think I'm crazy if I share my problems with them" or that sharing their feelings and emotions would be burdensome for others. One woman said,

> I try to talk about it but a lot of times you feel like people get tired of hearing your problems, you know. And people don't want you around if every time you come around you've got a problem. So you just keep it to yourself.

The women also discussed that they simply did not know how to express their emotions. Women from professional backgrounds talked about emotional suppression in the workplace:

> And it's always at the times when I'm most stressed. People always say, "Oh, you look so calm and you know, you're just so rosy and"—and I'm thinking I'm just about to crumble in two seconds and I think a lot of people don't know when Black women are stressed because of the Superwoman syndrome and especially in the workplace, where other women might be able to show their stress. I think for us, it's harder for us to acknowledge that stress, especially at the workplace when you're supposed to be extremely productive.

Resistance to being vulnerable or dependent. A clear theme emerged about being resistant to vulnerability. Women in all eight groups reported that it was not uncommon for them to "put up my defenses." Some participants shared that they did this because they did not know how to accept help. Others reported that vulnerability or dependence would cause them to get hurt. One woman said, "People take my kindness for weakness"; others echoed this sentiment. Women shared that they did not want to give others the opportunity to think that they could not do something; there was a feeling of mistrust: "If I were to open up to somebody they would take my feelings and use them to their advantage: 'Okay well she's weak right now, let me attack her.'" Others said that they could make it on their own and wanted to prove it to others, or that people had ulterior motives for offering help:

> It's hard to accept the support, because of the things that are attached to it. … Somebody asked the question about being able to let other people help you. And it's not so much that I don't want the help, but I don't want to give you an opportunity to think that I can't do it.

Because of their desire to resist vulnerability or dependence on others, some of the women expressed that they either preferred to be a leader or that they had difficulty not taking the lead. This was a factor across groups, but was more common in the groups of older women. Some stated that they had had to do for themselves for a long time, and that taking the lead or being in control of situations felt normal for them. Others echoed feeling most comfortable in a leadership position. A number of women spoke of being in charge in relationships to protect themselves from getting hurt. One woman stated, "If I want things done right, I'll do them myself." This seemed to be out of concern for things getting done properly. One woman said,

> Control, yeah. Because I've been taking care of myself since I was 16. I bought my own cars. I never had Daddy do anything. I mean, I have to help Daddy sometimes. So, I've never had that man to depend on. And I'm like, even if I do ever get married, I'm not going to close any of my accounts! [laughter] Oh no! I have trouble with that. I'm going to pay the bills. Like you can give me your paycheck, but I'm the one controlling the bills … 'cause that's what I do, and I'm not going to trust you to do it. 'Cause I've been doing it, and I can't give up that control.

Another woman verbalized internal conflict with her take-charge approach: "It's difficult to relinquish that control. But … you know, I still want the people to want to support me." Some women reported not asking for help until they felt extremely overwhelmed and admitted that this way of living caused them to go through "unnecessary struggles."

Determination to succeed despite limited resources. Another important theme for some of the women in the focus groups was an intense motivation to succeed despite limited resources. The women who participated in the focus groups were overall an ambitious group, expressing hope for being their best and overcoming any obstacle that they faced. This was common across the groups, particularly for the 18- to 24-year-olds in college and the college-educated group of women aged 25 to 45 years. Some acknowledged that they believed they could reach their goals even if they didn't have everything needed to do so. A number of women expressed a sense of pride related to achieving more than others expected from them.

Participants discussed that they routinely worked late, neglected taking breaks, sacrificed sleep, and put their health in danger to reach their goals. There was a sense of having to work harder than others to reach their goals. These women expressed a great deal of drive and ambition to "be the best." One expressed that the only way to be successful was to work hard constantly. These women had high personal standards, some expressing things like, "I want to retire before the age of 50," "I feel like I can do everything," and "I want it all." Others stated things such as, "I do not feel like I've done enough," and "There is always more that I want to achieve." For some, these feelings were stated with a tone of disappointment or even frustration:

> It's been very important to me to be the best. My coworkers get on me all the time, my significant other gets on me all the time, about slowing down, and I haven't managed that. Because I feel like I can do everything. I work two jobs, not because I have to financially, but because for career-wise, it's something that's important to me to build my resume. … Because I'm used to being the best at everything that I do, and knowing exactly what it is I'm supposed to be doing. So being even below the top is difficult, and I literally get stressed out. … Because at 45, I want to be able to retire. And the only way to do that is to constantly go now, but then I have no time for myself.

Some women were the first in their family to attain certain educational and professional achievements and, as a result, expressed that they could not rely on their family members to provide the extra boost of resources that other, more privileged, individuals might have. Several women reported that their determination to succeed despite limited resources came from a strong desire to provide for their children. For many, succeeding meant balancing the simultaneous demands of raising their children, completing their education, and working full time, without the assistance of a husband or their children's father.

Although a number of study participants were intrinsically ambitious and goal oriented, some of these women expressed that they also experienced pressure from others to be successful. Some made statements such as, "My family expects me to do more than I have time to do," and expressed that these expectations were burdensome. Others spoke more with a sense of regret that they weren't meeting the expectations of others, with statements such as, "I feel like I have not achieved what others expect of me," and "I feel like I have let others down."

Obligation to help others. The women discussed feeling obligated to meet the needs of others. Some described it as a need to nurture others and stated that this is a common trait of women. This theme was prevalent in all of the groups. Women reported believing it was their responsibility to make sure that everyone else's needs were met. Women reported that it was "my job to make others happy," and "The only thing I know how to do is make sure everybody else has [what they need]." Another stated, "I think I just take care of everybody and I don't know why." Several women described how taking care of the needs of others caused stress. One woman stated, "The problems of other people feel like excess baggage for me." Some women, particularly those who were between the ages of 18 and 24 years with at least some college education, talked about desires to provide financially for their families despite not having enough for themselves. It gave these women pride and satisfaction to be helpful to their parents especially; they felt strongly about their responsibility to give back. However, they acknowledged that doing this sometimes resulted in challenges to their own financial well-being.

Women discussed how their commitment to helping others led them to take on multiple roles and responsibilities and have difficulty saying no. Participants across age groups and educational backgrounds reported feeling overwhelmed by multiple roles and responsibilities in their families and community and church organizations. Some reported that they took on additional roles even when they knew that they were overcommitted. These sentiments were discussed most commonly in the older groups and the groups with college education.

> I wish I could learn to say no because just about everything, all the organizations, my church, family, whatever, I find myself being delegated or assuming, one or the other, more and more responsibility. And I guess I'm not saying no strongly enough.

The single women in the 25 to 45 age group believed that because they didn't have spouses and families, others expected them to have more time, and they were uncomfortable finding themselves delegated to more roles and responsibilities. One retired woman felt that she, too, was expected to volunteer more, because others perceived that she had more free time to do so.

Some women expressed that carrying the burdens of others gave their lives a sense of purpose. Meeting the needs of others seemed to help these women feel valued. One woman in the group of 25- to 45-year-old college-educated women stated, with group agreement (i.e., heads nodding), "I don't know how my life would be if I wasn't like putting out fires all the time, that this just seems like that's just normal."

Contributing Contextual Factors

Four contextual factors were identified as contributors to the Superwoman role, including a historical legacy of racial and gender stereotyping or oppression; lessons from foremothers; a past personal history of disappointment, mistreatment, or abuse; and spiritual values.

Historical legacy of racial and gender stereotyping or oppression. A number of women across groups discussed how racial or gender stereotyping and oppression contributed to the Superwoman role. One woman in the group of college-educated participants more than 45 years of age stated, "Well, you know what? We can take it back, way back. You can take it all the way to slavery times. The Black woman had to take charge many times, and we still do that." One young college student, in particular, discussed that her ambition and drive for success were related to others' expectations that she would fail in life because she was African American:

> They're all ready to write you off. They already tell you what you're going to be. They already tell you how far you're going to get in life. And so I felt like that added to a lot of

stress, because I refuse to be another statistic. I refused to drop out of high school. I refused to have a child.

A younger participant from the group of college-educated participants between 18 and 24 years of age said,

I think it's just, I feel like it was more of a motivation, like, not to become what everybody thought I was going to be or everybody had already, was already in the process of putting in the category. I think that was, it was more of a motivation for me.

Another in that group observed,

It just makes you upset to think that people could go around saying negative stuff about African Americans, you know, [they say things like] "You're not gonna be anything." "You're not gonna graduate." "You're gonna drop out have kids," and stuff like that.

Women, particularly those from the college-aged group and those with terminal degrees, discussed how the historical legacy of racial and gender inequality resulted in difficulty obtaining resources and mentoring from more experienced professionals, which they deemed as necessary for survival in the professional arena. One woman in the group with terminal or advanced degrees discussed how stereotypes about Black women might limit access to those supportive resources:

So I think for us, it's almost a double-edged sword to have that stereotype because it sort of masks when we actually might want to get assistance or begin to develop the support networks that we need to survive. … I think for other groups, the support system is already in place for them to achieve. But for us, we normally are probably the only [African American] ones. And if you are the only one, then who do you look to for your support, especially when the support might not be given to you wherever you may work, if it's in a law firm or if you're in the academy or if you're out in the business sector?

One of the college-educated women in the age 18 to 24 group noted,

I think that's why we have a little more stress 'cause we don't have people who are there for us as much when you get higher up. There's not that much of us there. It's kind of scarce. … We feel that we have to do more because [compared to others] there's no one else who's going to take up the slack for us or show us the right direction, or say here, this is already laid out for you.

Lessons from foremothers. Discussions developed across groups regarding how women patterned their lives after how they had seen their foremothers (e.g., mothers, grandmothers) live. Several described that their mothers and grandmothers explicitly taught them to be self-sufficient. One college student stated,

It's, you know, it's a trickle effect. Big Momma went through a struggle so she taught her daughter how to handle that struggle so she wouldn't have to worry about it. And then so her daughter has a daughter, she teaches her daughter. It continues. And then when a man comes around, we like, "Well, Big Momma taught us this a long time ago," and we tell them, "Forget you," 'cause we can prove a point. We don't need [you].

A number of women described never seeing their mothers cry or outwardly express their emotions. Many described their mothers as stoic and able to endure challenges with strength. A comment from the focus group with college-educated women aged 18 to 24 years demonstrates this:

I see it more now as an adult than I did as a child. One thing about Black women, they don't let you see their stress. … I never knew my mom's burden. Never, like she would never put on a sad face for us.

Another in that group observed,

I know my mom. She smokes. So that was her big stress reliever and for a while I didn't realize why Mom smoked but then after I got in high school I'd say, "Why are you smoking?" It's stress. It's stress. … If it wasn't a cigarette it would be something else and I never like, I knew we didn't have everything but it was me and Mom so we made it. Sometimes she had to work three jobs and she went back to school and, like, or she would keep busy, never sit down and I find that I do that now. When I'm stressed out, I just have to do something. I can't sit still.

A past personal history of disappointment, mistreatment, or abuse. Participants discussed that their reluctance to express emotions or seek assistance from others was related to past experiences of feeling let down by family members or friends who should have been able to provide support or guidance. Several participants across groups shared stories about their parents not being a source of tangible or emotional support. The theme of being let down by family or friends was most prevalent in the groups of women without college education. One woman in the group of women aged 18 to 24 without college education shared, "Nobody was there for me. And because nobody was there to tell me, 'It's okay to be afraid,' and everything … I just keep it right in my heart. I don't think I really express it." Another in the group of women aged 25 to 45 years without college education observed,

I'm so used to not asking people. I'm so used to people either saying, "No, no, no, no, no, no," you know, or … I guess I stopped hearing it when I was little. I closed that out. You know what I mean? I just started getting [things] however I could get it.

Another participant in the same group discussed how despite being generous to others, her favors were not returned frequently when she was in the position of needing assistance: "I would always, always extend myself … but then when I needed help, no one ever called me."

A number of participants, most commonly from the groups of women without college education, discussed experiences of being victims of emotional, sexual, and physical abuse. Some also described experiencing childhood distress as a result of their mothers being in abusive relationships. Women discussed how these experiences with abuse created suspicion, fear, apprehension, and mistrust, which led to the development of resistance to depending on others or being placed in a vulnerable position. One participant in the group of women aged 25 to 45 years without college education described how past experiences with abuse in romantic relationships caused her to put up her "defense shield" and be more emotionally guarded: "We don't want to let our guard down because we're scared to be hurt."

Another participant in the group of college-educated women over 45 years of age shared that to avoid staying in an abusive situation, she chose the path of single motherhood. She discussed her experiences of distress as a strong single mother:

I raised my daughter on my own [and] refused to get in a marriage where I was going to be mistreated and abused. So I decided that I was going to have my daughter and raise her on my own. I would have loved to have just had some "me" time, you know, to not have to be the only one worrying about bills. My parents, of course, helped me; but to have a partner and someone there that would have understood me and that would have helped me and that we would have made it without me and my daughter having to go through some of the things that we went through, that's what I miss. You know, you don't want to be strong all the time. You want to be able to be weak sometimes.

Spiritual values. Women in the focus groups discussed that faith, religion, and spirituality helped them to manifest strength to reach their goals and help them overcome challenges without the help of other people. They specifically discussed how relying on God offered encouragement in the context of inadequate tangible resources. Women discussed that faith strengthened their determination and resolve to succeed despite limited resources. The topic of spirituality was discussed most commonly among the college-educated women aged 18 to 24 years. One woman's discussion of religion in that group demonstrated religion's influence on perceptions of strength and fortitude: "I can do all things through Christ. That strengthens me. That motivates me and I think I can do anything that I set my heart to." Another woman observed, "When I was coming up I was raised in church and I was raised to believe that you just don't really give up. You just keep on doing the best that you can." Another participant summarized the role of faith in providing support by discussing what she learned from her grandmother in regard to relying on faith: "Be strong. Give it to God. Just pray about it. What doesn't kill you makes you stronger."

Perceived Benefits of the Superwoman Role

Preservation of self and survival. One of the most salient benefits of the Superwoman role was survival despite personal obstacles, perceived inadequacy of resources, and unique life experiences attributed to the double jeopardy of being African American and female. Women discussed the importance of being able to survive in the workforce, romantic relationships, the home environment, and society at large. When discussing the benefit of survival, they emphasized the importance of being able to survive while maintaining their self-worth and dignity.

Preservation of the African American family. Women discussed that a benefit of Superwoman characteristics was that it helped them to support their family members, particularly their children or parents. Women discussed that the benefit of working so hard was helping their children to be "better people." One woman in the group of women aged 25 to 45 years without college education stated, "We're like a lioness pride … and we're out there fighting and just like you would see on the TV the women are out there just tearing the world apart to survive for their children." Another woman in the group of women aged 25 to 45 years with college education observed,

> My children are never going to know what it's like not to have lights, or not to have food. So I work hard, but I hate my job … all to maintain my children's stability and happiness, and making sure they don't see me fall apart. So, that's a lot, to me.

Preservation of the African American community. Community preservation is related to the concept of fundamental philanthropy, a "'basic or natural philanthropy" that involves using one's "own 'natural' resources, such as talents, skills, knowledge and opportunities to perform an altruistic act" (Boles, 2008). A consistent theme throughout the majority of the focus groups was using one's efforts to improve the lives of others. Participants talked about the needs of the Black community and the importance of giving back. This was discussed across groups, but was discussed in greatest detail by the groups of college-educated women aged 18 to 24 years and women older than 45 years. One of the younger college-educated women said,

> You don't want to open a door for yourself and close it behind you … keep the door open and give someone else, who might not have had the same chances and opportunities as you, a chance because everyone needs help. Well, not everyone but a lot of African Americans don't see that door and you have to be the light for them and go back and tell them, "Okay, this is how I did it."

Perceived Liabilities of the Superwoman Role

The women discussed liabilities of the Superwoman role. These liabilities fell under three major categories: strain in interpersonal relationships, stress-related health behaviors, and embodiment of stress.

Strain in interpersonal relationships. Participants reported that the Superwoman role, particularly fear of vulnerability, was a source of strain in interpersonal (e.g., romantic) relationships. Resisting vulnerability prevented some participants from allowing themselves to "love fully" and be loved. One woman shared that she tried to dominate relationships, because, "I don't want to be the vulnerable one."

Another concurred and stated that her fear of vulnerability was a source of interpersonal conflict. Participants reported a strong need to be self-sufficient and not to accept help from others, particularly men. Many stated that they were used to doing things alone, without asking for help. Some stated that following the advice of their foremothers to be self-sufficient and independent in relationships might cause significant others to either feel frustrated, unneeded, or less motivated to provide support.

Stress-related health behaviors. Women discussed stress-related health behaviors such as emotional eating, smoking, dysfunctional sleep patterns (e.g., regularly staying up late to finish tasks), and postponement of self-care. This was most prevalent among the group of women aged 25 to 45 years with college education, but was discussed across groups. One participant in the group of college-educated women aged 25 to 45 years discussed how excessive work habits resulted in dysfunctional and excessive eating:

> Normally during the workweek, I'm always running, running, running, and so I don't eat until late at night. And I just, I don't know. I know I overdo it. I'm trying to eat to make up for the two or three meals I might have missed during the day. And I just sit there and I just eat, and I get fat, and that's what I do. That's so pathetic.

A woman in the same group discussed how characteristics related to the Superwoman role contribute to inadequate sleep: "I still have issues with not getting enough sleep when I'm stressed. 'Cause I feel like, while I'm asleep I could be doing this, this, and this." Another revealed that she developed a smoking habit in adulthood to help relieve the frequent tension that she faced.

Postponement of self-care was particularly relevant for the group of women with terminal or professional degrees, the college-educated women aged 25 to 45 years, and the group of women without a college education who were older than 45 years. Some women reported feeling physically drained, and that they did not have time for self-care because they are always taking care of others. One woman acknowledged the physical and emotional harm that this way of life was causing her when she stated, "I have been going too long doing too much." Some talked of consistently making self-care a last priority, such as one woman who said, "I feel like I have to be everything to everybody, and I'll come later on." Another woman expressed that her "life is tied around everyone else, and I forget about myself." Women reported feeling out of touch with themselves; one even stated, "Sometimes I wonder if there is a me." Another participant in the college-educated group of women 25 to 45 years old described how she commonly worked through meal times and did not eat until midnight. Many women agreed that taking time for themselves resulted in feelings of guilt.

Embodiment of stress. Participants shared stories related to what Krieger (2005) described as embodiment. According to Krieger (2005), bodies tell stories. Similarly, in response to the statement from one participant that, "What doesn't kill you makes you stronger," another woman said, "What doesn't kill you will make you sick." Throughout all of the focus groups, women made connections between undesirable health symptoms and the Superwoman role, particularly in the context of significant stress. Participants discussed a range of health issues including migraines, hair loss, panic attacks, weight gain, and depression. These health issues were discussed most explicitly in the focus group of college-educated women 25 to 45 years of age, but both younger and older participants made connections between stress, coping, strength, and health. Several women discussed physical symptoms related to feeling overwhelmed. One highly educated woman stated, "I don't notice that I haven't been taking care of myself until I see physical signs." Another woman in the group with a terminal degree stated, "I don't even recognize that I've been going so long with doing so much that it's not until my face breaks out that I say, 'Okay, wait a minute. What is really important?'" Another in the group of women aged 18 to 24 years with college education shared the following:

> Well I just feel like I'm just drowning in stuff. Like I feel like there's probably somebody sitting on my chest. That's what it feels like. So like when I need to talk to somebody about something, I don't. So I blow up all the time 'cause it's like I hold a lot of stuff inside me and I never, ever let it out, and that leads to this big ball of stress that it end up exploding, you know, on somebody else.

Some women discussed the effects on their mental health. One woman in the college-educated, 25- to 45-year-old group stated, "Last weekend, I had a breakdown just because I started realizing that I have so much stuff, and I was overwhelmed." One participant in the 25 to 45 years, college-educated group discussed how she thought that stress adversely affected her pregnancy:

> I have no doubts about the fact that the stress was toxic to my pregnancy, because when the autopsy was done, there was nothing found but fetal distress, and so I think about that a lot when I get overly stressed out. If that can happen to a pregnancy, what is happening to my body?

One woman reflected on how her grandmother's exterior strength might have been a cause of several undesirable health conditions:

> But about this strong woman thing, I never saw my nana cry. I saw my mom cry a couple of times, but I never saw my nana cry … and my nana had diabetes, and she was obese, and she suffered from breast cancer, and she had a double mastectomy. … And also my nana was younger, when she was a little closer to my age, she had a nervous breakdown. … I mean, my nana had gone through a lot of physical pain. It wasn't until I was older, I was able to look back and evaluate her life after she passed, that I realized that a lot of these things that she had gone through, might not have happened if she would have learned to cope with what she was going through. I mean, a nervous breakdown? That's something that's simple sometimes as just finding someone to talk to, or getting some things off your chest. But she internalized so many things. … I mean, she let it tear her apart, internally. So, then I thought about it, like, was that really a strength, if it weakens you physically?

Discussion

Summary of Findings

Presented in this article are African American women's perspectives of the Superwoman role, what it is, what contributes to it, and the benefits and liabilities of the role. Results of this study indicate that the Superwoman role is a multidimensional phenomenon encompassing characteristics such as obligation to manifest strength, emotional suppression, resistance to vulnerability and dependence, determination to succeed, and obligation to help others. According to the women in this study, the Superwoman role involves sociohistorical and personal contextual factors as well as themes of survival and health status.

Findings from this study corroborate and extend previous examinations of concepts of strength, perseverance, and self-reliance among African Americans (Beauboeuf-LaFontant, 2007; James, 1994; James, Hartnett, & Kalsbeek, 1983; Mullings, 2006; Shambley-Ebron & Boyle, 2006). Some of the previous empirical, data-based publications about the phenomenon of strength among African American women result from incidental insight on the topic only in the process of investigating other psychological or health-related phenomena. For instance, in one interview study, 12 African American women with postpartum depression discussed that obligations to exhibit strength, modeled by the women in their families, resulted in disregard for their physical and mental health, dissonance between their "real self" and "ideal self," and frustration when they were unable to live up to social expectations to be strong (Amankwaa, 2003). In another qualitative study, responses to adversity and psychological distress during pregnancy, childbirth, and early motherhood in Black Caribbean women were investigated. Women in that study shared that the exhibition of a strong exterior enabled them to maintain control and withstand otherwise insurmountable challenges (Edge & Rogers, 2005).

The findings in the current study closely parallel those of Beauboeuf-Lafontant (2007), who drew on two theoretical frameworks—feminism and Black feminist critique—to conduct and analyze 44 interviews with a nonclinical sample of African American women to investigate the links between strength and depression. She uncovered several themes, including the cultural mandate of strength, self-silencing, excessive attunement to the needs of others, and denial of one's own needs; similar to the current study, she identified positive characteristics of showing strength (e.g., enhancing success with goals, assertiveness, and moral character). However, for a majority of the women (particularly those in the midst of childrearing and those who served as caretakers for their loved ones), being strong contributed to levels of selflessness, powerlessness, and self-silencing that contributed to psychological distress and heightened risk for depression (Beauboeuf-Lafontant, 2007). The similarity of the findings from the current focus group study and the research of Beauboeuf-Lafontant and others strengthens the argument that the Superwoman/ Strong Black Woman role is an important factor in understanding stress and health in African American women.

Similar to the work of Beauboeuf-Lafontant (2007) and Mullings (2006), the current research is related to James' (James et al., 1983) landmark John Henryism Hypothesis (JHH), in which health effects of chronic, high-effort coping among individuals with inadequate resources are described within the historical social context of systematic discrimination and oppression of African Americans. The preliminary SWS framework shares elements of strength and determination postulated by the JHH; however, the SWS framework provides more nuanced details about women's suppression of negative emotion and difficulty with accepting emotional support. Other important components of the SWS framework not addressed explicitly by the JHH include (a) obligation to help others, which includes difficulty saying no to multiple roles and responsibilities; (b) resistance to being vulnerable or dependent; (c) obligation to suppress emotions; and (d) postponement of self-care. In addition, in the current study sociohistorical experiences of discrimination and oppression were identified as contributors to this phenomenon, but also revealed were the ways in which more proximal (and often gender-related) life experiences shape an African American woman's propensity toward the Superwoman role. These include personal experiences of mistreatment and abuse, single motherhood, and challenges associated with being an African American woman who has achieved a high level of education or professional success, as well as perceived benefits of the Superwoman role such as protecting the well-being of African American children.

Limitations

One limitation of this study was the sample population. Although efforts were made to include a sample of African American women who were diverse in age and educational background, all of the participants lived in the southeastern United States. It is possible that participants from other regions of the United States might have different experiences that might be used to expand the current framework of SWS. Furthermore, in recruitment materials, women were invited to participate in a focus group to discuss issues of stress and coping in African American women. It is likely that this method of recruitment resulted in a sample of women with higher levels of stress compared to the general population. African American women who were not attracted to the study advertisements might have had lower levels of stress and might be less likely to identify with the characteristics of the Superwoman role identified from the analysis of this study. In addition, the focus group environment might have promoted a tendency to express opinions in agreement with the rest of the group, which might have limited discussion of unique, but important, alternative experiences.

Implications for Clinical Practice and Future Research

Findings of this qualitative focus group study have implications for clinical practice and research and are consistent with research on embodiment and health disparities among African American women (Lende & Lachiondo, 2009). An embodied approach to investigating health disparities moves beyond rational explanations and incorporates contextual factors emphasizing how an individual's subjective experience influences health behaviors (Lende & Lachiondo, 2009). Cultural and psychosocial factors of the Superwoman role, such as focusing on the needs of others and making personal health a secondary or tertiary priority, might explain delays in health-seeking behaviors, limited adherence to recommendations made by health care professionals, and lower rates of screening procedures for conditions that are treatable if caught in the early stages (e.g., breast cancer screening, colonoscopies). Health care practitioners who are aware of the potential influence of the Superwoman role on health behaviors might have an enhanced ability to understand the lived experiences of their patients and the ability to integrate appropriate methods of patient education and counseling into their clinical practice. The stress-related coping strategy of strength might mask distress and make it more difficult for health care professionals to assess health status accurately and recommend effective interventions for health promotion and stress management in this population (Edge & Rogers, 2005).

It is reasonable for practitioners and researchers to examine how the Superwoman role might contribute to underutilization of mental health care among African American women when compared to the general population (Boyd, 1997, 1999; Gillespie, 1984; Greene, 1994; Martin, 2002; Mitchell & Herring, 1998; Romero, 2000; Shorter-Gooden & Jackson, 2000; Thomas et al., 2004; Thompson, 2000; Warren, 1994). Superwoman schema characteristics, such as resistance to dependence on others and emotional suppression, might prevent African American women from seeking help for emotional distress (Thomas, Speight, & Witherspoon, 2005). Verbalization of emotional distress or seeking professional mental health counseling might be interpreted as signs of weakness or as a failure to uphold the image of strength (Amankwaa, 2003; Curphey, 2003).

The preliminary SWS framework might enhance existing explanatory models of stress, coping, and physical or mental health among African American women. For example, emotional suppression has been found to influence excessive intake of alcohol (e.g., Ehrmin, 2002) and undesirable physiological processes that result in detrimental changes in immune functioning and illness (Petrie, Booth, & Pennebaker, 1998; Petrie, Fontanilla, Thomas, Booth, & Pennebaker, 2004; Smyth, Stone, Hurewitz, & Kaell, 1999). Emotional inhibition in African American women has been associated with higher sleep diastolic blood pressure (DBP) and smaller drops in DBP from day to night (Steffen, McNeilly, Anderson, & Sherwood, 2003). In addition, African American women who kept silent about unfair treatment were found to have higher blood pressure (Krieger, 1990) than those who did not keep silent. Future research can be used to explore how the Superwoman role might be related to these health conditions in African American women.

Furthermore, future research might be focused on how the Superwoman role might contribute to the disproportionate rate of obesity (Wang & Beydoun, 2007) and obesity-related illnesses among African American women. Excessive intake of food has been reported as a method used to relieve unresolved psychological distress in some African American women (Walcott-McQuigg, 1995). Even though emotional eating or stress-related eating might contribute to short-term relief from distress, in a survey of 148 African American women, those who felt that "[i]t is best for me to deny or hide personal conflicts or difficulties to present an image of strength for my family, friends, and community" (24% of those sampled) reported higher levels of distress, were more likely to report being unable to get rid of bad thoughts or ideas, were more likely to use food to cope with stress, and were more likely to have extreme obesity (Giscombe, 2005). Based on this evidence, a Superwoman ideal accompanied by emotional suppression might place the health and well-being of African American women who use this strategy at risk.

It is reasonable to assume that an isolated characteristic of the Superwoman role might not be, in and of itself, a risk factor for undesirable health outcomes. However, specific combinations of Superwoman characteristics and varying degrees of available resources might influence a woman's risk for impaired health. For example, a tendency to suppress negative emotions in the context of inadequate resources and responsibilities in multiple life domains might place a woman at greater risk for adverse health compared to a woman who has a great deal of determination to succeed, but also has the ability to express distress as a result of abundant tangible and emotional support from family and friends. Additional research might result in the identification of Superwoman characteristic profiles to identify women who are most at risk for undesirable health effects.

Also, in future research, differences could be explored between women who do and do not endorse the Superwoman role. As was the case with findings from a recent study investigating the concept of strength among African American women (Beauboeuf-Lafontant, 2007), varying degrees of endorsement of Superwoman characteristics among focus group participants were found in the current study. Another topic of exploration involves the applicability of the SWS conceptual framework in cross-cultural research. Existing literature suggests that the concept of strength is relevant to women from diverse backgrounds (Hayes, 1986; Herrera & DelCampo, 1995; Lim, 1997; Mensinger, Bonifazi, & LaRosa, 2007; Whitty, 2001). Future researchers might examine SWS in other ethnic groups (e.g., in European Americans, Latinas, Asian Americans, or Native Americans) to determine how ethnicity and cultural experiences influence links between the Superwoman role and health outcomes.

Findings from the current study suggest several directions for future research that might help researchers investigate stress-related health issues among African American women. However, it is important to first confirm and validate the components and organization of the preliminary SWS conceptual framework. It is also important to investigate the potential of additional concepts or factors that make a contribution to the development of the Superwoman role in African American women. To make more concrete empirical conclusions, a method of assessing SWS (e.g., the development of an SWS instrument) is needed to examine these hypothesized relationships. Once validated and confirmed with additional research, the SWS conceptual framework might be used to inform the development of culturally relevant educational programming, community-based interventions, and clinical practice and health-promotion strategies for African American women.

Acknowledgments

The author wishes to thank the participants for sharing their views and acknowledges the mentorship of Faye Gary, Margaret Miles, Joyce Roland, Linda Beeber, Debra Barksdale, and Merle Mishel during work on this project. Gratitude is extended to Margarete Sandelowski and Paul Mihas for consultation on qualitative methodology and to Teneka Steed, Valerie Parham-Thompson, Lee Smith, and Jennifer Leeman for technical and editorial support.

Declaration of Conflicting Interests

The author declared no conflicts of interest with respect to the authorship and/or publication of this article.

Funding

The author disclosed receipt of the following financial support for the research and/or authorship of this article: The National Institute of Nursing Research and the National Center on Minority Health and Health Disparities [grant number P20 NR 8369, 2006–2008]; the National Institute of Nursing Research [grant number T32NR007091, 2005–2007]; the National Institutes of Health Loan Repayment Program for Health Disparities Research [2007–2009]; and the Substance Abuse and Mental Health Services Administration Minority Fellowship Program at the American Nurses Association [2007–2009].

References

Amankwaa, L. C. (2003). Postpartum depression among African-American women. *Issues in Mental Health Nursing,* 24(3), 297–316.

Angelou, M. (1978). Phenomenal woman. In *And still I rise* (pp. 8–10). New York: Random House.

Banerjee, M. M., & Pyles, L. (2004). Spirituality: A source of resilience for African American women in the era of welfare reform. *Journal of Ethnic & Cultural Diversity in Social Work,* 13(2), 45–70.

Beauboeuf-Lafontant, T. (2003). Strong and large Black women? Exploring relationships between deviant womanhood and weight. *Gender & Society* 17(1), 111–121.

Beauboeuf-Lafontant, T. (2007). You have to show strength: An exploration of gender, race, and depression. *Gender & Society,* 21(1), 28–51.

Beauboeuf-Lafontant, T. (2009). Behind the mask of the strong Black woman : Voice and the embodiment of a costly performance. *Philadelphia: Temple University Press.*

Black, A. (2008, December). *Strength, resilience, and survivorship: A content analysis of life management strategies as reflected in African American women's magazines.* Poster presented at the National Institutes of Health Summit: The Science of Eliminating Health Disparities. National Center on Minority Health and Health Disparities, National Harbor, MD.

Boles, N. (2008). *Back to basics: Volunteerism and fundamental philanthropy.* Retrieved April 24, 2008, from http://www.worldvolunteerweb.org/news-views/viewpoints/doc/back-to-basics-volunteerism.html

Boyd, J. A. (1997). *In the company of my sisters: Black women and self-esteem.* New York: Dutton.

Boyd, J. A. (1999). *Can I get a witness? For sisters, when the blues is more than a song.* New York: Dutton.

Collins, P. H. *(2000). Black feminist thought: Knowledge, consciousness, and the politics of empowerment.* New York: Routledge.

Curphey, S. (2003). *Black women mental-health needs unmet.* Retrieved January 15, 2004, from http://www.womensenews.org/article.cfm/dyn/aid/1392

Cutrona, C. E., Russell, D. W., Hessling, R. M., Brown, P. A., & Murry, V. (2000). Direct and moderating effects of community context on the psychological well-being of African American women. *Journal of Personality and Social Psychology, 79*(6), 1088–1101.

Davis, R. E. (1998). Discovering "creative essences" in African American women: The construction of meaning around inner resources. *Women's Studies International Forum, 21*(5), 493–504.

Edge, D., & Rogers, A. (2005). Dealing with it: Black Caribbean women's response to adversity and psychological distress associated with pregnancy, childbirth, and early motherhood. *Social Science & Medicine, 61*(1), 15–25.

Ehrmin, J. T. (2002). "That feeling of not feeling": Numbing the pain for substance-dependent African American women. *Qualitative Health Research, 12,* 780–791.

Farquhar, C., & Das, R. (1999). Are focus groups suitable for "sensitive" topics? In R. S. Barbour & J. Kitzinger (Eds.), *Developing focus group research: Politics, theory, and practice* (pp. 47–63). London: Sage.

Frankland, J., & Bloor, M. (1999). Some issues arising in the systematic analysis of focus group materials. In R. S. Barbour & J. Kitzinger (Eds.), *Developing focus group research: Politics, theory, and practice* (pp. 144–155). London: Sage.

Geronimus, A. T. (2001). Understanding and eliminating racial inequalities in women's health in the United States: The role of the weathering conceptual framework. *Journal of the American Medical Women's Association, 56*(4), 133–136, 149–150.

Geronimus, A. T., Hicken, M., Keene, D., & Bound, J. (2006). "Weathering" and age patterns of allostatic load scores among Blacks and Whites in the United States. *American Journal of Public Health, 96*(5), 826–833.

Gillespie, M. A. (1984). The myth of the strong Black woman. In A. M. Jaggar & P. S. Rothenberg (Eds.), *Feminist frameworks: Alternative theoretical accounts of the relations between women and men* (pp. 32–35). New York: McGraw-Hill.

Giovanni, N. (1996). Ego-tripping. In *The Selected Poems of Nikki Giovanni: 1968-1995* (pp. 92–93). New York: William Morrow.

Giscombé, C. (2005). *The association of race-related, gender-related, and generic stress with global distress and coping among African American women.* (Unpublished doctoral dissertation). State University of New York at Stony Brook.

Giscombé, C. L., & Lobel, M. (2005). Explaining disproportionately high rates of adverse birth outcomes among African Americans: The impact of stress, racism, and related factors in pregnancy. *Psychological Bulletin, 131*(5), 662–683.

Greene, B. (1994). African American women. In L. Comas-Diaz & B. Greene (Eds.), *Women of color: Integrating ethnic and gender identities in psychotherapy* (pp. 10–29). New York: Guilford.

Hamilton, B. E., Martin, J. A., & Ventura, S. J. (2009, March 18). Births: Preliminary data for 2007. *National Vital Statistics Reports, 57*(12), 1–23. Retrieved January 5, 2010, from http://www.cdc.gov/nchs/data/nvsr/nvsr57/nvsr57_12.pdf

Hamilton-Mason, J., Hall, J. C., & Everette, J. E. (2009). And some of us are braver: Stress and coping among African American women. *Journal of Human Behavior in the Social Environment, 19*(5), 463–482.

Harris, T. (2001). *Sinners and saints: Strong Black women in African American literature.* New York: Palgrave.

Harris-Lacewell, M. (2001). No place to rest: African American political attitudes and the myth of Black women's strength. *Women & Politics, 23*(3), 1–33.

Hayes, L. S. (1986). The superwoman myth. *Social Casework: The Journal of Contemporary Social Work, 67*(7), 436–441.

Herrera, R. S., & DelCampo, R. L. (1995). Beyond the super-woman syndrome: Work satisfaction and family functioning among working-class, Mexican American women. *Hispanic Journal of Behavioral Sciences, 17*(1), 49–60.

hooks, b. (1993). *Sisters of the yam: Black women and self-recovery.* Boston: South End.

James, S. A. (1994). John Henryism and the health of African-Americans. *Culture, Medicine and Psychiatry, 18*(2), 163–182.

James, S. A., Hartnett, S. A., & Kalsbeek, W. D. (1983). John Henryism and blood pressure differences among Black men. *Journal of Behavioral Medicine, 6*(3), 259–278.

Jarrett, R. L. (1993). Focus group interviewing with low-income minority populations: A research experience. In D. L. Morgan (Ed.), *Successful focus groups: Advancing the state of the art* (pp. 184–201). Newbury Park, CA: Sage.

Kitzinger, J., & Barbour, R. S. (1999). Developing focus group research: Politics, theory, and practice. London: Sage.

Krieger, N. (1990). Racial and gender discrimination: Risk factors for high blood pressure? *Social Science & Medicine, 30*(12), 1273–1281.

Krieger, N. (2005). Embodiment: A conceptual glossary for epidemiology. *Journal of Epidemiology and Community Health, 59*(5), 350–355.

Kwate, N. O., Valdimarsdottir, H. B., Guevarra, J. S., & Bovbjerg, D. H. (2003). Experiences of racist events are associated with negative health consequences for African American women. *Journal of the National Medical Association, 95*(6), 450–460.

Lende, D. H., & Lachiondo, A. (2009). Embodiment and breast cancer among African American women. *Qualitative Health Research, 19,* 216–228.

Lim, I.-S. (1997). Korean immigrant women's challenge to gender inequality at home: The interplay of economic resources, gender, and family. *Gender & Society, 11*(1), 31–51.

Martin, M. (2002). *Saving our last nerve: The Black woman's path to mental health.* Roscoe, IL: Hilton.

McEwen, B. S. (1998). Protective and damaging effects of stress mediators. *New England Journal of Medicine, 338*(3), 171–179.

Mensinger, J. L., Bonifazi, D. Z., & LaRosa, J. (2007). Perceived gender role prescriptions in schools, the Superwoman ideal, and disordered eating among adolescent girls. *Sex Roles, 57*(7-8), 557–568.

Merton, R. K., Fiske, M., & Kendall, P. L. (1990). *The focused interview: A manual of problems and procedures* (2nd ed.). London: Collier McMillan.

Mitchell, A., & Herring, K. (1998). *What the blues is all about: Black women overcoming stress and depression.* New York: Perigee.

Morgan, D. L., & Krueger, R. A. (1998). *The focus group kit.* Volumes 1–6 (box set). London: Sage.

Morrison, D. H. (2006). *Even Superwoman needs to cry sometimes: An intimacy guide for men partnering with strong Black women.* Charleston, SC: Booksurge.

Mullings, L. (2006). Resistance and resilience: The Sojourner Syndrome and the social context of reproduction in Central Harlem. In A. J. Schulz & L. Mullings (Eds.), *Gender, race, class, and health* (pp. 345–370). San Francisco: Jossey-Bass.

Nyamathi, A., Wayment, H. A., & Dunkel-Schetter, C. (1993). Psychosocial correlates of emotional distress and risk behavior in African American women at risk for HIV infection. *Anxiety, Stress & Coping: An International Journal, 6*(2), 133–148.

Petrie, K. J., Booth, R. J., & Pennebaker, J. W. (1998). The immunological effects of thought suppression. *Journal of Personality and Social Psychology, 75*(5), 1264–1272.

Petrie, K. J., Fontanilla, I., Thomas, M. G., Booth, R. J., & Pennebaker, J. W. (2004). Effect of written emotional expression on immune function in patients with human immunodeficiency virus infection: A randomized trial. *Psychosomatic Medicine, 66*(2), 272–275.

Pons-Estel, G. J., Alarcon, G. S., Scofield, L., Reinlib, L., & Cooper, G. S. (2009). Understanding the epidemiology and progression of systemic lupus erythematosus. *Seminars in Arthritis and Rheumatism.* Epub ahead of print. DOI:10.1016/j.semarthrit.2008.10.007

Romero, R. E. (2000). The icon of the strong Black woman: The paradox of strength. In L. C. Jackson & B. Greene (Eds.), *Psychotherapy with African American women: Innovations in psychodynamic perspectives and practice* (pp. 225–238). New York: Guilford Press.

Sandelowski, M. (1986). The problem of rigor in qualitative research. *ANS: Advances in Nursing Science,* 8(3), 27–37.

Shambley-Ebron, D. Z., & Boyle, J. S. (2006). In our grandmother's footsteps: Perceptions of being strong in African American women with HIV/AIDS. *ANS: Advances in Nursing Science,* 29(3), 195–206.

Shorter-Gooden, K., & Jackson, L. C. (2000). The interweaving of cultural and intrapsychic issues in the therapeutic relationship. In L. C. Jackson & B. Greene (Eds.), *Psychotherapy with African American women: Innovations in psychodynamic perspective and practice* (pp. 15–32). New York: Guilford Press.

Smyth, J. M., Stone, A. A., Hurewitz, A., & Kaell, A. (1999). Effects of writing about stressful experiences on symptom reduction in patients with asthma or rheumatoid arthritis: A randomized trial. *JAMA,* 281(14), 1304–1309.

Steffen, P. R., McNeilly, M., Anderson, N., & Sherwood, A. (2003). Effects of perceived racism and anger inhibition on ambulatory blood pressure in African Americans. *Psychosomatic Medicine, 65*(5), 746–750.

Substance Abuse and Mental Health Services Administration, Office of the Surgeon General, United States Department of Health and Human Services. (2009). *Surgeon General's report. Fact sheets: African Americans.* Retrieved October 16, 2009, from http://mentalhealth.samhsa.gov/cre/fact1.asp

Thom, T., Haase, N., Rosamond, W., Howard, V. J., Rumsfeld, J., Manolio, T., et al. (2006). Heart disease and stroke statistics—2006 update: A report from the American Heart Association statistics committee and stroke statistics subcommittee. *Circulation, 113,* e85–e151. DOI:10.1161/CIRCULATIONAHA.105.171600

Thomas, A. J., Speight, S. L., & Witherspoon, K. M. (2005). Race and ethnicity in psychology. In J. L. Chin (Ed.), *The psychology of prejudice and discrimination: Bias based on gender and sexual orientation* (pp. 113–132). Westport, CT: Praeger/Greenwood.

Thomas, A. J., Witherspoon, K. M., & Speight, S. L. (2004). Toward the development of the stereotypic roles for Black women scale. *The Journal of Black Psychology,* 30(3), 426–442.

Thompkins, T. (2005). The real lives of strong Black women: Transcending myths, reclaiming joy. *Evanston, IL: Agate.*

Thompson, C. L. (2000). African American women and moral masochism: When there is too much of a good thing. In L. C. Jackson & B. Greene (Eds.), *Psychotherapy with African American women: Innovations in psychodynamic perspectives and practice* (pp. 239–250). New York: Guilford Press.

Walcott-McQuigg, J. A. (1995). The relationship between stress and weight-control behavior in African-American women. *Journal of the National Medical Association,* 87(6), 427–432.

Wallace, M. (1990). Black macho and the myth of the superwoman. *London: Verso.*

Wang, Y., & Beydoun, M. A. (2007). The obesity epidemic in the United States—Gender, age, socioeconomic, racial/ethnic, and geographic characteristics: A systematic review and meta-regression analysis. *Epidemiological Review, 29,* 6–28.

Warren, B. J. (1994). Depression in African American women. *Journal of Psychosocial Nursing and Mental Health Services, 32*(3), 29–33.

Whitty, M. T. (2001). The myth of the superwoman: Comparing young men's and women's stories of their future lives. *Journal of Family Studies, 7*(1), 87–100.

Woods-Giscombé, C. L., & Lobel, M. (2008). Race and gender matter: A multidimensional approach to conceptualizing and measuring stress in African American women. *Cultural Diversity & Ethnic Minority Psychology, 14*(3), 173–182.

Unit IV. Finding Purpose at the Crossroads of Race, Gender, Class, and Culture

Introduction: Finding Identity and Purpose

To be all that we can be, embracing our fullest identities as Afrikan women, is the charge that Fanon poses in his quintessential question: *Am I all I ought to be?* From our ancient past through the horrific and devastating conditions posed by the Maafa, a persisting reality shaping the experiences of Africana women even in the 21st century, Afrikan American women have demonstrated the ability to transcend our physical lives, to transform the environments we enter, and to create institutions, organizations, and settings that enliven our spirits and uplift our families, communities, and society. In this unit, the authors explore the ways that Afrikan American women have dealt with the challenges posed by race, gender, and class, integrating their appreciation of their Afrikan cultural heritage and, consequently, rising above the obstacles presented by the omnipresence of White supremacy over the past five centuries.

Becoming all that we are meant to be—achieving our highest possibilities—is a dynamic, life-long mission that is supported by knowing ourselves and being who we are authentically. Knowing that we are divine; that we are the mothers of humanity; that we have been heads of state, warriors, healers, and religious leaders, among many other roles and positions; and that we are resilient provides us with a defense system that is indestructible in the face of the interlocking oppressions that emerge due to our race, gender, class, age, sexual orientation, religion, or other demographic characteristics. The lives of women such as Sojourner Truth, aka Isabella Baumfree, and Fannie Lou Hamer provide exemplary models of the transformative process that some of us have experienced in middle age, revealing aspects of our identity previously unknown, the *not-yet self.*

In the chapters that follow, in numerous ways, the authors illustrate how Afrikan/Black women transcend their interlocking oppressions and find hope, tranquility, and purpose that go far beyond their individual existences. Opening this unit, Marva Lewis's analysis of mother–daughter hair-combing rituals reveals the sacred nature of a task that is too often viewed as a mundane daily routine. This ritualistic interaction provides a unique opportunity for bonding, cultural socialization, and transmission of family history between mother and daughter. The salutary benefits of positive attitudes about the texture of Afrikan hair on the mother–daughter relationship are identified and contrasted with the deleterious effects that negative attitudes about our hair have on these relationships. Neico Slater-Sa-Ra provides an enlightening overview of the historical and cultural practices of rites of passage (ROP) in Afrikan and Afrikan American societies and communities. ROP honor the transitions from one stage of life to the next and prepare girls/women for the assumption of their new roles, using cultural rituals and processes. Through the reclamation of ROP in Black communities, Afrikan/Black girls receive assistance in overcoming ancestral trauma; increase knowledge of who they are; and develop an authentic sense of their identity and appreciation of their sacredness. The transformative role of grief for Afrikan/Black mothers who have lost children to violence is the focus of Al'Uqdah and Adomako's chapter. From Mamie Bradley Till—mother of Emmett Till, tragically murdered at 14 years of age by the KKK—to the contemporary Mothers of the Movement, the authors examine the role of grief as a catalyst for social justice activism by mourning mothers. The theme of activism is further explored by Tameka Hobbs. In her chapter, she pays tribute to Afrikan/Black mothers, daughters, sisters, and friends, lifting them up as models of what it means to be an Afrikan woman and exemplifying the essence of being all that we ought to be. By unearthing these stories, Hobbs reveals to us the commitment to social justice that Afrikan American women have historically exhibited, the fearlessness of Black women who were unconstrained by gender-role prescriptions and proscriptions, and the tremendous power that Africana women hold when they embrace their identity in an authentic manner and carry out their divinely sanctioned life purpose as the mothers of humanity. Hobbs

275

shares poignant stories of Afrikan American women from the colonial period to the modern era who defiantly resisted the barriers of racism, sexism, and classism, demonstrating their courage, faith, and perseverance, and standing up against phenomenal odds. Closing this final unit, Linda James Myers offers a chapter on healing, coping, and transcending the legacy of intersecting oppressions, an allegory on the divinity of Afrikan women. She asserts that everything that Afrikan/Black women need is already in our possession and that, through alignment with our cultural legacy and optimal worldview, we can overcome the devastations wrought by the Maafa and achieve our traditional greatness.

Reading 4.1. Black Mother–Daughter Interactions and Hair-Combing Rituals

Marva L. Lewis

Introduction

One of the most intimate rituals performed by African American[17] women with their daughters is the task of combing hair. When a mother combs her daughter's natural hair once a day from ages 0–12 years, the routine of combing hair provides 4,380 opportunities for interaction between mothers and daughters.[18] This daily task provides a mother with a routine and rituals that may develop both the verbal, physical, and emotional aspects of their relationship and the gender identity of her daughter (Lewis, 1999). I propose that this interaction contributes to the quality of their attachment relationship. Research findings from a series of studies conducted over the past decade suggest that the positive or negative emotions associated with this task will remain forever imprinted in the childhood memories of the daughter. The thesis of the research that serves as the basis for this chapter is that a mother's approach to the everyday task of combing her daughter's hair embodies the larger toxic emotional symbolism surrounding race and gender identity (Lewis, 2000b, 2001; Lewis et al., 1999). Seen through the lens of a cultural-practices approach (Miller & Goodnow, 1995), the simple task of combing hair also builds on an untapped cultural strength of African Americans.

The hair-combing ritual reflects both cultural strengths and painful legacies of the history of African Americans' sociocultural experiences in the Americas. I will argue that the relationship dynamics evident when some African American women interact with their young daughters while combing their hair may also include modern-day unresolved psychological issues of the historical trauma of slavery. For other African American women, the daily ritual offers a relaxing and loving time of nurturing bonding with their daughters. The task may offer a positive emotional oasis for mothers or daughters facing other challenges or stressors in their lives.

African American women have historically faced, and currently battle, a multitude of psychosocial risk factors and challenges in their everyday lives (Collins, 1990; Dill, 2013; Jones & Shorter-Gooden, 2003; Thornton, 1987). In a racially stratified society, African Americans are frequently on the top or bottom of a long list of sociological and health-risk factors, reflecting high disproportionality and racial disparities due to individual and institutional racism. This list includes the highest rates of mass incarceration, infant mortality, and premature birth and low-birth-weight babies, as well as the highest number of children in foster care (Alexander, 2012; Williams et al., 2003). For example, in 2007, the infant mortality rate for non-Hispanic Black women was 2.4 times the rate for non-Hispanic White women (MacDorman & Mathews, 2008). Currently, African American women across all socioeconomic and age groups have the highest rates of infant mortality and low-birthweight (LBW) babies of all racial groups in the United States. Black women with excellent access to health care, who are over the age of 18 and who are in excellent health, are also part of these alarming inequities in LBW infants. In other words, the babies of these well-resourced, highly

---

[17] The nomenclature of *African American* is used to refer to the broader culture and traditions of African-origin people descended from slaves. In the United States, the term *Black* is a sociopolitical term used to identify the race of any person of African phenotype.

[18] Though other caregivers such as grandmothers, aunts, or older sisters may perform the task of hair-combing with both young girls and infant boys, in this chapter we focus primarily on the relationship dynamics of mothers with their young daughters.

educated women are also more likely to be born prematurely and small, and more likely to die before their first birthday. Not only are there heart-rending risks for an African American woman's birth outcomes, but Black women also have a shorter life expectancy and higher rate of death from heart attacks and other life-threatening illnesses than women in other racial groups (B. Avery, personal communication, October 15, 2012). Each of these abstract statistics may be accompanied by unexamined psychological responses of grief and loss in African American women.

The following questions led to the initial research question on the hair-combing task as a valid observational context for research. How, in the midst of these challenging life circumstances and the accompanying stress, could African American women nurture and love their infant children? How could a positive emotional bond form between a mother and child in the context of legacies of historical trauma and modern-day racism? The interaction that takes place while women comb their daughters' hair provides a more intimate psychological context to understand how the Maafa may impact interpersonal family relationships based on intergenerational legacies from this chronic historical trauma. First, I present a brief background to contextualize the attitudes of some members of African American communities who value straighter hair and lighter skin as modern-day legacies of the historical trauma of slavery Davis et al., 1998; Hardy, 1989). I discuss how the historical legacies of the Maafa—the great tragedy of the enslavement of Africans in the Americas—may shape individual differences in modern-day attachment relationships of African American mothers with their daughters. I call this distinct aspect of an African American woman's developmental history her *ethnobiography* (Lewis, 2001). An ethnobiography is the story of an individual's developmental experiences related to intergenerational legacies of their family, ethnic, cultural, and racial groups.

Next, I briefly present concepts from John Bowlby's (1969) attachment theory and Mary Ainsworth and colleagues' (1978) description of the maternal behavioral components needed in order for secure attachments to form between mothers and their infant children. I use findings from research using the hair-combing task to suggest how factors from the racialized and historical–sociocultural context may influence the development of individual differences in the formation of Black women's relationships with their daughters. These findings suggest there are powerful psychological processes and emotions surrounding the hair-combing task. I then describe the relationship "dance" that takes place between Black mothers and their daughters during hair combing in the early years of their relationship. Two major research findings are presented: 1) The identification of six distinct stages of hair-combing interaction; one stage, labeled *positional proximity*, includes the neurobiological implications of how the mother positions her daughter during this daily task; and 2) A typology of four types of African American mothers' perceptions of the hair-combing task and the relationship dynamics that may flow from these attitudes.

Finally, I discuss the implications of these findings for practice with African American women: the potential of using the hair-combing task for assessment and intervention, and possible directions for future research.

The Impact of the Maafa on African American Family Relationships

Complex sociocultural determinants affect African American mothers' relationships with their children (Meyers, 1999). For an African American mother, these determinants may include cultural expectations about what constitutes good behavior in children and her perception of a "good enough" parent (Benasich & Brooks-Gunn, 1966; Lewis, 2000a; Murry & Brody, 2002; Yeh et al., 2004). In addition to the well-known risk factors that impact parenting behaviors, analysis of risk must also include the chronic stressors associated with the compelling sociological inequities in which African American families are disproportionately represented (Bluestone & Tamis-LeMonda, 1999; Jewell, 2003; Middlemiss, 2003; Murry et al., 2001). Each of these risk factors includes highly charged emotions. Yet there are few research studies that address the historical and sociocultural determinants of African American parenting styles and parent–child attachment (Nsamenang, 1992; Peters, 2002; Rosser & Randolph, 1991).

The psychological impact of the Maafa has been under-studied regarding the formation of intimate, interpersonal family relationships. To understand the significance of this history to mother–daughter interaction during hair combing, I will first examine the psychological residuals of this tragedy and the implications for African American family relationships. A legacy of the Maafa is the social hierarchy that evolved first as a means of survival in slave communities (Stuckey, 1987) and now functions as an under-recognized factor in modern African American interpersonal relationships (Davis et al., 1998; Hardy, 1989). *Colorism*—the valuing of one skin color over the other—in addition to the practices of teasing and devaluing of "nappy" hair —natural, kinky African hair—are evident during hair-combing interactions and are the specific legacies of the Maafa that will be the focus of this chapter (Okazawa-Rey et al., 1987; Rooks, 2001; Russell et al., 1991).

The biography of the majority of African American families begins with the trauma of the brutality of forced separation from their loved families and friends, the familiar surroundings of their communities, and the ancient beliefs and culture of their ancestors (Bennett, 1982; Eyerman, 2004; Hill, 1972). Europeans and others created the business and politics of the enslavement. Over the span of several hundred years, more than 25 million Africans were captured, chained, and shipped as cargo to the Americas. External violence, fear for life, and the systematic eradication and loss of cultural identity permeate these original biographies (Burton, 2006; Taylor, 2005). The historical trauma of chattel slavery (where humans became the legal property of their owners for life) included a psychological tactic designed to separate and oppress the Africans captured at gunpoint or sold into slavery by other Africans (Eyerman, 2004; Stuckey, 1987). The primary social and legally sanctioned psychological tool used by slave owners was to classify the enslaved Africans as human property. Slave owners needed widespread social support for the institution of slavery from all levels of the United States society, including from non-slave-owners. They gained this support by intentionally and systematically devaluing the color of Africans' skin and by associating all things negative and physically painful with the color black (Blassingame, 1972). Called the "mark of oppression," the most visible differences between slave owners and enslaved people were the visible contrasts in their skin tone. The pale, almost colorless skin tone and straight hair of the European Americans contrasted sharply with the rich, dark skin tones and tightly curled hair of the enslaved Africans. These two features—dark skin color and coarse, kinky hair—became the embodiment of vicious negative stereotypes of any person with "one drop" of African blood (Bennett, 1982).

In addition, these physical features represented the volatile legacy of the issue of miscegenation, the mixing of Black and White races, and the sexually charged implications of varying skin tones in slave families (Burton, 2006; Pinderhughes, 1989; Rooks, 2001). The rainbow of skin tones that characterize African American communities and families is the evidence of a horrific practice during slavery—the legal and repeated rape of enslaved African women by their White slave owners. The complicated relationships between the White slave owners and their Black progeny resulted in some slaves being valued for their skin color and hair because of being their owner's descendant. The complicated roles of President Thomas Jefferson—as a philosopher and central author of the *Declaration of Independence* of the United States, as a slave owner, and in his purported long-term sexual relationship with an enslaved African woman, Sally Hemings—remain a source of controversy (Gordon-Reed, 1997). This well-documented relationship, which took place within the context of slavery, is an example of the historical origins of the modern schizophrenic-like relationship between Blacks and Whites (Stampp, 1956). The privileges and opportunities associated with being able to "pass" for White and escape the horrors of slavery then became the source of conflict *within* slave communities (Fanon, 1968). These conflicts remain with us today in the form of issues of "good hair" and acceptance or rejection of some African Americans because of their light or dark skin tones (Hardy, 1989; Lewis et al., 2008; Porter, 1991; Russell et al., 1992).

These same physical features have become the symbol and target of centuries of painful stereotypes and the basis for economic and social discrimination and emotional trauma (Davis et al., 1998; Eyerman, 2004; Fanon, 1968). Over the past century, the emotional baggage associated with hair and skin color has been a recurrent theme in popular movies, books, and articles, and a recurrent topic in church and professional seminars, in Black communities around the United States (e.g., Byrd & Tharps, 2001; Harris & Johnson, 2001; Russell et al., 1992; Straight, 2000; Tyler, 1990). The modern-day valuing of light skin color and devaluing of dark skin tones and nappy hair textures are direct legacies of the period of enslavement that currently insinuate themselves into the everyday interactions of African American mothers with their children.

Legal and social policies and practices used to preserve the institution of chattel slavery in the United States also contributed to modern-day factors that impact 20th-century African American family relationships. These macro-level social structural policies began with the designation of each enslaved African as the chattel property of the slaveholder for life and worth "3/5's" of a man. A complex set of social laws and a constitutionally based legal framework were created to preserve the business of the Atlantic African slave trade (Bennett, 1982). With the formal dissolution of the practice of slavery by the *Emancipation Proclamation* in 1865, the former slave laws were transformed into slave codes in the post-reconstruction era. These rigid laws dictating social status and rules for Blacks and Whites were secretly resurrected and enforced with the creation of the clandestine nightriders organized into the terrorist Ku Klux Klan, a White supremacist group that currently exists in the U.S.A.

Social practices developed to preserve the institution of chattel slavery provide the historical structure of modern racism and internalized oppression (Fanon, 1968; Healey, 2012). As late as the 1960s within some Black communities, the "brown paper bag test" was practiced to assign members social status (Pinderhughes, 1989; Russell et al., 1992). In this practice, admission to the elite Black upper-class social organizations, churches, and schools was determined by skin color. That is, if the applicant's skin color was lighter than a brown paper bag, admission was granted.

The collective silence, both in the larger society and within segments of African American communities, has served to prolong the necessary healing from these traumas and wounds of slavery (Eyerman, 2004). The inner conflicts and collective rage of African Americans originally identified by psychiatrists Grier and Cobbs (1968) in the mid-60s may be an unrecognized risk factor and influence on the most intimate relationship of a mother with her child. In the United States of America, race-related traumas are the target of modern-day racism, prejudice and discrimination, and historical stereotypes, and they generate powerful emotional responses in African Americans (Rankin, 1988). The intersection of race, gender, class, and culture in these race-based experiences and collective traumas may result in depression, paranoia, and aggression in African American women (Dill, 2013; Jones & Shorter-Gooden, 2003). The emotional responses to these everyday instances of microaggressions associated with race and gender may range from anxiety, worry, and irritation to fear, anger, and rage (Grier & Cobbs, 1968; Sue, 2010). Within African American communities and families, feelings of acceptance or rejection based on colorism and rejection of "nappy hair" may impact family and interpersonal relationships (Boyd-Franklin, 1989). Feelings of racial acceptance or rejection reflect intergenerational legacies of internalized stereotypes of Blacks. These toxic and unrecognized legacies include disconnection from and lack of identity with African American culture, shame and internalized stereotypes of Black Americans and Black families, and self-destructive ways of coping with modern-day racism (Eyerman, 2004; Hardy, 1987; Taylor & Grundy, 1996).

Historical Trauma and African American Family Relationships.

Eyerman (2004) argues that it is the collective memory of slavery that currently defines the identity of the descendants of slavery. He proposes that "… the past is a collectively articulated, if not collectively experienced, temporal reference point that shapes the individual more than it is reshaped to fit generational or individual needs" (p. 67). The manifestations of the Maafa in African American parent–child relationships may be in relation to socialization practices that highlight cultural histories, stories, and myths related to the minority group status (Thornton, 1997). More likely, in the collective narrative there may be silence and omission of sections of history related to painful memories and traumatic events of the group. For example, in my personal family history, when asked about her memories of slavery, my grandmother, the granddaughter of a slave, would say only, "no one wants to talk about that."

For African American women, the psychological legacies of the historical trauma of the Maafa are compounded with the intersection of race, gender, and socioeconomic class (Healey, 2012; Coner-Edwards

& Edwards, 1988). The intersectionality of these unrecognized forces may be a powerful factor in the behaviors of African American women during the hair-combing task—a singular ritual embodying this complex social history.

Next, the theory of parental acceptance and rejection and its importance to parent–child attachment are briefly described. These theories are used as a conceptual framework to understand the significance of African American women's behaviors and manifestations of intergenerational legacies of the Maafa during the hair-combing task, and the significance of the protective role of secure attachment for children's development. A new theory is presented, informed by the racial context of family relationships about childhood experiences of racial acceptance and rejection (CERAR) and its role in the maternal behaviors during hair-combing interactions (Lewis, 1993).

The Hair-Combing Ritual as a Cultural Practice That Strengthens Mother–Child Attachment

Parental acceptance and rejection of children. Consistent findings from studies of early experiences of parental acceptance and rejection and adult attachment style suggest that the caregiver's attachment history is associated with their caregiver-behavioral responses and the quality of attachment with their child (Rohner, 1975, 1986). From the developing infant's perspective, unconditional love and acceptance by a primary caregiver form the earliest template for psychological growth and development, and for healthy self-esteem and self-concept formation (Ainsworth et al., 1978; Bowlby, 1969; Rohner, 1975). Rohner (1986) argues that two domains consistently emerge in studies of children's perceptions of parenting practices: a behavioral domain in the form of parental control (ranging from strict to permissive); and an affective domain related to the child's feelings of acceptance and rejection (the warmth/coldness dimension). Consistently identified across many cultural groups, warm parents are those who show their love or affection toward children physically or verbally, but not excessively, and within standards for emotional display defined by their culture or community (Rohner, 1986; Thoits, 1989). Rejecting parents are defined as those who dislike, disapprove of, or resent their children. Rejection is seen in parental behavior as hostility and aggression or parental indifference and neglect. Parental warmth results in a child's feeling loved or accepted. On the other hand, parental rejection leads to a child's feeling unloved or rejected. The behaviors that lead to a child's feeling acceptance and warmth also promote secure attachment to the caregiver (Ainsworth et al., 1978).

The racial context that permeates the lives of African American women in their role as mothers has not been fully examined by developmental psychologists and social science researchers (Rosser & Randolph, 1991; Spencer & Markstrom, 1990). Specifically, we know little of how the racial context impacts the socioemotional domains in which African American women develop attachment relationships with their children. A critical aspect of the racial context is the set of historical racial stereotypes associated with indelible phenotypic features of race—skin color, hair texture, and nose and lip size.

These features of parental responsiveness, and their implications for the formation of secure attachment, have been studied from a cultural context in groups around the world (Bretherton, 1987). What has not been addressed is the more politicized racial context of racial features and the acceptance or rejection of children.

In parent–child attachment relationships, the affective domain is characterized by an exchange of positive and negative affect between the mother and child and includes the mother's emotional availability and the child's temperament (Biringen & Easterbrooks, 2012). The behavioral domain includes maternal behaviors that are sensitive and responsive to the child's cues and bids for attention (Ainsworth et al., 1978). The cognitive domain includes parental beliefs about children, knowledge, and attitudes. Both the mother and child operate from a mental representation of the stored history of their interactions (Bowlby, 1969, 1973). The mother's subjective representation of the child guides her behavioral and affective responses to the child (Biringen & Easterbrook, in press). The child develops an emerging sense of self and relatedness to others as his or her cognitive capacities mature and the capacity for symbolic thought becomes consolidated (Stern, 1985). Ongoing interactions between mother and child contribute to the child's evolving sense of self, including the child's capacity to form gendered and racial concepts of self (Branch & Newcombe, 1986; Bretherton, 1987; Murray & Mandara, 2002; Stern, 1985).

The developing attachment relationships between Black parents and young children are also vulnerable to the legacies of racism and internalized oppression. Specifically, a Black parent's early childhood experiences of negative messages associated with racial features of skin color and hair type may influence their beliefs and expectations about Black children. The parent may accept or reject children based on their skin color or hair texture. Further, unexamined early negative experiences may seep into a parent's everyday interactions with their child.

A finding from clinical research studies with adult Black women provides evidence of the emotional impact of more distal sources of early childhood messages of racial acceptance or rejection. Black women describe feelings of being accepted or rejected by Black peers and the Black community due to their light or dark skin tone (Pinderhughes, 1989). In various regions around the United States, typical issues addressed in therapy, with Black families and individual women across a range of socioeconomic classes, center on issues of skin color (Boyd-Franklin, 1989; Coner-Edwards & Edwards, 1988). In both group and individual therapy with Black women and girls, anger and resentment over the discrimination practiced in the Black community about the issue of skin color frequently occurs (Boyd-Franklin, 1989; Green, 1990). In a privately published memoir of growing up as a "colored Creole" in the city of New Orleans in the late fifties, Aline St. Julien (1987) writes, "My mother says I am Creole. My teacher said I am Negro. Some Europeans say I am Colored and others call me 'nigger.' Who am I?" (p. 2). She writes of experiences of racial acceptance and rejection of the children in her family within her own extended family group.

> Creole ranged in color from white to dark brown with a lot of yellow and "teasing tans" in between. Hair texture, if straight, is described as "good hair" and kinky hair is considered "bad hair." A dark child in a Creole family is "better off" with straight hair, which means he is more acceptable. If he has kinky hair and dark skin, he is usually the butt of family jokes, like, "where did you get that one from?" or "someone must have slept in the woodshed with a nigger." (St. Julien, 1987, p. 2)

She also writes of the developmental emotional residue and life choices influenced by these early painful experiences of skin color.

> Sometimes the older people would talk in French so that we children couldn't understand, but we knew they were talking about the "odd ball" of the family. Most of these children grew up with much more self-hate than their lighter sisters and brothers. They usually chose the lightest friends and quite frequently married that type also. ... The older people were not afraid to tell us when choosing a spouse to think of our children. This affected me, because I certainly didn't want my little monkeys to have kinky hair like me. Therefore my husband just had to have straight hair. By the time we reached the social age, we were ready to choose a spouse who met all the requirements of the typical Creole family ... because my husband is darker than a brown paper bag ... I was warned by one of my relatives that I could have a child as dark as the darkest member of his family and with my "bad hair." But the only thing I couldn't understand was why would this handsome man want to marry a kinky headed woman like me. Were "fine features" my only asset in attracting a husband? (St. Julien, 1987, p. 3)

Thus, experiences of racial acceptance or rejection may originate with people at all levels of the ecological niche (Lewis, 2000a, 2001). The most intimate-level messages may come from primary attachment figures and siblings, as well as extended family such as grandparents and cousins. At the outer levels of the ecological niche are same-race peers, same-race teachers, and other adults in the neighborhood and community. At a more distal level are advertisers and the public media, who communicate messages of racial acceptance and rejection based on European standards of beauty and stereotyped portrayals of dark,

African-featured individuals. Skin color is only one of the phenotype racial features that readily distinguish Black Americans from other groups. The indelible racial features include skin color; hair texture and length; nose size; and hip, lip, and buttock size and shape.

The Formation of the Parent's Ethnobiography

Perhaps a child was called Black and ugly, or light-skinned and pretty, by his or her father, mother, grandmother, or cousins. Perhaps she was always passed over by her Black teachers in her elementary school classroom when her hand was raised or harassed on the playground by her peers because of her ebony black skin and ruby-red lips. Perhaps she was always asked on dates with reference to her long silky hair and light skin tone. These race-related memories and experiences form the *ethnobiography* (Lewis, 2001) that helps shape a child's emotional sense of who she or he is in the most intimate family and social relationships (Emde, 1989; Stern, 1985). These experiences are summarized in Table 3.1.1.

These same childhood experiences lay the framework for the evolving individual ethnobiographies of parents and for their beliefs about beauty and beliefs about "good" or "nappy" hair in children. An ethnobiography is defined as an individual's developmental experiences related to their ethnic, cultural, and racial groups. Individuals may embrace or reject these experiences and cultural practices as they go through their process of identity development, including ethnic and racial identity development, as adolescents and young adults (McAdoo, 1985; Phinney, 1996; Sellers et al., 1998).

Black parents' individual *ethnobiographies* may influence their everyday interactions with their developing infants and toddlers. Further, this ethnobiography provides the foundation for beliefs about children related to their racial features. A parent's ethnobiography includes childhood experiences of racial acceptance and rejection, socialization into African American culture, current racial and ethnic identity, and the number of internalized stereotypes they believe about Blacks (Lewis, 2001).

The emotionally toxic residue of these early childhood experiences of racial acceptance and rejection may shape brain development (Botbol, 2010; Shore, 2000) and contribute to the template of personality related to self-concept, self-esteem, and ethnic identity (Lewis, 1993). These intense, emotional, race-related experiences serve to expand Rohner's theory of parental acceptance and rejection, and theories of racial socialization.

The emotional responses to these experiences become part of the parent's ethnobiography and subsequently may be projected onto their relationships with their children. A parent who has a poor racial self-concept and intense negative or unresolved emotions associated with the racial features of her child, such as skin color and hair texture, may have difficulty responding to the natural cues of her infant. Behavioral evidence is available from the everyday task of combing hair, a focus of stereotypes, racial pride, and shame (Lewis, 1999). The mother may perform this task in a perfunctory manner or simply assign the task to someone else if she has negative associations with kinky hair and has a young daughter with kinky hair. Thus, assessing an adult's recollection of statements made to them in their childhood in relation to racial factors of skin color, hair texture, and nose and lip size may be an additional index of childhood feelings of acceptance, rejection, or denigration. An adult's self-concept and ethnic and racial identity formation—that is, their ethnobiography—may include the emotional residue of childhood experiences of racial acceptance or rejection and form a flash point for racial and ethnic identity.

To examine the questions posed earlier, this chapter next discusses findings from a series of research studies that used the hair-combing task as a context to videotape the interactions of African American mothers with their daughters. A brief description of the research design of these studies is given. The findings suggest the presence of the intergenerational legacies of the historical trauma of slavery in current interactions of mothers with their daughters.

Table 3.1.1. Development of the Individual Ethnobiographies of African American Women

Childhood Characteristics and Experiences	Adult Ethnobiography
Phenotype of biological racial group	• Phenotype heritage: skin color, hair texture, nose and lip size
• Historical trauma of group—chattel slavery • Status of racial group within the host society	• Cultural practices of strength and survival • Group vulnerabilities to historical trauma response group • Social and economic power associated with minority or dominant status of racial group • Stereotypes or privileges associated with status of group
Acculturation to African American culture	• Degree of socialization into traditions • Beliefs and customs of childcare within family and community
Ethnicity	• Subjective identification with group • Emotional display rules
Family legacies and ethnobiographies: • Family secrets • Physical characteristics of family heroes/scapegoats/ spouse • Family stress (financial, social, marital/partner violence, mental health)	• Quality of attachment to primary caregivers • Birth order • Toxic physical resemblance to specific family members or absent parent
Experiences associated with gender and sex including bullying, same-sex aggression ("mean girls"), sexual abuse, gender-based discrimination	• Post-historical trauma response • Psychological resolution and stages of healing • Personality style and emotional coping responses
Intergenerational legacies of women in family's hair-combing experiences (grandmother, great-grandmother, etc.)	• Internal working model of mother–daughter hair-combing interactions
Racial and gender stereotypes	• Degree of internalization of stereotypes about group—"good hair," "nappyisms," and "colorism"
Childhood experiences of racial acceptance and rejection	• Positive, negative, ambivalence from proximal and distal sources • Perception of hair-combing task

Research Design of the African American Mother–Daughter Interaction Study (AMDIS)

In this research study,[19] the primary goal was to evaluate the efficacy of Hair-Combing Interactions (HCIs) as a viable method to conduct research on African American mother–child interactions. (See Lewis et al., 1999, for a detailed description of this study.) A non-clinical sample (N = 42)[20] of low- to middle-income African American mothers was recruited from four privately owned daycare centers in a metropolitan city of the southern United States. The mothers completed a set of standardized measures to assess their ethnicity, depressed mood, and internalized stereotypes (Taylor & Grundy, 1996). They were videotaped interacting with their toddler daughters while completing three standardized interactional tasks (Chase-Lansdale et al., 1989). These tasks were a graduated teaching task designed to increase frustration in the child, 10 minutes of free play, and the hair-combing task.

Additional data from other, smaller studies was also used for the overall findings reported in this chapter. The current study used mixed methods including standardized questionnaires, focus groups, and careful analysis of over 65 videotaped interactions of African American mothers, who ranged in age from 22 to 46 years and represented a range of socioeconomic statuses from several regions of the United States. The participants in these various studies had daughters ranging in age from six months to 18 years. The ages of the mothers were from 16 to 60 years. Some of the teenaged mothers were residents of a local shelter for homeless adolescents. The adult mothers recruited from daycare centers included women with little education to some with master's degrees. The regions of the country where the studies were conducted included a large urban city in a midwestern state, an urban city in a western state, and a mid-sized city in the southern region of the United States. The professions of the women in the studies ranged from custodian to attorney to psychologist. Several findings emerged from the analysis of 65 videotaped interactions conducted with the hair-combing task.

Summary of Major Findings of Research on the Hair-Combing Task

Two of the findings from the analyses of videotaped HCIs between African American mothers and their daughters suggest there are discrete stages of the hair-combing task as an everyday routine and ritual. In addition, the findings suggest a typology of caregivers' emotionally based perceptions of the task of hair combing. These two findings are labeled *The Relationship-Based Stages of Hair-Combing Interaction and A Typology of Mother Perception of the Hair-Combing Task*.

Based on the videotaped data from the AMDIS study, the entire HCIs lasted from 2 minutes and 10 seconds to 39 minutes and 18 seconds, with an average time of 8–10 minutes to complete the task. The stages of hair combing represent the actions of the mother to prepare for the task, the verbal interactions of the mother with her daughter, and the rituals associated with the task. Each stage was labeled according to the relationship-based goal needed to accomplish the task. The next section will give a brief description of each stage of the interaction. Quotes from the semi-structured interviews of the AMDIS mothers, completed after the videotaped HCIs, will be used to illustrate some of the findings. First, the *Six Stages of Hair-Combing Interaction* will be described.

The Relationship-Based Stages of Hair-Combing Interaction (HCI)

Based on the systematic analysis of all 65 videotapes, distinct stages were identified that occur during the HCIs between African American mothers and their young daughters. Each stage is characterized by the relationship dynamics evident during the videotaped interaction between the mother and the child. In each

---

[19] Funding provided by the National Institute for Mental Health Grant No. 1 R03 MH55736-0, and a Tulane University Summer Grant.
[20] In this sample of 42 mothers, one had a set of twins; thus, they completed questionnaires for their 43 children.

stage, either the mother or the child may dominate the interactions or set the tone of the stage. These stages are labeled according to the primary goal leading to the accomplishment of the hair-combing task. Six distinct stages were identified. The following descriptions will briefly define each stage of the hair-combing task and describe how the interactions that occur during this stage suggest the quality of the relationship that may be remembered by the young daughter.

Stage I: Preparation. Like an artist preparing to paint her canvas and create a work of art to last for all time, the mother organizes the utensils and ointments she will need to accomplish the task of combing hair. During the preparation stage of the hair-combing task, the mother organizes the utensils—such as combs and brushes—and supplies—such as hair ointment, or a water spritzer to moisturize her daughter's dry hair—that she will need as she works. In addition, many Black infants' hair texture may change during these early years, from straight or wavy and easy to manage to a coarse and tightly curled texture that requires more attention, time, and patience to style.

The mother may have a specially designated basket or bag of combs of different sizes, and a variety of brushes, bows, and barrettes. Like an artist, she selects the specific instruments she will need to style her child's hair.

During the interview after the end of the videotaped hair-combing session, the mothers were asked to describe a typical hair-combing session. One mother describes her routine, which involves her daughter's active participation in getting prepared to have her hair combed:

> … I start off with letting her get the comb and the brush. I kinda get her involved in, in getting all of the stuff, you know her bowrettes, um … picking out the color that she may need, that she's gonna wear … and let her get the comb and brush. 'Cause sometimes she'll tell me, I'm not ready to get my hair combed. … Right after we get the bowrettes and everything, the, like I said, you know I work through my procedures of combing, determining how many bowrettes she have, and how many ponytails she'll have for the day, and then all we do is we, we talk about, like I said, her typical day, and you know I, I want her to respond back.

Stage II: Invitation and Negotiation. The major goal of this stage of the HCI is the engagement of the child into the task. During this stage, the mother and child may engage in a process of negotiation and begin what appears to be the dance of their relationship routine. Bowlby (1969) describes the attachment relationship as a partnership that forms over the first few years of the child's life. During this stage of the HCI, the partnership takes on the form of the dancers. The mother extends the invitation to the child to join her in the task. The child, in turn, may accept the invitation or rebuff the mother. At different ages, the mother may require a different set of negotiation skills. As a child's temperament, personality, verbal skills, and cognitive awareness develop, this phase may include negotiations that take on the characteristics of a United Nations peace settlement between warring countries. For older children, the child may express, or the mother may inquire about, style preferences.

Some moms use no negotiation but use a simple command statement, "Come here to get your hair combed." Or, "OK, I'm ready to comb your hair." Or they may give a terse command, "Get over here so I can comb your hair." Some mothers may plead and cajole their reluctant daughters to sit down for the task. Some mothers may resort to threats or bribery.

The length of time a mother spends in this stage of the HCI may be reflective of other aspects of the mother's personality or the child's temperament, or it may simply be a pragmatic reflection of the time the mother has to accomplish the task before performing her other parental duties.

Stage III: Positioning for Proximity. According to attachment theory, as the infant grows and the attachment behavioral system is consolidated, proximity-seeking behaviors of the infant to the mother increase during stressful crises (Bowlby, 1969; Bretherton, 1987). In his formulation of attachment, John Bowlby (1969) identified proximity-seeking behaviors as a critical feature of the developing attachment relationship between mothers and infants. In Bowlby's formulation of proximity behavior, it is the child who seeks closeness to the mother during times of crisis. Ainsworth (1964) first noticed the African children in Uganda who clung to their mother's legs in the presence of the crisis she presented, as a white-skinned stranger, to the young children. They clung to their mothers as a secure base in the face of this unknown threat—the presence of the stranger who looked so different from members of their families and communities. During the hair-combing task, a unique manifestation of this parent–infant attachment behavior is labeled *positional proximity*.

In this relationship dynamic, it is the mother, not the child, who first establishes the proximity she allows her child to have to her as she carries out this task. I propose that this positional proximity of the child to the mother is an important source of physiological regulation distinct to the hair-combing task.

The mother's choice of the degree of proximity available to her child may be based in part on the mother's early experiences of racial acceptance or rejection, and on the levels of internalized stereotypes she has not resolved about natural nappy or kinky hair. The unconscious and unexamined negative stereotypes associated with African-origin hair and dark or light skin may intensify the messages of acceptance or rejection by some Black parents. These early experiences may interfere with the mother's recognition of the infant's normal developmental social and esteem needs for autonomy and exploration.

From an attachment perspective, the child's proximity to the mother during hair combing may provide an additional source of sensory stimulation and an opportunity for physical and emotional availability of the mother to the child (Biringen & Easterbrook, in press; Botbol, 2010).

Analyses of the videotapes revealed distinct groups that could be reliably coded as three different positions of proximity: functional, moderate, and close physical proximity. The infant may sit on her mother's lap, sometimes faced away, and sometimes faced toward her. In the closest position and proximity to the mother, the infant may have the optimal opportunity for multi-sensory stimulation during this task. As the infant increases in age, the positions chosen by the mother also change. Their relative positions during the task may range all the way from the daughter sitting between the mother's legs, for a maximum amount of opportunity for touch, to the child sitting on a chair and the mother standing or sitting in a separate chair, with no contact between their bodies. The degree of proximity between the mother and her infant during the hair-combing task may have determinants in both the mother and the developing child.

Each of these positions is labeled according to the increasing distance between the mother and child. "Functional proximity" is the position with the least amount of contact between the mother and child. In this position, the only type of touch is the contact created between the comb, brush, or hand and the scalp.

This mid-range position provides "moderate contact" between the child and the mother. In this position, the mother may hold a toddler comfortably between her legs as she sits on a chair or on the floor. The child easily sits and moves around in the fulcrum of the mother's legs. Or the child may be seated in a chair between the mother's legs. The child may lean against the mother's knee in a relaxed fashion, with easy physical access to her mother.

The third position is labeled "close proximity." With this degree of proximity, the child sits or lies on her mother's lap throughout the entire hair-combing task. Her body is comfortable and almost molded to the mother's body. The mother and child are both relaxed and move easily with each other throughout the interaction.

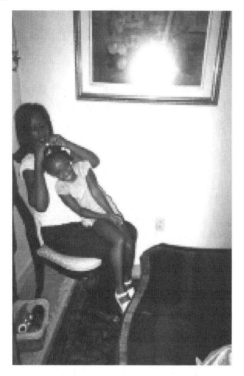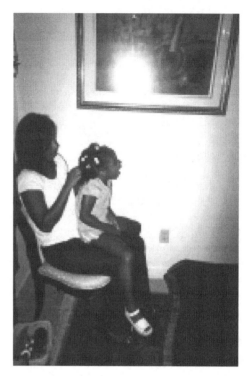

Figure 3.1.1a and b Illustrations of Different Types of Positions for Proximity of Mother to Child During Hair-Combing Interactions

A "mixed" category was also created, in which the child begins the session sitting on the mother's lap but ends up on the floor, through the child's initiation. Figure 3.1.1 presents pictures of each of these proximal positions.

Stage IV: Combing Hair. During this stage of interaction, the actual task of hair combing occurs. The mother parts the hair, spritzes water or uses some other solution to detangle and moisturize the hair, and applies ointments. This stage may last as long as it takes to comb through the hair and achieve a style to the mother's satisfaction. As noted earlier, the entire sequence of the videotaped HCI may last from 2 minutes to 39 minutes, so the time actually spent combing hair may be even shorter.

Talk, touch, and listening interactions while combing hair. During the actual process of hair combing, a rich set of activities occurs that may enhance the neurobiological development of the child and affect the attunement necessary for the synchrony of the mother's sensitive response to the infant's cues (Shore, 2000). These interactions may also serve as the mechanisms for emotionally charged memories of the mother having her hair combed and may compose the future attachment-related memories of the daughter (Botbol, 2010). Verbal interactions between the mother and child may be complex conversations or simple quiet time for both the mother and daughter. The physical touch that occurs during the mechanics of hair combing includes stroking, patting, or pulling on the hair.

When hair is conceptualized as skin (Montagu, 1971), the tactile sensations received during the HCI between an adult and a child may contribute to emotions of warmth and security of attachment. In the videotaped HCI of a mother combing her 13-year-old son's hair in a shelter for homeless women, the other mothers at the shelter observing the video identified a novel behavior by the mother that they termed "cupping." The mother cupped her son's head in her hands as she gently stroked his scalp with a soft brush. The boy's pleasurable physical response was evident as he closed his eyes and enjoyed the physical touch from his mother.

In order to successfully complete the task, it is necessary for the mother to listen to the cues of the child. Is she combing or brushing the hair too hard? Is she holding the hair too tight? Is the child physically tired from sitting in one position too long? This listening and responsiveness during HCI parallels the sensitive maternal behaviors that contribute to secure attachment (Nicholls & Kirkland, 1996).

Stage V: Relaxation/Playtime. After the hair combing commences, an established rhythm is evident as the mother sets about her task. Other activities that involve the mother and daughter interacting, either together or alone, take place. Teaching, singing, reciting ABC's, and chattering about the latest episode of a reality television show all go on during this phase. The verbal interactions may be directed to others who might come in and out of the room. In one dyad, the infant calmly sucks her pacifier as her mother deftly brushes her hair. In another dyad with a five-year-old, the child picks up the nearby toys the mother had placed near her at the outset of the task. The verbal interactions include topics about upcoming family events, the latest news from school, or instructions for behavior.

Stage VI: Ending Rituals. Feelings of accomplishment, pride, or sighs of relief are some of the emotions that may be expressed at the completion of the hair-combing task. The mother may simply state, "I'm done." After placing a final adornment such as a ribbon or barrette, some mothers may turn the child around, give her a final pat of approval with the hand, look her in the eye, and pronounce, "You look pretty!" In this case, the interaction during hair combing as an everyday routine takes on the element of a family ritual.

Hair Combing and Family Rituals.

Family rituals serve as powerful means to organize family life (Fiese, 2006). Steven Wolin and Linda Bennett (1984) describe the function and universality of family rituals. A function of rituals is to provide meaning and organization to the collective lives of a group, in this case a family. Rituals may protect the mental health of practicing members in times of great stress and transition, such as a divorce or natural disaster, and under high-risk conditions such as war (Salloum & Lewis, 2010). Though they vary in significant ways across cultures, rituals are universally practiced across many cultural settings. I propose that the hair-combing task may take on the properties of a ritual in some mother–daughter relationships.

Wolin and Bennett (1984) identified three types of family rituals, distinguished according to the setting in which they are practiced and the degree to which they are connected to cultural practices. *Family celebrations* typically represent culturally determined holidays. Weddings, graduations, Christmas, Passover, and other rites of passage are examples of this type of ritual. The second type of family ritual, *family traditions*, are less culturally specific but link family members together through designated family activities, such as an annual camping trip to Yellowstone National Park that the family has done for decades. Family members are able to strengthen their connections to each other and to identity with their family as a group as they participate. They are able to proclaim: "Every year we travel to Yellowstone Park for our summer vacation; it's our tradition!" The third category of rituals is *patterned routines*. They occur on a regular basis within the family but are the least consciously planned. Examples of patterned routines include dinner times, bedtime routines, or methods of washing and putting away dinner dishes.

Although the hair-combing task may readily be recognized as a routine of daily life, it may not at first appear to fit the definition of a formal family ritual. Fiese (2006) distinguishes family routines from family rituals by looking at the degree of communication involved, the commitment needed, and the level of continuity provided for family members. I argue that the hair-combing task may be characterized as both a family routine and a family ritual. This routine task only becomes a family ritual, with all its attendant psychological power, based on individual differences in the dyad and depending on the mother's approach to the task. Further, it is the ritual aspects of the HCI that may support the developmental needs of the child and ultimately strengthen their attachment relationship and partnership.

A mother who approaches the task in a perfunctory or rigidly prescribed way ("I only do the basics in getting her hair combed," or "I follow a precise order in carrying out this task") would fit the definition of the hair-combing task as just that, a routine task that must be accomplished each day for a variety of personal or perhaps socially sanctioned reasons ("My family will see me as neglectful if I don't comb my daughter's hair every day"). Mothers who practice *hollow rituals* are characterized by a lack of meaningful affect in this dyadic activity with their daughters, emphasizing the routine aspect of family rituals without the symbolic component. The rich elements of a ritual described earlier (the ritual as a means of communication, as an opportunity to reinforce commitment to the family, and as a form of continuity between generations) would not be part of a routine performance of this task by the mother. When the HCI is performed as a routine, only instrumental and functional communication occurs during the task. For example, the mother gives a command for her daughter to "sit still," or the daughter communicates information, such as "ouch, that hurts." Once the hair-combing task is completed, there is little if any afterthought about the task.

However, as a ritual, the hair-combing task provides an opportunity for the mother to communicate with her daughter about any number of topics during the time in which she is combing her hair. The mother and daughter may use the HCI time to have conversations with each other that include inside jokes, symbolic objects, and acts meaningful only to the dyad. For example, during a parent group in the homeless shelter using a program which I designed, *Talk, Touch & Listen While Combing Hair*, each mother is videotaped combing her child's hair. The group then views the videotape and identifies the strengths of the mother and daughter during the interaction. One mother refused to be videotaped combing her daughter's hair. She declared, "That time [during hair combing] is our special time. Not for everyone to see!"

There is sometimes an affective reaction at the conclusion of the activity that may be as subtle as a satisfied sigh, or as obvious as a deep breath of accomplishment. When the HCI is performed as a ritual, the mother demonstrates her commitment to her daughter's appearance and identity as a female member of her family group. Pleasant memories of having her own hair combed may drive the mother's pride and careful performance of this task.

There may be many sources that predict the individual differences in mothers as they accomplish the hair-combing task. These may include the length of time the mothers stay in each of these six phases, the number and type of verbalizations of the mother and child during the task, and their non-verbal styles of communicating during the task. For example, in one dyad, the mother of a 39-month-old daughter had the child hold each utensil and hand them to her as she requested them. These exchanges were the only talk during the otherwise silent interaction.

Another mother describes a very defined, ritualistic end to the hair-combing session during her interview. Asked if she has any routine that she completes with her 25-month-old daughter, she responds:

> Um, yeah, after I comb it, you know, as I'm combing it, I say, "We're gonna make Penny[21] look beautiful today" because she likes that, you know she wants that attention. Um, it's like, so I do that prior to even the complete hairdo is finished. Once it's finished, then I say, "Oh, you look so pretty!" And, um, I tell her, you know, "I'm proud of Penny for allowin' momma to comb her hair. You did a good job." And you know once you praise her, then that makes combing, getting her hair combed a lot easier. Then she looks forward to it.

The next section will discuss the second major finding from the research: individual differences in the mother's perceptions of the task of combing hair and their meaning for her relationship with her daughter.

Typology of Caregiver Perceptions of the Task of Hair-Combing

A sub-sample of 11 of the 42 mothers who participated in the original African American Mother Daughter Interaction Study (AMDIS-I) in 1998 were interviewed after they completed their hair-combing

---

[21] "Penny" is a pseudonym for the participant in the research study.

task. Each mother was asked a series of semi-structured questions about the typicality of the hair-combing session that had just been videotaped, the meaning of the hair-combing task to her, and the experiences she had when getting her hair combed as a child. Open-ended questions about the relationship of the mother with her own mother were asked, such as: *"What memories do you have getting your hair combed?"* The interview addressed the mothers' childhood experiences of racial acceptance and rejection. Some mothers recounted experiences of being either prized or discounted as children, and of negative and painful attributions made to their behavior based solely on their skin color and hair texture. These early race-based experiences were suggestive of later adult attachment styles. Each participant was also given a brief paper-and-pencil test to determine her adult attachment style (Bretherton, 1987), in which she chose which of three attachment categories best described her pattern of close relationships as an adult.

These interviews were transcribed and analyzed using qualitative methods of grounded theory (Glaser & Strauss, 1967) and identification of emergent themes. Relationship themes emerged as an important finding. A typology was developed to describe four types of emotional perception and approach to the hair-combing task seen in the mother. After being labeled, the four styles included one *Connected* and three *Disconnected* types.

Type 1. Connected. In this style, the mother approaches the task as *"A time for bonding."* This behavioral style is one that includes a lot of warmth, talking, listening, and responsiveness to the daughter during hair combing. A 24-year-old single mother of a 22-month-old, with an income of under $10,000, was then a college student who had not yet completed her undergraduate degree. When asked, "What does the activity of combing hair mean to you?" she readily responded, "I think of it as a time for like, um how can I phrase this, bonding, and we talk. Most of the time there's a conversation." Later in the interview, she was asked about the memories she has of getting her hair combed. Smiling, she described in detail her hair-combing experiences with her mother. "It was a long process, I remember that, it as a long process, and I used to like it because I used to like the way my mom combed my hair." This mother checked Pattern C as the adult attachment style that best describes her. The statement reads, "I am comfortable with closeness, and find it relatively easy to trust and depend on others. I don't worry about being hurt by those I'm close to."

Type 2. Disconnected: "It's my duty." This behavioral style is one of efficiency and lack of touch during the hair-combing task. There is little warmth, though the mother may be very responsive to the daughter during the hair-combing task.

To illustrate, a mother who will be referred to by the pseudonym of "Varianna," age 30, reported an income bracket of $31,000–$40,000 in 1997 dollars, which would place her solidly in the middle class. Her daughter, age 48 months at the time of the study, was an only child. Varianna reported her marital status as "living together" (unmarried), and for her education level, she reported that she had received "some college." A practicing Catholic, she reported attending church weekly. Growing up as the oldest of five children, Varianna checked that Pattern A was "very much like me." This pattern was described as "It is important to me to be independent and self-reliant. I'd rather not depend on others or have others depend on me. I am comfortable without a lot of closeness."

During the interview at the end of the videotaped hair-combing session, Varianna was asked about the meaning of the hair-combing activity to her. Her response typifies the dutiful nature of this type of attitude about the task of combing hair. She reported, "Um, it's basically a method of preparedness for the day. It's just another activity. Um, not a lot of thought goes into it. It's routine. We just do it for grooming purposes." She was then asked, "What would it mean if you didn't comb your child's hair?" as a means to determine the cultural value each participant held about the task. Her response was "… with a girl, I always feel they should be neat in appearance at all times. So, that would be a big problem for me if her hair weren't combed."

Type 3. Disconnected: "Let someone else do it." This type of mother typically finds someone else to comb her daughter's hair. An example of one 31-year-old mother's relationship with her own mother is illustrated in the following quote. Her mother had someone else comb her hair throughout her elementary school years, until about fourth or fifth grade.

> The only memories I have of getting my hair combed is that I can remember one plait up here [she points to the top right side of her head], and down here [she points to the bottom left side of her head]. Because my mother never could get the parts straight. She never could part hair, she never could comb hair. And my aunt lived around the corner and I would get up early and run by my aunt's house so she could comb my hair.

When asked in the interview how her experiences of getting her hair combed influence, if at all, how she combs her 24-month-old daughter's hair, she responded, "the only thing I thought was to make it better than what my mother did mine. More than anything I just practiced to make sure that it was always straight and even and that was it."

Another 30-year-old mother of a 29-month-old daughter who was classified in this category described her hair-combing memories from her childhood with dispassion and forgetfulness. "I don't have any bad memories. … I don't have any vivid specific moments where I can say, I know we did this routine at home. I don't remember that." She then revealed that her aunt who lived with them (one of her mother's four sisters) was the primary person who combed her hair as a child. When asked how she felt about someone else combing her hair, she stated, "I can't remember. I don't think I had a problem with it."

Type 4. Disconnected: "I don't know how to do it." This type of mother attempts to comb her daughter's hair but with generally poor results, which characterizes this type of relationship. The mother oftentimes gives up, and the daughter's hair typically looks uncombed. This group of mothers typically experienced the early loss of their mother due to death or had an emotionally unavailable or substance-abusing mother.

Additional findings suggest there were a variety of predictors of individual differences for women, categorized according to their approach to the task. For example, one mother in the study who was placed in this category provided what were concluded as rather "incoherent" and disorganized responses to questions about her early experiences of getting her hair combed. This 24-year-old mother of a three-year-old daughter reported her income as less than $10,000 per year. She had already given her three-year-old daughter a chemical permanent relaxer for her kinky hair. When asked what memories she had of getting her hair combed, her answer seemed inappropriate. She stated:

> Oh, I can recall one day, I didn't want to, um, go to church. Oh, I used to hate putting on them stockings on, so my mom, as a matter of fact, it was Easter I didn't want to go to church. "When was I gonna go serve the lord?" I just was mad at my momma because she bought me an ugly dress. I went into the bathroom, and my curls just fell. "You gonna have me late for church, but you going" and she just flicked my hair like once, and "Baby," she said, "you gonna go the way you look because you messed it up." I didn't like the dress—with polka dots. A lot of people said I looked cute. I looked ugly. It was one of those sailor's polka-dot dress and I thought that was ugly.

Later in the interview, when asked how she felt about the type of hair she had as a small child, she reported, "I always wanted, like, you know, like Creole people? I always wanted to be light [skinned]." Her answers were charged with emotions, but almost invariably were not quite a direct answer to the question.

Implications for Theory, Practice, Interventions, and Policy

Hair-combing interaction (HCI) offers a naturalistic, cultural-practices approach to study African American mother–child relationships (Lewis, 1999; Miller & Goodnow, 1995) that seems especially well-suited for evaluating the interactions between Black mothers and their children. HCI provides the opportunity for touch, verbal interaction, affect exchange, and maternal sensitivity to the child's cues. The task often elicits intense emotions that may influence the evolving parent–child relationship. These intense emotions may contribute in important ways to children's internal working models of current and future relationships. Further, issues of self-efficacy and self-esteem may be developmental outcomes for the daughter that are reinforced during the daily ritual of hair combing.

Mental health practitioners may use the hair-combing task as a clinical tool to assess gender and racial identity development, and as a vehicle for intervention in troubled parent–child relationships (Pinderhughes, 1989; Zeanah et al., 1997). The HCI may facilitate the transmission of a culturally meaningful and positive sense of self. Practitioners may support the mother in teaching her child to manage a variety of emotions and physical behaviors in order to accomplish the HCI task. The HCI may increase the mother's empathic awareness of her child's unique temperament and personality. The findings from research suggest there are individual differences in how a mother approaches the task of combing hair. Further, intergenerational themes may be explored with a mother, using questions related to the mother's memories of her own experiences getting her hair combed. Understanding the internalization of stereotypes and helping individual women recognize how these legacies of the Maafa may seep into their most intimate interactions with their daughters may facilitate the healing needed by African American families. The findings of these studies on HCIs between African American mothers and their children support the proposal that Black populations, arbitrarily classified into a racial category, do not form a homogeneous group. Rather, there are wide within-group differences driven by a large variety of cultural and racial experiences, including early childhood experiences that contribute to individual differences.

The role of race, culture, and ethnicity as sources of variability, or risk, or protection, will enrich our understanding of the complex set of factors that may result in insensitive behavior with young children. More importantly, understanding the role of culture and the racial context in parenting beliefs and behaviors will serve to build on the strengths of Black families and foster the use of culture and ethnicity as protective factors.

Directions for Future Research

These studies need to be replicated with larger samples and rigorous research designs, in a variety of regions of the country, to test the generalizability of these findings. Assessments of developmental outcomes for the daughters and associations with the mother's ethnicity will be the next step. Further, the use of conceptually derived measures of ethnicity using an Afrocentric framework will offer further validity to the role of racial identity (Moore, 1985; Parham, 1989).

The strengths of this study are the strong theoretical framework used to design the study and the use of widely used standardized measures, in addition to new, theoretically derived measures. Another strength of these studies was the use of normative, non-clinical samples of adult African American mothers. This same race sample allowed an exploration of the variability within the group of women, who all self-identified as "Black" or "African American." Future comparisons should be made with other racial groups, to test the robustness of the findings.

Further, studies of variability within groups could look at how childhood messages of racial acceptance and rejection from a variety of people who are important to a developing child (parents, extended family, peers, etc.) predict levels of self-esteem and depression in both women and men.

Findings from research in this area will enrich our understanding of the complex set of factors that result in insensitive behavior with young children and the maltreatment of children. Further, work in this area can address intergenerational legacies, family myths, and secrets that may unconsciously contribute to scapegoating, rejection or neglect, and abuse or conditional acceptance of infants and young children, based on their phenotypic racial characteristics. More importantly, understanding the role of race and ethnicity in parenting beliefs and behaviors will serve to build on the strengths of Black families (Hill, 1972; Norton, 1993). Culture and ethnicity may be used as protective factors and as basis for child abuse prevention programs. Further, understanding the role of ethnicity in children's development may support efforts for children's neurobiological and cognitive growth and learning.

Future studies using the HCI could examine the impact of internalized stereotypes on parental beliefs and behaviors and on a variety of developmental outcomes for children. In addition, the HCI offers an opportunity to study the positive, protective role that racial pride and strong racial identity can play in self-esteem and self-concept formation in young Black children.

There is much potential for use of the hair-combing task as a culturally valid clinical tool and an observational context for research. This methodology will enrich our understanding of normative socioemotional, attachment-related aspects of developing mother–child relationships and the developmental processes of young African American children.

References

Ainsworth, M.D. (1964). Patterns of attachment behavior shown by the infant in interaction with the mother. *Merrill-palmer Quarterly.*

Ainsworth, M. D., Blehar, M. C., Waters, E., & Wall, S. (1978). *Patterns of attachment: A psychological study of the strange situation.* Lawrence Erlbaum.

Alexander, M. (2012). *The new Jim Crow: Mass incarceration in the age of colorblindness.* The New Press.

Benasich, A. A., & Brooks-Gunn, J. (1996). Maternal attitudes and knowledge of child rearing: Associations with family and child outcomes. *Child Development, 67,* 1186–1205.

Bennett, L. (1961). *Before the Mayflower: A history of Black America.* Johnson Publishing.

Biringen, Z., & Easterbrooks, M.A. 2012). The integration of emotional availability (EA) into a

developmental psychopathology framework: Reflections on the special issue and future directions. *Development and Psychopathology, 24*(1), 137-142.

Bluestone, C., & Tamis-LeMonda, C. S. (1999). Correlates of parenting styles in predominantly working- and middle-class African American mothers. *Journal of Marriage and the Family, 61,* 881–893.

Blassingame, J. W. (1972). *The slave community: Plantation life in the ante-bellum South.* Oxford University Press.

Bowlby, J. (1969). *Attachment and loss, vol. 1: Attachment.* Basic Books.

Bowlby, J. (1973). *Attachment and loss, vol. 2: Separation, anxiety and anger.* Basic Books.

Botbol, M. (2010). Towards an integrative neuroscientific and psychodynamic approach to the transmission of attachment. *Journal of Physiology,* 263–271.

Boyd-Franklin, N. (1989). *Black families in therapy: A multi-systems approach.* Guilford.

Branch, C., & Newcombe, N. (1986). Racial attitude development among young Black children as a function of parental attitudes: A longitudinal and cross-sectional study. *Child Development, 57,* 712–721.

Bretherton, I. (1987). New perspectives on attachment relations: Security, communication and internal working models. In J. D. Osofsky (Ed.), *Handbook of infant development* (pp. 1061–1100). Wiley.

Burton, A. L. et al. (2006). *Women's slave narratives.* Dover Publications.

Byrd, A. D., & Tharps, L. (2001). *Hair story: Untangling the roots of Black hair in America.* St. Martin's Press.

Chase-Lansdale, P. L., Brooks-Gunn, J., & Zamsky, E. (1989). *Puzzle task coding manual: Parent–child interactions in young African American multi-generational families* [Unpublished manuscript]. Harris Graduate School of Public Policy Studies, University of Chicago.

Collins, P. H. (1990). Black women and motherhood. In *Black feminist thought: Knowledge, consciousness, and the politics of empowerment* (1st ed.). Unwin Hyman.

Coner-Edwards, A. F., & Edwards, H. E. (1988). Relationship issues and treatment dilemmas for Black middle-class couples. In A. F. Coner-Edwards & J. Spurlock, *Black families in crisis: The middle class* (pp. 227–238). Brunner/Mazel.

Davis, K. B., Daniels, M., & See, L. A. (1998). The psychological effects of skin color on African Americans' self-esteem. *Journal of Human Behavior in the Social Environment*, *1*(2–3), 63–90.

Dill, B. T. (2013). Our mothers' grief: Racial, ethnic women and the maintenance of families. In M. L. Andersen & P. H. Collins (Eds.), *Race, class and gender: An anthology* (pp. 314–326). Wadsworth.

Emde, R. N. (1989). The infant's relationship experience: Developmental and affective aspects. In A. Sameroff & R. N. Emde (Eds.), *Relationship disturbances in early childhood* (pp. 33–51). Basic Books.

Eyerman, R. (2004). Cultural trauma: Slavery and the formation of African American identity. In J. C. Alexander, R. Eyerman, B. Giesen, N. J. Smelser, & P. Sztompka (Eds.), *Cultural trauma and collective identity* (pp. 60–110). University of California.

Fanon, F. (1968). *The wretched of the Earth*. Grove Weidenfeld.

Fiese, B. H. (2006). *Family routines and rituals*. Yale University.

Glaser, B. G., & Strauss, A. L. (1967). *The discovery of grounded theory: Strategies for qualitative research*. Aldine.

Gordon-Reed, A. (1997). *Thomas Jefferson and Sally Hemings: An American controversy*. University of Virginia.

Green, B. A. (1990). Racial socialization as a tool in psychotherapy with African-American children. In L. A. Vargas & J. D. Koss-Chion (Eds.), *Working with culture: Psychotherapy interventions with ethnic minority children and adolescents*. Jossey-Bass.

Grier, W. H., & Cobbs, P. M. (1968). *Black rage*. Basic Books.

Hardy, K. V. (1989). *The psychological residuals of slavery* [Video]. Psychotherapy.net. https://www.psychotherapy.net/video/psychological-residuals-slavery-kenneth-hardy

Harris, J., & Johnson, P. (Eds.). (2001). *Tenderheaded: A comb-bending collection of hair stories*. Pocket Books.

Healey, J. F. (2012). *Race, ethnicity, gender, and class: The sociology of group conflict and change*. Sage.

Hill, R. (1972). *The strengths of Black families*. Emerson Hall.

Jewell, K. S. (2003). *Survival of the African American family: The institutional impact of U.S. social policy*. Praeger.

Jones, C., & Shorter-Gooden, K. (2003). *Shifting: The double lives of Black women in America*. HarperCollins.

Lewis, M. L. (1993). *Factors influencing the interpretation of emotions in infants by African American mothers* [Unpublished dissertation]. University of Colorado, Boulder.

Lewis, M. L. (1999). The hair-combing task: A new paradigm for research with African American mothers and daughters. *American Journal of Orthopsychiatry*, *69*, 1–11.

Lewis, M. L. (2000a). The cultural context of infant mental health: The developmental niche of infant–caregiver relationships. In C. H. Zeanah (Ed.), *Infant mental health* (2nd ed., pp. 91–107). Guilford.

Lewis, M. L. (2000b). The emotional lives of African American parents and their interpretations of emotions of Infants. In J. D. Osofsky and H. Fitzgerald (Eds.), *The world association of infant mental health handbook* (pp. 59–63). Guilford.

Lewis, M. L. (2001, April). *The childhood experiences of racial acceptance and rejection scale: Development, reliability and validity* [Poster presentation]. Biennial Meeting of the Society for Research in Child Development, Minneapolis.

Lewis, M. L., Diaz, L., Taylor, S., & Turnage, B. (1999, April). *Ethnicity predicts parenting styles in African American mothers* [Poster presentation]. Biennial Meeting for the Society for Research in Child Development, Albuquerque.

Lewis, M. L., Turnage, B., Taylor S. T., & Green, J. (2008). *Nappy-haired ghosts in the nursery: Intergenerational legacies of hair texture and skin tone and African American mother–child proximity during the hair-combing task* [Unpublished manuscript]. Tulane University, New Orleans.

MacDorman, M. F., & Mathews, T. J. (2008). *Recent trends in infant mortality in the United States* (NCHS data brief, No. 9). U.S. Department of Health and Human Services, Centers for Disease Control and Prevention, National Center for Health Statistics.

McAdoo, H. P. (1985). Racial attitude and self-concept of young Black children over time. In H. P. McAdoo (Ed.), *Black children*: *Social, educational, and parental environments* (2nd ed., pp. 213–242). Sage.

Meyers, S. A. (1999). Mothering in context: Ecological determinants of parent behavior. *Merrill-Palmer Quarterly*, *45*, 332–357.

Middlemiss, W. (2003). Brief report: Poverty, stress, and support: Patterns of parenting behavior among lower-income Black and lower-income White mothers. *Infant and Child Development*, *12*, 293–300.

Miller, P. J., & Goodnow, J. J. (1995). Cultural practices: Toward an integration of culture and development. In J. J. Goodnow, P. J. Miller, & F. Kessel (Eds.), *Cultural practices as contexts for development* (pp. 5–16). Jossey-Bass.

Montagu, A. (1971). *Touching: The human significance of the skin*. Harper & Row.

Moore, E. G. (1985). Ethnicity as a variable in child development. In M. B. Spencer & G. K. Brookins (Eds.), *Beginnings: The social and affective development of black children* (pp. 101–115). Lawrence Erlbaum.

Murry, V. M., & Brody, G. (2002). Racial socialization processes in single-mother families: Linking maternal racial identity, parenting, and racial socialization in rural, single-mother families with child self-worth and self-regulation. In H. P. McAdoo (Ed.), *Black children*: *Social, educational, and parental environments* (2nd ed., pp. 97–118). Sage.

Murray, C.B. & Mandara, J. (2002). Racial identity development in African American children: Cognitive and experiential antecedents. In H. P. McAdoo (Ed.), *Black children*: *Social, educational, and parental environments* (2nd ed.). Sage.

Murry, V. M., Bynum, M. S., Brody, G. H., Willert, A., & Stephens, D. (2001). African American single mothers and children in context: A review of studies on risk and resilience. *Clinical Child and Family Psychology Review*, *4*(2), 133–155.

Nicholls, A., & Kirkland, J. (1996). Maternal sensitivity: A review of attachment literature definitions. *Early Child Development and Care*, *120*, 55–65.

Norton, D. (1993). Diversity, early socialization, and temporal development: The dual perspective revisited. *Social Work*, *38*, 82–90.

Nsamenang, B. (1992). *Human development in cultural context*. Sage.

Okazawa-Rey, M., Robinson, T., & Ward, J. V. (1987). Black women and the politics of skin color and hair. *Women & Therapy*, *6*(1), 89–102. http://search.proquest.com/docview/216253869?accountid=10913

Parham, T. A. (1989). Cycles of psychological Nigrescence. *The Counseling Psychologist*, *17*, 187–226.

Peters, M. (2002). Racial socialization of young Black children. In H. P. McAdoo (Ed.), *Black children*: *Social, educational, and parental environments* (2ⁿᵈ ed.). Sage.

Phinney, J. S. (1996). When we talk about American ethnic groups, what do we mean? *American Psychologist*, *51*, 918–927.

Pinderhughes, E. (1989). *Understanding race, ethnicity, and power: The key to efficacy in clinical practice*. The Free Press.

Porter, C. P. (1991). Social reasons for skin tone preferences of Black school-age children. *American Journal of Orthopsychiatry*, *61*(1), 149–154.

Rankin, F. E. (1988). Identification of responses to emotional stress. In A. F. Coner-Edwards & J. Spurlock, *Black families in crisis: The middle class* (pp. 157–162). Brunner/Mazel.

Rohner, R. P. (1975). *They love me, they love me not: A worldwide study of the effects of parental acceptance and rejection*. HRAF Press.

Rohner, R. P. (1986). *The warmth dimension: Foundations of parental acceptance–rejection theory*. Sage.

Rooks, N. (2001). Wearing your race wrong: Hair, drama, and politics of representation for African American women at play on a battlefield. In M. Bennet & V. D. Dickerson (Eds.), *Recovering the Black female body: Self-representations by African American women* (pp. 279–283). Rutgers University Press.

Rosser, P. L., & Randolph, S. M. (1991). *Black American infants: The Howard University normative study*. Howard University, Washington, DC.

Russell, K., Wilson, M., & Hall, R. E. (1992). *The color complex: The politics of skin color among African Americans*. Harcourt Brace Jovanovich.

Stampp, K. (1956). *The peculiar institution: Slavery in the ante-bellum South*. Vintage.

St. Julien, A. (1987). *Colored Creole: Color conflict and confusion in New Orleans*. Originally printed as "Colored Creoles of New Orleans," ca. 1972, in *Freeing the Spirit*, a quarterly magazine sponsored by the National Office of Black Catholics.

Sellers, R. M., Smith, M. A., Shelton, J. N., Rowley, S. A. J., & Chavous, T. M. (1998). Multidimensional model of racial identity: A reconceptualization of African American racial identity. *Personality and Social Psychology Review*, *2*(1), 18–39.

Salloum, A., & Lewis, M. L. (2010). Parent–child coping and service needs post-Hurricane Katrina. *Journal of Traumatology*, *16*(1), 31–41.

Shore, A. (2000). Attachment and the regulation of the right brain. *Attachment and Human Development*, *2*(1), 23–47.

Spencer, M. B., & Markstrom-Adams, C. (1990). Identity processes among racial and ethnic minority children in America. *Child Development, 61*(2), 290–310.

Stern, D. N. (1985). The representation of relational patterns: Developmental considerations. In A. Sameroff & R. N. Emde (Eds.), *Relationship disturbances in early childhood* (pp. 52–69). Basic Books.

Straight, S. (2000, December). Talking heads: With this simple ritual we braid our lives together. *Reader's Digest*, 59–64.

Stuckey, S. (1987). *Slave culture: Nationalist theory & the foundations of Black America.* Oxford University Press.

Sue, D. W. (2010). Micro aggressions, marginality and oppression: An introduction. In D. W. Sue (Ed.), *Micro aggressions and marginality: Manifestation, dynamics, and impact* (pp. 3–24). Wiley & Sons.

Taylor, Y. (Ed.). (2005). *Growing up in slavery: Stories of young slaves as told by themselves.* Lawrence Hill Books.

Taylor, J., & Grundy, C. (1996). Measuring Black internalization of White stereotypes about African Americans: The Nadanolitization scale. In R. L. Jones (Ed.), *Handbook of tests and measurements for Black populations* (Vol. 2, pp. 217–226). Cobb & Henry.

Thoits, P. (1989). The sociology of emotions. *Annual Review of Sociology, 15*, 317–342.

Thornton, M. C. (1997). Strategies of racial socialization among Black parents. In R. J. Taylor, J. S. Jackson, & L. M. Chatters (Eds.), *Family life in Black America* (pp. 201–215). Sage.

Tyler, B. M. (1990). Black hairstyles: Cultural and socio-political implications. *Western Journal of Black Studies, 14*(4), 235–247.

Williams, D. R., Neighbors, H. W., & Jackson, J. S. (2003). Racial/ethnic discrimination and health: Findings from community studies. *American Journal of Public Health, 93*, 200–208.

Wolin, S.J. & Bennett, L.A. (1984). Family rituals. *Family Processes, 23,* 401-420.

Yeh, M., Hough, R. L., McCabe, K., Lau, A., & Garland, A. (2004). Parental beliefs about the causes of child problems: Exploring racial/ethnic patterns. *Journal of the American Academy of Child & Adolescent Psychiatry, 43*, 605–612.

Zeanah, C. H., Boris, N., Heller, S. S., Hinshaw, S., Larrieu, J., Lewis, M., Rovaris, J. M., & Valliere, J. (1997). Relationship assessment in infant mental health. *Infant Mental Health Journal, 18*(2), 182–197.

Reading 4.2. Marking the Coming of Age

Raising Our Daughters Through the Sacred and Ancient Practice of Age Grade Rites of Passage

Neico "Nkoso" Slater-Sa-Ra

Introduction

African-centered rites of passage are a process of *Sankofa*, returning to that which was lost. Under normal, natural conditions/circumstances, African girls, women, and elders develop in a holistic, thorough age grade cycle of learning, lessons, tasks, and tests as markers for each stage of development to a full person. The Maafa ripped African women from their cultural-spiritual source and disconnected African women from the wellspring of this critical cultural-spiritual process. African American women, however, have continued to strive for cultural, racial, and spiritual authenticity in an oppressive reality through the process of Sankofa.

The critical process of Sankofa allows African women to go back and return to their sacred way. *Rites of passage* provide direction for social development and are one of many cultural-spiritual processes that allow African women to replenish their spirit and reclaim their cultural-spiritual identity. The process of Sankofa, through implementing African-centered rites of passage, challenges African women to put their spiritual power to proper use.

Contextualization of Rites of Passage

African cosmological, axiological, ontological, and epistemological knowledge is critical in assuaging the psychological, social, economic, health, and identity problems that Africans across the Diaspora face. Africology, Black Psychology, and African-centered theory speak to the critical need to create, study, and utilize African knowledge to Deconstruct-Reconstruct-Construct (DRC) perspectives of the African in the world (Banks, 1982; Hotep, 2008). Understanding the historic and contemporary science of African coping, resistance, and role manifestation through the African worldview lens allows us to understand how the African has persevered in the face of unimaginable atrocities throughout modern times.

The African in America exists in comfortable captivity (Hotep, 2008), embracing European cultural reality while repudiating traditional African axiology, epistemology, and cosmology. This reality often leads to sickness and limited and poor psychosocial development. Divergence from traditional personhood development is cited by Akanbi and Jekayinfa (2016) as a reason for a decrease in ethical and moral behavior across the African Diaspora. To address issues of poor development, immorality, and unethical behavior, Akanbi and Jekayinfa (2016) suggest that Africans increase the utilization of the traditional models of personhood development through the implementation of rites of passage.

Rites of passage processes must be specifically situated within the cultural context of the initiate (Afrik, 1993; Akoto, 1992; Goggins, 2012; Nobles, 2013). For the African man, woman, and child, Africentric rites of passage must be implemented with a theoretical model consistent with the African worldview. The Africentric perspective refers to a Black perspective, a theoretical worldview centered in Africa as a historical point of generation (Asante, 1987; Floyd, 2011; Hill, 1999). Additionally, Afrik (1993),

Akoto (1992), Goggins (1996), and Nobles (2013) detail a rites of passage process that socially integrates African American students, which must be congruent with the African worldview perspective and operate clearly as African-centered.

The African worldview expresses the nature of the African as communal, cooperative, and interdependent. Several scholars' analyses (Diop, 1974; Kambon, 1998; Nobles, 1976) reveal a dichotomy between the African and European worldviews. Their work frames these two worldviews as irreconcilable cultural realities containing diametrically different conceptions of the spirit of beings. The African worldview lens contextualizes the roles, responsibilities, and structure of African existence that are critical to understand in conceptualizing the current and historic reality of the state of the African.

The African worldview establishes the lens through which the African should view the world. Throughout the Diaspora, Africans were dispossessed from their traditions and were required to accept the culture, religion, mores, and folkways of non-Africans. In this vein, African people lost some traditions; however, they held on tightly to others. African people have begun to reclaim the traditions of rites of passage in their various communities in the past hundred years.

African-centered rites of passage are a ritualized process whereby members of a particular society engage in African, cultural-centered, age set development (from birth to death) with the community, to cultivate and develop the initiate into a whole person. African-centered rites of passage are concerned with the development of the whole person, through understanding age grade responsibilities in each critical stage of development. African men and women have gendered role responsibilities in the community to ensure its optimal functioning and the survival of the nation state.

The intricacies of African-centered rites of passage reflect placing Africa at the center and utilizing tools from the African Diaspora to understand societal roles and to implement the rites of passage process. Warfield-Coppock (1992) suggests that rites of passage can be considered a social-cultural "inoculation" process that facilitates healthy, African-centered development among African American newborns, youth, adults, and elders to protect them against the ravages of a racist, sexist, capitalist and oppressive society.

Scholars Akoto (1992), Shujaa (1994), and Warfield-Coppock (1992) additionally state that African-centered rites of passage mentally, physically, and emotionally prepare African American youth for active resistance and struggle against the seductive lure of the American way while training them to embrace the core components of the African worldview and African survival thrust.

"Rites of passage shaped who I am through the emphasis on embracing my identity as an African woman in America, encouraging me to not conform to the beauty standards of Eurocentric figures and rather accept natural skin, hair, and style without fear of judgement."

—A.B., 2012 Rites of passage graduate, Southern United States

---

The *implementation and practice of rites of passage* have their origins in ancient Africa; however, they are not a phenomenon unique to the continent of Africa. The Jewish, Mexican, Samoan, and Polynesian peoples go through rites of passage processes. Thus, implementation of age set development in rites of passage is consistent in cultures across the world; however, it may look a little different or very significantly different, depending on the culture and region. The purposes and goals of rites of passage vary, based on regions and the type of rites processes.

The *purpose of African-centered rites of passage* is education for whole-person development. Typically, Western models of education differ from the African-centered models. The African historic model of education emphasized practical and spiritual development to teach personhood. Conversely, Western models of education primarily teach learning for the acquisition of employment. Morality, emotional maturity, and behavioral and spiritual development are explicitly removed from the American process of education, while they are emphasized in African and African-centered processes of education.

Rites of passage ritually celebrate the various stages of transformations in the life cycle (Ezenweke, 2016) and are an intensive educational tool that develops the person across the life span. African-centered rites of passage are a deeply structured, well maintained, ancient knowledge of history, codes of behavior, and rituals passed on from generation to generation. Traditional African rites of passage implement rituals as a formal procedure for transitioning into the next stage of life (Ezenweke, 2016).

Warfield-Coppock (1990) delineates traditional African models of rites of passage, utilizing *five stages of development across the life span*: birth, puberty, marriage, eldership, and death. The traditional African spiritual *life cycle of birth* represents a passage from the spiritual world to the physical world. Secondarily, and perhaps most significantly, the *puberty rites* mark the passage from childhood to adulthood. This stage emphasizes the education and training needed to become a full member and contributor, as an adult in the family, to community, society, and the nation state. This stage of development comes with a critical responsibility to contribute to the whole development of community and to maintain a flourishing existence. Third, the *rite of marriage* is the passage from individual to communal interdependent life.

The next stage of development in the life cycle is that of the *transition to elderhood*. The elder stage is a passage into a stage of wisdom. This stage affirms the significant work the adult has done throughout their life as comprehensive progression toward developing into a whole person. By making significant contributions to the society, family, and nation and fulfilling the individual spiritual mission, the adult is able to transition to elder.

African Proverb

An elder sitting on the ground can see further than a child even if s/he sits atop a tree.

This proverb speaks to the necessity of youth understanding the role of the elder in the community.

The final stage of development explicated by Warfield-Coppock (1990) is the *transition to death or ancestor.* This stage is the return to the spiritual world and is highly significant in African cosmology and ontology because it reflects the cultural manifestation of a completion of a life cycle. At this stage we seek to understand if the person's life reflected a fulfillment of their life mission and development into whole personhood.

Table 4.2.1. Transitional Stages of Development Across the Life Span

Stage	Age	Developmental Process	Skill/Item Task
Birth	Birth to 1 year	Secure the time on earth	• Naming • Rituals of beading to secure • Physical body in earthly realm
Pre-Puberty	6–12 years	Identity development as youth	• Teaching of culture and norms • Roles, Iwa character development • Preparation for rites
Puberty	12–16 years	Initiation into womanhood/manhood	• Womanhood training • Intense personhood and identity development • Lineage understanding
Marriage	Adulthood	Family building	• Marital training • Parenting in context of community
Elderhood	50–69 years	Embodiment of full personhood	• Impart wisdom to youth • Model age-appropriate behavior
Ancestralhood	70+ years	Death ritual initiation to ancestorhood	• Transition to ancestral realm, where spiritual work continues

This table additionally details the developmental process rituals and specific tasks at each stage.

Nation-states in Africa that are relevant to America and that facilitate rites of passage are: the Yorùbá (Ezenweke, 2016), Akan, and Mende. Among the Yorùbá and Ibo of Nigeria, the Akan of Ghana, and the Mende of Sierra Leone, rites of passage are cultural-spiritual rituals and ceremonies that highlight transitions into different phases of life. Specific to Africa is the development of personhood as "becoming." The development and maturation of a whole person is a foundation for rites of passage. The concept *Omoluabi* denotes a full person and is the standard, which determines the morality and immorality of an act in Yorùbá society in Africa (Akanbi & Jekayinfa, 2016). The process of African-centered rites of passage expressed in Omoluabi is to teach whole, moral person development through *Iwa*, or "character," development (Akanbi & Jekayinfa, 2016) along with teaching the embodiment of truth, justice, righteousness, propriety, reciprocity, harmony, balance, and order. The Yorùbá concept of *Eniyan* (a person) expresses that in order to be a whole person, each individual must process through and *ritualize* each age set development with specific ceremonies and actions that signify understanding of that particular developmental stage. In the Yorùbá perspective of personhood development, the emphasis is on Omoluabi —a moral, fully functioning human being who is a blessing to her family and a positive contributor to society (Akanbi & Jekayinfa, 2016).

The goal of ancient African rites of passage is to emphasize morality, personhood, and character development; these goals are similar to those of African American rites of passage. African American rites of passage, however, should additionally address the unique challenges of cultural oppression and being removed from the African nation state, and should explicitly deal with African cultural identity.

Rites of Passage Program Components

The components of rites of passage programs are specific to the nature and type of rites process. Birth, puberty, marriage, elder, and ancestral rites all have significantly different processes, depending on the phase of development and the type of program. Warfield-Coppock (1990) refers to the rituals of rites as symbolic acts that convey stability, ease of transition, groundedness, balance, and order.

African Proverb

A child who is not raised by her mother is raised by the world.

This proverb speaks to the necessity of female rites of passage.

Rites of Passage Programmatic Models

Warfield-Coppock (1992) details that African American rite of passage programs have functioned in the United States for several decades, and that the numbers are steadily increasing. More than 25 years later, rites of passage programs continue to be prevalent in communities, schools, and churches and have made their way to college campuses. Culturally conscious rites of passage realize that African American youth experience unique circumstances in their lives due to their African/African American background (Floyd, 2011).

Contemporary Examples of Puberty Rites

Puberty rites or adolescent rites of passage, throughout the world, have been documented by anthropologists, sociologists, historians, philosophers, and religious scholars (Boone, 1986; Diallo & Holt, 1989; Eliade, 1958; van Gennep, 1960; Warfield-Coppock, 1992). The adolescent rite of passage is a supervised, developmental, and educational process whose goal is to assist young people in attaining knowledge and accepting the responsibilities and privileges and duties of being an adult member of society (Warfield-Coppock, 1992).

Several researchers offer components of the traditional puberty rites that suggest the process begins with separation from the community (Delaney, 1995; van Gennep, 1960). Warfield-Coppock (1992) distinguishes the components most congruent with the African-centered model of rites of passage explicated by Eliade (1958): 1) preparation of the sacred area in which the initiates' education takes place; 2) separation of the initiates from the familiar (especially the mother); 3. a symbol of initiatory death; 4) the presentation of ordeals and challenges to the initiate; and 5) initiator rebirth or return to the community (Eliade, 1958).

Rites of passage prepare young girls, women, and elders for the: practical skills of "homestead skill development" (cooking, cleaning, childrearing, industry development, growing food), emotional development, strength testing, comrade/unity, elder respect, ancestral identity, personal identity, and knowledge of women of the world. Additional activities central to most rites of passage programs in Africa and the African Diaspora include a spiritual inculcation, rituals of libations and prayer, establishment of the ritual area through cleaning it out, and the utilization of African and African American proverbs to communicate and understand better the African ethos, beads, symbolic talisman, and cultural adornment. Puberty rites signify the specific age set development into adulthood. Oftentimes puberty rites will reflect all the significant things occurring during puberty—the start of the menses for girls, for example.

African Proverb

A girl may have as many clothes as her mother but never as many rags.

This proverb speaks to the relationship between mother and daughter as well as the necessity of clear understanding of roles based on age and relationship.

African Worldview

The author of this chapter suggests seven core steps to the African-centered rites of passage process for females:

1. Sequestering: The secret and quiet removal of the initiate from the home into an unknown environment.

2. Ordeal–Rituals: Specific, crafted events to challenge the initiate to struggle in an unfamiliar place.

3. Induction: The ritual process of commitment to the rite of passage—symbolically and spiritually binding the initiate to progress and development.

4. Intensive Development: Holistic education and study of African cosmological, ontological, epistemological, and axiological praxis.

5. Rituals: Sacred processes of ancestral cultural-spiritual knowledge taught to the initiate.

6. Seclusion: Restricted engagement symbolizing death of the old and spiritual embodiment of the new, with concentrated learning of the new role in the society (Ezenweke, 2016).

7. Outdooring (Community Presentation)—Final Step: an affirmation by community that the initiate has effectively completed all tasks associated with the process.

The African American adolescent rites of passage process is aimed at instilling a strong positive sense of self and achievement in African American youth and returning a sense of empowerment to African American families and communities (Warfield-Coppock, 1992). While the education process of the African-centered rites of passage addresses whole-person development, it most critically engages ancestral work.

African Proverb

Where you sit when you are old, shows where you stood in your youth.

This proverb explicates the necessity of elder work toward full personhood in order to fit the criteria to transition to ancestor.

Rites of passage work is not for the faint of heart, as it is hardcore ancestral work for Africans in America. *Ancestral work* in an African-centered rites of passage program addresses the issues of the family and the challenges of survival, while encouraging the building of a specific mission towards betterment, self-development, and becoming a whole person. This effort addresses lineage trauma by clarifying the intergenerational issues (drug use, violence, sexual abuse, cultural misorientation) and blessings (academic and artistic intelligence, physical strength, cultural-spiritual intergenerational knowledge) of the family clan, while working to increase understanding of, and address the challenges manifesting in, the present time. Simultaneously, the initiate in an African-centered rite of passage learns the lineage blessings and utilizes those blessings to understand who they are as individuals and who they ought to be.

The family ancestral research and lineage work is a critical component of personhood development and of the rites of passage process. This lineage work is not limited to puberty rites and is also seen as critical in other developmental stages.

I am able to understand the challenges of my family clan, my lineage, and myself through African glasses. Rites of passage helped me work with my family to begin to deal with issues. I am forever grateful for doing Rites of Passage as an adult; I wish I had done it younger. Maybe I could've dealt with some of these issues earlier.

—N. W. C., Southern United States

The requirements for this work include the development of a community where elders, adults, and youth know or learn their role and practice it. Rites additionally require a detailed structure in which the family community organization establishes a working society to develop into. A rites of passage process implies passing into something—in the case of African and most other societies, all members pass into key developmental categories based on their age set. Ideally, there are well-established organizations, institutions, and societies for the initiate to pass into. For example, Mende female graduates become Sande women (Boone, 1986).

Contemporary Examples

Across the United States, rites of passage programs have been and are being implemented to give guidance and development in the age set. Several programs and processes across the United States are known for the development of age grade rites in general and puberty rites in specific. Some major cities across the United States that maintain rites of passage include Washington DC, Oakland, Richmond, Chicago, New York, Atlanta, Philadelphia, and Tallahassee. While African American models of rites of passage lead to improvements in academics, self-esteem, and self-concept (Monges, 1999; Warfield-Coppock, 1992), traditional African, Yorùbá rites facilitate improvement in the critical development of the age set, increasing understanding of roles and moral development (Ezenweke, 2016). Addressing roles and moral development is also consistent with African-centered rites facilitated in America.

African Proverb

A wise woman who knows proverbs reconciles difficulties.

This proverb speaks to the critical importance of understanding proverbs in women's work.

Women's Work

Women's work reflects healing, emotionally nurturing, strengthening, pushing, and challenging the child and/or young adult woman, encouraging her to develop in both difficult and easy places. Both historic and contemporary models of rites of passage suffer from issues of opposition to their relevance. Often, traditional and modern African-centered rites of passage are considered inferior because they embrace an Africentric, matriarchal, non-Christian perspective. As a result, we must continue to challenge this dismissive notion in the commitment to this work, while embracing comprehensive perspectives of rites that may even come out of the church.

Women's work challenges girls/women to unearth their authentic selves under the layers of oppression, abuse, violence, image oppression, and familial disruption, and to undergo *decorticating*, or stripping down, to reveal who they really are. This strength-building happens in the arduous and spiritual moments. This work is intensive and critical, as it strives to awaken a dormant consciousness that has been dulled by negative media images of Black girls as video vixens, and by the "othering" of African women as only welfare moms.

Rites of passage work *creates a space for healing the trauma of abuse and is designed to prevent future abuse.* African-centered rites of passage *challenge negative images of self, instill an African aesthetic, and promote a positive self-image.* Additionally, African-centered rites of passage *actualize a cultural-spiritual space* where an African woman can contribute to those who come after her, disallowing her sister, daughter or cousin to go through the struggles of not knowing who she is. The female initiate is encouraged to show strength and to face the fears of a society of double negatives: being Black/African and being a woman. In this instance, strength represents the embodiment of fortitude, courage, tenacity, and vulnerability, which is counter to the narrative of the myth of the Strong Black Woman. Women's rites of passage improve self-efficacy and self-esteem developed through education and empowerment (Harvey & Hill, 2004).

Character (Iwa) development, self-concept improvement, and cultural understanding are accomplished through the work of rites of passage: the work of prayer, the work of sacrifice, the work of study, the work of learning, the work of healing, the work of singing and dancing, the work of calling on African gods and ancestors, the work of knowing what it takes to become a whole person.

Rites of passage are celebrated through ceremonies of initiation honoring natural developmental stages, connecting individuals to self, others, environment, and morality (Grimes, 2000). The success of these programs continues to pave the way for women's work and for a stronger African female self-identity.

African Proverb

Advise and counsel her; if she does not listen, let adversity teach her.

This proverb speaks to learning from ancient African wisdom to improve functionality in modernity.

The Necessity of Rites of Passage for Modernity

American culture highlights issues young African American women face in modernity, including the question of identity. Erikson (1968) suggests that the primary task of adolescence is the search for and development of identity, answering the question, "Who am I?" Answering the question of identity requires understanding and developing processes to address the issues of modernity. Nobles (2013) articulates that raising our children requires well thought-out strategies, procedures, and processes, intentionally designed to result in spirit beings characterized by confidence, competence, a full sense of responsibility, and unlimited potentiality. Essentially, to address the primary task of adolescence, we must use strategic tools such as rites of passage.

The knowledge of self and culture is crucial for these young people to successfully address the problems they face in today's world, and programs oriented toward achieving knowledge of self provide alternatives. Rites of passage programs for African American girls are essential to promote healthy development and self-confidence at a time when their self-esteem may be waning based on developmental challenges, negative media images, and social pressures (Green, 2013).

Research on rites of passage as education (Akoto, 1992; Shujaa, 1994; Warfield-Coppock, 1990) articulates the following key reasons for instituting rites programs in modern society: increasing cultural awareness; encouraging and prompting academic success; providing an alternative to, or disengaging youth from, violence, crime, and drugs; decreasing school dropout; enhancing cultural identity; and dissuading youngsters from early sexual activity. Warfield-Coppock (1990) identifies rites of passage as providing an additional support network, improving knowledge of the state of African Americans, and countering the effects of low socioeconomic status.

Rites of passage processes have significant psychological implications—increasing emotional maturity and coping. Working to identify and heal lineage trauma provides additional psychological coping and improves familial relationships while increasing understanding of ancestral contributions to the family clan. The rites' initiate is able to learn techniques for how to solve problems, build relationships, resolve conflict, and decrease conflict (Warfield-Coppock, 1992). Rites' graduates often experience improvements in their concepts of the self (Monges, 1999; Warfield-Coppock, 1992). After completion of the rites of passage process, knowledge of the self, self-esteem, self-worth, and self-concept improve. Rites of passage strengthen: appropriate socialization with peers, sense of maleness and femaleness, relationships with elders and with members of the opposite sex, interest in attending college or vocational school, and responsible attitudes and behaviors (Floyd, 2011; Warfield-Coppock, 1992).

In modernity, interactive applications of African wisdom traditions, history, culture, philosophy, and deep thought illuminate, inform, and develop both the spiritness of the person (Iwa/personal character) and their environmental character (Nobles, 2013). The design of modern rites programs should re-establish and/or restore harmony and optimal human functioning (Nobles, 2013). Essential to the task of womanhood growth and development is the requirement that the developmental process be congruent with African and African American philosophy, beliefs, culture, and customs (Nobles, 2013).

In conclusion, African-centered rites of passage are an ancient process utilized in modern times to continue the process of personhood development and society development in communities of Africa and abroad. The imperative of continued implementation of rites of passage is affirmed in the success of the process and in the impact each age grade rite has in maintaining the society in which the people exist. Graduates of rites of passage programs should be able to assert that we are who we ought to be. Prior to completion of the process, the initiate should be able to provide concrete (historic and modern) examples of how African women have coped with, resisted, and implemented roles as mothers, sisters, and activists, to manifest all that they can be.

References

Afrik, M. H. T. (1993). *The future of Afrikan American education: A practitioners view.* Council of Independent Black Institutions.

Akanbi, G., & Jekayinfa, A. (2016). Reviving the African culture of 'Omoluabi' in the Yoruba race as a means of adding value to Education in Nigeria. *International Journal of Modern Education Research, 3*(3), 13–19.

Akoto, K. A. (1992). *Nationbuilding: Theory & practice in African-centered education.* Pan African World Institute.

Asante, M. K. (1987). *The Afrocentric idea.* Temple University Press.

Banks, W. (1982). Deconstruction falsification: Foundations of a critical method in Black psychology. In E. Jones & S. Korchin (Eds.), *Minority mental health.* Praeger Press.

Boone, S. A. (1986). *The radiance from the waters: Ideas of feminine beauty in Mende art.* Yale University Press.

Delaney, G. H. (1995). Rites of passage in adolescence. *Adolescence, 30*(120), 891–897.

Diallo, Y., & Holt, M. (1989). *The healing drum: African wisdom te*achings. Destiny Books.

Diop, C. A. (1974). *The African origin of civilization: Myth or reality* (M. Cook, Trans., 1st ed.). [Translation of sections of *Antériorité des civilisations négres* and *Nations nègres et culture*]. Lawrence Hill.

Eliade, M. (1958). *Rites and symbols of initiation: The mysteries of birth and rebirth.* Harper & Row.

Erikson, E. (1968). *Identity and the life cycle: A reissue.* W. W. Norton.

Ezenweke, E. (2016). Rites of passage and sustainable development in traditional Africa: Reflections for a contemporary society. *Journal of Religion and Human Relations, 8*(2).

Floyd, D. C. (2011). Impact evaluation of a rites of passage mentoring program [Dissertation]. Olivet Nazarene University.

Goggins, L., II. (2012). *Bringing the light into a new day: African-centered rites of passage* (2nd ed.). Saint Rest Publications.

Green, J. (2013, Summer). Rites of passage: The "Rite to success" for African American Girls. *Black Child Journal.* National Rites of Passage Institute.

Grimes, R. (2000). *Deeply into the bone: Re-inventing rites of passage.* University of California Press.

Harvey, A., & Hill, R. (2004). Africentric youth and family rites of passage program: Promoting resilience among at-risk African American youth. *Social* Work, *49*(1), 65–74.

Hill, P. (1999). *Rites of passage, forward to the past: Adolescent rites of passage.* East End Neighborhood House.

Hotep, U. (2008). Intellectual maroons: Architects of African sovereignty. *The Journal of Pan African Studies, 2*(5).

Kambon, K. K. K. (1998). *African/Black psychology in the American context: An African-centered approach.* Nubian Nation Publications.

Monges, M. (1999). Candace rites of passage program: The cultural context as an empowerment tool. *Journal of Black Studies, 29*(6).

Nobles, W. (2013). Our sacred responsibility: The raising up of the Black child. *Black Child Journal.* National Rites of Passage Institute.

Sarpong, P. (1977). *Girls' nubility rites in Ashanti* Ghana Publishing Corp.

Shujaa, M. (1994). *Too much schooling, too little education: A paradox of Black life in White societies.* African World Press.

van Gennep, A. (1960). *The rites of passage.* The University of Chicago Press.

Warfield-Coppock, N. (1990). *Afrocentric theory and applications: Adolescent rites of passage.* Baobab Associates Inc.

Warfield-Coppock, N. (1992). The rites of passage movement: A resurgence of African-centered practice for socializing African American youth. *Journal of Negro Education, 61*(4), 471–482.

Reading 4.3. From Mourning to Action

African American Women's Grief, Pain, and Activism

Shareefah Al'Uqdah and Frances Adomako

On July 26, 2016, nine African American women appeared in a semicircle on stage at the National Democratic Conference (Ross, 2016). Despite hailing from various parts of the United States, they are inextricably linked by their children being "killed under questionable circumstances directly connected to their race" (Ross, 2016, p. 1). They coined the term "Mothers of the Movement" to represent their reason for involvement in social justice activism (Drabold, 2016). During their speech, they relayed their grief regarding their children and how their grief inspired their activism in the movement for Black lives (Ross, 2016). Furthermore, they discussed the important role grief played in their transformation from mourners to social justice activists (Ross, 2016). While these women represent a new wave of African American mothers who turn to activism following the death of a child in questionable race-related circumstances, they are not the first. Mamie Bradley Till may have been the first widely known African American woman social activist following the unconscionable murder of her son, Emmett Till. In August of 1955, 14-year-old Emmett traveled from Chicago to Mississippi to visit his uncle (Pool, 2015). About a week into his visit, Emmett went to the corner store with his cousins, where he allegedly "talked fresh" or "whistled" at a White woman, Carolyn Bryant (Pool, 2015). Four days later, four men appeared at Emmett's residence in the middle of the night, dragged Emmett to their car at gunpoint, tortured, and killed him (Pool, 2015). He was found three days later with a cotton gin fan tied around his neck in the Tallahatchie River (Pool, 2015). Mamie Bradley Till, in an act of civil disobedience and social justice, insisted her son have an open casket at his funeral.

The four-day memorial service that followed allowed press and major television network coverage of Emmett's open casket. During the next month, tens of thousands of people viewed young Emmett's body (Pool, 2015). By showing the world the violence enacted upon her son and her subsequent grief, she contributed significantly not only to the civil rights movement but also to the sensitivity of the White majority (Pool, 2015). Following the acquittal of her son's murderers, the National Association for the Advancement of Colored People (NAACP) recruited Mamie to speak about her son's life and his brutal death. She also became a spokesperson for the unequal treatment of African Americans in the south.

Mamie Bradley Till and the Mothers of the Movement highlight the often unspoken experience of African American motherhood that involves trauma and violence enacted upon themselves and their children, and their subsequent experience of grief. These experiences relay a need for an exploration into the impact of grief on the lives of African American mothers. Significantly, African American women remain underrepresented in bereavement literature and research (Piazza-Bonin, Neimeyer, Burke, McDevitt-Murphy, & Young, 2015). In an effort to address the paucity of literature in this area and explore grief within the African American community, we will discuss African American mothers, their grief, and their grief-inspired activism. We also provide recommendations on how practitioners working with African American mothers can promote activism.

Motherhood in the African American Community

Motherhood is a significant, yet complex role in the African American com- munity (Collins, 2000). In the African American community, motherhood involves not only bloodmothers, those related biologically to the child/ren, but also othermothers, those who assist in the child-rearing responsibilities of non-biological child/ren

(Collins, 2000). Community othermothers, those women who may not be involved in direct child-rearing tasks but who feel connected to all African American children and responsible for their general well-being are also included as mothers (Collins, 2000). In fulfilling this pivotal role in the community, African American mothers contend with sexism and racism, which increase their experiences of discrimination (Collins, 2000).

Often these experiences may combine to oppress African American women (hooks, 2000) and subject them to various forms of trauma. Researchers suggest that African American women are more likely to experience intimate partner abuse than any other ethnic group (Al'Uqdah, Maxwell, & Hill, 2016; Oliver, 2000). They disproportionately reside in low-income neighborhoods, thus increasing their risk of being a victim to community violence (Al'Uqdah, Grant, Malone, McGee, & Toldson, 2015). Moreover, the leading causes of death for African American children between the ages of 1 and 19 are homicide and unin- tentional injuries (Centers for Disease Control, 2015). Thus, African American mothers may experience direct trauma as victims of abuse and crime. They may also experience grief and trauma from the unexpected loss of their child. These compounding traumatic experiences may contribute to the unique experiences of grief faced by African American mothers (Laurie & Neimeyer, 2008).

Burdened by oppressive forces that contribute to various forms of trauma, African American mothers' experience of grief and loss is substantial. Goldsmith, Morrison, Vanderwerker, and Prigerson (2008) found that African Americans have a higher prevalence rate of complicated grief than their Caucasian counterparts. For African American mothers, the loss of a child from community violence can lead to complicated grief, posttraumatic stress disorder (PTSD), and prolonged depression (Bailey, Hannays-King, Clarke, Lester, & Velasco, 2013). Moreover, Piazza-Bonin et al. (2015) asserted that being a mother of a deceased child might prolong the grieving process and increase the likelihood of developing complicated grief. Thus, the death of a child may leave African American mothers struggling to cope and adapt.

Examining Grief in the African American Community

While grief is a universal process that aids in people healing from the loss of a loved one (Piazza-Bonin et al., 2015), researchers indicated that people fundamentally change following the death of a significant loved one (Lebel & Ronel, 2009). One process that may promote change and healing in African American mothers is meaning making. Meaning making is a process by which mourners reevaluate their self-identity, heal, and move toward increased psychological well-being (Bailey et al., 2013). The meaning-making process following the loss of a child is an active cognitive and emotional process (Bailey et al., 2013). It is a critical step in not only minimalizing pre- and post- loss conflicts that may occur, but also in making sense of one's reality during bereavement (Neimeyer, 2000). Through meaning making, African American mothers may become more politically active. Such increased political activity following the loss of a loved one may be termed political mourning (Cheng, 2000). Political mourning involves mobilizing and utilizing the grief of ordinary citizens as a political tool of social change (Cheng, 2000).

Political mourning asserts that grief and its public expression has social and political implications for the individual and for the marginalized group (Cheng, 2000). Specifically, for African American mothers, grief is transformed into grievance such that their mourning becomes public and therefore displayed for the benefit of the larger society (Cheng, 2000). A mother's grief can transform the marginalized, racialized, and oppressed person "from an object bearing grief to being a subject speaking grievance" (Cheng, 2000, p.174). Moving grief to the public sphere to be shared by others allows for agency. This sense of agency is significant in the healing process of African American mothers.

Healing, Empowerment, and Activism

Another important aspect of healing is empowerment (Goodman, Fauci, Sullivan, DiGiovanni, & Wilson, 2016). Empowerment is feelings of personal control over all facets of one's life (Samuels-Dennis, Bailey, Killian, & Ray, 2013). Christens (2012) linked a sense of empowerment to increased civic participation and engagement and reduce depressive symptoms. Furthermore, for African Americans, research has indicated that empowering oneself and others may increase psychological adaptation, function, self-esteem, and achievement (Carter, 1991; Parham & Helms, 1985; Searle & Ward, 1990). Due to the unique sociocultural and sociopolitical position of African American mothers, activism allows African American mothers to enact their sense of agency, experience empowerment, and effect social change.

Activism may increase psychological well-being, in particular, in the domains of empowerment and social support (Ramirez-Valles, Fergus, Reisen, Poppen, & Zea, 2005; Samuels-Dennis et al., 2013). Activism provides social support in the form of linking individuals to their larger community or society (Brown & Brown, 2003). Thus, through activism, African American mothers are able to move toward psychological empowerment (Brown & Brown, 2003). While in some instances activism may produce burnout, research suggests that it may also aid in the resiliency of participants dealing with various stressors (e.g., discrimination, community violence, loss, etc.) and their negative outcomes through social support (Ramirez-Valles et al., 2005). African American women's activism arises from their race, ethnicity, class, sexual orientation, and community of residence (Naples, 1992). Therefore, involvement in social justice activism can lead to empowerment and social support.

African American mothers' social justice activism connects their role as a mother within and outside of their home. Martin Luther King, Jr., in a letter to Septima Clark, a prominent civil rights activist and mother, expressed that the struggle of the "southern negro woman is to realize her role as a mother while fulfilling her forced position as community teacher, intuitive fighter for human rights and leader of her unlettered and disillusioned people" (Robnett, 1996). As explained by hooks (2000), "Black women's struggle against racism infuses their mothering practices inside and outside the home" (p. 41). Thus, for African American mothers who have lost children, mothering the community is a form of social justice activism. Therefore, the home and community is not only a site of resistance, but also a place where "our beings, our blackness, our love for one another is necessary resistance" (hooks, 2000; p. 46).

For many African American women, this form of resistance aids their heal- ing process and simultaneously strengthens the broader African American community. An important component of Mamie Bradley Till's healing process was her involvement in the civil rights movement. For her and for many mothers who lose their children to violence, activism becomes a way in which they can make meaning of their lives and role as mothers (Bailey et al., 2013). Moreover, grieving African American mothers have transformed the education, social, political, and economic welfare of their communities (Gutierrez & Mattis, 2014). Many African American women, especially mothers, strengthened the civil rights movement. Mothers such as Mamie Bradley Till, Myrlie Evars, Fannie Lou Hammer, Corretta Scott-King, Betty Shabazz, and now the Mothers of the Movement have worked to reform communities. Additionally, African American mothers have founded organizations, such as Mothers in Charge, following the loss of their child (Mothers in Charge, 2016).

Many grieving African American mothers learn that prosocial involvement in the African American social movements involves supporting or engaging in behaviors that benefit African American communities (Naples, 2012). This includes engaging or volunteering through political participation, organizational membership, mentoring, or other social justice behaviors that enhance and advance the lives of African Americans and their families (Bailey et al., 2013; hooks, 2000; Naples, 2012). Through these activities, an inherent strength emerges as they realize that in order to cope they must not only survive themselves but fight for others to do the same (Naples, 2012).

Recommendations for Promoting Social Justice Activism in African American Women

Examining ways that African American mothers heal from loss is important. Current research is limited regarding experiences of African Americans' grief and their unique ways of healing (Piazza-Bonin et al., 2015). Research may want to examine how activism and other forms of active coping may help African American mothers heal from traumatic loss. We recommend that research exploring African American mothers acknowledge and recognize African American mothers' sociopolitical location, the historical significance of their struggle for liberation, and experiences with trauma and loss. Thus, the use of longitudinal studies, qualitative studies, and possible group comparison studies may accurately assess African American mothers' experiences of grief and the ways in which they heal.

Despite the paucity of research, there is a long history of African American women's involvement in activism. Given this and the role of activism in their healing from trauma, individuals working with African American women can foster activism in African American women prior to the loss of a child. A way in which activism could be fostered is through the implementation of social issues courses in high school and middle school. A social issue course could highlight various critical social issues affecting the local, national, and international communities. Students can learn about the various forms of activism and then develop and engage in activism activities. Additionally, community service initiatives can include involvement in social activist activities as credit for community service hours. School districts should also allow students to be representatives on local school boards and other governance boards.

Community and religious organizations that work with African American women may want to connect with activist groups (or local members) to host informational sessions. Such sessions will educate attendees about ways they can be involved in social activism and how social activism may improve their current conditions. Schools can also include activism as a part of their parent organizations (e.g., Parent Teachers Organization). Parents can be encouraged to advocate for their needs both within their school and within their local community. School districts, city councils, and other local governance boards should allow parents to be members in order to promote political and social activism. Research asserts that including information in children's doctor appointments is an easy way to inform parents about relevant information (Kogan et al., 2004). Thus, pediatrician offices could include social justice magazines, pamphlets, or leaflets. Pediatricians that work with predominately African American or Latino clients may want to post dates of local social justice organizations meetings and events. Pediatricians may also suggest activism as a way to address health concerns that relate to systemic oppressive forces. For example, patients who develop asthma due to poor living conditions (i.e., mold exposure, roach infestation, etc.) may be advised to join or start a tenant association to address the issue.

Broadly, grief and loss can be a tumultuous experience. For African American women, their healing may be further complicated, given their experiences of racism and sexism. Because social activism is related to several positive benefits that include increased social support, positive self-identity, and healthy psychological adjustment following traumatic experiences, we assert that social activism can be used as a healing tool for grieving African American mothers. Given its positive outcomes, activism should become an integral part in daily lives of women, especially women who are disproportionately impacted by negative social forces (i.e., racism, sexism, and classism).

Notes on Contributors

Shareefah Al'Uqdah, PhD, is an assistant professor and Director of Training for the Howard University Counseling Psychology program. She earned her BA and MA from North Carolina Central University. She is an avid researcher of issues that affect urban families, which includes intimate partner abuse, community violence, and parenting behaviors. Dr. Al'Uqdah is also committed to exploring the intersectionality of the African American Muslim identity. Through her research, she hopes to increase awareness and skills related to working with African American Muslims and African American families.

Frances Adomako, MA, is a PhD student in the Counseling Psychology program at Howard University. She earned her BA from St. John's University and her MEd from Teachers College of Columbia University. Her research focuses on activism, racial identity, and psychological well-being. Currently, her work aims to explore the relationship between activism and the mental health of African Americans. Through scholarship, she not only hopes to gain further insight into the way in which activism is marginalized in the academy, but also develop and understand activism as an intervention in healing from trauma.

References

Al'Uqdah, S. N., Grant, S., Malone, C. M., McGee, T., & Toldson, I. A. (2015). Impact of community violence on parenting behaviors and children's outcomes. *The Journal of Negro Education*, *84*(3), 428–441.

Al'Uqdah, S. N., Maxwell, C., & Hill, N. (2016). Intimate partner violence in the African American community: Risk, theory, and interventions. *Journal of Family Violence*, *31*(7), 877–884.

Bailey, A., Hannays-King, C., Clarke, J., Lester, E., & Velasco, D. (2013). Black mothers' cognitive process of finding meaning and building resilience after loss of a child to gun violence. *British Journal of Social Work*, *43*, 336–354.

Brown, R. K., & Brown, R. E. (2003). Faith and works: Church-based social capital resourcesand African American political activism. *Social Forces*, *82*(2), 617–641.

Carter, R. T. (1991). Racial identity attitudes and psychological functioning. *Journal of Multicultural Counseling and Development*, *19*(3), 105–114.

Centers for Disease Control. (2015). Leading causes of death by age group, black males—United States, 2011. Retrieved September 28, 2017, from https://www.cdc.gov/healthequity/lcod/men/2011/LCODBlackmales2011.pdf

Cheng, A. A. (2000). *The melancholy of race: Psychoanalysis, assimilation, and hidden grief*. New York, NY: Oxford University Press.

Christens, B. D. (2012). Toward relational empowerment. *American Journal of Community Psychology*, *50*(1–2), 114–128.

Collins, P. H. (2000). *Black feminist thought: Knowledge, consciousness, and the politics of empowerment*. New York, NY: Routledge.

Drabold, W. (2016). Meet the mothers of the movement speaking at the Democratic Convention. *Time Magazine*. Retrieved September 22, 2017, from http://time.com/4423920/dnc-mothers-movement-speakers/

Goldsmith, B., Morrison, R. S., Vanderwerker, L. C., & Prigerson, H. G. (2008). Elevated ratesof prolonged grief disorder in African Americans. *Death Studies*, *32*(4), 352–365.

Goodman, L. A., Fauci, J. E., Sullivan, C. M., DiGiovanni, C. D., & Wilson, J. M. (2016). Domestic violence survivors' empowerment and mental health: Exploring the role of the alliance with advocates. *American Journal of Orthopsychiatry*, *86*(3), 286–296. doi:10.1037/ ort0000137

Gutierrez, I. A., & Mattis, J. S. (2014). Factors predicting volunteer engagement among urban-residing African American women. *Journal of Black Studies*, *45*(7), 599–619.

hooks, B. (2000). *Feminist theory: From margin to center* (2nd ed.). London, England: Pluto Press.

Kogan, M. D., Schuster, M. A., Yu, S. M., Park, C. H., Olson, L. M., Inkelas, M., … Halfon, N.(2004). Routine assessment of family and community health risks: Parent views and what they receive. *Pediatrics*, *113*(6), 1934–1943.

Laurie, A., & Neimeyer, R. A. (2008). African Americans in bereavement: Grief as a function of ethnicity. *Omega-Journal of Death and Dying*, *57*(2), 173–193.

Lebel, U., & Ronel, N. (2009). The emotional reengineering of loss: On the grief-anger-socialaction continuum. *Political Psychology*, *30*(5), 669–691.

Mothers in Charge. (2016). Retrieved from http://www.mothersincharge.org/

Naples, N. A. (1992). Activist mothering: Cross-generational continuity in the communitywork of women from low-income urban neighborhoods. *Gender & Society*, *6*(3), 441–463. Naples, N. (Ed.). (2012). *Community activism and feminist politics: Organizing across race, class, and gender*. New York: Routledge.

Neimeyer, R. A. (2000). Searching for the meaning of meaning: Grief therapy and the processof reconstruction. *Death Studies*, *24*(6), 541–558.

Oliver, W. (2000). Preventing domestic violence in the African American community: The rationale for popular culture interventions. *Violence against Women*, *6*(5), 533–549.

Parham, T. A., & Helms, J. E. (1985). Relation of racial identity attitudes to self-actualizationand affective states of Black students. *Journal of Counseling Psychology*, *32*(3), 431.

Piazza-Bonin, E., Neimeyer, R. A., Burke, L. A., McDevitt-Murphy, M. E., & Young, A. (2015). Disenfranchised grief following African American homicide loss: An inductive case study. *OMEGA-Journal of Death and Dying*, *70*(4), 404–427.

Pool, H. (2015). Mourning Emmett Till. *Law, Culture and the Humanities*, *11*(3), 414–444.

Ramirez-Valles, J., Fergus, S., Reisen, C. A., Poppen, P. J., & Zea, M. C. (2005). Confrontingstigma: Community involvement and psychological well-being among HIV-positive Latino gay men. *Hispanic Journal of Behavioral Sciences*, *27*(1), 101–119.

Robnett, B. (1996). African-American women in the civil rights movement, 1954-1965: Gender, leadership, and micromobilization. *American Journal of Sociology*, *101*(6), 1661–1693.

Ross, J. (2016). Nine *grieving mothers came to the Democratic National Convention stage*. *Washington Post*. Retrieved from: http://www.washingtonpost.com/news/the-fix/wp/2016/07/26/nine-grieving-mothers-came-to-the-democratic-national-convention-stage/?utm_term=.0a57b31c25bb

Samuels-Dennis, J., Bailey, A., Killian, K., & Ray, S. L. (2013). The mediating effects of empowerment, interpersonal conflict, and social support on the Violence–PTSD processamong single mothers. *Canadian Journal of Community Mental Health*, *32*(1), 109–124.

Searle, W., & Ward, C. (1990). The prediction of psychological and sociocultural adjustmentduring cross-cultural transitions. *International Journal of Intercultural Relations*, *14*(4), 449–464.

Reading 4.4. A Vital Cohesion

African American Women as Activists in the Family and Society

Tameka Bradley Hobbs

The goal of this chapter is to explore a range of activism instituted by women of African heritage in America from the colonial to modern eras, as they have experienced the unique intersection of race, gender, and class. The term "activism" has necessarily been interpreted very broadly and ranges from the more visible "community" activities that were public and organized for the benefit of the larger community, to examples of personal activism and individual agency. During most of the 300 years that they have lived on these shores, African American women have faced limited choices in meeting challenges. Because they lacked power, resources, or standing, it is necessary to dissect the individual choices of Black women to gain insight into the larger, collective struggles they faced in American society by examining the lives and circumstances of exemplary Black women, as well as groups of unnamed activists. Several questions will guide the investigation: How have women of African heritage in America crafted lives as mothers, partners, daughters, sisters, employees, and entrepreneurs, despite the limitations and stereotypes? What tools have Black women used to successfully navigate the intersection of racism, sexism, and classism? What survival skills and resources have they used to aid their communities in the face of oppressive conditions?

Incidents in the Lives of Enslaved Women: Black Women in Early America

From the beginning of the Transatlantic Slave Trade, or Maafa, not only have African women experienced abuse and exploitation, but their bodies became the foundation upon which the institution of slavery was constructed in the 17th century in North America. Scholars estimate that there were over 100,000 African women brought to colonial North America, who, by 1860, were responsible for birthing an enslaved population of nearly four million (Klein, 2010, pp. 135–160).

In addition to undergoing the traumatic disruption of life in the western and central regions of the African continent wrought by the increasing demands of the slave trade, African women suffered the humiliation of sexual exploitation. They endured the physical trauma of being captured, shackled, and marched long distances to the Atlantic coast, only to then have their humanity reduced to a commodity as they were inspected, sold, and branded. Upon boarding the slave ships for the months-long journey to the so-called New World, Africans experienced horrendously unsanitary conditions, but it was also on these voyages that European sailors subjected African women to forcible rape and sexual abuse.

As slavery grew in North America, the bodies of Black women became the terrain upon which racial domination and White hegemony were built, as evidenced by laws defining legal status by birth, the destabilization of the Black family unit, and the categorization of Black female labor. As the usefulness and affordability of enslaved Africans outpaced that of English indentured servants, legislators in the British colonies gradually created laws that made it increasingly difficult for Blacks to achieve social and civic equality with Whites. These steps would transform the labor regime from temporary and non-discriminatory into a racialized system of perpetual oppression. In 1643, Virginians made a seemingly subtle reclassification of "titheable" labor, for the first time taxing the labor of Black women, and not White women, in the same way that the labor of White and Black men was already calculated (Brown, 1996, pp. 116–118). Such laws served fiscal purposes, but they also established a segregated femaleness that separated White "ladies" from Black "women," a cultural dynamic that would govern the status and condition of Black women for the next 300 years. Later, in 1662, the Virginia General Assembly instituted the legal principle of *partus sequitur ventrem*, which determined the legal status of an infant according to the status of its mother, not its father, contrary to English custom and to the customs of many other countries in the world. This sinister twist of cultural norms ensured a perpetual supply of enslaved labor. Further, the legislature outlawed interracial marriage and began punishing interracial sex, in order to forestall the thorny issue of mixed-raced progeny by cutting off Black men's access to the White female body.

As the system of slavery became entrenched in North America, Black women's value, in the words of historian Jacquelyn Jones (1985), was derived from their abilities as producers and reproducers. While the experience of Black men in America is often central to explorations of African American people during slavery, it is important to remember that the circumstances of enslavement experienced by Black women— the defeminization, the exploitation of the Black female body, and the disruption and disfigurement of Black family structure—burdened Black women differently than Black men. Black women received none of the respect given to English women. Gender differences, save those of pregnancy, were given little consideration. Black women worked alongside their men as field hands, where the sole differentiation was physical strength, not gender. Whether in the tobacco or rice fields, or processing indigo and later cotton, women hoed, chopped, plowed, weeded, and harvested the same as men; on average, seven of eight enslaved women worked in the fields. Many of the others served in the homes of their masters, attending to a seemingly never-ending cycle of duties—cooking, cleaning, laundering, nursing, scrubbing, changing linens, setting tables, and sewing, to name a few. There was little relief from the constant demands of the master's family. Contrary to the belief about the relative ease of life in the "big house," enslaved women in these positions faced numerous challenges, not the least of which was sexual harassment and abuse. Additionally, female house servants suffered the fiery tempers of their White mistresses, frequently becoming the targets of their violent temper tantrums and sadistic whims (Gaspar & Hine, 1996; Jennifer Morgan, 2011, pp. 144–165; Schwalm, 1997).

Despite the harsh demands placed on them as workers, enslaved Black women, as well as men, possessed survival skills that have been greatly underappreciated. Black women's work did not end when they put down their hoes at the end of the day. They returned to their cabins to prepare meals for their families, to embrace their children and their mates, and to find fellowship with the other members of the enslaved community. Enslaved men and women shared the goal of providing for their families and provided guidance and support for each other and their children. Together with Black men, Black women worked to create and sustain families. In some ways, the experience of bondage equalized the importance of women's contributions to the household, and this yielded an increased level of respect for them within the family and the enslaved community. This more balanced level of gender relations in the slave cabin, and the mutual respect it engendered, differed greatly from the male domination and sexism that was a part of Western culture and would have ramifications for centuries to come as Black and White women reevaluated their station in American society.

The condition of the Black family during slavery, especially the relationship between enslaved men and women, has been the subject of heated scholarly debate. Intellectual sparks flew in the aftermath of Daniel Moynihan's (1965) publication *The Negro Family in America: The Case for National Action*. A sociologist at Harvard University and advisor for then-President Lyndon B. Johnson, Moynihan described the Black family as "a tangle of pathology," tracing its dysfunction back to slavery. In his view, bondage created a matriarchal culture among African Americans that undermined the institution of marriage and the necessary influence of Black men in the home, relegating them to subordination or absenteeism in the family. While Moynihan's assertions were widely accepted as accurate, a number of Black intellectuals and scholars disagreed. A historian, Herbert Gutman, provided the most useful rebuttal to Moynihan in his book, *The Black Family During Slavery and Freedom, 1750–1925*. Through careful analysis of slave censuses, plantation records, and marriage records created during and after the U.S. Civil War, Gutman documented the remarkable persistence of a two-parent, nuclear family structure among the enslaved population, despite the forces continually pulling them apart. In some cases, the rates of two-parent homes were as high as 75%. Twenty years after Reconstruction, some areas in the South averaged a two-parent home rate of 61% among African American married couples (Gutman, 1976, pp. 10–15, 427).

Despite the reality of bondage, Black women defied the expectations of White society through legal and intellectual endeavors. Though they were victimized and often voiceless, in that there are scant records reflecting the personal thoughts and feelings of women in bondage, there are examples of enslaved women challenging the system of slavery. They sought freedom—defined in many ways—for themselves and their family members. Elizabeth Freeman offers one such example. Inspired by the rhetoric of the American Revolution, "Mum Bett," as she was also known, sued for her freedom after learning of the terms of the new Massachusetts state constitution. "I heard that paper read yesterday, that says, 'all men are born equal, and that every man has a right to freedom,'" Freeman noted. "I am not a dumb critter; won't the law give me my freedom?" Her owner, Colonel Ashley, had been active in the American Revolution, and he frequently held meetings in his home where the men discussed the abuse and "slavery" they experienced at the hands of the British government. Certainly this would have sparked Freeman to consider her own plight, and reminded her of the physical abuse she'd received at the hands of her mistress. After securing counsel, Freeman and another enslaved man by the name of Brom successfully challenged their bondage and won their liberty in 1781, paving the way for complete emancipation of all enslaved people in Massachusetts. Hers was one of the earliest such successful suits during the Revolutionary period, and one that was based on the legal principle of human rights, as opposed to individual genealogy or circumstance (Banks, 1993; Zilversmit, 1968).

The continued territorial expansion of the United States, and the concomitant increased arable land, most notably after the Louisiana Purchase in 1803 and the conflict with Mexico in 1848, fueled increasing demand for enslaved labor in the Deep South and the West. Since the nation legally banned its participation in the Transatlantic Slave Trade in 1808, this meant that Black women became the main "suppliers" of new Black bodies that would join the ranks of the laboring class. The subsequent growth of a massive domestic slave trade would have tragic consequences for enslaved women and their families, as demand for enslaved labor increased with the territorial expansion of the United States. It became increasingly common for families to be broken up at the auction block. Faced with the increasing threat of separation through sale, enslaved women initiated and participated in more dramatic expressions of rebellion, ranging from running away to committing homicide and suicide.

Recognizing that valuable terrain of their own bodies, as valued by their owners, some enslaved women attempted to "reclaim" themselves from bondage, demanding, sometimes viciously, some level of authority over their lives and those of their children. These challenges are evidenced in the life of Margaret Garner. In the winter of 1859, Margaret Garner and her husband Robert fled the Kentucky plantation of their respective owners with her four children in tow, along with Robert's parents. Under cover of night, the group traveled over land in a stolen sled and then walked across the frozen Ohio River to freedom. Upon discovering the whereabouts of the family in Cincinnati, Margaret's owner, Colonel Archibald Grimes, went to retrieve his "property," bringing slave catchers along with him. Faced with the prospect of returning to bondage, Margaret killed her two-year-old daughter, Mary, nearly decapitating her with a butcher knife. She then turned to her three remaining children, intending to give them the same treatment, but was overpowered by slave catchers before she could execute her intentions. Margaret later claimed that her intent was to kill all of her children, and then herself, to prevent them from being re-enslaved.

The reverberations of Margaret Garner's act shook the nation. The elements of this unimaginable tragedy captured the attention of the reading and movie-going public in the 20th century, first in 1987 with Toni Morrison's Pulitzer Prize-winning novel, *Beloved*, and again in 1999, when the novel was transformed into a film by the same name starring Oprah Winfrey. At the time of the event, pro-slavery advocates pointed to Garner's actions as proof positive of the animalistic nature of enslaved people, and the lack of maternal feeling among Black mothers. These claims supported the narrative of slavery as a "positive good," a benevolent and paternalistic institution that protected African Americans from their innately primitive behaviors. The truth, however, is a tragic combination of fear and pain, forged in the fires of bondage, and yielding a nearly incomprehensible pathological behavior in this one slave woman.

Contemporary newspaper reports help to untangle some of the threads of Garner's experience under slavery. The murdered child, Mary, was described as very light-skinned and possessing a "rare beauty." Her other siblings—Samuel, Priscilla, and an unnamed girl who was in utero during the escape and trial—were described as very fair-skinned or mulatto, with the exception of Garner's oldest son, Thomas, who was born shortly after her union with Robert. Robert Garner was noted to have very dark skin. While there is not conclusive evidence, it would not be beyond the realm of possibility to assert that Colonel Grimes, the only White male with a consistent presence at the Maplewood plantation where Garner lived, was indeed the father of the younger children. Other details from the press indicate that Grimes was ill-tempered and abusive to the enslaved people on his plantation. Margaret Garner bore a scar along her forehead and cheek. When asked about the source, she simply said it was made by a White man. Additionally, in her interviews with reporters, Garner cited abuse by Grimes as the reason for their escape attempt. While these data are circumstantial, they do paint a clearer picture of what might have been on Margaret Garner's mind when she assaulted her children. More than just an individual incident, her act of infanticide was "a masterstroke of rebellion against the whole patriarchal system of American slavery." Garner's pathological actions embody a significant pillar of the African American female experience during slavery—a woman's inability to control her fate and her body, or those of her children (Weisenburger, 1998).

Forcible rape was a near-constant reality for enslaved women. Harriet Jacobs, who had formerly been enslaved in North Carolina and took extreme measures to escape the undesired sexual advances of her owner, testified to the high price that accompanied beauty for an enslaved woman: "If God has bestowed beauty upon her, it will prove her greatest curse. That which commands admiration in the white woman only hastens the degradation of the female slave" (Jacobs, 1861/1987, p. 46). One southern White woman, despite the material benefits reaped from slavery, claimed that

> [o]urs is a monstrous system, a wrong and iniquity. Like the patriarchs of old, our men live all in one house with their wives and their concubines; and the mulattos one sees in every family partly resemble the white children. Any lady is ready to tell you who is the father of all the mulatto children in everybody's household but her own. Those, she seems to think, drop from the clouds. (Chesnut, 1905)

"The Moses of Her People": Activist Harriet Tubman

While Margaret Garner's example encapsulates many of the tragedies faced by enslaved women, the remarkable life of Harriet Tubman offers a divergent illustration. Born Araminta Ross around 1821 in Dorchester County, Maryland, Tubman experienced the severity of enslaved life in her youth, from poor diet, sickness, strenuous work, routine physical abuse, and the sale of family members. After the death of her owner in 1849, fearing that she would be among the slaves sold to settle her master's debts, Ross fled north of Philadelphia. She changed her first name to Harriet, her mother's name, and retained the last name of her free husband, John Tubman, although he opted to remain behind in Maryland. Within a year, she made another journey into Maryland to rescue other family members. Over the next decade, Harriet Tubman made an average of two trips into the South each year, mainly to Virginia and Maryland, leading an average of ten people out of bondage with each voyage. She made it her goal to free all of her family members, including her elderly parents. Earning the nickname "Moses," in reference to the biblical hero of the Old Testament, Tubman was famous for her bravery, determination, and a mystical sense of cunning that she credited to the voice of God. Other workers on the Underground Railroad, including William Garrett and William Still, held Tubman in high esteem, collaborating in and assisting her on her missions.

A dedicated freedom fighter, when she wasn't conducting rescue operations, Tubman worked to raise money to support herself and to fund future trips into the South. It was only due to illness that she was not with John Brown at his famous and ill-fated raid on Harpers Ferry, Virginia, in October of 1859. While other abolitionists, most notably Frederick Douglass, thought Brown's plan to be foolhardy, Tubman considered him a fellow-traveler, and the two bonded over their deep hatred of slavery. Thinking counterfactually, it is not farfetched to assert that, given her gift for strategy and her knack for covert communication with members of the enslaved community, Tubman's assistance would have greatly enhanced John Brown's chances of success.

Tubman is especially unique considering her gender. Scholars have documented the fact that it was most often young and unattached enslaved men who comprised the majority of fugitives from slavery. Unlike women, they were less likely to be burdened in their journey by noisy and slow-moving children. Additionally, they often worked in capacities that allowed them to gain valuable knowledge about geography and possible routes of escape. Tubman's risky decision to return for others after her own successful escape speaks of a very high level of selflessness and daring. Despite the potential danger, she traveled with infants and the elderly, and used her sidearm to ensure the cowardly did not jeopardize her mission.

Harriet Tubman's full array of talents would be brought to bear during the U.S. Civil War. At the outbreak of the conflict, she headed south to perform work she was intimately familiar with: assisting the formerly enslaved in their transition to being free people. She worked with the Union army as a cook and nurse, earning the respect of the military elite and soldiers alike for her use of herbs to heal. Secretary of State William Seward, a long-time friend, encouraged Union generals to employ Tubman's scouting skills to aid the military. At his urging, she was charged with organizing and leading a group of Black spies for the dangerous mission of gathering intelligence behind enemy lines. In 1863, Tubman took charge of leading a raid into Port Royal, South Carolina. The information gathered by her and her agents, along with her use of the communication "grapevine" in the local enslaved community, ensured a brilliant victory over the Confederates at the Battle of Combahee, resulting in the liberation of over 750 people from slavery.

Until the end of her life in 1913, Harriet Tubman continued to support others in need. Her openness meant that her home in Auburn, New York had a virtual revolving door for individuals seeking aid, guidance, or both. Of utmost concern to her were the most vulnerable elements of society: orphans and the elderly. Her vision was manifested with the opening of the Harriet Tubman Home for the elderly. The range of her life—from bondage to lifetime of continued self-sacrifice for the sake of others—stands as a remarkable legacy of human determination and resilience (Clinton, 2004).

Enslaved Without Fetters: Free Black Women in Antebellum America

While not subjected to the same circumstances as their enslaved sisters, free Black women broke the boundaries of both race and gender in challenging slavery and sexism. These women demonstrated their leadership abilities and intellect, despite the prevailing belief that they were members of the "fairer sex" and of a supposedly inferior race. Black women actively sought to both mitigate and end slavery in the United States, through bold truth-telling in pen and on podiums. A member of Boston's Black middle-class community, Maria W. Stewart became the first American-born woman to speak publicly in the United States in 1832. Her speeches and writing, published frequently in William Lloyd Garrison's abolitionist newspaper, *The Liberator*, reflected a deep commitment to moral living and self-determination as the path to success for the race. Her eloquent but direct criticism of Black male leaders ended her speaking career shortly after it began. In a speech delivered in February 1833 at the African Masonic Hall in Boston, Stewart threw down the gauntlet: "I would ask, is it blindness of mind or stupidity of soul or the want of education that has caused our men … never to let their voices be heard nor their hands be raised in behalf of their color?" (Stewart, 1879). Her outspokenness came with a price, as she was shunned and shamed away from future public speaking engagements. Stewart's silencing stands as evidence of the unique double burdens of racism and sexism faced by African American women.

Despite Stewart's short-lived career as a public speaker, Frances Ellen Watkins Harper maneuvered through the door that her predecessor cracked open. Over the course of her lengthy career, Harper worked as a lecturer, poet, and author who lent her talents to a myriad of social and political causes including the abolition of slavery, women's suffrage, temperance, and civil rights for African Americans. Orphaned at the age of three, Harper was taken in by an uncle who ran the prestigious William Watkins Academy for Negro Youth in Philadelphia, giving her the opportunity to cultivate her natural intellect and achieve an education rare for women of the day, regardless of race. Harper also faced hard choices when it came to the breadth of her activism. After the debate over the ratification of the 15th Amendment (which gave Black men the right to vote), she broke ties with her White colleagues, who adopted racist rhetoric to advance the cause of women's suffrage. The choice Harper encountered at this juncture—having to choose between advocating for her race OR her gender—would be faced again and again by African American women over the next century, as it would take that long for Black women to successfully recognize and articulate the unique "double jeopardy" they faced. While she opted not to break ranks with Black men, her loyalty did not stem her criticism. She, like Maria Stewart before her, noted "that while men talk about changes, the women [were] implementing them."

In addition to doing her advocacy work, Harper used her creative talents to capture the struggles and aspirations of African American people. Critics note not only her lyrical skill, but also her ability to convey the humanity of Black people. Both before and after emancipation, Harper worked to counter the negative portrayal of Blacks as shiftless, ignorant, and dangerous, and to provide a more accurate, and decidedly more positive, representation of the race. Her crowning achievement in this area would be the 1892 publication of her novel *Iola Leroy, or Shadow Uplifted*, which follows the life of her mulatto protagonist from her experience of passing as a White southern belle through the ordeal of slavery, the devastation of war, and her fight to establish a meaningful life in the post-Civil-War South (Bacon, 1989; Harper et al., 1990; Washington, 1988).

Transitioning From Slavery to Freedom

With the advent of emancipation and the official death of slavery, Black women underwent a range of transitional and transformative experiences as they attempted to make meaning of their newfound freedom. Of great importance to freedpeople, male and female, was the reunion of their families and the stabilization of their marriages. Black women became pawns in the battle to redefine race relations in the post-Civil-War South, as their mates asserted their newfound patriarchy, modeled on the example from White society, in attempts to keep them in place and protect them within the domestic sphere of the home. Meanwhile, Whites sought ways to continue exploiting their labor in White homes and fields.

African American women, individually and collectively, mobilized during the era of Reconstruction (1863–1876) to address the special needs of their communities, specifically in the areas of education, medical care, and the care of the elderly and orphans. Moreover, this era gave Black women occasion to flex their well-worked muscles of survival and resourcefulness, in order to take advantage of new opportunities for activism and leadership. Lucy Goode Brooks used a painful experience in her own life as motivation to help those in need. While she was in bondage, her young daughter was sold away from her family. After emancipation, Brooks assuaged her pain by providing care for orphaned children in her community, founding the Friends' Asylum for Colored Children in 1872. The legacy institution, the Friends' Association for Children, still operates today as a child-placement agency in Richmond, Virginia (Kneebone, 1998).

Access to education became one of the most steadfast demands of freedpeople as they emerged from enslavement. It is no accident, then, that a number of African American women focused their talents and energies on teaching, and on establishing schools throughout the South. In her desire to aid freedpeople who were living in the area of Fortress Monroe near Hampton, Virginia, Mary Peake began conducting school, in the absence of a property structure, under the shade of an oak tree. The site of her open-air school later became the home of Hampton Institute (now Hampton University), founded in 1868.

Charlotte Forten Grimké, a member of the distinguished free Black Forten family of Philadelphia, also traveled south, in her case to South Carolina, to provide educational opportunities to the adults and children of the Sea Islands (Grimké, 1988). Another Black woman found her stride, not in the South, but the North. Born into slavery, Fanny Jackson Coppin escaped bondage with her family and went on to graduate from Oberlin College in Ohio. After the conclusion of the Civil War, she led classes for freedpeople who had migrated to the area. In 1869, Coppin was appointed president of the Institute for Colored Youth in Philadelphia, making her the first Black woman in the nation to achieve such a position. An innovative and visionary educator, Coppin developed instructional models focused on the psychological needs of students that would not become popular until the twentieth century. Although Booker T. Washington is most closely associated with the concept of industrial education, Coppin incorporated the idea into her curriculum and opened an exceedingly popular trade school, the only one in Philadelphia open to Blacks, in 1889. Coppin State University in Baltimore, Maryland is named in her honor (Perkins, 1993).

Even though the 15th Amendment to the U.S. Constitution granted the right to vote only to Black men, Black women were greatly concerned with political affairs and exercised considerable influence on the electoral decisions of Black men. Using the indirect methods of rallying, praising, and shaming, Black women became the "neck that turns the head" when it came to political matters. White men interpreted this behavior as evidence of the lack of manhood in Black men, and the lack of femininity among Black women. It was a clear misreading of the unique formation of gender roles born under the yoke of slavery. These myopic interpretations would be reflected in the predominant stereotypes of Black women in American society during the late 19th and early 20th centuries—the overbearing "Mammy" and the sharp-tongued "Sapphire."

Fighting for Our Men, Fighting for Ourselves

During the latter part of the 18th and the beginning of the 19th centuries, African Americans were experiencing the "nadir" of race relations in the United States. By the turn of the century, southern legislatures found creative ways to circumvent the rights and protection of the Reconstruction Amendments, effectively reestablishing White supremacy throughout the region. Where the law failed, southern Whites employed brutal violence to discourage Black advancement. The loss of the franchise deprived Black men of the most critical tool to protect the fruits of emancipation as well as their families and communities. In 1896, the U.S. Supreme Court's decision in the *Plessy v. Ferguson* case solidified this reality by sanctioning the practice of racial segregation. Facing limited access to political and economic resources, coupled with social stigma of race, Black people found that the bright promise of emancipation seemed to be in full eclipse. These circumstances would draw Black women into the public sphere on behalf of themselves and their communities. African American women advocated for the most vulnerable and abused among them— the young, the ill, the aged, and those who were victims of lynching in the South—and, most importantly, for themselves. Their concentrated energies represented a high-water mark for Black women's activism. It is the height of irony that one of the most well-known defenders of Black men was a Black woman, Ida B. Wells-Barnett. Perhaps the most recognized activist of this period, and a journalist, author, and lecturer, Wells-Barnett uniquely illustrates the possibilities and limitations of Black women's activism during these years. Wells-Barnett drew both national and international attention to the crime of lynching in the U.S., effectively disproving the excuses White leaders used to defend the practice. Her three books, *Southern Horrors* (1892), *A Red Record* (1896), and *Mob Rule in New Orleans* (1900), and international speaking tours helped to educate the public about the horrific brutality and civil rights abuses visited upon Blacks in the South. Wells-Barnett placed herself in physical danger: she traveled to the scenes of lynching incidents to investigate and gather the information she needed to accurately record the true motives and horrific brutality of lynching; her press was destroyed in Memphis, Tennessee; and her life was threatened for her fiery contestation of White Southern fallacies about the rape of White women. There were also detractors in the African American community who criticized Wells-Barnett for being "unsexed" in a time when women were still expected to be seen and not heard. Wells-Barnett symbolized the potential of Black women to lead, once liberated from the narrow constraints of gendered spheres of influence. Paradoxically, the anti-lynching activities of Ida B. Wells-Barnett, primarily in the defense of African American men, resulted in public attacks that led to the formation of organizations to defend the reputation of Black women. What has come to be known as the Black Women's Club Movement was born of efforts of Black women to celebrate

Wells-Barnett's accomplishment and to defend her, as well as the image of all Black women, from character assassination. A testimonial dinner for Wells-Barnett was held on October 5, 1892, organized by other Black women to provide audience for her work and to assist her with publishing her findings. Within a few months of this gathering, inspired by Wells-Barnett's achievements and the potential for Black women as leaders, several important clubs were organized: the New Era Club in Boston, under the leadership of Josephine St. Pierre Ruffin, who also published *The Woman's Era*, the first publication created by and circulated for Black women; the Women's Loyal Union of New York City, led by Victoria Earle Matthews; and the Colored Woman's League of Washington, DC. The focus of much of their work was local in scope, including the organization of kindergartens for local children, raising funds to support Black schools, and providing aid to the sick and elderly (Bay, 2009; McMurray, 1998; Schechter, 2001). The complexity of the challenge Black women in America faced was crystallized by comments from a prominent White journalist aimed at denigrating Wells-Barnett and all Black women—deriding them as hypersexual and devoid of virtue. In response to this vicious and very public attack, Josephine Ruffin reprinted the letter in her journal and called for Black women to organize in defense of their reputations. "Too long," proclaimed Ruffin, "have we been silent under unjust and unholy charges; we cannot expect to have them removed until we disprove them through *ourselves.*" Her call led to the convening of the First National Conference of Colored Women of America, and gave birth to the National Federation of Afro-American Women in 1895. The group later merged with the Colored Women's Clubs to form the National Association of Colored Women (NACW) in 1896, and elected Mary Eliza Church Terrell as its first president. Starting with 54 member clubs at the time of its founding, the NACW grew into a nationwide network that claimed nearly 400 member organizations by 1916 (Giddings, 1984, pp. 75–117). The network shared news and information about the work of member organizations, and held biennial conferences to bring the members together.

This spirit of cooperation provided models of community aid and reform activism that helped Black women sustain their local work. Members cheered examples of successful programs like Victoria Earle Matthews's White Rose Mission in New York City, founded in 1897 to provide resources and shelter to Black women who were relocating to the city, and the Phyllis Wheatley Home in Chicago, which provided care for the elderly. Led by women like Mary Church Terrell, Josephine St. Pierre Ruffin, and Margaret Murray Washington (the wife of Booker T. Washington), the NACW and other clubs used the "politics of respectability" not only to provide uplift to the needy in their communities but also to rehabilitate the public image of the race. Much of their work, however, was colored by classism and a desire to sanitize the image of all Blacks in the public eye. These women operated from a worldview firmly rooted in the middle-class values of strict morality, piety, chastity, family, and education. Their efforts to lift up "the least of these" were sometimes motivated by less-than-altruistic reasons, as middle-class African Americans recognized that the entire Black community would be judged collectively by the most negative activities and behaviors exhibited by individuals of their race. Naturally, these pressures for conformity led to harsh judgments and meddling, causing friction between African American reformers and the people they sought to aid. Working within the Black women's club movement cultivated a cadre of very capable advocates, able to effectively articulate both the hope of the race and the place of the Black women in the struggle.

Fannie Barrier Williams of Chicago, a contributor to Ruffin's *The Woman's Era*, gave a speech in May 1893 at the Departmental Congress of the National Association of Loyal Women of American Liberty at the World's Congress of Representative Women, chiding Whites for discriminating against Black women, no matter their education, modesty, or personal character. The highly educated (she was the only woman invited to join the American Negro Academy), eloquent, and forceful Anna Julia Cooper not only advocated for the advancement of the race but also celebrated Black women as the linchpins of the future success of the Black community. It was in the hands of the Black woman, Cooper wrote, to "stamp weal or woe on the coming history of this people," declaring that "when and where the black woman excelled, the fate of the race excelled as well" (Cooper, 1892).

While social uplift was important, bread-and-butter issues did not escape the attention of Black women activists. Both individually and collectively, Black women worked for the economic advancement of themselves and their communities. In the early days of Reconstruction, Black couples desired to keep women and girls from under the control of White bosses. Financial pressures, however, eventually overturned their efforts. Black women, no strangers to work, once again returned to the soil and to the kitchens in White homes, to help provide for their families. This reversal of fates once again placed these women in circumstances that mimicked the power relations established during slavery, leaving them vulnerable to exploitation. Even so, these arrangements did not go unchallenged. Some Black women attempted to control the conditions and terms of their labor, choosing to work as laundresses outside of White homes, as opposed to maids inside of them. They also gave birth to a new struggle for fair labor compensation. Historian Tera Hunter has written about an impressive but ultimately unsuccessful effort of African American laundresses in Atlanta, Georgia, to strike for higher wages in 1881. Using the social network within the Black churches of the city, the Black women, in a remarkable demonstration of unity and economic self-determination, stood together in an effort to improve their collective lots. Their actions spoke of an increased appreciation of the value of their work, and a desire to empower themselves to protect it (Hunter, 1997).

There are also stunning examples of individual women who contributed to the economic advancement of their communities. Maggie L. Walker was one of them. She dedicated much of her life's work to the Independent Order of St. Luke's, a mutual aid society. Organizations like St. Luke's institutionalized the culture of communal support and self-reliance that enabled African Americans to survive slavery. Membership guaranteed money for a decent burial or aid to surviving family members after the death of a household's breadwinner. Walker joined the organization as a young woman and continued to rise through the ranks over the years, serving as Right Worthy Grand Outside Sentinel, Inside Sentinel, Grand Messenger, Vice Chief, and, by 1890, Chief. Then, from 1891 through 1898, Walker worked as a recruiter for the organization, and assumed the helm at the Right Worthy Grand Secretary of the Independent Order of St. Luke's in 1899. During Walker's 35-year tenure, the Independent Order of St. Luke's membership grew to 100,000, including 20,000 children, in 22 states, with a strong presence in Washington, DC, Baltimore, Philadelphia, and New York. Walker not only saved the group from near economic failure, but took the additional step of organizing the group's resources in order to capitalize a number of businesses, including a bank, a dry goods store, and a newspaper. Walker's business savvy, her sincere concern for the uplift of African Americans, and her folksy style engendered respect in the male-dominated world of finance (Marlowe, 2003).

Similarly, Sarah Breedlove, better known as Madame C. J. Walker, created a line of hair care products and tools for the care of Black women's hair that would make her a millionaire. Her innovations were born of her attempts to address her painful scalp condition and the hair loss it caused. Walker's struggle mirrored those of other Black women who, enduring the harsh physical and temporal demands of slavery, deprioritized self-adornment. As a practical matter, Black women lacked the time and resources necessary for beautification. Moreover, the legal defeminization of Black women under the yoke of bondage reached into the cultural realm, manifesting in the suppression, or outright rejection, of Black women's beauty. During the antebellum period some cities, Charleston and New Orleans in particular, took the unusual step of outlawing fancy headdresses for unfreed women. Under such pressures, the maintenance and care of kinky hair became a lost art. Walker's products—shampoos, pomades, and her straightening comb—not only made her a millionaire but also enabled thousands of African American women to expand beyond the drudgery of domestic work to become entrepreneurs in their own right. Black women who would otherwise be relegated to work as maids or laundresses, as Walker herself once was, could now achieve financial independence by selling hair products door to door, or by opening their own hair salons offering services developed by Madame Walker. Her business model, and her personal example for determination and drive, offered a useful example to other African American women (Bundles, 2001).

Finding a Place, Finding a Voice: 1920–1950

Black women were caught between the decline of civil rights for African Americans on the one hand, and the promising portal of the franchise that was opened by the ratification of the 19th Amendment on the other. While racism and sexism limited the trajectory of their lives, African American women continued to participate in public life and leadership within their communities. At the same time, as millions of Blacks left their traditional homeplaces in the South for the opportunities and excitement of northern cities, Black women had to negotiate the benefits and challenges of urban life. These women, particularly the unmarried, demonstrated a great deal of agency in striking out into what was for them unchartered territory, seeking better jobs and improved access to education for themselves and their children. Unfortunately, the change in geography sometimes left little unchanged; for those who were not working in agriculture in 1920, 80% of Black women were employed as domestics, cooks, and laundresses (Jones, 1985, p. 167).

If they were able to escape the kitchen, one of the professional fields open to Black women was education. In 1886 in Augusta, Georgia, Lucy Craft Laney, with the support of the Presbyterian Church, established the Haines Normal and Industrial Institute. Its mission was to provide educational opportunities for young Black girls. Over the course of its existence, the school focused on industrial training and expanded from offering primary and secondary education to becoming a normal school with programs in nursing, teaching, and printing. Similarly, noted speaker and activist Nannie Burroughs founded the National Training School for Women and Girls in Washington, DC, in 1909. Another significant voice during this period was that of Anna Julia Cooper, a much-sought-after writer on the condition of Black women in the South. She demonstrated a lifelong dedication to education, as an instructor and one-time principal of the famous M Street Academy in Washington, DC, and earned her doctoral degree from the Sorbonne in France at an advanced age.

Perhaps the most dynamic of all these educators was Mary McLeod Bethune. The daughter of formerly enslaved Africans, Bethune developed a passion for education and for serving others that led her to found the Daytona Educational and Industrial Institute in Daytona, Florida in 1904. Beginning with "five little girls, a dollar and a half and faith in God," the school merged with the Cookman Institute in 1923 to become the coeducational Bethune-Cookman College, with Bethune as president. A leader of great talent, Bethune also served as president of the Florida Federation of Colored Women's Clubs, and later as the president of the National Association of Colored Women in 1924. Under her guiding hand, the organization opened its national headquarters in Washington, DC. Perhaps Bethune's greatest achievements of her career would come through her work with the National Youth Administration, a New Deal program specifically designed to aid youth in surviving the economic downturn of the Great Depression. In 1939, Bethune was installed as head of the agency's Negro division, and during her tenure she worked to provide equal opportunities and funding to Black youth and educational programs. Her personality and determination endeared her to a number of the Washington elite, including no less than President Franklin Roosevelt and his wife, Eleanor. In spite of her gender, which had limited the public careers of Black women before her, Bethune became a major power broker for African Americans, assuming the role as the spokesperson for the race during the World War II era. It was Bethune who organized the Federal Council on Negro Affairs, also known as the Black Cabinet, which included 30 members who worked in the federal government and offered the president advice on addressing the needs of the nation's Black citizens. Her position within the national government would be succeeded only by Black women who were elected to public office during the 1960s (Smith, 1980).

The early 20th century also witnessed a resurgence of Black nationalism among African Americans, centered mainly within the Universal Negro Improvement Association. Part of the credit for the tremendous rise in UNIA membership (it would go on to become the largest African American organization in the nation's history) belongs to a Black woman, Henrietta Vinton Davis. After joining the UNIA, she used her reputation as an actress and entertainer to draw crowds in order that Marcus Mosiah Garvey, the organization's Jamaican founder, could recruit them into his movement. She went on to serve as a director of the Black Star Line, and to hold the posts of International Organizer and Fourth Assistant President General, the highest rank achieved by any female member. Garvey praised her as the "greatest woman of the Negro race today." Also instrumental to Garvey's work and legacy was his second wife, Amy Jacques Garvey. She traveled extensively with her husband as he worked to recruit membership and wrote a women's column for the UNIA newspaper, the *Negro World*. After her husband's conviction by the U. S. Government in 1923 for mail fraud in connection with his ill-fated dream of starting a shipping company and his subsequent deportation in 1927, Amy Jacques Garvey proved to be a capable leader and continued to advocate for self-determination for Black people, but also to encourage the leadership potential of Black women specifically. When Marcus Garvey died in London in 1940, she kept the flame of Black self-determination alive, publishing *The Philosophy and Opinions of Marcus Garvey* (1923 and 1925), *Garvey and Garveyism* (1963), and *Black Power in America* (1968). Her efforts in preserving the legacy and work of the UNIA helped to connect it with the burgeoning civil rights and Black Power movements of the 1960s.

In the early 1930s, as the economic crisis of the Great Depression deepened, Black women struggled to stay afloat. With job opportunities becoming increasingly scarce and racism hampering access to relief, Black women came together in search of solutions. Their years of work in Black women's clubs had groomed them to successfully organize themselves in defense of their communities. They took the lead in organizing economic boycotts in cities like Detroit, Cleveland, Chicago, and Harlem, pressuring White store owners to hire African Americans. Fannie Peck of Detroit founded the Housewives' League in 1930, which encouraged Black women to harness their spending power to support Black businesses, recognizing that they "were the most strategically positioned group to preserve and expand the Black internal economy" (Hine, 1993, p. 585). Within four years, the group's membership grew to 10,000. With efforts like these, as well as boycotts organized under the banner of "Don't Shop Where You Can't Work," historian Jacquelyn Jones (1985) estimates that, collectively, women in these organizations created 75,000 jobs.

Other activists took steps to draw attention to the suffering and exploitation Black women experienced during the economic downturn in the 1930s. Social scientists Ella Baker and Juanita Williams published a piece in *Crisis* magazine about what they called the Bronx "slave markets"—the street corners where Black women gathered to negotiate daily employment with White women who, due to high unemployment, offered these women as little as $2.00 a day. Desperate to feed their families, Black women agreed to work for these low wages, yet it was not uncommon for them to be exploited, either being required to perform more work than they had agreed to or being dismissed without pay altogether. Adding insult to injury, these street corners also attracted White men soliciting women for sex work, and undercover policemen attempting to arrest Black women who agreed to such arrangements.

Truth and Power: Black Women in the Civil Rights Era

In the years before and after World War II, African Americans continued to pursue their agenda for inclusion in American society and access to the prosperity around them. During the war years African Americans championed a campaign for winning the Double V—victory over fascism abroad and against racism at home—stiffening their resistance to discrimination. Membership in the NAACP, the nation's oldest civil rights organization, grew at a rapid pace. Steeped in organizing, communicating, and executing programs through their work in the Black church and women's clubs, Black women were well prepared to serve as leaders and foot soldiers in the burgeoning Civil Rights Movement.

Many historical timelines mark the beginning of the Civil Rights Movement with the 1955 murder of Chicago teen Emmett Till, who was brutally executed by White men in Money, Mississippi for breaking the rules of Southern racial etiquette by speaking to a White woman. The true horror of his death, however, was brought to the American public because of a decision made by Till's mother, Mamie Till Bradley. She made an intentional choice to open her son's casket and to allow the image of Emmett's bloated, bludgeoned corpse to be photographed and filmed. The images shocked and outraged African Americans around the country. Seeing those pictures became a formative experience in the minds of many young Blacks, and convinced many others that racism and segregation needed to be confronted in a more immediate and direct manner. Despite her grief over the murder of her son, Mamie Till Bradley became the face of the struggle for racial justice in America. With poise, dignity, and determination, she told and retold the story of her son's murder before audiences across the nation, and bore witness at the sham of a trial given to Roy Bryant and J. W. Milam.

As the movement progressed, a number of Black women entered the forefront of the fight against Jim Crow. Organizers like Jo Ann Robinson and Mary Fair Burks of Montgomery, Alabama conceptualized and planned the Montgomery Bus Boycott, a fact that is often left out of the history books in favor of highlighting the beginnings of the Rev. Dr. Martin Luther King, Jr.'s civil rights career. Newspaper publisher and NAACP leader Daisy Bates helped publicize and strategize the movements of the Little Rock Nine as they battled daily to survive their matriculation at Central High School beginning in 1957. Women like Ella Baker, Ruby Doris Smith, Septima Clark, and Marian Wright Edelman were also instrumental in providing the leadership and organizational skills within groups like the Southern Christian Leadership Conference (SCLC), the Student Nonviolent Coordinating Committee (SNCC), and the Congress of Racial Equality (CORE). Scholar Kimberly Springer defines women like these as "bridge leaders" who, while excluded from formal leadership positions within the movement because of their gender, carried the grassroots messages of students and laypeople into the realm of the mostly male decision-makers (Robinson, 1987).

Black women played integral parts not only in the grassroots movement, but also in outlining and implementing legal and political challenges to the Jim Crow system. As a member of the NAACP's Legal Defense and Education Fund team, Constance Baker Motley led court challenges to segregated education in the South, often facing great personal risk and racist and sexist treatment in court. Political activists like Evelyn Butts-Thomas and Fannie Lou Hamer both offered bold challenges to the electoral system. Beginning in 1963, Butts-Thomas not only served as plaintiff in a case that officially ended the poll tax in Virginia, but also went on to become a Democratic party leader and elected official in Norfolk, Virginia. Hamer, a sharecropper, experienced brutal treatment when she attempted to register to vote in Sunflower County, Mississippi. Undaunted, she became a leading spokesperson with SNCC and their Mississippi Freedom Summer campaign during the summer of 1964. Her plainspoken and moving speech during the National Democratic Convention that same year, about her fight to participate in politics, cemented her public image as a courageous freedom fighter.

The late 1960s and early 1970s witnessed great transformation in America, as well as within the ranks of those working to improve the lives of African Americans. Tired of "mainstream" civil rights leaders they perceived as a weak and slothful, younger activists with SNCC began to forge their own path. Under the leadership of Stokely Carmichael and his mantra of "Black Power," SNCC purged its ranks of White members and, inspired by the teachings of the late Malcolm X, took a much more confrontational stance in dealing with White racism. It was also during Carmichael's tenure as director that women, both Black and White, began to complain about the rampant sexism within the movement. Women were routinely overlooked for leadership positions and relegated to the roles of secretaries, housekeepers, and coffee-makers. Disenchanted, White women from SNCC and the Students for a Democratic Society (SDS) joined to confront these realities and started what became the "second wave" of the Women's Rights Movement. Some Black women, like Pauli Murray and Eleanor Holmes Norton, did participate in the mainstream feminist movement, becoming active members of the National Organization for Women (NOW). Many African American women, however, found it difficult to identify with White feminist prerogatives—their middle-class bent (White women were campaigning for the right to work outside the home, which most Black women did not see as novel), their view that family life was burdensome and stifling, and their vilification of men. Faced with the conundrum of choosing whether to fight for the uplift of Black people or fight against the sexism they were experiencing, the vast majority of Black women chose to stay within the ranks of the Civil Rights Movement and maintain their focus on the target of racism, albeit with much bitterness and growing resentment (Anderson-Bricker, 1999).

The tone and tenor of the Civil Rights Movement changed dramatically in 1966 with the founding of the Black Panther Party (BPP) in Oakland, California by Huey Newton and Bobby Seale. Angela Y. Davis, a scholar and intellectual of great renown, became one of the group's most visible members, especially after she was charged with aiding the escape attempt of George Jackson. Despite the BPP's goals of self-defense and the autonomy of Black communities, the group, along with other Black nationalist organizations, adopted a worldview that confined Black women to the supporting roles of child-bearers, attending to the affairs of the household while the men led the movement. Ironically, these ideas coincided with Daniel Patrick Moynihan's theories about the corrupting influence of strong Black matriarchs on Black family structure. As a result, African American women were labeled as problematic, within both the Black community and American society as a whole.

This limited view of the role of Black female revolutionaries naturally became a source of tension within these groups, although the perspectives of former members vary on the subject. Black women were the majority of the members—in the case of the BPP, as many as two thirds of the members—but they had trouble achieving and maintaining leadership within the group. The exception would be Angela Y. Davis, known for her arrest and trial for kidnapping, conspiracy, and murder in relation to Jonathan Jackson's attempted jailbreak in 1970, but her time with the BPP was limited in scope. Elaine Brown, the only woman ever to lead the BPP, testified to the difficulties she experienced within the group's ranks around issues of gender roles and sexuality. Kathleen Cleaver (2001), then married to BPP leader Eldridge Cleaver, is less critical of the gender dynamics within the group. While she worked in the party as Director of Communications, she recalls that it was common for women to hold positions of leadership, noting that:

> Some women worked with the newspaper, like Shelley Bursey, who became a grand jury resister when she was jailed because she refused to respond to one of the investigations into the Black Panther Party newspaper. Some of us, like Ericka Huggins, saw their husbands murdered, then were arrested themselves. In Ericka's case, she was jailed along with Bobby Seale and most of the New Haven chapter on charges of conspiracy to commit murder. She was later acquitted, but imagine what happens to an organization when fourteen people at once get arrested on capital charges. That doesn't leave much time to organize, or to have a family life. Maybe that was the kind of pressure that they hoped would force us to give up. (Cleaver, 2001, p. 125)

In reflecting on her time in the BPP and the reputation the group has since garnered as a bastion of sexism, she draws a thread between the sexism and exploitation that women experienced in American society in general during that time. In Cleaver's view, such discussions shift focus away from the vital work the women and men in the BPP performed in their quest to recreate their communities.

It was in this vacuum between White feminism and Black male chauvinism that Black feminist, or womanist consciousness, was born. Scattered and relatively short-lived, these Black feminist organizations and the women who articulated their points of view represented new levels of vocality and visibility. Frances Beal founded the short-lived Black Women's Liberation Committee under the umbrella of SNCC, and later led the Third World Women's Alliance, organized in 1970. Their activism coalesced around many issues, some of which were worked out on local turf—daycare for working mothers, medical care, shelters for battered women, and access to birth control and safe, legal abortions. These groups would also splinter on the issue of sexual orientation. Such disagreements resulted in the birth of the Combahee River Collective, based in Boston, Massachusetts and named for the successful battle organized and led by Harriet Tubman during the U.S. Civil War. Their statement of purpose, issued in 1982, still stands as one of the most eloquent articulations of visionary Black womanhood:

> Black women are inherently valuable, that our liberation is a necessity not as an adjunct to somebody else's but because of our need as human persons for autonomy. ... We realize that the only people who care enough about us to work consistently for our liberation is us. Our politics evolve from a healthy love for ourselves, our sisters, and our community which allows us to continue our struggle and work. (Combahee River Collective, 1977)

Other voices from the period were not so tame. Michele Wallace's fiery *Black Macho and the Myth of the Superwoman*, published in 1978, threw down the gauntlet on the perception and reality of the relationship between Black men and women:

> I am saying, among other things, that for perhaps the last fifty years there has been a growing distrust, even hatred, between black men and black women. It has been nursed along not only by racism on the part of whites but also by an almost deliberate ignorance on the part of blacks about the sexual politics of their experience in this country. (Wallace, 1978/1990)

Can You See Me Now?: Black Women's Visibility in the Modern Era

As the twin barriers of racism and sexism showed signs of weakening in the 1980s, Black women moved forward to capitalize on the expanding avenues to power and influence. One of the main battlefields has been within the influential realm of the American media. No single individual embodies this turn of events better than Oprah Winfrey. She is one of the most famous, wealthy (self-made), and influential women of any race in America and the world, based around the cult of personality she built during her years as the host of *The Oprah Winfrey Show*, and now at the helm of the Oprah Winfrey Network. Her power as a media mogul has helped not only to democratize the images of African American people to America and the world, offering a much more diversified and in-depth exploration of Black people, but also to humanize the public image and lived experiences of Black women. Winfrey's influence on television, film, and prose has helped shed much-needed light on African American artists and stories of the African Diaspora. She even threw her influence behind the presidential candidacy of fellow Chicagoan, Barack Obama. Perhaps more importantly, Winfrey has used her wealth to fund and support efforts to uplift Black people in the United States and South Africa.

Winfrey's success has not come without a price. Her very public struggle with her weight and body image reflects the continuing struggle for many African American women to value themselves despite the European standards of beauty that pervade American culture. As her success blossomed, many in the African American community criticized Winfrey for abandoning her Black fan base in order to appeal to middle-class White women. Mainstream African Americans have also questioned her life choices: remaining childless; opting for a long-term relationship with her partner, Stedman Graham, instead of getting married; and exercising spiritual beliefs that operate outside of Christian norms. While Winfrey's non-traditional lifestyle may be judged critically by some, her ability to define the terms of her life for herself as a woman of African ancestry, when considered in light of history, is a remarkable commentary on the possibilities available to other women like her.

Television also served as the canvas upon which a serious contest involving the intersection of politics, race, and gender played out in the 1990s. In 1991, Clarence Thomas, an African American, was nominated to the U.S. Supreme Court to fill a vacancy left by the retirement of Thurgood Marshall, the first African American to sit on the bench. Thomas, a noted conservative nominated by President George H. W. Bush, was accused by his former employee, Anita Hill, a Black woman, of sexually harassing her while the two worked together. The seamy details were laid bare before the nation during the televised confirmation hearings—something that had not occurred before—and they gripped the nation's attention. Many leaders in the Black community came to Thomas's defense, publicly supporting his nomination. Hill, conversely, was vilified as a traitor to her race who was being used as a pawn to bring down a "brother," or worse, a dreaded radical Black feminist. Not all members of the African American community felt that way. A group of 1,603 Black women took out a full-page advertisement in the *New York Times* to make public not only their support for Hill, but also their rejection of the sexism and misogyny being directed against Black women. The statement placed Hill's ill treatment in the context of the historical dismissal of abuse suffered by Black women:

> We speak here because we recognize that the media are now portraying the Black community as prepared to tolerate both the dismantling of affirmative action and the evil of sexual harassment in order to have any Black man on the Supreme Court. We want to make clear that the media have ignored or distorted many African American voices. We will not be silenced. … This country, which has a long legacy of racism and sexism, has never taken the sexual abuse of black women seriously. Throughout U.S. history black women have been sexually stereotyped as immoral, insatiable, perverse, the initiators in all sexual contacts—abusive or otherwise. The common assumption in legal proceedings as well as in the larger society has been that black women cannot be raped or otherwise sexually abused. As Anita Hill's experience demonstrates, Black women who speak of these matters are not likely to be believed (The Proclamation, 1991).

Despite Anita Hill's claims, Clarence Thomas was confirmed to the court. The ordeal, of course, sharpened the nation's dialogue on the topic of sexual harassment, and soured the conversation around gender relations between African Americans, exacerbating tensions left over from the 1970s (Smitherman, 1995).

At the same time that the Hill–Thomas controversy was playing out in Washington, DC, another contest was brewing that would have broader implications for a younger generation of Black women. This time it involved one of the most dominant forces in the entertainment industry, rap music. Miami-based rap trio 2 Live Crew's 1989 album, *As Nasty as They Wanna Be*, was banned in Broward County for its sexually explicit lyrics. The group challenged the ban in court, which included an appeal to the U.S. Supreme Court, and the rappers were victorious. Hailed as a victory for free speech, this paved the way for the increased use of sexually graphic and misogynistic lyrics in rap music. This fact, coupled with the rising popularity of music videos, meant that Black women's bodies would become visual tools used to convey the hypersexual messages in the music.

These developments did not go unnoticed or unanswered. C. Delores Tucker, head of the National Congress of Black Women, chastised record company executives for the content of the rap artists they promoted, and she encouraged boycotts of stores that sold "gangsta rap" albums. Largely unsuccessful, Tucker paid the personal price of being vilified in the lyrics of the very artists she spoke out against, most notably Tupac Shakur and Lil' Wayne. The battle over the representation of Black women in rap music and culture exploded again, garnering a great deal of public attention, in the spring of 2004. This time it was a group of young women at Spelman College, the best-known college for Black women in America, who would lead the challenge. Upon learning that rapper Nelly was planning to hold an event to promote bone marrow donation in the Black community on their campus, student leaders planned a protest to decry the images of Black women featured in his most recent music video, "Tip Drill." It featured scantily clad Black female strippers, simulating sex acts while money is being thrown at them. In one of the more outrageous scenes, Nelly runs a credit card between one woman's buttocks. The controversy drew national media attention and resulted in several public dialogues between rap artists and Black women, one mediated by hip-hop mogul Russell Simmons, about the representation of women in hip-hop culture. In the midst of these tensions, several critical studies and commentaries have been written by women of the hip-hop generation, including Joan Morgan's (1999) *When Chickenheads Come Home to Roost: My Life as a Hip Hop Feminist*. Morgan gives poignant insight into the conflict young Black women have with young Black men, simultaneously articulating frustration and hope. Morgan offers an observation that echoes the reality of gender relations from generations past:

> I love black men like I love no other. And I'm not talking sex or aesthetics, I'm talking about loving y'all enough to be down for the drama—stomping anything that threatens your existence. Now only a fool loves that hard without asking the same in return. So yeah, I demand that black men fight sexism with the same passion they battle racism. I want you to annihilate anything that endangers sistas' welfare—including violence against women—because my survival walks hand in hand with yours. (Joan Morgan, 1999, p. 44)

The fight to improve the public image of Black women and girls in American society also includes more proactive initiatives. In the fall of 1997, between 500,000 and 750,000 women gathered on the streets of Philadelphia to participate in the Million Woman March (MWM). Inspired by the Million Man March that had been sponsored by the Nation of Islam in Washington, DC the previous year, organizers Phile Chionesu and Asia Coney sought to bring women of African ancestry together to stand in solidarity. They issued a 12-point plan to outline the goals of the group. Atypically in comparison to other "march" movements, the leaders stayed away from the typical silos of Black social and political influence, namely the NAACP, Black churches, and Black elected officials. Their belief in the power of grassroots organizing paid off, not only attracting thousands of women to the event, but also garnering national media coverage and raising the consciousness of thousands of other women who were not able to attend but sympathized with the MWM's mission and goals. Other efforts seek to boost the self-esteem of young Black women and expand their worldview. The fight to improve the public image of Black women and girls has also encompassed movements to boost their self-esteem. This is the mission of Beverly Bond, model-turned-disc jockey and founder of *Black Girls Rock!* Her vision started as a summer camp for urban girls in Queens, New York, but in partnerships with *Essence* magazine and Black Entertainment Television (BET), she created a televised awards show by the same name, whose mission is to "celebrate the brilliance and beauty of Black women."

Outside the cultural sphere, one of the most significant signs of Black women's advancement in American society has been their ability to achieve high political office. In those roles, African American women have worked to remedy the effects of racism and sexism. In 1968, Shirley Chisholm became the first Black woman elected to the U.S. Congress in the nation's history and, in 1972, the first Black woman to run for the presidency on the ticket of a major party. Her staunch rejection of the status quo in favor of championing causes and people in the margins of the American democracy inspired others to follow in her footsteps. A contemporary of Chisholm's, Barbara C. Jordan became the first African American woman from the South to serve in the U.S. Congress when she was elected in 1972. She won political note for her work to expand the 1965 Voting Rights Act to include Mexican Americans, as well as for her role in the impeachment trial of Richard Nixon. Twenty years later, in 1992, Carol Mosley Braun became the first African American woman elected to the U.S. Senate. She remained the only African American woman ever elected to the U.S. Senate until Vice President Kamala Harris was elected in 2020. In recent decades, African American women in the U.S. Congress have participated in and led a number of initiatives, drawing attention to the continuing inequality and injustice in American society. Their work and advocacy has focused on protecting affirmative action, preserving women's rights, and promoting inclusion for minority-owned businesses. U.S. Representative Cynthia McKinney (D-Georgia) stood in opposition to the war in Iraq. Due in part to her vocal opposition, she lost her seat during the next election. U.S. representative Maxine Waters (D-California) focused attention on the Iran-CONTRA scandal, demanding a federal investigation to determine if drugs were intentionally being funneled into the African American community as a part of the arrangement. Often criticized as angry or obstructionist, these women are the torchbearers in the tradition of truth-tellers, tenaciously advocating for their communities (Wright, 1999).

African American women have also served in appointed positions at the national level. They walk in the path that Mary McLeod Bethune started before them, but have a greater ability than she did to exercise power and make decisions that affect millions of lives, both nationally and internationally. The first Black woman to serve officially as a member of the president's cabinet was Patricia Harris, who served as secretary of Housing and Urban Development under then-President Jimmy Carter. Hazel O'Leary (Secretary of Energy) and Joycelyn Elders (U.S. Surgeon General) served under President Bill Clinton. A Republican president, George W. Bush, was the first to elevate an African American woman to a high-level position in the cabinet, as he did when he selected Condoleezza Rice to serve as his Secretary of State in 2005. After his election in 2008, President Barack Obama included African American women in his inner circle, namely Valerie Jarrett (Senior Advisor to the White House), Lisa Johnson (Director of the Environmental Protection Agency), and Susan Rice (U.S. Ambassador to the United Nations).

Despite these welcome additions, it was President Obama's wife, First Lady Michelle Obama, who became the most visible and influential African American woman in the country during the Obama presidency. As the wife of the first African American president to be elected in the United States, she became both a light and lightning rod by which people attempted to judge the progress of Black women in the country. Michelle Obama proved to be an incredibly popular First Lady, and a capable surrogate for her husband, but she was also heavily criticized by conservatives in the media who attacked her patriotism, her temperament, and even her physical appearance. Starting in the early days of the 2008 presidential campaign, distractors attempted to characterize her as an "angry Black woman" with an "un-American" chip on her shoulder, citing comments on the campaign trail and writings from her undergraduate days at Princeton University. This line of thought came to life on the July 2008 cover of the *New Yorker*, which pictured Candidate Obama in Muslim garb, and an afro-wearing, machine-gun-toting Michelle Obama giving her husband a fist bump while the U.S. flag burned in a fireplace, over which hung the framed image of Osama bin Laden. In 2011, Jodi Kantor published a book on the First Couple, *The Obamas*, which painted Michelle Obama as angry, domineering, and at odds with her husband's staff. No doubt seeking to sensationalize rather than document, the author played the keys of centuries-old tunes about emasculating and abrasive

Black women that the American public knows so well. So disturbed was she by Kantor's assertions that the First Lady took to the media in defense of herself.

In spite of the harsh spotlight, Michelle Obama continued to blaze her own trail, both during and after the Obama presidency. Her fashion sense—a unique combination of bold, sporty, and feminine—has caught the attention and approval of the fashion world. Likewise, her choices about her family offer an interesting window into Michelle Obama's personal values. While she is as highly educated and accomplished as her husband, instead of jumping into the political fray as a policymaker, à la Hillary Clinton, Michelle Obama has prioritized her role as a mother to her two daughters above advancing her own career. The issues that she has chosen to involve herself in are decidedly domestic and family-centered. She used her influence to encourage children and parents to eat better as she cultivated a garden at the White House, and to get more exercise through her "Let's Move!" campaign. Michelle Obama's example as an African American woman is, in many ways, a litmus test for the progress and challenges that Black women continue to face in American society.

Conclusion

There is no simple way to encapsulate the role of Black women activists in American society, as there is no easy way, nor any single way, to navigate successfully through a society that is based on racial and gender inequality. The progress achieved by Black women over three centuries has required a unique balance of mental, physical, and spiritual strength, undergirded by the core value of survival and the ability to "speak truth to power," even to those who preferred their silence. African American women have exuded these qualities as they have fought for their families, their communities, and for themselves—for space to simply "be" and for the freedom to define themselves, for themselves, outside of struggle. It is with this magic mix that Black women have found the ability to steady themselves and provide the vital cohesion necessary to allow the survival of African-heritage people in America.

The latter fact is no accident or coincidence; it is the legacy of African cultures that valued the collective over the individual, understood the interconnectedness of the parts to the whole, and valued the discourse between the human and the divine. As the experience of enslavement shattered these cultural structures, Black women gathered the shards and fashioned a framework to shelter and care for their families, physically, spiritually, and psychologically. They developed these survival skills and imbued their daughters and granddaughters with them, providing future generations with the critical skill of *functioning through dysfunction*.

This survival, however, has not come without a price. At times the burden has been too great, and many have broken beneath its weight. The twisted growth of Black womanhood has sometimes choked the growth of Black manhood, as they both sought to survive in limited spaces. The necessary language of survival learned by Black women in America has often been ignored, misunderstood, and misinterpreted by those outside of their unique experience. Sadly, some African-heritage women have failed to understand and appreciate their own unique history, and struggle through a morass of conflicting internal desires and external expectations, sometimes leading to depression, drug addiction, and suicide.

In summary, it is important to recognize that Black women in modern America are the beneficiaries of their foremothers' struggles. The opportunities before them are vast and have been bought for a hefty price, a debt that must always be remembered. By acknowledging and understanding this legacy—the long distance between Margaret Garner and Michelle Obama—today's Black women can fully appreciate the double burden of racism and sexism, and use the valuable toolkit their history provides as a source of strength, motivation, and strategies for creating a better future.

References

Anderson-Bricker, K. (1999). "Triple jeopardy": Black women and the growth of feminist consciousness in SNCC, 1964–1975. In K. Springer (Ed.), *Still lifting, still climbing: African American women's contemporary activism* (pp. 49–69). New York University Press.

Bacon, M. H. (1989, January). "One great bundle of humanity": Frances Ellen Watkins Harper (1825–1911). *Pennsylvania Magazine of History and Biography, 21*(35).

Banks, T. L. (1993). Freeman, Elizabeth. In D. C. Hine, E. B. Brown, & R. Terborg-Penn (Eds.), *Black women in America* (pp. 469–470). Indiana University Press.

Bay, M. (2009). *To tell the truth freely: The life of Ida B. Wells*. Hill and Wang.

Brown, K. M. (1996). *Good wives, nasty wenches, and anxious patriarchs: Gender, race and power in colonial Virginia*. University of North Carolina Press.

Bundles, A. (2001). *On her own ground: The life and times of Madam C. J. Walker*. Simon and Schuster.

Chesnut, M. B. *A Confederate Lady's Diary*. (Original work published 1905)

Cleaver, K. (2001). Women, power, and revolution. In K. Cleaver & George Katsiaficas (Eds.), *Liberation, imagination, and the Black Panther Party: A new look at the Panthers and their legacy* (pp. 123–127). Routledge. pp. 125.

Clinton, C. (2004). *Harriet Tubman: The road to freedom*. Little, Brown.

The Combahee River Collective. (1977). *The Combahee River Collective statement*. http://americanstudies.yale.edu/sites/default/files/files/Keyword%20Coalition_Readings.pdf

Cooper, A. J. *A voice from the South by a Black woman of the South*. (Original work published 1892 by the Aldine Printing House)

Gaspar, D. B., & Hine, D. C. (Eds.). (1996). *More than chattel: Black women and slavery in the Americas*. Indiana University Press.

Giddings, P. (1984). *When and where I enter: The impact of Black women on race and sex in America*. William Morrow.

Grimké, C. L. F. (1988). In B. Stevenson (Ed.), *The journals of Charlotte Forten Grimké*. Oxford University Press.

Gutman, H. G. (1976). *The Black family in slavery and freedom, 1750–1925*. Vintage Books.

Harper, F. E. W., Foster, F. S., & Cairns Collection of American Women Writers. (1990). *A brighter coming day: A Frances Ellen Watkins Harper reader*. Feminist Press at the City University of New York.

Hine, D. C. (1993). Housewives' League of Detroit. In D. C. Hine, E. B. Brown, & R. Terborg-Penn (Eds.), *Black women in America*. Indiana University Press.

Hunter, T. W. (1997). *To 'joy my freedom: Southern Black women's lives and labors after the Civil War*. Harvard University Press.

Jacobs, H. A. (1987). *Incidents in the life of a slave girl: Written by herself*. Harvard University Press. (Original work published 1861)

Jones, J. (1985). *Labor of love, labor of sorrow: Black women, work and family, from slavery to the present*. Basic Books.

Klein, H. S. (2010). *The Atlantic slave trade: New approaches to the Americas*. Cambridge University Press.

Kneebone, J. T. (1998). Brooks, Lucy Goode. In J. T. Kneebone et al., *Dictionary of Virginia biography* (Vol. 2, pp. 272–273). The Library of Virginia.

Marlowe, G. W. (2003). *A right worthy grand mission: Maggie Lena Walker and the quest for Black economic empowerment.* Howard University Press.

McMurray, L. O. (1998). *To keep the waters troubled: The life of Ida B. Wells.* Oxford University Press.

Morgan, J. [Jennifer]. (2011). *Laboring women: Reproduction and gender in New World slavery.* University of Pennsylvania Press.

Morgan, J. [Joan]. (1999). *When chickenheads come home to roost: My life as a hip hop feminist.* Simon & Schuster.

Moynihan, D. P. (1965). *The Negro family: The case for national action*. U.S. Department of Labor, Office of Policy Planning and Research.

Perkins, L. (1993). Coppin, Fannie Jackson. In D. C. Hine, E. B. Brown, & R. Terborg-Penn (Eds.), *Black women in America*. Indiana University Press.

Robinson, J. A. G. (1987). *The Montgomery bus boycott and the women who started it: The memoir of Jo Ann Gibson Robinson*. University of Tennessee Press. http:// nationalhumanitiescenter.org/pds/maai3/protest/text5/robinsonbusboycott.pdf

Schechter, P. A. (2001). *Ida B. Wells-Barnett and American reform, 1880–1930.* University of North Carolina Press.

Schwalm, L. A. (1997). *A hard fight for we: Women's transitions from slavery to freedom in South Carolina.* University of Illinois Press.

Smith, E. M. (1980). Mary McLeod Bethune and the National Youth Administration. In M. E. Deutrich & V. C. Purdy (Eds.), *Clio was a woman: Studies in the history of American women.* Howard University Press.

Smitherman, G. (Ed.). (1995). *African American women speak out on Anita Hill-Clarence Thomas.* Wayne State University Press.

Stewart, M. W. Throw off your fearfulness and come forth! *Meditations from the pen of Mrs. Maria W. Stewart.* (Original work published 1879)

The Proclamation (1991). https://www.sisterstestify.com/about/the-proclamation/

Wallace, M. (1990). *Black macho and the myth of the superwoman*. Verso. (Original work published 1978)

Washington, M. H. (Ed.). (1988). *Invented lives: Narratives of Black women, 1860–1960.* Anchor.

Weisenburger, S. (1998). *Modern media: A family story of slavery and child-murder from the Old South.* Hill and Wang.

Wright, S. D. (1999). Black women in Congress during the post-Civil Rights Movement era. In K. Springer (Ed.), *Still lifting, still climbing: African American women's contemporary activism* (pp. 149–163). New York University Press.

Zilversmit, A. (1968). Quok Walker, Mumbet, and the abolition of slavery in Massachusetts. *William and Mary Quarterly.*

Additional Resources

Bambara, T. C. (Ed.). (1970). *The Black woman: An anthology*. New American Library.

Bates, D. (1962). *The long shadow of Little Rock, a memoir*. David McKay Co.

Brown, E. (1994). *A taste of power: A Black woman's story*. Anchor/Doubleday.

Brown, K. (1996). *Good wives, nasty wenches, and anxious patriarchs: Gender, race, and power in colonial Virginia*. University of North Carolina Press.

Clark, S. P. (1962). *Echo in my soul*. E. P. Dutton.

Collier-Thomas, B., & Franklin, V. P. (2001). *Sisters in the struggle: African American women in the civil rights-Black power movement*. New York University Press.

Collins, P. H. (1990). *Black feminist thought: Knowledge, consciousness, and the politics of empowerment* (1st ed.). Unwin Hyman.

Crawford, V. L., Rouse, J. A., & Woods, B. (Eds.). (1990). *Women in the civil rights movement: Trailblazers and torchbearers, 1941–1965*. Carlson.

Davis, A. Y. (1974). *An autobiography*. Random House.

Davis, A. Y. (1983). *Women, race and class.* Vintage Books.

Evans, S. (1979). *Personal politics: The roots of women's liberation in the civil rights movement and the new left*. Vintage Press.

Gilmore, G. (1996). *Gender and Jim Crow: Women and the politics of White supremacy in North Carolina, 1896–1920*. University of North Carolina Press.

Grant, J. (1998). *Ella Baker: Freedom bound*. Wiley.

Guy-Sheftall, B. (Ed.). (1995). *Words of fire: An anthology of African-American feminist thought.* The New Press.

Harley, S., & Terborg-Penn, R. (Eds.). (1978). *The Afro-American woman: Struggles and images*. Kennikat Press.

Higginbotham, E. B. (1993). *Righteous discontent: The women's movement in the Black Baptist Church, 1880–1920*. Harvard University Press.

Hine, D. C. (1994). *Hine sight: Black women and the re-construction of American history.* Carlson.

Hine, D. C., & Thompson, K. (1998). *A shining thread of hope: The history of Black women in America.* Broadway Books.

hooks, b. (1981). *Ain't I a woman: Black women and feminism*. South End.

Hull, A. G., Bell-Scott, P., & Smith, B. (1982). *All the women are White, all the Blacks are men, but some of us are brave: Black women's studies*. Feminist Press.

Jones, C., & Shorter-Gooden, K. (2003). *Shifting: The double lives of Black women in America*. HarperCollins.

Lerner, G. (1972). *Black women in White America: A documentary history*. Pantheon Books.

Lorde, A. (1982). *Zami: A new spelling of my name*. Crossing Press.

Lorde, A. (1984). *Sister outsider: Essays and speeches*. Crossing Press.

Moody, A. (1968). *Coming of age in Mississippi*. Dial Press.

Moraga, C., & Anzaldua, G. (Eds.). (1981). *This bridge called my back: Writings by radical women of color*. Persephone Press.

Olson, L. (1997). *Freedom's daughters: The unsung heroines of the civil rights movement from 1830 to 1970*. Simon and Schuster.

Omolade, B. (1994). *The rising song of African American women*. Routledge.

Ransby, B. (2003). *Ella Baker and the Black freedom movement: A radical democratic vision*. University of North Carolina Press.

Shaw, S. J. (1996). *What a woman ought to be and to do: Black professional women workers during the Jim Crow era*. University of Chicago Press.

Springer, K. (2005). *Living for the revolution: Black feminist organizations, 1968–1980*. Duke University Presses Books.

Stack, C. (1974). *All our kin: Strategies for survival in a Black community*. Harper & Row.

White, D. G. (1999). *Aren't I a woman? Female slaves in the plantation*. W. W. Norton.

White, D. G. (1999). *Too heavy a load: Black women in defense of themselves, 1894–1994*. W. W. Norton.

White, E. F. (2001). *Dark continent of our bodies: Black feminism and the politics of respectability*. Temple University Press.

Yee, S, J. (1992). *Black women abolitionists: A study in activism, 1828–1860*. University of Tennessee Press.

Yellin, J. F. (1989). *Women and sisters: The antislavery feminists in American culture*. Yale University Press.

Reading 4.5. Healing, Coping, and Transcending the Legacy of Racism, Classism, and Sexism

Linda James Myers

When I dare to be powerful—to use my strength in the service of my vision, then it becomes less and less important whether I am afraid.

—Audre Lorde

The Empress – Our Story

Imagine this. What if you were an Empress (or Emperor, as the case may be, but we will focus on Black women at this time) with full and sole authority over your wonderful kingdom? Your kingdom is invaded by the evildoers, whose goal it is to take over your kingdom and control, exploit, and enslave you and your future generations for their benefit. Over time, you succumb to the invaders' deception and manipulations, and begin to lose any memory of yourself as the Empress. Becoming accustomed to responding to the dictates and definitions of your captors as if they were your own and having internalized their false ideas of your inferiority and their superiority, you fall unconscious and enter the nightmare state of existence in which you are continually subjected to terrorism and violence.

Fear, insecurity, guilt, shame, anger, and self-destruction become the hallmarks of your trauma. As you survey the landscape, there is no relief in sight. You vaguely remember the stories of your ancestors and their glory days—how they too had been overrun and captured but fought back and achieved what they thought was the beginning of a new day. Their sense of liberation was short-lived (as in the 60s Black Power and Civil Rights movements), as they found themselves a few decades later only further immersed in the structures and systems of the oppressor and having internalized the oppression. What you need is a magic potion to awaken the Empress from her sleep, to bring her to awareness of her greatness and her ability to wield her divine inheritance. In order to regain her power, the Empress must plug back in to her power source with her time and attention.

Clearly this allegory is about what has happened to Black people in general, and Black women in particular, as we have experienced the Maafa, the African Holocaust, and now seek to regain our power. Distress, dysfunction, and disorder are the negative and harmful manifestations of a people living under terrorism and trauma for generations. In addition to individual subjective distress and behavioral problems, dysfunction in relationships and roles, families, groups, and communities signals the need to attend to and make the psychological changes necessary for health, wholeness, and sustainability. Identifying and confronting the source of the trauma and difficulties is the first step towards healing. As the Ethiopian proverb says, "he who conceals his disease cannot be cured."

This chapter was first published by Linda James Myers, Ph.D. (2010) in L. Rodgers-Rose & Z. Zai'mah (Eds.), *Healing Black Women from Violence: Reclamation and Peace*. Norfolk, Va.: Traces Publications. The current revision was done with the assistance of Kristee Haggins, Ph.D., California Institute of Mental Health.

The Truth of Who We Were

The foundation of our beliefs, as the authors of this chapter, is that all that we need, we have. We are not victims, but rather triumphant survivors, and if there is a role that we have played in our own victimization, we are now able to confront and transform its outcomes. The best news is that our ancestors left the solutions, tools, and roadmap for us to go forth and conquer all demons. Among the other places where they left this knowledge, wisdom, and understanding are their ancient sacred texts, including the Holy Bible, when interpreted from the cultural frame of reference of the people who originally wrote it. Most importantly, they left it, and we carry it with us in our souls; our charge is now to use the keys left us to unlock this hidden treasure in our hearts, minds, and souls that it might free us, individually and collectively, from the pain and sorrow, liberate us from the mechanisms of abuse and violence, and uplift us to the heights of our true being.

Yes, we are indeed truly Divine Spirit having a human experience. Given the power to create, we determine our experience on its most essential level outward. How so, you say, in that you know some of the things that have happened to you were most certainly not what you would have created for yourself. Agreed, of course they may not have been your preference. However, the success of the power to create is not measured by what happens to you; it will be assessed by how you respond to what has happened to you. At all times you will have at least two choices—to try to see the good, that is, get the lessons the so-called negative might bring and master them, or to focus on the negative. With the first choice you will remain aligned with the infinite positive energies of the universe, thereby drawing into manifestation the blessings and favor of alignment with that Divine Energy which is always there, whether or not we are aware of it, and experience the peace, love, and joy it brings.

Understanding the Problem—Diagnosing the Disease

There are also equally abundant negative forces, which gain power when we supply them with our time and attention. Fear, guilt, shame, anger, anxiety, depression, regret, jealousy, and envy are among those negative energies most frequently overtaking our hearts, minds, and souls. They abound because of the way we have been mis-socialized and mis-educated by virtue of the Maafa and its derivative outcome, mentacide, the systematic destruction of our culture and minds. However, each of us still holds the keys to the kingdom of our own consciousness, and we can at any time transform our experience, one thought and one feeling at a time.

So how have these negative forces of the Maafa impacted Black women? The mindset that has resulted in the development of racism, classism, and sexism has also resulted in violence and abuse directed toward African American women. The Justice Department estimates that one in five women will experience rape or attempted rape during their college years, and that less than five percent of these rapes will be reported (Karjane et al., 2005). If this is the experience of educated women in an educational environment, what is likely the experience of women in other environments? Income is also a factor: the poorer the household, the higher the rate of domestic violence—with women in the lowest income category experiencing more than six times the rate of nonfatal intimate partner violence as compared to women in the highest income category. When we consider race, we see that African American women face higher rates of domestic violence than White women do (Bachar et al., 2010).

Disenfranchisement is accomplished by shifting our awareness to a suboptimal cultural worldview steeped with the illusion that we are not good enough by virtue of some external criteria (e.g., white skin, male gender). Our negative feelings set up a bioenergetic or electromagnetic field of energy, attracting like energy. This reality gives birth to and shapes perception, so that what we perceive, the meaning we make of it, and what we think, feel, and do about it, if anything, are programmed by the set of cultural assumptions derived from the social context within which we find ourselves. At the core of the system are suboptimal assumptions antithetical to the health and sustainability of all people, but particularly to persons acknowledging African ancestry, who are not privileged by the assignment of value and opportunity given to Whites (and for women, the privilege given to males). The structures of oppression are layered from the system's innermost core, shaping perceptions, informing thoughts, feelings, and behaviors, and dictating social policies and practices that are rooted in the institutions carrying out the socially engineered agendas.

How to Cope

In light of these grim realities and statistics, what can we do to reduce violence against women, and to mitigate racism, classism, and sexism? With a deeper understanding of the psycho-cultural and psycho-social factors accounting for the prevalence of these -isms, we can learn what forces are at our disposal to prevent and protect against them, as well as how best to militate against their likelihood from a psycho-cultural perspective. The key will be in providing a culturally syntonic psychology and psychological analysis grounded in the tradition of wisdom and deep thought of our Ethiopian (Black, African) ancestors, so that our right minds, true identities, and rightful place can be restored as Ethiopian women.

The need for a theory of optimal psychology emerges from the unique experience of non-immigrant Africans in the Americas, as they were for centuries forced to live under a system of chattel enslavement that denied their humanity. Subsequently, they were forced to continue living under social conditions that both deemed their healthy, efficacious behaviors insane and sanctioned their abuse by their captors as legitimate and civilized (Myers, 1993). The mental health professionals of the days of slavery considered African captives who tried to escape to freedom mentally ill and prescribed extra physical abuse as the most effective treatment for captives appearing not to work with enthusiasm. Mistrust of the culture of the captors and their descendants is warranted by this history. In addition, the need to determine the characteristics and parameters of true mental health and illness, to say nothing of moral and spiritual development, is also warranted.

Optimal theory evolved in the vein of the wisdom tradition to seek to predict how human consciousness can be structured with observation and reason to be in union with the divine or supremely good. The records left by our ancestors (the African mothers and fathers of all human culture and civilization) reinforce a conception of the timelessness of the universe and a holistic perspective which recognizes the interrelatedness and interdependence of all things. This orientation is paradigmatically distinct from Western psychology, emphasizing a perspective that is holistic and integrative rather than fragmented and disintegrative (Myers & Speight, 2010).

We now have a better understanding of the context and history that impact Black women in terms of the obstacles designed to control, exploit, and oppress us. Having properly diagnosed the problem, which is the first step in healing, we can manage and transcend these obstacles. This next step is administering the cure, which includes recovering important information necessary to regain our power, liberating our consciousness, and fostering positive well-being and functioning. As rulers of the realm of our own consciousness, we must engender the return of the divine feminine which we are, showing ourselves the love and respect, we deserve, cherishing the sacred vessels which are our bodies, and healing our spirits, individually and collectively. Black/ African/ Africana psychology, based on our ancestors' teachings, can provide us with the analysis and tools needed to overcome that which would hold our consciousness captive.

Healing Our Spirits

...spirituality is a way of life based on a society's belief systems and moral values as they relate to a higher being. A spirituality is all of what you define yourself to be and is intertwined with your everyday actions. Your spirituality cannot be separated from your being. Egyptians believed that God is everything and everything is God as did many other Africans, not the idea that God is just in everything. Spirituality is also the relationship between you and your ancestors. When a person dies, the "spirit" returns to a higher being. Your ancestors then become your link with that higher being. Symbolism is a way of expressing that spirituality through individual aspects of your culture. Therefore spiritual

symbolism means your relationship with a higher being and your ancestors who are parts of the higher being through the individual aspects of your culture in everyday life.

—Africana Research Center Writing Project, Cornell University

Africana psychology has examined the influences of cultural and intellectual imperialism on the human psyche, and within the field of psychology, on the production of psychological knowledge (Myers, 2009). The cultural worldview currently prevailing has influenced the shift from psychology as a study of the soul to a psychology in service to particular dominant groups in societies. Traditional, Western psychology is problematized as a discipline whose knowledge production appears to narrowly serve the interest of the dominant group rather than the collective good within our society. Optimal Theory conceives of a reality that is a spiritual/material unity, is focused on the highest good for all, is holistic and integrative, and is based upon the wisdom tradition of the ancient Egyptians.

Language in the classical African culture of ancient Kmt (Black Land, later known as Egypt) was called Mdw Ntr, or words of the Divine or God. Thus, consciousness of God was lived, and life was organized around giving thanks and praise to The Most High in all of its manifestations. The natural order of the universe was acknowledged and honored, with each aspect respected for its contribution to the greater good of the whole. When Djehuti, also known as Thoth and Hermes, said that the first cardinal principle is that "all is Mind" or consciousness, he was reporting knowledge that had been established over the ages and was passing it on to future generations. As the proverb says, "if you do not know where you are going, any path will get you there." In the wisdom tradition of Ethiopian deep thought, we know who we are and where we are going; however, the Maafa has moved us away from knowledge of our Oneness with the Divine and turned our time and attention to a suboptimal reality constructed to enslave us to the service of the negative forces. Our challenge now is to disrupt the forces taking us away from our Divine connection and inheritance.

Ntr is the life force energy in every element. Characterized by being everywhere present (omnipresent), all knowing (omniscient), and all powerful (omnipotent,) that energy or Spirit is known as God, also called Supreme Being, The Most High, Holy Spirit, Creative Life Force, and many religious names, such as Jesus, Allah, Buddha, and so on. Committing to the intention to experience conscious awareness of or union with the Divine Spirit, individually and collectively, will yield true mental health and generate the capacity to create a healthy, supportive socio-cultural environment. Much like our ancestors did, we will have the ability to accomplish feats that were once perceived as impossible to the carnal mind. Though much detail can be and has been given in other writings, suffice it to provide here one example of what I am suggesting with the intention of telling like it is, in the height of the Ethiopian cultural tradition.

As a Divine Spirit having a human experience, our purpose for incarnating is to come to realize more and more about our true Self, until we achieve full and conscious awareness of ourselves and all that is as Divine Spirit. Achieving this Oneness of Being in human form is the Christian religion's equivalent of becoming a Christ. The African wisdom tradition teaches that we will all have ample opportunity to achieve this aim, with each incarnation designed to provide exactly the lessons needed to ensure and further proper progress. Teachings have it that we choose not only parents to come back through, but also the best location, time, environment, and others to come with us to accomplish our aims. The goal is to produce the circumstances most likely to give us the experiences that we need, as has been determined and selected by us and by those working on behalf of The Most High. Though the ultimate purpose for all of humanity is as described, we each also have come with our personal purpose, which is designed to contribute to the greater good of the One, and with the gifts and talents needed to fulfill our specific purposeful contribution.

How do you know your specific purpose and the issues you came to work on? In traditional culture, we had healers, priests, priestesses, and shaman to divine for us, as it was built into the cultural fabric. We had appreciation for how the planetary energies were aligned at the time and location of birth, as well as awareness that all around us at all times are signs and symbols to guide us along our paths. Today those same resources still exist, but we have often been socialized to negate and fear them, and to see them as something other than Divine. It is also true that some charlatans or imposters have infiltrated Divine space to dupe and exploit us, but they are not true emissaries of the Divine, and we must develop the spirit of discernment to avoid any traps they might set.

What one author notes in her interactions with diviners is that they seldom tell her something she does not already know or have some sense of, and if their information is true, it resonates in her heart as true. In terms of your personal purpose, it will likely be related to something you are good at and enjoy; you would be unlikely to come to this plane without the talents you need, though effort and hard work may be required. Relative to your particular lessons, you will recognize them because they will be issues that likely keep coming up in your life in one form or the other. The signs and symbols of nature provide an excellent gauge and guide for your endeavors once you learn how to interpret them.

However, what we have found most helpful on our journey has been working on our own personal relationship and alignment with The Most High. It ignites a self-correcting, self-perpetuating system which is experienced, and also can be observed and shared with others, for the greater good of the whole. Depending on the stage of soul development, the lessons and experiences encountered may be for the growth and benefit of others as well as oneself. The sequence of development and progression, which I call the optimization process, is cyclic, spiraling in nature much like the double helix of DNA. This process is so essential to the grand system of organization that whether or not you make the commitment consciously, you will be propelled forward in the cycles toward union.

Demonstrating that you are an eager learner by consciously making the commitment maximizes the potential for a more positive experience of the process and more immediate goal achievement. For example, when you decide you believe you are one with the Divine Infinite and your patterns of interpreting reality and the designs for living align with that belief, in a fragmented, suboptimal socio-cultural context such as this society, you will bring into your experience something to test or challenge your sense of unity consciousness. You will know that you are being challenged because you will feel one of the negative emotions. Since the purpose of negativity in human experience is to provide the opportunity for edification and growth, your charge will be to bring the negative emotions to conscious awareness and interrogate them. Examine what your thoughts, what your self-talk, has been. Ninety-nine percent of the time you will find that you have been caught up in a sense of self defined by the dominant, suboptimal socio-cultural context. Your focus has been on an externalized sense of self defined by what you think other people might think or by socially engineered notions of your worth based on your looks, income, education, position, and so on.

Cut to the chase through all of that suboptimal programming to the bottom line, which is this: either you are Divine Spirit and part of a Divine Order, even though you may not fully see it or understand it at the time, or you are not. If you believe that you are, use your faith to master the lesson the sense of separation has come to teach you, about the areas of your life you need to secure, and come back to your true self, clearer, stronger, and more capable than you were before the "crisis." Over time your heart mind will be re-programmed to see the crisis as a challenge, then an opportunity, and ultimately a blessing. At the latter stage you will have unified, contained, and transcended the oppositions of life, a characteristic of achieving consciousness union with the Divine, or God.

The universe by its nature is built on polarities and dualities, which are complementary, and without which neither could be. In order to know good, you must at least have a sense of not quite as good, otherwise everything is the same and indistinguishable. Both positive and negative are needed. However, because the negative forces are generated by mankind as conceived separate from the Divine, they are illusory in nature and will dissipate once the light of the eternal Divine Force is shined upon them. The Divine, whose nature has historically been characterized as love, is the most powerful force in the universe and is beyond eternal time and space. While this knowledge may be good to know, if it is only in your head, it becomes theoretical. As our ancestors so clearly voiced, the key is to know it in your heart, and practice living it through your heart mind. At the point and time that we are able to feel a sense of peace, love, and well-being, we can know that we are aligned in consciousness with the righteous forces. Over time we develop a deep sense of gratitude for The Most High, which becomes a beacon ensuring the good into which we are immersed. Such a state of health becomes difficult to achieve without knowledge of its nature, processes, and functioning. The nature of knowledge is infinite, so the potential for growth, which means more lessons, does not cease. How we experience the lessons changes with growth, such that with mastery, over time the most horrible thing becomes the challenge, which becomes the opportunity, which becomes the blessing.

What is the first step to heaven, where the Divine resides? Going within and finding that place of peace, of joy, of love, of truth is the first step. For this step, the tune and words "I don't care how you get there, just get there if you can …" become the most appropriate directive. Be it in the form of any practice that awards awareness of the presence and power of the Divine—meditation, prayer, singing, dancing, running, writing, whatever can facilitate taking you to the awareness of the place of which I speak—it will become your anchor on a stormy sea, your centering device in the face of wrath, and your blessed assurance in your time of need. The truth of the matter is that there is nowhere, no time that the Divine is not in you and you in it. Learning to practice awareness of this spiritual presence, individually and collectively, creating sacred space through intention, ritual, and praise, has been a centerpiece of Ethiopian cultural tradition. Our systems of social organization and functioning were imbued with cosmological appreciation of the natural order of the universe and our role in it and relationship to it.

Western scholarship has only recently become aware of what our ancestors have known for thousands of years, and research across cultural groups has begun to confirm the same ideas. For example, the heart as mind and its role in human experience is greater than that of the brain as mind. The heart mind generates an electromagnetic field that projects around 10 feet from a person. In addition, we now know that it is the emotions that determine how information is processed by the brain and the body. The body does not distinguish between what is imagined to be true and what is true; it will go with whatever you are believing at the time. It is not surprising that in classical African civilization the wise was defined as the one whose heart is informed about things we otherwise do not know. Use your heart mind to heal your spirit.

Recovering Ourselves

Ethiopians wake up and see yourself coming into the glorious light of the Sun. Prosperity is howling every day, will you accept it, for it will be peace, joy and health to the soul. Think for yourself then you will create what you think.

—Prophet G. W. Hurley, 1923

To progress beyond the limits of the prevailing suboptimal cultural worldview, we must educate ourselves about the construction of a new reality grounded in our Ethiopian ancestors' cultural traditions and embrace their optimal psychology. Rejecting the definitions of the cultural reality from which the deplorable history of racism and racialization that has characterized American social policy and practice emerged, we must embrace our own patterns of interpreting reality and designs for living. The mindset that fostered racism is also responsible for sexism, classism, elitism, and so forth. Regaining our power, healing our spirit, and recovering ourselves are made possible by the resilience and truth of our ancestral worldview. It is that worldview that brought us through almost 400 years of the most brutal, vicious, dehumanizing form of enslavement and terrorism ever practiced in the history of humankind, to become this nation's moral and spiritual leaders. Realizing that the potentials for both optimal and suboptimal functioning exist within us, it only makes sense for us to choose to pursue divine consciousness. Faith is the substance of things expected, the evidence of things not seen. An optimal psychological analysis enables us to get beyond the fragmented, self-destructive worldview imposed upon us through the brainwashing of our ancestors' captors and their offspring.

A Black psychology and analysis worthy of its name must explore all of the facets of the energy spectrum made evident in classical African ontology, epistemology, and axiology. Its assumptions about the nature of reality, about knowledge and how one knows, and about what is of highest value, all have to be consistent with the ancient writings and sacred texts. It must begin with classical African cosmological principles and beliefs about the nature of the universe. So developed, such praxis will allow us to interrogate the Totality, fearlessly studying the metaphysical and physical aspects of being which account for our strength and resilience in the face of ceaseless onslaughts, as well as other aspects of the shadow (negative) side of life.

We are required to examine and make sense of that which dominant Western culture, with its intellectual imperialism and epistemic violence, has told us and trained us to believe is of no value, unknowable, or not of God. This psychological and cultural injustice and violence presents the worst aspect of the enslavement of African people as chattel, the capstone of our dehumanization. We have begun to see the fullness of its impact and the devastation it brings. But despite the disruption of the normal modes of cultural transmission and the ongoing development and refinement of cultural practice, the potential loss of our cultural consciousness could not be completed. The shift toward the cultural consciousness of the captors and their progeny was only achieved by virtue of a long-standing pattern of brainwashing, and in more contemporary times, by the relentless social engineering via media and often via formal education. Irrespective of these formidable forces, we still rise.

Despite every effort that has been made and continues to be made to destroy African Americans, despite the racism, sexism, and classism that exist in the lives of African American women, Black cultural consciousness has not been lost. Nor can it ever be, by virtue of its comprehensive, cohesive, and coherent nature. Although it appears we are at our lowest ebb of Black cultural consciousness since having given over the education and socialization of our children more than 50 years ago to de-segregation, and the organization of our communities to "urban renewal," there have always remained among us the keepers of the culture. Their commitment, insights, and diligence have ensured successful transmission and resistance to assimilation into the captor's cultural frame, often referred to as integration. We have now come into the time when we are able to reignite our collective movement toward health, wholeness, and sustainability, as the cultural consciousness of our forebears' captors has been exposed for what it is and is not. It is bankrupt, toxic, and pathological, having pushed the world and humanity to the brink of collapse and destruction. The salvation of humanity requires that we come into the light of the amazing resilience and strength that are our inheritance.

Returning to Our Truth—Black Cultural Consciousness

It is the spiritual or metaphysical aspects of being, which our ancestors understood so well and incorporated as their Black cultural consciousness and praxis, that have been and continue to be our saving grace. That is why, despite every attempt at cultural disruption and dehumanization, we non-immigrant Africans in America emerge out of the Maafa as the moral and spiritual leaders pushing this nation that enslaved us as chattel to live up to its word of equal civil rights for all. Where did that moral and spiritual acumen, courage, and drive come from? Most certainly not from our captors. We contend that it came from our Black cultural consciousness, which from classical civilization to date has understood its connection to something greater than what appears, has been aware of the necessity to look within oneself, and has trusted in that Ntu, Life Force, to carry us forward, despite what might come against us. Let us give you an example, starting with the quote introduced at the beginning of this section of the paper.

Known as Prophet G. W. Hurley by his followers, George Willie Hurley had a vision in which a Black damsel by the name of Haggar came to him and instructed that he commit to instilling the Ethiopian spirit in the children. He was charged with the mission of starting a school of mediumship and psychology to teach Black people that God is Spirit, as are they—the essence which is them, within them, and within which they are. White supremacists of the day, both White and Black (having internalized oppression and become mentacidal), tried to destroy Hurley and his movement, forcing him to start (under the weight of much persecution) a church, rather than a school. Disparaged for teaching about the spirit realm, including what Western Christianity regarded as the forbidden and wicked occult, Hurley managed to keep his mission alive of instilling the Ethiopian spirit in the children.

The Universal Hagar Spiritual Association continues today, still teaching: how to become a healer; how to become a medium in the spirit realm (i.e., develop psychic abilities of clairvoyance and clairaudience, which Western operatives call remote viewing, and other spirit-based skill sets); and how to master other aspects of African metaphysics, much like what has been seen among healers and shaman throughout the continent among groups such as the Zulu, Akan, Yorùbá, Dogan, Dagara, Shona, and Wolof. How did the transmission of such Black cultural consciousness occur? It was transmitted through the spirit realm, which has no limitations of time and space. Western science, through quantum physics and neuroscience, has only recently become cognizant of and learned to respect those dimensions and their power. Consistent with the classical African knowing that all is energy, Ntr, Divine, Spirit, God, our ancient ancestors' understandings reemerge despite every effort to prevent it. This historical reality gives us a sense of the charge, challenges, and triumph that Black psychology and psychological analysis must uncover. In this light, the central question is no longer the identity question of who we are. Our ancestors have answered that, almost uniformly, across the board—we are Divine Being. The new question for us is, how are we Divine, and how can we be so in this day and time?

As Africana psychologist and educator Asa Hilliard so aptly cautioned us, we must have a psychology and psychological analysis that leave people of African ancestry fully knowledgeable of themselves, familiar with and immersed in the best of their cultural traditions, and conscious of their condition. We must bring a syntonic, or culturally congruent, understanding of what it means to be human to their experience (Hilliard, 1997, p. xiii), and we now have that. Embracing knowledge from the ancient wisdom of our Ethiopian (Black) ancestors to the heights of present-day research, optimal psychology and psychological analysis have over the past 40 years developed a holistic, integrative understanding of human functioning. As a result, a comprehensive, cohesive, and coherent multi-dimensional examination of the human condition and human development has been created. The outcomes of the resulting probes have been phenomenal, literally and figuratively speaking. All knowledge seems to be converging around the same assumptions, as each cultural group has approached the subject of humanity and divinity from its own perspective. Black/ African/ Africana researchers have been consistent and clear over the generations in terms of the causes of our demise and its cure.

The major factors which have tremendous implications for our optimal health and well-being, individually and collectively, are metaphysical in nature. That is, they are of a higher order behind, yet beyond and encompassing, the physical. For all practical purposes on the human plane of existence, that would mean such forces as thoughts, feelings, intuitions, revelations, insights, dreams, visions, and so forth, which are the substance of reality. When aligned with the Divine, these are forces we control and can therefore use to overcome the psychological oppression and its resultant mental bondage and mentacide.

As we engage in the processes of regaining our power, healing our spirits, and recovering our inheritance, we acknowledge the psychological and cultural violence that has been and continues to be inflicted on us, but we also use it for our growth. The special challenge to Ethiopians, Black people throughout the world, in this spiritual war is that we have been forced to survive and develop in suboptimal socio-cultural contexts founded on and infused with structural biases that by their nature can render us disenfranchised, exploited, disadvantaged, labeled, and treated as inferior, if not less than human. However, it is the deep structures of culture that determine the patterns of interpreting reality and designs for living which individuals internalize to shape their consciousness and experience, and we have the power to define those. The metaphysical core of the system of White supremacy is steeped in beliefs and values that would lead us to believe that we are separate from our divinity. This lie is perpetuated on several psycho-social levels and dimensions, which we can dismantle. Let us begin with the emotional reactions informed by the heart mind.

Summary

What does all of this mean in terms of recovering ourselves and healing from racism, sexism, and classism? It means developing an awareness that almost everything that we have been taught is true about ourselves, the world, and the way things work is actually false. Often, the absolute opposite is true. We must return to the African-centered paradigm and holistic conceptual system based on the oneness of spirit and matter. We must recognize that everything is interrelated through networks of human and spiritual processes and that each person is an expression of the energy and essence that flows through all life. The importance of self-knowledge and consciousness of the unified self (consciousness is connection to the energy that permeates everything) is essential to good health. Liberation comes from freeing our minds and making contact with the consciousness of Oneness. Through interventions such as analysis of our belief systems, our consciousness can be transformed, and the quality of life can be improved for ourselves and others. The solution is to learn to express our authentic selves within contexts that actively work against our validation and affirmation, recognizing the truth of the matter, which is that we are one with the Divine.

References

Bachar, K. J., Campbell, R., Fisher, B. S., & Rumburg, D. (2010). *Sexual violence research 15 years after VAWA – Panel at the 2010 NIJ conference* (NCJ 234785). National Institute of Justice. https://www.ojp.gov/ncjrs/virtual-library/abstracts/sexual-violence-research-15-years-after-vawa-panel-2010-nij

Hilliard, A.G.,III (1997). *SBA: The reawakening of the African mind.* Gainesville, FL: Makare Publishing.

Karjane, H. M., Fisher, B. S., & Cullen, F. T. (2005). *Sexual assault on campus: What colleges and universities are doing about it* (NCJ 205521). National Institute of Justice, Research for Practice. https://www.ojp.gov/pdffiles1/nij/205521.pdf

Myers, L. J. (1993). *Understanding an Afrocentric world view: Introduction to an optimal psychology.* Kendall/Hunt.

Myers, L. J. (2003). *Our health matters: Guide to an African (Indigenous) American psychology and cultural model for creating a climate and culture of optimal health.* Ohio Commission on Minority Health.

Myers, L. J. (2009). Theoretical and conceptual approaches to African American psychology. In H. Nevelle, S. Utsey, & B. Tynes (Eds.), *Handbook of African American psychology.* Sage Publications.

Myers, L. J., & Speight, S. L. (2010). Reframing mental health and psychological well-being among persons of African descent: Africana/Black psychology meeting the challenges of fractured social and cultural realities. *The Journal of Pan African Studies, 3*(8), 66–82.

Contributor Biographies

Jasmine Abrams, Ph.D. Dr. Abrams's work as a behavioral research scientist is conducted with the goal of utilizing culture as an avenue to better understand and reduce health disparities among women of African ancestry via health promotion. As the Director of the Global Community Health Promotion Network, Dr. Abrams conducts domestic and international research in collaboration with community-based organizations. Importantly, Dr. Abrams is fiercely dedicated to sexual health promotion among women of African ancestry.

Valerie N. Adams-Bass, Ph.D. Dr. Valerie N. Adams-Bass is an Assistant Professor of Youth and Social Innovation, a faculty affiliate of the Youth-Nex Center to Promote Effective Youth Development, and a faculty affiliate of The Center for the Study of Race and Public Education in the South, in the Curry School of Education at the University of Virginia. Dr. Adams-Bass's research centers on Black children and youth. She is most interested in examining how media exposure influences inter-personal interactions and self-concept and how racial/ethnic socialization experiences are related to the process of identity development through social and academic experiences. Dr. Adams-Bass regularly trains youth development professionals to use culturally relevant practices when working with African American children and youth.

Frances Adomako. Frances Adomako is a current Counseling Psychology Ph.D. candidate at Howard University who was recently awarded a two-year APA Minority Postdoctoral Fellowship. She holds an Ed.M. from Teachers College of Columbia University in Counseling Psychology as well as a B.A. in Sociology from St. John's University. Adomako's work explores race-based stress and trauma through the lens of social activism, emphasizing the use of digital media in Black activism and psychological well-being. With a commitment to bridging the divide between the academy and the community, Adomako's work engages with community organizations, research, and public policy. Adomako's clinical work is also heavily focused in the area of trauma, specifically Race-based Trauma + Post-Traumatic Stress Disorder.

Shareefah Al'uqdah, Ph.D. Dr. Shareefah N. Al'Uqdah started her doctoral program when her oldest son was seven months. While earning her Ph.D. she had to learn how to manage school, work, life, and parenting stress. Throughout graduate school, Dr. Shareefah gained invaluable skills to help families and individuals residing within urban communities. Her training has included working in DC public and charter schools, DC Superior Courts, St. Elizabeth's Hospital, community mental health clinics, and college counseling centers. Dr. Shareefah completed a Substance Abuse Mental Health Services Administration (SAMHSA)-sponsored training in co-occurring disorders aimed at improving clinicians' ability to address mental health and substance abuse issues. She has also conducted mental health trainings internationally. She is a licensed clinical psychologist in private practice in the DC metro area.

Faye Belgrave, Ph.D. Dr. Belgrave is Professor of Psychology at Virginia Commonwealth University and the Founding Director of the Center for Cultural Experiences in Prevention. Her programmatic and research interests are in the areas of drug and HIV prevention among African Americans and other ethnic minorities. Dr. Belgrave's research also focuses on the role of culture and context in prevention interventions and on gender- and female-related issues. Much of her work has been conducted in collaboration with community-based organizations. Dr. Belgrave has published extensively, including five books and close to 100 papers, and is an invited speaker on the topics of African American culture, female issues, and community-based evaluation and research. Dr. Belgrave has received numerous awards and recognition for her research, teaching, and service including awards from the American Psychological Association, the Association of Black Psychologists (Distinguished Psychologist), Virginia Commonwealth University, The State Council of Higher Education in Virginia, and the Substance Abuse and Mental Health Services Administration.

Keisha Bentley-Edwards, Ph.D. Dr. Keisha L. Bentley-Edwards is an Associate Professor at Duke University's School of Medicine, General Internal Medicine Division, and the Associate Director of Research/Director of the Health Equity Working Group for the Samuel DuBois Cook Center on Social Equity. Dr. Bentley-Edwards is a developmental psychologist whose interdisciplinary research focuses on how race, gender, and racism stress influence social, health, and academic outcomes. Her work has particularly focused upon the development of culturally relevant measurement and research that addresses racial/ethnic socialization, racial cohesion and dissonance, and the intersection of race and gender throughout the lifespan. She has provided expert commentary to national and regional media outlets on issues relating to race, social justice, and disparities in health and education. Overall, she uses research to guide parents, policy makers, and practitioners to support healthy functioning.

Yolanda Bogan, Ph.D. Dr. Yolanda K. H. Bogan is a professor of psychology and recent past associate dean for research and assessment in the College of Social Sciences, Arts and Humanities at Florida A&M University. A licensed psychologist, she has been engaged in sexual assault research and education for over 30 years. Her interest in colonial America is based on her work in genealogy. She has traced her paternal line to the late 1600s, and her Native American sixth great-grandfather was an American Revolutionary War patriot.

Sheriden M. Booker, Ph.D. Dr. Booker is Director of the Beyond Identity Scholar Activist Program at The City College of New York. She received her doctorate in Sociocultural Anthropology from Yale University. An entrepreneur and experienced cultural strategist, she leverages her training as a social scientist and her global experience in development, media, and philanthropy to strategize client relationships, impact, and operational sustainability. In addition to her academic pursuits, she is an artist and creative producer in her own right, performing under the moniker Chéredyn. Singing in different dialects, she continuously infuses new sounds from her global treks and has conceived her own diasporic sound, one in which R&B gets engaged to Afro-Caribbean rhythms.

Moesha Ciceron. Moesha Ciceron is a second-year Community Psychology master's candidate at Florida A & M University. As a first-generation, Haitian American college student, Moesha is currently researching the deconstruction of European beauty standards as it interacts with the epidemiology and cultural identity of Afro-Caribbean people. When not writing, she's involved in local grassroots organizations in her hometown of Charlotte, NC, geared toward mobilizing communities of color and advancing topics of Black mental health.

Patricia Hill Collins, Ph.D. Dr. Patricia Hill Collins is a Distinguished University Professor of Sociology at the University of Maryland, College Park specializing in race, class, and gender. She is also the former head of the Department of African-American Studies at the University of Cincinnati, and a past President of the American Sociological Association (ASA). Collins was the 100th president of the ASA and the first African American woman to hold this position. Her work primarily concerns issues involving feminism, gender, and social inequality within the African American community. She first came to national attention for her book *Black Feminist Thought*, originally published in 1990.

Kyla Day Fletcher, Ph.D. Dr. Kyla Day Fletcher is the Lucinda H. Stone Associate Professor of Psychology at Kalamazoo College. She teaches courses in adolescent development, sexuality, psychology of the African American experience, and research methods. Dr. Fletcher's research employs mixed methods to understand sexual socialization, substance use, intimacy, and sexual health from a comprehensive and strengths-based perspective. She earned her bachelor's degree from Howard University and a Ph.D. in Developmental Psychology from the University of Michigan. Dr. Fletcher is involved in several college initiatives, including those focused on inclusion, excellence, and sexual assault prevention.

Barbara Haile, D.S.W. Dr. Barbara J. Haile is a retired Associate Professor and Coordinator of the social policy sequence for the M.S.W. Program at Florida A&M University. She received a B.A. at the University of Kentucky, M.A. in sociology at Indiana University, M.S.W. at Howard University, and D.S.W. from the University of Pennsylvania. Her research interests have focused on HIV/AIDS in both the American and South African contexts; the social, economic, and psychological conditions that confront and challenge African American women and families; and the role of social work advocates in effecting policy changes for the empowerment of oppressed communities. Recent research and publications direct attention to utilizing the concept of "cultural policy," which involves a recalibration of norms, standards, and expectations of Black children that are held by the Afrikan American community.

Brooklynn K. Hitchens, Ph.D. Dr. Brooklynn K. Hitchens is a postdoctoral associate and Assistant Professor at the University of Maryland, College Park in the Department of Criminology and Criminal Justice. She is a sociologist and urban ethnographer who specializes in race, class, and gender inequities in crime and victimization, urban violence and trauma, and policing. Her work centers the marginalized experiences of urban, street-identified Black women and girls, particularly those with personal and vicarious experiences with victimization, and those who are "homicide survivors," or have experienced the loss of a loved one to homicide. She is a community-engaged researcher who uses an innovative methodological framework called Street Participatory Action Research (Street PAR). This method shifts the location of power in the research paradigm by including members of the population under study in each phase of the research process.

Tameka Bradley Hobbs, Ph.D. Dr. Tameka Bradley Hobbs, Associate Provost for Academic Affairs at Florida Memorial University, attended Florida State University, where she earned her doctoral degree in United States History and Historical Administration and Public History in 2004. Since that time, she has taught courses in American history, African American history, oral history, and public history at Florida A&M University, Virginia State University in Petersburg, Virginia, and John Tyler Community College in Chester, Virginia. In addition to her teaching experience, she has served as a researcher, writer, consultant, and director for a number of public and oral history projects in Florida and Virginia, including the African American Trailblazers in Virginia History Program, a statewide educational program focused on celebrating African American History. She joined the faculty of Florida Memorial University in Miami Gardens, Florida, in August of 2011. Hobbs is currently working on a manuscript on lynching violence during the era of World War II in Florida.

Kristina Jean-Baptiste. Kristina Jean-Baptiste is currently a Community Psychology Master's candidate at Florida A&M University with professional interests in the topics of body image, race, and clinical psychology. While obtaining her bachelor's degree at Stetson University in psychology, she completed a thesis focusing on the issue of Black women, body image, and racial identity. She plans to continue researching minoritized groups and body image after obtaining a doctorate.

Mawiyah Kambon, Ph.D. Dr. Mawiyah Kambon is an internationally acclaimed psychologist, traditional healer, and community elder in service to our community for 30+ years. Though many call her by her professional title, Dr. Kambon prefers her community names of Nana Efia (as bestowed through her initiation into the Akan traditional spiritual system of Ghana, West Africa) and Mama Mawiyah, a name that generations of younger people in the community affectionately call her. As a community elder, she is passionate about helping children and younger generations. In her practice, she helps children, adults, couples, and families restore themselves in mind body and spirit. As the current Director of Onipa Psychological and Consulting Services, she does in-office and online teletherapy counseling. Additionally, she operates an online guided meditation practice that complements her therapy practice. She has specialized in mental health and community outreach for over 30 years. She is a Past President of the Association of Black Psychologists.

Marva L. Lewis, Ph.D. Dr. Marva Lewis is a sociocultural developmental psychologist, academic researcher, and educator in the area of infant mental health, parent-child relationships, and diversity awareness. She is a committed, experienced, and successful trainer for child welfare social workers and early childhood consultants on diversity issues and services to African American families. Her innovative program of research builds on the strengths of families and communities, based on a cultural practices approach. She has obtained private, state, and federal funding for research and is skilled in conceptualization and development of culturally valid, community-based research methods. Her research on African American mother–daughter relationships uses the hair-combing task as a naturalistic intervention to strengthen parent–child attachment behaviors and build community connections among parents.

Morgan Maxwell, Ph.D. Dr. Morgan Maxwell is a Health Prevention Specialist and Researcher. She obtained a doctorate in Social Psychology from Virginia Commonwealth University. Her primary interests involve improving the physical and psychological well-being of communities of African ancestry worldwide and addressing the prevalence of colorist ideologies. Through evidence-based preventive programs, she strives to examine society's influence on individuals' sexual practices and to decrease the incidence of HIV within minority populations.

Afiya Mbilishaka, Ph.D. Dr. Afiya Mbilishaka is a therapist, research scientist, and hairstylist. She is the owner of Ma'at Psychological Services, a private practice in Washington, DC focused on promoting balance and restoring order to the lives of her clients. Her work focuses on understanding and using traditional African cultural rituals for contemporary wholistic mental health practices. Dr. Mbilishaka innovated the practice and research of "psychohairapy," where she uses hair as an entry point for mental health services in beauty salons and barbershops, as well as through social media. She has now gone international, leading a cultural and mental-health-focused trip to Cuba and to various African countries. She is the former Association of Black Psychologist (ABPsi) DC chapter president and a recent recipient of the ABPsi Research Award. Dr. Mbilishaka is a natural hairstylist at N Natural Hair Studio in Silver Spring, Maryland, where she loves creating art with locs, twists, and afros.

Linda James Myers, Ph.D. Dr. Linda James Myers (Ph.D.), retired professor of psychology at Ohio State University's Departments of African American and African Studies and Psychiatry, specializes in psychology and culture; moral and spiritual identity development; healing practices and psychotherapeutic processes; and intersections of race, gender, and class. Internationally known for her work in the development of a theory of Optimal Psychology, Dr. James Myers has conducted lectures and trainings in England, South Africa, Ghana, and Jamaica. She is the author of numerous articles, book chapters, and five books, including: *Understanding an Afrocentric World View: Introduction to Optimal Psychology* (1988); *Blessed Assurance: Deep Thought and Meditations in the Tradition and Wisdom of Our Ancestors* (2004); and *Recentering Culture and Knowledge in Conflict Resolution Practice* (2008, co-editor). Dr. Myers was named Distinguished Psychologist by the Association of Black Psychologists and has received numerous other honors and awards for excellence in research and scholarship, including the Bethune/Woodson Award for Outstanding Contributions in the Development of Promotion of Black Studies from the National Council of Black Studies; the Oni Award from the International Black Women's Congress; the Building to Eternity Award from the Association for the Study of Classical African Civilization; and the O.S.U. College of Arts and Sciences Outstanding Teaching Award, among others. Professor James Myers is a past president of the Association of Black Psychologists and Elder of Elders.

Helen A. Neville, Ph.D. Dr. Helen Neville is a professor of Educational Psychology and African American Studies at the University of Illinois at Urbana-Champaign. She is a past Associate Editor of *The Counseling Psychologist* and of the *Journal of Black Psychology*. Her work on race, racism, and racial identity has been published in a wide range of peer-reviewed journals. Dr. Neville has been recognized for her research and mentoring efforts including receiving the APA Graduate Students Kenneth and Mamie Clark Award, the APA Division 45 Charles and Shirley Thomas Award for mentoring/contributions to African American students/community, and the Winter Roundtable Janet E. Helms Mentoring Award. She was honored with the Association of Black Psychologists' Distinguished Psychologist of the Year award and the APA Minority Fellowship Award, Dalmas Taylor Award for Outstanding Research Contribution. She is a past president of the Society for the Psychological Study of Culture, Ethnicity, and Race.

Nimot M. Ogunfemi. Nimot Ogunfemi is a doctoral student in the Counseling Psychology program at the University of Illinois at Urbana-Champaign. She uses her social justice orientation to inform her work and organization style. Her primary research interests are the expression of spirituality in everyday spaces and spiritual well-being among people of African descent. As the current graduate assistant for the Sankofa Black Student Outreach Team at the University Counseling Center, she does psychoeducational community work in collaboration with Black students. She is also the co-facilitator for the transgender and queer support groups on campus. She is a member of the #PowerUp youth participatory action research project, where she works with young people to actualize change around gun violence in their community. She is the 2017–2019

Wanda Taeschner Babcock Fellowship awardee as well as the 2019 winner of the Champaign Area Psychological Society's Arnie Miller and Barb Bremer Memorial Scholarship.

Yasser Arafat Payne, Ph.D. Dr. Yasser Arafat Payne is an Associate Professor in the Department of Sociology and Criminal Justice and the Department of Africana Studies at the University of Delaware. He has written and published extensively in peer-reviewed journals. His research addresses the experiences of urban Afrikan Americans, particularly Black men, and focuses on themes of street life, resilience, and social justice. His research relies on the use of community-engaged and participatory approaches. He has received numerous awards for his work and is a sought-after speaker.

Michell Pope. Michell Pope is co-founder and CEO of Research Unlimited, a a full-service research assistance firm that specializes in helping researchers increase their productivity and maximize their efficiency. She received her doctorate in Health Psychology from Virginia Commonwealth University in Richmond, Virginia, where she also received her Bachelor of Science degree in Psychology. Her research interests are social and cultural influences affecting African American and Latino adolescents' body image attitudes and behaviors, sexual health, and mental well-being.

Amorie Robinson, Ph.D. Dr. Amorie Robinson is a licensed clinical psychologist. She is the Behavioral Health Lead Therapist at the Ruth Ellis Center in Highland Park, Michigan. She served just under 15 years at the Third Circuit Court (Juvenile/Family Division) Clinic for Child Study in Detroit, providing psychotherapy and assessments. She also sees clients of all ages at the Radical Well-Being Center. Dr. Robinson earned her B.A. in Psychology at Oberlin College and her doctorate in Clinical Psychology at the University of Michigan, where she has taught women's studies and psychology courses, including Introduction to LGBT Studies and Gender and Group Process in a Multicultural Context. Dr. Robinson conducts cultural competency workshops and is a trainer for the Michigan Department of Education. Published articles include domestic violence in Black lesbian communities, Black lesbian youth resiliency, and Black LGBT and gender-nonconforming youth in juvenile justice. Dr. Robinson coined the term "attractionality" to replace "sexuality" when referring to one's identity. She is a co-founder of the Ruth Ellis Center for at-risk LGBT+ youth who experience homelessness. The Center recently opened a specialized program for lesbian/queer women and girls called "Kofi House," based on Dr. Robinson's African name, Kofi Afua Adoma. She has received awards for community service from the Association for Women in Psychology and the Association of Black Psychologists and served on both boards. Dr. Robinson's self-care includes playing her violin and djembe drums, as well as hustle line-dancing and ballroom dancing.

Neico N. Slater-Sa-Ra, Ph.D. Dr. Neico Slater-Sa-Ra is currently a Visiting Professor of Psychology at Florida A&M University. She holds a bachelor's degree in Psychology, a master's degree in Community Psychology, and a doctorate in Educational Leadership. Dr. Slater-Sa-Ra has worked as a Clinical Therapist with adults and children in the field of Psychology for over 15 years. As an educator and clinician, she is a strategic thinker who takes calculated risks, and a visionary who works well in diverse business environments. Dr. Slater-Sa-Ra has extensive experience in organizational and educational leadership. Her interests are in analysis of the explicit and implicit intentionality of curriculum, culturally relevant pedagogy, and African-centered education.

Anita J. Thomas, Ph.D. Dr. Anita Thomas is the executive vice president and provost at St. Catherine University. She has more than 20 years of experience in academia, both as faculty and an administrator. Her research interests include racial identity, identity socialization, and using culturally affirming counseling approaches with African American families. She has conducted training seminars and workshops on multicultural issues for state and national professional organizations in counseling and psychology, hospitals and corporations, and human service organizations. Her background is in Counseling Psychology.

Khia A. Thomas, Ph.D. Dr. Khia A. Thomas is an Associate Professor of Psychology at Broward College, where she has served as a full-time faculty member since 2011. She has earned distinction for excellence in teaching and as a faculty advisor for the Psychology Club. She earned her bachelor's degree from Florida Agricultural and Mechanical University and her master's and doctorate in Developmental Psychology from the University of Michigan. Her research interests center on gender and sexual socialization of African American youth, specifically messages communicated by parents, peers, and the media; community-based prevention or interventions that engender healthy sexual outcomes; and Strong Black Woman ideology and its linkages with traditional gender scripts, romantic relationships, and mental health correlates.

Tiffany G. Townsend, Ph.D. Tiffany G. Townsend is the Chief Diversity Officer at Augusta University and Associate Professor of Psychological Science in Augusta, Georgia. She is also a Health Equity Researcher. Her research addresses race-related stress and race and ethnic socialization. She received her doctorate in Clinical Psychology from George Washington University, and is the former Senior Director of the Office of Ethnic Minority Affairs for the American Psychological Association (APA). Dr. Townsend's work involves the implementation of community-based research and prevention programs to decrease health and mental health disparities among ethnic minority women, children, and families. Her most recent NINR-funded project, entitled *Aza Sisters: An HIV Prevention Program for African American Girls*, was designed to develop an HIV prevention intervention that can empower African American girls who may have experienced some form of child sexual abuse or interpersonal trauma. She has served as the Associate Editor of the *Journal of Black Psychology* and on the Editorial Board for the *Psychology of Women Quarterly*. In addition, she has served as an ad-hoc reviewer for over 12 other academic journals and has authored or co-authored numerous peer-reviewed journal articles and book chapters.

Cheryl L. Woods-Giscombé, Ph.D., RN. Dr. Cheryl L. Woods Giscombé is the Melissa and Harry LeVine Family Professor of Quality of Life, Health Promotion and Wellness. Her program of research focuses on understanding and reducing stress-related health disparities among African Americans. Her research incorporates sociohistorical and biopsychosocial perspectives to investigate how stress and coping strategies contribute to stress-related psychological and physical health outcomes. Dr. Giscombé has a particular interest in the potential for integrative approaches to reduce mental-health-related disparities among African Americans.

Credits

Fig. 1.0.2: "Sankofa" © bagaball, (CC BY 2.0) at: http://www.flickr.com/photos/33756523@N05/3298844364.

Fig. 1.0.3: Source: http://commons.wikimedia.org/wiki/File:Akindra.jpg. Copyright in the Public Domain.

Fig. 1.1.1: Adapted from "Nguzo Saba: The Seven Principles," by Dr. Maulana Karenga.

Fig. 1.1.2: Source: http://commons.wikimedia.org/wiki/File:Ahmose-Nofretari.jpg. Copyright in the Public Domain.

Fig. 1.1.3: "Queen Tiy" © Keith Schengili-Roberts, (CC BY-SA 3.0) at: http://commons.wikimedia.org/wiki/File:QueenTiy01-AltesMuseum-Berlin.png.

Patricia Hill Collins, "Black Women's Love Relationships," Black Feminist Thought: Knowledge, Consciousness, and the Politics of Empowerment, pp. 161-186. Copyright © 2009 by Taylor & Francis Group LLC. Reprinted with permission.

Brooklynn K. Hitchens and Yasser Arafat Payne, "Adapted from "Brenda's Got a Baby': Black Single Motherhood and Street Life as a Site of Resilience in Wilmington, Delaware," Journal of Black Psychology, vol. 43, no. 1, pp. 50-76. Copyright © by SAGE Publications. Reprinted with permission.

Cheryl L. Woods-Giscombe, "Superwoman Schema: African American Women's Views on Stress, Strength, and Health," Qualitative Health Research, vol. 20, no. 5, pp. 668-683. Copyright © 2010 by Sage Publications. Reprinted with permission.

Shareefah Al'uqdah and Frances Adomako, "From Mourning to Action: African American Women's Grief, Pain, and Activism," Journal of Loss and Trauma: International Perspectives on Stress and Coping, vol. 23, no. 2, pp. 91-98. Copyright © 2018 by Taylor & Francis Group. Reprinted with permission.